The Supreme Court of Florida

UNIVERSITY PRESS OF FLORIDA

Florida A&M University, Tallahassee
Florida Atlantic University, Boca Raton
Florida Gulf Coast University, Ft. Myers
Florida International University, Miami
Florida State University, Tallahassee
New College of Florida, Sarasota
University of Central Florida, Orlando
University of Florida, Gainesville
University of North Florida, Jacksonville
University of South Florida, Tampa
University of West Florida, Pensacola

THE

SUPREME COURT OF FLORIDA

A JOURNEY TOWARD JUSTICE, 1972–1987

NEIL SKENE

UNIVERSITY PRESS OF FLORIDA
Gainesville / Tallahassee / Tampa / Boca Raton
Pensacola / Orlando / Miami / Jacksonville / Ft. Myers / Sarasota

This book may be available in an electronic edition.

22 21 20 19 18 17   6 5 4 3 2 1

Library of Congress Cataloging-in-Publication Data
Names: Skene, Neil, author.
Title: The Supreme Court of Florida : a journey toward justice, 1972–1987 /
   Neil Skene.
Description: Gainesville : University Press of Florida, 2017. | Includes
   bibliographical references and index.
Identifiers: LCCN 2017016662 | ISBN 9780813054483 (cloth)
Subjects: LCSH: Florida. Supreme Court—History—20th century. | Justice,
   Administration of—Florida—History—20th century.
Classification: LCC KFF512 .S593 2017 | DDC 347.759/03509047—dc23
LC record available at https://lccn.loc.gov/2017016662

The University Press of Florida is the scholarly publishing agency for the State
University System of Florida, comprising Florida A&M University, Florida
Atlantic University, Florida Gulf Coast University, Florida International
University, Florida State University, New College of Florida, University of
Central Florida, University of Florida, University of North Florida, University
of South Florida, and University of West Florida.

University Press of Florida
15 Northwest 15th Street
Gainesville, FL 32611-2079
http://upress.ufl.edu

Dedicated to my friends
Mathewos, Temesgen, Yousef, Dawit
and other journalists of Eritrea—
imprisoned since 9/18/2001 without counsel or trial
for want of due process and an independent judiciary

Non nobis solum nati sumus.
(Not for ourselves alone are we born.)

Marcus Tullius Cicero

CONTENTS

FIGURES

Figures follow page 233.

PREFACE

Justice Harris Drew remarked more than four decades ago that justices of the Florida Supreme Court were not household names, and that was a good thing, he said, because it indicated that the court was looked upon as an institution and not as a group of individuals. I dissent. One of the most interesting and compelling aspects of the institution is the people who bring their different personalities, philosophies, intellects, and experiences to the state's highest court.

This book, the third in a series that began with the earliest court of territorial Florida, describes a judicial institution evolving in a time of deep political and social change: the 1970s and 1980s. This volume of the story begins amid the upheaval of the civil rights movement, the Vietnam War, and the Watergate scandal, along with a youth-driven revolution in music and morality. Sometimes embracing change and sometimes embracing tradition, the justices of the Florida Supreme Court reflected the cultural conflicts in the cases that came before them. Each new justice changed the course of the law, sometimes in subtle ways, sometimes in very noticeable and significant ways.

Their personal interactions changed too. Ben Overton arrived in 1974 as Mr. Clean in a time of scandal, and his early tenure was guided by advice to be careful of the other justices and avoid close relationships. Arthur England came next and told his staff to talk to no one outside their chambers. But after the old guard was gone, things changed. Some of the justices developed close lifelong friendships. England would drop in on law clerks' after-work social events. He and Sundberg, who had met only once in passing before their arrival on the court, became the closest of friends for the rest of their lives. Ray Ehrlich would eat his health-food lunches in the court's small lunchroom and chat with court staff that came in. Overton's backyard backed up to Steve Grimes's backyard, and they even cut a gate in the fence so they could go back and forth easily. Ehrlich lived almost across the street.

Rosemary Barkett, who arrived in late 1985, saw her years on the court as a time of camaraderie despite sometimes sharp 4–3 divisions on cases. "We literally lived together," she said. "We were together every day at the court. We would have conferences every single week almost. We would go to events together—the legislative events, the events you have to go to in Tallahassee." The socializing leavened the differences on cases. "If you've been singing songs at a piano with Parker Lee McDonald while Ruth [his wife] is playing," Barkett recalled, "you can't get all that mad at him when he disagrees with you about something, or at least you can't get mad at him on a personal basis."

Part 1 of this book, "The Reformation," focuses on the refurbishing of Florida's judicial system over a period that began in 1966 with the Constitution Revision Commission and extended through major jurisdictional change in 1980. The goals of this Reformation were to create a more effective buffer between the court system and political pressures and to achieve greater openness, provide accountability, and concentrate the attention of the state's highest court on the issues of greatest significance.

Part 2, "The Life of the Law," borrowing a phrase from Oliver Wendell Holmes (who went on to say that the life of the law "has not been logic, it has been experience"), is about Job #1 at the court, deciding cases. This longer section of the book returns to the beginning of the period and examines a large sample of the court's decisions illustrating the justices' continual effort to draw lines between conflicting interests in society and between stability in the law and adaptation to change. Time after time, we see that cases are not just logical extensions of other cases but reflect the experiences and philosophies of the justices and their own sense of what justice calls for.

As with my coverage of the court for the *St. Petersburg Times* in the 1980s, the book is written for people who are not lawyers as well as for lawyers and judges. A primary goal, particularly in Part 2, is to describe the justices at work. The spotlight widens beyond the justices, however, to lawyers and lower-court judges, whose arguments and opinions shaped the thinking of the justices. I have included exchanges from oral arguments, the one part of the job that is done in public—and today, unlike the days of this book, is live on camera.

A popular impression is that justices decide cases largely on the basis of their own political leanings. This view is simplistic. High-profile decisions produce reactions from high-profile losing parties blaming decisions on justices' political views, while winners consider the same decisions learned and wise. These remarks appeal to public opinion, but they do little to enhance public judgment about the issues or the courts. Like other professionals, judges reach their judgments within a framework of rules and conventions as well as institutional awareness.

Decisions are a hybrid of many factors for each justice. A decision may reflect an explicit or poorly written statute, or inadequate evidence, or clear precedent. On the other hand, the philosophies and experiences of individual justices clearly matter, as they draw on a personal sense of justice. They even yield to their own suppositions—whether, for example, it harms family relationships to let one spouse sue the other's insurance company over an automobile accident. The collective decision making of seven justices reflects society's investment in a rule of law and not a rule of a single judge. After all, fundamental to the workings of both business and personal relationships is the expectation that the law will apply the same way to all and won't change with every new case that comes along. Judges, then, ideally are chosen for their judgment and perceptiveness as well as their ability to delve into all the evidence and law to produce a body of law that is consistent and predictable while open to the inevitable evolution of society.

The approach and style of this volume are different from the two preceding volumes of Florida Supreme Court history. Those first two volumes, by Walter W. Manley II and Canter Brown Jr., are panoramic in telling the story of the court from the state's territorial days to 1917 and then from 1917 to 1972, each far more years than this volume covers. This volume is more telescopic. People who had a role in the events of that era, including most of the justices themselves, were alive to tell their story. My goal was to harmonize these individual accounts with documents, articles, and cases to produce both a permanent record and a deeper understanding of how Florida's legal system and case law changed through that turbulent time.

Previous volumes established a particularly high standard in biographical material on the justices, and I have sought to sustain that standard. As was true in the earlier volumes, the biographies sometimes include uncomfortable aspects of the lives of the men and women who served on the court. Omitting the negative would diminish the credibility of the positive, whether in the assessment of their work or the story of their lives.

The formal boundaries of this volume, 1972 to 1987, reflect the period beginning with the year a major revision of Article V of the Florida Constitution was approved and ending as Justices Jimmy Adkins and Joe Boyd concluded their eighteen-year tenure and as Governor Bob Graham left office. There is never a precise moment where one era ends and another begins, however, and this book occasionally breaks the confines of the calendar to complete a story or provide additional perspective. On the other hand, there is always the prospect of a sequel, and some stories are "to be continued."

My goal was not to produce an encyclopedia or a law review but an institutional memoir, telling stories of people who made a difference in the life of the court, brushing lightly over many episodes and cases, omitting hundreds more entirely, and pausing to contemplate some in detail. Each topical chapter is a blend of the important, the anecdotal, and the unexpected. Some cases get a lot of attention because they had a dramatic effect on the law and some because there was something about the way the case was decided that transcends its value as precedent.

Sometimes I include the seemingly trivial or quirky. The passage on "Dog Day" at the court is included not to pander shamelessly to dog lovers (or at least not solely for that purpose) but to illustrate through two prosaic cases the tension between what justice or common sense requires and what a statute seems to require. The attention to death penalty cases is extensive, but it is also the highest-profile activity of the court; the topic is about a tenth of the book but consumed perhaps a third of the justices' workload. There will undoubtedly be criticism about omissions or even inclusions. There is little coverage of discipline cases against lawyers and judges, for example. Those are worthy subjects, but the facts and context require a certain commitment of time for relatively little additional insight into the decision-making of the court. Some will object that I put more emphasis on obscenity and nudity cases than on advisory opinions to governors. Others will be grateful.

Chronology is subordinated to topic. In general, the topics are in an order roughly corresponding to the key episode in the chapter, but necessarily each chapter covers overlapping segments of the entire period. The chapters are designed to stand largely on their own, though with some assumption of familiarity with the main characters, the justices. To counteract any "time tunnel" disorientation, the book contains a chronology of cases and the dates justices and governors arrived and departed.

There is nothing in the footnotes except references to source material. If it is worth saying, the reader should not have to go looking for it in the footnotes. In quotations, I made purely typographical changes without the intrusion of brackets or the finger-wagging "*sic*." My rare explanatory additions to quotations are in brackets; parentheses in quotations are in the original material. My deletions are shown with ellipses.

I have tried diligently to avoid acronyms and to explain legal terms as they are used, but a couple are common enough to warrant brief advance explanation. I often use "DCA" to refer to a District Court of Appeal, the mid-level appellate court between the trial courts and the Supreme Court. A "per curiam" opinion is one with no designated author; the Latin label literally means "for the court." Justices may choose the "per curiam" label if multiple justices contribute significantly to an opinion, if the case is in a designated category such as a Bar case or capital case, or if the opinion is brief or relies heavily on a lower-court opinion. "Per Curiam Affirmed," or PCA, is a term of art for a one-word unsigned opinion that simply affirms (upholds) a trial court decision without explanation. This type of decision is explored in chapter 10.

I hope even careful students of the court will discover in this book information they did not know, find humor here and there, and gain new insights into the third branch of Florida government and its role in the checks and balances of our democracy. I also hope that everyone will come to know better the individuals who are not household names but who have left an indelible mark on the Supreme Court of Florida.

ACKNOWLEDGMENTS

As Ruth McDonald and I walked together out of the old Silver Slipper Restaurant one day after a monthly luncheon of the Capital Tiger Bay Club, she asked if I would be interested in writing a third volume on the history of the Florida Supreme Court. She was then the longtime treasurer of the Florida Supreme Court Historical Society, and she and her husband, Parker Lee McDonald, had known me since 1980, when I began covering the Florida Supreme Court for the *St. Petersburg Times*. It is likely that this book, at least with my name on it, would not exist without Ruth McDonald's encouragement.

Ben Hill, Bob Ervin, John DeVault, Mark Hulsey, and Dexter Douglass formed the society's book committee that got this project going, and Ed Guedes took the lead once the work began. Ed, along with Kelly O'Keefe, the president of the Historical Society during the two years of completion and publication, were consistent supporters of my approach to the book and managed to somehow exhibit both understanding of the long process of research and writing and eagerness to see it published. I am grateful to all of the trustees of the Historical Society for their support as the years of research and writing progressed.

And at the other end of this project are the editors and designers of the University Press of Florida, whose experience took a manuscript and made a book of it.

My first interview was with Martin Dyckman, my longtime colleague at the *St. Petersburg Times* and a walking Wikipedia on Florida's political history and the Florida Supreme Court. His book on the Supreme Court scandal of 1974–75, *A Most Disorderly Court*, documents the most significant scandal in the court's history, while his biographies of LeRoy Collins and Reubin Askew describe the lives and governorships of Florida's two greatest governors. Martin's reporting and columns as well as his voice as a longtime member of the *Times* editorial board have shaped the Supreme Court and all of Florida's government for half a century. Martin is a state treasure, and it is a privilege to count him as a friend and colleague for these many, many years.

Many justices and former justices, former law clerks, and lawyers generously shared their time and knowledge with me. All of those interviewed are listed in the bibliography. Although some are not directly quoted or footnoted, all added abundantly to my understanding of the court and the justices and the era covered by this volume. Four deserve special mention: Ben Overton, Arthur England, Parker Lee McDonald, and Sandy D'Alemberte. Each of them endured multiple in-person interviews as well as phone calls to ask "one more question" that would turn into yet another hour of conversation. I was privileged to have them not just as sources but as friends since my earliest days in Tallahassee. I also have to mention Governor Reubin Askew. There was nothing quite like a conversation with Askew, who was full of stories and mischievous humor.

Without the *St. Petersburg Times*, this book would have been far more difficult and perhaps very different. Eugene Patterson, the great editor and CEO of that news organization in the 1970s and 1980s, hired me out of law school because he believed in having reporters as knowledgeable as possible about the subjects they covered. He made the decision to send me to Tallahassee and encouraged reporting and writing that made the law understandable to readers of the *Times*. I never knew Gene Patterson to make an unprincipled decision, and his own writing was both wise and eloquent. Around me at the *Times* and later at Congressional Quarterly were terrific researchers, reporters, and editors, whose work I admired and learned from every day.

I confess that I have cited my own *Times* articles with some frequency and have used the *Times* as a source far more often than other newspapers. This was largely a factor of availability and convenience. I have a file drawer full of clippings, now yellowed, and the *Tampa Bay Times*, as it is now known, generously provided me access to the news library that was so familiar to me in bygone days.

Other journalists, historians, and analysts have done some remarkable work on the court and this era in Florida history, and I have tried to give them visible credit in the text itself. One very special and continuing resource and supporter was the Supreme Court's archivist, Erik Robinson. His job is to safeguard and organize the vast archival material of the court, and he cheerfully found materials I needed and secured the consent of the court for access to draft opinions and vote sheets and other materials the court deems confidential.

While the Historical Society provided a financial grant to support the preparation of this book, neither the society nor the justices nor anyone else imposed any requirements or censorship on its contents. The responsibility for conclusions and imperfections in this book is entirely mine.

Five law students from four different law schools bore an important part of the research load on this book. In the early stages were Lindsay Wells (Grogan) of Florida State University Law School and Hayley Curry of the University of Pennsylvania Law School. Involved later in the project were Hallee Moore of Mercer University Law School, Curtis Filaroski of FSU Law School, and my daughter Jennifer Skene of Yale Law School.

The longest-serving research assistant, however, was my wife, Madelyn Miller Skene, a graduate of American University Law School who came to Tallahassee in 1983 as a reporter for the Associated Press and also covered the Florida Supreme Court before we were married (in 1984 by Justice McDonald). She not only gathered cases and wrote summaries of several areas of the law but also read multiple drafts of chapters with a keen eye. She has endured the highs and lows of this project. This project obviously permeated the whole household, and though their role in the book was less direct than Jennifer's and Madelyn's, son Christopher and daughter Katie certainly are part of this book in spirit.

I cannot complete a book about the law without noting also the influence of my dad, George N. Skene, who went to night law school and occasionally took me along when I was about nine years old. He was a fifty-year member of the Georgia Bar before he retired, and my mother, Louise Pate Skene, was his office manager and sometime paralegal during his many years of insurance defense and workers' comp practice. They made a lot of things possible for me.

This book happened because of my parents' confidence and encouragement in anything I wanted to pursue, and because of the support and sacrifices of my wife and children in this and so many other ventures.

To all of those who made this book possible, I am deeply grateful.

CHRONOLOGY OF CASES AND IMPORTANT EVENTS

Date	Petitioner/Appellant (or Event)	Respondent/Appellee	Topic	Chapter
11/5/1968	*Voters approve new Florida Constitution without revision of Art. V*			4
4/29/1970	Time Inc.	Firestone	Media Law	12
1/5/1971	*Reubin O'D. Askew replaces Claude R. Kirk Jr. as Governor*		Governor	1
1/21/1971	Advisory Opinion to the Governor (Corporate Tax)		Corporate Tax	2
1/27/1971	City of Miami Beach	Berns	Open Government	27
2/22/1972	State	Silva	Criminal Law	29
3/14/1972	*Voters approve Article V court restructuring*		Article V	4
5/17/1972	Bassett	Braddock	Open Government	27
6/29/1972	Branzburg	Hayes	Media Law	12
6/29/1972	Furman	Georgia	Death Penalty	16
7/1/1972	*Office of State Court Administrator opens*		Article V	5
7/17/1972	Donaldson	Sack	Death Penalty	16
9/8/1972	Anderson	State	Death Penalty	16
9/26/1972	Baker, In re		Death Penalty	16
12/20/1972	Firestone	Time, Inc.	Media Law	12
2/28/1973	Florida Bar	Amer. Legal & Business Forms Inc.	Legal Services	9
4/6/1973	Canney	Bd. of Public Instr'n of Alachua Co.	Open Government	27
6/6/1973	Pierce	Piper Aircraft Corp.	Jurisdiction	10
7/10/1973	Hoffman	Jones	Personal Injury	11, 24
7/11/1973	Kluger	White	Personal Injury	11
7/18/1973	Tornillo	Miami Herald Pub. Co.	Media Law	12, 28

(continued)

Date	Petitioner/Appellant (or Event)	Respondent/Appellee	Topic	Chapter
7/26/1973	State	Dixon	Death Penalty	16, 24
7/31/1973	Williams	Seaboard Airline Railroad Co.	Personal Injury	11
9/19/1973	Rhodes	State	Constitutional Rights	22
10/10/1973	A.R. Moyer, Inc.	Graham	Personal Injury	11
11/14/1973	Florida workmen's compensation rules of procedure, In re		Jurisdiction	10
1/10/1974	Gilliam	Stewart	Personal Injury	11
1/30/1974	Florida Bar Examiners (Ben Ervin)		Bar Regulation	31
1/30/1974	Gulf Power Co.	Bevis	Corporate Tax	2
2/27/1974	State ex rel. Turner	Earle	Judicial Ethics	3, 6
2/28/1974	*Chief Justice Vassar Carlton resigns from court*		Justices	2
3/1/1974	*James C. Adkins becomes Chief Justice*		Justices	1, 2
3/27/1974	*Askew appointee Ben F. Overton becomes 62nd Justice*		Justices	2
4/10/1974	Jones	State	Constitutional Rights	22
4/25/1974	Ernoznik	City of Jacksonville	Constitutional Rights	22
5/1/1974	State	Aiuppa	Constitutional Rights	22
5/1/1974	State ex. Rel. Gerstein	Walvick Theatre Corp.	Constitutional Rights	22
5/1/1974	Town of Palm Beach	Gradison	Open Meetings	27
5/15/1974	Taylor	State	Death Penalty	16, 17
6/13/1974	Gulf Power Co.	Bevis	Corporate Tax	2
7/17/1974	Florida Bar	Stupica	Legal Services	9
9/10/1974	*Arthur England beats Sam Spector to replace Richard Ervin*		Justices	2
9/10/1974	*Ben Overton wins election to keep seat on Supreme Court*		Justices	2
10/16/1974	Bucolo	State	Constitutional Rights	22
10/24/1974	Scholastic Systems, Inc.	LeLoup	Jurisdiction	10
11/6/1974	Lamadline	State	Death Penalty	16
11/27/1974	Sullivan	State	Death Penalty	16
12/11/1974	Firestone	Time, Inc.	Media Law	12
12/11/1974	Hallman	State	Death Penalty	16
1/6/1975	*Richard Ervin retires*		Justices	2
1/8/1975	*Arthur J. England Jr. becomes 63rd Justice*		Justices	2

Date	Petitioner/Appellant (or Event)	Respondent/Appellee	Topic	Chapter
1/29/1975	Alford	State	Death Penalty	16
1/29/1975	Florida Bar	Thomson	Judicial Ethics	3
2/4/1975	In Re Boyd (reprimand)		Judicial Ethics	3
2/4/1975	In Re Dekle (Fitzpatrick Case)		Judicial Ethics	3
2/4/1975	In Re Dekle (Mason Case) (reprimand)		Judicial Ethics	3
2/19/1975	Spinkellink	State	Death Penalty	16
2/20/1975	Austin	State ex rel Christian	Ethics	3
2/26/1975	Gardner	State	Death Penalty	17, 28
3/10/1975	*Hal Dekle announces resignation from court*		Justices	3
3/20/1975	State ex rel. Tindel	Sharp	Public Records	27
3/26/1975	Finn	Finn	Divorce	14
4/28/1975	*David McCain announces resignation from court*		Justices	3
5/28/1975	Proffitt	State	Death Penalty	16, 17, 24
6/2/1975	*Alan C. Sundberg becomes 64th Justice*		Justices	3
6/23/1975	Ernoznik	City of Jacksonville	Constitutional Rights	22
7/8/1975	*Askew appoints Joseph Hatchett as first black justice*		Governor	1. 3
7/15/1975	Bennett	State	Criminal Law	29
7/30/1975	Lincenberg	Issen	Personal Injury	11
9/2/1975	*Joseph W. Hatchett becomes 65th Justice*		Justices	1, 3
9/3/1975	Songer	State	Death Penalty	24
9/3/1975	Swan	State	Death Penalty	17
9/17/1975	Alvord	State	Death Penalty	17
11/19/1975	Tedder	State	Death Penalty	17
1/15/1976	Florida Bar	Mason	Ethics	2
1/28/1976	Petition of Post-Newsweek Stations I (Cameras)		Cameras in Court	8
2/18/1976	Darden	State	Death Penalty	24
3/1/1976	*Ben Overton becomes Chief Justice*		Justices	6
3/2/1976	Time, Inc.	Firestone (U.S.)	Media Law	12
3/8/1976	Bucolo	Adkins	Constitutional Rights	22
5/12/1976	National Airlines	Edwards	Jurisdiction	10

(*continued*)

Date	Petitioner/Appellant (or Event)	Respondent/Appellee	Topic	Chapter
6/23/1976	Advisory Opinion to the Governor (Sunshine Law)		Open Government	27
6/30/1976	Nebraska Press Association	Stuart	Open Courts	27
7/1/1976	Planned Parenthood of Central Missouri	Danforth	Personal Privacy	23
7/2/1976	Gregg	Georgia	Death Penalty	16
7/2/1976	Proffitt	Florida (U.S.)	Death Penalty	17
7/2/1976	Roberts	Louisiana	Death Penalty	16
7/2/1976	U.S. Supreme Court declares Florida death penalty constitutional		Death Penalty	16
7/8/1976	Cooper	State	Death Penalty	24
7/21/1976	West	Caterpillar Tractor Co.	Personal Injury	13
7/30/1976	Morgan	State	Media Law	12
7/30/1976	State ex rel Miami Herald Publishing Co.	McIntosh	Open Courts	27
9/23/1976	Spears	State	Constitutional Rights	22
10/11/1976	Weber	Smathers	Constitution Amendments	6, 26
10/14/1976	Moffett	State	Constitutional Rights	22
11/2/1976	*Fred Karl elected, Sundberg reelected to Supreme Court*		Justices	6
11/2/1976	*Joe Hatchett becomes only black to win a contested statewide election in Florida in twentieth century*		Justices	6
11/2/1976	*Voters approve merit selection of appellate judges and justices*		Art. V	6
11/12/1976	Florida Bd. Of Bar Examiners, In re		Bar Regulation	31
11/24/1976	Florida Bd. Of Bar Examiners, In re		Bar Regulation	19
11/30/1976	Odom	Deltona Corp.	Growth Management	15
1/4/1977	*Frederick B. Karl becomes 66th Justice*		Justices	6
2/10/1977	Laird	State	Privacy	27
2/25/1977	News-Press Pub. Co.	Wisher	Public Records	27
3/17/1977	Barclay	State	Death Penalty	24
3/22/1977	Gardner	Florida	Death Penalty	17
4/7/1977	Elledge	State	Death Penalty	16

Date	Petitioner/Appellant (or Event)	Respondent/Appellee	Topic	Chapter
4/7/1977	Harvard	State	Death Penalty	17
4/7/1977	Petition of Post-Newsweek Stations II (Cameras)		Cameras in Court	8
4/21/1977	Florida Greyhound Owners & Breeders Assn.	West Flagler Associates Ltd.	Jurisdiction	10
5/27/1977	Wald Corp.	Metropolitan Dade County	Growth Management	15
6/30/1977	Cardenas	Smathers	Reapportionment	20
6/30/1977	Milton	Smathers	Reapportionment	20
7/14/1977	Occidental Chemical Co.	Mayo	Open Meetings	27
9/16/1977	Spenkelink	State	Death Penalty	16
9/29/1977	Florida Bd. Of Bar Examiners, In re		Bar Regulation	19
9/30/1977	McArthur	State	Criminal Law	24
11/17/1977	Shor	Paoli	Family Tort Immunity	14
1/10/1978	Florida Bar	Brumbaugh	Legal Services	9
1/15/1978	Florida Bar	McCain	Judicial Ethics	3
3/2/1978	Florida Bd. Of Bar Examiners, In re		Bar Regulation	19
3/2/1978	State	Walls	Search and Seizure	21
4/5/1978	*Fred Karl resigns from Court*		Justices	6
4/5/1978	Willinsky	State	Criminal Law	29
4/11/1978	*James E. Alderman becomes 67th Justice*		Justices	7
6/15/1978	Florida Bar	McCain	Judicial Ethics	3
6/29/1978	Proffitt	State	Death Penalty	24
6/30/1978	Hargrave	State	Death Penalty	16, 17
7/1/1978	*Arthur England becomes Chief Justice*		Justices	10
7/3/1978	Lockett	Ohio (U.S.)	Death Penalty	16
7/27/1978	Matthews	State	Constitutional Rights	22
7/28/1978	Clark	State	Criminal Law	29
9/7/1978	Washington	State	Death Penalty	17
9/14/1978	Myers	Hawkins	Financial Disclosure	10

(*continued*)

Date	Petitioner/Appellant (or Event)	Respondent/Appellee	Topic	Chapter
10/12/1978	First Amendment Foundation of Florida, Inc.	State	Constitutional Rights	22
1/2/1979	*D. Robert Graham replaces Reubin Askew as Governor*		Governor	15, 16
1/25/1979	Menendez	State	Death Penalty	17
2/1/1979	Tribune Co.	School Bd. of Hillsborough Co.	Open Government	27
3/29/1979	Kampff	State	Death Penalty	17
3/29/1979	McArthur	Nourse	Criminal Law	24
4/12/1979	Petition of Post-Newsweek Stations (Cameras Final Order)		Cameras in Court	8
4/19/1979	Commercial Carrier Corp.	Indian River County	Sovereign Immunity	25
5/10/1979	Florida Bar	Furman	Legal Services	9
5/22/1979	Spenkelink	Wainwright (U.S.)	Death Penalty	16
5/24/1979	Interest on Trust Accounts, Matter of		Legal Services	9
5/24/1979	Wainwright	Spenkelink (U.S.)	Death Penalty	16
5/25/1979	Spenkelink	Wainwright	Death Penalty	16
5/29/1979	*John Spenkelink becomes first person executed in Florida since 1964*		Death Penalty	16
6/14/1979	Lucas	State	Death Penalty	17
6/25/1979	Proffitt	State	Death Penalty	24
6/29/1979	Advisory Opinion to Governor (5th DCA)		Courts	10
7/2/1979	Gannett Co. Inc.	Pasquale	Open Courts	27
7/18/1979	*Joseph Hatchett resigns from court*		Justices	7
7/26/1979	Rutledge	State	Death Penalty	17
10/26/1979	*Parker Lee McDonald becomes 68th Justice*		Justices	7
12/20/1979	Raisen	Raisen	Family Tort Immunity	14
1/17/1980	Shevin	Byron, Harless, Schaffer, Reid	Privacy of Records	27
1/24/1980	Norman	State	Search and Seizure	21
1/31/1980	Canakaris	Canakaris	Divorce	14
1/31/1980	Duncan	Duncan	Family Tort Immunity	14
2/14/1980	District School Bd. Of Lake County	Talmadge	Sovereign Immunity	25

Date	Petitioner/Appellant (or Event)	Respondent/Appellee	Topic	Chapter
3/11/1980	*Voters approve revision of Supreme Court jurisdiction*		*Art. V*	*10*
5/6/1980	Magill	State	Death Penalty	24
5/8/1980	King	State	Death Penalty	17
6/12/1980	Gafford	State	Death Penalty	24
6/26/1980	Jenkins	State	Jurisdiction	10
7/1/1980	*Alan Sundberg becomes Chief Justice*		*Justices*	
7/2/1980	Richmond Newspapers, Inc.	Virginia	Open Courts	27
7/24/1980	Witt	State	Death Penalty	17
9/11/1980	Hetland	State	Search and Seizure	21
10/23/1980	Milton	Smathers	Reapportionment	20
12/11/1980	Johnson	State	Death Penalty	17
12/18/1980	Perry	State	Death Penalty	24
12/18/1980	Robinson	State	Constitutional Rights	22
1/8/1981	Spaziano	State	Death Penalty	17
1/15/1981	Brown	Wainwright	Death Penalty	17
1/15/1981	State	Daley	Death Penalty	17
1/15/1981	State	Sarmiento	Search and Seizure	21
1/21/1981	Chandler	Florida (U.S.)	Cameras in Court	8
1/21/1981	*U.S. Supreme Court upholds Florida's rule allowing cameras in courtrooms*			8
2/12/1981	State	Tsavaris	Search and Seizure	21
3/5/1981	State	Green	Cameras in Court	8
3/5/1981	State	Palm Beach Newspapers Inc.	Cameras in Court	8
3/26/1981	Jacobs	State	Death Penalty	24
4/16/1981	Graham	Estuary Properties, Inc.	Growth Management	15
4/20/1981	In Re Florida Bar (Chap. 119)		Open Government	27
4/30/1981	Florida Bar (Public Records)		Public Records	27
4/30/1981	Hoberman	State	Search and Seizure	21
6/4/1981	Barclay	State	Death Penalty	24
6/18/1981	Florida Bd. Of Bar Examiners Re N.R.S.		Bar Regulation	19

(continued)

Date	Petitioner/Appellant (or Event)	Respondent/Appellee	Topic	Chapter
6/18/1981	Smith	Brantley	Impeachment	2
6/25/1981	Dept. of Transportation	Knowles	Sovereign Immunity	25
7/16/1981	Cauley	City of Jacksonville	Sovereign Immunity	25
7/23/1981	State	James	Evidence	22
7/30/1981	Goodwin	State	Death Penalty	24
7/30/1981	Petition of Diez-Arquelles		Bar Regulation	19
8/9/1981	*Arthur England resigns from Court*		Justices	18
10/15/1981	State	Brady	Search and Seizure	21
12/3/1981	*Raymond Ehrlich becomes 69th Justice*		Justices	18
1/7/1982	Vaught	State	Death Penalty	16
1/19/1982	Eddings	Oklahoma	Death Penalty	16
2/25/1982	Hitchcock	State	Death Penalty	24
3/4/1982	Breedlove	State	Death Penalty	17
3/11/1982	Scott	State	Death Penalty	17
3/27/1982	Florida Senate	Graham	Reapportionment	20
4/6/1982	Florida Senate	Graham	Reapportionment	20
4/15/1982	Francis	State	Death Penalty	24
4/15/1982	Harvard	State	Death Penalty	24
4/29/1982	Ard	Ard	Family Tort Immunity	14
4/29/1982	Joseph	Quest	Family Tort Immunity	14
4/29/1982	Roberts	Roberts	Family Tort Immunity	14
4/29/1982	West	West	Family Tort Immunity	14
4/29/1982	Woods	Withrow	Family Tort Immunity	14
6/7/1982	Tibbs	Florida (U.S.)	Death Penalty	24
6/24/1982	State	Bobbitt	Castle Doctrine	22
7/1/1982	*James Alderman becomes Chief Justice*		Justices	27
7/8/1982	Jaramillo	State	Evidence	23, 24
7/15/1982	Department of Educ.	Lewis	Free Speech	19

Date	Petitioner/Appellant (or Event)	Respondent/Appellee	Topic	Chapter
9/2/1982	Miami Herald Pub. Co.	Lewis	Open Courts	27
9/14/1982	City of St. Petersburg	Collom	Sovereign Immunity	25
9/14/1982	Department of Transp.	Neilson	Sovereign Immunity	25
9/15/1982	*Alan Sundberg resigns from Court*		Justices	23
9/19/1982	Proffitt	Wainwright (Fed.)	Death Penalty	24
9/23/1982	Morningstar	State	Search and Seizure	21
10/21/1982	Askew	Firestone	Constitution Amendments	26
10/28/1982	DeMontmorency	State	Search and Seizure	21
10/28/1982	Williams	State	Search and Seizure	21
11/8/1982	*Voters approve constitutional amendment on search and seizure*		Constitution Amendments	21
12/16/1982	Florida Bar in re Kimball		Bar Regulation	19
12/16/1982	Osterndorf	Turner	Constitution Amendments	26
12/22/1982	Middleton	State	Death Penalty	17
1/10/1983	*Leander J. Shaw Jr. becomes 70th Justice*		Justices	23
2/17/1983	Ralph	City of Daytona Beach	Sovereign Immunity	25
3/10/1983	Magill	State	Death Penalty	24
5/12/1983	Florida Bar In re Mandatory Pro Bono		Legal Services	9
5/23/1983	United States	Hasting	Criminal Law	29
5/26/1983	Spaziano	State	Death Penalty	17, 24
6/15/1983	Planned Parenthood Association of Kansas City, Missouri, Inc.	Ashcroft	Personal Privacy	23
7/7/1983	Harrison	Escambia County School Bd.	Sovereign Immunity	25
7/7/1983	State	Lavazzoli	Search and Seizure	21
8/25/1983	Harich	State	Death Penalty	17
8/25/1983	Teffeteller	State	Death Penalty	17
9/1/1983	Arango	State	Death Penalty	24
9/8/1983	Mason	State	Death Penalty	17
9/22/1983	Routly	State	Death Penalty	17

(continued)

Date	Petitioner/Appellant (or Event)	Respondent/Appellee	Topic	Chapter
11/3/1983	Florida Bar Examiners (63161)		Privacy of Records	27
11/10/1983	Florida Bar Examiners (60550)		Privacy of Records	27
11/20/1983	*Robert Sullivan becomes second man executed under 1972 law*		Death Penalty	24
11/21/1983	Sullivan	State	Death Penalty	24
12/8/1983	Florida Bar In re Rules (Dissolution of Marriage)		Legal Services	9
12/8/1983	State	Williams	Search and Seizure	21
1/12/1984	Murray	State	Criminal	29
1/12/1984	State	Murray	Criminal Law	29
1/19/1984	Barclay	Wainwright	Death Penalty	24
1/26/1984	Lusk	State	Death Penalty	17
2/2/1984	Rembert	State	Death Penalty	17
3/27/1984	Fine	Firestone	Constitution Amendments	26
4/12/1984	Insurance Co. of North America	Pasakarnis	Personal Injury	13
4/19/1984	Department of Transp. Of State of Fla.	Nalven	Growth Management	15
4/26/1984	Florida Bar	Furman	Legal Services	9
5/3/1984	Belcher Yacht, Inc.	Stickney	Personal Injury	13
5/3/1984	Florida Bar In re Rules (Dissolution of Marriage)		Legal Services	9
5/17/1984	Grapin	Grapin	Divorce	14
5/24/1984	James	State	Death Penalty	24
7/1/1984	*Joseph Boyd becomes Chief Justice*		Justices	28
8/30/1984	Forsberg	Housing Authority of Miami Beach	Privacy of Records	27
9/6/1984	Tribune Co.	Cannella	Open Government	27
9/13/1984	Smith	Russell	Media Law	12
9/13/1984	Tribune Co.	Levin	Media Law	12
9/27/1984	State	Neil	Criminal Law	29
10/3/1984	Evans	Firestone	Constitution Amendments	26
10/4/1984	Andrews	State	Criminal Law	29

Date	Petitioner/Appellant (or Event)	Respondent/Appellee	Topic	Chapter
10/18/1984	Moffitt	Willis	Open Government	27
10/22/1984	Pulitzer	Pulitzer	Divorce	14
11/21/1984	Hardwick	State	Death Penalty	17
12/13/1984	Nodar	Galbreath	Media Law	12
1/31/1985	Songer	State	Death Penalty	24
1/31/1985	State ex rel. Quigley	Quigley	Divorce	14
2/14/1985	Johnson	State	Death Penalty	24
2/21/1985	Michel	Douglas	Open Government	27
2/28/1985	DeMontmorency	State	Search and Seizure	21
2/28/1985	State	Brady	Search and Seizure	21
3/7/1985	Champion	Gray	Personal Injury	13
3/7/1985	Jones	Utica Mut. Ins. Co.	Personal Injury	13
4/4/1985	Carter	City of Stuart	Sovereign Immunity	25
4/4/1985	City of Daytona Beach	Palmer	Sovereign Immunity	25
4/4/1985	Everton	Willard	Sovereign Immunity	25
4/4/1985	Reddish	Smith	Sovereign Immunity	25
4/4/1985	Trianon Park Condominium Ass'n., Inc.	City of Hialeah	Sovereign Immunity	25
4/18/1985	Florida Bar	Hawkins	Bar Regulation	31
5/16/1985	Patient's Compensation Fund	Von Stetina	Personal Injury	13
8/15/1985	Bertolotti	State	Death Penalty	24
8/15/1985	Wilson	Wainwright (Fed.)	Death Penalty	24
8/16/1985	Songer	Wainwright (Fed.)	Death Penalty	24
8/29/1985	Snowten	U.S. Fidelity and Guar. Co.	Family Tort Immunity	14
8/30/1985	City of Daytona Beach	Del Percio	Constitutional Rights	22
8/30/1985	State	Kinchen	Criminal Law	29
8/31/1985	*James Alderman resigns from Court*		Justices	30
11/15/1985	*Rosemary Barkett becomes 71st Justice*		Justices	30
2/6/1986	Harvard	State	Death Penalty	24
3/20/1986	State	Castillo	Criminal Law	29

(*continued*)

Date	Petitioner/Appellant (or Event)	Respondent/Appellee	Topic	Chapter
4/3/1986	City of Miami	Florida Literary Distributing Corp.	Constitutional Rights	22
4/30/1986	Batson	Kentucky (U.S.)	Criminal Law	29
5/15/1986	Coastal Petroleum Co.	American Cyanamid Co.	Growth Management	15
5/15/1986	Maxwell	State	Death Penalty	24
7/1/1986	*Parker Lee McDonald becomes Chief Justice*		Justices	28
7/3/1986	Lucas	State	Death Penalty	24
7/10/1986	VMF to the Florida Bar, Application of		Bar Regulation	19
7/17/1986	State	DiGuilio	Criminal	24, 29
9/25/1986	Marr	State	Criminal Law	18
1/6/1987	*Bob Martinez replaces Bob Graham as Governor*		Governor	14
1/30/1987	*Gerald Kogan becomes 73rd Justice*		Justices	14
1/30/1987	*Stephen H. Grimes becomes 72nd Justice*		Justices	14
3/19/1987	Florida Bar in re Rules (Continuing Education)		Legal Services	9
4/22/1987	Hitchcock	Dugger (U.S.)	Death Penalty	24
6/29/1987	Proffitt	State	Death Penalty	24
7/9/1987	Proffitt	State	Death Penalty	24
9/24/1987	King	State	Death Penalty	17
1/7/1988	Bernie	State	Search and Seizure	21
3/10/1988	Blackshear	State	Criminal Law	29
3/10/1988	Perry	State	Death Penalty	17
3/10/1988	State	Slappy	Criminal Law	29
3/10/1988	Tillman	State	Criminal Law	29
3/24/1988	Sturiano	Brooks	Family Tort Immunity	14
7/1/1988	*Raymond Ehrlich becomes Chief Justice*		Justices	18
10/20/1988	Hawkins, In re		Bar Regulation	31
1/23/1989	Florida	Riley (U.S.)	Search and Seizure	21
5/25/1989	Songer	State	Death Penalty	24
6/15/1989	Kibler	State	Criminal Law	29
7/6/1989	Roundtree	State	Criminal Law	29

Date	Petitioner/Appellant (or Event)	Respondent/Appellee	Topic	Chapter
8/31/1989	State	Singletary	Criminal Law	29
10/5/1989	T.W., In re		Personal Privacy	23, 30
11/30/1989	Bostick	State	Search and Seizure	30
12/21/1989	Cox	State	Death Penalty	23, 30
7/1/1990	*Leander Shaw becomes Chief Justice*		Justices	23
9/27/1990	Agriculture and Consumer Services, Dept. of	Bonanno	Jurisdiction	10
1/7/1991	*Raymond Ehrlich retires*		Justices	18
1/15/1991	Douglas	State	Death Penalty	24
1/28/1991	*Major B. Harding becomes 74th Justice*		Justices	14
6/6/1991	Norris, In re		Judicial Ethics	23
7/1/1992	*Rosemary Barkett becomes Chief Justice*		Justices	30
1/9/1994	*Charles T. Wells becomes 75th Justice*		Justices	
4/21/1994	*Chief Justice Rosemary Barkett resigns from court*		Justices	30
5/31/1994	*Parker Lee McDonald retires*		Justices	
8/29/1994	*Harry Lee Anstead becomes 76th Justice*		Justices	
4/17/1997	State	Spaziano	Death Penalty	17
12/10/1997	*Barbara J. Pariente becomes 77th Justice*		Justices	
12/7/1998	*R. Fred Lewis becomes 78th Justice*		Justices	
12/8/1998	*Peggy A. Quince becomes 79th Justice*		Justices	
1/4/1999	*Ben Overton retires*		Justices	
3/11/1999	Weiand	State	Castle Doctrine	22
9/24/1999	Provenzano	Moore	Death Penalty	23
12/2/2004	Amendments to rules of workers' comp. procedure		Jurisdiction	10

I

THE REFORMATION

1

FOUR HORSEMEN
OF THE REFORMATION

On the sunny Tuesday morning after Labor Day in 1975, a sea of black Floridians full of pride and hope filled the wooden pews, stood in the aisles and alcoves, lined the vanilla-colored walls, and flowed into the marble rotunda at the Supreme Court of Florida. They had come by the busload. Never before, as far as anyone could remember, had black Floridians been more than a scattered presence in this courtroom.[1]

The center of attention that September 2 was Joseph Woodrow Hatchett, who had grown up in a segregated black neighborhood of Clearwater and attended a segregated black public high school there. His father had died in 1949 while Joe was still in high school. Joe's mother would remember, as she sat in the courtroom that morning at the age of ninety-one, that Joe came to her then and said, "If you let me stay in school, I'll make you proud of me."[2]

He had indeed made her proud. Today he would put on the robe of a justice of the Supreme Court of Florida and become the first black justice of a state supreme court anywhere in the states of the old Confederacy.

Eighty of the spectators had come from Jacksonville on two buses chartered by the Bethel Baptist Church. Hatchett was part of the congregation there, along with his wife, Betty Lue, and their two daughters, fifteen-year-old Cheryl and twelve-year-old Brenda. Another bus had brought family and friends from Clearwater. No longer just the kid down the street, Joe Hatchett personified the dreams of black Floridians for equal opportunity in America.

For decades, the Florida Supreme Court had thwarted efforts to end segregation and discrimination. As he looked out over the crowd that morning from the chair next to the one Hatchett would occupy, Justice Arthur J. England Jr., who nine months earlier had become the court's first Jewish justice, wondered if a black person had ever felt welcome in this room before.

Sitting four chairs away from Hatchett's, at the right hand of Chief Justice

James C. Adkins Jr., was a man who had been defending the old way of life from the time he was appointed to the Florida Supreme Court in 1949: Justice B. K. Roberts. He had been part of the unanimous court that in 1950 upheld the conviction of the black "Groveland Boys" on doubtful evidence by an all-white jury in Lake County.[3] He had invoked a states' rights theory from the old Confederacy in the court's resistance to integration of the University of Florida Law School in the 1950s. He had orchestrated the closing of historically black Florida A&M Law School in Tallahassee in 1965 to be replaced by a new law school on the white side of the railroad tracks, at Florida State University. The Florida Legislature named the new law school's main building after Roberts, which was a matter of continuing dismay for many students; his name disappeared during a refurbishing of exterior signage in 2013.[4]

Roberts was an extraordinary man of many accomplishments, including leading roles in creation of the state's public defender system in the 1960s and in restructuring the court system in the 1970s. Late in his life he was recognized as a "Great Floridian," and he would end his speeches with a homily to "the proposition that all men are created equal under the law."[5] His dedication to that proposition had not been so clear when it mattered most. Florida's U.S. senators of the 1950s, Spessard L. Holland and George A. Smathers, had argued (as Roberts did) to keep universities segregated. Roberts's admirers would explain his resistance to racial integration as reflecting "a man of his time," born in 1907.

Just below the imposing mahogany rostrum where the justices sat were the dignitaries taking part in this historic investiture. First among them was Governor Reubin O'Donovan Askew, a teetotaling, moralistic, straight arrow of a man from the conservative Florida Panhandle. Askew had stood against segregation almost as long as Roberts had been protecting it. Born in Muscogee, Oklahoma, in 1928, Askew came to Pensacola at the age of nine, so he was not immersed in the Southern segregationist culture. He was a generation younger than the old segregationists who held the top offices in Florida. As president of the Student Government Association at Florida State University in 1951, Askew had pushed the statewide student government association to support desegregation of universities, an effort that earned him an inquisition in the office of FSU President Doak S. Campbell.

In choosing Hatchett for this Supreme Court vacancy, Askew had passed over six politically prominent and well-connected white lawyers and judges. Decades later, after his hair had turned white and his walk had grown feeble, and as leaders in both parties called him one of Florida's greatest governors, Askew would often say that his appointment of Joe Hatchett was the most satisfying decision of his administration.

Hatchett's investiture marked much more than a racial transformation, however. The Supreme Court by then was beginning to embrace the expansion of rights for women, minorities, and gays. Government was opened to public view. It was, as journalist Martin Dyckman labeled it, a "golden age" in state government as young, progressive, public-minded professionals from the cities moved into power in government, replacing populists and so-called good ol' boys who were beholden to utilities, agribusiness, and corporate interests and who secured their political standing with pork-barrel spending and appeals to racial prejudice.

The court itself was experiencing a renaissance after a dark age of scandal. Askew and others were succeeding in their years-long crusade to create a legal system as removed as possible from political pressures, with judges chosen for ability and integrity rather than political connections. Judges and justices often saw themselves as politicians. Until the 1970s, candidates for the Supreme Court would run for office as Republicans or Democrats. There was popular speculation that a lawyer's failure to make a campaign contribution to a judicial candidate might not be good for his clients in that judge's courtroom. When there were mid-term vacancies, the governor filled them for the rest of the term, usually by appointing a friend or political supporter.

Like other politicians, the justices of the Florida Supreme Court had traditionally welcomed visitors to their offices. Youngsters selling cookies, politicians and lobbyists dropping in for coffee, or campaign supporters with cases pending could walk through the silver front doors of the Supreme Court building and up the curved staircase to the justices' office suites on the top floor.

There were more courtly customs, too. Each morning until the early 1970s, a black butler in a white coat bearing a silver tray brought around coffee in china cups, then resumed his main duty of rolling file carts from office to office as justices shared the one file on each case in those days before efficient copiers. The justices would eat lunch together a couple of times a week at Morrison's cafeteria just up the hill. On Wednesdays they would ride together to lunch at the Capital City Country Club, once a city-owned segregated golf facility. After lunch, the justices would linger to watch Justice Richard W. Ervin tee off with a 150-yard shot almost identical to the one the week before and the week before that.

The rotten apple that spoiled the barrel in the early 1970s was Justice David L. McCain, who had lost an election bid for the court in 1968 but won a lame-duck appointment from Governor Claude R. Kirk Jr. in December 1970, less than a month before Kirk left office. Florida Bar President Burton Young had vehemently opposed the appointment. Other justices fell into McCain's ethos of easy virtue. Vassar B. Carlton and James C. Adkins, both elected in 1968, came to the court with good reputations as circuit judges but were weakened by their separate addictions: Carlton's to gambling, and Adkins's to alcohol. Joseph A. Boyd Jr. and Hal P. Dekle thought of themselves as politicians, were intellectually unexceptional, and acquiesced in a little outside help on a difficult and politically sensitive case. The resulting scandals drove away Carlton, Dekle, and McCain. Ervin, known for his liberal dissents, reached mandatory retirement.

The newcomers of the Askew era—Ben F. Overton, Arthur J. England Jr., Alan C. Sundberg, and Joseph W. Hatchett—became the Four Horsemen of a judicial reformation. Only one of them remained on the court longer than eight years, and they often disagreed with each other on cases or policy; however, they shared a powerful commitment to personal and judicial integrity.

Joe Hatchett was born during the Depression. "We were poor but didn't know it," Hatchett recalled.[6] His father, John Hatchett, was the first black field foreman for Bilgore Groves in Pinellas County, with a crew that picked oranges, grapefruit, and tangerines. In the evenings at home, he would compile the accounting of how much his crew had picked that day. For the nine months of the year when there was no fruit to pick, the family would move to a different house on property owned by a winter resident in the exclusive Harbor Oaks section on Clearwater's waterfront. John Hatchett worked as a caretaker.[7] Lula Hatchett, almost fifty when Joe was born in that house, worked as a maid there for twenty-four years. The woman she worked for would hire the Hatchett boys as chauffeurs and handymen during summer vacations.

John and Lula Hatchett had ten children in all, but only five survived—four boys and a girl over a span of more than fifteen years. Joe, born September 17, 1932, was the youngest. He was seven years behind Paul, the next-youngest, who would be Joe's high school shop teacher and, years later, a city commissioner and vice mayor of Clearwater. Their father enforced discipline in the household, even with a whipping from time to time. "And I'm glad he did," Hatchett claimed many decades later.

Joe was nine years old when the United States entered World War II at the end of 1941. His father became a proud and patriotic neighborhood "warden," enforcing nightly blackouts ordered by the government as a precaution against enemy air raids. Hatchett remembers "a lot of religion" in the family, and they were taught to "stand up for something, do the right thing." But in those days, long before civil rights, they also learned that you didn't break the rules.

Joe attended Pinellas High School, the separate public school for Negroes, which would graduate its last class in 1968. He played trombone in the school band, played piano for his Sunday school class at Mount Carmel Baptist Church, played basketball, and after school earned money doing yard work and running the elevator at the Coachman office building in Clearwater or washing towels and linens for a nearby Presbyterian church.

He graduated second in his small high school class of about thirty students. He went to Florida A&M on a scholarship, majored in political science, and played trombone in the Marching 100 band ("They were the Marching 99 until I arrived," he liked to joke). Legendary band director William Foster "had a great ability to build pride in young people," Hatchett recalled many years later. "When I came to FAMU, I had never been a part of anything really good, but that changed with the band. I remember how proud I was to be a part of something this good, this sharp."[8]

Hatchett remembered that during his sophomore year at Florida A & M, political science professor Emmett Bashful, a future chancellor of Southern University of New Orleans, took the class over to the Florida Supreme Court to watch an oral argument. Virgil Hawkins, a middle-aged black man, had petitioned the court in 1949 to order him admitted to the segregated University of Florida Law School. The state hastily created a new "separate and equal" law school for blacks at Florida A&M, but Hawkins rejected that option. The Florida Supreme Court turned Hawkins down four times between 1950 and 1957, unanimously in the first two and 5–2 in the two after *Brown v. Board of Education*. Each time, Hawkins would appeal to the U.S. Supreme Court and win, only to see the Florida Supreme Court devise pretexts for stalling.[9]

Hatchett took ROTC in college to defer being drafted for the Korean War, so he had a two-year military obligation after graduation. Since the war had ended, he spent most of the time in West Germany as a lieutenant in anti-aircraft artillery. It was the first time in his life that he lived without segregation.

After his honorable discharge from the U.S. Army in 1956, Hatchett went to law school. He traced his desire to be a lawyer to an eighth-grade civics teacher, who told him the courts would change America. Avoiding the continuing controversy over integration of the UF law school, Hatchett enrolled at Howard University Law School in Washington, D.C., the nation's preeminent black law school. He remembers that Thurgood Marshall, who had led the NAACP Legal Defense Fund for two decades and successfully argued *Brown v. Board of Education* in 1954, would walk the halls at Howard, his old law school (Class of 1933), and engage students in discussions about the ongoing civil rights litigation. Many of the faculty at the school had worked on the briefs for *Brown*.

Among Hatchett's new friends at Howard was third-year student Leander J.

Shaw Jr. from Virginia, who graduated in 1957 and soon landed in Tallahassee as an assistant professor of law at Florida A&M, where Shaw's father had become dean of graduate studies. After graduating with honors in 1959, Hatchett returned to Florida. He and Shaw studied together for the bar exam in 1959 and rode together to Miami to take it.

This was five years after the *Brown* decision. But it was five years before President Lyndon B. Johnson pushed through Congress one of the most transformative laws in American history, the Civil Rights Act of 1964, which outlawed segregation in hotels, restaurants, and other commercial businesses. Denied a room at the segregated DuPont Plaza Hotel, where the exam was being administered, Hatchett and Shaw stayed at a hotel for Negroes down the street. They could not even eat lunch at the DuPont Plaza unless they ate by themselves on the mezzanine.

Florida had admitted just sixty-six black lawyers in the previous ninety years.[10] In all of America, there were only about 2,100 black lawyers, or less than 1 percent of the legal profession.[11]

Shaw went into law practice in Jacksonville. Twenty years later he would become the second African-American appointed to the Florida Supreme Court.

Hatchett started his law practice in Daytona Beach with a well-known black lawyer named Horace Hill, another Howard Law graduate (class of 1948), who had been arguing the Virgil Hawkins case that day years earlier when Hatchett and his classmates visited the Supreme Court. Soon Hatchett opened his own practice. Along with a typical small law practice he advised civil rights protesters on what they could and couldn't do and how to behave if they were arrested. Then he started filing lawsuits to desegregate public facilities like swimming pools and golf courses and restaurants. When racial protests in St. Augustine became national news with a visit from Martin Luther King Jr., donations poured in from across America to lawyers like Hill and Hatchett. One check Hatchett wishes he had kept instead of cashing was made out to him by perhaps the biggest black entertainer of the era: Sammy Davis Jr.

Much of Hatchett's civil rights practice was in the federal district court, and his work attracted notice in federal circles. In 1966 Hatchett was hired by U.S. Attorney Edward F. Boardman, whose Middle District of Florida sprawled along the Atlantic beaches from the Georgia line, down through Brevard County, and then across central Florida to the Gulf beaches, stretching from Citrus down to Charlotte counties. (Boardman later became a judge on Florida's Second District Court of Appeal.) The U.S. Justice Department had no black prosecutors anywhere in the South in 1966, Hatchett recalled. He commuted to Jacksonville from Daytona, where his wife was teaching. In

August 1967 Hatchett became the chief assistant U.S. attorney. After Richard Nixon was elected president in 1968, John L. Briggs replaced Boardman and asked Hatchett, whom he considered "extremely capable," to stay on in his role. Briggs said Hatchett was able to relate to the North Florida jurors and had "a sense of justice and fairness [that] permeated everything he did." In 1969 the *Daytona Beach News-Journal* wrote a profile of Hatchett and called him "a man on the move—going up."[12]

Among the federal judges Hatchett worked with was William A. McRae, a former Rhodes Scholar appointed in 1961 by President John F. Kennedy. McRae, a 1933 law graduate from the University of Florida, had practiced in Jacksonville and was teaching law at Florida when World War II began. He became a colonel in the Army Air Corps and then resumed teaching before joining Senator Holland in the Bartow firm Holland & Bevis. Four years later, in 1950, McRae lured to Holland, Bevis & McRae another war vet who had been one of his star students and had been practicing law in nearby Arcadia for two years. That young lawyer was Chesterfield H. Smith, who would later push the law firm to international status, lead the rewriting of Florida's Constitution, and become president of the American Bar Association.

McRae's eye for talent was drawn to Joe Hatchett. McRae and the other federal judges oversaw much of the civil rights litigation as well as the federal criminal cases handled by Hatchett and his fellow lawyers in the U.S. Attorney's Office. One day, Hatchett read that Congress, to address the growing caseload, might create the position of federal magistrate to handle pretrial matters and non-jury cases. Hatchett alerted McRae, who had become chief judge in 1971. After the magistrate law passed, McRae, with the support of the other federal judges in the Middle District, appointed Hatchett. Briggs cautioned Hatchett that it might be a "dead end" job.

McRae died on January 27, 1973, but not before giving Hatchett's career another boost. Chesterfield Smith, an early supporter of Askew's campaign for governor, recalled years later that "my former law partner and perhaps my best friend Bill McRae encouraged me to support then-magistrate Joe Hatchett, who served in Jacksonville, for significant judicial advancement."[13]

The 1970 elections in Florida elevated to the state's highest offices two little-known state senators who came from rural areas but reflected progressive values.

In the election to replace retiring Senator Holland, Lawton Chiles from Lakeland garnered attention by rejecting big campaign donations and walking a zig-zagging thousand miles from Century on the Alabama line down to the Florida Keys. He bested former governor Farris Bryant in the Democratic primary and powerful Republican Congressman William C. Cramer in November to win a seat in the U.S. Senate. For governor, Floridians chose Reubin Askew from Pensacola, who had promised government reform and a 5 percent tax on corporations' profits. A respected but largely unknown state senator, Askew won the Democratic primary ahead of the attorney general, the Senate president, and the Dade County mayor. Then he won in November against incumbent Governor Kirk.[14]

Askew despised politics in the selection of judges. He felt judges should not have to seek contributions and make speeches to win elections. But if judges are to be appointed, Askew argued, the appointments shouldn't go to political cronies of the governor. Instead, they should be chosen through a nonpolitical process with the expectation they would rule on the facts and law of each case, without regard to politics or personal relationships. Askew chose a "merit selection" approach that Missouri had adopted in 1940,[15] widely referred to as the "Missouri Plan." Prospective judges would apply for a vacancy and be screened by a "nominating committee," which would send its top choices to the governor, who had to choose from the names on the list.

Efforts to create such a system for all judgeships had failed during the Constitution Revision process of 1968 and were still stalled in the legislature. The governor, however, had the sole constitutional power to fill mid-term vacancies by any method he chose, and Askew seized that opportunity to ensure his appointees had integrity and superior legal ability. In September 1971, he created judicial nominating councils by executive order. He allowed the Florida Bar to appoint three members, the governor would appoint three, and those six would choose three more. They would solicit applications for vacant judgeships and recommend at least three they considered best qualified. Appointed judges still had to face a contested election within two years.

It was a time when political liberalism and investigative journalism were powerful forces. A youth culture focused on sexual freedom and the social use of drugs divided the nation generationally and politically. Racial conflicts, protests against the Vietnam War, and a campaign for equal rights for women and minorities divided Americans intensely and sometimes violently. The U.S. Supreme Court struck down the death penalty in 1972 and most restrictions on abortions in 1973. A voter backlash against liberalism had elevated Republican Richard M. Nixon to the presidency in 1968. He won a landslide reelection in 1972, but a media-driven Watergate scandal over abuses of presidential power led to Nixon's resignation in August 1974 in the face of likely impeachment.

Scandals in Florida during the same period drove from office not only three

Supreme Court justices but also the lieutenant governor and three of the six elected members of the Florida Cabinet—the education commissioner, the treasurer/insurance commissioner, and the comptroller/banking commissioner. Chief Justice Adkins complained in an interview with the *Florida Bar Journal*, "We on the court realize that many of the Florida newspapers would like to have a Florida Watergate if they could." He went on, "Anything we do is magnified in hopes it will bring down something on the court."[16]

With ethics, accountability and judicial reform already a prominent theme in Florida politics, the *Tampa Tribune* in August 1973 published the first story in what became a long and memorable scandal focused on the Florida Supreme Court. The newspaper reported, based on an anonymous, unsubstantiated report, that bribery had influenced the Florida Supreme Court's decision in a racetrack case.[17] A few days later, the *St. Petersburg Times* followed with a story saying Justice McCain had unsuccessfully tried to influence two judges on the Second District Court of Appeal to overturn the criminal conviction of a campaign supporter and then voted with a majority of the Supreme Court to do what the court of appeal had refused to do.[18]

In November, newspapers revealed a months-old investigation of Justice Dekle for trying to influence a circuit judge presiding over a trial involving a campaign supporter. In December, the *Times* revealed questionable contacts between a utility lawyer and Justices Boyd and Dekle as the court considered a multimillion-dollar utility case. That case would determine whether the new corporate profits tax Askew had championed would be treated as a business expense and passed on to utility customers through higher electric rates. Askew had promised voters they would not be stuck with the tax. Utilities appeared to be secretly influencing the court to thwart Askew's promise.

The chief justice serving when the scandals began unfolding, Vassar B. Carlton (a distant cousin of former governor Doyle Carlton), became caught up in the scandal as well. Once a popular circuit judge who served for twenty-seven years on county and circuit courts in Brevard County, Carlton had won election to the Florida Supreme Court in 1968 along with Adkins and Boyd.[19] Carlton's problems were largely personal ones. His second wife, Grace, had died of leukemia on January 17, 1973. Her death appeared to devastate him. One of his research assistants later testified that Carlton left opinion writing to his aides and mostly sat in his office with a cigar. He also loved gambling and was a regular and shrewd bettor at the dog track in Jefferson County, just east of Tallahassee.

In the fall of 1973, a reporter for WPLG-TV in Miami, Clarence Jones, trailed Carlton to Las Vegas and came back with video of Carlton gambling in a casino as two women looked on. Jones reported a source's tip that the junket had been subsidized by gambling interests. Not long after, in January 1974, sixty-two-year-old Carlton married Sue Collins. He described Collins as a friend of the family, and reporters noted that she was half his age. He also announced his retirement, effective February 28, with the explanation that he was weary of court work and would make $8,953 a year more from retirement pay than from his current state paycheck after the deductions. What Carlton did not say, and what a statement from the chairman of the Judicial Qualifications Commission (JQC) carefully obscured, was that the commission had been investigating Carlton but dropped the case when Carlton decided to retire.[20] (He lived another thirty years and died August 31, 2005.)

Adkins became chief justice a year ahead of schedule on March 1, 1974, and was unopposed for reelection to the court that November. Not long after the election, newspapers revealed that, three years earlier, the JQC and Adkins had entered into an odd probation-style agreement. Adkins had appeared drunk at the morning investiture of U.S. Circuit Court of Appeals Judge Paul H. Roney in St. Petersburg in 1972. JQC Vice Chairman Richard T. Earle was there. A Democrat, Adkins had been a longtime and respected circuit judge in Gainesville. He had beaten Republican McCain in the 1968 election for the Supreme Court by positioning himself as such a hardline conservative that the liberal *St. Petersburg Times* had endorsed McCain. In Tallahassee, though, another part of Adkins's past caught up with him. He brought a varied and unhappy marital history with him. He had married during law school in 1937, got a divorce the same year, was married again the next year, and had been through two more marriages by 1950. His marriage to Ethel May Fox endured for twenty-three years, but by 1969 he was unhappy at home and liked hanging out at bars after work. After five failed marriages, Adkins made alcohol and the bar scene a part of many evenings.

The JQC posed to Adkins a difficult choice: face an inquiry that might result in a reprimand or removal from office, or sign an undated letter of resignation that the JQC would send to the governor if Adkins were ever caught drinking again. After a stern lecture from B. K. Roberts,[21] Adkins signed the letter. He'd still go to bars with law clerks and friends, but he never drank. No one ever saw him drink alcohol again. He went on to serve a total of eighteen years on the court until mandatory retirement in 1987.

2

1974

Overton and England

The resignation of Chief Justice Carlton at the end of February 1974 created Governor Askew's first opportunity to bring his philosophy of judicial integrity and independence to the Florida Supreme Court. Using his new merit-selection process for the first time in the selection of a justice, Askew appointed Ben F. Overton, the chief judge of the Sixth Judicial Circuit in St. Petersburg and chairman of the Florida Conference of Circuit Judges.[1]

Overton was an ideal first appointment. Tall and stocky, with a no-non-sense demeanor and a reputation for integrity, Overton was clearly not going to become a captive of the court's ethical casualness. Yet he also had good political sense in dealing with public issues. He had chaired U.S. Senator Spessard Holland's reelection campaigns on Florida's west coast in 1958 and 1964. He also knew, and was known by, most of the circuit judges in the state.

He understood and even enjoyed judicial administration. When he was chief judge, he would have a problem-solving breakfast once a month with the other three elected officials with major responsibilities for criminal justice in Pinellas County: Sheriff Donald Genung, State Attorney James T. Russell, and Public Defender Robert Jagger. Pinellas was one of the first counties where a criminal judge would use "adjudication withheld" and probation instead of finding defendants guilty. Russell supported pretrial intervention programs and the guardian ad litem. Stetson Law Dean Harold L. "Tom" Sebring, a former Supreme Court justice, created the first clinical programs for third-year students to work as public defenders in criminal cases—a program that won Supreme Court approval when Sebring paid a return visit to the Supreme Court building and walked from office to office getting justices' signatures, according to Overton.

When the legislature was considering court reforms in 1971, then-Representative H. Talbot "Sandy" D'Alemberte as House Judiciary chairman had asked staff director Janet Reno to look at statistics and find a judicial circuit that would be a good model. Reno singled out the Sixth Circuit, where Overton was chief judge. Overton became an unofficial advisor to the Judiciary Committee.[2] More important, he helped neutralize the circuit judges' long-standing opposition to court consolidation and nonpartisan elections. D'Alemberte called Overton's leadership "spectacular."

Overton was born December 16, 1926, in Green Bay, Wisconsin, but the family moved to Duluth and later Winona in Minnesota, then to La Crosse, Wisconsin. His father was an expert on transportation rates and the Interstate Commerce Commission. He worked for various trucking and railroad firms seeking higher rates or for local governments seeking lower rates. With trucking businesses struggling during the fuel shortages of World War II, the elder Benjamin Overton in 1944 got a job in Florida working to get better transportation rates for the City of St. Petersburg and Pinellas County. Ben's mother stayed behind in La Crosse until Ben finished high school in 1945, and Ben went into the army as a private a few weeks before Japan's surrender.

He spent two years "stateside," came out of the army in March 1947, and had already registered at the University of Wisconsin when his mother, by then in St. Petersburg, encouraged him to enroll at the University of Florida instead. Even before finishing his undergraduate degree, Overton started taking law school classes. He received a B.A. in business administration in 1951 and his law degree in 1952. He moved to St. Petersburg with his wife, Marilyn, whom he had met on a double date (each was with someone else) and married during law school. His early law practice included the role of city attorney for St. Petersburg Beach. Eventually he joined the law firm of Henry C. Baynard and William McLeod, whose clients included banks and the *St. Petersburg Times*.

Baynard had been a respected state senator when Spessard Holland was governor (1941–45), and the two remained close after Holland became a U.S. senator in 1946. Baynard made Overton the Holland campaign manager for the west coast of Florida—first in 1958 (when Holland was challenged in the Democratic primary by Claude Pepper, who had lost his U.S. Senate seat in 1950) and again in 1964 (when Holland was challenged by Republican newcomer Claude Kirk). In 1960 Overton was active in the campaign of Democrat Farris Bryant for governor.

In 1961 Overton's reserve unit was called back to military duty during the Berlin Wall crisis. Overton was a captain then. The company clerk was Martin Dyckman, whose reporting for the *St. Petersburg Times* a decade later would inspire public support for the judicial reforms Overton championed.[3] After returning to the law firm, Overton handled property condemnations for some of the county's major new transportation projects.[4] He also taught civil procedure and trial practice as an adjunct professor at Stetson Law School.

One day in 1964, Sebring called Overton, invited him to lunch, and told him to bring Marilyn. Sebring knew Governor Bryant was about to offer Overton a new judgeship in the Sixth Circuit, and Sebring told Overton he should take it. If he did, Sebring added, Overton should think of the judiciary as a lifetime commitment and "not a stepping-stone to a better law practice." The Overtons had three children and would see Ben's salary drop from $32,000 that year to $22,000. "You are going to have to learn to wear Schwobilt suits," Sebring said, referring to a chain of discount men's stores.

As a judge, Overton was surprised by the inadequacy of some of the lawyers he saw in his courtroom. Overton had been in a firm with highly competent lawyers. Now he found himself calling his old law firm for some extra research that he thought the lawyers on the case had failed to provide. Later, the tougher canons of ethics Overton helped establish in 1973 would prohibit that kind of help unless the judge notified the parties. Oddly enough, the old practice Overton had followed was cited by Justices Boyd and Dekle in defending against charges of improper contacts on pending cases. (Overton, however, wasn't getting the undisclosed help from parties to the case.) The experience helped propel his interest in legal training and legal ethics as well as his reputation among other justices and law clerks for citing obscure out-of-state cases that weren't cited in briefs.

In 1971 Overton was selected chief judge of the Sixth Circuit. He replaced Richard Kelly, whose behavior had been so erratic that two-thirds of the lawyers in Pasco County, where Kelly was assigned, routinely asked that he disqualify himself in their cases. The Florida House of Representatives even impeached Kelly in 1963 for what it considered a pattern of harassing lawyers and others, but the Senate would not remove him. That episode had inspired the creation of the Judicial Qualifications Commission in 1966, so there could be a process other than impeachment to investigate and punish judges' misbehavior.

A year into his role as chief judge, Overton began a one-year term as chairman of the Florida Conference of Circuit Judges in 1972. It was a fateful step in his life. A determined advocate of court reform and a stronger code of judicial ethics, neither of which was universally popular among circuit judges, Overton impressed Governor Askew. He also impressed Pensacola lawyer Dixie Beggs, who was the vice chairman of the special committee that developed the new ethics code and later became the first chairman of the Supreme Court Nominating Commission.

Overton almost didn't apply for the Carlton vacancy. Overton's mother was very ill (she died three weeks after he joined the Supreme Court). But he said others in his family encouraged him, and he changed his mind at the last minute. His close friend Alan C. Sundberg, also of St. Petersburg, was a little late finding out and also applied. Sundberg had been manager of Overton's campaign to retain his judgeship in 1966—an unopposed election, as Sundberg would often add wryly to emphasize his meager political experience.

Twenty-three others also applied for the appointment. Only three would make the final list of nominees forwarded to the governor. One applicant was former Gov. LeRoy Collins, a revered moderate governor (1955–61) who later served as President Lyndon Johnson's chief mediator on racial conflicts, then ran for the U.S. Senate in 1968 and lost. Members of the nominating commission considered the effect of a Collins nomination on Askew, who idolized Collins. As a college student at FSU in 1950, Askew had worked on Collins's reelection campaign for the state Senate. It would be awkward for him to deny Collins a seat on the Supreme Court. Yet, after all his criticism of cronyism, it would be even more awkward for Askew to give his first appointment to a former governor and recent political candidate who had no judicial experience. Some commission members also saw Collins as more politician than lawyer: at sixty-five years old, he was just five years from the mandatory retirement age. Collins was stung not to make the list of nominees. Askew, who said he forbade contact between his staff and the nominating commissions, said he did not know of Collins's application.[5]

The commission nominated both Overton and Sundberg, along with Miami lawyer Mallory Horton, who had served on the Third District Court of Appeal but stepped down because he found the salary inadequate at a time when four of his six children were in college. It was an easy choice for Askew. He was deeply appreciative of Overton's role in judicial reform and respected Overton's integrity and his administrative ability. Overton started his duties on special assignment from Chief Justice Adkins even before his formal investiture on March 27, 1974.

When Overton arrived at the court, he, like other outsiders, was unaware of the extent of the scandals that were just beginning to unfold. But he knew enough to keep his distance from others on the court. Baynard, a former classmate of B. K. Roberts, warned Overton not to become indebted to anyone. And he didn't. Roberts called Overton to offer temporary living quarters in a cottage behind Roberts's main house, but Overton declined and lived in his motor home in a trailer park until he and Marilyn could buy a house.

Overton did have a strong connection to Justice Ervin. As attorney general,

Ervin had hired Overton right out of law school to a one-year position as special assistant attorney general. Ervin always reserved a spot for a graduate of the University of Florida Law School. A ten-year veteran on the court when Overton arrived there, Ervin had shared a room with Roberts during his senior year of law school, and their offices were across from each other at the court. But now they rarely spoke to each other except in formal court conferences. Ervin also cautioned Overton to "be careful."

Overton kept even Ervin at some distance. For one thing, Ervin was more liberal than Overton, but Overton really didn't trust anyone at the court except his own clerks. As the scandals began unfolding, and Overton kept to himself, he came to be isolated at the north end of the corridor on the top floor. Along with his old tendency to cite obscure cases from other jurisdictions when he wrote opinions, Overton left clerks in others' offices thinking of him as remote and arrogant. Others had the impression that he saw himself as Askew's white knight. Overton saw himself as simply heeding those early warnings: "Be careful."

Ervin himself was not above politics when it came to the selection of his successor. He had been reelected without opposition in 1972 for a term lasting six years, but the Florida Constitution's mandatory retirement for judges at age seventy would force him out on January 26, 1975. Two floors below the justices' offices in the Supreme Court building was the First District Court of Appeal, and one of the judges on that court, Sam Spector, aspired to the Supreme Court. Spector had been an assistant attorney general under Ervin, and he had even been assigned to the big reapportionment case at the U.S. Supreme Court in 1965–66. Ervin saw him as "one of his boys," in Overton's words. Spector also was close to Roberts. Spector had recently written a controversial opinion allowing Roberts's longtime big client and patron, the influential industrialist Ed Ball, to keep a fence across the Wakulla River to exclude boaters from his Wakulla Springs resort (which came into state ownership years later).[6]

Though a respected DCA judge, Spector could not count on an appointment from Askew, even if he made it through the nominating commission. An election, on the other hand, with the support of Roberts and Ervin, had a high probability of success. Ervin, who had gotten on the court through appointment, told others he preferred the election system and suspected the merit-selection process would allow lawyers from big law firms to control the appointments.

Ervin undertook to control his own succession. A vacancy on January 26 clearly would create a mid-term vacancy to be filled by appointment. Ervin instead picked January 6 to retire—the same day the terms of Adkins, Boyd, and new appointee Overton would end. All three had to be elected to new six-year terms. So Ervin molded his mid-term departure to coincide with the end of the others' terms. He wrote the governor a letter of resignation in February 1974—even before Overton's arrival—to be effective January 6. He declared his decision was irrevocable, to ensure that the seat could be "filled by the person who will be elected in the 1974 judicial election."

There was no direct evidence of an orchestrated effort on behalf of an election in general or Spector in particular. Certainly Ervin's letter gave plenty of notice to other possible candidates to prepare for an election. The word around the capital, however, was that Spector had the inside track for the seat and was the preferred candidate of Roberts and Ervin. That alone would be enough to discourage most prospective candidates.

As the July qualifying period neared, Attorney General Robert L. Shevin issued a formal opinion that the vacancy should be filled by appointment. Shevin, a former state senator from Miami, was another reformer in the Askew mold who had won election to the State House from Dade County in 1964 and won his statewide office in 1970, when Attorney General Earl Faircloth ran unsuccessfully for governor. In Shevin's view, the term for which Ervin was elected (without opposition) in 1972 ran until January 1979. Mandatory retirement rules intervened to force his retirement on January 26, 1975, but either a resignation or a mandatory retirement would create a mid-term vacancy, which under the Constitution was to be filled by appointment. However, there was no "vacancy" until the resignation took effect, Shevin declared, because any resignation effective in the future could be withdrawn. Ervin's resignation letter, however, seemed to anticipate that argument in declaring his decision irrevocable.

Arthur England kept hearing the rumor that, despite Shevin's opinion, Spector would file candidate qualifying papers and, if refused, petition the Supreme Court, which would then vote in favor of an election. Whatever orchestrated effort there might have been on Spector's behalf, it didn't reckon on the determined intervention of England or the political impact of the unfolding court scandal.

A tax lawyer from Miami, England had been a key draftsman of Askew's corporate profits tax legislation, which the voters had approved in 1971. Askew had promised voters the tax would not increase utility rates. The Public Service Commission, then an elected body, partly adopted that position in setting utility rates. Gulf Power Company and other utilities appealed to the Supreme Court. England was Askew's counsel in the case. As months went by with the justices closely divided, Edward L. Mason, a former Dade County commissioner and former public service commissioner who represented Gulf Telephone Company and St. Joseph Telephone Company, had given Dekle and Boyd a secret memorandum that was in effect a draft opinion.[7]

In January 1974, a month after the *St. Petersburg Times* revealed Mason's secret contacts with Dekle and Boyd, the court ruled against Askew and the PSC in a 4–1 decision, written by Dekle, with Ervin dissenting.[8] As the scandal over Mason's secret memo grew, the court reversed itself on June 13. Ervin's dissent turned into a majority opinion supporting the PSC and preserving Askew's partial victory.[9]

England had left Askew's staff but was frequently in Tallahassee for work on the Administrative Procedure Act for the Law Revision Council. Because of his earlier role in drafting the corporate profits tax that was now the centerpiece in the PSC case, England was following with particular interest both the scandal and the politics of the Ervin retirement.

England tried to recruit other lawyers to run against Spector, but he invariably got the response, "I practice law in this state. No thanks." The message was that lawyers did not want to make an adversary out of the incumbent justices and challenge a likely winner. England didn't have that problem. His practice was in federal tax law. Except for his role with Askew, he did not appear in state courts. "What have I got to lose?" he told himself. Decades later he said, "It was my wild idea. Nobody else would do it."[10]

England enlisted friend and former law partner D'Alemberte as his lawyer in the maneuvering over the vacancy. When the candidate qualifying period for fall elections opened in July, England showed up at the state's Division of Elections to qualify. Secretary of State Dorothy Glisson declined to take the qualifying papers because of Shevin's opinion that the vacancy was to be filled by appointment. England got her to put her decision in writing, then waited.

On the next-to-last day of qualifying, July 22, Spector showed up to qualify, got the same refusal from Glisson, and immediately went across the street to the Supreme Court. He filed a petition seeking a writ of mandamus to compel the Secretary of State to accept his qualifying papers. England and D'Alemberte filed a motion to intervene in the case and argued that the vacancy should be filled by appointment, but if an election were held, England should be allowed to qualify and run. England also asked the court to establish when the term would end if the seat were filled by election. Focusing on the termination date would underscore the mid-term nature of the vacancy.

Time was short—just fifty-two days until the September 10 election (when non-partisan judicial elections were being held statewide for the first time).

The court set a hearing for August 2. Immediately after the hearing, it ordered the seat filled by election.

It was not until December—after the election—that the court explained its decision.[11] Justice Dekle's opinion for a 5–2 majority noted Ervin's "magnanimous" gesture in leaving office early "to accommodate the electorate." The constitutional ambiguity should be resolved in favor of election, Dekle wrote. He also noted that the governor's appointment power had been narrowed when merit selection came into the Constitution in 1972; before, appointments were for an entire unexpired term, but now judicial appointees had to stand for election at the next statewide election.

Justice Boyd, in dissent, countered that he had "searched in vain for a constitutional provision which would permit the vacancy . . . to be filled by popular vote. There is simply no such language in the Florida Constitution." It was a striking position for Boyd, a product of the political system who tended toward populist positions. Overton dissented, too, but he did not explain why.

Overton's vote certainly reflected his support for the merit-selection process that had brought him to the court. But it turns out that Overton stopped the majority from cutting England's term short. Overton's role is revealed in a box of archived files England later assembled in preparation for presiding, as chief justice, over the Senate impeachment trial of Judge Samuel Smith, which also raised an issue over when a "vacancy" occurred.[12]

An early draft of Dekle's opinion in *Spector v. Glisson*, being prepared after England had beaten Spector, declared that the term of Ervin's successor would extend to the end of the term for which the departing justice was originally elected. That meant England's term would end in January 1979, since Ervin had been reelected to a six-year term beginning in January 1973. The selection was not being treated as a mid-term vacancy for purposes of how the successor was chosen but was being treated as a mid-term vacancy in determining the length of the term. The Spector allies thus were limiting England's term to four years. It is sheer speculation whether their view of the term would have been different had their friend Spector won.

Upon seeing Dekle's draft, Overton wrote a private memo to "the Court" and said Dekle's view conflicted with an opinion of the attorney general that an election was for a full term. More significantly, it "will adversely affect up to thirty-seven county judges, forty-seven circuit judges, five district courts of appeal judges, and one Supreme Court justice in addition to Justice England, who were successful candidates in the 1974 election." That other Supreme Court justice was himself. It is not clear why he thought so, since his predecessor, Carlton, would have been up for election in 1974 anyway. If the court were going to decide the term England would serve, Overton said, he would have to recuse himself and the court should have counsel brief and argue the issue.

Dekle backed off. The issue went unmentioned in the published opinion. The court denied D'Alemberte's request for a rehearing to address the issue. D'Alemberte and England did not know they were better off letting that sleeping dog lie.

Losing on the election issue proved lucky for England. Askew later told him he would not have appointed one of his staff members—including England—to the court because it would look like cronyism. England also later concluded that his lack of trial or judicial experience might have blocked him from a recommendation from a nominating commission. As for the length of the term, the question never came up again. England served a full six-year term before standing successfully for retention in 1980.

At least the 1974 election was nonpartisan. In 1970 the legislature had tried to change the judicial elections from partisan ones held in November to nonpartisan ones held in September along with the party primaries. But Governor Kirk vetoed the legislation. The next year, the legislature passed it again, and Askew happily signed it.[13] Ervin ran unopposed in 1972. McCain, who had two opponents in 1972, won with the help of four-figure contributions from a number of special-interest organizations.

In 1974, however, three seats besides Ervin's were up for election. Adkins and Boyd, first elected in 1968, were finishing their first six-year terms. Adkins drew no opposition. Boyd, who was in the headlines because of the Ed Mason memorandum, was opposed by Spector's brother-in-law, Tallahassee lawyer Rivers Buford Jr., who had run against McCain in 1972 and whose father had served on the Supreme Court for twenty-three years. A prolific glad-hander who had previously been a Dade County commissioner, Boyd got 64 percent of the vote.

Overton, who had been in office only a few months, drew opposition from Miami Circuit Judge Shelby Highsmith, who years later would be appointed a federal district judge by President George H. W. Bush. Highsmith's candidacy was boosted by his visible role a few years earlier on Governor Kirk's "war on crime" commission.

Overton had a secret weapon in his campaign: his connections to the old Spessard Holland campaign organization. Overton called Senator Holland's former chief aide in Florida, Merrill Winslett, who agreed to come out of retirement and run Overton's campaign for nothing but expenses. Winslett prescribed a $100 limit on contributions, called Holland's local campaign chairmen, and essentially resurrected the old Holland organization on Overton's behalf.

Overton went to almost every county, where he would speak at a civic club, visit the local radio and TV stations, and pay special attention to weekly newspapers. Winslett's view was that daily papers would be in the trash by dinner time, but the small weeklies would be around all week, probably with Overton's picture on the front. Overton won with 65 percent of the vote, barely better than Boyd.

And then there was the England-Spector campaign. Spector had both political and judicial experience, while England had never been a judge or seriously involved in a campaign. D'Alemberte was strategic advisor, and the campaign staff consisted of England's former secretary, a young law associate, England's wife DeeDee, and their four daughters—all working out of his house. Intellectual and formal without a trace of a cracker accent or attitude, England was not a natural politician. Overton remarked with a chuckle that England was "a fish out of water." One of England's key supporters in Jacksonville, after interrupting a debate over the death penalty that England was having with a voter at a campaign rally, encouraged England to spend his time elsewhere and let his local supporters handle the campaign there.

England's former law partner Joseph P. Klock Jr. of Steel, Hector & Davis, upstairs from England's office at Paul & Thomson, had a plane and would fly England around the state. Sometimes England, a pilot himself, would take the controls. Askew was running for reelection that year, and Askew supporters, including newspaper editorial boards, were reliable England supporters. In St. Petersburg, England met one of Overton's key supporters, Alan Sundberg, who declined to work for England lest it dilute his efforts on behalf of Overton. After Sundberg joined the court, the two became close friends and allies.

Born December 23, 1932, in Dayton, Ohio, and raised in Shaker Heights, England had an Ivy League education from the University of Pennsylvania. After getting a B.S. from Penn's Wharton School of Finance in 1955, he spent two years in army counter-intelligence in Munich, Germany, returned to Penn Law School, and graduated *magna cum laude* in 1961. He joined one of New York City's premier law firms, commonly known as Dewey Ballantine. In 1964 England moved to Florida to join the Miami office of the tax-law firm headed by Hugh Culverhouse, who was on his way to making multiple fortunes from investments and who in 1974 was awarded the Tampa Bay Buccaneers expansion football franchise. Culverhouse credited England with the strategy and arguments that persuaded the U.S. Tax Court to make a landmark decision treating works of art as an investment—a boon to many wealthy clients.

England became part of a circle of politically active, progressive lawyers in Miami. Among them were Richard Pettigrew, a state legislator, and Sandy D'Alemberte, who would take advantage of court-ordered reapportionment in 1966 to win his own seat in the legislature. England helped in D'Alemberte's campaign. In 1969 England left the Culverhouse firm to become the lead tax lawyer at the firm where D'Alemberte was a senior partner: McCarthy, Steel, Hector & Davis.

Meanwhile, in Tallahassee, some young legislative aides, including an FSU law student and future Pettigrew chief of staff named Eugene Stearns, developed an argument for a "fair tax" on corporations to reduce the disproportionate sales tax burden on poor and middle-class Floridians. They wanted it to be a major campaign theme for a candidate for governor in 1970. The candidate they had in mind was D'Alemberte. When D'Alemberte declined to run, they took the idea to Askew, who had shown no previous interest in tax reform but needed something to catapult him out of political obscurity. Askew seized the idea and made it the centerpiece of his campaign for governor. The plan called for a "corporate profits" tax, so named to avoid the dreaded term "income tax."[14] After Askew won the election, Pettigrew asked England, the Ivy League tax lawyer, to come to Tallahassee as special tax counsel to the House to turn the idea into law.

At Askew's inauguration, England was sitting next to Stearns. They heard Askew announce that "today" he would ask the Supreme Court for an advisory opinion on whether a constitutional amendment was needed for the "corporate profits" tax. The Florida Constitution prohibited an income tax on "residents and citizens" and said nothing about corporations. England turned to Stearns. "Who is drafting that?" he asked. Replied Stearns: "Oh, I forgot to tell you. You are."[15]

Although England formally was working for Speaker Pettigrew, not Askew, he left in the middle of Askew's inauguration speech and had the formal letter to the court drafted and filed by 5 p.m. The state was projecting a revenue gap of more than $200 million in the next fiscal year, a gap that could be closed by a corporate income tax. Corporate interests, hoping to have the court declare a corporate income tax a violation of the Florida Constitution unless the voters approved an amendment, filed their own briefs with the court. Among them were the St. Regis Paper Company, the largest employer in Askew's hometown of Pensacola, and Associated Industries, an aggressive lobbyist for Florida business, which was represented by one of the candidates Askew had beaten in the governor's race, outgoing Senate President John E. Mathews Jr.

The pro-business court quickly ruled 6–1 that corporations were "citizens" protected by the constitutional provision forbidding income taxes.[16] Ervin's dissent argued that the words "resident" and "citizen" "plainly bring to mind only natural persons." After the loss, England drafted not only the tax legislation itself but also a constitutional amendment, which was passed by the legislature and ratified by voters by a 2–1 margin in a special election in November 1971. England then moved to Askew's staff as consumer advisor and drafted the 1973 Florida Deceptive and Unfair Trade Practices Act.

These roles, plus an easy manner with journalists, got his name in Florida newspapers often. He returned to private practice in Miami, with the media-connected law firm headed by Dan Paul and Parker Thomson, but kept a hand in public affairs as the Law Revision Council "reporter" (meaning principal draftsman) for rewriting the Florida Administrative Procedure Act in 1974.

Opening his campaign for the court on August 6, 1974, England remarked, "Over the years, the Florida high court has been accused of being 'political' as much as it is 'judicial.' In recent months a majority of the court seems to have justified those charges."[17] He cited a decision admitting Ervin's brother, Ben, to the Bar even though he had failed the Bar exam four times; decisions limiting investigations of judges and Cabinet members; and the Spector decision itself, thus associating Spector with the shenanigans of the Supreme Court even though he was not on it.

Spector fired back that England had authored the corporate income tax and was from "the McGovern wing" of the Democratic Party, referring to the party's liberal nominee for president in 1972. Someone anonymously filed a Bar ethics complaint against England for criticizing a sitting judge after he told an editorial board that Spector had written an opinion for the appellate court limiting press access. The complaint went nowhere.

England's favorite story of the campaign was his effort to win the support of the heavily Jewish condo residents in Broward County. Annie Ackerman, a political force among condo residents, invited England and Spector to speak, but only England showed up. Soon she called to tell him the association had decided to endorse Spector because Spector was Jewish and England was not. England was stunned. "You've got it backwards," he said. The condo residents thought "Spector" sounded more Jewish than "England," and the "Jr." in his name had misled the association, since it is rare for a Jewish baby to be named after a living person. Ackerman invited England back, and England made sure this time to mention his service as president of Temple Israel in Tallahassee. Perhaps parts of Florida less inclined to support Jewish candidates never suspected.

England had no previous judicial experience, was not active in the Bar, had no Florida alumni network from his university or law school, had no personal wealth, no political consultants. He would show up at political events along with Overton, see people coming over to greet Overton, and remark to his colleague, "They don't know who I am." D'Alemberte gave England a ride to a television station on election night and confided for the first time that he thought England "didn't have a chance in hell" of winning.

But he did win, with 58 percent of the vote. England joined the Supreme Court on January 6, 1975, and became its first Jewish justice. He moved into Ervin's old office across the hall from Roberts in the south wing of the top floor, at the opposite end of the corridor from Overton. Like Overton, England avoided a close relationship with Roberts or the other justices and felt hostility from Roberts in particular. "I had to be very careful," England said. "He had cousins in the post office, in the marshal's office, on the Judicial Council, everywhere." England told his staff not to have conversations about court matters with other court staff except to carry out their responsibilities. He told them, "We are an island."

Among the less consequential changes he instigated during his tenure, this first Jewish justice eliminated what he called the "archaic" use of "A.D."—the abbreviation for Anno Domini, Latin for "Year of our Lord"—in writing dates in opinions and orders. It was Supreme Court Clerk Sid J. White who would have to implement his request. "I promised Sid White," England said, "that if there's ever any confusion between the opinion of January 1985 A.D. and the one of the same year B.C., I personally assume the responsibility."[18]

3

1975

Sundberg and Hatchett

As the 1974 campaigns moved forward, so did the JQC investigations of Mc-Cain, Dekle, and Boyd—and so did investigations of two Cabinet members by State Attorney Ed Austin of Jacksonville, who had been appointed by Askew as special prosecutor. The court itself was thwarting both sets of investigations at every opportunity.

In February 1974 the court declared that judges are immune from ethics charges over misconduct that happened more than two years before their current terms began.[1] One year later, the court upheld a lower-court decision that invalidated a criminal indictment of one of the Cabinet members.[2] In between, in the summer of 1974, Chief Justice Adkins generated widespread criticism by issuing an order, without notice or any hearing or even consultation with the full court, stopping a grand jury investigation of a Cabinet member up for reelection that fall. The order was rescinded after a hearing and after pressure from Overton and others, but it was widely viewed as another sign of the court protecting the traditions of easy political virtue.[3]

The ruling in February 1974 immunizing judges from accountability for older ethics violations called into question the JQC inquiry into the most serious charges against McCain. One concern was a pattern of decisions favoring parties represented by McCain's friend and supporter Joseph D. Farish Jr., a plaintiffs' lawyer in West Palm Beach. Another focused on McCain's effort to influence the two judges on the Second District Court of Appeal, Robert T. Mann and Joseph McNulty, to reverse the bribery conviction of Richard Nell, president of a union local in Ft. Lauderdale. McNulty and Mann were particularly unlikely targets of influence because of their reputations for integrity. As a prominent legislator, Mann had urged passage of ethics legislation with the observation, in a speech on the House floor: "We're all agreed that no member of this chamber can be bought. The purpose of these rules, however, is to assure the public that a legislator can't be rented for a few months."[4] Mann and McNulty reported McCain to the JQC.

The court's creation of a "statute of limitations" on ethics cases would not, however, protect McCain from an allegation that Nell had bribed McCain with $10,000 two days before the court issued a 5–2 decision reversing the conviction. Nell had been convicted, interestingly enough, of bribing local officials over a permit. The Nell appeal originally was heard by a panel of five justices, but the court was split 3–2, with Roberts writing an opinion joined by Adkins and Dekle that was a creative limitation on the crime of bribery. It said there was no bribery because they did not actually need the license they were trying to get. Bribery happens "only when the object sought to be accomplished comes within the scope of the official's public capacity or duty."

Boyd and Ervin in dissent echoed Judge Mann's lower-court opinion: the "scurrilous peddling of one's influence" is what the law prohibits, and the ability of a public official to influence outcomes is not limited to his actual authority. The 3–2 split in a five-justice panel meant that the other two justices would join the case. Carlton and McCain came in, and both sided with the majority. (The legislature later neutralized the ruling by creating the separate offense of "unlawful compensation."[5])

As for Dekle, he faced two accusations. One involved Ed Mason's memo in the corporate tax case. The other went back much further, to a conversation Dekle had with a trial judge in Panama City, W.L. Fitzpatrick, on behalf of a campaign supporter involved in a case in Fitzpatrick's court. Shocked by this obvious effort at influence, Fitzpatrick first delayed his ruling, then after a second contact from Dekle, recused himself entirely. He explained why privately to his fellow judges and to counsel in the case (well-known Tallahassee lawyer Dexter Douglass was on the opposite side from Dekle's supporter), but the judge did not talk to the JQC until JQC members heard about it and contacted him. The JQC gave Dekle formal notice of the investigation on May 3, 1973. Dekle responded with a letter that apologized "if I were in any violation." Two months later, Mason handed Dekle the envelope containing the secret memorandum that would be the center of the second case against Dekle.

In February 1974 the JQC voted 8–4 that Dekle had committed conduct unbecoming a judge in the Fitzpatrick case, but it could not produce the supermajority vote need to recommend punishment. The case sat in limbo.

The one case against Boyd, like the second against Dekle, was over the Mason document. Boyd's connection with the document became known several months after Dekle's, but his involvement was the most memorable episode of the entire scandal. While the Mason and Boyd accounts differed in many respects, Boyd most likely received the document after the two men played golf. He was the justice assigned to write the opinion, which was to overturn the PSC's decision and adopt the utilities' position. After a law clerk noticed the unusual document in the case file, Boyd testified that he realized its impropriety, took the document (and his law clerk) to the justices' restroom at the court, tore the document into "seventeen equal parts," and flushed it down the toilet.[6] Later he told journalist Thomas R. "Ray" Reynolds that the comment, which stuck with Boyd the rest of his life, was "carefully intended" to illustrate that "you're certainly not going to be using it."[7]

The cases against McCain, considered to contain the most serious violations, were stalled by their complexity, including the effect of the court-imposed bar against pursuing older ethics violations, and by the limited resources of the JQC, which relied almost entirely on volunteers.

The Boyd and Dekle cases on Mason's secret document and the Dekle case on the effort to influence Fitzpatrick all moved simultaneously from the JQC to the Supreme Court, which is the final authority on ethical discipline for all lawyers and judges. Ervin was assigned to write the opinions. Boyd and Dekle as well as four justices serving with them at the time recused themselves. Ervin recused himself in the Fitzpatrick-related case against Dekle because his brother Robert Ervin, a former president of the Florida Bar, was representing Dekle. He did not recuse himself in the Dekle case over the Mason document.

Overton, who had successfully advocated a tougher judicial ethics code before he joined the court, recused himself, too—at Dekle's request, Overton said. He did not require Dekle to give a reason but felt the new judicial canons allowed Dekle to make the request. It was something of a relief for Overton, burdened over the summer with both his court workload and his campaign and now facing additional work that fell to him as Dekle and Boyd abstained from all other cases.

A "special panel" of substitute judges selected to rule on Boyd's and Dekle's Mason-related cases consisted of retired Justice Alto Adams, who had first served as a justice 1940–51, then had been reappointed by Kirk in 1967 to a placeholder appointment until Kirk confidant Wade Hopping could qualify for appointment in August 1968; First District Court of Appeal Judge Dewey Johnson, who had been State Senate president when the "pork chop gang" ruled Florida politics; Harvie S. DuVal, a circuit judge from Miami who had long ties to Roberts and would run against Hatchett in 1976; Ninth Circuit

Judge Parker Lee McDonald, who had become chair of the Conference of Circuit Judges and would be appointed to the Supreme Court by Governor Bob Graham in 1979; Seventh Circuit Judge James T. Nelson; and First Circuit Judge Ernest Mason. Tenth Circuit Judge Clifton M. Kelly substituted for Ervin in the Dekle case related to Fitzpatrick.

The opinions were issued a month after England arrived, but Ervin stayed on the case, as retiring justices often do. Newcomer England was disqualified from participating in the Mason-related cases because of his role as Askew's counsel in the related Gulf Power litigation.

In the Fitzpatrick-related case against Dekle, the court voted 5–2 to dismiss the case and not discuss it on the merits.[8] The dissenters were Judges Mason and McDonald, who wrote without elaboration that they would have decided the case on the merits.

In the Mason-related case, the majority rejected the JQC's recommendation of removal and voted only to reprimand Dekle. The unsigned opinion, which law clerks later said was written primarily by Ervin, said Dekle was "lax, obtuse, and insensitive" in failing to either recognize "the memo was improper when Mason gave it to him" or have "the memo checked out to determine if it was proper for him to use it."[9] But the panel also said Dekle's "status as an outstanding jurist" must be taken into account, along with his lack of a "corrupt motive."[10]

DuVal wrote a dissent, joined by Adams and Johnson, saying the JQC had failed to establish "conduct unbecoming a judge." The three would have imposed no punishment.[11] So Dekle came just one vote away from getting off without even a reprimand.

The Boyd opinion was released the same day, February 4, 1975.[12] The panel's language about Boyd was much harsher. It called his actions "bumblingly bizarre" and his judgment "execrably bad,"[13] but in the end ordered only a reprimand. As with Dekle, the panel found no "corrupt motive," which they saw as the standard required for removing a judge.[14] They said Boyd was a "friendly affable fellow" who was "a politician first, and a justice second."[15]

The decision to let Boyd and Dekle remain on the court was not well received. The Tampa Tribune in an editorial said the panel's decisions were the true "execrably bad" judgment. The Orlando Sentinel said the court "treats the judiciary and the legal profession as a private club."[16] Across the street in the Capitol, where the unfolding of events over the past year or more had been watched with growing frustration, the special panel's focus on a lack of a "corrupt motive" was particularly grating. JQC Chairman Richard T. Earle Jr. said, "The objective doesn't really matter. It's the conduct."[17]

Over the weekend after the decisions, JQC member Thomas Barkdull briefed legislative leaders. In light of the court's decisions, it seemed futile for the JQC to pursue a McCain investigation. Instead, House Speaker Donald Tucker, a distant cousin of B. K. Roberts, launched an impeachment inquiry. He chose as outside counsel Frederick B. Karl, a former state senator whose stature and knowledge of procedure would demonstrate that Tucker and House Judiciary Chairman William J. Rish were serious. Rish said the "corrupt motive" standard would not apply in impeachment proceedings.

The hearings began immediately, and the embattled justices did little to improve their position. Dekle described his communication with Fitzgerald as "an opportunity to strike a blow for justice," which was taken as something close to a confession. When Karl, who had been making inquiries of other judges about similar contacts from Dekle, asked Dekle about communications with other district or circuit court judges, Dekle responded, "I just don't know." His attorney, Robert Ervin, jumped in to advise him to say no more.

Dekle decided to give up the fight. Just five weeks earlier, he had come within one vote of exoneration by the Supreme Court. Now the bad headlines were starting all over again with new hearings, and he would have to face a reelection campaign in 1976. Dekle announced his resignation on March 10, 1975, effective April 30, and explicitly reserved his pension rights. He and many supporters felt "an aggressive liberal press" had targeted conservative judges to give Askew a chance to pack the court with his own appointees.[18] Even Rish said Dekle was "basically a good man that made some mistakes."[19]

Boyd, whose appearance at the hearing was equally acrimonious but who was just two months into a new six-year term, refused to resign. He said he had "both the black-hat and white-hat boys after me." The "white hat boys" were the media and Askew, whom he accused of an attempt at court-packing out of a desire for "some new faces on the court." The "black hat boys" included Roberts, who later privately said he had hoped Dekle would stay on the court but hoped Boyd would leave. Roberts testified that he had once urged Boyd to leave the court and run for secretary of state. And in reaction to Boyd's impulsive behavior and allusions to having "mob connections," Roberts persuaded Boyd to go for a psychiatric examination at the Ochsner Clinic in New Orleans.

Particularly after a former law clerk lectured Boyd in impertinent prosecutorial tones during the impeachment hearings, some members of the impeachment committee had "the uncomfortable feeling that they were harassing someone who was emotionally or mentally ill,"[20] Dyckman reported at the time. The committee took some weeks off because Karl needed surgery. By the time they returned on May 5, Sandy D'Alemberte had replaced Karl as the impeachment counsel and Dekle had left the court. The focus turned to Boyd and McCain.

When Dekle announced his resignation, the nine-member Supreme Court Nominating Commission went back to work again. Alan Sundberg was again one of the three names sent to Askew, along with Stephen H. Grimes, then a judge on the Second District Court of Appeal, and Mallory Horton, who had been nominated along with Sundberg for the vacancy Overton filled. Askew picked Sundberg.

The youngest of the three, at forty-one, Sundberg was a graduate of Harvard Law School and a prominent figure in the Florida Bar. Born June 23, 1933, he came from a middle-class background in Jacksonville, where his father, Robert C. Sundberg, was vice president of a cigar company. One day he went with his father to the federal building to mail some Christmas packages, and with a little time to spare, his father took him to a courtroom to see a trial. "I don't know what there was about it, but from that day forward I never had any doubt that I wanted to be a trial lawyer," Sundberg remarked during an interview for the *Florida Bar Journal*.[21] He was always the bright student and even skipped a grade or two, said his older brother, Richard.[22]

After graduating from Andrew Jackson High School, Alan went to Florida State University, where his brother was a junior. Popular as well as bright, Alan became president of the inter-fraternity council his senior year. The council signed black jazz great Duke Ellington and his band for its annual dance in 1955. FSU had never allowed blacks on campus except as hired help. Dyckman, then a reporter for the college newspaper, recounted that the paper was preparing a story, but Sundberg and the dean feared segregationist politicians would try to ban the event if they found out. The compromise was to omit from the story any reference to Ellington's race or to the historic nature of the event.[23] But alongside the story was Ellington's picture.[24]

At FSU Alan met Barbara Lester, whose father was a successful rancher and furniture retailer in Pinellas County. After his graduation in 1955, she went to art school at Syracuse University, and Alan went to Harvard Law. They married during his first year. Brother Richard recalled that Alan had always said he was going to Harvard Law School, and it was the only law school he applied to. He just assumed he'd get in. "I guess I was a little naïve," Sundberg said in the *Bar Journal* interview. But he got in. Sundberg, who toward the end of his life served as general counsel and a trustee at FSU, spoke more fondly of FSU than Harvard and would often say that Harvard taught him to think like a lawyer, but FSU taught him to think.

With law degree in hand in 1958, the Sundbergs moved to Barbara's hometown, St. Petersburg. Sundberg practiced first with the corporate-oriented law firm of Mann, Harrison, Mann & Rowe, then joined with plaintiffs' lawyer Barney Masterson in Masterson, Sundberg & Rogers. Standing an imposing six-feet-five inches tall, Sundberg was a commanding courtroom presence with a devilish wit and an exuberant personality. A frequent response to a "How are you?" greeting was, "Virtually perfect." Sundberg was popular in the Bar and became a Sixth Circuit representative on the Florida Bar's board of governors to succeed Paul H. Roney, appointed by President Nixon to the U.S. Fifth Circuit Court of Appeals in October 1970.

Barbara Sundberg and Marilyn Overton were both active in the Junior League, and the Overtons' three children and the Sundbergs' five children were close in ages and often went to the same schools. Years later, Mrs. Sundberg (under her maiden name Barbara Lester) painted a number of the portraits of the justices that hang in the alcoves and corridors of the court building.

Fifteen months after losing the appointment to his friend Overton, Sundberg joined the Supreme Court on June 2, 1975. In the courtroom, his chair was to the chief justice's far left, next to Overton. England was at the opposite end. Now there were three of what law clerks began calling "the young bucks." Overton, at forty-seven, was the eldest of them, but still more than a decade younger than Adkins and Boyd and nearly a quarter-century younger than Roberts.

By the time Sundberg took his seat, it was already clear that yet another new justice would be arriving soon. Boyd was determined to survive the scandal. But McCain had finally given up.

The House impeachment committee, once outraged that the court panel had let Boyd stay, was now reluctant to pursue his removal. The committee proposed that Boyd be allowed to remain on the court if he would undergo a new psychiatric examination. He did. Two psychiatrists and a psychologist at Shands Hospital in Gainesville found no evidence of a mental disability, although there were "some minor personality problems." "Being an honest, conscientious and hardworking individual, Judge Boyd tends to suppress many of his more negative feelings and he exerts an almost super-human control over his emotions." The doctors recommended he take a vacation.[25]

McCain was another matter. Many who knew McCain described his legal brilliance, but he also was, as Roberts had confided to Askew months earlier, a "falling-down drunk." The hearings would show far worse behavior.

Both D'Alemberte and a new volunteer investigator at the JQC, a municipal judge and future Fourth District Court of Appeal Judge Gavin K. Letts, pursued leads and new evidence. The Supreme Court unanimously rejected McCain's petition to stop the impeachment proceedings.[26] More lower-court judges came forward to say McCain had tried to influence them on pending cases. Supreme Court Clerk Sid White and research aides testified about McCain's rigging the assignment of cases involving his friends. And there was testimony about the effort to influence Mann and McNulty in the Second DCA decision. D'Alemberte had evidence that Nell bribed McCain, and while he believed the evidence was sound, didn't find it convincing enough to use in the impeachment.

The committee voted unanimously for impeachment and directed D'Alemberte to prepare articles of impeachment for "bias and favoritism," "undue use of judicial office," and taking either illegal campaign contributions or illegal compensation. D'Alemberte, who had an unrelated meeting scheduled in California, holed up in the waterfront town of Tiburon, just across the Golden Gate Bridge from San Francisco, to draft the formal charges.

On his return, he saw a newspaper story describing the impeachment process and noting that the chief justice, who was then Adkins, presides at impeachment trials in the Senate. D'Alemberte called Adkins and asked to see him. He went to Adkins's office and told him, "Judge, I don't think you're going to be presiding. You're going to be a witness." D'Alemberte explained that McCain likely would defend himself on the bribery charges by saying he was part of a collegial court and could not do anything without the other justices. So D'Alemberte would have to question the other justices involved in those cases. The senior justice who would not be a witness would be Overton, who presumably would preside in the Senate.

Adkins relayed the conversation to Roberts, who, according to his former chief aide and future law partner, Fred Baggett, had been distressed by the entire scandal.[27] Roberts had not chosen these justices, but he needed to protect the court as an institution. Roberts was not going to have his court and his own reputation further tarnished by a public inquisition in the Senate chamber. Roberts considered it demeaning to his office as chief justice even to appear at legislative committee hearings. He had supported a consolidation of trial courts and a number of other changes in the judicial article of the Florida Constitution because he wanted to clearly establish the courts as an independent branch of government. Well before the scandals entered the headlines,

Roberts had confided to Askew that he was thinking of resigning because some of the current justices did not measure up to those who had once served with Roberts. And now this.

Roberts went to McCain and told him he had to resign.[28] Adkins began brokering the terms of the resignation. He was a consummate politician and had credibility with McCain. "He knew how to find people a graceful exit," said John Newton, who became an Adkins research assistant the next year and later became an administrative law judge.[29]

First, Adkins asked that McCain be granted immunity from further disciplinary proceedings by the Florida Bar. D'Alemberte rejected that and insisted on an unconditional resignation, and added that the legislature should not suggest what the Bar should do. Then Adkins asked that the effective date of a resignation be delayed long enough for McCain to qualify for a pension. Dekle was keeping his pension, which had already vested. Pension payments of about $10,200 a year for McCain's lifetime were still less than the cost of a drawn-out impeachment trial in the Florida Senate, which, after all, had never in history produced the two-thirds vote necessary to remove an official from office. D'Alemberte and the committee agreed. The governor went along, too, after Adkins promised that McCain would get no new cases, would write no more opinions, and would not vote on cases if his vote changed the outcome.

McCain's resignation letter of April 28 defiantly declared that he "cannot conceive of any wrong or misdoing on my part."[30]

The deal to delay the effective date until August 31 ended up being worthless. McCain was expecting passage of legislation that would allow judges to qualify for a pension after eight years of service, as other elected officials did, rather than the ten years then required for judges. But when the legislation passed, an amendment delayed the effective date to the following January 1, intentionally too late to help McCain.[31]

There was one last gasp of the old court just before McCain resigned. With McCain and Boyd joining Adkins and Roberts, the Court reaffirmed, 4–3, a decision announced in January that allowed disbarred attorneys to work as paralegals for other lawyers.[32] Overton, in dissent, said the difference in roles would not be clear to clients and others outside the legal profession.

McCain's troubles did not end. In October 1976 McCain was arrested for drunk driving and was convicted the next year. In 1978 he pleaded guilty to assault for threatening a teenage girl with a .38-caliber revolver. That same year he was disbarred,[33] though he was able to work as a paralegal because of the court's decision two years earlier.

In 1983 McCain was indicted for conspiracy to import fifteen tons of marijuana after undercover agents taped his conversations with other smugglers. He fled while under a million-dollar bond. Investigators got tips about sightings of him in Costa Rica, Colombia, Panama, the Bahamas, and even Fort Pierce, where he had been an Eagle Scout and had given a high school valedictory speech saying, "Friends, may you recall only our virtues, forgetting our faults."[34]

He wound up living under the name Thomas Sam Mills at his daughter's small apartment in a large suburban complex on Cedar Creek near the St. Johns River in southwestern Jacksonville. He had cancer but kept smoking. His daughters took turns caring for him, and he spent time with his grandchildren.[35] The bondsman had long ago quit looking for him. After cancer surgery in Jacksonville in October, according to *Miami Herald* reporter David von Drehle, McCain debated turning himself in, and actually wrote a letter to U.S. Attorney Leon Kellner in Miami wondering if he could make a deal. McCain died on November 11, 1986, still a fugitive after 1,390 days.[36] A day or two later, Kellner got his letter.[37]

When McCain announced his resignation, Joe Hatchett was enjoying being on the other side of bench as the U.S. magistrate after years as a lawyer. But he really wanted to be a full federal judge, with its constitutional status, life tenure, and power to enforce change. While state courts like Florida's had often obstructed the civil rights movement, federal judges were boldly ordering compliance with desegregation rulings and new legislation. Federal judges were the ones who turned the civil rights movement into actual results.

A federal judgeship requires a presidential appointment and confirmation by the U.S. Senate. The Senate by custom required concurrence of the senators from the appointee's home state. Hatchett knew he could not become a federal judge without the support of Florida's two U.S. senators, Lawton Chiles and Richard Stone. They had set up a nominating commission modeled on the one Askew was using, and Hatchett would have to get through that process.

As a dry run, just to get experience with the nominating process, Hatchett decided to apply for the vacancy created by McCain's resignation from the Supreme Court. "If I make the list," he thought, "I'll look good. I'm not going to be appointed, but I want to go in and be interviewed and see if I can make that list."[38] Hatchett was one of fifty-three people who applied. He wasn't well known in Florida, since most of his sixteen-year legal career had been spent in the federal system in northeast Florida. Black lawyers and white lawyers didn't socialize much, even in professional settings. No more than one or two members of the Supreme Court Nominating Commission knew Hatchett before he arrived in Boca Raton for an interview, recalled Miami attorney Robert L. Parks, a member of the commission at the time.[39]

The commission members readily agreed on two names they would send to Askew. Hatchett was not one of those. But they were required to nominate at least three, and one thing was on the commission members' minds: if Hatchett were among the nominees, Askew surely would not miss the opportunity to appoint Florida's first black justice.

The governor had made clear his determination to appoint highly qualified black people to state offices and had no concern for the possible political backlash of supporting racial equality. He had won his own State Senate seat from the western Florida Panhandle in 1962 against a well-connected white incumbent after appealing to black clergy and criticizing the incumbent's segregationist voting record. Heckled as a "nigger-lover," he responded, "The trouble is that I don't love them enough. The difference between you and me is that I'm trying to overcome my prejudices and you're not."[40] In 1972, as segregationist Alabama Governor George C. Wallace was on his way to sweeping Florida's presidential primary, Askew was speaking out against a statewide referendum opposing busing of students to achieve school desegregation. The referendum wasn't even binding. It passed despite Askew's opposition, but the episode removed any lingering doubt about Askew's commitment to the cause.

No wonder nominating commission members who preferred other applicants were reluctant to put Hatchett on the list. Stories persist even forty years later that a list without Hatchett's name came out of the nominating commission but was returned by Askew with insistence on Hatchett's name. Askew denied it in a conversation with the author. Askew's chief of staff at the time, James W. Apthorp, does not remember any such incident, although he believes the nominating commission was well aware of Askew's desire for a black person on the court. Dyckman did not know of any such move at the time. In fact, when the nominations were made public, Dyckman was surprised to learn that one of the nominees was black. Dyckman later examined archival records from Askew's office and found no written communication between the nominating commission and Askew's office except the final nominating list.

The story was first spread by Harvie DuVal in his 1976 campaign against Hatchett. In a question-answer session on Miami television station WCKT on August 13, DuVal said Askew rejected two sets of three nominees each. Hatchett, also on the program, said nothing at the time and explained later, in denying DuVal's charge, that he understood that speaking up on the air would violate the ground rules of the forum. Hatchett said DuVal's claim was "absolutely false." After Askew press secretary Paul Schnitt promptly called it "absolutely false" and commission vice chairman Julian Clarkson called it "totally false," DuVal backed off. "If they deny it, then I'm in error," DuVal said that evening.[41]

The commission's final secret vote produced a five-way tie for the third spot. Parks said commission rules did not provide for breaking ties, so seven names went to Askew.

All but Hatchett were well known. One was Fred Karl, the former state senator who had been the first special counsel to the House impeachment committee; he would win a seat on the court by election the next year. The others were Woodie A. Liles, the public counsel representing consumer interests before the Public Service Commission; District Court of Appeal Judges Guyte P. McCord Jr. of Tallahassee and James A. Walden of West Palm Beach; Circuit Judge Alan R. Schwartz of Miami (later appointed to the Third District Court of Appeal); and Circuit Judge Howell L. Melton of St. Augustine (appointed a U.S. district judge in 1977).[42]

Letters came to the governor from all over the state supporting one nominee or another. Most boosted a nominee from the letter writer's community. Some objected to the idea that Askew would choose Hatchett because of his race rather than choosing the "most judicially deserving" or "best" candidate. Others urged Askew to take the opportunity to "prove to the nation that racial prejudice has been overcome in Florida, and that we are finally beginning to believe in the brotherhood of all men," in the words of Clearwater lawyer Ralph Richards, who knew Hatchett as he grew up and was revered in that city for his commitment to the community.[43]

Askew took longer in making his choice this time. As with Sundberg a few months earlier, Hatchett was the only nominee Askew invited for an interview. On the first Saturday in July, Hatchett drove over from Jacksonville, pulled up in front of the two-story white-columned Governor's Mansion, and rang the doorbell. (Those were days of less security and no security fence.) At first there was no answer. Then Hatchett saw a man in tennis shorts come around the corner of the house with two Cokes in his hand. It was the governor, and they sat by the pool and talked. It was really a "get-acquainted session," Askew told reporters a few days later. "I had pretty much made up my mind."

Askew already had consulted the two federal judges in Jacksonville, Charles R. Scott and Gerald Tjoflat. Both praised Hatchett. Chesterfield Smith, heeding the dying exhortation from his old friend and law partner Judge Bill McRae, urged Askew to choose Hatchett. Clarkson, the nominating commission vice chairman, was Smith's law partner. "The obvious traits that Joe Hatchett had to offer—diversification, legal qualifications and experience, and integrity—led me to enthusiastically support his nomination to fill that vacancy," Smith recalled a quarter-century later.[44]

As they talked by the pool, Askew wanted to be sure Hatchett would run the next year in the statewide election to defend his seat on the court. It was an intimidating prospect. Black representation in elected state offices consisted of just two members of the 120-member Florida House of Representatives. Florida had no black senators, no black Cabinet members, no black circuit judges, and no black federal judges. No black person had won a statewide election in Florida since Josiah Thomas Walls had been elected to a statewide congressional seat in 1870, 1872, and 1874, during Reconstruction, when many whites loyal to the Confederacy had been excluded from voting.[45] A century later, in 1970, a young black lawyer from Fort Lauderdale, Alcee L. Hastings (the future federal judge and congressman), had run for the U.S. Senate and gotten only 12.5 percent of the vote among five candidates in the Democratic Primary.

Hatchett told the governor he didn't have much hope of winning, but he would run.

On Tuesday, July 8, Askew announced his choice. In future years, it would be commonplace for governors and presidents to act as if it didn't matter to them that their appointee was black. Askew forthrightly said race was "a major consideration." He added, "Beyond that, Mr. Hatchett is, I think, a remarkable person. . . . For a black person in the professional world . . . to get ahead as much as Hatchett has, (he) really has to have something extra."[46] No Florida governor had ever before made the visible commitment to black representation that Askew made with Hatchett's selection over so many well-connected white lawyers.

Two months passed before Hatchett took his seat. As the only federal magistrate within 100 miles of Jacksonville, he felt he could not resign until the six federal judges chose his successor. He spent the time studying state court issues, "starting with jurisdiction," a matter decidedly different from the federal system where Hatchett had been working for many years.[47]

Hatchett's investiture "was electric," recalled Robert T. Benton II, Hatchett's first law clerk and a future judge on the First District Court of Appeal. Even Benton didn't have a place to sit.

From Daytona Beach came Richard V. Moore, chancellor of Bethune-Cookman College, a revered private college for blacks. Moore told the audience that Hatchett gave "inspiration and courage to millions of black people all over the world."

John Briggs, the former U.S. attorney, called Hatchett "a black man of great courage yet without bitterness." Judges Scott and Tjoflat were part of a delegation of five federal judges. Tjoflat and Hatchett would later serve together on the U.S. 11th Circuit Court of Appeals, and Hatchett would succeed Tjoflat as its chief judge.

Chesterfield Smith brought his country oratory and his new national reputation. As president of the American Bar Association in the middle of the Watergate scandal the previous year, Smith had shocked the establishmentarian ABA by calling for President Nixon's resignation and declaring, "No man is above the law."

Virgil Hawkins was there, too—but not down front with the dignitaries. He still was not a member of the Florida Bar these twenty-six years after he first tried to integrate the University of Florida Law School. He was just one of the throng in the spectator seats, where college sophomore Joe Hatchett had sat to watch Hawkins's case being argued a quarter-century ago. As Hatchett's friends and admirers drifted out into the midday sun, Hawkins remarked, "I wouldn't have missed this for anything."[48]

4

ARTICLE V

Architects of Change

Like many other changes in Florida government and policy during the last quarter of the twentieth century, the transformation of Florida's court system probably would not have happened without the reapportionment of the legislature in the 1960s. The reallocation of legislative seats from rural to urban counties attracted new legislators who shared an urgency about better government, better education, fairer taxation, and more social and economic equality. These impulses had been bottled up since the end of World War II. The financial power of Social Security and veterans' benefits made the temperate climate of Florida's peninsula attainable for more and more people and dramatically shifted the distribution of Florida's population to the southern half of the state.

When Florida's legislative seats were allocated in the Constitution of 1885, roads and cars and planes and air-conditioning had not opened up the peninsula. The turn of the century brought an economic boom, but the 1920s brought a bust that stunted growth through World War II. After it ended, the needs of growing urban areas and the more progressive attitudes prevalent there created dissatisfaction with the segregationist, rural, complacent politics of the dominant legislative faction known as the "Pork Chop Gang." Repeated efforts by Governor LeRoy Collins and others in the late 1950s to shift more legislative power to southeast Florida and the Orlando and Tampa Bay regions met fierce resistance.

Before 1962 less than a fifth of the state's voters elected a majority of both houses, paid just 15 percent of the state's taxes, and received 30 percent of state spending. Jefferson County east of Tallahassee, with ten thousand citizens, had its own senator and representative, while Dade County, with fifty times as many people, had one senator and three representatives. Many narrowly focused state agencies were largely under the sway of their special-interest constituencies. Those whose votes were diluted were not just liberal urban Democrats. Republicans, who also saw a bloated and corrupt government in Tallahassee, were closed out as well. After the 1960 elections, the Florida Senate had just one Republican—newly elected C. W. Bill Young from St. Petersburg, protégé of one of the state's most powerful Republicans, Congressman William C. Cramer.

On July 26, 1962, two months after the U.S. Supreme Court's decision in *Baker v. Carr*[1] authorized federal courts to hear lawsuits over legislative apportionment, a three-judge panel of the U.S. District Court in Tallahassee declared Florida's rural-dominated apportionment "prospectively null, void and inoperative" and ordered reapportionment.[2] A special session of the legislature was set for January 30, 1963. The day before the session began, W. Reece Smith, an assistant city attorney for Tampa and a future president of the Florida Bar and the American Bar Association, filed a new federal lawsuit in Tallahassee on behalf of five Florida cities. It was consolidated with another lawsuit filed by Richard H. Max Swann of Dade County under the name *Swann v. Adams*.[3] When Swann was appointed to the Third District Court of Appeal in 1965, he recruited attorney Dan Paul to continue the case under Swann's name.[4]

The legislature, which in the mid-1950s had stayed in session for two years without passing a reapportionment plan, passed one in that 1963 session after two days. Special elections afterward sent to Tallahassee the first vanguard of reformers, including future House Speakers Richard Pettigrew of Miami and Terrell Sessums of Tampa and future Senate President Louis de la Parte, also from Tampa. Another court-ordered reapportionment brought more seats to urban areas in the 1964 elections; among the newcomers was future Attorney General Robert L. Shevin of Miami. In mid-1965 a court ruling led to a "temporary" reapportionment and special elections that fall, and there was a less hurried reapportionment in the regular session of 1966. But it took one more reapportionment, in 1967, to satisfy the population equality for districts that the U.S. Supreme Court required.

Even by 1965 there was enough legislative force behind the idea of reform that conservative Governor Haydon Burns and the legislature established a Constitution Revision Commission to rewrite the state's constitution for the first time since 1885, when Florida had one-twentieth as many people. The 1885 Constitution, passed when memories were still fresh of heavy-handed, centralized government during Reconstruction, had been amended 129 times when the new commission started its work.

A strong and eloquent proponent of rewriting the Constitution had been Chesterfield H. Smith, president of the Florida Bar in 1964–65 and head of the law firm then known as Holland, Bevis, Smith, Kibler & Hall. In the 1965 legislative session Smith pushed successfully for a constitutional amendment establishing the Judicial Qualifications Commission to investigate ethical charges against judges. It was approved by voters in 1966, by a vote of 533,974 to 142,863. That same 1965 legislature approved another amendment that expanded the number of Court of Appeal districts from three to "four or more," and even authorized an "emergency election" in November 1965 to win voter approval. The Second District was split and a Fourth District Court of Appeal was created with headquarters in Vero Beach.[5]

Smith also pushed the 1965 legislature to establish a constitution revision commission. The thirty-seven members of the Constitution Revision Commission were appointed by the heads of the three branches of government—Governor Burns, the presiding officers of the House and Senate, and Chief Justice B. Campbell Thornal. Members included young, reform-minded legislators like future governors Reubin Askew and Lawton Chiles and more conservative ones like Republican future congressman Bill Young and former "Pork Chop Gang" governor Charley Johns. Justice Roberts and former justices Tom Sebring and Stephen C. O'Connell were members. Burns asked Chesterfield Smith to serve on the commission, but Smith said no. About three weeks later the governor called back to ask him to be chairman, and he said yes.

The commission met between January and December 1966. It was nearing the end of its work when the statewide elections of November 1966, after court-ordered reapportionment earlier that year, brought another large wave of new legislators. Among them were Bob Graham, who later became governor and U.S. senator, and three future members of the state Cabinet: George Firestone and Gerald Lewis of Miami and William Gunter of Orlando. Other reform-minded newcomers included Sandy D'Alemberte, who later chaired the 1978 Constitution Revision Commission, became president of the American Bar Association, 1991–92, and was president of Florida State University, 1994–2003. People long shut out of government by unequal apportionment had a "common agenda," Graham recalled fifteen years later as he sat in the Governor's Mansion. "Not to say everybody agreed what the solutions were, but everybody agreed what the questions ought to be."[6]

At the same time, voters elected Claude Kirk, the state's first Republican governor since Marcellus L. Stearns, who had succeeded to the governorship at the death of Republican Governor (and former Supreme Court Justice) Ossian B. Hart on March 18, 1874. Kirk won in 1966 with votes from conservative Democrats, who abandoned their party's nominee, liberal Miami Mayor Robert King High, after High defeated incumbent Burns in the primary.

A big, self-confident, flamboyant man, Kirk had first made a name for himself in 1964 as the long-shot Republican challenger to longtime U.S. Senator Spessard Holland. Kirk was an insurance man and loved the promotional value of bold strokes. Kirk often did not want the same changes the urban liberals did, but he joined the urban Democrats and Republicans in attacking the corrupt, patronage-laden bureaucracy. He proved to be a Faustian mix of crusading government reformer, antic attention-getter, environmental protector, anti-union and anti-spending conservative, and race-baiting populist.

He embraced constitution revision as a way to strengthen the governorship (he repeatedly referred to the Cabinet as the "Six Dwarfs") and to gain more control over political appointees. After his election, and even before being sworn in, Kirk sat day after day in the clerk's chair at the front of the Senate chamber, where Smith was presiding over the commission's final decision making. He simply watched. "I just wanted to help by being interested," he explained in an interview on the twentieth anniversary of the commission's final vote. "This was the number one priority for the state, as far as I was concerned."[7]

Kirk quickly came to like and respect Chesterfield Smith, the stocky, self-confident, and bold reformer-lawyer with the cracker drawl. In Smith's obituary many years later, in 2003, the *Sun-Sentinel* of Fort Lauderdale would say Smith "bestrode Florida's legal landscape like a colossus."

Born July 28, 1917, to parents in little Arcadia, Chesterfield Harvey Smith went by his middle name through high school because "Chesterfield" was not exactly a cool name for a teenager and, besides, his uncle Stanhope Chesterfield Smith, who owned the local drugstore, already was using the name. Harvey's father was elected superintendent of schools but, ambitious for DeSoto County's growth, built more new classrooms than the county needed after the boom went bust and was voted out in 1928. In 1934 Harvey's father was elected to a term in the legislature, and young Harvey went up to be a page. His mother, though, was the real force in his life. She was "a very, very smart woman, a quick and aware woman who was caring and purposeful and knew how to handle all people, including me," Smith told an interviewer in 2000.[8] The family finances were always strained, but Harvey was at the top of his class in school most of the time. In high school he worked for Uncle Chesterfield at the drugstore. After graduation at sixteen, he went off to the University of Florida but would take semesters off to work.

When the military draft was imposed in 1940, he joined the National Guard. That, Smith said, is when he first starting feeling a sense of leadership. It was also when the military, whose insistence on uniformity did not indulge those who went by their middle names, rebranded him as "Chesterfield." Smith was promoted gradually from private to master sergeant. After the Pearl Harbor attack on December 7, 1941, he was accepted to officer candidate school. In January 1943, he came back to Arcadia on furlough and married his high school sweetheart, Vivian Parker. In June he was ordered to London. A captain, he commanded an artillery unit and went to Normandy a month or so after D-Day in 1944. At some point his unit became part of General George S. Patton's legendary Third Army in France and Germany. He rose to the rank of major. "I was in charge of most everything I did," he recalled. "I would go out and be in charge and I think it made me a leader. . . . It did not take me long to decide or do things, and I learned that in World War II."[9]

On the transport home he made enough money gambling to stake himself to law school on the G.I. Bill at the University of Florida. He finished first in his class in 1948 and joined a small law firm back in Arcadia. He was thinking of running for the legislature, but his uncle jumped in ahead of him. Thwarted in this early ambition, he was ready when his old law school professor, William McRae, invited him to join Holland, Bevis & McRae in Polk County, which was ten times bigger than little DeSoto County down the road.

Smith had great ambition for himself and the firm. He was made a partner after three months. The next year he started hiring the top graduates from his old law school—Henry Kittleson the first year, then future Florida Bar president William O.E. Henry, and after that future Supreme Court Justice Stephen H. Grimes. He and these other three young lawyers, Smith said, planned the firm's growth path. By 1955 Smith was managing partner.

Smith wanted to build a firm with a national reputation. One step was for him, as its leader, to become president of the Florida Bar, which in turn became his pulpit for constitutional reform. As he began leading the revision commission, he also began the subtle but determined campaign to become president of the American Bar Association.

Between the conclusion of the revision commission's work in December 1966 and the statewide vote on November 5, 1968, Smith concluded a merger of the Holland firm with Tampa's Knight, Jones, Whitaker & Germany. The managing partner there was Smith's boyhood friend from DeSoto County, John Arthur Jones, who still referred to Smith as "Harvey." Smith told his partners that becoming a national law firm meant it could not keep changing its name as partners changed. They needed a simple, enduring name. The founder of the Bartow firm, Holland, was in the U.S. Senate and not practicing. The founder of the Tampa firm, Peter O. Knight, was dead. Smith and Jones jointly agreed to name the merged firm Holland & Knight. If their partners didn't like that, Smith told Jones with his typical wit, they would call it "Smith & Jones." According to Smith, when he told Senator Holland the news on a conference call with all the partners, Holland objected that he would not be in a firm that did not have Smith's name in it. Smith said he replied, "Senator Holland, where are you going to practice?"[10]

Smith was no less ambitious and self-confident in leading the Constitution Revision Commission. As he saw it, the commission was going to clean out the silt from eighty years of constitutional amendments, streamline the government, recognize equality of political rights, and create an effective government for a state that was growing faster than almost any other state in America. Smith presided with firmness and determination, to the point that he was sometimes referred to (mostly but not always in good humor) as "Lord Chesterfield."

One of the most contentious issues was judicial reform under Article Five, the section of the Constitution dealing with the judiciary (referred to with a Roman numeral, Article V). [11] Smith made Askew the chairman of that committee; B. K. Roberts, who surely wanted the role, instead became chairman of Human Rights. Commission member Richard T. Earle Jr. of St. Petersburg said later, "My good friend Reubin Askew had his ideas of how it ought to be done, with which a few people agreed. I had [my ideas] as to how it ought to be done. We collided. Then we added in the [opposition of] constables, the JPs [justices of the peace], the circuit judges. . . . There really was no way to accomplish it."[12]

Over the decades, a motley collection of local courts had developed, because the Florida Constitution's formula, passed in 1934, set the number of circuit judges at one for every fifty thousand people, which came to be interpreted as a cap. This proved grossly inadequate for growing caseloads, so other types of courts had sprung up—a dozen different courts in some urban counties. There were separate traffic courts, municipal courts, justice of the peace courts, and civil courts of record as well as the county and circuit courts. Many judges, including some county judges, did not have legal training. The courts had overlapping jurisdiction, so parties could choose the judge more likely to rule in their favor. Each court had its own marshals and clerks, so they were sources of patronage. When voters in 1956 approved creation of the district courts of appeal and streamlined Article V by consolidating fifty-four sections of the Constitution into twenty-six, no change was made in the trial courts.[13]

Legal issues for the first half of the twentieth century were not complex. Most court proceedings involved wills or deeds or court proceedings for traffic tickets or accidents. There were few laws related to growth management, economic regulation, pollution, securities, or other such emerging issues. The U.S. Supreme Court had barely begun establishing constitutional standards for "due process" in criminal and civil cases. But the 1960s were producing a "law explosion," as Ben Overton later described the situation in his address to the legislature as chief justice in 1977. His list of factors: "(1) new theories in the law evolving from consumer and environmental actions; (2) the expanded use of old theories such as malpractice; (3) the substantial increase in new legislation which requires construction and interpretation by the courts; (4) new regulatory legislation which requires a review within the appellate courts such as the Administrative Procedure Act; (5) the increase in crime and changes in criminal due process requirements; and (6) new citizen awareness of the availability of the courts."[14]

As mostly liberal forces won more victories at the national level in these areas, they were often frustrated by local judges, who obstructed these gains through inertia, ignorance, or sometimes active resistance. For advocates of judicial reform, elevating competence and integrity was the first order of business, and keeping up with growing caseloads and growing population was a close second. However, many advocates were also seeking effective implementation of their hard-won changes in the law.

The revision commission's debate over Article V was complicated by the need to get the plan through the Legislature. One provision of the new Constitution would allow future revision commissions to place their proposals directly onto the ballot, rather than having to go through the legislative process. But this first commission had to get its proposals through the legislature with a three-fifths vote, and the body had limited enthusiasm for consolidation of trial courts. The commission's recommendations were delivered on December 13, 1966. The Article V proposal included nonpartisan rather than partisan election of judges and justices, merit selection with nominating commissions for filling vacancies, and four types of trial courts—county and circuit courts, magistrate courts, and municipal courts.

On January 3, 1967, Kirk called a special session of the legislature to move the proposed constitution forward. As the session opened on January 9, House Speaker Ralph Turlington appointed himself chairman of a special committee on constitution revision and personally introduced the legislation to approve the Revision Commission's proposal.[15] But that morning, the U.S. Supreme Court threw out the reapportionment plan used in the 1966 election.[16] Now legislators were distracted by thoughts of their own political futures.

Nevertheless, on the morning of January 10, Chesterfield Smith addressed the House, including his "Uncle Chesterfield" from Arcadia.[17] He said the existing constitution from 1885 created a weak legislature and a weak governor because Floridians distrusted the "carpetbaggers" who had just been routed from control of state government. "Framed to provide the basis of state government for a rural society, before the discovery of electric lights, automobiles, television or jet aircraft," Smith declared, "the existing document has become increasingly inadequate to meet the pressing needs of the most rapidly growing state of the nation, which is now predominantly urban in nature." He noted that thirteen amendments had been submitted for voter approval in November 1966 alone.

Smith offered six standards for a constitution, which he said the commission had met: It has to be consistent with the U.S. Constitution. It should have a bill of rights. It should establish a framework of government with "a sound balance of power among the various branches." It should state the rules and adequate authority to exercise those powers. It should have "clear, simple language, readily intelligible to the average citizen." Finally, it "should be confined to matters of a fundamental nature," unlike the existing constitution, which "contains a mass of details dealing with temporary matters." Smith told the legislators that "the most difficult thing you will have to do is to face up to the reality that someone else besides you has intelligence," so that legislators of the future have "the flexibility to meet the needs of government under then existing conditions."

In part because legislators got caught up in producing another reapportionment plan, and in part because of their intense feud with Kirk over taxes and spending, consideration of the new constitution took eighteen months, including four special sessions, with numerous compromises. Finally, on July 2, 1968, the legislature produced the needed three-fifths majority to put the new Constitution on the statewide ballot in November 1968. The voters' approval produced the sixth constitution in the state's history, known as the Constitution of 1968.

One important element was missing, though: a new Article V. The changes the revision commission proposed in the judicial article ran into staunch resistance in the legislature, which was besieged by objections from the local judges, clerks, and bailiffs whose fiefdoms would be abolished. Even the surge of reformers from the 1966 elections and another reapportionment and election in 1967 could not get the judicial reforms onto the ballot. The old judicial article dating back to 1885 remained in force, with partisan elections of judges and the rules that promoted the proliferation of local courts.

With the revision commission now history, the Florida Bar's board of governors took up the cause under the leadership of Dick Earle, who would later be a key figure as a member and chairman of the Judicial Qualifications Commission in the investigation of Supreme Court justices Adkins, Boyd, Carlton, Dekle, and McCain. Earle said later that his committee was the originator of the two-level trial court system, county courts and circuit courts, without the additional magistrate and municipal courts in the revision commission proposal. That, he added, was important in winning over the circuit judges and helped clear a path to legislative passage.[18]

Justice Roberts, while no longer the political force he once was, still had connections with many of the veterans remaining from the "Pork Chop Gang" era. Proud of his role as a revision commission member, he wrote in the Judicial Council's 1968 report that the council "has, from a practical standpoint, become an extension of the Constitution Revision Commission." One issue in particular that Roberts kept pushing was non-partisan election of appellate judges, which did not require a constitutional amendment. In 1969 the change was nearly accomplished through legislation, without a constitutional amendment. The bill passed the Senate but failed by two votes in the House.

But the judicial reformers that year managed to win near-unanimity for amending Article V—just one nay vote in the House and three in the Senate. It would be on the ballot November 3, 1970. The proposed amendment included the two tiers of trial courts for large counties, but smaller counties would be able to have three types of trial courts. That was one of many compromises made in quest of passage—too many compromises, in the view of many reformers. The compromises "left to the discretion of future legislatures an unnecessarily large number of actions considered mandatory to a complete new system of courts," as Roberts's Judicial Council put it in its 1971 report. [19] Neither the Florida Bar nor the Judicial Council endorsed it.

There was still another legislative session before the 1970 elections, and that time around the legislature passed the bill for nonpartisan election of both trial and appellate judges. Governor Kirk vetoed it and argued that the issue should be deferred until after the Article V vote that fall.

Attention turned to the fall elections. Clearly the political winds were blowing harder in the direction of reform, but by then the reformers were focused more on their own political ambitions—Askew most of all. Dismayed with both the hard-drinking lifestyle and political chicanery of Governor Kirk, straight-arrow Askew had been thinking of running for governor and declined to sign a pledge endorsing Senate President John E. Mathews Jr. for governor. In retaliation, Mathews assigned Askew to the chairmanship of Senate Judiciary but with little likelihood that anything Askew wanted would get through the Senate. Though he considered Mathews well qualified for governor, Askew made the decision to run against him.

Askew won the governorship, but despite support of newspaper editorials, the Article V proposal failed. It was close: 503,992 for, 526,328 against.

One of the reformers discouraged by the defeat of even this "pabulum" of reform was Representative Sandy D'Alemberte, whose ambition was turning elsewhere as well. Besides his legislative work, D'Alemberte had worked on Senator Robert F. Kennedy's presidential campaign in 1968, which had ended with Kennedy's assassination. Now, after four years in the House, D'Alemberte was realizing that the salaries in big law firms like Steel Hector were increasing dramatically. Some of his partners were restless about the time D'Alemberte was devoting to politics and government instead of billable hours. D'Alemberte told his friend Pettigrew that he was not going to run again.

Pettigrew, who had been designated the next Speaker of the House with the power to choose committee chairmen, told D'Alemberte he could have any committee he wanted if he'd stay one more term. What D'Alemberte wanted was one more chance to change Article V. He wanted to chair Judiciary, and he wanted to name his own committee staff. Pettigrew agreed.

D'Alemberte's interest in the legal system was genetic. A great-uncle on his mother's side, James B. Whitfield, served for thirty-nine years on the Florida Supreme Court, earned a reputation as a scholar and statesman, and left his name on the building that housed the court from 1902 to 1949. Justice Whitfield's father was a Leon County judge, and Whitfield's half-brother, George Talbot Whitfield, served as clerk of the Supreme Court and was Sandy D'Alemberte's grandfather. Jimmy Adkins, who arrived at the court as law clerk shortly before George Whitfield's death, remembers that his "stiff collar attached to his shirt with collar buttons and his mannerisms gave him an air of elegance and formality, but he was friendly and helpful."[20] D'Alemberte's grandmother Rebecca "Ruby" Whitfield had been married previously to the father of Park Trammell, the governor and U.S. senator.

Herbert Talbot D'Alemberte, who would become "Sandy," was born in Tallahassee on June 1, 1933, in a house at 502 South Adams Street, where the twenty-two-story capitol building now stands. It was his grandmother Whitfield's house, and D'Alemberte calculated that her front porch was where the Great Seal in the floor of the capitol rotunda now rests. Justice Whitfield and his family lived on the other side of what is now called the "old capitol," across Monroe Street. D'Alemberte's father, Daniel D'Alemberte, the state purchasing agent, eventually moved his wife and son to Chattahoochee, where Sandy's brother Richard was born. After retiring from state employment, while his son was in law school, Dan D'Alemberte had a small-town law practice where food or other in-kind payments might be found at the office door some mornings.

Young Sandy graduated from Chattahoochee High School and went off to the University of the South in the hills of southern Tennessee, largely because the Episcopal priest visiting at Sunday dinner one day declared he should go there. Sandy spent a summer at the University of Virginia and another at Florida State and then did military service in the U.S. Navy Reserve. After a year at the London School of Economics, he went to the University of Florida Law School. There he was captain of the moot court team, president of the Student Bar Association, articles editor of the law review, and at his graduation in 1962 was named the outstanding law graduate. At the age of twenty-nine, he became the eleventh lawyer at Miami's Scott, McCarthy, Preston & Steel, which later became Steel, Hector & Davis. In 1966, when nineteen legislative seats were being voted on countywide in Dade County and more than two hundred candidates were running, D'Alemberte distinguished himself from the pack with billboards bearing the slogan, "REMEMBER THE NAME THAT'S HARD TO REMEMBER: D'ALEMBERTE."

As the 1970 political season approached, a few admirers thought he'd be a good governor. The legislative staffers who had drafted the concept of a corporate profits tax had liberal D'Alemberte in mind to carry that banner. Never shy about floating new ideas, D'Alemberte as a legislator had proposed things like changing to a one-house legislature and making Florida a better choice than Delaware as the home of corporations, especially those expanding internationally. But running for governor was too far-fetched an idea. Eventually the corporate tax plan was pitched to Askew, who made it the populist centerpiece of his campaign.

Within a few blocks of where Pettigrew and D'Alemberte lived in south Miami were other new legislators who shared their enthusiasm for government reform. Murray Dubbin became chairman of the Rules Committee, the gatekeeper for legislation. Maxine Baker, elected along with Dubbin and Pettigrew in 1963, never gained the stature or influence of her male colleagues from Miami, but her legacy was the Baker Act, which created the first meaningful due process in the commitment of people with mental illness and emphasized community services instead of institutionalization. Bob Shevin, elected to the House in 1964, would become attorney general in 1978. Marshall Harris, elected in 1966, later chaired Appropriations. Gerald Lewis didn't live in the neighborhood, but he too won election to the House in 1966. Bob Graham from up in Miami Lakes decided he, too, would run.

Two others in the circle of friends were never legislators but would have roles in judicial reform. One was John Edward Smith, a tax lawyer who had joined the Holland firm after law school but, chafing at life in Polk County, moved to Steel Hector & Davis in Miami and was D'Alemberte's law partner. Another was Janet Reno, whose mother and father were both newspaper reporters, her mother at the *Miami News* and her father at the *Miami Herald*. Reno had been a debate champion and valedictorian at Coral Gables High School, went off to college at Cornell, then graduated from Harvard Law School in 1963, a year behind Bob Graham. She returned to Miami, interviewed with the Scott McCarthy Law Firm, a forerunner of Steel Hector, and was told there was no chance the firm would hire a woman.

As Pettigrew was luring D'Alemberte back to the legislature in 1970 for one more term, Reno was practicing law with Gerald Lewis, a 1960 Harvard Law grad who was running for the State Senate. Lewis, whose family wealth made him less dependent than his friends on making money as a lawyer, gave priority to his political career. Reno felt she was carrying the load of the law practice. One night soon after the November election, when D'Alemberte was at the Smiths' home, Sarah Smith told D'Alemberte he should think about Reno for the Judiciary Committee staff. "The next day," D'Alemberte said, "I was driving down Dixie Highway in my Mustang convertible with the top down, and heard the horn from the car next to me. I looked to my right, and it was Janet. I motioned to her to follow me home. Before we finished our second drink, she agreed to be my staff director."[21]

It almost didn't last. Just after New Year's, a Miami legislator pleaded guilty in a federal fraud case and resigned. Reno quit her job and announced she would run for the vacancy. Just three days later, Askew decided to just let the seat stay vacant, because Dade County already had twenty-one legislators and it would cost $280,000 for a special election. Reno took the news with good cheer. D'Alemberte quickly gave her back her old job, which paid $17,500 a year.[22]

Reno soon won the regard of Sen. Dempsey J. Barron, D'Alemberte's counterpart in the Senate as chairman of the Judiciary-Civil Committee. In addition to being a lawyer in Panama City with a heavy insurance-defense practice, Barron owned a ranch near Bonifay, up near the Alabama line, and a 3,000-acre ranch in Wyoming, which he once called "a leftover dream from cowboy movies when I was a little boy."[23] He often sported western-style attire. His portrait as Senate president (1975–76) shows him not in a traditional pose but in an open-necked western-style shirt atop his palomino horse.

Barron had once been a law clerk to Jimmy Adkins when Adkins was a circuit judge. Adkins had joined the Supreme Court just three years before the legislature took up the Article V revisions. Like B. K. Roberts, Barron had grown up in a poor home in the Panhandle. Unlike Roberts, who had been certified as a teacher at the age of thirteen and charmed patrons like business magnate Ed Ball, Barron quit school in the sixth grade, though he later got a GED diploma and went to college at Florida State. Barron joined the navy at seventeen and spent World War II in the Pacific, where a boat was torpedoed out from underneath him.

As a freshman House member in 1955, Barron was one of four North Florida legislators to support Governor Collins's veto of legislation closing public schools to preserve segregation—a veto sustained by one vote in the House. Despite the unpopularity of such a position in the Panhandle, Barron won another term in the House and then served twenty-eight years in the Senate. He had a libertarian streak that led him to resist higher taxes but also support a constitutional amendment legalizing marijuana and oppose one relaxing standards for police searches.

Barron's enduring power in the Senate came from an uncanny ability to exploit whatever other legislators wanted. He said the secret to his power was not wanting anything. He rarely sought earmarks for his own district. He rarely had legislation he wanted to pass. But he knew every nuance of parliamentary rules and used them to save or block legislation, depending on which outcome he preferred. He knitted together Republicans and conservative Democrats to dominate the Senate long after the south Florida liberals like D'Alemberte and Graham had surged into the legislature in the 1960s. He cultivated reporters from the big-city newspapers but often said that criticism in the *St. Petersburg Times* would get him ten thousand more votes in Panama City. He did protect the interests of insurance companies. Eventually it was the Florida trial lawyers who raised campaign funds to support a challenger in 1988—a challenger who won but lasted just one term.

Barron and Reno both loved lowbrow western mysteries; they would swap books amid talk about judicial reform. B. K. Roberts also pushed Barron and other senators on reform, but his uptown formality clearly didn't nurture the kind of easy relationship that Barron and Reno had. While unrelenting about preserving local elected judges and frequently challenging Governor Askew on other issues, Barron moved the Article V changes through the Senate as D'Alemberte and Pettigrew were moving them through the House.

It took all of 1971 behind the scenes to get the Article V amendment ready for a legislative vote. Askew called a special session of the legislature starting November 29, 1971. The major items were passage of a corporate income tax, which the voters had approved as a constitutional amendment in the November 2 special election, and proposing revisions to Article V for voter approval in 1972.[24]

The most significant Article V changes that came out of that special session:

- In place of the special local courts, judicial power was vested in a supreme court, district courts of appeal, circuit courts and county courts, and "no other courts may be established."
- In place of a formula for adding local judges as populations grew, the Supreme Court was directed to establish new "uniform criteria" for adding or reducing judges and "certifying" the result to the legislature for approval.
- Governor Askew's method for filling vacant judgeships through the nominating process became a constitutional requirement binding future governors, but—significantly many years later—allowed the appointment and makeup of the nominating commissions to be changed by general law.
- The state took over the salaries of all judges, something politicians could describe as providing relief for local property taxes. State attorneys and public defenders were required to be full time and could not have private law practices on the side.
- County judges in counties of less than forty thousand people still were not required to be licensed lawyers. (The provision was changed by statute in 1978 amid growing concerns about a lack of due process when non-lawyer judges were deciding some cases. After that, all trial judges had to be lawyers, except that the twenty-five nonlawyer judges already in office were protected even through future elections.[25] The requirement of Bar membership "unless provided by general law" was put into the Constitution in 1984. Existing county judges were grandfathered, and as late as 2003 Florida still had five nonlawyer judges, in the Panhandle counties Santa Rosa, Jackson, Holmes, and Madison.)
- Though it was a subtle change understandable only to lawyers, there was a provision intended to eliminate long-standing technical rulings that could destroy a lawsuit. The new article in Section 2 said, "No cause shall be dismissed because an improper remedy has been sought."

The constitutional changes did not specify nonpartisan election of judges. Kirk had vetoed legislation to accomplish that in 1970, but the legislature had come back in its spring session of 1971, months before completing the Article V revisions, and passed the bill again.[26] The new governor, Askew, signed it.

Merit selection of all judges continued to elude the reformers. Local elected judges had blocked that change with the help of the Republican Party, which did not want a Democratic governor to control all the judgeships, with or without "merit" screening.

The House-Senate conference committee that worked out the final Article V changes included not only D'Alemberte and Barron but Reno's former law partner, Senator Gerald Lewis, and future Supreme Court justice, Senator Fred Karl. The result, Senate Joint Resolution 52-D, was approved on December 11, 1971, by the three-fifths vote of both houses needed to go on the ballot (72 needed in the 120-member House, twenty-nine in the forty-eight-member Senate). The House vote, with eleven members absent, was 75–34; in the Senate, 34–10.

A separate vote produced the three-fourths vote (ninety and thirty-six needed) to put the amendment on an earlier ballot, the 1972 presidential primary on March 14, 1972.[27] That early approval was critical, because it meant the changes would take effect before the reelection of the many local judges in the November 1972 elections. Otherwise, consolidation of the courts would effectively be delayed for four years as these judges served their new terms. There was another incentive for speed: If the constitutional revisions were passed in March, before the regular session began in 1972, the legislature could create additional circuit and county judgeships to be filled in the 1972 elections. The vote to put it on the March ballot was 90–19 in the House—not a single vote to spare—and 42–2 in the Senate.

In contrast with the narrow loss for the tepid 1970 proposals, voters gave the new, more ambitious Article V overwhelming approval—969,741 for, 401,861 against. Legislators followed up in their spring session by creating twenty-six new circuit judgeships and 135 county judgeships, many of which went to judges of the abolished local courts.

Reno soon went to work for Pettigrew, who was elected to the State Senate in 1972, and took part in a major revision of Florida's criminal code. She returned to Miami in 1974, joined the state attorney's office, then in 1976 became a partner with D'Alemberte at Steel Hector. In 1978 Governor Askew appointed her the state's first woman state attorney, for the Eleventh Circuit in Dade County.

Reno was still in that role in early 1993 when newly inaugurated President Bill Clinton was looking for an attorney general. His two previous nominees, Zoe Baird and Kimba Wood, had withdrawn after disclosure that they failed to pay withholding taxes on their nannies. D'Alemberte, who was then president of the American Bar Association, was a member of Clinton's Justice Department transition team and suggested Reno's name to Peter Edelman, a Georgetown law professor and Clinton confidante. Hillary Clinton's brother,

Hugh Rodham, was an assistant public defender in Miami assigned to an innovative drug court program, widely emulated later, that had been created by Reno, Public Defender Bennett Brummer, and Circuit Judge Gerald Wetherington.

Had Reno been President Clinton's initial choice in December 1992, when Baird was nominated, Reno likely would have declined, because her mother, Jane Wood Reno, was very ill. (She died on December 21, 1992.) After Zoe Baird withdrew in January and Kimba Wood withdrew in early February, Reno was nominated on February 11, 1993, and won Senate confirmation on March 11, 1993. The first woman to be U.S. attorney general, she served through both of Clinton's terms and had the second-longest tenure of any U.S. attorney general.

As for D'Alemberte, he was voted Most Outstanding House Member in 1972 after the new Article V passed. Keeping his promise to his law partners, he did not run again. Over the next half century, as a lawyer, as chairman of the 1977–78 Constitution Revision Commission, as dean of the Florida State law school, as president of the American Bar Association and the American Judicature Society, as president of Florida State, and as an activist lawyer into his eighties who was always ready to file a petition against a governor or another state official, he had a rare level of influence on the Florida Supreme Court and the state legal system.

Article V itself permanently transformed the legal system of Florida, but some of its provisions that had seemed so innovative and promising proved disappointing. It was as if the drafters of Article V expected to have a governor like Askew and a House speaker like Pettigrew in perpetuity. But the reformers also faced a political reality: there were only so many specifics they could load into Article V before it would collapse under its own weight in the face of opposition.

Although the court system is well under 1 percent of state spending, the courts remained entirely dependent on legislative appropriations. In older times, courts were supported mainly by filing fees, but these came to be moderated by concerns that fees discouraged access to courts. Article V banned local supplements to judges' salaries and began a move toward state funding of the court system, including prosecutor and public defender offices.

On spending and other matters, the legislature showed bursts of hostility toward the third branch, whose decisions it could not control in the way that it controlled executive branch agencies. The 1972 provision on certifying a need for more judges was an improvement over the old formula, but it proved disappointing to court reformers. The legislature often did as it wished in funding new judgeships.

Article V had established the merit selection process, including the use of nominating commissions, but had not specified the makeup of the nominating commissions. That was left to statute and the good intentions of the governor and the Florida Bar. The shared appointment of commissioners by the Bar and the governor lasted until 2001. That was the year after Supreme Court rulings in the 2000 general election delayed the certification of the governor's brother, George W. Bush, as the winner in Florida and the next president of the United States. (Most of the key circuit judge rulings, however, supported the Bush position.) Governor Jeb Bush and Republicans began viewing the Supreme Court with much more animus.

Another contributor to this animus was a backlash against the Florida Academy of Trial Lawyers, the organization of plaintiffs' lawyers whose members and allies dominated the nominating commissions and the governor's appointments under Governor Lawton Chiles and his general counsel, Dexter Douglass. Supreme Court appointees Charles T. Wells and Harry Lee Anstead in 1994 and Barbara J. Pariente in 1997 were strongly supported by the plaintiffs' bar in preference to Republican, defense-oriented nominees.

Early in his administration Governor Jeb Bush successfully asked the Republican-controlled legislature to give him sole appointment power over the nominating commissions, with the Bar simply recommending members. To opponents, this was a reversion to cronyism. The governor could stack the commissions with allies. To Bush and Republicans, the Chiles administration had started it, and now it was their turn. They could not undo trial lawyers' influence in the Bar, so they simply bypassed the Bar in the selection of the commission members.

"If I could do anything over, it would be to have a constitutional nominating commission," Askew remarked in 2006, meaning that his formula for the makeup of the nominating commissions would be part of the Constitution.[28]

No one else would receive the accolades that followed Askew for the rest of his life for his devotion to the cause of judicial independence. Askew's successor as governor, Bob Graham, said Askew viewed the court scandals early in his administration "not as a tragedy but an opportunity." On receiving a lifetime achievement award from the Supreme Court Historical Society in 2013, a year before his death, Askew said the independent judiciary was the issue on which he spent more time than any other. "As an old man of 84, which I am right now, I want to tell you, if you're looking to protect your rights, don't look to the executive, don't look to the legislative, look to the courts and the judiciary, because they're the only ones that'll stand up [for] absolute fairness."[29]

5

THE THIRD BRANCH

B. K. Roberts had long wanted the state's judiciary to be seen as a real third branch of government, equal to the executive and legislative branches and independent of them—not just a "department," as the 1885 Constitution called it. Article V, unifying the court system, and the simultaneous creation of the Office of State Court Administrator under the chief justice finally gave Roberts the structure to make his goal a reality.

For many years, through sheer political will and personal influence, Roberts had exercised some measure of administrative control over the Florida court system through the Florida Judicial Council, which Roberts often chaired even when he was not chief justice. In part, the council buffered the court from legislative intrusion on its independence by handling lobbying on matters of judicial administration. When Roberts lobbied personally, he might be asked about some pending case a legislator had an interest in (usually on behalf of a constituent or contributor). That kind of pressure was avoided when local judges, as members of the council, would go and speak for the judicial system. And local judges could be particularly persuasive with their local legislators.

In the mid-1950s, Roberts had supported creation of the district courts of appeal, which would handle the majority of appeals and expand as population and caseloads grew. Their creation was the first major initiative of the Judicial Council, created by the legislature in 1953 with Supreme Court Justice Elwyn Thomas as chairman. The council stagnated after that until the summer of 1962, when Roberts, then in his second tenure as chief justice, replaced O'Connell as council chairman and enlisted help from Governor Bryant to revive the council. It had an instantaneous new mission: by the first meeting on September 15, the U.S. Supreme Court had accepted an appeal from Clarence Earl Gideon, serving time for a burglary in Panama City and arguing that the Sixth Amendment right to counsel required the state to provide a lawyer to people who could not afford one. Florida's Attorney General, Richard Ervin, was on the other side, but 22 attorneys general in other states were actually supporting Gideon. Roberts, at that September meeting, began anticipating what was coming.

Gideon had prepared a handwritten petition from Florida's Raiford Prison. Standing over his shoulder and giving advice as he wrote was a famous fellow inmate, Joseph A. Peel Jr., a former attorney and municipal judge convicted in the murder of Palm Beach Circuit Judge Curtis E. Chillingworth and his wife, Marjorie, in 1955.[1] Roberts's court summarily rejected the petition in October 1961 and did not even bother to request a response from the attorney general's office first. Gideon sought review at the U.S. Supreme Court, which took the issue quite seriously and appointed a nationally prominent lawyer, Abe Fortas, to represent Gideon. A year after Roberts and his court had blithely dismissed the issue, it was now one of Roberts's consuming interests.

On March 18, 1963, the U.S. Supreme Court ruled for Gideon and declared that every defendant facing a serious criminal charge had a right to counsel paid by the state if the defendant couldn't afford one. Roberts had anticipated the decision and led the Florida Judicial Council in drafting a plan for a state-wide public defender system. Just fifteen days after the ruling in *Gideon*, bolstered by the work of the Judicial Council's finished report, Governor Bryant addressed the opening session of the legislature and asked for creation of the public defender system. The legislature agreed, although the political and financial reality at the time was that counties had to share in the funding.

The *Gideon* case was really the beginning of the upheaval in the legal system of Florida (and the nation). Not only were there now public defenders, but they had a growing arsenal of "due process" rights that had never been extended to criminal defendants before. The new procedural standards drove structural changes, and the more complex legal structure drove a need for stronger administration of this third branch of government under the chief justice. This, too, B. K. Roberts had anticipated.

As legislators were preparing for another attempt at revising Article V after the 1970 elections, it was time for the regular rotation of leadership down the hill to the west at the Supreme Court building. The normal rotation of the chief justice position every two years, to the most senior justice who had not previously been chief, would have made Vassar Carlton next in line. But he had joined the court just two years earlier, as had Jimmy Adkins and Joe Boyd. David McCain had been on the court for a month after replacing Campbell Thornal, who had died on November 4, 1970. Hal Dekle was just joining the court after winning election in November to replace Harris Drew, who retired after nearly twenty years.

Except for Roberts, every possible successor to Chief Justice Ervin had been on the court just two years or less. Roberts had been on the court since 1949, the year his childhood friend, Fuller Warren, became governor. Roberts had been on vacation with his wife, Mary, in Hot Springs, Arkansas, when Warren called him and told him he had just announced his appointment to the Supreme Court. Roberts served as chief justice in 1953–55 and again in 1961–63. After the death of Chief Justice Glenn Terrell on January 12, 1964, Roberts was clearly the court's dominant political force. Others of considerable intellectual ability served on the court—among them Elwyn Thomas, E. Harris Drew, and future University of Florida president Stephen O'Connell. But not even Thomas had the concerted interest in judicial administration that Roberts had.

As progressive spirit and more talk of judicial reform filled the air of the 1970 election season, Roberts was eager to take the chief's chair one more time. He clearly saw the opportunities and challenges if the judicial reforms came about. If he were ever again to serve as chief justice, this was the time. So the court went back to its most senior justice to begin a new seniority rotation, something last done in 1957. On January 5, 1971, B. K. Roberts became chief justice for the third time.

Soon after losing to Askew in the 1970 Democratic primary for governor, Attorney General Earl Faircloth asked one of his rising young lawyers, Fred Baggett, how he'd like to work for Justice Roberts over at the Supreme Court. Baggett, working in the prestigious criminal division, might have once had hopes of moving to the governor's office with Faircloth, but that prospect was gone. Baggett was told he had an appointment with Roberts that afternoon. Roberts offered him a job as a research aide, "starting tomorrow," assuring him that General Faircloth had already gotten adequate notice.

Baggett, who had been in the second class to arrive at Florida State's law school in fall of 1967, said he doesn't know how the appointment with Roberts came about. The two talked less about the job of research assistant and more about politics and policy. "He did not hire me for my academic achievements," Baggett wryly recalled. "But he was totally like a father to me." Baggett found himself working for a man with a phenomenal memory of cases and a fondness for jokes and stories. "He was always happy with people," Baggett recalled. Fuller Warren would visit frequently. The two were best friends. Warren was known as a storyteller, but he called Roberts the best storyteller since Abraham Lincoln. "You would hear this laugh," Baggett said. "It would start at Governor Warren's toes and sort of rumble out and fill the whole place."

As summer came in 1971, and the work on Article V grew more intensive, the chief decided that he needed a chief of staff for the third branch of government just as the governor and the House speaker and the Senate president had. Administration of the court itself and the court system was going to become more complex. Askew provided $18,000 from the governor's discretionary account, and Roberts made Baggett the first "executive assistant" to the chief.

Baggett had two main jobs: monitoring the development of the judicial reform legislation and preparing for the creation of a new office to manage the unified court system, which would become known as the Office of State Court Administrator, or OSCA. Besides consolidating multiple trial courts into two, Article V unified governance of all the courts under the Supreme Court, with the chief justice as the head of that branch of government. The Supreme Court would make administrative rules for the system, and the chief would issue administrative orders to the lower courts. The legislature could overturn an administrative rule by a two-thirds vote of both houses.

Baggett and Roberts obtained a $44,000 grant from the Law Enforcement Assistance Administration in Washington to create the Office of State Court Administrator. After voters approved the Article V revisions in March 1972, the Legislature formally created OSCA and authorized a new administrator to run it at $30,000 a year. The office opened July 1, 1972, ten weeks after voter approval of the new Article V of the Constitution.

From a national search, Roberts made an interesting and somewhat mysterious choice to head the new office—the deputy general counsel of the Central Intelligence Agency, James B. Ueberhorst, a forty-three-year-old graduate of the University of Michigan Law School with no Florida connections. Ueberhorst had recently finished a program at the National Center for State Courts, which had been founded just a couple of years earlier at the urging of U.S. Supreme Court Chief Justice Warren E. Burger as part of his effort to create a central administration for the federal courts.

Roberts announced the Ueberhorst appointment on May 31 to a hostile audience—the circuit court clerks, elected at the circuit level and accustomed to substantial authority over the budgeting and administration of the local courts. The clerks had seen the entire Article V movement as a dilution of their authority and independence as elected constitutional officers. Now there would be court administrators at the local level as well as OSCA at the state level. Roberts stressed that Ueberhorst would not be a "boss" to the clerks but that his duties would include "assignment of judges, adjustment of caseloads, keeping up with dockets and the general administration of the court system" on behalf of the chief justice.[2]

OSCA was a small office in the sub-basement of the Supreme Court's twenty-seven-year-old building, two floors below ground from the front of the building but with an exit to the rear of the building on the steeply sloping block west of the capitol. The First District Court of Appeal had its courtroom and offices one floor above OSCA on what was called the "basement" floor, to the dismay of the First District judges, who thought their floor should be called the "second floor." The Supreme Court's big courtroom was on the third floor (which then was called the first floor, as it appeared from the front). The floors were indeed renamed years later—after the First DCA moved out.

Only OSCA's administrator and deputy had private offices. Several people shared one big conference table or just used the desk of someone who wasn't there. They were building an organization almost from scratch, without computers, with just paper files, with typewriters and white-out correction fluid, with budgets from multiple courts in 20 judicial circuits and 67 counties. "We spent most of the time trying to determine its new role in the existing judicial structure, meeting the many players and related organizations, and beginning to establish a rudimentary case inventory system," recalled Sue K. Dosal, whom Ueberhorst hired as deputy administrator from a job at the Institute for Court Management in Colorado.[3] (She became state court administrator in Minnesota in 1982 and served there for more than thirty years.)

Eventually the centralization of information and authority began. The first reference to the state court administrator in the records of justices' conferences was on July 26, 1972, when Ueberhorst and Baggett presented "a brief explanation of the new Florida uniform case reporting system," including proposed forms that were being sent to local court clerks for their "comments." The Legislature was working on a personnel system to transfer employees of local clerks or court and circuit administrators to a state-funded system. Unfortunately, that all coincided with the Supreme Court scandals, which bolstered local resistance toward the state's intrusion into local courts. Mike Bridenbach, later court administrator in the Thirteenth Judicial Circuit (Hillsborough), who joined OSCA in 1976, called it a "rebellion" over Ueberhorst's "attempt to centralize authority and control."

Ueberhorst had not helped matters by declaring early on that court clerks should be appointed, not elected. "No reform more threatens these officials," wrote Larry C. Berkson and Steven W. Hays in a study of the early years of court administrators.[4] At the same time, new court administrators were being hired in each circuit to take on some duties previously performed by the clerks of court, who felt they answered to the voters, not the chief judge. Although clerks of court had less education and less management experience than the new court administrators, the clerks were elected constitutional officers, and they had strong local political ties and wide-ranging duties.

More than half the court clerks in a survey said they did not even communicate with the new court administrators. Chief judges viewed their own roles as primarily mediators among their fellow judges and viewed management from Tallahassee as intrusive. So they gave little authority to court administrators, even though they were supposed to bring greater efficiency to the management of the court system. "With the exception of two or three court administrators," Berkson and Hays wrote in 1976, "court administrators have become highly paid valets, chauffeurs, legal researchers, personal secretaries and/or statisticians."

As local court administrators struggled to find their footing, so did Ueberhorst. "Unfortunately, the first state courts administrator had almost no experience in the area of court management," Berkson and Hays commented in their 1976 study. "More important, he was not a Floridian, and consequently was ignorant of the local political ethos." It did not help that Chief Justice Carlton, who succeeded Roberts in January 1973, had little interest in court administration and was distracted by his wife's terminal illness and death. After Carlton's resignation from the court on February 1, 1974, Adkins became chief. He likewise lacked the intense interest in developing the central administration that Roberts envisioned and was preoccupied with the growing scandal enveloping the court.

This inconsistent leadership in the chief's office and the hostility of local clerks doomed Ueberhorst. On May 19, 1975, he resigned. His public statement said the Supreme Court had "weathered the storm of derision and unfair criticism with dignified success."[5] The resignation drew little public attention at the time, and Ueberhorst went to work at a newly created job as chief of the Division of Management Review in the administrative office of the U.S. court system. A month later, though, the *St. Petersburg Times* revealed that Ueberhorst's resignation was preceded by an internal audit showing he used a Supreme Court credit card to pay for his wife, stepdaughter, and mother-in-law to go with him to the American Bar Association convention in Hawaii in 1974.[6]

That disclosure was only the beginning of criticism of the financial practices of the fledgling Office of the State Court Administrator. State Auditor General reports for 1975 and 1976 noted a lack of documentation for a wide range of expenditures. Merely an "oral agreement," for example, supported $90,000 in payments to the University of Florida Law School to train non-lawyer judges. Overton, in an interview decades later, called one of the audits "scathing." Adkins, as chief justice, commented in a response to the 1975 audit that the court has "not regarded standard purchasing procedures . . . as practical necessities."[7]

In contrast with the outsider who focused on the other courts of Florida's judicial system, the man who administered the Supreme Court's internal work had a long history with the court. Sid J. White was a native of Clearwater and was a sergeant in the Marine Corps until 1952, graduated from the University of Virginia in 1955, and in 1960 earned a law degree from Stetson Law School in St. Petersburg. He was briefly an assistant attorney general under Richard Ervin, then in 1961 he became the law clerk for Justice Thomas.

On October 1, 1964, upon the retirement of longtime Supreme Court Clerk Guyte McCord Sr., White got the job. It was nine months after his old boss, Ervin, had joined the court. White became the only person besides the justices themselves who participated in the justices' regular conferences.

Unfailingly polite and accessible, White also acquired a certain heroic stature as he navigated the scandal-ridden months that followed the triumphs of 1972. In the impeachment hearings of 1975 over the conduct of Boyd, Dekle, and McCain, White, who held his job at the pleasure of the justices, provided key testimony about Justice McCain's unusual requests for assignment to nine different cases.[8] "Always with class, with courtesy, with distinction," Justice England said, White "provided me and a lot of others with wise counsel and unfailing assistance."[9]

White served as Clerk of the Supreme Court for nearly thirty-five years, the longest tenure in the court's history. He retired on April 14, 1999, at age sixty-eight,[10] and died on August 13, 2016.

6

THE SPIRIT OF 1976

Reformers Take Control

On December 18, 1975, Justice England hand delivered to the other six justices an envelope marked "personal." Inside was an eight-page memo on "the matter of the selection of the chief justice." Adkins would finish his tumultuous two-year term as chief in less than three months. The traditional successor, next in seniority, would be Joe Boyd, but he had been reprimanded ten months earlier for unethical conduct.

For months there had been an assumption that Boyd would take himself out of consideration, but he had shown no indication of doing so. England took the initiative to get a court majority to skip Boyd and elect Overton as chief in 1976. Because of "events" the past two years, including Boyd's reprimand for "impropriety in office," England wrote in the memo, "the prestige of the court" required this extraordinary break from tradition. Furthermore, he said, the meeting to vote on the next chief should be opened to the public.

There was a time in the court's history when the choice of chief had been much simpler. The 1885 Constitution called for the chief to be chosen "by lot in such manner as they [the justices] may determine," and the justices did this by going around the table with each justice opening the Bible or a new law book. The chief would be the one whose right-hand page had the highest last digit, or perhaps a first word beginning with the letter closest to "Z." Even that produced mischief. When Adkins was a law clerk in 1938, Justice William H. Ellis told him that as a new justice in 1915 he had drawn a very promising "7," then senior Justice R. Fenwick Taylor (Ellis's father-in-law) had opened the Bible, declared "I have a 9," and shut the book quickly before anyone could see. Ellis had to either challenge the honesty of his father-in-law and colleague, or acquiesce. So Taylor, who had served eight straight years as chief 1897–1905, became chief again for the 1915–17 term. He won it one more time, in 1923. Only once more in the twentieth century did a chief serve consecutive two-year terms: Jefferson B. Browne of Monroe County, who became chief in January 1917 and served three terms, until January 1923.

After Florida's lottery for chief justice attracted national ridicule in 1925, a constitutional amendment let justices choose their own method of selecting a chief. The seniority system with the traditional two-year term began then and continued for fifty years without interruption other than occasionally restarting the seniority rotation.

Roberts had restarted the rotation in 1971. Next in line in 1973 was Vassar Carlton, one of the three justices elected in 1968, who was considered the most senior because of his seventeen years as a circuit judge in the Seventh Circuit. With Carlton's resignation halfway through his term as chief in February 1974, Adkins' fifteen years as a circuit judge in the Eighth Circuit put him next in seniority, and the biennial rotation shifted permanently to even-numbered years, with a March 1 start date instead of January. Boyd, the third of the 1968 group of justices, had no prior judgeship and would ordinarily follow Adkins.

Boyd struck back at England's memo with one of his own. He argued that he had been vindicated by the investigations and reaffirmed by the voters in his 1974 reelection. Perhaps overconfident or perhaps bluffing, he proposed that the public session be in the largest conference room available. Roberts weighed in as well with a memo challenging England's version of court history.

There was now an "Askew majority" on the court that could control the choice of chief if they voted together. England felt sure that Sundberg and Hatchett would support Overton, Askew's first appointee to the court. Overton agreed that Boyd's selection would embarrass the court but was unwilling to be the deciding vote for himself. Boyd had the support of Adkins and Roberts. Adkins argued forcefully that any person sitting on the court was qualified to be chief. England suspected that Roberts, though he was talking about retiring, would love to be the compromise choice and have a fourth term as chief. Roberts had won the job ahead of Carlton in 1971 by arguing that Carlton's two years on the court were inadequate experience for a chief justice, and Overton likewise had been there just two years. To prevail, though, Roberts would need the support of Adkins and Boyd as well as one of the Askew justices. That didn't seem likely.

England figured his only leverage was to seek a public session, with the implicit threat that it would generate a media reprise of the Boyd reprimand. England thought Roberts would not publicly oppose the three justices supporting Overton by voting for either himself or Boyd, and like Overton, would not want to be publicly elected by a divisive 4–3 vote.

Sure enough, Roberts relented. "I will not be a candidate, but select Ben," he told England.[1]

The selection of the chief had been publicly announced for January 19, and Chief Justice Adkins had left open the option of making it a public session. But five days ahead of schedule, on January 14, the justices met in a private conference. Adkins explained afterward that he "decided not to have a public meeting and get it over with in a hurry." Hatchett, according to Adkins at the time, still had not committed his vote to Overton when the conference began. Adkins nominated Boyd for chief. Boyd complained that the proceeding was an exercise in "raw power," but the momentum was against him. He relented. The official minutes, making no reference to the internal differences, reported that Boyd nominated Overton and the court elected him unanimously. The *St. Petersburg Times* called it a "harmony and unity compromise set up by the withdrawal of two more senior colleagues."[2]

At the unanimous direction of the justices, Clerk Sid White collected copies of the memos to burn them. England explained later that before the meeting ended, "someone" suggested this action because "there is a responsibility to let bygones be bygones . . . to say the work of the court is more important." At least one copy of England's memo apparently survived, however, and was leaked to *Miami Herald* reporter Mike Baxter, who then got the rest of the story from interviews with England and Adkins.[3] Boyd would not talk to Baxter about what happened but showed him a plaque some friends had given him bearing the words "To JUSTICE JOE BOYD AT HIS 'PASSOVER.'"

On March 1, Overton succeeded Adkins as chief. Adkins, surrounded by boxes as he packed up the previous Friday afternoon, reflected on his turbulent two years and called it "an interesting experience."[4] There was no gavel-passing ceremony in those days. Over the weekend, the new chief simply moved into the chief's suite next to the atrium with the view of the capitol out the window.

Overton said the first goal would be to speed up the handling of cases and to catch up on the backlog lingering from the recusals, vacancies, and distraction of the investigations in 1974–75. He said the justices had agreed to curtail public appearances until the backlog was reduced. He added, in an interview with his hometown newspaper, the *St. Petersburg Times,* that he would also focus on long waits for trial in circuit courts in some parts of the state.[5]

The selection of the new chief launched a contentious political year for the court. For one thing, Overton was a taskmaster, a contrast to Adkins's easy-going, deferential style. Overton wanted to move cases along. At one point, realizing that a number of death-penalty cases were stalled by the same two or three issues, he put twenty-five death cases on the agenda for one conference. That produced a lot of grumbling, but he said the cases got resolved more quickly as a result.

Overton also had to contend with the chaos in court administration and the resignation of the first state court administrator, Gerald Ueberhorst (chapter 5). After the resignation, Overton and Roberts became a two-person search committee to hire a new state court administrator. The job was posted, but Overton had an idea about who he wanted: John F. "Jack" Harkness Jr., who was in private practice with his father in North Miami but who had been staff director of the House Judiciary Criminal Committee. Harkness was a polar opposite of Ueberhorst. He knew the new court reorganization plan intimately and had worked with Adkins while the legislature was rewriting the state's criminal laws. Harkness was known and respected on both the legislative and judicial sides of court administration.

When Harkness started work on December 1, 1975, he found that office equipment consisted of one big photocopier and a word processor. The twenty or so people working there shared no more than four phone lines.[6] But he had connections not only with the legislature but with another network of great importance in those years: Florida Blue Key, the club for politically ambitious students at the University of Florida. The organization fostered a lifelong fraternal spirit, and perhaps a fourth of the legislators at that time were Blue Key alums. "I never got surprised at the Legislature," Overton recalled with a chuckle.

Harkness clearly had managerial ability. With Overton's selection as chief shortly after Harkness arrived, Harkness also worked for a chief who had a strong aptitude for judicial administration, a no-nonsense attitude about the changes needed, and strong connections with the local courts and chief judges.

Soon after becoming chief, Overton received a call from Governor Askew's budget director, Joseph P. Cresse, whose good-ol'-boy manner masked deep knowledge about the state budget. The two men had been fraternity brothers at the University of Florida and were neighbors in Killearn Estates, a suburb in northeastern Tallahassee where a number of top state officials lived. Cresse told Overton the statewide account for paying jurors was $1 million overdrawn. Funds could be reallocated to cover the overrun, Cresse said, "but I thought you ought to know."

Overton was meticulous about financial records. As a circuit judge, he would write personal checks to reimburse the county for personal calls on his office phone at ten cents a call. He put Harkness to work on the jury money. It turned out, Overton recalled decades later, that jury duty was a form of patronage in many counties. County commissioners or elected court clerks were putting chosen supporters onto the list of people called for jury service (back when $5 or $10 a day was more meaningful than today), but it turned out that some smaller counties would pay jurors for an entire week even if they were excused the first day. The elected court clerks would even hand the checks personally to the jurors.

Overton became chief just in time for the 1976 annual legislative session, where reformers were trying one more time to establish merit-selection of all judges in Florida, not just for filling vacancies between elections. Supreme Court justices and county judges had been elected since early statehood, but for a hundred years, circuit judges were appointed by the governor with confirmation by the Senate. In 1948 that changed, and circuit judges also were elected unless a vacancy happened in midterm, in which case the governor made the appointment. All judicial elections were partisan ones. A return to an appointive system had first been proposed in 1956, alongside the constitutional provision creating the mid-level courts of appeal. It was also part of the unsuccessful package of proposals from the Constitution Revision Commission in 1966.

The use of nominating commissions to screen applicants for appointment by the governor had become part of the Florida Constitution with the Article V amendments in 1972, but only for vacancies. Judicial elections had become nonpartisan after that, but the compromise that got that amendment on the 1972 ballot eliminated "merit selection" for all judgeships. The Florida Bar president, William Reece Smith, continued to be a strong advocate for merit selection of all judges, but the Bar itself was divided. So was the legislature. Smith and others kept trying, but on May 16, 1973, the House killed the idea.

Now, three years later, the appetite for judicial reform was revived by the court scandal. The Supreme Court itself unintentionally stirred new reformist sentiment when it ruled in 1974 that the Judicial Qualifications Commission had no jurisdiction to investigate a judge who had been indicted but acquitted on bribery charges before becoming a circuit judge.[7] The legislature responded immediately with a constitutional amendment to make clear that the JQC could investigate misconduct "during term of office or otherwise occurring on or after November 1, 1966," the date the JQC was created.[8] Voters approved the amendment in November 1974.

In the 1976 session, a second-term House member named C. William Nelson, a Democrat from Melbourne, who would later become U.S. Senator Bill Nelson, dug into the research on Florida judges. A fifth-generation Floridian, he had been a political science major at Yale, wrote his honors thesis on "The Impact of Cape Kennedy on Brevard County Politics," was the class orator at graduation in 1965, and went on to the University of Virginia Law School. After two years as an army captain, he came back to Florida, served briefly as a legislative aide to Governor Askew, and then ran for the House in 1972. His research showed that incumbent judges were unopposed for reelection 85 percent of the time during the previous twenty years. Only one Supreme Court justice had been defeated in fifty years: Republican Wade S. Hopping, a Kirk appointee who had served six months before being defeated by Democrat Vassar Carlton in the 1968 election. The previous defeat was Robert S. Cockrell, who lost the 1916 election after fourteen years on the court. Only one district court of appeal judge had been defeated in twenty years.

"Our present system is a fiction as an elected system," Nelson said.[9] He was the lead sponsor of the merit-selection proposal in the House. Another supporter, Representative Helen Gordon Davis, a Democrat from Tampa, argued that the election of judges was not part of any democratic tradition—the U.S. Constitution does not provide for it, and no other democracy except Switzerland elects judges. Judges, she added, were not supposed to reflect majority opinions. "Many times they must represent and protect the minority," she said.

Among the opponents was the chairman of the House Judiciary Committee, William J. Rish, a Democrat from Port St. Joe widely known as "Billy Joe." He said he was "unalterably opposed" to merit retention and said it would perpetuate mediocre judges. Florida Bar lobbyist Richard C. McFarlain responded that mediocre judges, "if there are any," will go on the ballot so that voters can vote them out of office. "As it is now, lawyers don't run against them," he said. "Therefore, they never go on the ballot. Therefore, you've got them for life."

House Speaker Donald Tucker refused to let Rish kill the bill in committee. He told Rish he wanted a vote on the floor of the House. He also overruled Rules Chairman Gus Craig, who did not want to take the legislation to the floor.[10]

Some Republicans held back support because they thought Askew had been appointing too many Democrats. But Sen. David McClain, a Republican from Tampa, co-sponsored the proposal in the Senate along with Democratic Sen. Kenneth M. Myers of Miami.

Compromises continued. Most significantly, the provision would apply only to judges of the district courts of appeal and the Supreme Court. Trial judges would continue to be elected. Further, legislators had been miffed that all three of Askew's appointments to the Supreme Court came from Pinellas County, although Hatchett had spent his professional years in Daytona Beach and Jacksonville. One price of putting merit selection on the ballot was a provision that there be at least one justice from each of the appellate districts. And nominating commissions would nominate exactly three candidates, not "at least" three, as had happened with Hatchett appointment. (The provision was changed twenty years later to allow six nominees for a seat.)

The compromises cleared the way for merit selection to be on the ballot in November for voter approval. If the proposal were ratified, 1976 would be the last year in which opposing candidates competed for Supreme Court seats.

Sundberg and Hatchett had to stand for election in 1976, as all appointed judges had to do at the first statewide election after their appointment.

Roberts's term was ending as well. In the midst of (or shortly after) the chief selection in early 1976, Roberts began preparing for his own departure. He did not have to leave. The constitutional provision establishing mandatory retirement for judges at age seventy explicitly excluded any justice appointed before the provision took effect on July 1, 1957. But his influence with the other justices was fading. No one thought of this as B. K. Roberts's court anymore.

Fred Karl, the former state senator who had applied for the McCain vacancy on the court along with Hatchett in 1975, said he got a call in "late 1975" from Roberts, who told him he was calling the finalists for that appointment to alert them to his intention not to seek reelection that year.[11] Like Justice Ervin in 1974, Roberts said he would time his departure so that the voters, not the governor, would fill the vacancy. Roberts told his colleagues the same thing. But he continued in public to toy with running again. "I'll tell you this," he told a reporter in an article published February 8, 1976, "I'm getting lots of encouragement to run."[12] Roberts was going to urge the legislature one more time to support merit selection, and he did not want to be a lame duck. He most assuredly did not want them to know he was timing his own departure to avoid the very thing he was advocating.

Not until June 12, after the legislative session was over, did he announce his retirement. "The four new members of the court, they're all young," Roberts said.[13] "They are entitled to an opportunity to impress their philosophy on the record of the court. After twenty-seven years, I decided it was time to move over." Without mentioning a desire to see his successor chosen by election rather than appointment, Roberts said he would stay until the end of his term so he could promote merit retention. "I've been working ten years to get that," he said. "I believe I can be more successful in office than out."

Roberts's successor would be chosen in a non-partisan election held alongside the party primaries in early September, when Sundberg and Hatchett would also be on the ballot if they had opposition.

Hatchett drew fierce opposition very early. Even as the drama over the chief justice was unfolding in secret during January, longtime Roberts ally Harvie DuVal announced he would challenge Hatchett. Many people suspected Roberts actually encouraged the challenge, but there was no evidence of that. DuVal had been appointed a circuit judge in 1960. His great-granduncle was Florida's first territorial governor, William Pope DuVal, for whom Duval County is named. DuVal said he had not applied for the seat when Hatchett won it because "you've got to put your hat in your hand and politic with the governor to get the appointment."

Bob Benton, the future judge who was Hatchett's law clerk at the time, remembered riding with Hatchett to very conservative Panama City, where Benton grew up, for a candidate forum one day. DuVal talked about his ancestors and noted that Duval County was named for them and so was a street in Key West. Then, in a striking and poignant contrast, Hatchett stood up and said his family too had been in Florida since the 1800s and had nothing named for them. He went on to talk about becoming a lawyer and a prosecutor. "He was good. He had good presence," said Benton, and he connected with all those people who didn't inherit anything and had nothing named for them, either.[14]

DuVal ran a negative campaign that continually alluded to race. He said Hatchett was "completely unqualified" for the job and that Askew had tampered with the nominating commission and used "reverse discrimination" in appointing Hatchett. Askew and leaders of the nominating commission denied any tampering. DuVal withdrew the charge, but continued to note Askew's statement that "race played a major consideration" in the appointment and claimed it was Askew's "only reason." Noting that Hatchett had been federal magistrate before his appointment, DuVal said, "What in the world is a magistrate? He tried the traffic cases in the naval base, [found] probable cause and set bonds."

DuVal used Hatchett's post-appointment celebrity against him. The *Orlando Sentinel* reported that Hatchett, much in demand as a speaker, spent up to 25 percent of his days away from the court on court-paid trips. Soon after DuVal announced, however, or at least after Overton became chief, Hatchett charged very few trips to the state. DuVal claimed Hatchett was behind in his work, attributing the information to "a source" on the court, generally assumed to be his friend Roberts. Overton would not reveal internal workload figures but did say the court had cut its backlog in half by disposing of more cases in the first half of 1976 than in all of 1972. DuVal also said Hatchett had "no state court trial experience," even though Hatchett had practiced law for seven years handling everything from murder cases to civil lawsuits before joining the U.S. Attorney's office.

Hatchett's supporters in Askew's office enlisted a prominent young lawyer as finance chairman and day-to-day manager of the Hatchett campaign. Howell L. Ferguson had come out of Yale University and the University of Florida Law School, served as an assistant attorney general under Robert L. Shevin 1971–72, then served as an aide to Askew 1973–74. Askew's staff figured Ferguson could take some time off from making a living to run the campaign, because his mother was Louise Lykes Ferguson, of the Lykes Brothers business empire—Lykes cattle and meatpacking, Lykes citrus, Lykes steamship lines, plus major holdings in utilities and banks and other businesses, and one of Florida largest landowners, including the 7L Ranch near the Everglades created by Howell T. Ferguson and his seven sons in 1895. Young Howell would eventually become the empire's CEO and then chairman of the board.

Askew aide Hugh MacMillan took five weeks of vacation time to work in the Hatchett campaign, though he said Askew did not ask him to do it. Another former Askew aide, future Attorney General James C. Smith, would also write a fund-raising letter. Unlike DuVal, Hatchett limited contributions to $100. Askew himself helped Hatchett raise money and campaigned actively for Hatchett. Askew's chief of staff, James W. Apthorp, said Askew's role did not violate the separation of powers between executive and judicial branches. "He appointed the man," Apthorp said.[15]

Hatchett also had most of the state's newspaper editorial boards on his side, and news reporters dug into DuVal's own record. *Miami Herald* reporter Tom Fiedler wrote that DuVal had been reversed on appeal sixty-eight times during his thirteen years on the bench—not fewer than twenty times, as DuVal had claimed. (DuVal counted only final judgments, not pretrial or mid-trial rulings or dismissals.) Another report was that DuVal had been a lawyer's guest on a trip to New Mexico at the same time he was presiding over a major case that the lawyer won. Sitting by special appointment in the Dekle reprimand case at the Supreme Court, DuVal had dissented from any reprimand.[16]

When the Bar poll of its members rated Hatchett qualified and DuVal not qualified, the challenger claimed Askew had rigged the poll. The poll rated DuVal fortieth out of forty-four circuit judges in Dade County in integrity and temperament.

Hatchett still had some things working against him, in the view of campaign strategists. DuVal's name was familiar and would be ahead of Hatchett's on the ballot. And it was an open question whether Floridians would elect a black man over a white man. A smaller turnout could also favor DuVal, and the nonpartisan judicial elections were now in September, alongside the party primaries, rather than in November, when the presidential race pulled people to the polls.

Sundberg, too, faced opposition. Shortly before the noon closing of election qualifying on July 20, Fort Lauderdale lawyer John V. Russell showed up at the secretary of state's office in Tallahassee still uncertain whether to challenge Palm Beach lawyer Gavin Letts for the Fourth District Court of Appeal or Sundberg for the Supreme Court. Letts was there; Sundberg was across the street at the court. Russell decided to challenge Sundberg. "It's the pinnacle of my profession," he said later.

Sundberg had been on the Florida Bar's governing board and a prominent trial lawyer and corporate lawyer in St. Petersburg. He was well liked and highly respected even before his appointment by Askew gave him statewide visibility. Russell knew, therefore, that "we won't have the Bar" on his side, as he was quoted as saying in a newspaper article shortly after qualifying. When the Bar was holding a news conference in August to announce the results of a poll of Bar members on the qualifications of the candidates, Russell sent an aide with a written statement saying, "Regardless of the outcome, the real question is not what the organized Bar thinks of me or my opponents, but rather what the public thinks of the organized Bar."[17]

Russell had served as a Fort Lauderdale city commissioner in the 1950s, gone to Indiana to become an executive in a bank controlled by his in-laws, then returned to Broward County to be in law practice again. He had eschewed involvement in Bar activities. Four years earlier he had run "not very hard," in his words, against Fourth DCA Judge Gerald Mager, a Kirk appointee, and had come close to winning.

Sundberg left the elections office and called his longtime friend Robert L. Parks, a Miami lawyer who had been a member of the Judicial Nominating Commission for all three of the Askew appointments of the past two years. "Bobby, we have got opposition, and we have to run a statewide campaign, and I don't know what to do."[18] Sundberg had never run for office and had little political experience. Parks was not that much more experienced, but he had run a local legislative campaign for Sandy D'Alemberte. Parks had to work to persuade Sundberg to visit Miami to campaign ("I suggested to him that there were an awful lot of folks down here that voted"). Sundberg took with him a huge supply of new campaign materials, all printed without the obligatory union seal—"an unpardonable sin" in statewide politics—so they had to be thrown away.

Parks's favorite story from the campaign was about a pre-dawn drive up LeJeune Road in Coral Gables to get Sundberg to a very early flight. They were running late, and six-foot-five Sundberg threw his luggage into the back seat and quickly stuffed himself into Parks's sporty little Datsun 240Z, only to hear a tearing sound. "Oh God, Bobby, I have torn my pants from the waistline all the way down," Sundberg told him. Sundberg rejected the idea of a Supreme Court justice walking into the Miami airport "showing from stem to stern," so he decided to climb into the tiny back seat and change clothes there. "You keep driving," Sundberg said, then somehow twisted his way to the back—"it was not pretty, but it was definitely unique," as Parks put it. Parks drove through "some green lights and the rest of them" and was seeing the speedometer approach eighty. Sundberg told him, "If you don't get me to the plane on time, your appellate career is history." Parks returned the humor. "If I get stopped doing 80 miles an hour with a half-clothed Supreme Court justice in the back seat, we are both history."

Although he lacked campaign sophistication, Sundberg also won the support of newspapers and the Bar. As with DuVal, a majority in the Bar poll rated Russell unqualified. Sundberg was rated qualified by 95 percent of those responding, higher even than Hatchett's 82 percent approval.

And then there was the Roberts seat.

Tipped off by Roberts, Karl records in his memoir that he wondered "if this was what I had been waiting for."[19] He would not have to unseat an incumbent, as he had to do when he first ran for the Florida Senate. And because of Roberts's call, he would have the advantage of announcing early and perhaps discouraging others. On the other hand, "there were many negative factors to consider." He had been forced to quit his special counsel role in the impeachments of the justices earlier in 1975 because of surgery that had not gone well, and his health still was not good. "I convinced myself that I was feeling good," his memoir says, though he "probably fudged a bit on that issue."

Personal finances were also a problem. In private law practice he was making about $150,000 a year. A Supreme Court justice made $40,000 in 1976. "Could I reduce my needs and obligations to my children for their education," he wondered, or draw enough from his "modest assets" to make up the difference? He decided it was "doable," and his family "was in accord that I should go for it."

He thought judges should not have to get their seats by election. He felt campaigning "diminishes judicial candidates" by making them go "hat in hand looking for money" and "kiss the ring of professional politicians to induce them to help." Part of his concern was practical. A lawyer in private practice can't keep much of a practice going while he campaigns, so even if he loses, his law practice is likely to be "in shambles." He figured a lot of lawyers simply didn't run. "It follows that we should expect to have a better set of judges if they are appointed instead of elected."

Karl was also a victim of his own ethical standards. He put a $100 limit on contributions, and he was not getting a lot of those, especially with competition from two high-profile incumbent justices also running in contested elections. Karl says one lawyer "familiar with my financial situation" offered to underwrite the entire campaign, but Karl rejected the offer. "I don't know exactly what he had in mind or what the quid pro quo would have been, but I was glad I wasn't so desperate to win that I was tempted to go against my better judgment." Another lawyer offered $5,000 or nothing. Karl took nothing.

He soon drew his first opponent: Charles R. Holley, a plaintiff's lawyer from Naples who had been in the legislature and sought the Republican nomination for governor in 1964, when Karl was unsuccessfully seeking the Democratic nomination for governor. Holley had been a circuit judge in St. Petersburg from 1966 to 1972. Just before the qualifying period closed, a third candidate joined the race: Richard H. Max Swann from Miami. Unlike Karl, Swann had appellate experience as a judge on the Third District Court of Appeal for eight years before returning to law practice in 1972. "It was now a whole new contest with the very real possibility of a runoff," Karl recalled.

Neither of the other two candidates put any limits on contributions, so Karl made that an issue in the campaign. Since it was a nonpartisan race, he could not identify himself as a Democrat. Like most candidates for judgeships, he talked mainly about his own experience. He was not supposed to talk about his position on issues, but he pointed people to his positions as a legislator. "I made them understand that I was not trying to hide behind the rule that limits what judicial candidates can do in their campaigns, and that I was actually inviting them to look at my past activities and use them as points of reference."

In the Bar poll, more than 80 percent of those responding rated Swann qualified, just a little behind Karl. Swann actually came out ahead of Karl in the Dade County poll. Two-thirds of those responding rated Holley unqualified for the Supreme Court. In response, Holley said it was "fascinating" that 647 lawyers out of more than a thousand had rated the quality and clarity of Karl's opinions as acceptable "when he's never written one."

Karl relied heavily on his family in the campaign. His wife, Mercedes, known as Merci, managed the campaign logistics. Their son Rick was chauffeur and baggage handler.

Health remained a challenge. Karl's surgery a year earlier, for a ruptured esophagus, seemed to be having the permanent effects that doctors had warned about. "I had little strength, no endurance, considerable pain, and I felt rotten most of the time," he wrote. But he had "some form of campaign organization" in every county and began thinking he might avoid a runoff.

"A justice is the sum of his past," his uninspiring campaign slogan said. At fifty-two, he was no stranger to politics and government. He had been elected to the Florida House of Representatives from Volusia County in 1956, the same year LeRoy Collins was running for governor. In his first year he spotted a local bill that would make it a felony to attend an integrated athletic event and alerted Collins, who vetoed it. Karl supported John F. Kennedy for president in 1960. He ran for governor in 1964. He called education "the closest thing we'll find as a panacea for all ills . . . the best way to attack the racial problem, the economic problem, other social problems."[20] Other parts of his platform sound like a preview of Florida policymaking for the next two decades: fair apportionment of the legislature, open government, a program to protect natural resources, a new state constitution, tax reform to more equitably share the costs of government, an aggressive campaign to attract clean industry, strict enforcement of highway safety laws, but also adding "an end to promiscuous borrowing and a return to true fiscal conservatism."

Karl did not win the Democratic primary; Haydon Burns of Jacksonville did. Four years later, in 1968, Karl won a seat in the State Senate against an incumbent, Republican Ralph R. Clayton of DeLand. The Senate when he arrived had an exceptional membership—people who would go on to statewide office and political careers of integrity, among them Reubin Askew, Lawton Chiles, Robert L. Shevin, and Bill Gunter. Karl became chairman of the Commerce Committee and of the Select Committee on Executive Suspensions. He also was a member of the conference committee that in 1971 produced the final version of the Article V revisions that went on the 1972 ballot.

Karl had grown up in a political family. His father, Fred J. Karl, served on a county commission in Michigan. His mother, Mary Brennan Karl, was a crusader for vocational education. She was visiting her parents in Daytona Beach when Frederick Brennan Karl was born on May 14, 1924. The Karls moved to Daytona permanently before Fred entered kindergarten.

Mary Karl was a first cousin of U.S. Supreme Court Justice William Francis

"Frank" Murphy, who Fred Karl said was an inspiration in his life. Murphy had been a Depression-era mayor of Detroit, governor-general of the Philippines and then governor of Michigan (1937–39). President Franklin Roosevelt appointed him U.S. Attorney General in 1939 and to the Supreme Court in 1940. Murphy, generally considered liberal, is most remembered for a powerful dissent in *Korematsu v. United States*.[21] Murphy said the confinement of Japanese Americans after the Pearl Harbor attack "falls into the ugly abyss of racism."

In Daytona, Mary Karl founded and led the Mary Karl Vocational School, which eventually became Daytona State College. (Although she died in 1948, in 2011 she was inducted into the Florida Women's Hall of Fame. As her son accepted the award on her behalf, Governor Rick Scott remarked that Fred Karl "basically had every job other than mine in this state."[22]) Her son was student council president at Seabreeze High School. In 1942 he enrolled at the University of Florida, but almost immediately enlisted in the army as a private, went to officer candidate school, and was commissioned as a second lieutenant at age eighteen. Those were, of course, the early days of World War II, and Karl became a tank platoon leader, fought in the Battle of the Bulge, and was awarded a Silver Star, a Bronze Star, and the Purple Heart. After the war, he went to Stetson Law School and got his law degree in 1949.

In his campaign for the House of Representatives in 1956, Karl won the Democratic nomination in a runoff, had no Republican opposition, and became part of an exceptional class of freshman representatives whose notable members also included future Senate presidents Dempsey Barron and John E. "Jack" Mathews Jr. and future longtime congressman Sam Gibbons. After his run for governor in 1964 and his return to the legislature as a senator in 1968, Karl moved to Tallahassee in 1972 and was counsel to the House committee handling the impeachment investigation of Boyd, Dekle and McCain. He then served as public counsel advocating the consumer side of utility rate cases.

Karl was well known and respected by reporters and editorial boards as a result of his visible roles in state government, but Swann tried to turn the media against him in the 1976 election by associating Karl with Pat Tornillo, executive director of the Dade County Teachers Association. As a legislative candidate, Tornillo had sued the *Miami Herald* to require the newspaper to publish verbatim his reply to two editorials attacking Tornillo (chapter 12). The newspaper refused, lost at the Florida Supreme Court, but eventually won on First Amendment grounds at the U.S. Supreme Court. Swann said Tornillo's public support of Karl raised questions about Karl's commitment to the

First Amendment. But by the time Swann entered the race, Karl had already visited every editorial board at least once in his eight-month campaign and had largely won their support. He said the editors tested his knowledge of Article V and court jurisdiction and asked about his favorite U.S. Supreme Court justice and his assessment of cases on integration, reapportionment and other big topics. They asked "whether I would be a conservative justice and limit my rulings to interpretations of the constitution, or be an activist justice and legislate matters expanding the power of government."

Turnout in the September 1976 election was "pathetic," in the view of State Elections Director Mary Singleton, but it ended up working in favor of the more motivated progressives and activists who wanted to continue the Askew reforms.

Karl came close to crossing the 50 percent mark, but Swann, running in third place with less than 25 percent of the vote, had drawn away just enough votes, mainly in Miami, to force a runoff against Holley, the most conservative of the candidates, who took about 32 percent of the vote. Karl had to campaign for another three weeks before winning the Supreme Court seat in a runoff election. He would refer to himself afterward as the last justice to join the Supreme Court by election.

Sundberg won 56 percent of the vote to dispatch John Russell.

The truly historic result, however, was Joe Hatchett's victory over Harvie DuVal. It had been 102 years since a black person won a statewide election in Florida, and the last time had been during Reconstruction, when many whites who had supported the Confederacy were not allowed to vote. DuVal lost his home county, Dade, as well as the county that bore his family name. Hatchett was the only black person elected in a statewide contested election during the twentieth century. (The next time it happened was when Barack Obama won the 2008 presidential primary.)

It was an election year dominated by moderation and ethical government. In contrast with the vicious 1972 national campaigns that produced what President Gerald R. Ford would call the "national nightmare" of the Watergate electioneering scandal, 1976 at the presidential level pitted two low-key politicians with reputations for ethical, bipartisan government—Republican President Gerald Ford and Democratic challenger Jimmy Carter, the former governor of Georgia. The post-Watergate mood undoubtedly bolstered the ethical, reform-oriented candidates for the Florida Supreme Court.

But so did the memories of judicial scandal, which had generated sustained prominent headlines throughout 1975 and echoed in the judicial campaigns of 1976. Without those memories to motivate voters, it is very possible that Hatchett and perhaps others would not have survived the onslaught of old politics.

There were also some big policy issues affecting the judiciary that the voters had to decide that November.

The legislature had approved a constitutional amendment overturning one of the key Supreme Court rulings in the JQC cases against Boyd and Dekle: that removal from office was appropriate only for a judge who had a "corrupt motive." The voters overwhelmingly approved the amendment.

Another was Askew's "Sunshine Amendment," the first proposed amendment to get on the ballot through voter signatures. That process had been created in the 1968 Constitution (chapter 26). Askew launched the initiative after the legislature rejected his call for candidates and officeholders to file personal financial reports for public perusal. His "Sunshine Amendment" was ratified by one of the most lopsided votes in Florida history, 1,765,626 votes for, 461,940 against. The amendment took effect on January 1, 1977.

It was widely speculated that Roberts's early retirement on November 30, 1976, was prompted by a desire to avoid the need to disclose financial information, as he would have had to do if he stayed until his term ended on January 4. Roberts joined with former executive assistant Fred Baggett and other partners, and they practiced law together until the firm merged with Miami-based Greenberg Traurig.

And there was merit selection. Finally, after so many years and so many failed efforts, the proposal had made it onto the ballot for voter approval. The voters embraced it almost as enthusiastically as the Sunshine Amendment: 1,600,944 votes for, 527,056 against.

7

UNEXPECTED REPLACEMENTS

Alderman and McDonald

Even before Fred Karl took his seat on January 4, 1977, as the sixty-sixth justice, the court sent him a three-feet-high stack of files from a death-penalty case that would be his responsibility. On arrival, he was presented a bucket and mop, a tradition that Sundberg and Overton remembered as well, as a reminder that he was the least senior justice and a grim allusion to the perpetually leaky roof on the court building. Overton recalled that the tradition stopped with Hatchett; Sundberg said he simply was not going to give a bucket and mop to the first black justice, whose mother spent her working life as a maid. But the tradition was resurrected one last time for Karl. "I knew it was a humorous routine," he recalled in his memoir, but it was also a reminder that "no matter how important the position of justice was or how critical the work of the court might be, there was still a ranking order, and I was ranked below everyone else."[1]

Karl had known Adkins a long time, and Overton was not a stranger either. Karl saw Sundberg as a legal scholar who "genuinely loved the law and was content to spend his time among the books in the library." Sundberg also was well known for drinking martinis and "could hold more of them than anyone I had ever known." Karl "envied Arthur [England] because of his brain," and he was "at least a cut above the rest of us." Hatchett, who had been chosen over Karl the previous year, was "a fine justice and a fine human being."

The relationship with Boyd was more awkward. Karl, after all, had been the counsel to the House Judiciary Committee during the first portion of the impeachment investigation of Boyd, Dekle, and McCain. "I had interviewed the person who was alleged to have drafted an opinion for Boyd," Karl wrote, referring to utility lawyer Ed Mason. "I knew a different version of the facts of that incident than was accepted by the committee after I left." Karl seemed to say he accepted Mason's account, and the facts as he saw them "somewhat poisoned my mind and were ever present as I worked with Joe."[2]

Karl had one fundamental disagreement with England—over oral arguments. After England's arrival and Sundberg's, the court became a "hot" court, as lawyers call it, peppering advocates with question after question during oral arguments. Both England and Sundberg, who went to Ivy League law schools a decade after Karl had finished at Stetson, believed that oral arguments were to let justices ask questions, test positions the lawyers were taking, and resolve issues troubling the justices. Sometimes the questions took the entire allotted time, and the lawyer had little time to summarize his case his way. Karl had a more traditional view. "I contended that the purpose of oral arguments was to give lawyers an opportunity to make their most important points and briefly explain why they ought to win on them," he said in his memoir. "We should not interrupt them unless they strayed or seemed not to know what to do." But his view did not prevail. The other justices "would follow Arthur's lead so they could be as involved in and knowledgeable about the issues, but often it was hard for any of us to get a question in edgewise."[3]

Overton recalled an oral argument while he was chief in which England, on one side of the bench, and Sundberg, on the other, disagreed on the case and peppered the lawyers with questions essentially arguing their own different views. When time expired, Overton told the lawyers he would give each of them five more minutes, "uninterrupted," to summarize their case. "They were the closest of friends," Overton said of England and Sundberg. "They enjoyed each other's intellectual abilities."[4]

Overton remembered Karl as a considerate person who "did really enjoy in part the monastery existence," because "you can quietly without interruption really think about what you're going to do. It was so much different from what he'd been involved with before."

But Karl's tenure did not last long. All his plans about how to accommodate his personal finances to the lower pay at the Supreme Court fell apart. He remembered the shock at his first paycheck at the court, less than $2,000 a month after deductions, out of the $43,200 annual salary of a justice. As a well-paid private lawyer, he "had been accustomed to wasting as much money as the net of my new take-home pay." His wife, Merci, had gone back to work, and they had sold their second car. But he had children in college. He had a $115,000 house, "extravagant" in the 1970s, with 4,000 square feet and six bedrooms that cost $1,000 a month in upkeep, but he could not find a buyer.[5] "The economy was in a slump; the value of my stock was down; and there was no market for a block of shares we owned in a bank," he wrote. "I just decided

I would not let them go into default," he said later. "I would not let a member of the Supreme Court be sued." He had hoped the legislature would raise the justices' pay, but it had not. He could have lived on his court salary, he felt, if he had been able to get the equity out of his house.

Unable to pay his bills, and unwilling, he said, to seek loans from banks that might be looking for his favor, he decided to resign. He managed to line up a new position, at substantially higher but undisclosed pay, as full-time legal counsel for the Florida Association of Insurance Agents. He withdrew from participating in any insurance-related cases when his discussions with the organization began.

He had tears in his eyes when he met with Chief Justice Overton on the morning of February 8, 1978, and gave him a formal resignation letter to the governor setting his departure for April 5. Overton knew Karl's resignation would be big news immediately, so he wanted to give Askew a heads-up before walking across the street to deliver the letter to the governor's office, where it would be a public record. "Reubin was never in the office before 10—don't even try to ask him anything before 10," Overton recalled later. He called his wife, Marilyn, who was a close friend of Donna Lou Askew, and got the First Lady's private phone number. He called Mrs. Askew, told her the news, and asked her to be sure the governor got the message as soon as possible.

Meanwhile, Karl told the other justices, who took the news with unusual emotion. Karl had been part of the rebuilding of the court system, as a senator serving with Askew and a collaborator on judicial reform, as counsel in the impeachments, as a two-time candidate for the court who had persevered through lingering health problems to win a seat on the court, and as a person of unquestioned integrity before and during his judicial service. "I was absolutely shocked," Sundberg told a reporter. "I am sick about it. I know that doesn't sound very judicial, but that's the way I feel." Overwhelmed by the emotional response from the other justices and the pain of giving up a job he had worked so hard for and loved, Karl left the building and secluded himself in a motel room in Thomasville, just across the Georgia line, to compose himself for a day before meeting with reporters.

Karl's parting lament was about judicial salaries. Without higher salaries, he said, the judiciary would be dominated by "career" judges who adapt their lifestyles to judicial salaries, or exceptionally wealthy lawyers who were not concerned about the pay. Most successful lawyers, though, would avoid the judiciary.

Sure enough, the other two new justices who came directly from successful private practices resigned from the court in the next five years. Like Karl,

England and Sundberg had children heading off to college and were attracted by the fast-growing salaries in private practice. They left after seven years or so on the court. Karl and Sundberg were both replaced by district court judges. England was replaced by a well-to-do lawyer from private practice who was already sixty years old, was a longtime bachelor who married late and had no children of his own, and would reach mandatory retirement in ten years.

Upon Karl's resignation, the nominating commission again went to work, and for the first time since Overton's appointment six years earlier, Askew turned to a sitting state court judge. This time it was a judge Askew himself had appointed two previous times, first to the county court and later to the Fourth District Court of Appeal, where his nominee was now chief judge. No other justice then serving had served at all four levels of the court system; in fact, four of them had never served as state judges before.[6]

James E. Alderman came from a ranching family. Another James Alderman, his great-great-grandfather, had migrated in the 1830s from Georgia to northern Florida, where Judge Alderman's great-grandfather was born, then in the 1840s to Manatee County, then to Basinger, a crossroads town east of the Kissimmee River between Sebring and Okeechobee. Soon after the turn of the century, the future justice's grandfather, B. E. "Teat" Alderman, moved to Fort Pierce and raised a son and two daughters and built his own herd of cattle.

Back then cattle grazed on an open range, but grandfather Alderman had the foresight to realize that the open range would not last forever. In 1937, more than a decade before "fence laws" were passed under Governor Fuller Warren, Teat Alderman began buying land west of Fort Pierce for $2 an acre and moved a herd of cattle there. He started putting up fences long before the law required it. The path out to the ranch, which straddled the boundary of St. Lucie and Okeechobee counties, is now Orange Avenue. The eastern end was paved, then there was dirt road, and the rest was cross-country. The judge's granddad would ride a horse or later drive a pickup truck out there. B. E. Alderman Jr. worked for the Post Office, and on November 1, 1936, he and his wife, Frances, had a son they named James E. Alderman.

Young Jim Alderman grew up in Fort Pierce, but he would be part of the ranching business during periods like round-up time. Jim would join the cowboys out on the range, where they killed a yearling for beef to eat during the round-up and slept under mosquito netting. At Fort Pierce High School, he was in the Future Farmers of America, known as the FFA, and raised steers and bulls as FFA projects. The "fence laws" his grandfather had anticipated came to pass about the time young Jim was finishing high school.

After graduation he headed to the University of Florida, where he made a fateful decision to become a lawyer. "My grandfather and father were running the ranch, and there wasn't room for another partner," he told interviewer Nancy Dale. In the summer before his junior year, when he would have to declare a major, he worked in the law office of longtime family friend John McCarty, a future president of the Florida Bar, and Charles R. M. Brown. Alderman was hooked on law after that and, after earning a bachelor's degree in 1958, went on to the UF law school.

Over at the new medical school in Gainesville, in the microbiology lab, was a young woman named Jean Thompson, who had recently moved there from Winston-Salem. She was a few years older than Jim, but a young woman Jim knew from Fort Pierce worked with Jean and thought Jean, the newcomer, and Jim, the shy student, would make a nice couple. A blind date was arranged. They dated for two years, and on Friday afternoon, March 3, 1961, they went down to the county judge and got married. They spent the weekend in St. Augustine, and Jim was back for class Monday morning. He returned to St. Lucie County with his new wife, was admitted to the Bar in October 1961, and practiced law in a firm initially known as McCarty, Brown, Cooksey & Alderman, "helping whoever came through the door." Over the next decade he had a term as president of the St. Lucie County Bar Association and served as part-time federal magistrate for the Southern District of Florida. He wanted to be a judge.

In 1971 soon after Askew became governor, a vacancy opened up on the St. Lucie County Court. Askew had not put his nominating commission system into place, so Alderman met with the local Democratic committee, which was Askew's patronage committee, and won the appointment. In 1972, after the Article V amendments reorganized the trial courts and created new circuit judgeships, Alderman ran for one in the nineteenth circuit against two opponents, won in a runoff, and took office in January 1973. In 1976 he applied for a vacancy on the Fourth District Court of Appeal, went through the still-new nominating process, and again won an appointment from Askew.

With Fred Karl's resignation in the spring of 1978, Alderman applied for the vacancy. The last Fourth DCA judge who had served on the Supreme Court was the infamous David McCain. The applicant pool was limited this time. The 1976 constitutional amendment expanding merit selection to every appellate judgeship also required that the Supreme Court have one justice from each appellate district. There had been no justice from the Fourth District since McCain's resignation.

One of the other applicants was Parker Lee McDonald, a circuit judge in

Orlando who had succeeded Overton as chairman of the circuit judges conference, knew Overton well, and wanted to follow Overton's path to the Supreme
Court. McDonald had applied for the previous vacancy but was not among
the seven on the list of nominees from which Askew had chosen Hatchett.
McDonald made the nomination list this time, but Alderman won the appointment and took his seat on the court on April 11, 1978, a week after Karl's
departure.

Alderman would prove to be more conservative and traditional than anyone else who joined the court in the Askew era. He took a hard line on criminal cases, Bar discipline, and procedural requirements. He was quiet, unpretentious, more of a loner—perhaps that stereotypical cowboy with little to say.
He rarely initiated a conversation with the other justices, though he would
make strong points during the conferences themselves. The justices liked and
respected him. He and Overton sometimes carpooled from their homes near
each other in Killearn Estates and would be joined by Alderman's senior law
clerk, Marguerite "Ditti" Davis. Jean Alderman, more outgoing than her husband, is remembered partly for her spinning wheel and her ability to spin wool
sheared from sheep on the Alderman ranch.

Shortly before his death in 2014, on the way to what would be his final
public appearance at a memorial service for Arthur England, Askew was asked
about his selection of this more conservative justice. "I didn't appoint him for
his ideology," Askew said. "I appointed him for his integrity."

Joe Hatchett's tenure lasted four years. The election that kept him in office in
1976 had also produced the first Democratic president in eight years, Jimmy
Carter, who had campaigned as a progressive southern governor and Washington outsider. It might well have been Reubin Askew who won that presidential election, but unlike Carter, who had been limited to one term as governor, Askew was still governor in 1976 and did not want to run for president
yet. Askew's appointment of the first black state Supreme Court justice in the
South made Hatchett a prospect for a lifetime presidential appointment to the
federal bench.

In 1979 Congress created an additional judgeship on the U.S. Fifth Circuit
Court of Appeals, which covered the gulf states of the Deep South, from Texas
to Florida. The nominating commission established by Florida U.S. senators
for filling federal judicial vacancies was headed by one of Tallahassee's leading
attorneys, DuBose Ausley. This was a lifetime federal judgeship on a court of
appeals, even better than the district judgeship Hatchett had envisioned as he
sat as a magistrate in Jacksonville.

As with the Florida Supreme Court vacancy in 1975, the field of nominees was impressive: District Court of Appeal Judges Robert P. Smith Jr. and Stephen H. Grimes; Public Service Commissioner and former legislator Robert T. Mann; U.S. District Court Judges C. Clyde Atkins, Joe Eaton, James Lawrence King and John A. Reed Jr.; and Carlton Fields partner Thomas A. Clark. Carter nominated Hatchett. He would become the first black person appointed to the Fifth Circuit Court, which through the 1960s and 1970s had aggressively ordered desegregation through the region. At a hearing of the U.S. Senate Judiciary Committee on June 25, 1979, Hatchett was one of seven nominees for federal judgeships who were questioned together.

Hatchett's appearance before the Senate committee was overshadowed by questions about the membership of two other nominees in country clubs that excluded blacks, Jews and women. U.S. Senator Howell Heflin, a former chief justice of the Alabama Supreme Court who was the Judiciary chairman, asked each nominee about such memberships. Had Hatchett, he asked, been a member of any club or organization that was "exclusively black?" "Mr. Chairman, I am not and have never been," Hatchett said. He also told the committee, "I am ready to get to work."[7] His confirmation, never in doubt, soon followed, and Hatchett resigned from the Florida Supreme Court on July 18, 1979.

Notably in light of Karl's financially motivated resignation the previous year, Hatchett was trading a Florida Supreme Court salary of $45,000 and a six-year term for a lifetime federal appeals court appointment with a salary of $57,500. Two years later, the Fifth Circuit was split in two, and a new Eleventh Circuit was created covering only Florida, Georgia and Alabama. Hatchett transferred to the new circuit on October 1, 1981, and served as its chief judge from September 1996, until his retirement on May 14, 1999.

Filling the Hatchett vacancy fell to Governor Bob Graham, who had succeeded Askew the previous January on a day so cold it actually snowed in Tallahassee. (Graham would joke that people always said it would be a cold day in hell when someone from Dade County became governor.)

By this time, Florida had a new Fifth District Court of Appeal, covering an area stretching from Orlando to Daytona. The temporary chief judge, assigned by the Supreme Court, was Ninth Circuit Judge Parker Lee McDonald. He had applied for a permanent judgeship there before Hatchett's confirmation as a federal judge. Since no one already on the court was from that area, the new justice had to be from the twelve-county Fifth District. McDonald applied. It was his third try for the Supreme Court.

McDonald grew up not far from Alderman but was a dozen years older.

He was born on May 23, 1924, in Sebring, though he joked that he was "bred" in South Carolina, since his mother was seven months pregnant when she came from South Carolina to join her husband. McDonald's father, Monroe R. McDonald, had been a state representative in South Carolina and met his wife, Mattie Etheredge, when she was attending Columbia College for Women in the capital. Florida's boom offered a new land of opportunity. His mother's cousin, E. J. Etheredge, was in DeSoto City and became a state senator in 1923, and said he'd help the family settle there. So the McDonalds moved to Sebring. Parker Lee was the third of five children.

His father was a country lawyer in a solo practice and did well until the boom went bust, which was before the economic collapse that gripped the rest of the nation in 1929. Their nice house got foreclosed on, and they moved into a little two-bedroom house with one bathroom on a fifty-foot lot. Parker Lee picked fruit to make money during high school—eight cents for a box of oranges, four cents for a box of grapefruit—and worked in a grocery store. Customers gave him a shopping list, he retrieved the goods, then wrote down the price and did the math to add up the total.

Parker Lee went off to college at the University of Florida in 1942, but as with others of his generation, World War II interrupted his studies. After a stint in anti-aircraft, he wound up in the Twentieth Armored Division during the last six months of the war in Europe, and was preparing for deployment to the invasion of Japan when the dropping of the atomic bombs brought the Pacific War to an end. He was a corporal when he left the service.

McDonald returned to Florida, and like Overton he simultaneously pursued an undergraduate business degree and a law degree, awarded in February 1950. One weekend he went to visit his younger sister Martha at Florida State College for Women in Tallahassee and met a sorority sister, Velma Ruth Wilkie, from Jacksonville, who was getting her degree in music education. They dated for three years, and in 1949, just after her graduation and six weeks before his, they married. It was timed so they could have a two-week vacation together at Christmas. His mother was dying of cancer, so the couple moved to Sebring, where McDonald joined his father in law practice.

After his mother's death, McDonald joined J. Thomas Gurney in Orlando, which five years later became Gurney, McDonald, and Handley. The firm primarily represented insurance companies, but McDonald also had cases on the plaintiffs' side. He remembered going all the way to the Florida Supreme Court to win a lawsuit against a man who was taking advantage of blacks with outrageous loan practices. McDonald's cracker accent and easygoing manner proved deceptive. McDonald earned a reputation for being prepared and aggressive. The firm flourished.

But he wanted to be a judge, and in 1961, a new circuit judgeship was available in Orange County. Governor Farris Bryant made him his first appointee to the circuit bench. As with Overton, appointed three years later, the judgeship meant significantly lower pay. He had been making a much larger income for just three years or so, and he fortunately had not gotten used to it. His family was growing; he and Ruth eventually had four children. His trial practice took a lot of time away from them. As he saw it, he could have a comfortable life as a judge if he were careful with the money, and it was a job his family could be proud of.

As a judge, he said, he tried to prepare carefully and told lawyers he expected an "intelligent presentation of the case." His reputation was for being tough and demanding but fair in his decisions. Over the next decade he served in every division of the circuit court and often sat on courts of appeal by special appointment. He became secretary-treasurer of the Circuit Judges Conference in 1973, the year Overton became chairman. Two years later McDonald became chairman and was also named the outstanding trial judge in Florida by the Young Lawyers Section of the Florida Bar. By then his friend Overton had been on the Supreme Court for five years.

McDonald made points with the Supreme Court Nominating Commission, concerned about the departure of Fred Karl over financial pressures, by noting that he had been doing fine on a judge's salary for eighteen years. The key, he told them, was to "keep yesterday's car and yesterday's house and stay married to yesterday's wife." Out of eight applicants, McDonald became one of three nominees, all white males. At fifty-five, McDonald was the oldest. The other two were Warren H. Cobb of Ormond Beach, another circuit judge who was also applying for the Fifth District Court of Appeal, and a relatively unknown but respected real estate and business lawyer, L. Pharr Abner.

On Friday afternoon, October 7, 1979, Governor Graham called and offered McDonald the appointment—Graham's first to the Supreme Court. In interviews afterward, McDonald described himself as "a relative conservative—moderate would be a better word" from a legal standpoint—and said he was "a reasonable scholar, but I'm no Phi Beta Kappa." At the Supreme Court he would quickly be recognized as plain-spoken.

McDonald was sworn in on October 26, 1979, although like most new justices, he actually started work at the court several days before the investiture ceremony. He was keenly aware that he was a white guy replacing the court's first black justice. At his investiture, the speakers include Paul Perkins of Orlando, a prominent black lawyer who had worked alongside Thurgood Marshall in the "Groveland Boys" case in Lake County in the late 1940s.

He found the Supreme Court a collegial place. "We were friends," he said. Most of the justices would eat lunch together frequently, although Alderman rarely joined them. Justices, wives, and aides would be invited out to the McDonalds' home overlooking Lake Jackson, with plenty of yard for outdoor games. They created what they called the "Olympic" games, consisting of things like an "opinion toss," to see how far a court opinion could be thrown (some chose to make it a paper airplane), and relay races with a *Southern Reporter* casebook balanced on the runner's head. Ruth played piano while people sang, as she also did at Kiwanis Club luncheons and at the Florida Bar president's reception at Bar conventions.

Just as Karl remembered England and Sundberg dominating oral arguments, McDonald remembered their "ping-pong match" style in conference as they similarly dominated internal debates. McDonald said he didn't try to bring others around to his view but simply told them why he decided as he did. "I think it is important to have a mixture of real academic scholarship and people who are cognizant of the real world," McDonald once remarked.[8] He was known for communicating likes and dislikes with a smiley-face or frowny-face drawing on internal drafts of opinions.

Like Karl, McDonald had an awkward relationship with Boyd. McDonald had sat on the Supreme Court by special assignment to determine the punishment for Boyd and Dekle in the court scandal and had voted with the majority to reprimand Boyd. McDonald rarely had interaction with Boyd outside the conferences of all the justices.

McDonald and Overton had a strong friendship and professional relationship that grew out of their long service on the trial court before joining the Supreme Court. They clearly influenced each other in some areas of the law. Despite their moderate, establishment leanings, McDonald brought Overton to give greater significance to mitigating factors in the backgrounds of murder defendants facing the death penalty. The two generally favored defendants in personal injury cases, as did Alderman—a reflection, McDonald said, of their preference for stability in the law. "I don't mean it should be rigid and not subject to change when there are sociological changes," he once remarked. "But on the other hand it's important for people to know what their rights and their obligations and responsibilities are, and we get those from existing case law."[9]

McDonald on the bench had an acerbic air about him when he didn't like something. Overton called him "the enforcer" for his impatience with lawyers he felt weren't being straightforward. "Parker Lee would lean back in that chair, and you'd think he was asleep," Overton once remarked, his smile expanding into a toothy grin. "Another justice would ask a question, and the lawyer was evading the answer, and you'd hear, like it was out of a deep hole, 'Answer the question!'"

McDonald was the last appointee of the 1970s. He and Alderman would prove distinctly more conservative than the justice each replaced. The switch would have consequences in a number of 4–3 decisions in the years ahead.

8

PLAYING CHICKEN
WITH COURTROOM CAMERAS

Television cameras made their first appearance in Florida's courtrooms on July 1, 1977, but how they came to be there and how Florida's courts became a national model for televised court proceedings goes back to a determined CBS News sketch artist named Aggie Whelan. She showed up in U.S. District Judge Winston E. Arnow's courtroom in Gainesville in June of 1973 for a case known as the Gainesville 8 conspiracy trial.

The trial that summer and the atmosphere around it had become an extension of the protests against Watergate, the Vietnam War, race discrimination, and other high-profile conflicts of the day. Like other contemporary multidefendant conspiracy trials growing out of political protests, the Gainesville 8 trial was presided over by a no-nonsense judge with little patience for politicization of the case. Judge Arnow, who had been the Florida Supreme Court's sole law clerk in 1934–35 and was a municipal judge in Pensacola before President Lyndon Johnson appointed him to the federal court, had previously ordered desegregation of Escambia County schools, banned the high school's use of the Confederate flag and the nickname "Rebels" in 1973, and ordered the U.S. Air Force to hire and promote more black civilians at Eglin Air Force Base.

The Gainesville 8 were members of a protest group called Vietnam Veterans Against the War. They were charged with conspiring to disrupt the 1972 Republican National Convention in Miami Beach, where President Richard Nixon was to be nominated for a second term. The defendants argued that their "conspiracy," including gathering weapons like slingshots and crossbows, was actually fomented by an FBI undercover agent, who told them there was a secret effort by the FBI to instigate violence and make the protesters look bad. The undercover agent, the defendants said, inspired their preparation to thwart the FBI's effort. There was never any actual assault on the convention.

The trial produced evidence of electronic surveillance of the antiwar protestors by the FBI. This was the same year that burglars led by a White House operative had bugged the Democrats' offices in the Watergate office complex, which later would lead to Nixon's resignation. Former U.S. Attorney General John Mitchell, indicted in the Watergate scandal, was subpoenaed by the Gainesville 8 defense and, when he arrived late, was admonished by Judge Arnow for being tardy. At one point during the trial, two FBI agents with telephone and electronic gear were discovered in a broom closet at the courthouse. Disputing defense lawyers' accusations that their purpose was to eavesdrop on the defense lawyers, the agents asserted that they were trying to be sure the FBI's phones weren't tapped.[1] From a perspective four decades later, the whole episode seems like outlandish parody.

In the earliest days of electronic media, there were few restrictions on court coverage. The first radio broadcast of a trial was the 1925 coverage, by WGN Radio in Chicago, of the John Scopes "Monkey Trial" in Dayton, Tennessee, over the teaching of evolution. But photographs and intrusive reporting fell into disrepute in 1935 with the boisterous atmosphere of the trial of Bruno Hauptmann, accused and ultimately convicted and executed for the kidnapping and murder of aviator Charles Lindbergh's baby. In 1965 the U.S. Supreme Court had focused on media intrusion in overturning the swindling conviction of Billy Sol Estes, a financier who had business ties to Vice President and President Lyndon Johnson. After that, television cameras were rarely allowed in any courtroom anywhere in America.

Sketch artists, then, provided the only way for television to show a court proceeding.

In the Estes case,[2] Chief Justice Earl Warren had quoted at length from a *New York Times* story on a pretrial hearing in the small courtroom in Tyler, Texas. Though it was only a pretrial hearing, the report formed the widespread perception of what television coverage of trials was like: "A television motor van, big as an intercontinental bus, was parked outside the courthouse, and the second-floor courtroom was a forest of equipment. . . . With photographers roaming at will through the courtroom, petitioner's counsel made his motion that all cameras be excluded. As he spoke, a cameraman wandered behind the judge's bench and snapped his picture."[3] Justice Tom Clark's separate opinion in the Estes case speculated on the trial participants' "awareness" that the proceedings were being broadcast and the effect it might have had on them. He said the use of cameras was "inconsistent with our concepts of due process"[4] and noted that "all but two of our states" banned cameras in the courtroom.[5]

Photographs and broadcasting during trials had been declared a violation of judicial ethics as far back as 1937, when the American Bar Association (ABA) adopted Judicial Canon 35 in response to the Hauptmann trial. While ABA canons of ethics are not binding, states tend to adopt them as their own ethical standards. In 1952 the ABA amended Canon 35 to ban television coverage, and reaffirmed the ban in 1972 when the ethical rules were rewritten. Florida adopted the ABA rules in what was known as Canon 3A(7) of the Florida Code of Judicial Conduct.

And so it was that on June 20, 1973, Aggie Whelan showed up at the federal courthouse in Gainesville along with CBS correspondent Jed Duvall for pretrial proceedings in the Gainesville 8 case. When he saw Whelan, Judge Arnow declared that no sketches in the courtroom would be permitted. That afternoon, Whelan sat in the courtroom without her sketch pad watching for about two hours, then left the courtroom, took a seat in the hallway, and began sketching from memory. A marshal saw her and reported to Arnow. The judge summoned both Duvall and Whelan to his chambers and said no publication of sketches would be permitted, regardless of where the sketches were drawn. The next day, the president of CBS News sent the judge a telegram protesting the order, to no avail. Defying Arnow's directive, Whelan made sketches in her hotel room, and four of them were shown on the CBS Morning News on June 22.

On June 27, after the Gainesville 8 pretrial proceedings were over (ultimately all eight were acquitted), Judge Arnow issued an order to show cause why CBS should not be held in contempt of court. The network hired Sandy D'Alemberte to lead its defense.

The contempt hearing was on Saturday, July 7, in Pensacola. Judge Arnow himself presided. Since there was no written order, D'Alemberte and law partner Joseph Klock insisted that the content of the order be proven in court, so the U.S. attorney called the judge's law clerk and secretary to testify. The judge joined in the questioning of his staff to ask if "he," referring to himself, had also said something they had not yet mentioned. D'Alemberte, who was on crutches after a motorcycle accident, had brought along a stack of forms for notices of appeal and a checkbook, and every time the judge would try to block one of D'Alemberte's maneuvers, Klock would get up and hand the clerk a notice of appeal and a check for the filing fee, right in front of the judge. Klock remembered filing about sixteen notices of appeal during the five-hour contempt hearing. Arnow found CBS guilty of contempt, then was told by D'Alemberte that, since he denied CBS a jury trial and an independent judge, the maximum fine he could impose for contempt was $500. Arnow imposed it. Even as the judge was orally pronouncing his decision and chastising

D'Alemberte and his clients, Klock got up and filed another notice of appeal with the clerk.[6]

Arnow also issued a new rule of court declaring that "hereafter" no sketch of the courtroom "or its environs or any proceedings therein" could be made, "regardless of the place where such sketch is made." He said the eyes of the sketch artist were as intrusive as the eye of the camera had been in *Estes v. Texas.* "It is clear," the judge went on, "that defendants are actively seeking publicity and in so doing are trying to place before the public, including persons who are potential jurors, their own version of the merits of the case . . . That this conduct, if continued, might be prejudicial to a fair and impartial trial cannot be doubted."

On emergency appeal, the U.S. Fifth Circuit Court of Appeals almost immediately suspended the ban on sketch artists. A year later almost to the day, its final ruling sympathized with the judge's challenge in managing the Gainesville 8 trial but overturned the contempt citation and the fine and, in a separate opinion, overturned the "overbroad" directives against sketching and publication.[7] The opinion, written by Judge David W. Dyer, noted that publication of the sketches could be censored only if there were "an imminent, not merely a likely, threat to the administration of justice." There had been "no showing whatsoever that sketching is in any way obtrusive or disruptive," so Judge Arnow's ban on in-court sketching was overturned.

Back in Miami, D'Alemberte was talking about the CBS case one day with his clients at WPLG-TV, including news director Gregory Favre, who later became the top news executive of McClatchy Newspapers. WPLG, owned by the Washington Post Company, was named for Philip L. Graham, the late husband of Post chairwoman Katharine Graham and the older half-brother of Bob Graham, who had recently become a Florida state senator. WPLG had won renewal of its broadcast license against a challenge by friends and supporters of President Nixon of the Post-Newsweek broadcast licenses in Florida. That challenge came the same month that Nixon declared, as recorded on White House tapes, that the Post Company would have "damnable, damnable problems" in its license renewals because of its aggressive coverage of Nixon's role in the Watergate scandal.[8] The station's investigative reporter, Clarence Jones, had done the stories that led to the resignation of Chief Justice Carlton a year earlier.

As they talked with D'Alemberte about the sketch-artist case, Favre and his staff showed D'Alemberte a brand new low-light camera, which could shoot high-quality video without extra lighting. With no noise or lights, a television camera could operate with even less distraction than the motion and sound of a court sketch artist, which the Fifth Circuit had now explicitly allowed in the courtroom. The low-light camera made a light bulb go on for D'Alemberte. "We ought to seek access for cameras," D'Alemberte said. "The rationale of *Estes* no longer applies, because technology now allows the non-disruptive presence of cameras."[9]

The cameras-in-court petition was filed at the Florida Supreme Court on January 24, 1975. It was not a propitious moment. The court was under siege by media reporting of its scandalous inner workings. The next month the court would reprimand two of its own members for misconduct. Chief Justice Adkins, although enthusiastic about open government, was clearly unhappy with current stories about the justices.

D'Alemberte, joined by Steel Hector law partner Donald M. Middlebrooks, the future federal judge, asked the Supreme Court to permit cameras or at least to launch a reexamination of the ban. On May 21, the court invited responses. Opposition poured in—from the Florida Bar and its Trial Lawyers section, from the Conference of Circuit Judges, represented by its chairman, Parker Lee McDonald, and from the chairman of the Judicial Qualifications Commission. The Florida Association of Broadcasters and the Society of Professional Journalists supported the petition. On December 18, Adkins designated Justice Roberts to convene a conference of all the counsel "to discuss the feasibility of such a program" and later added recent arrival Alan Sundberg to the meeting as well.

The group met on January 15, 1976, almost a year after the petition was first filed. Roberts indicated that the court was ready to approve experimental use of cameras. The Bar pressed its argument that television would put pressure on lawyers, witnesses, and jurors. Circuit Judge Ben C. Willis, chief judge of the Second Circuit based in Tallahassee, agreed to conduct two experimental trials, one criminal and one civil, with television cameras present under guidelines agreed to at the meeting. On January 28, the court formally launched the experiment.[10] In April the court added still photographers to the experiment.

Nine months went by with no trial, because one of the conditions was that "the parties to the litigation, jurors and witnesses must consent to the televising of their participation in the trial." On September 17, the court expanded the pilot to the Ninth Circuit under Chief Judge McDonald.[11] Still no trial. In December, two more circuits were added—the Fourth and the Eighth in northern Florida.

Finally, a trial with all the necessary consents was scheduled in Jacksonville, which happened to be the home of another Post-Newsweek station, WJXT.

At the station's invitation, the court dispatched Sundberg and England to observe, but while they were en route, one attorney in the trial withdrew his consent. Since there were no cell phones back then, the justices found out about the cancellation only after they arrived.

The failed journey to Jacksonville proved to be a breakthrough. England and Sundberg got a demonstration of the low-light camera set up in the courtroom. As they drove back to Tallahassee, the two justices concluded that it was futile to try to obtain the consent of all parties.[12] They persuaded their colleagues to drop the consent requirement and simply open up courtrooms statewide for one year.

Fred Karl later said there was "a substantial difference of opinion" in the court's private conference. All agreed that cameras would change the decorum of the courtroom, but they disagreed whether changes would help or hurt litigants. Sundberg's opinion, Karl said, "went as far as the majority of the court was willing to go at that time."[13] Karl wanted more openness and fewer restrictions, but clearly Sundberg, who was writing the opinion, wanted a unanimous opinion for such a bold and dramatic experiment. Five of the seven justices were Askew-era justices, untainted by scandal and riding a wave of post-scandal admiration. Roberts had retired. Adkins and Boyd, though they had suffered in media coverage of the scandal, went along as well. The order was released on April 7, 1977.[14] For the first time in decades, virtually every court proceeding in a state would be open to cameras, starting July 1, 1977.

How would the U.S. Supreme Court view Florida's experiment? Chief Justice Warren E. Burger was openly hostile to television coverage even of his own public speeches. Especially in televised criminal cases, scores of Florida convictions might be overturned if that court rejected cameras as it had in the Estes trial. Fred Graham, the lawyer-journalist who covered the U.S. Supreme Court for CBS News, remarked, "The Florida Supreme Court is playing chicken with the United States Supreme Court."

Televised trials in Florida began immediately. Newspaper photographers found still cameras with silent shutters. Television cameramen had to cover the little red light on their cameras that showed the camera was running. There could be only one video and one still camera in a courtroom, so local media worked out press pools. Cameras were fixed in positions beside the jury box, so jurors would not be in the line of sight. Overton, as chief justice, got some calls from trial judges with one excuse or another for keeping cameras out of their trial, but he was unyielding and told them he would issue a direct order if the local judge did not allow the cameras.

Most media voluntarily avoided photographing children, rape victims, and police confidential informants. The rules allowed judges to ban cameras if they would have a "substantial effect" on trial participants beyond the normal reactions to cameras. And of course, the federal courts were a separate system and still did not allow cameras.

Perhaps the most unusual consequence of the experiment was that it led to Justice Adkins's sixth, final, and happiest marriage. In early 1978 Adkins sat as the trial judge in a capital murder case, *State v. Goodwin*, in Panama City, after the original judge recused himself (chapter 24). Beth Lawrence was covering the trial for WJHG television. Adkins got legal aide John Newton to invite her to join them for dinner one evening during the trial. She and Adkins married a few months later, and they were together until Adkins's death on June 24, 1994.

In Miami, five months into the experiment, two police officers went on trial for a burglary at Piccolo's, a well-known Miami Beach restaurant, in the wee hours of the morning on May 23, 1977. The floor safe with the previous day's receipts had been "drilled" and was empty.

Although no one realized it at the time, the case would be the one that challenged Florida's experiment at the U.S. Supreme Court. Joel Hirschhorn represented the two officers, Noel Chandler and Robert Granger, and tried multiple times to block television coverage of their trial, without success. As the trial began, he questioned each prospective juror about the ability to be "fair and impartial" despite the cameras, then unsuccessfully asked the judge to sequester the jury because of the likely television coverage. The judge refused but instructed the jurors to watch only national news, not local news stations.

Only one significant piece of evidence linked the two officers to the crime: a tape recording made by an amateur radio operator, who became the state's chief witness. He said he awakened in the middle of the night, turned on his ham radio, and happened to overhear the officers' conversations on their police walkie-talkies talking about a burglary. He decided to record what he heard. But he could not be sure of the date it happened. Chandler, who had investigated an earlier burglary at the restaurant, admitted the conversation but said he and Granger were staging a bogus burglary on a wager over whether anyone heard them, and it was not the night of the Piccolo's burglary. The officers' wives both testified that they were at home the night of the burglary.

The coverage of the Chandler-Granger trial hardly lived up to the aspirations of the proponents of cameras. A television camera was at the trial for the testimony of the ham radio witness and for closing arguments, but in just under three minutes of television broadcast, only the prosecution's side was shown. The jury found the defendants guilty, and they were sentenced to five years apiece on the burglary and an additional year for grand larceny, as well as a year in county jail for the misdemeanor of conspiracy to commit a felony.

A year after the trial, as the justices were weighing the results of the one-year experiment with cameras, the Third District Court of Appeal rejected the Chandler-Granger appeal. It would not second guess the Supreme Court's implicit decision that television coverage did not violate defendants' constitutional rights.[15] Hirschhorn appealed again, this time to the Florida Supreme Court.

Meanwhile, a Florida trial caught national television attention with the defense claim of "television intoxication," which supposedly had led a fifteen-year-old boy, Ronny Zamora, to kill his eighty-two-year-old neighbor, Elinor Haggart, when she caught him and a friend burglarizing her home in Miami Beach. Zamora was represented by flamboyant Miami lawyer Ellis Rubin, who became known for his innovative defenses and lost causes. Rubin had defended the wife of a sheriff's deputy on prostitution charges by arguing that the antidepressant Prozac made her a nymphomaniac. He had pioneered the "battered woman" defense in Florida. He once served thirty-seven days in jail for refusing to represent a murder suspect he said was intending to lie in court.

Zamora's defense was that he was so obsessed with the television cop show *Kojak* that he was unable to tell the difference between fantasy and reality. A prominent expert on the insanity defense, Michael M. Gilbert, testified that Zamora had been exposed to "tremendous" television violence since the age of five and that his fixation on violent shows had caused him to shoot reflexively when caught in the burglary. (Years later, Gilbert himself was accused of bribing a police officer and tried the insanity defense in his own case. His own lawyer called him a "lunatic" in his own televised trial. Gilbert's conviction was overturned on appeal.) Rubin's "TV intoxication" defense didn't work. Zamora was found guilty and sentenced to life in prison with a minimum term of twenty-five years. (He was released after twenty-seven years, on June 1, 2004, and deported to his native Costa Rica.)

As Florida's experiment unfolded, at least fourteen states began some kind of experiment in electronic coverage of courts. On August 2, 1978, at a meeting in Burlington, Vermont, the National Conference of State Chief Justices voted 44–1 in favor of state-by-state standards for electronic coverage. Other reaction was more skeptical. In February 1978 the American Bar Association's Committee on Fair Trial-Free Press proposed approving televisions in courtrooms under standards set by local judges. The proposal won support from the ABA's committee on Criminal Justice Standards but in 1979 was rejected by the ABA's governing body, the House of Delegates.

In Florida, the experiment was going well—so well that in April 1979, D'Alemberte asked the judges to continue to allow cameras after June 30 while the court pondered the results of the one-year experiment. The justices, 4–3, refused. Overton, Adkins and Boyd said the experiment should keep going. "Lawyers, jurors, witnesses, news reporters and the viewing public have grown accustomed to cameras in court," Boyd wrote. "The temporary termination of such activity, with the probability of its renewal within a few weeks, would tend to disrupt and frustrate the program which at this time appears to be generally accepted in this State." But England and Sundberg, who would eventually get most of the national recognition for the cameras initiative, rejected the request to continue the experiment. Joining them were Hatchett and new arrival Alderman.

So after June 30, 1978, cameras disappeared from Florida courtrooms.

More than 2,750 people had participated as lawyers, judges, witnesses, or jurors in trials covered by electronic media, according to the Supreme Court. A survey was sent to all except the judges, and a remarkable 62 percent responded. From those, the Supreme Court concluded that the presence of electronic media "had little effect upon the respondents' perception of the judiciary or of the dignity of the proceedings . . . [and] disrupted the trial either not at all or only slightly." Respondents said the cameras made them "slightly self-conscious" but also made them "feel just slightly more responsible for their actions." They reported little distraction and little urge "to see or hear themselves" on television. Court personnel and attorneys considered attorneys "more flamboyant only to a slight extent," said witnesses were "slightly inhibited" by the cameras, and thought jurors "were made slightly self-conscious, nervous, and distracted, but also slightly more attentive."

Florida's Conference of Circuit Judges surveyed its own members and got responses from about half. Two-thirds said they had some experience with electronic media during the experiment; thirty-six were positive, twenty-nine were negative, and thirty-seven neutral.

Sundberg began drafting a final opinion by hand on a yellow legal pad—twenty-five pages, with his own footnotes and few editing changes as he went. He began with the ending: "It is our conclusion, then, that, without demonstration of prejudice, there is no per se proscription against electronic media coverage of judicial proceedings imposed by the 14th amendment to the U.S. Constitution nor by Art. I, Section 9, Florida Constitution."[16] His formal published opinion picked up the theme:

Electronic media coverage of all other branches and subdivisions of Florida government exists and apparently has served not only to inform the public about the operation of their government but has made the representatives of government act more responsibly. . . . The court system is no less an institution of democratic government. . . . Ventilating the judicial process, we submit, will enhance the image of the Florida bench and bar and thereby elevate public confidence in the system.[17]

Sundberg recited the fears about grandstanding and other "mischievous potentialities," as U.S. Supreme Court Justice John Marshall Harlan II had called them in his concurring opinion in *Estes*, but Sundberg said they were "but assumptions unsupported by any evidence. No respondent has been able to point to any instance during the pilot program period where these fears were substantiated."[18]

The opinion was released on April 12, 1979, with all six of his colleagues joining in. Television cameras would return to Florida courtrooms on May 1, 1979. The Florida Bar's lawyer, Richard McFarlain, who had argued against cameras, was wryly philosophical. "The court says what goes on in the courtrooms, and if they like cameras, we like cameras." The chief judge in the Sixth Circuit, Harry W. Fogle, expressed concern about the imminent trial of Theodore Bundy, accused of murdering two young women from St. Petersburg. "It would be disturbing if his trial should result in a finding of guilt, to have it reversed on cameras in the courtroom."[19]

There was still that little problem of Hirschhorn's Chandler-Granger appeal. The Florida Supreme Court rejected it as moot after the *Post-Newsweek* final order, but the U.S. Supreme Court accepted the case. Fred Graham had said Florida was "playing chicken," and now the chickens might be coming home to roost.

On Wednesday, November 12, 1980, Attorney General Jim Smith personally appeared for oral argument at the U.S. Supreme Court to defend the Chandler and Granger convictions and Florida's new program for cameras in courts. It was his only oral argument at the nation's high court during his eight years as attorney general. Assistant Attorney General Calvin L. Fox of Miami, five years out of Tulane Law School, was lead counsel on the case.

Hirschhorn, a criminal defense lawyer from Miami who would try hundreds of major cases during his career, argued first. Almost immediately Justice William H. Rehnquist interrupted to ask what evidence was in the record to show that cameras had affected the fairness of the trial. "Common sense tells us that being on television is different than any other type of public trial,"

Hirschhorn said, "and . . . behavioral scientists tell us that people act differently, posture differently, pose differently when they know they're on TV."

Was there any evidence, though?

"No, we were not permitted to introduce any evidence."

"Did you tender such evidence?"

"No, Mr. Justice Rehnquist. The trial judge determined that he had no discretion; it was mandatory." But evidence shouldn't be necessary, Hirschhorn added quickly. The court had not required evidence before concluding it was "inherently prejudicial" for a defendant to appear in court in prison garb, for example.

"You're also saying, really, I think, that there's a bit of ham in all of us, including jurists," interjected Justice Harry Blackmun.

"I know television will make a cocky witness more cocky," Hirschhorn said. "I certainly know it will make a timid witness more timid."

Chief Justice Burger interrupted him. "When you say you know these things, do you get them by osmosis, or how do you know?"

Hirschhorn tried to shift the burden of proof to the Florida Supreme Court, which had imposed the mandate "without the benefit of testimony." He said twenty-seven states permitted televising at that point, and seventeen of them required the consent of the defendant.

Fox's turn came. "The state's position in this case is quite clear," he declared. "The defendants received a fair trial. . . . They make no effort whatsoever to discuss how Noel Chandler and Robert Granger did not receive a fair trial."

Justice John Paul Stevens wanted to know why the *Estes* decision "is not squarely in point" in this case. Like a law professor sneaking up to pounce on a student in class, Stevens referred coyly to "the holding in that case, based specifically on the one question the court granted certiorari to consider."

Fox, missing Stevens's subtlety, noted that it was a plurality opinion, not a majority. Stevens shot back, "I'm talking about the judgment of the court on the facts of the case. Why isn't that directly in point? In fact, why isn't that a stronger case because there the jury was sequestered?"

It still wasn't clear what Stevens was getting at. "It IS a stronger case, Your Honor. . . . The facts—"

"A stronger case for ALLOWING the television," Stevens stated.

Whoa. The cameras had been excluded in *Estes* even though that was a STRONGER case for allowing cameras? The *Chandler* situation was actually WORSE than *Estes*? That was not good for Fox's argument. "Pardon me, Your Honor?"

"I said it's a stronger case for allowing television because the jury [in *Estes*] was sequestered."

Fox tried again. "But on the other hand, the extreme fact circumstances in that case—"

"There were no extreme fact circumstances," said Stevens, known as a stickler for the facts of cases. The cables all over the floor and photographers walking around were all at a pretrial hearing, not at the trial itself. At the trial, Stevens said, there was "a thing built up there so you couldn't notice the television cameras. . . . There was no disorder during the trial."

But the opinions in *Estes* focused on the pretrial facts, Fox said.

"I asked you why wasn't the HOLDING specifically in point here?"

Fox was struggling. This was like a nightmarish law school inquisition, but it was a real case in the highest court of the land. Fox had arrived ready to distinguish the circus atmosphere described in the *Estes* case with the serene setting of the Chandler trial. But Stevens was arguing that cameras had been ruled unconstitutional in the Estes trial itself even though it was as serene as the Chandler trial. And, what's more, the Estes jurors had not been influenced by TV reports because they had been sequestered.

"I think the court was concerned with the infection that had preceded the trial—"

"The court declined to grant certiorari on that very question," Stevens shot back.

The opinions, Fox said, did not talk about "the serenity which prevailed at the trial."

So why then, Justice Potter Stewart chimed in, "isn't my brother Stevens exactly correct?"

Uh-oh. Stewart had actually been part of the *Estes* decision, and now he seemed to be siding with Stevens on what it meant. But Fox found his footing. "Most respectfully, by your leave, Mr. Justice Stewart, I'd submit to you that Mr. Justice Harlan would not have joined in a per se rule [banning cameras in every case], and in fact he did not. And he states quite clearly in his opinion that he restricts . . . his support of the majority opinion to . . . the extreme—"

An interruption by another justice changed the subject. Eventually Justice Lewis Powell, who often looked for a middle ground, wondered: could a judge in Florida actually keep a camera out of a trial?

"Yes, Your Honor," said Fox. "There's a case, *Palm Beach Newspapers* . . . in which the cameras were excluded. . . . A prisoner had objected to being filmed because of the fact that he felt his life would be in jeopardy if he testified. And the trial court closed the trial. . . . We're in a frontier area here, Your Honor. There have been very, very few cases with respect to closure or the media appealing a closure."

Have you had a case, Powell asked, where a witness after being sworn says to the judge, "I've been camera-shy all my life, I just don't think I can possibly testify fairly and honest with cameras on me."

A defendant did make a claim like that, Fox replied. The trial judge ruled against her, but the Third District Court of Appeal had overturned the conviction and said the judge should have held a hearing on the matter.

"You're saying, as I understand it, that the judge has full discretion to exclude cameras from the courtroom . . . if a witness or a juror persuaded him that it was in the best interests of justice?"

"Yes, Your Honor."

Would that include a "camera-shy lawyer?"

Fox laughed at the very idea, but went on to say that is what a case-by-case evidentiary proceeding would be for.

With that Fox quickly handed off the rest of the argument to Attorney General Smith.

Rehnquist immediately picked up Powell's theme about the camera-shy lawyer. What about a lawyer used to being in a small courtroom suddenly finding himself in a large courtroom? The lawyer would obviously be expected to perform, Smith said.

"What if it was Yankee Stadium?" Stevens chimed in. "How do you differentiate this from Yankee Stadium?"

Equating television cameras in a courtroom with trying people in a stadium was not a friendly question. Smith tried to redirect the focus. "The presence of the media in the courtroom and your recent judgment in the Richmond case[20] recognized the surrogate responsibility that the media has . . . in bringing to the attention of the public any kind of trial that is newsworthy."

"Are you telling us, Mr. Attorney General, that broadcasting 2 minutes and 55 seconds of the prosecution's case only, just one side of the case, has contributed something significant to the improvement of the administration of justice in Florida?" Burger asked Smith.

"I submit that it is better for the citizens of our state . . . to see the actual image and hear those portions of the testimony as it has happened, rather than have to depend on the interpretation that a news commentator might like to give it."

Justice Byron R. White, once an All-American football halfback known as "Whizzer White," then created a big opening for Smith to run through. "In any event, Mr. Attorney General, we don't need to, and we mustn't, decide whether or not this is a good idea. The question is whether what Florida has done is constitutionally permissible."

Smith ran for the goal line. "That's correct," he said. "The Florida rule [is] well within constitutional bounds and well within the encouragement this court has given states to experiment with novel ideas. The experiment has proved successful in Florida. We have had literally hundreds of trials where the cameras have been present in the courtroom, reported generally very few situations where there's been an objection. And I submit the big reason for that is the government-in-the-sunshine policies that we have in our state, the fact that in our state, when our citizens go to a county commission meeting or a city commission meeting, even our clemency meetings in capital cases, they see the television camera. . . . It has become commonplace in Florida and commonplace in our daily lives."

Hirschhorn got the last word. "Being around television and watching television is different than being ON television," he said. A trial is "the very nerve center of the fact-finding process, the life-blood of the system, the defendants' right to a fair and impartial trial." Jurors in the Chandler-Granger trial could see that the cameras were there for the prosecution witness and not for defense witnesses. The Palm Beach case required cameras be turned off for two witnesses, not all of them. Injecting a "mini-trial" over issues like that could disrupt trials further.

As divided as the court seemed at oral argument, it was not divided when *Chandler v. Florida* came out on January 26, 1981.[21] It was 8–0, with Burger writing the opinion. Stevens did not participate. He and D'Alemberte, who had filed an amicus brief in *Chandler*, had both participated in an Aspen Institute program a few weeks after the oral argument, and one discussion was about cameras in the courtroom. Stevens apparently decided to avoid the appearance of an extraneous influence on his decision. He wasn't needed for a majority, and he might well have dissented.

Burger's opinion declared that the *Estes* case "does not stand as an absolute ban on experimentation with an evolving technology." Any criminal case that generates a lot of publicity "presents some risk that the publicity may compromise the right of the defendant to a fair trial," but a defendant can still "demonstrate that the media's coverage . . . compromised the ability of the particular jury that heard the case to adjudicate fairly."[22] Burger added, "Florida admonishes its courts to take special pains to protect certain witnesses—for example, children, victims of sex crimes, some informants, even the very timid witness or party—from the glare of publicity and the tensions of being on camera."

The Florida Supreme Court had won its game of chicken. But the justices in Florida also took seriously the concerns of the justices in Washington, especially Powell's focus on the authority of trial judges to exclude cameras. Just five weeks after *Chandler* was decided, the Florida Supreme Court ruled against cameras in the two pending cases Fox had mentioned at oral argument.

The Third DCA had called it "reversible error" when a trial judge allowed cameras when faced with a "borderline competent defendant" and allegations that cameras would unsettle her to the point of reducing her mental function. An evidentiary hearing should have been held. The Florida Supreme Court upheld that decision in *State v. Green*.[23] It was a rare reversal of a criminal conviction because of cameras, and Overton used the occasion to emphasize judges' responsibility to assess claims of a "qualitatively different" effect of cameras on certain people involved in the case.

In the *Palm Beach Newspapers* case the same day, two prisoners testifying for the prosecution in a trial over the torching-murder of another inmate had said they feared reprisals and would not testify unless cameras were removed. D'Alemberte argued that the prisoners' names would be in the papers anyway, even if their faces weren't shown. He said judges should not rely on assumptions instead of evidence about whether a witness would be uniquely affected by the presence of cameras. Assistant Attorney General Robert Bogen replied that affidavits about a fear of cameras coupled with a judge's "common sense" should be enough.

England's opinion for the court said the issue was not whether the witnesses were justified in their fear but whether each side can fully present its case with the cameras present. While cautioning judges not to abuse their discretion, England said it "remains more important that a trial go forward with the testimony of witnesses than that the media be permitted to cover their testimony."[24]

Despite limitations like those, cameras became more and more commonplace in the courtrooms of Florida. D'Alemberte was frustrated, though, that television coverage for the most part was still short snippets on the evening news shows that offered little real insight or education. In late 1984 the Florida State University Law School, where D'Alemberte had become dean, in concert with WFSU public television, began recording every oral argument at the Florida Supreme Court.

During a renovation and expansion of the Supreme Court building in the 1990s, lighting in the courtroom was improved and four barely noticeable small cameras were permanently installed—two atop columns on either side of the spectator seats aimed at the justices' bench, and two covered by tinted glass and tucked into the paneling behind the justices, aimed at the attorneys and the spectators. From a control room upstairs, a producer could choose camera angles and zoom in or out. Any broadcaster could plug into the feed. Oral arguments were streamed live over the Internet as well as on the state-supported Florida Channel on cable television. WFSU archived the recordings.

At the national level, the proliferation of courtroom cameras and the large television audience for the William Kennedy Smith rape trial in Palm Beach County in 1991—memorably featuring a blurry blue dot blotting out the victim's face during her testimony—led to the launch on July 1, 1991, of a new cable channel, Court TV, devoted to televising trials. Eventually every state allowed cameras in courtrooms, although the scope varied widely.[25]

The use of cameras wreaked havoc on sketch artists, who were left to eke out a living bringing the remaining untelevised courtrooms to life through the art of the freeze-frame drawing.[26] The federal courts remain their refuge, their colored pencils and pastels a "technology" dating back to the Salem witch trials.[27] The Judicial Conference of the United States, the administrative body for the federal courts, eventually allowed the federal circuit courts of appeals to permit cameras in oral arguments, but only two circuits had done so as of 2014. The Eleventh Circuit, which includes Florida, was not one of them.

In September 2010 the U.S. Judicial Conference created a pilot project to allow cameras in some federal trial courts, under substantial control and discretion of each trial judge, including delayed release of the video.[28] As with Florida's failed first effort at its cameras experiment, the federal experiment allows any party to veto use of cameras. So the pilot produced very little.

Chief Justice Burger's personal hostility toward cameras was unabated. In November 1984 he said television was "the most destructive thing in the world" and he would never mix "show business and judicial business" in the courtroom of the U.S. Supreme Court.[29] Burger's tolerance of Florida's innovation as constitutional had a supporting vote from his eventual successor as chief justice, William Rehnquist, whose own successor as chief justice, John G. Roberts Jr., was Rehnquist's law clerk when *Chandler* was decided. The court makes audio recordings of its oral arguments, and they became publicly available largely as a result of the huge interest in the arguments surrounding the court's resolution of the 2000 presidential election. That's as far as the court would go. The U.S. Supreme Court continued to reject any video of its own proceedings well into the twenty-first century.

9

ACCESS TO LEGAL SERVICES

Who Will Serve the Poor?

On his way home to Vancouver from a Canadian Bar Association meeting in Jamaica in March 1976, Sholto Hebenton stopped in Tallahassee for a visit with his old friend Arthur England. When they were just out of law school fifteen years earlier, in 1961, "Heb" and Arthur were both first-year associates at the Dewey Ballantine law firm in New York City; Heb was in litigation, mainly antitrust, and Arthur was in tax. They were also neighbors in Brooklyn Heights, and their oldest children were born a day apart. In 1964 England moved to Miami, and Hebenton moved back to his hometown of Vancouver, British Columbia. "What's new in British Columbia?" England asked casually over a glass of wine.[1]

Hebenton's answer transformed legal aid in Florida and led to an initiative that produced an estimated $400 million over the next thirty-five years to support legal aid and legal reform programs in the state, spread rapidly to all fifty states, and was producing $350 million a year nationwide by 2013.

Remember the time back at Dewey Ballantine, Heb said to Arthur, that we were talking about all the money sitting in law firm trust accounts without drawing interest because the government wouldn't allow interest on checking accounts? "We solved that," Heb said. "In British Columbia we have a program where the interest goes to a foundation for law libraries and legal services."

Until 1964 in England and Scotland, Hebenton explained, checking accounts paid interest. Solicitors who were holding money in a bank escrow account on behalf of clients—for a real estate closing, to take a familiar example—kept the interest earned on the money. The interest might be just a dollar or two for an individual client, whose money was on deposit only a few days, but could be considerable for the lawyer with significant continuing balances in those days of rapidly rising interest rates.

In 1964 the British House of Lords had declared that the interest didn't belong to the lawyer. But calculating interest for an individual client for just a couple of days was a lot of work for very little benefit. So a lawyer in British Columbia proposed a foundation be formed to gather the interest and use it to support legal aid for the poor. New South Wales in Australia did just that in 1967, and British Columbia got its foundation started in 1969. Its income the first year was $50,000 and within three years had grown to $250,000. The money went to legal aid, law libraries, and projects for law reform. Other provinces had followed British Columbia's model.

So that's what was new in British Columbia.

Justice England was intrigued. Concern had been growing for many years about the lack of affordable legal services for poor and even middle-income people. Public defenders for criminal cases had been created in the 1960s in response to *Gideon v. Wainwright*, and President Johnson's "War on Poverty" programs had provided federal funds to create legal services organizations with paid lawyers to help eligible people in civil matters. There were some private local efforts in some of Florida's more urban counties. But services were grossly inadequate. A report in 1970 showed that only twenty-one of Florida's sixty-seven counties had any organized legal help for the poor and recommended a statewide program for that purpose.[2]

Here was an idea to generate money without relying on legislative appropriations or the charity of individual lawyers, but from money that was sitting in bank accounts not drawing interest and basically enriching the bankers. At England's request, Hebenton agreed to assemble a group knowledgeable about the British Columbia program, and England would fly out there after an American Bar Association meeting coming up in Chicago. (State Comptroller Gerald Lewis later balked at paying the cost of the trip, since Vancouver was not on the way back from Chicago, but eventually relented.)

After his return to Florida, England met with the Florida Bar's board of governors in July 1976 and outlined the specifics of a program that would rely on interest on lawyers' trust accounts to fund legal aid and programs to improve the legal system in Florida. He learned that Bar staff counsel Norman C. Faulkner had explored such a program as far back as 1971, but the idea had not progressed beyond research. England asked that the Bar take up the issue and present a plan to the Supreme Court. It would be known as IOTA, for Interest On Trust Accounts.

The Bar filed an initial petition at the court for adoption of the program in December 1976, but opponents soon came forward—among them the Florida Bankers Association. There was an oral argument in April 1978, but another year passed before the court issued a decision. On March 16, 1978, just before he became chief justice, England wrote an opinion for the court approving the IOTA program and designating the Florida Bar Foundation to administer the program. England noted later, with a smile, that the elements of the program were remarkably similar to those he had outlined in his speech to the Bar's governing board in 1976.[3]

But the work was only beginning. There were three big hurdles still ahead.

The first problem was who would manage the money that would start flowing in. British Columbia had set up a foundation to receive the interest payments and make grants. Florida already had a foundation, the Florida Bar Foundation, but England described it as largely a social organization of older lawyers who gathered for social events and collected money for law school scholarships. It had to be restructured as a serious grant-making organization with a professional staff.

The Bar and a group of bankers had to develop details of a system of interest-bearing trust accounts that would remit interest directly to the Bar Foundation rather than to lawyers who controlled the accounts. Banks would have to sign on to take part in the program.

Then there was the Internal Revenue Service, which had to be convinced that interest on a lawyer's trust account, paid to the foundation under the IOTA program, would not count as taxable income to the lawyer or the client. The IRS held the position that the interest, though tiny, was taxable to the individual clients, who were said to have simply "assigned" the interest to the Bar Foundation. "Assignment" of income was a big deal to the IRS, which viewed it as tax avoidance by high-income taxpayers and saw in the IOTA program "a breeding ground for yet unborn tax avoidance schemes," as England later put it.[4]

England, who had an LL.M. in tax, had once won a great victory for Hugh Culverhouse's law firm by persuading the IRS to treat an art collection as a business with deductible expenses, not as a hobby. He had drafted Florida corporate income tax laws in 1971. But he was a judge now and could not handle this crucial piece of getting his idea implemented. So the Bar Foundation recruited a prominent D.C. tax lawyer, Henry G. Zapruder, born in Brooklyn and raised in Dallas. He was the son of Abraham Zapruder, who achieved enduring fame when he captured the assassination of President John F. Kennedy on film in 1963.

The IOTA concept was one of just many controversies facing the Bar in the late 1970s over the issue of access to legal services and to the courts. Critics sought to break the self-protective habits of the organized Bar and create greater access to legal services and more meaningful protection for consumers through new avenues of litigation.

The most prominent controversy was lawyer advertising. Having already declared that "commercial speech" had constitutional protection[5] and that fixed pricing and bans on advertising did not serve the public interest,[6] the U.S. Supreme Court struck down state bans on lawyer advertising in 1977.[7] Then in two cases on the same day in 1978, the U.S. Supreme Court declared a First Amendment right of a nonprofit organization to solicit clients for litigation[8] while also upholding Ohio's right to discipline a lawyer for in-person solicitation of a client.[9] The Florida Bar was moving in fits and starts toward allowing advertising while avoiding misleading advertising.

By the time it considered formal rules for advertising in 1980, the Florida Supreme Court was ready to enter this brave new world. With the Florida Association of Broadcasters as an active participant in the rulemaking proceedings, the court went beyond what the U.S. Supreme Court had done and beyond the Florida Bar's desire to limit advertising to print media. The court made Florida one of the most permissive states toward lawyer advertising by permitting ads in "electronic media" as well.[10] Misleading ads and misleading trade names would be prohibited.

Electronic advertising drew an objection from Sundberg, who said he knew he had to permit advertising but he didn't have to like it. He agreed with the Bar that there were "special problems" in broadcast advertising that needed more study and more specific rules. "I question the effects of advertising upon a great and noble profession and the resultant ability of the legal profession to fill the role it is obliged to perform in our society," wrote Sundberg, who was joined by Alderman. "It is my firm conviction that the practice of law is first and foremost a profession and only incidentally a means of earning a living."[11]

Sundberg went on, "I recognize that the deficiency in delivery of legal services remains a persistent problem, one to which this court and the Florida Bar must be dedicated to alleviate. I am not convinced, however, that unlimited lawyer advertising is the solution many proclaim it to be."

A lot of forces were driving toward a goal of making legal services more accessible and reducing the impediments to the legal process for the middle class. Florida's legislature, for example, had created no-fault divorce. Now the new right to advertising was giving lawyers a chance to offer inexpensive handling of routine matters, including wills and uncontested divorces, for $200 or so with the idea that they were largely a matter of using basic legal forms and adding a little bit of individualization.

That in turn led to the creation of non-lawyer services run by secretaries and notaries to fill in the forms and show people how to file them on their own, without the need for lawyers at all. Again, the Bar raised objections. As early as 1973, Florida's justices had granted an injunction against a business forms company owned by a notary public. It sold a "divorce kit" containing forms, helped people fill them out and even filed the papers for them, all for $187.[12] The next year the court unanimously declared that selling a written summary of the law, even when no individual advice was given, also amounted to "unauthorized practice of law."[13] "The advice given in the 'Divorce Kit' as to use of the forms is quite comprehensive and specific. It parallels much of what an attorney would customarily advise his clients who seek dissolution of marriage," Justice Ervin wrote.

As concern grew about access to legal services, the court became slightly more tolerant. It rebuffed a Bar complaint against Marilyn Brumbaugh, who offered services as a legal secretary and typed forms for her clients for $50. The court said that was okay as long as she did not advise clients on remedies available or assist them in determining what to put on the forms or how to file the forms or how to present their cases in court.[14]

For another legal secretary, however, that was not good enough. Rosemary Furman said the ruling in the *Brumbaugh* case was "so narrow that it deprives citizens of equal protection of the laws" and restricted her right to disseminate information that let indigent litigants effectively have access to the states' divorce courts.

Represented by Albert J. Hadeed of Southern Legal Counsel in Gainesville and Alan B. Morrison, the co-founder with Ralph Nader of the Public Citizen Litigation Group in Washington, Furman said she could not stay within the *Brumbaugh* guidelines because customers who came to her, as the court summarized it, "are not capable for various and sundry reasons, mainly not being familiar with legal terminology or illiterate, and were unable to write out the necessary information." Furman gave detailed instructions on how papers should be filed and hearings arranged and told clients the questions and answers they should be prepared for at the hearing.

A retired judge assigned as "referee" declared that Furman presented "a grave danger to the people of Florida," should be held in contempt of court, and should be prohibited from typing legal papers. He said she had "shielded" herself "behind the cloak of Northside Secretarial Service," which she had never registered as a business name, and engaged in the unlicensed practice of law for three years. "The fact she is an expert stenographer does not give her any legal right to engage in divorce and adoption practice any more than a nurse has the right to set up an office for performing tonsillectomy or appendectomy operations or a dental assistant to do extractions or fill teeth," the referee wrote.

When the report reached the Supreme Court, the justices acknowledged the problem of legal services. "Devising means for providing effective legal services to the indigent and poor is a continuing problem," the court said. "In spite of the laudable efforts by the bar, however, this record suggests that even more attention needs to be given to this subject." The court even declared, "Without question, it is our responsibility to promote the full availability of legal services." It directed the bar to "determine better ways and means of providing legal services to the indigent" and file a report by January 1, 1980.[15]

Support for Furman's cause did little for Furman's case. The justices embraced the referee's findings against Furman and said their decision in Brumbaugh's case "could not have been clearer." They enjoined Furman from "unauthorized practice of law," and Alderman wanted to make her pay for the costs of the proceedings against her.

While the controversies over lawyer advertising and access to legal services had been getting most of the public attention in the late 1970s, England's idea about interest on trust accounts had been jumping over each hurdle in its way. Coincidentally, banking regulators gave final approval to what were called NOW accounts, interest-bearing checking accounts, so that finally in America people could earn interest on checking balances as well as "savings" accounts.

The biggest hurdle for the IOTA program had been the IRS, whose skepticism effectively blocked the program. First, the IRS declared that several of the foundation's new goals would disqualify it from 501(c)(3) charitable status. Its goal of providing access to legal services for everyone had to be changed. But it was okay to fund legal services for the poor and to support legal scholarships and projects to improve the legal system.[16] At last the IRS told Zapruder it would approve the tax-exempt status of the IOTA program as long as clients had no control over where the interest income went.

The IRS concerns about the program had the odd effect of boosting the Bar Foundation's desire that the program be mandatory for all lawyers, not merely voluntary. The Supreme Court invited one last round of comments on the program before final approval, and they came in abundance, most of them still hostile to the program and its mandatory nature. In the court's opinion on July 16, 1981, England listed the objections in some detail: the program was an unconstitutional "taking" of clients' property. It interfered with "attorney-banker relations." It created administrative burdens for law firms. "It has been suggested that the Foundation's proposal is not only outside our constitutional authority, being a legislative function (taxation), but is unconstitutional (taxation without representation, among other reasons), is unwarranted (because some attorneys can now get interest for their clients on their individual accounts), is unwise (because the Foundation is selected as sole recipient of any earnings which are generated), and is unjust (bankers complain that they cannot even earn interest on their own funds which are escrowed with attorneys)."

Then England's opinion offered a hint of his own frustration after the five years of effort since he first conceived of the program—and ten years since the Bar's Norman Faulkner first started studying the idea. "In its persistently careful effort to bring about a trust account interest program which can at last see the light of day, the Foundation has filed a response with the Court which has met virtually every legitimate concern and problem with either an answer, an accommodation, or an acknowledgment of the difficulties. It urges us, nonetheless, not to send the program back into studied oblivion. On this point we are in complete accord with the Foundation. The time has come either to implement this concept, or to scrap it. We choose to implement."[17]

It was a 5–2 decision. Boyd and Adkins dissented. Boyd noted that he had supported the program in 1978 but now agreed with a number of the concerns, including the "taking" of clients' interest income and the mandatory nature of the program.

L. David Shear, a Tampa lawyer and former Florida Bar president, chaired a commission to oversee the details of implementation and promote the new program in Florida.[18] Among other things they worked with a group of bankers to create a simple program that would remit interest directly to the Bar Foundation. Jane Curran became executive director of the Bar Foundation, a position she held for more than thirty years, and continued to expand the foundation's revenue streams and promote legal services and initiatives in the administration of justice.

There was one more key figure in giving life to the program in 1981: a banker named Charles Zwick. He was the CEO of Southeast Banks of Miami, a client of Steel Hector's John Edward Smith. His was the first major bank to establish IOTA accounts, and his embrace of the program set the standard for the rest of the banks.

The Supreme Court's approval of IOTA was one of England's last opinions on the court. Financially burdened by his daughters' education and recent hospital bills for his wife, DeeDee, England resigned from the court effective August 9, 1981, and went back to Miami to practice law—not tax law now, but appellate practice. Still, he and others who had developed the Florida program wanted to take it national for one very practical reason: the faster the idea went into practice, the less likely it was that further challenges could undo it. And many other states were indeed interested. The name of the program morphed into "Interest on Lawyer Trust Accounts," or IOLTA.

There was an organization in place to move the idea forward. Even as the first opinion in 1978 was authorizing the accounts, an organization called the Florida Justice Institute was coming into being in Miami to undertake major litigation on behalf of the poor. It was the creation of Roderick N. Petrey, who at the time was executive vice president of the Edna McConnell Clark Foundation in New York City, an early proponent of legal services programs. The initial board included Chesterfield Smith of Holland & Knight and John Edward Smith, as well as Askew legal counsel Eleanor Mitchell, who would soon become a law clerk to England at the Supreme Court.

The institute hired Randall C. Berg Jr. as executive director. As the Bar Foundation prepared for final approval of the IOTA program in 1981, Berg was asked by Bar Foundation president Russell Carlisle and Legal Services president Don Middlebrooks to help with the petition and coordinate amicus briefs in other states. He later created what became known as the "IOLTA Clearinghouse" to provide information to other legal organizations in other states to help get similar programs going there. Zapruder, whose family sold the famous Zapruder assassination film to the federal government for $16 million, joined the volunteer advocacy team as well and went state to state promoting the program. So did England.

There would be one more round of challenges to the new IOLTA programs. The conservative Washington Legal Foundation challenged the constitutionality of the program in the late 1990s. The U.S. Supreme Court, by a 5–4 vote, ruled against the Texas IOLTA program and said the interest was the property of clients, but the case was returned to a lower court to determine whether the program was a government confiscation of property without compensation.[19] The issue was put to rest in 2003 in a challenge from Washington state. Justice Sandra Day O'Connor switched sides and voted with the more liberal justices to uphold the IOLTA program.[20] Justice John Paul Stevens quoted Oliver Wendell Holmes from nearly a century earlier saying, "The question is what has the owner lost, not what has the taker gained." The interest—$4.96 for one of the challengers—would be less than the administrative costs of paying it, the court reasoned, so the owners of the funds had lost nothing. The 5–4 decision, two decades after the Florida Supreme Court approved the program, put an end to challenges to IOLTA.

IOLTA came along just in time to counter national budget cuts in legal services, reversing the expansion that began under President Johnson in the

1960s. In 1982 the national Legal Services Corporation suffered a 25 percent cut in its federal funds as President Ronald Reagan's administration led a Republican attack on pro-consumer litigation filed by legal aid programs. Berg called the IOLTA program "a blank check for the public good." The implementation of the program did not, however, end the concern over funding for legal services.

In 1983 Miami lawyer Neil Chonin, a former chairman of the Pro Bono Legal Services Commission, which had led the IOTA effort, tried to persuade the court to require every Bar member to donate twenty-five hours of professional services each year, participate in IOLTA, or donate $500 to the Bar Foundation. Florida Bar President James C. Rinaman of Jacksonville argued against it. On May 12, in a unanimous decision written by Justice McDonald, the court said no. "Every lawyer, regardless of professional prominence or professional workload, should find time to participate in serving the disadvantaged," McDonald wrote, but added, "We have been loathe [sic] to coerce involuntary servitude in all walks of life; we do not forcibly take property without just compensation; we do not mandate acts of charity. We believe that a person's voluntary service to others has to come from within the soul of that person."[21]

Rosemary Furman remained dissatisfied. Four years after her first case at the Supreme Court, Furman was back at the court on contempt charges for continuing her legal services business.

Rejecting her claim that she was entitled to a jury trial before being put in jail, the court held her in contempt, sentenced her to thirty days in the Duval County jail, suspended another ninety days if she quit giving "legal advice," and ordered her to pay $7,802.14 in court costs. The justices, who were enduring significant scorn in newspaper editorials and articles over the legal system's persistence against Furman, took pains to say that Furman was not merely giving legal advice but giving wrong advice and encouraging her clients to offer false information in court proceedings. Far from taking business away from lawyers, the court said, "It may well be that respondent adds to the workload of properly licensed lawyers and judges by her unauthorized and maladroit attempts to practice law."[22] Her customers, however, had not complained. The ones interviewed by reporters gushed at the results they got. And people continued to see her as a hero for taking on the club of well-paid lawyers.

A week after holding her in contempt, the court approved a rule allowing no-lawyer divorces for couples married for fewer than five years without minor or dependent children as long as they had lived in Florida at least six months.[23] It was nicknamed—not by the court, of course—the "Furman Rule." The new rules came complete with legal forms, which would be distributed and notarized by court clerks, just as Rosemary Furman and Marilyn Brumbaugh had done for their clients.

The debate over those rules reflected the tension between providing more lawyers and avoiding lawyers altogether. Nancy Smith, a lawyer from Kissimmee, told the court at oral argument on February 10, 1983, that general-practice lawyers were overwhelmingly opposed to the new no-lawyer divorce rules. Justice McDonald asked if they were not just concerned about their own economic interests. "No, sir," Smith replied. She objected to the assumption that some people just don't need a lawyer. "These are people who need at least the opportunity to be informed of their rights," Smith said. And Stephen Sessums of Tampa, head of the Bar's Family Law Section, expressed concern that some spouses might be so dependent on the other spouse that they would have no real chance to assert their rights if they did not have a lawyer. Boyd made that point in his lone dissent.[24]

Frank D. Newman of Miami, who chaired the Bar committee that developed the proposed rules, noted the continued popularity of "do it yourself divorce." One company had sent the court a two-page brief claiming to have sold twenty-thousand kits over the previous ten years. "Obviously there are people out there who want to get a divorce without a lawyer."

The "Furman Rule" was a major step, because divorce cases accounted for about a third of the civil cases filed in Florida courts. Overton noted in a preliminary opinion that the court had taken a similar step in providing forms for small claims and small probate estates.[25]

The U.S. Supreme Court refused to hear Rosemary Furman's appeal, but a clear sign of the popularity of her cause was that Governor Graham, using his clemency powers, excused her jail term. "For millions of people, Rosemary Furman stands for the idea that you shouldn't have to pay a fortune for a simple legal matter," said Graham, himself a lawyer. "Her case has raised the fundamental right of access to the courts. I don't think we've heard the last of her."[26]

He was right about that. Her notoriety put her on national news. She was featured on the CBS news magazine *60 Minutes*. Furman also spawned a separate case in federal courts by telling an illiterate customer, Serena Dunn, that since Furman could not help her directly in obtaining a divorce, she should sue the Florida Bar and claim that its rules on unauthorized practice of law violated her constitutional right to access to the courts. That case was filed in

March 1983 by Alan Morrison, who was also Furman's lawyer. U.S. District Judge Howell Melton allowed the lawsuit to proceed as a class action. Four years later, with the suit still pending, the Bar relaxed its rules to allow non-lawyers like Furman to provide "oral communication to assist individuals in the completion of legal forms approved by the Supreme Court of Florida" under certain conditions.

During the Florida Supreme Court's review of the Bar proposal, Morrison submitted comments to the Supreme Court saying the standards were too strict in allowing only communication "essential" and "necessary." That should be loosened to a standard of reasonableness. Morrison also wanted it made clear "that non-lawyers may tell the individuals, for example, how many copies must be filed, what the filing fees are, what is the proper method of payment, how long the typical period is before a hearing will be scheduled, and other matters of a routine administrative nature."

The court adopted the changes Furman and her lawyer wanted.[27]

In 1985 another commission after another study actually recommended a mandatory contribution of legal services by all lawyers. In 1989 Sandy D'Alemberte led another petition effort whose signatories again included prominent members of the Bar, including England and Sundberg, who were by then back in private law practice and had not been on the court for the 1983 petition.[28] This time the effort was not mandatory legal services but simply mandatory reporting of the extent to which a lawyer engaged in pro bono work. The effort eventually won approval through the work of a committee led by future First DCA Judge William A. Van Nortwick.

Efforts continued through the years. Eugene Pettis, the first black president of the Florida Bar, highlighted the problem of access to legal services in 2013–14 but took the different approach of urging it as a state responsibility, not simply a responsibility to be borne by the Bar. In 2014 the new chief justice, Jorge Labarga, echoing Pettis's theme, appointed yet another commission but included legislators and representatives of private companies.

10

"SAVE THE SUPREME COURT"

As he prepared to succeed Ben Overton as chief justice less than four years after his election to the court, nothing was more important to Arthur England than narrowing the scope of the Supreme Court's jurisdiction. The District Courts of Appeal, created in 1957, were supposed to be the last stop for the vast majority of appeals. England thought the Supreme Court had violated that principle in recent years by stretching its own jurisdictional rules. The Supreme Court, in England's view, needed to spend less time deciding which cases to take and more time deciding important questions of law. It was a matter of increasing the court's importance by limiting its discretionary power, so more of its work had significance beyond the individual case.

Caseloads throughout Florida's legal system had grown rapidly over the past decade. The population was growing faster than in almost any other state, and there were many more rights to litigate over. Total case filings tripled from 1958 to 1972. A 1972 statute restoring the death penalty in Florida was bringing thirty-five or forty new death cases every year and was occupying a third or more of the court's time on direct appeals and requests for stays of execution. To keep up, the Supreme Court had created a pool of law clerks to summarize petitions, started sitting in five-justice panels to relieve the load on each justice, and limited oral arguments to cases where the justices thought them essential rather than upon request of the lawyers. Yet, to England's chagrin, a majority of justices had continued an expansive view of the court's jurisdiction.[1]

"It is my duty to advise you that the courts of Florida are no longer capable of satisfying the demands placed on them by the people and the laws of this state, and that unless certain steps are taken now, the public's confidence in the judiciary will be seriously imperiled," England wrote on April 2, 1979, in his first annual report to the legislature as chief justice.[2]

England had a broader agenda than just jurisdiction. England also wanted a clearer separation of powers and a stronger position for the judiciary as an independent third branch of government. He wanted better judicial salaries, which he said ranked twenty-sixth in the nation among appellate courts and twenty-first among trial courts, even though Florida was then the eighth largest state in population. He wanted to take advantage of technology—a need illustrated by the fact that his annual report on the judiciary included charts created on a typewriter with hand-drawn lines on the charts.

First, however, England had to win his colleagues' vote to become chief justice. In 1976 he had led the revolt against the normal rotation by seniority so that Overton would become chief instead of scandal-tainted Joe Boyd (chapter 6). In 1978 England had to persuade the other justices to bypass Boyd once again and elect him, as next in seniority behind Overton. Adkins, a consistent supporter of Boyd, at one point talked about calling for a public session where he would reveal England's efforts to manipulate the process. Adkins had argued since 1976 that any justice of the court was qualified to be chief. He also had expressed public support for holding justices' conferences in public. England also supported a public session, again believing that the predictable news stories would diminish justices' support for Boyd.

On March 27, 1978, the week before Fred Karl was to leave the court, the justices met in a hastily called public session to choose Overton's successor. It would be the only time in the court's history that the chief was chosen in public. The justices sat, without their robes, at a conference table below the justices' bench in the big courtroom, with reporters in the audience. There were only subtle hints of the posturing and negotiations beforehand.

As he had two years earlier, Adkins nominated Boyd. Boyd declined the nomination and said he wanted to avoid a "schism" on the court. "There are some people on this court today who would vote for me for chief justice," Boyd said. "Some obviously would not. But I don't think my own political future, my own destiny, should be considered in this matter." Alan Sundberg, next in seniority behind England, then nominated England. "I abstain from the vote," Boyd announced. Adkins abstained, too. The five Askew-era justices were united for England. After the 5–0 vote, Karl looked at Boyd, whom he had prosecuted in impeachment hearings three years before, and said, "You are a big man, a strong man, a good man."[3]

Soon after becoming chief on July 1, England had an unexpected occasion to draw a line in the sand on separation of powers—or more accurately, the line was in Duval Street separating the court from the capitol. State work crews showed up one day to take down two large magnolia trees on either side of the front entrance to the Supreme Court building. Justices and their staffs were appalled. "You're the chief—do something!" they told England. He immediately summoned the head of Askew's Department of General Services to his office, told him that this city block was under the control of the Judicial Branch of government, not the governor, and work was to stop. It did. The magnolias remained for another quarter-century, until major repairs to the leaky foundation of the building forced their removal.

On the other hand, England experienced a unique melding of the branches of government when, as the Constitution dictates for the chief justice, he presided over the Florida Senate for the impeachment trial of Circuit Judge Sam Smith of Lake City, who had been convicted of conspiracy to sell marijuana. Overton had presided over pretrial sessions in May 1978, but the Senate trial itself was in September. England had never even tried a case as a lawyer and had never presided over a trial. But he immersed himself in impeachment law as well as rules of evidence and procedure. The legislature itself was not new to him, since he had served as special tax counsel to the House of Representatives in the drafting of the corporate income tax in 1971. Fortified by orange juice provided by the Florida Citrus Commission from a seemingly bottomless dispenser on the president's rostrum, England presided for three days that produced the only impeachment and removal of a public official from office in Florida's history at that time.[4]

"Justice should be done, but not overdone," Justice Elwyn Thomas had written in *Lake v. Lake*[5] shortly after the new district courts of appeal came into being in 1957. Thomas, often viewed as the father of the DCAs because of his advocacy for their creation when he was chairman of the Judicial Council, was determined that the mid-level courts would relieve "intolerable" congestion from growing appellate caseloads and not just become "way stations on the road to the Supreme Court." Justice Campbell Thornal had later carried the torch, mostly in dissent as the court abandoned that principle. Now England made their crusade his own. Although his vision for the court was expansive, England was determined to narrow its reach on its most fundamental constitutional role, the review of cases from lower courts.

The constitutional amendment creating the district courts of appeal allowed the Supreme Court to review cases "in direct conflict" with cases from another district court or the Supreme Court. In *Lake v. Lake*, Thomas had written for a 5–0 court that the court would not review district court decisions that simply declared a trial court decision was "Affirmed" without any opinion explaining the decision. It did not matter if a party claimed some conflict. Such decisions were known as "Per Curiam Affirmed" decisions, or PCAs (not to be confused with the DCAs, or district courts). Only in an "exceptional case" would the Supreme Court "dig into the record" of the lower-court proceedings to find a conflict not apparent in the simple one-line Per Curiam Affirmed decision. "When a party wins in the trial court, he must be prepared to face his opponent in the appellate court, but if he succeeds there, he should not be compelled the second time to undergo the expense and delay of another review," Thomas wrote. "We assume that an appeal to a district court of appeal will receive earnest, intelligent, fearless consideration and decision."[6]

It turned out that the justices were not as determined on this point as their 5–0 decision suggested, and the rule began to erode. Seven years later, Thomas and two other justices who had joined his opinion in *Lake* found themselves in the minority when the issue arose again. Richard Ervin had replaced Justice W. Glenn Terrell, their fourth vote, in 1964. B. K. Roberts and Harris Drew, who had been on the court but not part of the five-justice panel in *Lake*, now led a majority for the opposite view, joined by Ervin and Justice Millard Fillmore Caldwell (a former governor, 1945–1949) in a case called *Foley v. Weaver Drugs Inc.*[7]

Roberts's opinion for the new majority said that hundreds of decisions had come to the court under the "direct conflict" jurisdiction, a large number of them PCAs claiming to be the "exceptional case" that Thomas allowed for. Most were denied, some were remanded with a request that the court explain its decision, and in at least one case the court had dug into the record and found a conflict. Roberts said Supreme Court review of such decisions was necessary "to keep the law harmonious and uniform."[8]

The complexity of that duty is illustrated by the supposed "conflict" in the *Foley* case. James M. Foley had gone to Weaver Drugs and bought a bottle of Revlon's "Thin Down" reducing pills for his wife, and when she started to unscrew the top of the glass jar, it broke into pieces and cut her wrist. Foley sued both Revlon and the retailer. The trial judge let Weaver Drugs out of the case on a summary judgment and allowed the suit to proceed against Revlon. The Third District Court issued a summary Per Curiam Affirmed decision upholding that ruling. But the Foleys said that ruling was inconsistent with a decision a few years earlier from the Second DCA in a lawsuit by a woman hurt when she tried to open a glass bottle of Canada Dry with a bottle opener on the wall at a Food Fair store.

Presented with the PCA decision against the Foleys, the Supreme Court first simply asked the Third DCA to write an opinion explaining its decision.[9] The Third DCA, which had acceded to a similar request in 1961 as the Supreme Court's backsliding was just beginning,[10] refused to capitulate again. "We are not inclined to reconsider the case on its merits," wrote Judge Charles A. Carroll. "And we do not feel it is essential or appropriate for us now to produce theories and reasons for the decision which we made in November of 1962 [30 months earlier]."[11]

Undeterred, Justice Roberts for the majority then said the conflict between the two cases was "clear," took jurisdiction of the case, and concluded that the Third DCA had been correct in dismissing the retailer from the case and the earlier Second DCA decision about Food Fair had been wrong and no longer reflected the law in such cases.

Thornal wrote a dissent on jurisdiction, joined by Stephen O'Connell and Thomas, reiterating Thomas's point from the *Lake* case. Long delays had been frustrating justice for litigants, Thornal said, and giving finality to DCA decisions was fundamental to the new court structure. "It seems to me that we now proceed to undo all of this," he said. "If I were a practicing lawyer in Florida, I would never again accept with finality a decision of a District Court. . . . There is always that potential opportunity to obtain another examination of the record by the Supreme Court with the hope that it will in some way differ with the District Court."[12]

Sure enough, England later observed that the *Foley* case had "a tremendous effect" on the growth of the caseload.

The Supreme Court's self-generated freedom to reach down and find ways to review cases also was a factor in the court scandals later, when Justice McCain was accused of leading the court to overturn cases that had gone against a political supporter. So England, who had just arrived at the court when the House was considering impeachment of McCain, had a special objection to this expansive approach to jurisdiction.

A stolen-cow case the year after he joined the court prompted England to express his view on jurisdiction for the first time. The defendant had been charged with stealing nine heifers. The victim could identify only seven as his, and the jury acquitted on the theft of six of the cows and convicted the defendant on just one. The district court of appeal upheld the conviction. Sundberg, along with Adkins and Boyd, joined Roberts's majority opinion overturning the conviction, which to them seemed clearly nothing more than an unjust compromise verdict. If the defendant did not steal six of the cows, he surely did not steal the seventh one either.

Overton and Hatchett joined England's dissent, which was tinged with sarcasm. "A majority of the court finds direct conflict between the district court's decision, which in its entirety read 'affirmed,' and two other Florida appellate cases. I cannot." England went on to observe that the dissenting opinion in the lower court began with the words "based on the facts of this case," which to him showed that "obviously no great legal principle separates" the judges— merely a difference based on "the peculiar facts of this case." Moreover, one of the cases in conflict had already been overruled. The other wasn't really relevant, as even the majority acknowledged. And one more thing: the stolen-cow statute in question had been repealed.

In 1977 England weighed in again in *Florida Greyhound Owners and Breeders Association Inc. v. West Flagler Association Ltd.*[13] "This case crystallizes my evolving concern and leads me to conclude that the time has indeed come to recede from *Foley* and its ill-conceived attempt to retain the last word on every matter brought to the Florida appellate courts," England wrote. The court had become "reflexive" in asking the DCAs to issue an opinion instead of their simple "affirmed."

Unable to persuade enough of his colleagues in the stolen-cow case or the *Greyhound* case, and eager for a fix that would not be undone by changing majorities on the court, England was ready for a new look at the basic jurisdictional structure of the Supreme Court.

England was keenly sensitive to the court's workload. After moving into Ervin's old office at the court, England struggled to keep up with the caseload and remembered Harris Drew telling him that while every case was important, all cases are not created equal. He would have to pick the cases that deserved more attention. To England, one way of doing that was to identify a category of cases that should not be at the court at all.

England and Sundberg disagreed again over a case called *National Airlines Inc. v. Edwards* in 1976.[14] It grew out of the spate of hijackings of airliners to or from Cuba during the 1970s, most of them resolved without death or even serious injuries. This case was over the hijacking of a National Airlines DC-8 on July 24, 1971, by a man born in Cuba. A flight attendant and a passenger were injured, but the claimant in the case, Theodora "Teddy" Edwards, sued because she got a "permanent illness" from the Cuban food and drink she consumed in Cuba.

A judge in Miami dismissed the case, but the Fourth District Court of Appeal reinstated it. Edwards had presented a legitimate claim that, as the court paraphrased it, "The airline knew or should have known that . . . its airplane containing plaintiff would be taken to Cuba and there detained by the Cuban authorities . . . [and] forced in order to sustain herself to consume dangerous and illness-causing food and drink provided by the Cuban government."[15]

National Airlines appealed to the Supreme Court, which took the case, and in an opinion by Justice Roberts, reversed the Fourth DCA and threw out the lawsuit on May 12, 1976. "The damages alleged by respondent to be a result of National's negligence . . . were too remote as a matter of law to be recoverable," Roberts wrote. Adkins, Boyd, Sundberg, and Hatchett joined him. England and Overton dissented, and England wrote another remonstrance against the acceptance of cases on flimsy jurisdictional grounds. There was no legal principle at issue, England said. The case was simply a disagreement between the Supreme Court majority and the Fourth DCA over whether there was a sufficient "intervening cause" of Edwards's illness to relieve the airline of responsibility.

"This is a case that came to the court at a time when Alan and I and Ben Overton and Joe Hatchett were striving to get the Supreme Court away from its long-standing habit of taking too many cases, which were not important to the people of the state, and . . . eroding the authority of the district courts of appeal," England recalled years later.[16] Sundberg voted to accept the case. "Why did he do it? Because the district court's decision was just plain wrong. He did not allow that decision to stand and become part of our jurisprudence in this state, because it was poorly decided, had the wrong principles applied and did not fit within the common law of this state."

The old friends continued to debate that case for the rest of their lives. It represented the core of the debate over the jurisdictional amendment.

Overton shared England's concerns and usually joined England's dissents. In his 1978 report to the legislature, shortly before his term as chief ended, Overton proposed a commission with a variety of people, including non-lawyers, similar to the group that produced the 1956 amendment creating the district courts. Among its topics was adding a fifth district court of appeal—after the original three in 1957, a fourth had been added in 1965—and assigning workers' compensation appeals to district courts rather than to the Supreme Court. Upon becoming chief, England created the Appellate Structure Commission with Overton chairing it. England added an agenda item that Overton had not mentioned: a review of the system in light of the 1956 goal "to ensure that the district courts of appeal are courts of final appellate review."

That November, however, members of Overton's commission were discouraged when voters rejected all of the recommendations of the 1977–78 Constitution Revision Commission. They saw it as public weariness with constitutional reform. The more widely accepted reason was that the recommendations were collateral damage from well-financed "no" campaigns against legalizing casino gambling and elimination of the elected executive Cabinet. The defeats prompted the Appellate Structure Commission to change its mind about proposing any constitutional amendment to limit the Supreme Court's jurisdiction. Any changes should be by court rule or statute, not constitutional amendment, the Overton commission said. The rules were indeed changed. One change let district courts sit "en banc," with all the judges, to resolve conflicting decisions among their own three-judge panels. Still, the changes fell considerably short of what England and Overton wanted to accomplish.

The justices would not let the issue drop. England and Overton finally produced a draft of a constitutional amendment that the justices unanimously endorsed. Unfortunately, their amendment, filed as Senate Joint Resolution (SJR) 714, was proposed late, as legislative cycles go—just as the legislature was beginning its 1979 session in April 1979, after much of the preparatory committee work was done. Under the pressure of time, England could not win the Florida Bar's official endorsement—only eighteen of thirty members of the Bar's board of governors voted yes, while twenty, or two-thirds, were needed for endorsement.

Sundberg, who had been a lobbyist and a member of the board of governors before joining the court, argued in support of the proposal before two sessions of the Senate Judiciary-Civil Committee, but SJR 714 went nowhere and was withdrawn. No companion proposal was even introduced in the House of Representatives. Sundberg reopened discussions with the Bar, and they worked out compromises, but they would have to wait for a later legislative session.

One major item that did pass during the regular legislative session of 1979 was the creation of a Fifth District Court of Appeal. Overton's commission had recommended a fifth district, carved out of the First, Second, and Fourth districts, with the Second's headquarters in Lakeland logically becoming the home of a new Fifth District stretching from Hardee and Polk counties northward straddling Interstate 4. The Second DCA, no longer including the Tenth Circuit with Polk County, would get a new headquarters in Tampa or St. Petersburg, more central to a district covering southwestern Florida and closer to more of its population.

But House Speaker Hyatt Brown and House Majority Leader Sam Bell were both from Daytona Beach, as was influential Senator Edgar M. Dunn, and they wanted the new court headquarters in their home town. The new headquarters held the prospect of new construction as well as more new judges appointed from their community. To justify a new headquarters in Daytona, though, they had to remove Lakeland, with its existing DCA headquarters, from the proposed Fifth District. And since districts are made up of complete judicial circuits, the only way to get Lakeland out was to exclude the entire Tenth Circuit, with Highlands, Hardee, and Polk, and leave it in the Second District. The Fifth instead would take the Seventh Circuit, north of Daytona, from the First District.

The Appellate Structure Commission and the justices had tried to equalize the population among the five districts, but leaving the Tenth Circuit in the Second District meant that the Second would have by far the largest population and workload, while the First District, with the loss of the Seventh Circuit in Daytona at the southeastern end of its territory, would have too little workload and too many judges.

The workload imbalance was a major impediment to passage of the Daytona plan. Sharyn Smith, a former assistant attorney general under Robert Shevin, was now working for Speaker Brown and was assigned the task of solving the imbalance. Since redrawing boundaries of individual circuits posed huge administrative and political challenges, she looked for a way to move some large category of cases into the First District. Since the Supreme Court wanted to move its workers' comp jurisdiction to the district courts, Smith proposed moving all workers' comp appeals to the First DCA, no matter where in the state they originated. It was inconvenient for lawyers, since most of the workers' comp cases originated at the other end of the state, but it better balanced the appellate caseloads. The Industrial Relations Commission was eliminated. (One of the commissioners, future justice Leander Shaw, was then appointed to the First DCA.) Moreover, with venue mandated in Leon County for cases against state government officials, the First DCA would receive those appeals as well.[17]

There was one problem with the idea: the First DCA judges didn't want workers' comp cases. To mollify them, Brown agreed that the First DCA could have its own new building, just like the Fifth, and move out of the basement of the Supreme Court building. The court ended up with a new white-painted brick building a block away between the Supreme Court and the FSU Law School.

England also wanted the legislature to eliminate the constitutional requirement, inserted in 1976, that at least one justice come from each appellate district. He argued that a statewide pool produced higher-quality nominees. The Senate, however, had not forgotten that just four years earlier, Askew's first three appointees to the court all had Pinellas County ties. (Hatchett, the third appointee, had not lived in Clearwater since high school and spent his entire professional life in the Daytona-Jacksonville area, but even the Supreme Court's own public listing of justices showed Hatchett as being from Clearwater.) England was told that if his change stayed in the legislation, it probably would not pass. He gave up.

The legislature passed the Daytona version of the new appellate district, but so contentious was the issue that eight senators asked Governor Graham to veto it. Instead, Graham simply let the bill become law without his signature. Graham also asked the court for an advisory opinion that the legislation, heavily modified by the legislature, met constitutional requirements for legislative deference to proposals from the Supreme Court. The requirements had been put in the Constitution in 1972 so the legislature could not simply ignore Supreme Court recommendations for the Judicial Branch of government.

In the court's response to Graham, three justices complained that Graham had failed to explain why he thought there was something unconstitutional about the statute and why he did not take part in the court's public hearing on his request for an opinion. "The judicial process is a precise issue-oriented process," Harvard Law grad Sundberg instructed Harvard Law grad Graham.[18] But a majority of the court upheld the result, no doubt content with whatever relief they could get in the district court workloads.

The matter of workers' compensation appeals was a little-noticed sideshow in the struggle over jurisdiction.

In the early part of the 1970s, the justices were growing weary of a system that sent to the Supreme Court all the appeals from the Industrial Claims Commission, whose members at the time were not lawyers. After the makeup of the Industrial Claims Commission was successfully challenged at the First District Court in 1969,[19] Justice Roberts and First DCA Judge Sam Spector began talking about a way to restructure the commission and improve the balance and credibility of its decisions with less appellate review. That effort coincided with Attorney Stephen M. Slepin's appointment by Askew to head the Division of Labor and Employment Opportunities and to chair the Industrial Relations Commission with a focus on greater professionalization.

As Slepin explained it, while Roberts was often viewed as an ally of business, he also had been a poor boy from Sopchoppy and "had a heart for mommy and the kids" and what they would have left after a breadwinner was injured. It also was an example of Roberts's expansive view of his place in the governance of Florida.

The legislature in 1971 created a new Industrial Relations Commission and a cadre of industrial claims judges who had the same qualifications as circuit judges. Slepin worked with Roberts to draft new workers' compensation rules of procedure. Although workers' comp was not part of the court system, the rules were "voluntarily submitted" to the court for approval, which was granted on November 14, 1973.[20] And for thirty years thereafter, the Supreme Court oversaw the workers' comp rules just as it oversaw rules of procedure for the various divisions of the court system such as juvenile and criminal and probate.

Roberts sought to underscore the higher status and ethical requirements by holding the investiture of the newly constituted industrial claims judges at the Supreme Court building in 1973. That same year, the court took the first step toward less aggressive review of workers' comp cases by declaring, in *Pierce v. Piper Aircraft Corp.*,[21] that the new judges of industrial claims were "somewhat akin to circuit judges" and would no longer be required to prepare detailed findings of fact.

It was an open secret that, while Roberts wanted professionalization of the workers' comp system, he and other justices considered comp appeals to be beneath the dignity of the Supreme Court. The creation of a stronger Industrial Relations Commission gave the justices a rationale to relieve their workers' comp workload by judicial fiat in 1974 *with Scholastic Systems Inc. v. LeLoup.*[22]

Justice Hal Dekle's opinion in that case compared the workers' comp system to congressionally created courts under Article I of the U.S. Constitution, such as the U.S. Tax Court, and explicitly recognized the commission as a "judicial tribunal" for purposes of meeting a constitutional requirement of access to the courts. Therefore, Dekle wrote, "there is no constitutional requirement for this court to review orders of the IRC as a matter of right." It would review cases only if the court found a "departure from the essential requirements of law." Overton, brand new on the court and eager to limit the court's jurisdiction and workload to the more important cases, joined Roberts, Adkins, Boyd, and McCain in signing on to Dekle's opinion.

Besides the unilateral redefinition of its workers' comp jurisdiction, the oddest thing in the opinion is Dekle's Orwellian view of *Foley v. Weaver Drugs*. Dekle claimed *Foley* illustrated that the court "has from time to time reconsidered the manner in which it can best utilize its judicial resources." He described *Foley* as "requiring that conflict certiorari must appear from the 'record proper' as a basis for a review." What was in fact an expansion of jurisdiction was recast as a limitation. "Record proper" could include something deep in the file of the case and not apparent on the face of the district court decision.

Ervin, who saw the Supreme Court as the ultimate protector of the working class in workers' comp cases, did not trust the comp system to protect them.

He dissented and sarcastically called the opinion "innovative." It was "a break from the past review policy of the court . . . which gave litigants seeking review the equivalent of a direct appeal" and deferred to comp judges' decisions only if there were "competent and substantial evidence" to support the decision. Ervin added, "I readily agree that this court is overloaded and overworked in this area of its review authority, but I do not believe the remedy for this onerous condition should be the deprival of the type of review now afforded workmen's compensation litigants."

The Askew-era justices later preserved the *LeLoup* decision. In 1976, in *Chicken 'N' Things v. Murray*, a 4–1 denial of review of a comp decision that was favorable to the employee, Hatchett wrote that accepting the case and drawing "our own factual conclusions de novo from the cold record" would lead to undesirable second-guessing of factual determinations, "create additional uncertainty both for claimants and employers," and disrupt the creation of a specialized tribunal for comp cases. Decades later, the case was a basis for denying appeals of landowners affected by the citrus canker eradication program.[23]

The outlier *LeLoup* decision also was a factor in an early test of Askew's Sunshine Amendment, which called for financial disclosure and banned legislators from representing clients at state agencies. The amendment permitted legislators to continuing representing clients in "judicial tribunals," a term not otherwise defined or even used in the Constitution but used in the *LeLoup* case. Askew's draft of the amendment said "courts," but the chairman of the Industrial Relations Commission asked Askew to include workers' comp. So the term "judicial tribunals" was substituted, apparently without reflection on what else the term might embrace.

State Senator Kenneth Myers, a prominent Miami Democrat, had a substantial law practice before the Public Service Commission while also chairing a Senate committee that handled PSC-related legislation. Before adoption of the Sunshine Amendment, he sought a formal opinion from Attorney General Shevin, who said Myers was prohibited from practicing before the PSC. After voter approval of the amendment, Myers then turned to the PSC itself for help.

The PSC had no interest in stopping Myers from practicing there and had no authority to ban him (that was an Ethics Commission matter), but the agency cooperated with Myers in a test case at the court. The PSC entered an order barring Myers. Myers then filed a petition at the Supreme Court against PSC Chairwoman Paula Hawkins (the future U.S. Senator) and the other two commissioners and argued that the PSC, like the Industrial Relations Commission, was a "judicial tribunal" where he could still practice. Myers asserted that the category logically also included the Public Employees Relations Commission and the Career Service Commission.

This was exactly the kind of conflict of interest Askew wanted to stop—legislators using their authority over state agencies' appropriations and substantive laws to gain an edge for their paying clients in the decisions agencies made. Recognizing that the PSC was not a motivated adversary to Myers, Askew not only filed his own amicus brief but asked Shevin to step in and argue the case. Shevin did so, along with Assistant Attorney General Sharyn Smith.

LeLoup was on a list informally compiled by a few lawyers in Shevin's office identifying Supreme Court decisions they considered unexplained outliers. *LeLoup* seemed to reflect no precedent or legal principle. Others on the list were suspected of being tainted by some extra-judicial consideration, usually connected with the pre-Askew justices and their relaxed attitude toward contacts with outsiders on cases. The list was internally referred to as "no cite-em cases," meaning the lawyers in the office should avoid citing them as precedents because the court knew their peculiarity and would give them little deference.

Shevin and Smith urged the court to overrule the *LeLoup* case. England, writing for the court in *Myers v. Hawkins*,[24] dismissed the *LeLoup* issue out of hand in a footnote, leaving it confined to comp cases but declining to overrule it. England personally disliked the whole notion of including these independent agencies as "judicial" agencies and did not want the Supreme Court handling workers' comp rules. Rather than focusing on *LeLoup*, though, he simply declared that while the PSC had some judicial-like functions, it was not a "judicial tribunal." That avoided having more "tribunals" as shadow functions of the judicial branch. Myers nonetheless dodged the ethical restriction on his PSC practice, because the court said the Sunshine Amendment could not be applied to those already in office when the amendment took effect on January 4, 1977, because that would amount to changing the qualifications for office. Myers, elected the same day the amendment passed, began his legislative term in November—before the January effective date.

It was not until 2004, during what was to be yet another routine update of the workers' comp rules, first shepherded through the court by B. K. Roberts in 1973, that the court suddenly declared that it had been acting unconstitutionally all this time.[25] The decision roughly coincided with another round of workers' comp legislation in 2003. The new legal provisions included caps on attorney fees and the shift of workers' comp judges into what business lobbyists considered the more neutral environs of the Division of Administrative

Hearings. The shift seemed to produce an epiphany at the Supreme Court. "The Workers' Compensation Rules of Procedure constitute an unconstitutional encroachment on the power of the executive branch to adopt rules of procedure for its own agencies," the court said in 2004. It repealed the rules effective immediately.

For all that was done in 1979, England's biggest priority remained undone—permanently reshaping Supreme Court jurisdiction. But he soon got another chance. In November, there was to be a special session on a number of tax proposals from the governor, and the matter of the court's jurisdiction was added to the agenda. Sundberg went back to negotiate further with the Bar. Overton reconvened the Appellate Structure Commission to rework the plan.

Under the commission's final proposal, the DCAs would have a major role as gatekeepers for the Supreme Court through the power to "certify" for Supreme Court review decisions "of great public importance" or "in direct conflict" with a decision of the Supreme Court or another DCA. A novel "pass-through" authority allowed a DCA to skip its own review and accelerate a trial court decision that needed "immediate resolution by the Supreme Court" and was "of great public importance" or had "a great effect on the proper administration of justice throughout the state." The pass-through role would be used many times, most feverishly two decades later as the First DCA received a flood of appeals during the presidential election recount of 2000. Overton remarked that Florida was the only state that used the mid-level appellate courts as part of the screening mechanism for the Supreme Court.

Without a constitutional amendment on jurisdiction, though, the Supreme Court was faced with relying more and more on a growing central staff of law clerks to screen cases—a "silent judiciary," Overton called them.[26]

The Supreme Court's blessing of the Fifth DCA headquarters in Daytona Beach no doubt made the legislature, particularly Speaker Hyatt Brown, more amenable to another try at a constitutional amendment. England recalled that the Speaker invited him over to the capitol to meet with the key House leadership and explain once again what the court was trying to achieve.

The problem for the court, England told them, was not simply the screening and review of the one-line Per Curiam Affirmed opinions. It was also the lawyers' frivolous inclusion of constitutional issues so they could justify a direct appeal to the Supreme Court and bypass the district courts.

It was the time spent sifting through filings—1,600 filings invoking the Supreme Court's "discretionary" jurisdiction, of which just fifty-eight were accepted for review.

It was the rise in the Supreme Court caseload, from 457 right after the DCAs were created in 1957 to more than two thousand in 1977.

It was the resulting backlog of cases of two years or more. It could take five months or more just for a decision whether to accept the case.

The House Speaker's leadership team asked questions and made comments, then, by England's account, the Speaker declared, "You've heard the Chief Justice. I think he's right. We're going to pass this."

And they did, by 38–2 in the Senate and 110–2 in the House, on November 28, 1979.[27] It would be on the March 1980 ballot alongside the presidential primary and a Graham proposal to raise the homestead exemption on property taxes from $5,000 to $25,000.

Tobias Simon, a longtime civil rights lawyer who had been on the Appellate Structure Commission, did not like the diminished opportunity for people to take their cases to the court. He set out on a campaign against the amendment. He and England were friends in Miami, and they ended up in speaking engagements that became debates of the jurisdiction issue all across Florida.

Simon had a flair for dramatic challenges to the Establishment. In 1961 he and fellow Miami attorney Howard W. Dixon had successfully challenged in the U.S. Supreme Court a state requirement passed in 1949 that teachers take an oath that they were not communists.[28] He had coauthored the American Civil Liberties Union's amicus brief in *Gideon v. Wainwright*. During the civil rights protests led by Martin Luther King Jr. in St. Augustine in 1964, Simon went there, began helping the protesters with their legal problems, and represented King when he was jailed. The St. Johns County Bar Association filed a complaint that he was soliciting legal business, and Simon recruited Fred Karl and onetime Florida Bar President Cody Fowler to defend him. They asked the Florida Supreme Court to order the grievance proceedings open to the public. The court refused, but eventually the complaint was dropped.[29]

Now Simon was turning his flair for the dramatic on the Supreme Court and the effort to narrow its jurisdiction. Keenly aware that victims of injustice often needed a high-profile case to win, Simon did not want such litigants stuck with a decision from the far less visible district courts of appeal. He believed litigants should be able to ask the justices to review any decision of a district court and not be arbitrarily foreclosed by a DCA's own failure to explain its decision. His organization, Floridians Against Limited Access, included former Attorney General Shevin, former Secretary of State Jesse McCrary, and former Dade State Attorney Richard Gerstein. (Retired Justice Roberts also publicly opposed the amendment.)

The last round of the collegial but intensely competitive jousting over jurisdiction started when England called a news conference in the large courtroom for February 29, two weeks before the vote. He had the clerk's office bring out the red file folders from every pending capital-punishment case and line them up on the justices' bench and on the side tables to illustrate the court's workload.

But as reporters arrived, Simon hijacked England's news conference with his own, on the front steps of the Supreme Court building. "It will be easier for Floridians to go to the Supreme Court in Washington than this court if the amendment passes," Simon said. As he finished his remarks, he tore open his shirt to reveal a T-shirt underneath that read, "Save the Supreme Court."

Then the reporters, along with Simon, went inside for England's event. Reporters and cameras filled the rows down front, while the file folders covered all the available table tops. Death cases alone, England told reporters, took nearly half the working hours of the justices. As he later put it, he wanted to stop lawyers who were "importuning for trivia" with appeals important to clients but not to the development of the law of Florida. England said he might have to come up with his own T-shirt. "I don't know what it will say. . . . It certainly will not say 'Save the court for certain lawyers who don't want their cases to end and who don't care how much it costs their clients.'"[30]

The campaign was one of Simon's last crusades. He died of cancer at age fifty-two on February 25, 1982. That year the Supreme Court began the annual presentation of a Tobias Simon Pro Bono Service Award to lawyers with extraordinary records of free legal services for the poor.

On March 11, 1980, Ronald Reagan and incumbent President Jimmy Carter won their respective party presidential primaries in Florida; Graham's higher homestead tax exemption passed; and the jurisdiction amendment was approved by a 2-to-1 margin—940,420 to 460,266.

Less than three months later, the Supreme Court issued an opinion saying that the new jurisdiction provision meant exactly what England had been saying it meant. The case, *Jenkins v. State*,[31] was over the legality of a police search made without a search warrant on the basis of third-hand statements from an informant. The trial judge had rejected the defendant's challenge, and the Fourth District issued a Per Curiam Affirmed decision. A dissenting opinion "recited the facts extensively and concluded that under prevailing law the search violated petitioner's Fourth Amendment rights," as Sundberg described it.

The dissent made this different from the old *Foley* case, because the Supreme Court could readily see what the lower-court decision was about and what the conflict might be. But it did not matter. The Supreme Court said it would accept a case for review only if the majority of the district court "expressly" said their decision "directly conflicts" with another appellate decision.

It was a 6–1 decision. Adkins, as fervent about access to the court as England was about limiting jurisdiction, was the dissenter, to no one's surprise. In interviews and civic club speeches during the campaign, he had often said, "The voters pay us to work, not to avoid working." In his dissent, Adkins noted that he had concurred with the majority in *Foley v. Weaver Drugs*. "We are embarking on a course which limits our jurisdiction to matters concerning deep questions of law, while the great bulk of litigants are allowed to founder on rocks of uncertainty and trial judges steer their course over a chaotic reef as they attempt to apply Per Curiam Affirmed decisions," Adkins wrote. He said voters did not fully understand the consequences of the amendment they approved.

A year later, in a review of the internal effects on the court, England noted the individual statistics of the justices in accepting cases in the first year after passage of the amendment. Before, the court was accepting about 5 percent of the discretionary appeals. Now, Justice Adkins was voting to accept 45 percent of the reduced filings, while Alderman—the only former DCA judge on the court—was voting to accept 10 percent, even lower than England's 11 percent. Overton and McDonald voted to accept 17 percent and 18.5 percent, respectively, and Boyd was at 20 percent. Sundberg was at 38 percent, but his percentage was probably inflated because of the way such cases flowed to the chief justice.[32]

Meanwhile the district courts of appeal had not materially changed the number of cases disposed of without opinions—ranging from a low of 10 percent at the Third DCA to a high of 49 percent at the Second DCA. England publicly emphasized "an increased obligation on district court judges who have some ability to control a party's right to Supreme Court review."

The view urged by Adkins and Toby Simon diminished in force but did not die. In 1983, not long after England and Sundberg had resigned from the court, Alderman, by then the chief justice, created a new commission (again chaired by Overton) to reexamine Article V a decade after the first major revision in 1972. Jurisdiction was a dominant issue, and Adkins in an interview vowed to continue to oppose the 1980 changes.[33] Lawyers noted the number of cases decided without opinion by the district courts and branded them a miscarriage of justice.

Twenty years after the amendment passed, the debate continued. This time, a new committee that included a judge from each of the district courts looked specifically at the decision without opinion, the PCA. While saying PCAs were not abused, the committee said many lawyers still believe the no-opinion decisions "leave the nearly unavoidable impression that the majority has acted in an arbitrary fashion." One member, Third DCA Judge Gerald B. Cope Jr., said Per Curiam Affirmed decisions not only impaired public confidence that the court is performing but also diminished litigants' "assurance that their cases have been thoughtfully considered." The Supreme Court subsequently changed appellate rules to allow lawyers who receive a PCA in their case to ask courts to issue an opinion in some circumstances.

II

THE LIFE OF THE LAW

11

PERSONAL INJURY

A Collision of Interests

Sammy Cacciatore was a year out of Stetson Law School on the Wednesday morning of May 24, 1967, when a NASA engineer named William Harrison Jones Jr. slammed into the rear of a large, slow-moving asphalt truck that pulled out in front of his little Karmann Ghia. Driving near the speed limit of sixty-five miles per hour on U.S. 1, possibly unable to veer left because of a Corvette off his left rear bumper, or possibly drowsy and inattentive, or maybe just lacking time to react, Jones plowed into the back of the fourteen-wheel truck about forty feet south of the intersection.

Jones died at the scene, but his accident produced an enduring legacy through Cacciatore's surprise landmark victory six years later on behalf of Jones's widow, Hazel J. Jones. Decided 6–1 by the Florida Supreme Court, *Hoffman v. Jones*[1] marked the beginning of an upheaval in the tort law of Florida with aftershocks as far away as California. Over the next dozen years, a see-saw of shifting majorities on the Florida Supreme Court, often 4–3 votes, opened up more avenues for plaintiffs to sue but then imposed new protections for defendants in cases of personal injury, known to lawyers as "torts."

When Jones had his accident, the long-standing rule in American law was that an injured person could not win a lawsuit if he contributed in any way to the accident. The doctrine was called "contributory negligence," and all a defendant had to do to win was show that some negligence, even minor, on the part of the injured plaintiff contributed to the accident. The theory was that if the plaintiff had not also been negligent, the accident wouldn't have happened no matter how negligent the defendant was. To make the case even tougher for Mrs. Jones, there was a widespread assumption that a driver who rear-ends another car, as her husband did, is the one at fault.

So Hazel Jones wasn't in a very good legal position a few weeks later when she went to see lawyer E. Thom Rumberger about suing the owner of the asphalt truck, Pav-A-Way Corporation, and driver Philip F. Hoffman. Rumberger took the case on a contingency fee; he would get paid only if Mrs. Jones won. Sammy Cacciatore, Rumberger's associate in his first year out of law school, had a brief role in the early preparation of the case, but left the firm on August 1, 1967, to become an associate with James "Booty" Nance in Melbourne. Late in 1967, when Rumberger became a circuit judge, he referred his plaintiff cases to his friend Nance. *Jones v. Hoffman* became Cacciatore's case.[2]

Cacciatore had wanted a case like this since the day he sat in Professor Frank E. Booker's torts class at Stetson Law School and heard Booker talk about the unfairness of the contributory-negligence doctrine. Booker, who counted Baptist preachers and Cherokee Indians as well as Missouri farmers among his ancestors and who later taught at Notre Dame Law School, was noted for his eloquent critiques of the law. "Remember," Booker would tell students, "the common law is no friend of the common man."[3]

Cacciatore's Supreme Court brief later traced the contributory-negligence doctrine back to 1809 in England. England abandoned it by an Act of Parliament in 1945. About a dozen state legislatures had done the same. But no state had abandoned the doctrine by judicial decree. Florida still followed the old rule, established by the Florida Supreme Court in 1886.[4]

The case went to trial on May 19, 1969, two years after the accident. At the halfway point, even before the defense put on evidence, Circuit Judge William Akridge directed a verdict for the defendant, because Jones's contributory negligence left nothing for the jury to decide. Cacciatore appealed to the Fourth District Court of Appeal and won a new trial. The appellate court didn't strike down the contributory negligence rule. It simply said the jury, not the judge, should have decided whether Jones could have reacted faster and avoided the accident.[5]

The case now was "perfectly framed," as Cacciatore saw it, for a direct challenge to the contributory-negligence doctrine. The Fourth DCA had said any negligence in Jones's reactions was for the jury to decide. So now Cacciatore had more reason to ask the judge to instruct the jury to compare the negligence of the two drivers. Akridge refused again, as the law at the time required him to do. He gave a traditional instruction about contributory negligence: if the jury thought the preponderance of the evidence showed the truck driver Hoffman was at fault, the next step was to consider whether there was enough evidence to prove that Jones was partly at fault, too. If he was, Mrs. Jones would lose.

Sure enough, the jury found for the defendant. Mrs. Jones got nothing. So Cacciatore went back to the Fourth DCA, and this time there was no avoiding the issue. The only way Mrs. Jones could get a new trial would be an appellate decision to abandon the contributory-negligence doctrine and replace it with a doctrine of comparative negligence. If a jury determined that a plaintiff bore 20 percent of the responsibility for an accident, the damages he suffered would be reduced by 20 percent in determining how much the defendant would pay. If both parties were injured and sued each other, the one most liable would pay the net between the proportionate damages.

On February 8, 1973, the district court issued its ruling.[6] All three judges on the panel agreed that the contributory-negligence doctrine was unfair and needed to be overturned, but one of the judges was unwilling to vote that way as a judge on a mid-level appellate court. Judge Gerald Mager, however, was not so reticent. Once a legal assistant to Governor Claude R. Kirk Jr., Mager had become the youngest appellate judge in Florida when Kirk appointed him in December 1970 to the Fourth DCA. He succeeded David McCain, whom Kirk had just appointed to the Supreme Court. Joining Mager's opinion was sixty-five-year-old Circuit Judge Russell O. Morrow, a former state senator appointed to the bench by Governor LeRoy Collins and now sitting as a substitute on the appellate court.

Drawing on Cacciatore's brief, Mager quoted the Florida Supreme Court from a year earlier when it in turn had quoted iconic former U.S. Supreme Court Justice Oliver Wendell Holmes: "The law is not static. It must keep pace with the changes in our society." Even when Florida's Supreme Court had affirmed the contributory-negligence doctrine in 1886, Mager noted, Chief Justice George G. McWhorter had been critical of it and called for the legislature to change it. Eighty years later, a mere four months before Jones's accident, Justice Stephen C. O'Connell had called the doctrine "primitive" and said it imposes "the burden of an accident on one of the parties in the face of evidence that both are to blame."[7] But again the doctrine had survived.

The Fourth DCA decision striking down the doctrine forced the Florida Supreme Court's hand. While the Supreme Court was likely to take the case anyway because of the Fourth DCA's certification of its "great public interest," the court certainly could not tolerate one part of the state following an entirely different principle of law in a major field like personal injury with thousands of pending cases. The Supreme Court would have to either overturn the Fourth DCA decision or accept comparative negligence and make it applicable statewide. Hundreds of cases statewide were suddenly frozen by uncertainty.

Although it had taken almost six years, two trials, and two appellate decisions to get the litigation to this point, the case began moving with astounding speed. Just one month after the Fourth DCA decision on February 8, 1973, the Supreme Court accepted the case. A month after that, the lawyers were standing before the court at oral argument. Things were moving so fast that on the day of argument, Cacciatore filed a "Notice," hand-written on lined yellow paper torn from a legal pad, citing an additional case he would use in support of his argument.

Edna L. Caruso, who had just been admitted to the Bar in 1970, was representing Pav-A-Way's insurance company. Defense lawyers from some of the state's leading law firms swarmed around to try to preserve the contributory-negligence doctrine, which had protected so many defendants for so long. Future Justice Raymond Ehrlich and James E. Cobb of Jacksonville filed an amicus curiae, or "friend of the court," brief on behalf of two insurance associations. St. Petersburg lawyers Sam H. Mann and John T. Allen of the Harrison, Greene, Mann firm filed a brief for Florida Power Corp., the electric utility that decades later became part of Duke Energy. William B. Killian of McCarthy, Steel, Hector, and Davis represented Florida Power & Light. Graham Carothers and DuBose Ausley of Tallahassee and Kenneth L. Ryskamp of Miami joined in on behalf of railroad interests. Even the Florida Defense Lawyers Association filed a brief.

Cacciatore wanted his own show of force and asked the Academy of Florida Trial Lawyers, the major organization for plaintiff lawyers, to come in as amicus. The "academy" declined. Its board figured the court took the case because it intended to reverse the Fourth DCA decision. Only one amicus came in on Mrs. Jones's side—Thomas W. McAliley of Miami, representing various railroad unions—or, as he colorfully put it in his brief, representing "Floridians who pay their insurance premiums, who drive the trains and the cars over some disgracefully protected crossings; who work around high voltage, and who are injured and killed on the streets and highways of this state with no recourse when someone adjudges them partially at fault." McAliley called the doctrine "an invalid that refuses to die."

Cacciatore's brief said the legislature had never actually created a rule of contributory negligence, as the court seemed to believe in 1886. On June 29, 1823, the legislature of the brand new Territory of Florida had sweepingly adopted the law of England as it existed before July 4, 1776. But contributory negligence, Cacciatore said, did not become the law in England until 1809. It was a judicially created doctrine then, had been sustained by the courts of Florida rather than the legislature, and could now be abolished by the justices without legislative action.

He listed other cases in which the court had overturned long-standing traditions and precedents instead of deferring to the legislature. In 1931 the court threw out the principle that a person's tort claims expired at the person's death.[8] In 1941 the court rejected a common-law doctrine that gave fathers a stronger claim than mothers to custody of children.[9] In 1957 the court over-turned a rule "steadfastly followed" in the past and held municipalities liable for the torts of their employees.[10] The defense lawyers countered that those decisions were prompted by new legislation or constitutional provisions, nei-ther of which was a factor this time.

Cacciatore and law partner Booty Nance were almost alone on their side of the Supreme Court's big courtroom at oral argument. This was the first Su-preme Court argument for thirty-year-old Cacciatore as well as for Edna Ca-ruso as they faced Chief Justice Carlton and Justices Roberts, Ervin, Adkins, Boyd, McCain, and Dekle. At one point, Cacciatore recalled, Adkins asked him why, if comparative negligence were such a good principle, the legislature had not already adopted it. "No offense, Your Honor, but if the court will look to the left side of the aisle at the number of amicus lawyers," the reason would be obvious, Cacciatore responded. Those powerful interests, he was saying, were an overwhelming force at the legislature as well. Adkins smiled. "No of-fense taken," he said.

Cacciatore's observation had some support in Killian's brief for the defense. In 1971 bills establishing comparative negligence were introduced in both House and Senate but didn't get out of committee. In 1972 a Senate bill was "indefinitely postponed" and a House bill failed 49–56. Another bill was pend-ing in the 1973 session, under way as the oral argument happened. To Killian, the legislation, even unsuccessful, showed the legislature "is alert to the issue," even though he conceded it would be something of an exaggeration to call it a legislative "determination."

Less than three months after oral argument, on June 28, Chief Justice Carl-ton sent a memo to the other justices attaching a draft opinion from Adkins and noting that the case was on the weekly conference agenda for July 2. "In the interest of filing an opinion as soon as possible in this case, it is my hope that we can delete any portions of this opinion to which the majority does not fully agree and make any additions or corrections which are unanimous," Carlton wrote. Any changes not unanimous "could be handled in short (hope-fully) special concurrences," to be prepared while the draft is being finished.[11]

On July 10, 1973, barely a week after that conference and barely five months after the Fourth DCA decision, the Supreme Court gave Cacciatore and Mrs. Jones a resounding 6–1 victory. Adkins later called it "the opinion I am most proud of" and said it "has affected more people than perhaps any other decision of the court during my tenure."[12] He would become the court's most consistent vote for plaintiffs during his eighteen years on the court.

"All rules of common law are designed for application to new conditions and circumstances as they may be developed by enlightened commercial and business intercourse," Adkins wrote. He noted that the Legislature had recently created a no-fault system for many automobile accident cases, and the concept of contributory negligence seemed at odds with that concept.

The doctrine appeared to have been created to protect "the essential growth of industries, particularly transportation," in the nineteenth century. "Modern economic and social customs, however, favor the individual, not industry," said Adkins. The strongest argument for change, he added, is "the injustice which occurs when a plaintiff suffers severe injuries as the result of an accident for which he is only slightly responsible, and is thereby denied damages."

Adkins added that if there are multiple defendants, "each should pay the proportion of the total damages he has caused the other party."[13] That simple statement gave no hint of the years of contentious legislation and appeals to follow over liability in cases with multiple defendants.

As for deference to the legislature, Adkins noted that the legislature had passed a law in 1887 applying the "comparative negligence" standard to railroad cases, but the Supreme Court had struck it down in 1965, at the urging of the railroads, as a violation of equal protection.[14] In 1943 the legislature had passed a bill replacing contributory negligence with comparative negligence, but it was vetoed by Governor Spessard Holland. "One man thus prevented this state from now operating under a much more equitable system of recovery for negligent personal injuries and property damage," Adkins said.

"Contributory negligence," he added, taking up Cacciatore's recitation of history, was a judicial creation, and "we feel the time has come for the court to join what seems to be a trend toward almost universal adoption of comparative negligence."

Adkins wrote years later that the issue of deferring to the legislature was "the most difficult question." He said his first impulse was to defer, until research showed that the doctrine "was initially created by the courts, the justifications for the theory had vanished, and the doctrine fostered unjust results."[15] He also said juries had a "routine practice of ignoring plaintiff's negligence and allowing a contributorily negligent party to recover," so the new rule would allow jurors to both "abide by the law and do justice."

In his memoir Adkins also noted that the *Hoffman* decision had an effect beyond trials themselves. The contributory-negligence doctrine had "virtually halted all forms of settlement," because insurance companies "would dig until they found something the plaintiff had done wrong, no matter how minor, and then end all settlement negotiations."

Many related issues would await future judicial resolution, but the court did eliminate a separate doctrine called the "last clear chance" doctrine. It had developed as a counterweight to contributory negligence and created a sort of ping-pong match for jury deliberations in some cases. After deciding whether the defendant had been negligent, then deciding whether the plaintiff had contributed to the accident through his own negligence, juries would be told to go one more step and determine if one party had missed a "last clear chance" to avoid the accident, regardless of other negligence in the case. The finer points of "last clear chance" were widely misunderstood and misapplied. Juries often used it as an excuse to make up for unfairness they perceived in the contributory-negligence doctrine. Justice O'Connell, in his 1967 opinion criticizing contributory negligence, went on for page after page explaining— "again," he said in palpable frustration—what "last clear chance" meant. It was a case the court decided it would not even review.[16]

Before his resounding affirmation of Judge Mager's conclusion, however, Adkins chastised Mager for deigning to decide a case contrary to precedents of the Supreme Court. "The District Court has exceeded its authority," said Adkins. The Fourth DCA created "confusion and much delay" in the trial courts. District judges "are free to express their disagreement with the law and certify a question to us," he said later in his memoir, "but must rule in accordance with Supreme Court precedent."

Two years later, the California Supreme Court cited *Hoffman v. Jones* in shifting to a comparative negligence standard in that state.[17] Other courts followed. Today, most states apply that standard through some combination of legislative and judicial decisions.

Five of the six justices in Florida's majority had been on the court less than five years. All six had run in statewide elections, which surely diminished their sense of deference to locally elected legislators. Ervin had served four terms as elected attorney general before his appointment to the court. Adkins and Carlton had been trial judges.

There was one dissenter: B. K. Roberts, who was approaching a quarter-century on the court. He had been on a statewide ballot only once in his life— in 1952, when he was the appointed incumbent justice. "My primary concern is whether this court is empowered to reject and replace the established doctrine of contributory negligence by judicial decree," he wrote. He insisted that contributory negligence was, in fact, part of English law before 1776 and traced it back to "A.D. 1606" and even to "imperial Rome." He said the "primary question" was not whether the doctrine should be changed "but who should do the changing."

With his appellate victory in hand, Cacciatore prepared for a third trial. On the morning of trial, the case was settled—for the limits of Pav-A-Way's insurance, $100,000.

From a gauzy perspective four decades in the future, it is often assumed that it was the much-heralded judicial reforms of 1972-1976, with judges appointed through merit selection rather than politics and cronyism, that launched Florida into an age of realism and reform in its jurisprudence. As the *Hoffman* case demonstrates, however, the court was responding to the zeitgeist of reform before Governor Askew's first appointee, Ben Overton, took his seat on the court in 1974. And it was not the Ivy League lawyers England and Sundberg who showed the way but the crusty, populist, unpretentious judge from Alachua County, Jimmy Adkins.

Adkins was a stark contrast to Roberts, who was an institutional reformer but not a man of the people in the way Adkins was. Roberts assiduously cultivated political and business relationships and lived a country club life. At the Roberts home, a white-gloved black butler served dinner, and after dinner the men would retire to one room and smoke cigars and drink brandy while the ladies went into another room for tea. Adkins preferred pub crawling.

Adkins grew up in the era when Florida politics was dominated by the "Pork Chop Gang" of legislators from rural areas. Gainesville, with its mix of university academics surrounded by small businesses and farms and ranches, helped make Adkins something of a transitional figure as the Pork Chop era faded and progressivism took hold. That was true as well for another Gainesville political figure, Ralph Turlington, a House member who became Speaker for 1967–68 as the only prospect acceptable to both Pork Choppers and progressives. Adkins wasn't caught up in philosophical debates about judicial activism. He figured people didn't really care whether the politician making a decision was a judge or a legislator. People only cared whether the result was good for them.

Adkins's father, the senior James Calhoun Adkins, had represented Alachua County in the Florida House and been elected state attorney. Great-uncle Andrew Zenas Adkins had served in the State Senate. The family was prominent and comfortable, but never amassed much wealth. In personality, Jimmy Adkins was unpretentious and gregarious. The conservative side of his populism emerged in his unwavering support of the death penalty. The liberal side was reflected in his support for government openness, for freedom from government intrusion through searches without warrants, for access to courts, and for easing the ability of people to sue insurance companies and other corporations for personal damages. "I have sympathy for everybody except the killers," he once said in explaining this record.[18]

Even before *Hoffman*, Adkins wrote for a unanimous court in *Gates v. Foley*,[19] throwing out another decades-old tort doctrine—one that seems far quainter, from the perspective of the twenty-first century. The court decided that women as well as men were entitled to sue for "loss of consortium," a legal concept often referred to as marital "companionship" but specifically including the loss of sexual relations after injury or death of a spouse.

Hilda I. Gates of Fort Pierce had filed the lawsuit after her husband was "totally disabled" in a collision with an automobile driven by the defendant in the case, Harry Edwin Foley. Mrs. Gates's only individual claim, distinct from her husband's, was for loss of consortium. She was represented by future circuit judge Philip G. Nourse and local attorney C. R. McDonald Jr.; Foley was represented by future Fourth District Court of Appeal Judge John R. Beranek. The trial judge dismissed the lawsuit, and Mrs. Gates appealed to the Fourth DCA, the court that would later support Cacciatore's attack on the contributory-negligence rule. But this was before Mager joined that court; his predecessor, future justice David McCain, was part of a 2–1 vote against Mrs. Gates.

Twenty years earlier, long before Adkins was a justice, the Supreme Court in *Ripley v. Ewell* had reaffirmed an old rule that a wife had no claim for loss of consortium—only the husband. The court back then referred to the wife as the "inferior" spouse whose interests were "merged" with those of the injured party, the husband. "It cannot yet be said that the law places the husband and wife upon an exact parity," the court said at the time.[20]

Assigned to Hilda Gates's case soon after his arrival at the Supreme Court in January 1969, Adkins took pen in hand and overturned the hoary tradition. Adkins came into the court's all-male private conference one day and joked that the fundamental issue in the case was whether women enjoyed sex as much as men, and he would need several weeks to research that. His opinion, however, was serious and thoughtful and perhaps a bit wistful. Consortium "means much more than mere sexual relation and consists, also, of that affection, solace, comfort, companionship, conjugal life, fellowship, society and assistance so necessary to a successful marriage," Adkins said. "Elements comprising a cause of action for loss of consortium are equally precious to both husband and wife. The classification by sex formerly made by this court discriminates unreasonably and arbitrarily against women and must be abolished."

The decision was unanimous, joined by justices Roberts, Ervin, Carlton, Boyd, and Dekle. New wording in the 1968 Florida Constitution was a factor. A clause that once referred to "all men" now read, "All natural persons are equal before the law." And a new provision said, "There shall be no distinction between married women and married men in the holding, control, disposition, or encumbering of their property, both real and personal."

While *Gates* is often viewed as a women's rights case, to Adkins, "*Gates* presented me with an opportunity to discuss the propriety of a court rejecting outmoded common law doctrines." In Adkins's old files is a November 4, 1971, clipping from the *Florida Times-Union* reporting that a seventy-eight-year-old woman had been awarded $30,000 from Seaboard Coast Line Railroad after a train collision. Says the article: "Attorney Pat Whitaker said he believed the case was the first in the state where a woman had sued successfully on the sole grounds of loss of consortium."[21]

The outcome of *Hoffman v. Jones* made clear what the *Gates* consortium case had only hinted: even before judicial elections were discarded in favor of "merit selection," even before scandal changed its personnel, the Florida Supreme Court was consciously taking an active role in the modernization of the law of Florida. As time went on, the court often would find itself in 4–3 or 5–2 votes on torts issues. Almost always there were at least two justices at each end of the plaintiff-defendant spectrum, and one or two justices in the middle would often determine the result.

"Activism" was already a political slur against the courts in 1973 as a result of political attacks on U.S. Supreme Court rulings in equal protection and criminal procedure. It was, and remains, a way of characterizing a judicial decision that departs from precedents or changes the balance between categories of parties, such as plaintiffs and defendants in civil cases. Many view it as an elevation of judicial authority over legislative authority when statutes are declared unconstitutional, although the famous U.S. Supreme Court case of *Marbury v. Madison*[22] in 1803 declared that the legislative body is subject to the Constitution and that it is the prerogative of the judiciary to declare what the Constitution means. From the earliest days under Madison's Constitution, that prerogative has been a fundamental part of the "checks and balances" in the American republic.

Justice Dekle spoke for those opposed to "activism" a few months after *Hoffman*, dissenting in a 5–1 decision, *A.R. Moyer Inc. v. Graham*. The case allowed a general contractor to sue an architect over defective plans for an apartment building.[23] "It is usually indicative of another departure from *stare decisis* [a Latin reference to precedent] when an opinion starts reciting at length from law reviews, trial courts and the more liberal jurisdictions, each reciting the other's authority for their new found doctrine," Dekle wrote. "It is not difficult to rewrite the law if one sets out on a determined course to depart from established precedent; what is difficult is to stand fast in support of the sound principles of fundamental law, against the onslaught of new and novel theories asserted to provide economic relief to the present unfortunate litigant, from some source which appears available to tap."

Adkins, however, shared the philosophy of Sammy Cacciatore's law school professor, Frank Booker, in seeing that sometimes the common law was no friend of the common man. Doctrines like contributory negligence were created in another era when winds were blowing a different way, toward industrialization and new machines. The 1970s were a time of reformation, sometimes violent and significantly cultural but also institutional and legal. Justice Ervin wrote eloquent dissents but did not seem to move the other justices. It was Adkins who created majorities among the other elected justices of the Florida Supreme Court and persisted in making the common law more about the common man.

The day after the decision in *Hoffman*, the court issued another pro-plaintiff opinion by Adkins striking down one element of a new no-fault insurance law, which Adkins had cited the day before as legislative action inconsistent with the old rule of contributory negligence. The Supreme Court was closely divided this time, but once again the court showed hostility toward a rule that kept a plaintiff from even trying to prove a claim. Adkins later said the case, *Kluger v. White*,[24] was "one of my most cited cases" because it put force behind the Florida Constitution's right of access to the legal process, which in its 1968 version said: "The courts shall be open to every person for redress of any injury, and justice shall be administered without sale, denial or delay."[25]

Clara Kluger had an old car worth about $250. With her son driving, it was in an accident with a car owned by Bernadette White. The cost of repairing the Kluger car was estimated at $775, but normally in such cases a car is "totaled" and the reimbursement limited to the value of the car, in this case the $250. The legislature had created the "no-fault" law to reduce litigation over smaller automobile accidents like this one, but Mrs. Kluger now had no collision insurance of her own to cover property damage (this is common with old, low-value cars) and was barred by the no-fault law from filing a claim against Bernadette White. The new law would have let her sue (or settle) if her claim were $550 or more, but not with a claim of only $250.

"I did not like the whole statute," declared Adkins in his memoir, but this case "fell through the cracks" in the new law and, in his view, deprived Mrs. Kluger of access to the courts for redress of injury. "Upon careful consideration of the requirements of society, and the ever-evolving character of the law," he wrote in his opinion, the court would not strike down the no-fault law, but also would not "allow the Legislature to destroy a traditional and long-standing cause of action upon mere legislative whim, or when an alternative approach is available." The legislature can abolish a cause of action, he said, only if it provides "a reasonable alternative to protect the rights of the people" or if it "can show an overpowering public necessity for the abolishment of such right" even without an alternative.

What kind of right might properly be abolished? In 1945, Adkins noted, the legislature abolished the right to sue for "alienation of affections, criminal conversation [adultery], seduction or breach of promise [to marry]." The court had later ruled that those laws had led to "extortion and blackmail." Adkins said that was an example of the "public necessity" for abolishing those rights.

Boyd wrote a dissent in *Kluger*, joined by Carlton and Dekle. He compared no-fault to workers' comp, an alternative approach for resolving on-the-job injuries. The court has upheld other restrictions on access to courts such as statutes of limitation on the time a lawsuit can be brought, Boyd said. He also said Mrs. Kluger had made the decision not to buy property insurance and had therefore accepted responsibility for damages up to the $550 threshold.

Three weeks after the *Hoffman* decision came an unusual ruling reaching back nine years and applying *Hoffman* to reinstate an original verdict for a plaintiff. The decision was all the more notable because the plaintiff's lawyer was Joseph D. Farish, whose cases before the Supreme Court became a center of attention during the investigations of Justice McCain starting later that year.

The plaintiff, Warren G. Williams, had won a jury verdict of $141,750 against Seaboard Airline Railroad over a collision at a railroad crossing in West Palm Beach. Williams was driving a milk van making retail deliveries about 5 a.m. on July 29, 1963. Municipal ordinances required automatic electric signal devices at railroad crossings, but there was none. However, there was also testimony that Williams had not looked carefully and may have been looking back at his milk inventory as he drove across the bumpy tracks. In those days when the "contributory negligence" doctrine prevailed, a special "comparative negligence" statute was still in place for railroad cases, and it led to the large verdict for Williams. While Seaboard's appeal was pending, the Florida Supreme Court held in a separate case that the special comparative-negligence treatment for railroads was unconstitutional because it unfairly burdened railroads more than all other defendants.[26] On that basis, the Florida Supreme Court reversed the jury verdict for Williams and ordered a new trial.

Along came *Hoffman* and flipped the law around, so that comparative negligence, instead of being unconstitutional for applying only to railroads, was now the law of Florida and applicable to everyone. Warren Williams, who had lost at the retrial under the contributory-negligence doctrine, appealed to the Fourth DCA. On a 2–1 vote on November 2, 1972, two months before its groundbreaking decision in Mrs. Jones's case, the Fourth DCA upheld the defense verdict against Farish's client, Williams. The dissenter was McCain, still participating in the Fourth DCA case nearly two years after his appointment to the Supreme Court. Farish appealed Williams's case to the Supreme Court.

On July 31, 1973, with comparative negligence now the law of Florida, Boyd authored an opinion for a 4–1 majority that reversed the results of the second trial and reinstated the original $141,750 verdict for Williams that the Supreme Court had previously overturned.[27] Boyd noted that the original trial had actually applied the principles of comparative negligence that the court had recently announced in *Hoffman*, so "both justice and common sense mandate that we simply reinstate the original judgment." Adkins, Carlton, and Ervin joined the opinion. Roberts dissented. McCain was not on the five-justice panel.

Hoffman turbocharged a societal trend toward more lawsuits with more defendants, and the allocation of liability among those defendants became a growing challenge.

For personal injury lawyers taking plaintiffs' cases on a contingency-fee basis, which compensated them only as a percentage of what they recovered from defendants, the incentive was to include more defendants with more ability to pay. Insurance covered more and more causes of injury, including the cost of defending those cases, so insurance companies were more interested in seeing cases through to establish precedents than an individual defendant might be. More and more, then, there was not just one "defense" side of the case but multiple defendants, and they were pointing fingers of blame not only at each other but at parties not even in the courtroom. Their jostling was making litigation more complicated and expensive for plaintiffs as well.

"Comparative negligence," once the bane of defendants, became their crusade once *Hoffman* was decided. As Adkins had suggested, it was not only the way to apportion damages more fairly between plaintiff and defendant but also the way to allocate the burden more fairly among multiple defendants.

One of the protections for successful plaintiffs under rules before *Hoffman* was the doctrine of "joint and several liability." It said that, in cases with multiple defendants sharing responsibility for an accident, each defendant was responsible not only for its own share of the damages but for the share owed by any other defendant that failed to pay. Winning plaintiffs were entitled to collect the entire amount from one defendant, usually the one with the "deepest pockets" in terms of ability to pay. Beyond that, another long-standing rule, known as "no contribution among joint tortfeasors," said that a defendant who paid could not then sue other defendants for a share, on a theory similar to contributory negligence: a wrongdoer could not sue another whose wrongdoing was no greater than his own.

If even a small degree of liability could make one defendant fully responsible for the entire payment, why wasn't that just as unfair as contributory negligence, in which even a small degree of fault made the plaintiff totally responsible?

The perennial defendants hurt by those doctrines were first and foremost the insurance companies but also the kinds of companies on the losing side of *Hoffman v. Jones*—big utilities, railroads, manufacturers. Now they too had to challenge some old doctrines that seemed inconsistent with the new era of comparative fault. In 1975 it became the defendants' turn to rebalance tort law in their favor.

Two years after *Hoffman v. Jones*, the lone dissenter in that case penned the majority opinion in *Lincenberg v. Issen*,[28] which began Florida's long and lurching transition away from joint and several liability and recognized a right of contribution among joint tortfeasors for the first time. Minnie Issen had been a passenger in Harry Lincenberg's car when it collided with another car. The jury awarded her $20,000 in damages, and declared that Lincenberg was 15 percent responsible and that the owners of the other car were 85 percent responsible. The judge wasn't sure whether to hold them all totally responsible, which was the traditional rule, or to enter a judgment for only their allocated percentage, as Adkins's comment in *Hoffman* had suggested. The Third District Court of Appeal in Miami said *Hoffman* had not changed the law on defendants' liability, so Lincenberg (or his insurance company) was responsible for the entire $20,000 if the other defendants (or their insurance company) did not pay.

The very acceptance of jurisdiction in *Lincenberg v. Issen*—declaring it in conflict with *Hoffman*—suggested where the Supreme Court was headed. Both sides turned out plenty of legal artillery. Future justice R. Fred Lewis was on Minnie Issen's side, in support of keeping the old rule, along with well-known plaintiff lawyers Robert Orseck and J. B. Spence on behalf of the Academy of Florida Trial Lawyers. Kenneth Ryskamp, the future federal judge who had opposed comparative negligence as a lawyer in the *Hoffman* appeal, represented the Florida Defense Lawyers Association in seeking expansion of comparative negligence to defendants.

To those on the plaintiffs' side, however, any departure from full liability of each defendant meant that the plaintiff would once again be the one who bore the loss, this time because one or more of the defendants did not pay. It would undo what they had just won in *Hoffman*. The defense side countered that a winning plaintiff already loses if there is only one defendant and that defendant doesn't pay. Why should it be different with multiple defendants?

To plaintiffs, the *Hoffman* case had nothing to do with shared liability among defendants. It was about relieving a plaintiff of bearing total responsibility when the defendant was also at fault. Period. Justice Roberts did not see it that way. Though he had questioned whether the court or the legislature should change the common law in *Hoffman*, in *Lincenberg* he declared that "the court may change the rule where great social upheaval dictates."[29] He cited Adkins's own words in *Hoffman*. "With emphasis, we restate that this court in *Hoffman* announced that when the negligence of more than one person contributes to the occurrence of an accident, each should pay the proportion of total damages which he has caused the other party. The same rationale eliminates justification for the no-contribution principle and dictates that this rule be abolished."[30]

Roberts had some legislative action to bolster his view. As the *Lincenberg* appeal headed for the Supreme Court, the defense interests—the ones Cacciatore had pointed out on the other side of the courtroom—had advocated legislation to accomplish what they were asking the Supreme Court to do in *Lincenberg*. The legislature passed the Uniform Contribution Among Joint Tortfeasors Act,[31] signed into law by Governor Askew on June 13, 1975. It took effect immediately and specifically applied to cases pending at the time.

The law was awkwardly worded. Justice Boyd, concurring in the *Lincenberg* decision six weeks after the law passed, noted a "conflict" among the factors listed for consideration in the apportionment of liability. "Relative degrees of fault shall not be considered," the statute said—seemingly a conflict with the concept of both Adkins and Roberts. But "principles of equity applicable to contribution generally shall apply." What the drafters of the statute apparently intended to accomplish, through this astoundingly oblique language, was that a number of longstanding rules of "equity" proceedings, such as the attribution of an agent's fault to the employer, would be applied as opposed to a simple percentage of fault. The complexity of the language, though, would trouble the courts and the legislature for years to come. Roberts had an inkling of that and permitted judges to create "special verdict" forms to guide juries.

Roberts was joined by Adkins, McCain, and recent arrival Overton, with Boyd concurring in a separate opinion. (The court was still frequently using five-justice panels.) The law "retains the full, joint, and several liability of joint tortfeasors," Roberts noted, "and provides for contribution between them on a pro rata basis."

More than three decades later, the Florida Legislature formally adopted the comparative negligence doctrine for most tort cases and eliminated the doctrine of joint and several liability, effective April 26, 2006.[32]

In between *Hoffman* and *Lincenberg*, the court took on another challenge to a long-standing tort doctrine, the "impact rule." It, too, was a broad constraint on lawsuits and money damages. This time, though, the court clung to tradition.

The impact rule was established in Florida in 1893, in a lawsuit by someone who claimed emotional suffering as a result of delayed delivery of a telegram. The goal of the doctrine was to avoid exaggerated or false claims of psychological or emotional injury by allowing those damages only if they resulted from physical impact.[33] At the time, medicine and psychology had little ability to assess a mental or emotional condition, and the impact rule became a convenient way of avoiding litigation where the results were likely to be speculative. A case in England had established the rule five years earlier, in 1888, but the rule was marginalized there a dozen years later.[34]

In Florida the rule persisted for a century. It was applied to reject a lawsuit over negligent handling of the bodies of dead family members and a lawsuit by a woman whose car had been trapped on the railroad track in heavy traffic and who fled to avoid an oncoming train. It was also applied to parents wanting damages for their mental anguish when a hospital sent their baby home with the wrong people. The rule did not apply, though, to the mental anguish allegedly suffered by the owner of a dog maliciously killed by a garbage collector; the dog owner won.

Into this legal environment came Jane R. Stewart. On January 20, 1970, two cars had collided outside the Stewart house and jumped the curb onto the Stewarts' property. One car hit an oak tree, and the other hit the house and chipped some masonry on the exterior. It was about nine in the morning. Mrs. Stewart was still in bed but not asleep. The thuds of the impacts were "enough that my cat . . . was running around like he was crazy." She went to the porch and saw a car up against her house with steam coming out of the radiator. The car was blocking her door, so she ran through the house and out another door to see if anyone needed help. Then she went back inside to use the telephone and allowed others in to use it as well. After fifteen minutes she began suffering chest pains, and two hours later at the hospital she was diagnosed as having a heart attack. She had no previous heart problems, and her doctor diagnosed it as a result of fright. She was in the hospital for nearly a month.

She sued the drivers of the two cars, Freddie LaVerne Gilliam and Robert Leo Bradley, but the trial judge granted a summary judgment for the defendants after noting that the cars had hit her property but not Mrs. Stewart herself. On appeal to the Fourth DCA, Judge Mager again was on the panel. Two months before his opinion striking a blow at contributory negligence in *Jones v. Hoffman*, Mager struck a blow against the impact rule. By then, Mrs. Stewart was dead, and her husband, J. Parks Stewart, was pursuing the claim.

Citing the Adkins opinion in *Gates v. Foley* as a precedent for overthrowing outdated doctrines, Mager recited the history of the impact rule in England and America as well as in Florida and concluded that "this state should now align itself with the overwhelming majority of jurisdictions," which rejected the impact rule. "The courts of this state have been able to separate the genuine from the bogus claims" in all sorts of cases, "and there is no reason to assume that this problem cannot be properly dealt with in instances where there has been no impact." Proving causation or injury may be more difficult with emotional injury, but Mager said the plaintiff should have a chance to try.[35]

Mager also noted that there was more than "emotional" injury to Mrs. Stewart; there was actual "bodily injury or illness": the heart attack. The Second District Court of Appeal recently had taken a similar approach in a lawsuit against Tampa Coca Cola Bottling Company after the plaintiff found in a Coke he was drinking something "resembling a rat with the hair sucked off" and "became nauseated and vomited."

Again the Supreme Court was compelled to consider the district court's departure from long-standing precedent. Unlike the fast and unified response to the Fourth DCA decision in *Jones v. Hoffman,* it took the Supreme Court a year to reach a sharply divided decision in *Gilliam v. Stewart.*[36] Roberts did not participate, and retired justice Harris Drew filled in and wrote the opinion. This time the court rejected Mager's view and retained the impact rule.

Joined by Carlton, Boyd and Dekle, Drew first lectured Mager, as Adkins had, for "openly overruling decisions of this court." On the merits, he wrote very little except to adopt the reasoning of the dissenter at the Fourth DCA, Chief Judge John A. Reed Jr., who concluded that "not every injury which one person may by his negligence inflict upon another should be compensated in money damages." Drew added, "There must be some level of harm which one should absorb without recompense as the price he pays for living in an organized society." He did disagree with Reed's view that only the legislature could change the rule. "The impact rule is a judicial creation just as are many other substantive rules of tort law and, since it was judicially created, we are of the view that if this Court should reach the conclusion that such rule was inequitable, impractical or no longer necessary, it may be, judicially, altered or abolished."

Adkins wrote a long and passionate dissent. So did Ervin. McCain dissented but wrote no opinion.

Ervin's dissent summarily adopted Mager's opinion and went on to defend Mager against Drew's lecture about the district court's subordinate role. "There is no supremacy clause in the Florida Constitution as there is in the Federal Constitution," Ervin wrote. "District Courts have final appellate jurisdiction except as otherwise provided in the Florida Constitution. Consequently District Courts must decide appeals according to the justice of the cause in keeping with controlling law from whatever source."

Adkins went straight to the issue. "Where a definite and objective physical injury is produced as a result of emotional distress proximately caused by defendant's negligent conduct," he wrote, "a plaintiff should be allowed to maintain an action and recover damages for such physical consequences to himself regardless of the absence of any physical impact." The impact rule would not apply if there were a "substantial physical injury" that "followed closely" in time after the fright. The plaintiff would have to prove that the injury was a "natural result" of the fright. And there would be no compensation for someone with "hypersensitive mental disturbance where a normal person would not have been so affected."

It would take eleven years, though, for Adkins to get the additional vote he needed to prevail.

12

MEDIA LAW

Satyrs, Beer Trucks, and Teachers

The end of 1974 was an inopportune time for a media company to be defending itself at the Florida Supreme Court. The most scandal-ridden months in the court's history gave the justices a sour attitude toward the media.

All year the court had been sitting on the appeal of Palm Beach socialite Mary Alice Firestone in her libel case against *Time* magazine over its one-paragraph account of her salacious divorce from tire company heir Russell Firestone. It was the second Supreme Court case arising out of the divorce: the first was Mrs. Firestone's appeal of the divorce decree itself.

The divorce trial was peppered with allegations of adultery and other domestic strife. The presiding judge was Circuit Judge James R. Knott of Palm Beach County, whose father, William Valentine Knott, has his name on a state building in Tallahassee after serving as state comptroller and an unsuccessful Democratic nominee for governor in 1916. In his final order granting the divorce on December 15, 1967, Judge Knott described testimony that Mrs. Firestone's "extramarital escapades" were "bizarre and of an amatory nature which would have made Dr. Freud's hair curl," and that Mr. Firestone was "guilty of bounding from one bedpartner to another with the erotic zest of a satyr." Although the judge was "inclined to discount much of this testimony as unreliable," he concluded that "neither of the parties has shown the least susceptibility to domestication, and that the marriage should be dissolved."[1]

The divorce trial naturally generated waves of national headlines. In its issue published on the Sunday two days after the judge's order (though dated the following Friday, December 22), *Time* magazine published a single paragraph on the judge's decision to appear in its "Milestones" column:

Divorced. By Russell A. Firestone, Jr., 41, heir to the tire fortune. Mary Alice Sullivan Firestone, 32, his third wife; a onetime Palm Beach schoolteacher; on the grounds of extreme cruelty and adultery; after six years of marriage; one son; in West Palm Beach, Fla. The 17-month intermittent trial produced enough testimony of extramarital adventures on both sides, said the judge, "to make Dr. Freud's hair curl."[2]

Judge Knott proved better at colorful writing than legal precision in the Firestone case, and *Time* was caught up in the confusion. Despite the abundant testimony about adultery and cruelty and the judge's titillating description of it, Mrs. Firestone objected that *Time* had been wrong in reporting that the divorce was granted on those grounds; it was based on "lack of domestication," she argued, even though that was not a legal basis for divorce in Florida. If the basis had been adultery, she went on, Florida law would have prohibited the award of alimony she received. She had sought "separate maintenance" from her husband—an old method of evading church bans on divorce—but opposed the actual divorce. She appealed the divorce decree and sued Time Inc. for libel.

Her lawyer was Joseph D. Farish Jr., a well-known plaintiff's lawyer in West Palm Beach, whose role created yet another complexity in the web of intrigue enveloping the Firestone cases. Justice McCain was said to have referred to Farish as a "benefactor" of his political career, and one of the subthemes of the ethics and impeachment investigations of McCain in 1974 was McCain's involvement in cases where Farish was counsel. Summoned to testify to the impeachment committee investigating McCain, Farish refused to give the committee any client files, which were privileged communications, and through his lawyer, Robert Montgomery, invoked the Fifth Amendment protection against self-incrimination. Montgomery insisted, however, that Farish's "ability, and his ability alone, have led him to the path before you." The Bar had no proof that Farish ever asked for or encouraged favoritism from McCain, and it never found any wrongdoing.[3]

While the libel case was just beginning in the circuit court, the appeal of the divorce decree went to the Fourth District Court of Appeal, where it sat for eighteen months. Chief Judge Spencer Cross and Judge James H. Walden were ready to uphold Judge Knott's divorce decree, but McCain, who was on the Fourth DCA then and was part of the three-judge panel, wanted to write a dissent in favor of Mrs. Firestone. McCain still had not gotten around to writing it when Governor Kirk appointed him to the Supreme Court in December 1970. McCain stayed on the Firestone case after he moved to Tallahassee, and Cross kept pressuring him to finish the dissent so that the decision could be announced.

Anne Parker, McCain's research assistant in West Palm Beach and then in Tallahassee, offered to draft a short dissent if McCain would tell her his reasons. McCain agreed; however, upon seeing her draft, he decided that he wanted something more comprehensive. Finally, pressed again by the chief judge, McCain signed off on Parker's draft, more than a year and a half after Mrs. Firestone's appeal had arrived at the Fourth DCA.[4] The evidence "overwhelmingly establishes that appellee-husband is not entitled to a divorce," the dissent said. "It is textbook law in this state that one may not come into court of equity with unclean hands and receive relief." Mr. Firestone's "unclean hands" were reflected in the testimony about his own extramarital adventures. By McCain's reading of the law at the time, the Firestones were stuck in their unhappy marriage.[5]

Since appellate courts normally defer to trial judges in divorce cases, Cross and Walden considered her appeal not even worth an opinion and entered a simple "per curiam affirmed" decision, accompanied by McCain's dissent, on May 14, 1971. Had this been 1981 instead of 1971, the Supreme Court would not have had jurisdiction to review a per curiam affirmed decision. But in 1971, the Supreme Court frequently took such appeals (chapter 10).

Farish appealed the divorce case to the Supreme Court. As co-counsel, Farish enlisted former governor Fuller Warren, who had appointed B. K. Roberts, his childhood friend, to the court in 1949. The Supreme Court accepted the case by finding a conflict with a 1940 case that had upheld a finding of "extreme cruelty," which Judge Knott had not found in the Firestone case.

McCain was not supposed to participate in the case under court rules, since he had ruled on the matter as a lower-court judge, but research aide Parker testified to the House impeachment committee that his secretary typed a memo about the case, apparently prepared by McCain to help Roberts in writing the court's opinion, which was identified as "per curiam" when it was published.[6] Roberts immediately tore up the McCain memo, according to his research aide at the time, Marguerite Davis, who worked on the opinion and said she never saw the McCain memo.[7] Later, David Smith, manager of McCain's 1968 campaign for the Supreme Court (he lost to Adkins), testified to the House Impeachment Committee that McCain solicited Mrs. Firestone for a campaign contribution that year and told Smith later that her contribution would be "substantial" if "her old man would just let loose of some of that dough."[8] There was nothing illegal in such a contribution; it was the inherent problem of judicial elections.

Mrs. Firestone won big at the Supreme Court, which delved into the details of the testimony and concluded that the trial judge had not properly taken into account considerable assets of Mr. Firestone. The judge had granted her

$750 a month in child support and $3,000 a month in alimony. The alimony "appears to be sufficient," the Supreme Court said, then went on to behave like trial judges. "We must examine the record to determine whether the award is such that it will permit the wife to live in a manner reasonably commensurate with that provided for her by the husband during coverture and whether the husband has the ability to pay the award."

Mr. Firestone's income was $521,888.47 in 1965, but the trial judge had emphasized his "debts totaling $1,400,000" and the obligations of his "individual business operations involving helicopters, airplanes, race horses and real estate, and taxes reaching the current maximum 70% bracket," which Judge Knott thought "tend to rob the financial picture of much of its rosy hue." The Supreme Court noted that Mr. Firestone received a $2.5 million trust distribution at age forty and would receive another at age fifty. Mrs. Firestone was accustomed to a clothing allowance of $5,000 a month and use of the automobiles, a plane, and a helicopter. "To say the least, the luxuries shared by these parties during cohabitation would equal the splendor of many of the sultans out of 'Arabian Nights,'" the Supreme Court said. Eight of the Firestones' thoroughbred horses should be treated as hers, the court said, and the husband should not have been allowed to keep for himself the $184,000 in insurance proceeds on Mrs. Firestone's 26½-carat diamond engagement ring, which had been taken from her during a robbery.

While the justices said there was no such thing as "lack of domestication" as a basis for divorce in Florida, they said there was enough evidence to uphold the divorce on the ground of extreme cruelty. The court made no mention of adultery, which by then was the centerpiece of the libel litigation against Time Inc. Had the court found adultery on her part to be an additional basis for the divorce, it would have devastated both of Mrs. Firestone's claims—her claim against her ex-husband for alimony and her lawsuit against Time Inc. for libel.

Time Inc. refused a retraction demand, so the lawsuit alleged that *Time* magazine had "maliciously" prepared and published the article. Eventually Palm Beach Circuit Judge Culver Smith granted a summary judgment in favor of Time Inc. Mrs. Firestone then appealed to the Fourth DCA. McCain, still a DCA judge at the time, was on the three-judge panel, along with Judges Cross and John L. Reed Jr.

In seeking a summary judgment, Time Inc. had filed an affidavit from one of its reporters saying Farish had told him that adultery was a basis for the divorce. Farish filed his own affidavit saying the reporter's statement was "a gross error" or "an outright falsehood." That made Farish a witness, so he withdrew as counsel, but his parry was enough to overcome the summary judgment for Time. The Fourth DCA unanimously declared there were material issues of fact and reinstated the case.[9] The Florida Supreme Court refused to take the publisher's appeal.[10] The case went to trial.

The jury was told that the news item amounted to accusing Mrs. Firestone of "unchastity." It should have been obvious to *Time* that there was no finding of adultery, jurors were told, because under Florida law no alimony was payable to an adulterous spouse. Time Inc. noted Judge Knott's own discussion of adultery, but the jury awarded Mrs. Firestone $100,000.

Now the libel case was going up on appeal to the same court that had summarily upheld the divorce decree—the Fourth DCA. Robert Montgomery, who had represented Farish at the McCain impeachment hearing, was now representing Mrs. Firestone. William S. Frates and Larry S. Stewart of Miami and Harold R. Medina Jr. of Cravath, Swaine & Moore in New York were representing Time Inc.

The argument turned on a decade of U.S. Supreme Court rulings designed to protect media defendants from legal challenges over mistakes made under deadline pressures. "Erroneous statement is inevitable in free debate," the U.S. Supreme Court had said in 1964 in *New York Times v. Sullivan*,[11] so a public official should not prevail in a libel suit without proving a statement was made recklessly or with knowledge of its falsity, a standard the court labeled "actual malice." The principle was subsequently extended to stories about public figures such as big-name college football coaches[12] and to a "false portrayal" by *Time* magazine of a person whose experience as a crime victim had been fictionalized in a play.[13] And in a case dealing with coverage of a police raid searching for obscene books, the Supreme Court had gone another step to protect media coverage of matters of "public interest."[14]

The Fourth DCA unanimously reversed the $100,000 judgment against Time Inc. "Given the divorce's inclusion as an event of great public interest," Judge Walden wrote, Mrs. Firestone could win only by proving malice on the part of *Time*. "We can find no malice. "*Time* had made a "rational interpretation" of the divorce judge's decree, Walden said. Judges Reed and William C. Owen Jr. joined Walden's opinion; McCain was not on the panel this time.

The Florida Supreme Court took Mrs. Firestone's appeal in the libel case just as it had with the divorce case, again overruled the Fourth DCA, and reinstated the $100,000 verdict in a 5–0 decision issued December 20, 1972. *Firestone v. Time Inc.*[15] was written by Judge Joseph P. McNulty of the Second District Court of Appeal, substituting for McCain.[16] "We are committed to the view that neither wealth, social position nor fame, of themselves, render the private affairs of those involved amenable to constitutionally protected un-bridled public scrutiny under the guise of public or general interest," McNulty wrote. "That the public was curious, titillated or intrigued with the scandal in the Firestone divorce is beyond doubt," but no real "public concern" was shown that would be "enhanced by 'free discussion' and 'robust debate' about the divorce of Russell and Mary Alice Firestone." [17]

But the libel case still was not over. The Supreme Court returned it to the Fourth DCA to resolve other issues. One was the possibility that the *Time* article, as a description of a judicial proceeding, was "privileged" under tra-ditional libel law. Judge Walden and his Fourth DCA colleagues responded sarcastically on June 20, 1973, that their earlier "multitude" of points included all the points the Supreme Court was asking them to address. If they had "known at the time that our Point III opinion would not survive, we would have chosen another point to discuss in depth as a basis for reversal." Walden dug in his heels about his court's freedom to write opinions as it wished and simply provided a one-sentence summary of each of the other reasons for overturning the libel verdict. The court stood by its decision for Time Inc.[18]

Mrs. Firestone returned once again to the Florida Supreme Court. Mont-gomery had a new partner on the appeal now. Edna L. Caruso, who had un-successfully defended the doctrine of contributory negligence in *Hoffman v. Jones* the previous year, was now on the plaintiff's side of a case. The court barely mustered the four votes needed to accept the appeal. The vote was tied 3–3, and Chief Justice Carlton allowed McCain to break the tie in favor of review even though he had participated in the summary judgment issue at the DCA. When McCain's participation became known, Adkins, who had suc-ceeded Carlton as chief, said McCain's participation seemed preferable to call-ing in a substitute justice merely to vote on accepting the case. McCain said his only participation at the Fourth DCA was on an "interlocutory" matter and was not a review of the entire case. He didn't sit on the full Supreme Court appeal. He told Martin Dyckman of the *St. Petersburg Times* it was because "I just got sick and tired of you writing about me and Joe Farish." His vote was not needed for Mrs. Firestone to win.

Eighteen months after the Fourth DCA had stood its ground, the Supreme Court once again reinstated the $100,000 award, this time on a 4–2 vote. By this time the court was in the throes of its own headline-grabbing scandal over outside influences on its decisions, and the court's irritation at the media was palpable in the opinion. It was a per curiam opinion, but Adkins appeared to be the principal author. He said reporting on judicial proceedings is protected only if it is "fair and impartial and also accurate in regard to all material matters." Falsely accusing a woman of adultery "is libelous per se," he added. "This is a flagrant example of journalistic negligence. . . . This erroneous reporting is clear and convincing evidence of the negligence in certain segments of the news media in gathering the news."

Ervin dissented without explanation. Overton's one-paragraph dissent said there was no conflict with existing case law and blandly said the Fourth DCA decision properly applied prior case law.

The 4–2 decision still did not end the seemingly endless Firestone saga. Time Inc. decided to ask for review by the U.S. Supreme Court, even though that court had begun pulling back from media protection in libel cases. John H. Pickering of Washington represented the publisher, and Edna Caruso continued to represent Mrs. Firestone. The U.S. Supreme Court's majority opinion against Time Inc., written by Justice William H. Rehnquist, was disparaging toward media coverage of judicial proceedings. "There appears little reason," he said, that individuals should forfeit their legal protection from defamation "simply by virtue of their being drawn into a courtroom."[19] The 7–2 vote was viewed as a major defeat for the media.

A decade later Mrs. Firestone returned to the headlines. In 1985, by then married to Kentucky oil executive John Asher, the former Mrs. Firestone, now Mrs. Asher, and her son Mark Firestone were charged with possession of cocaine, marijuana, and drug paraphernalia. Mrs. Asher pleaded guilty and was sentenced to five years' probation, while charges against John Asher and Mark Firestone were dropped. In 1989 Mrs. Asher filed court documents asking that Russell Firestone, her ex-husband, be held in contempt for failing to pay $519,750 in alimony, child support and other expenses unpaid since June 1976. In 1995 Mr. Firestone was ordered to pay $1.2 million in back alimony, child support, and interest. In 1998 Mrs. Asher was still trying to collect, and Farish, by then seventy-seven years old, was still her lawyer and lamented the money would never be collected unless he could find a judge to put Firestone in jail for contempt. Russell Firestone was four-times divorced. The son who was the subject of the child-support fight had turned thirty-five and had children of his own. *The Daily Business Review* reported at the time that the case docket had 1,800 entries and the file was eighteen volumes thick.

In a different case moving toward the Florida Supreme Court in the early 1970s, *The Miami Herald* fared no better than *Time* at winning a First Amendment argument at the Florida Supreme Court, but it became one of many occasions when the U.S. Supreme Court had a more generous reading of the Constitution.

Pat Tornillo, a longtime leader of the Miami-Dade teachers' union, was a candidate for the legislature in 1972 and had sued to force the *Herald* to print verbatim his replies to two critical editorials. He relied on a Florida statute making it a misdemeanor for a newspaper to fail to grant a candidate a "right to reply" to newspaper criticism. A circuit judge in Miami denied Tornillo's petition for a court order and declared the law unconstitutional.

At the time, jurisdiction allowed for a direct appeal of such an order to the Supreme Court. Tobias Simon was representing Tornillo; Dan Paul and James W. Beasley Jr. were representing the *Herald*. The case attracted a horde of amicus filings, most of them from newspapers but also from Attorney General Shevin and the American Civil Liberties Union of Florida.

The Florida reply statute was very broad—written, after all, by political candidates. "If any newspaper in its columns assails the personal character of any candidate for nomination or for election in any election, or charges said candidate with malfeasance or misfeasance in office, or otherwise attacks his official record, or gives to another free space for such purpose, such newspaper shall upon request of such candidate immediately publish free of cost any reply he may make thereto in as conspicuous a place and in the same kind of type as the matter that calls for such reply."

Four of the five Florida justices in the majority in *Tornillo v. Miami Herald Publishing Company*[20] had been candidates themselves in hard-fought elections within the past five years—Adkins, Carlton, McCain, and Dekle. (The fifth, substitute John S. Rawls, had been a state senator before being appointed to the First DCA in 1961.) Their 5–1 per curiam opinion went on for nine pages, not counting a long concurring opinion by Roberts, and was filled with quotations from cases and James Madison and others about the responsibility of the press and the goal of preserving what the court called "an uninhibited marketplace of ideas wherein truth will prevail rather than to countenance a monopolization of that market, whether by government or private enterprise."

They added, "What some segments of the press seem to lose sight of is that the First Amendment guarantee is 'not for the benefit of the press so much as for the benefit of us all.'" That comment slightly misquoted a 1967 U.S. Supreme Court decision, *Time Inc. v. Hill*,[21] and turned its context and meaning upside down. The *Hill* case had no relationship to a right of reply. Justice William J. Brennan was explaining why restrictions on the press were to be avoided. The losing attorney in the *Hill* case was a future president who had no peer in his animosity toward the media—Richard M. Nixon.

Florida's justices gave particular emphasis to a U.S. Supreme Court decision in 1969 that had upheld a portion of the Federal Communications Commission "Fairness Doctrine" requiring "equal time" in broadcasters' discussion of public issues.[22] The majority opinion did not mention a more recent decision of the U.S. Supreme Court declaring that broadcasters were not compelled to accept advertisements on public issues.[23]

On rehearing nearly three months after the original decision, the justices rejected the *Herald* complaint that such a broad and vague reply mandate was particularly out of place when a criminal penalty was being imposed for violation. "Our task is to preserve the prerogative of the legislative body unless it clearly contravenes the basic federal and state charters adopted by our citizenry," the justices declared.

Boyd dissented. He had also been a candidate—for Dade County commissioner and then for the Supreme Court—but he was skeptical about the whole idea of mandating publication of replies. "Does the law include both news stories and editorial comment? If a story mentions a situation, but does not mention the candidate by name, may he reply? When the publisher knows his statements are true, must he publish a statement from the candidate which he knows to be false?"

Boyd's closing comment in the dissent is poignant in light of his own media troubles that would arise within a few months and haunt him for the rest of his career: "Almost everyone whose name has been carried frequently in the news media has been offended, at one time or another, by stories or comments with which he disagrees. This is part of the price one pays for success and notoriety. If there exists a problem in this state of affairs, the muzzling of a free press is not the solution to such problem."

Herald Publishing took the case to the U.S. Supreme Court, which reversed the Florida decision and struck down the reply law—unanimously.[24] Chief Justice Burger, a persistent critic of the press, wrote the majority opinion. While recognizing the value of the "marketplace of ideas," he said, "press responsibility is not mandated by the Constitution and . . . cannot be legislated." The reply law was an "intrusion into the function of editors" and penalized the press on the basis of content.

Adkins later suggested that his court's *Tornillo* decision had prompted ill will toward the court among reporters and inspired what became the ethics scandal of 1974–75.[25] It was only later that it became known that the concern about the ethics of the justices began with the justices' own law clerks, who had leaked word of the ethics problems to the press.

Long before she won a Pulitzer Prize or became a star reporter in the state capital or had the Senate press gallery named for her, Lucy Morgan was a reporter in one of the more remote and underappreciated bureaus of the *St. Petersburg Times*. She had started her journalism career as a freelancer for the *Ocala Star-Banner*, a job she got when an editor knocked on her door and told her she would probably be a good reporter because the local librarian had said she read more books than anybody else in town. On her first assignment covering the city council, a member told the reporters not to write about what they were going to discuss, which was the police chief. "It didn't seem right to me not to write what they were talking about, so I did," she recalled many years later.[26]

Divorced with three children, Lucy Ware moved in 1968 to the small Pasco County bureau of the *Times* and eventually married the tough-minded bureau editor, Richard Morgan. With her Mississippi twang and a toughness inherited from her "fiercely independent" single mother, Lucy Morgan had a way of working sources that would become the envy of many of her colleagues and competitors.

And so it was that on November 1, 1973, in the section of the newspaper known as the *Pasco Times*, a headline over her byline read: "Jury Assails Dade City, Indicts No One." Morgan had been sitting in the hallway outside the grand jury room watching who went in and out. At one point, the Pinellas-Pasco State Attorney himself, James T. Russell, had stopped to talk to her.

Grand jury proceedings are secret, and any formal presentment, as opposed to an indictment, was kept secret for up to fifteen days so that anyone criticized had a chance to respond. Morgan's story did not wait. She reported among other things that the grand jury, which was looking into government corruption, "reportedly" criticized certain Dade City officials and decided to "keep a close eye" on the Pasco County building department.

The morning the story appeared, Morgan was served a subpoena to see Russell, who demanded to know where she got her information. His justification was that Florida law prohibits any grand juror from revealing the nature or substance of the deliberations or vote. When Morgan refused to tell him where the information came from, a judge waiting in the next room held her in contempt and sentenced her to five months in jail.

William C. Ballard, a former Overton law partner representing the newspaper, appealed the first contempt finding and the five-month sentence to the Second District Court of Appeal, which reversed the conviction on March 21, 1975. Judge Stephen H. Grimes, the future justice, wrote the short opinion. He was joined by Judges T. Frank Hobson Jr., son of a former justice, and John Scheb. "This case can be disposed of upon narrow grounds," Grimes wrote. Florida law authorizes a state attorney to summon witnesses to testify about a violation of "the criminal law," but the law on grand jury secrecy was not a "criminal law." It said grand jurors "shall not disclose" but did not make it a crime to do so. So Russell's investigation was "unauthorized."[27]

Russell started over. He got a subpoena from the grand jury itself, then held a formal grand jury proceeding on November 13. The grand jury said it was investigating "possible leaks" and granted Morgan immunity from prosecution. Again she was asked where she got her information, and again she refused to answer and said the confidentiality of her sources was protected by the First and Fourteenth Amendments of the U.S. Constitution. Russell hauled her into circuit court, and this time she was sentenced to ninety days.

The Second DCA saw no easy out this time. "The grand jury was clearly well within its proper authority in investigating matters which imperiled its own integrity or its entitlement to the secrecy," wrote Judge McNulty on December 3, 1975.[28] "Our own Supreme Court held fairly early on [in 1950] in *Clein v. State* that there was no privilege of confidentiality." The U.S. Supreme Court had recently established a reporter's privilege of confidentiality in *Branzburg v. Hayes*,[29] he added, but "it was determined there that a valid inquiry into criminal activity was of sufficient compelling nature as to override whatever conditional privilege was vested in the press."

Branzburg had suggested, as McNulty noted, that a reporter's privilege of confidentiality could be overridden only if society's interest is "immediate, substantial, and subordinating" and if there was "a substantial connection" between the information the reporter had and society's interest in it. And the means of getting the information could not be "more drastic than necessary."

Without any discussion of the facts or the need for secrecy in the Pasco case, McNulty declared those criteria met in Morgan's case and also concluded that a case did not have to be a criminal one to overcome the reporter's privilege. "We are of the view that preservation of the rule of secrecy in grand jury proceedings and preservation of the integrity of the grand jury as an arm of the judicial branch of government is of compelling public interest," he said. McNulty also said the sentence was within the limits allowed by law and would not be deemed excessive. The decision was unanimous, joined by Judges Grimes and Edward Boardman.

Morgan remained out of jail while seeking review at the Supreme Court. At the urging of many *Times* reporters, editor Eugene C. Patterson added Sandy D'Alemberte as attorney for the Supreme Court appeal. Patterson, who had been a tank commander in General George S. Patton's Tenth Armored Division in World War II, was an intrepid protector of the First Amendment. If reporters at small newspapers were caught up in legal challenges their employers couldn't afford to defend, Patterson would hire them and defend them. He had won a Pulitzer Prize as the anti-segregation editor of the *Atlanta Constitution*. As managing editor of the *Washington Post*, he had leaped onto a desk in the newsroom to announce that newspaper's victory in the Pentagon Papers case at the U.S. Supreme Court,[30] which relieved that newspaper of charges of contempt of court for publishing the previously secret history of the Vietnam War. Morgan's case was the first serious legal attack on the *St. Petersburg Times* or its reporters since Patterson arrived as editor in 1972.

The Florida Supreme Court had changed significantly since it decided the second *Firestone* appeal against *Time*. England, Sundberg, and Hatchett had replaced Ervin, Dekle, and McCain. Roberts was retiring and did not participate in the Morgan case. When the Morgan appeal arrived, Hatchett drew the assignment and turned *Morgan v. State* into a solid declaration of a reporter's right to keep confidential sources confidential. [31]

"These contempt proceedings were not brought to punish violation of a criminal statute and were not part of an effort to obtain information needed in a criminal investigation," Hatchett wrote. "Their purpose was to force a newspaper reporter to disclose the source of published information, so that the authorities could silence the source." Citing the Pentagon Papers case, Hatchett said, "Various governmental operations may be hampered by publicity, but the desirability of secrecy varies greatly, depending on the particular governmental function, and its sensitivity to publicity. A nonspecific interest, even in keeping the inner workings of the Pentagon secret, has been held insufficient to override certain First Amendment values."

Hatchett noted that *Branzburg* had featured grand jury investigations of drug trafficking, assassination attempts on the president, and "violent disorders.'" The Pasco grand jury was not investigating any crime at all. It simply criticized Dade City's police chief. "The only specific interest compromised by premature disclosure of the grand jury's presentment," Hatchett said, was that the chief didn't have a chance to ask a court to suppress the criticism. He may not have prevailed in such a request.[32] Hatchett also observed in a footnote the role of the state attorney himself in providing information to Morgan. He cited Morgan's confirmation that Russell personally told her that the presentment would be released "in a very short time" and also said the grand jury looked at the purchase of land by the mayor and others, who then approached the city to get city water and sewer services.

Adkins and Boyd, who had endured the slings and arrows of articles based on confidential sources, joined Hatchett's opinion. England concurred only in the result. Sundberg wrote a long opinion concurring "generally" with Hatchett's opinion but seemed to have a narrower view of the privilege. He also thought the case was about as simple as it was when Grimes overturned the first contempt finding: "Essentially, I see it as a matter of Ms. Morgan's having been found guilty of an offense which is not supported by the evidence in the record."

Overton's dissent was an example of his strong respect for and deference to government institutions, especially the judicial branch. He had been a law partner of *Times* lawyer Ballard. As chief judge in Pinellas-Pasco, he had worked closely with State Attorney Russell. "I am deeply concerned that the decision by the majority will allow individual grand jurors, prosecutors, court reporters, or other grand jury staff to divulge to the press with immunity the contents of secret grand jury proceedings," he said. "The secrecy of the grand jury has as its purpose the protection of jurors from retribution, assuring the grand jury's independence from outside influence, and the protection of the innocent from unjustified charges." He then added, provocatively, "If we are going to compromise the secrecy of its deliberations, it would be better to open them up entirely."

Besides boosting Hatchett's 1976 election campaign, the case dramatically boosted Morgan's statewide journalistic celebrity. "I think it immediately made people trust me more," she said, adding that it also discouraged subpoenas of other reporters.

Even as it gave new protection to reporters and their confidential sources, endorsed accountability of government, and awarded media companies victory after victory in public records cases (chapter 27), the Florida Supreme Court continued showing little tolerance for media companies in individuals' claims of unfairness and error. The *Tornillo* case set the tone, and *Firestone* applied it to libel cases. But when individuals rather than newspapers were the ones sued for defamation, the court was more forgiving.

In *Miami Herald Publishing Company v. Ane*, Aurelio Ane was suing because a *Herald* article had falsely identified him as a likely owner of an Old Milwaukee beer truck carrying three tons of marijuana when it was seized by Monroe County Sheriff's deputies on November 21, 1977. *Herald* reporter Greg Kirstein made concerted efforts to identify and confirm the owner of the truck. He called the company that had previously leased the truck, United Brands, checked with auto-registration and tag agencies, and repeatedly checked with the sheriff's department. He identified four possible owners, including the registered owner identified by the sheriff's office, but there were suggestions that the truck had just been sold. Kirstein could not confirm which was the actual owner and could not contact Ane, who was out of town.[33] The next morning, the *Herald* reported:

TRUCK ADVERTISED BEER, CARRIED MARIJUANA BALES

An "Old Milwaukee" beer truck, sold only last Thursday by a Miami firm to a Key West distributor, was confiscated early Monday carrying about three tons of baled marijuana on U.S. 1 in Marathon, Monroe County Sheriff's officials said. . . .

The large red-and-white truck, which Monday contained bales either wrapped in burlap or packaged in cartons from Colombia, had been purchased Thursday by Aurelio Ane, Key West Distributors Inc. president, according to Marvin Kimmel, president of Miami's Universal Brands Inc. . . .

Although Kimmell said Ane purchased the trucks, both sheriff's officials and state Motor Vehicle Department officials said the truck's plate was registered to another Key West resident, Lillian Fernandez. . . .

A day later, the newspaper definitively identified Fernandez as the owner and reported: "Police and a Miami beer distributor said Tuesday that Aurelio (Porky) Ane, president of Key West Distributors, Inc., was not involved in the purchase of the truck. They blamed earlier reports of his involvement on a 'misunderstanding.'"

Ane sued both the *Herald* and Kimmel, the one who first wrongly identified him as purchaser of the beer truck, and won $5,000 from the *Herald* and $10,000 from Kimmel. At one level, the *Ane* case was a simple decision: the *Herald* had wrongly identified Ane as the owner of a truck seized with three tons of marijuana, and anybody so accused would feel their reputation was damaged and suspect that the truth would never catch up with the falsehood. There was no sign that Ane suffered any significant damage to his reputation or psyche, which explains the relatively low damage awards. The *Herald* had relied on a named source; Kimmel simply had his facts wrong and was assigned two-thirds of the liability.

The *Herald* had tried to go beyond the police report on the marijuana seizure to track the ownership of the beer truck. The trail grew muddled as the day's reporting went on. The story the next morning described every source relied on and described the uncertainty. And when the truth emerged the next day, the newspaper immediately exonerated those it had listed as possible owners. To the Third DCA, that was not enough—and in fact became another demerit against the newspaper.

When *Ane* reached the Supreme Court, the justices were seeing a steady stream of media cases pitting openness against privacy (chapter 27). They naturally seized upon the differentiation by the U.S. Supreme Court on reporting about "private" citizens like Aurelio Ane—people who were not public officials or had not become public figures by virtue of their own voluntary actions, such as famous college football coaches. The U.S. Supreme Court, in the *Firestone* case and others, had said each state could determine for itself whether to make it easier for "private" persons to sue news organizations for defamation.

The media lawyers in the *Ane* case wanted the same high standard to apply to all people suing for libel. By a 5–2 vote, the Florida Supreme Court declined. "This Court has not previously held that there is a qualified privilege for a newspaper or a private person to defame a private person merely because the defamatory communication is directed to a matter of public or general concern, and we decline to do so now," said the per curiam opinion. "We find that reasonable care is not too much to expect and that it encourages responsible reporting while allowing breathing room for mistakes to occur."

Boyd, Adkins, Overton, Alderman, and the newest justice, Leander J. Shaw Jr., made up the majority. McDonald dissented, and England replacement Ray Ehrlich joined him. A news organization "should not have to defend its inadvertent and unintentional errors," McDonald wrote. Private individuals should have to meet the same standard as public individuals and should recover damages only by proving an error "was published with knowledge of its falsity or with reckless disregard for the truth."

The same day as the *Ane* ruling, September 13, 1984, the court also upheld a libel verdict in favor of a businessman, Leonard D. Levin, who had been the subject of articles about his association with a solar heating manufacturer. *Tribune Company v. Levin*[34] had the same 5–2 lineup of justices. McDonald wrote in dissent that the higher standard of proof should be imposed on "a commercial enterprise engaged in marketing and selling goods or services to the public," because people have "a right to know of the character and activities of such a business concern." He added, "In our free enterprise system a free and open exchange of information serves the best interest of the public," and the lower requirements for businesses to bring libel suits "will greatly retard investigative reporting of commercial enterprise."

Two other contemporaneous defamation cases were not against media companies but against individuals who had complained about public employees to their employer and others. Those defendants fared much better than media defendants.

One case, filed by a police officer, was decided the same day as *Ane* and *Levin* and reaffirmed the importance of the legal protection of citizens to raise concerns with their government. It is referred to as a legal "privilege," protecting people from erroneous statements as long as they were not "malicious." In *Smith v. Russell*,[35] St. Petersburg Police Officer Jeffrey K. Smith had stopped George P. Russell on suspicion of driving while intoxicated. Russell complained to the officer at the time, and later to a judge, about the arrest procedure and what the defendant claimed was unnecessary force. Russell wrote letters to the police chief, a county judge he knew, and others. At the libel trial, the jury awarded the officer $10,000, including punitive damages, over what Russell had written in those letters.

The Second DCA unanimously overturned the decision, and the Supreme Court unanimously agreed. The police officer "is a highly visible representative of government authority who has power over citizens and broad discretion in the exercise of that power," Justice Shaw wrote on behalf of the court. That made him a public official and required a stronger showing than the trial judge's jury instructions had called for.

Three months later, the court made a more thorough assessment of the protection citizens have to make complaints to government. A teacher in a tenth-grade gifted English class, Patricia Galbreath, gave young Joseph Nodar a B in the course. Unhappy about the grade, the father, also named Joseph Nodar, and his wife contacted the teacher. Obviously unsatisfied, they moved up the hierarchy of the school system and even to the governor's office. Nodar had his son keep a detailed log about the teacher's activities. It culminated in a short speech at a school board meeting about "the harassment my son has been receiving from this particular teacher because of our investigation or inquiry as to his grades and why his grades are going down. . . . And the only thing he gets is an unqualified teacher, that's all he's got, and that's all the rest of the children in that class have—an unqualified teacher."

Galbreath sued for slander, the spoken equivalent of libel in the broad category known as "defamation." At trial, the jury decided that Nodar's statements were not just opinion, which he could freely express, but were presented as facts, for which he could be held liable if inaccurate. The jury awarded the teacher $5,000 in damages for her injury and $5,000 in punitive damages. The trial judge determined that the jury wasn't unanimous on the punitive damages and eliminated that.

On appeal, Judge John A. Beranek wrote for a unanimous three-judge panel of the Fourth District Court of Appeal in upholding the verdict. He said the Florida Supreme Court had not ruled on whether teachers were "public figures" for determining the margin for error in a defamatory statement, but it didn't matter, he said, because the real question was whether the father's remarks were protected by a "qualified privilege" for statements anyone makes to government authorities. "Defendant was . . . speaking to the superiors of the teacher of his child about whom he had complaints. He had the privilege to make these statements with the proviso that they were true and made without malicious intent," which Beranek said means they were "made in good faith, that is, with a good motive, and not for the purpose of harming the subject of the defamation."

But then Beranek accepted the jury's finding that the statements were made with malice, which negated any privilege to speak. So Nodar still lost.

Nodar went to the Supreme Court and was supported by Sandy D'Alemberte for amicus Herald Publishing Company and George K. Rahdert for amicus Times Publishing Company. They won a reversal of the judgment against the father. Boyd wrote the opinion, which was distinctly more analytical and precise in outlining the law of libel than the per curiam decision in *Ane*. Boyd began by describing the situation more charitably toward Nodar, who he said had been "dissatisfied with the instruction his son was receiving in the class and believed that it was not in accord with the established curriculum."

Boyd also said Beranek should have distinguished the malice Nodar may have felt toward the teacher, which he labeled "express malice," from what the U.S. Supreme Court confusingly labels "actual malice," defined as exceptional carelessness about the truth. The two types of malice are very different. The courts say that "public figures" have to prove exceptional carelessness, or "actual malice," before they can win a libel claim. But the U.S. Supreme Court had not applied that higher burden to lawsuits brought by private individuals. So the "public figure" determination in the case of a teacher mattered a great deal. Boyd declared that teachers are not public figures or public officials. They do not make "the same kind of surrender of the right to vindicate defamation as does one who seeks or accepts an elected or policymaking position with a public body or government institution." That brought Patricia Galbreath to exactly the same status as Aurelio Ane and Mary Alice Firestone—that of private citizen.[36]

Then Boyd turned to whether an individual defendant like Nodar was entitled to the same level of protection from defamation claims as media defendants like the *Herald*. "The constitutionally protected right to discuss, comment upon, criticize, and debate, indeed, the freedom to speak on any and all matters is extended not only to the organized media but to all persons," Boyd wrote.

It did not matter whether Nodar had been "negligent" in his statements about the teacher, Boyd said. The important thing was the same issue Beranek focused on—the "qualified privilege" to speak to the government. Boyd cited a law review article—a rare thing for the court, but this one was co-authored by amicus lawyer Rahdert on the continuing significance of traditional defenses to defamation even with the new focus on constitutional protections.[37] "The remarks of the defendant . . . came within the scope of the privilege based on mutuality of interest of speaker and listener," Boyd wrote. "The concern of a parent for the welfare of his child provides a privilege for the occasion of speaking to one having the power or duty to take action for the benefit of the child."

Did Nodar have such a malicious feeling toward the teacher that it wiped out that right to speak? Boyd said Nodar's evidence about his feelings had been improperly excluded from the trial and the jury had been improperly instructed. "Strong, angry, or intemperate words do not alone show express malice," Boyd wrote. The repeated calls and letters do not show "malice" in a legal sense and actually "shows that defendant tried to seek redress of his grievances through private communications before he publicly revealed his complaints at the school board meeting." They show "a degree of parental concern for the effectiveness of public schools which our state, through its courts of law, should attempt to encourage rather than discourage."

McDonald and Ehrlich, who had been on the *Herald*'s side in *Ane*, remained on the defendant's side in *Nodar*. Adkins and Overton, who had sided with the plaintiff in *Ane*, remained on the plaintiff's side. But Boyd, Alderman, and Shaw switched to the defendant's side this time, apparently because Nodar's remarks were "privileged" regardless of error or fault—something not found with the *Herald* story.

13

PERSONAL INJURY

A Wrong Finds a Remedy

As the long yellow Caterpillar grader went past her down the street that was under construction, nineteen-year-old Gwendolyn West stood on the street corner waiting for a bus and talking with a friend. As her bus approached, Mrs. West looked to her left, toward traffic and away from the Caterpillar grader, then began crossing the street and looking in her purse, perhaps for bus fare. She did not look to her right, down the closed street, where the big Caterpillar had gone.

She was unaware that the grader had reached the end of the street and was backing up toward her. A large blind spot obscured the driver's vision over his left shoulder, and there were no outside mirrors. There was no beeping sound then, as there is today on large trucks and equipment. As Mrs. West continued walking and looking in her purse, the grader's huge left wheel, as tall as she was, struck her, knocked her down, and ran over her.

She suffered massive internal injuries and died six days later.

Four years after the accident, which happened September 1, 1970, and after a federal court trial in which jurors declared Mrs. West 35 percent responsible for the accident, her husband's claim over her death arrived at the Florida Supreme Court. *West v. Caterpillar Tractor Company*[1] became another landmark change in tort law, this time on the liability of manufacturers for defects and dangers in their products.

Mrs. West and her husband, Leon, were a young black couple living in a poor part of Miami. Mr. West sought the help of a young lawyer just a couple of years out of American University Law School, Philip Freidin. It was a tough case on a negligence claim: Mrs. West had not looked up to see the huge grader "backing up right in front of her," as Freidin put it many years later.[2] He managed to win a $35,000 settlement with Houdaille Industries, the contractor that employed the operator of the grader. But Freidin also thought of a novel claim that would bring Caterpillar into the case and perhaps avoid or reduce the effect of Mrs. West's own negligence. He would argue that a manufacturer like Caterpillar had "strict liability" for dangerous products like the huge grader.

"I read in the *Journal of the American Trial Lawyers* about a case in California adopting strict liability," Freidin said. "I had never really heard of it before except a law school professor saying this was going to be the future. I decided to draft the complaint, even though the theory was groundbreaking and not likely to succeed." It was such a long shot, Freidin said, that he proposed a $10,000 settlement and would have accepted $5,000, but Caterpillar said no. The case went to trial in Miami before U.S. District Judge Peter T. Fay, later a judge on the Fifth Circuit and Eleventh Circuit U.S. Court of Appeals.

Freidin's claim was this: The Caterpillar grader was negligently designed because it lacked an audible warning system for use when backing up, lacked adequate rearview mirrors, and had a blind spot for the operator looking to the rear while the grader was backing up. That made the grader unreasonably dangerous. At trial, Caterpillar's key witness talked confidently about the safety of the equipment and noted that the machine had a horn that could be used. On cross-examination, Freidin asked the witness to describe how to operate the grader. The operator would use his right hand to shift the gear into reverse, the witness said, gesturing, and would have his left hand over on the horn. "You have no hands on the steering wheel?" asked Freidin. To him, it was "the gotcha moment" every lawyer hopes for.

The larger point, of course, was that the operator could not see clearly when backing up. Freidin's expert witness, a navy veteran, described navy equipment that had an automatic audible warning when backing up. The expert said he could build one for a few dollars. "That was the key to every product design case—what was the risk vs. what was the cost to repair it," said Freidin.

The jury awarded Mr. West $125,000 against Caterpillar, but it was reduced because of the 35 percent fault attributed to Mrs. West. Caterpillar appealed to the federal Fifth Circuit. To protect this remarkable victory, Freidin turned to Robert Orseck, already legendary in Miami as an appellate lawyer for plaintiffs. He had also been co-counsel for Hilda Gates and written the amicus brief in *Lincenberg* on behalf of the Florida Trial Lawyers. James S. Usich of Coral Gables, a young lawyer at Papy, Levy, Carruthers, and Poole in Coral Gables, represented Caterpillar in the appeal.

The Fifth Circuit Court needed to apply Florida tort law, but as the court put it, "There appear to be no clear controlling precedents" on what the law is.[3] So that federal courts won't be declaring what Florida's law is, the Florida Constitution gives the Florida Supreme Court jurisdiction to respond to specific legal questions federal courts need answered in pending cases. The Fifth Circuit sent the Florida court a series of questions, jointly agreed to by the lawyers for West and Caterpillar, on the Florida law of strict liability in tort and its contract-law companion, "implied warranty."

The basic legal problem was that Mrs. West had no contractual or other direct relationship with Caterpillar, a relationship lawyers call "privity." The general rule was that a plaintiff had to have "privity" with the defendant to maintain a legal claim, but the requirement was widely criticized and evaded as consumers sought greater legal protection from defective and dangerous products.

"Florida's courts had strained so long in so many different ways to allow recovery for damages in the absence of privity that this court was left with a mess to clean up," Justice Adkins recalled later. He compared the court's task in *West v. Caterpillar Tractor* to cleaning the Augean stables, an episode in Greek mythology in which the Fifth Labor of Hercules was to clean the stables of King Augeas, which held three thousand cattle but had never been cleaned of the manure. The justices took well over a year to resolve the case. Adkins, who was chief justice when the case arrived, finally took over writing the opinion "when the others had reached a standstill."[4]

Adkins considered his task not a labor of Hercules, however, but "a labor of love." He remembered a case from his own law practice. A man had given an electric blanket to his sister, who then gave it to a friend. The blanket malfunctioned and burned the friend badly. She sued Sears but obviously had no direct relationship, or "privity," with Sears. Adkins said he got a good settlement from Sears by telling its lawyer that he would take the chance that the Supreme Court would "stretch that privity" to make Sears pay what Adkins vowed would be "one hell of a big verdict." The Supreme Court had been "stretching privity" for some time on a case by case basis to produce a result the justices thought just.

When Adkins assigned himself the *West* case, "I did not want to see others caught in the same situation." He wanted to resolve all the confusion that "results when the courts must stretch the law in order to reach a just result." He went on to say in his memoir, "I believe clear rules, set out for the benefit of the bench and bar, are much preferable to decisions based on a judge's feeling on a particular case."

The stretching in the past meant that the *West* decision was less a major departure from precedent, as *Hoffman v. Jones* had been, and more a culmination of a multitude of cases at the district courts of appeal since the Supreme Court's last incremental decision several years earlier.

Adkins's opinion on July 21, 1976, swept away privity as an issue in such cases and said exactly what Freidin had hoped for when he drafted his novel complaint: manufacturers have "strict liability" to anyone harmed by a dangerous product, even mere bystanders like Mrs. West (or like Adkins's one-time client with the Sears blanket). Manufacturers could not expect people to investigate for defects and dangers before using their products.

"The obligation of the manufacturer must become what in justice it ought to be—an enterprise liability, and one which should not depend upon the intricacies of the law of sales," Adkins wrote. "The cost of injuries or damages, either to persons or property, resulting from defective products, should be borne by the makers of the products who put them into the channels of trade, rather than by the injured or damaged persons who are ordinarily powerless to protect themselves. We therefore hold that a manufacturer is strictly liable in tort when an article he places on the market, knowing that it is to be used without inspection for defects, proves to have a defect that causes injury to a human being."[5]

The "foreseeable bystander who comes within range of the danger," Adkins added, does not have to prove a specific act of negligence. Adkins also harkened back, though, to the principles of comparative negligence he established in *Hoffman* three years earlier: "On the other hand, the consumer, user, or bystander is required to exercise ordinary due care."

That "ordinary care" was Caterpillar Tractor's point. It is one thing to protect consumers from devices with hidden dangers, Usich argued, but quite another to hold a manufacturer responsible for a danger so "blatantly obvious" to someone like Mrs. West as "a yellow road grader being approximately thirty feet long, nine feet wide, standing at its canopy fifteen feet high, and weighing approximately fifteen tons."

Alas, the emphasis on size of the grader just reinforced for the justices the enormity of the danger and the insignificance of the cost of a warning device. Justice England years later remembered the case for one simple element: Caterpillar could have avoided the harm by spending an extra dollar or two to install an audible automatic back-up warning on each machine.

Freidin couldn't say for sure that his case was the direct cause of the beeping warnings on trucks and equipment today, but they proliferated soon after the *West* decision. "So I'll take full credit," he said, "though my friends complain that it's a very annoying sound."

After the Florida Supreme Court decision, the case went back to the federal Fifth Circuit, which upheld the verdict for Mr. West but subtracted the 35 percent negligence for Mrs. West's failure to look both ways. Mr. West was awarded $81,250,[6] which was on top of the $35,000 settlement with the grading company.

"That was the era when you could see a wrong and make a new cause of action," Freidin said forty years after the decision. "That era is long gone."

No one would think of Jim Alderman as an innovator or a man ahead of his time. He was perhaps the most traditional and conservative of all the justices who served on the Supreme Court in the last quarter of the twentieth century. Even in 2014 he had no Internet service at his ranch and no e-mail account. But Alderman's opinion in *Insurance Company of North America v. Pasakarnis*[7] on April 12, 1984, provided a substantial financial incentive for people to wear seat belts at a time when just 14 percent or so of the American population regularly did so and long before Florida began imposing fines on people who were caught not wearing them.

Richard D. Pasakarnis was driving a Jeep convertible and not wearing a seat belt when John Menninger ran a stop sign obscured by trees and slammed into the Jeep at an intersection near Stuart. The Jeep skidded and rolled on its side, and Pasakarnis was thrown out and landed on his posterior and suffered a compression-type injury to his lower back. Menninger's insurance company brought in a seat-belt expert, who concluded that Pasakarnis probably would not have been injured at all if he had been wearing his seat belt and shoulder harness. But the trial judge, C. Pfeiffer Trowbridge, would not allow the expert to testify. All of the case law in Florida up to that point had declared that the failure to wear a seat belt was not admissible in a lawsuit. The jury awarded Pasakarnis $100,000 for his back injury.

The Supreme Court had never addressed the subject, but the First District Court of Appeal had set the standard in 1966, still during the reign of the contributory negligence doctrine, when any bit of negligence by a plaintiff effectively voided a claim against a defendant. In the 1966 case, teenager Diane Kendrick was injured in an accident while riding in a car driven by another teenager. The driver of the second car was adjudged not to be at fault. The father of Diane's friend who was driving argued that Diane should have been wearing a seat belt. The judge would not allow that defense, and the jury awarded $16,000 in damages to Diane and $1,341 to her father. The First DCA upheld the trial judge and said it was up to the legislature to create any seat-belt defense.[8]

Sixteen years later, the legislature had taken no action. On December 15,

1982, two different panels of the Fourth DCA, Alderman's former court, in two different 2–1 votes, followed the old rule and rejected a seat-belt defense. One was the *Pasakarnis* case. In the second case, *Lafferty v. Allstate Insurance Company*,[9] Circuit Judge Philip Nourse had admitted testimony about the plaintiff's failure to wear a seat belt, and the jury verdict of $3,700 was so low that Nourse actually increased it by $2,500. The plaintiff, Lorraine Lafferty, appealed nonetheless. Judge John Beranek, joined by Judge James C. Downey, gave Lafferty a new trial and said it was a matter for the legislature, which "has had two decades in which to enact a statute similar to that enacted in 1971 requiring motorcycle riders to wear helmets."

Beranek said Lafferty was acting lawfully, and a person driving lawfully is generally not held to be negligent. "People lawfully driving a car on New Year's Eve probably know there will be drunks on the road, but the innocent driver is not held negligent because he would have been safer at home." All kinds of "pre-accident conduct" could be dragged into the case, he went on. Large cars, for example, are safer than small cars. "Should a plaintiff be penalized for not taking this safety factor into consideration when purchasing a car?" Convertibles are dangerous, especially if the top is down. "We view such evidence of prior conduct as a Pandora's box which we decline to open.[10]

In the *Pasakarnis* case, Judges Gavin K. Letts and Hugh S. Glickstein upheld the exclusion of seat-belt evidence with a simple citation to Beranek's opinion. Third District Judge Alan R Schwartz, sitting temporarily on the Fourth DCA, dissented, as did Judge Daniel T. K. Hurley in *Lafferty*. Schwartz concluded that "the failure to expend the minimal effort required to fasten an available safety device which has been put there specifically in order to reduce or avoid injuries from a subsequent accident is, on the very face of the matter, obviously pertinent."[11]

At the Supreme Court, the Florida Trial Lawyers joined the case in opposition to the seat-belt defense. Joining the other side were the Florida Defense Lawyers Association, the Florida Safety Council, and the Motor Vehicle Manufacturers Association. The lawyers for the parties were West Palm Beach lawyers Marjorie Gadarian Graham for Insurance Company of North America and James C. Gavigan for Pasakarnis. At the time, only five other states allowed the seat-belt defense.

Alderman, as consistent in voting for defendants as Adkins was for plaintiffs, saw the defense as a logical extension of the comparative negligence doctrine that the court had established eleven years earlier in *Hoffman v. Jones*. It was not about relative fault for the accident, of course, but it was relative fault for the injury and financial loss suffered. He was not impressed by Gavigan's estimate at oral argument that the seat-belt defense could reduce jury verdicts by 10 or 20 percent. "What's wrong with that?" Alderman interjected.[12]

In his opinion for the court on April 12, 1984, Alderman said the Supreme Court "has not abdicated its continuing responsibility to the citizens of this state to ensure that the law remains both fair and realistic as society and technology change." In fact, he said, "The law of torts in Florida has been modernized, for the most part, through the courts."

Alderman noted that automobile manufacturers have to engineer their cars with collisions in mind, so drivers should likewise have to behave with the prospect of a collision in mind. "No recitation of authority is needed to indicate that this court has not been backward in overturning unsound precedent in the area of tort law," Alderman wrote. "Legislative action could, of course, be taken, but we abdicate our own function, in a field peculiarly nonstatutory, when we refuse to reconsider an old and unsatisfactory court-made rule." He added, "To abstain from acting responsibly in the present case on the basis of legislative deference would be to consciously ignore a limited area where decisions by the lower courts of this state have created an illogical exception to the doctrine of comparative negligence adopted in *Hoffman* and the underlying philosophy of individual responsibility upon which the decisions of this court succeeding *Hoffman* have been predicated."[13]

A defendant had to prove that the plaintiff's failure to wear a seat belt was unreasonable under the circumstances and that the failure to wear the seat belt had actually caused some of the plaintiff's injuries, said Alderman, noting there might be circumstances where not wearing a seat belt was reasonable. He did not list any examples, but Marjorie Graham had suggested at oral argument that a woman "nine months pregnant" or "a deliveryman jumping in and out" of a vehicle might reasonably not wear one.

The newest justices split on the issue. Boyd, Overton, McDonald, and England replacement Ray Ehrlich joined Alderman's opinion. This time, it was Adkins, along with Sundberg replacement Leander J. Shaw Jr., as the author of the dissent, wanting to wait for the legislature to act. Shaw said it was "an unwarranted and inappropriate use of judicial power to impose by fiat a debatable public policy on an unwilling public." He said he was "reluctant to tread on established legal principles and impose a new duty upon the Florida motoring public, absent legislative action." In fact, he said, the legislature had indeed spoken on the issue, to some extent, and "specifically prohibited, in any civil action, the admission of evidence that a parent or legal guardian of a child has not provided and used a child passenger restraint."[14] Shaw also predicted "the proliferation of this new species of expert witness, the seat-belt expert," who would complicate trials and overshadow the wrongful conduct of a defendant who caused the accident in the first place.

Two years later, in 1986, over objections about personal freedom, the legislature reacted to the decision. It made seat-belt use mandatory in most vehicles, established fines for violation, and then picked up the theme of Alderman's opinion: "A violation of the provisions of this section shall not constitute negligence per se, nor shall such violation be used as prima facie evidence of negligence or be considered in mitigation of damages, but such violation may be considered as evidence of comparative negligence, in any civil action."[15]

Three weeks after its landmark decision on seat belts, the Supreme Court was dealing with dogs.

"Dog Day" brought one of those odd pairings of cases that shows the mischief created by inadequately drafted statutes applied in unforeseen situations. The dog cases also show that Supreme Court cases sometimes aren't big landmarks.

On a summer day in 1980, Thomas J. Stickney had been walking from his car to his yacht, stored at the Belcher Yachts marina in Miami. The marina had a "BAD DOG" sign posted at the gate, but Stickney, as he so often did, walked past the guardhouse toward his boat. Alas, Duke the watchdog lived up to his marquee billing. Duke lunged at Stickney and, as the lawsuit put it, "severely injured his testicles." Stickney's case, however, had to overcome the state law that let a dog owner avoid responsibility for his dog's bites if he has "displayed in a prominent place on his premises a sign easily readable, including the words Bad Dog."[16]

There was no such sign in Roy G. Davis's yard back in 1974 when twelve-year-old Donnie Jones and two other children, including Davis's son Michael, tied the Davises' German Shepherd, Shane, to a red wagon and climbed in. Alas, Shane couldn't pull them, so the boys got out and were walking alongside when Shane saw Donnie's dog and gave chase with the wagon rolling along behind him. The wagon struck Donnie's leg and permanently injured his Achilles tendon. The case went to trial, and the jury awarded $7,600 to Donnie and $2,250 to his parents. The law that applied was awkwardly worded: "Owners of dogs shall be liable for any damage done by their dogs to sheep or other domestic animals or livestock, or to people." The part about people wasn't even in the original legislation long ago but was added by compilers of the statutes.

The case may have been small, but it attracted big-name lawyers—Joel D. Eaton and Joel S. Perwin of the Podhurst, Orseck, and Parks plaintiffs' firm in Miami and Timon V. Sullivan of Shackelford, Farrior in Tampa for the Utica

Mutual Insurance Company, which insured the Davis home. Sullivan argued that the law making dog owners liable applied only if the dog was acting like a dog, and pulling a wagon is not something dogs do.

Adkins, writing for a majority, didn't buy the argument. He said an owner is responsible for any harm caused by an "affirmative" or "aggressive" act by a dog. "Is it meaningful to conclude the dog in this case was exhibiting canine characteristics when it chased another dog but acting less like a dog because it was tied to a wagon? We think not." It was 5–2, with Boyd, McDonald, Ehrlich, and Shaw all joining Adkins.[17]

At oral argument in the case of old Duke, Stickney's lawyer, Edward Perse of Miami, also argued that the law didn't apply in this case. The sign law was intended to apply to residences, not places of business where people are expected to come onto the property. The lawyer for Belcher Yachts, James L. Dennis, responded that the law ought to mean just what it says. That brought surprise from Justice McDonald. Just by putting up a sign, a person could avoid any obligation to control the dog? "You don't think the court's going for that, do you?"[18]

But it did, by another 5–2 vote. Justice Shaw wrote that the court was "not disposed to revisit" earlier decisions to that effect.

So the court in both cases stuck with the wording of the statutes. The safe haven provided by the "BAD DOG" sign prevented even business customers ("invitees," in the word of tort law) from getting recovery from a dog bite. And when there was no "BAD DOG" sign, the dog owner was liable. McDonald went along with upholding the verdict for the Joneses but dissented in the Belcher Yachts case by saying every dog owner has to exercise reasonable care, sign or no sign.

Overton thought the court got the results backward. He dissented in both cases and wanted to back off from the earlier cases that Shaw did not want to reconsider. A basic problem in the red-wagon case was that Shane was not actually a bad dog. He was just a nice doggie that kids were playing with and suddenly did what even nice doggies do when he saw another dog and ran toward him. There was no reason for a sign. "The injury occurred because the wagon was tied to Shane, not because Shane was a dog," Overton wrote.

He added: "It does not appear reasonable to me that the legislature intended strict liability to apply for injuries which occur from little red wagons tied to dogs by small boys or, for that matter, from injuries which occur when a Saint Bernard is put in the back seat of a car and the dog causes a loaded shotgun also placed in the back seat to fire."[19]

Yes, that happened, too, when an eighteen-year-old returning from a hunting trip put his girlfriend's Saint Bernard in the back seat of a Volkswagen along-side a loaded twelve-gauge pump shotgun. The dog immediately bumped the shotgun, which went off and seriously injured a boy standing outside the car. The First District Court of Appeal held the dog owner liable, because it was "the affirmative act of the dog."[20] The case never reached the Supreme Court.

After a tragic hospital error that left a young woman in a coma for the rest of her life, after a malpractice trial against the hospital with dozens of witness, af-ter a final verdict of more than $12 million, and after extended argument over the constitutionality of Florida's efforts to tame a perceived crisis in medical malpractice insurance going back a decade, the Florida Supreme Court's deci-sion in *Patient's Compensation Fund v. Von Stetina*[21] turned on a single piece of evidence that required a new trial. The court was so closely divided that Justice Ehrlich, who had recused himself because of his former law partner's role as an amicus in the case, joined the consideration of the key issues other than the one of interest to his former partner just so the court could produce a majority opinion.

Susan von Stetina, the twenty-seven-year-old manager of a Sound Advice audio store, was seriously injured in a car crash and was admitted to Florida Medical Center in Lauderdale Lakes on November 26, 1980. She had surgery for internal injuries, including removal of her spleen and a portion of her liver and pancreas, and came through "very nicely," as the surgeon put it. She was put on a respirator to assist her breathing and eventually was entirely reliant on the respirator. In the early morning hours of December 3, a nurse noticed an extremely low heart rate and initiated a "code blue," but Von Stetina had by then suffered severe brain damage because of an extended interruption of her oxygen supply, resulting apparently from a malfunction of the respirator.

A jury ultimately awarded $12.5 million in damages, perhaps the largest verdict in Florida up to that time. Laws passed in 1976 and 1982, however, provided for a payout over a period of years through the Patients Compensa-tion Fund, and it eventually fell to the Supreme Court to decide if that law was constitutional. That part of the decision was unanimous. The court declared that the legislation was a reasonable way to provide malpractice insurance to physicians and hospitals when the private market dried up but also ensured "payment to malpractice plaintiffs." The reasonableness of attorneys' fees of more than $4 million, the issue that concerned former Ehrlich partner and former Senate President John E. Mathews Jr., was also unanimously upheld simply by citing a decision earlier that year.

The most divisive part was an obscure matter of the rules of evidence. Von Stetina's lawyers had shown jurors at the trial a fictitious account of a comatose patient's thoughts and feelings, which had been used as part of the hospital's training of its nurses. The hospital argued that the fictitious article had no relevance to Von Stetina's case and had simply inflamed the emotions of the jurors, who then inflated the verdict. With Ehrlich recused, the court was split 3–3. Overton and Adkins thought the evidence was justified as evidence of the standard of care set by the hospital for strict monitoring of respirators. Alderman, McDonald, and Shaw said it was inflammatory and wanted to grant a new trial. Boyd agreed that the evidence was unfairly prejudicial, but considered it "harmless error" in light of all the other evidence of the hospital's negligence. He proposed simply reducing the portion of the verdict for pain and suffering from $4 million to $2 million.

Since the lawyer-fee issue underlying Ehrlich's recusal was resolved unanimously, the other justices asked Ehrlich to step back in and break the tie on a new trial. If he joined Overton and Adkins, there would still be no fourth vote for simply upholding the verdict, since Boyd wanted to reduce it. Ehrlich, the one-time insurance defense lawyer, who nonetheless had frequently sided with plaintiffs in tort cases since his arrival on the court, this time agreed with the defense contention about the article. The Von Stetinas sought a rehearing over Ehrlich's ethical conflict, but in a second extended opinion on the matter, he rejected their complaint with the unanimous support of the other justices.

Facing the prospect of a new trial, Von Stetina's parents settled for a one-time payment of $6.7 million and payments of $20,000 a month, increasing yearly by 4 percent, for the rest of her life. Susan von Stetina, cared for by her family, lived in the coma for another eight years. A few days before her fortieth birthday on July 9, 1993, she suffered a respiratory infection, went to the hospital for treatment, and died there on July 15.[22]

Although the court was leaning toward defendants in the mid-1980s, the century-old impact rule (chapter 11) finally came up against facts so compelling that the court was unanimous in overturning it.

As fourteen-year-old Karen Champion and others gathered to watch police handle a minor traffic accident on State Road 50 around midnight on August 31, 1980, a Pontiac Firebird driven by twenty-one-year-old Roy Lee Gray Jr. suddenly came out of the darkness. The driver, later charged with drunk driving, saw the lane blocked by the accident, swerved, brushed past the cluster of onlookers, and smacked into the ditch.

"It's hit the little girl!" someone shouted. Karen, an eighth grader at Parrott

Junior High in Brooksville who sang in the chorus and preferred blue jeans to dresses, was dead. As the crowd hovered over her, the girl's mother, forty-four-year-old Joyce Champion, who had a history of diabetes, heart trouble, and high blood pressure, ran up. "It's my daughter!" Mrs. Champion screamed. People held the mother back. "I had her in my arms," her sister-in-law said. "Then she took a long, deep breath and fell backwards." She died a short time later.[23]

The husband and father, Walton Champion, sued Gray and included a claim for negligent infliction of emotional distress on behalf of his late wife. The circuit judge in Hernando County ruled that Gray could be held responsible for Karen's death but dismissed the claim over the wife's death because of the Supreme Court's decision in 1974 in *Gilliam v. Stewart*,[24] disallowing claims in the absence of actual impact on the victim. The Fifth District Court of Appeal upheld the decision.[25] Judge James C. Dauksch, joined by Chief Judge Melvin Orfinger and Judge Frank D. Upchurch, criticized the impact rule, endorsed Judge Mager's opinion in the *Stewart* case, and certified the issue as one of great public importance for Supreme Court review, just as the 4th DCA had done a decade earlier in *Stewart*. But the DCA judges felt that until that court ruled, precedent bound them to sustain the trial judge's ruling against Champion.

When it ruled, the Supreme Court essentially adopted Adkins's view from Mrs. Stewart's case that the obvious physical harm eliminated the concerns about speculative injury that originally justified the impact rule. But there was disagreement and compromise among the justices on the breadth of the ruling. The decision in *Champion v. Gray*[26] was published March 7, 1985, but was held up on rehearing until October 31.

It was one of the defense-oriented justices who wrote the majority opinion for the plaintiff. Even in the absence of physical contact with the plaintiff by the defendant, Justice McDonald wrote, an action for negligent infliction of emotional distress may be brought if there was a discernible physical injury as a result of psychological stress arising from a "sensory perception of" the death or injury of a loved one caused by another's negligence. McDonald cautioned, as Justice Drew had in *Stewart*, that individuals must bear some level of harm without recompense as the cost of living in an organized society. The justices refused to focus, as some courts had, on whether the injury was "foreseeable" and instead looked to three threshold elements: (1) there had to be a "significant discernible physical injury;" (2) the mentally injured claimant "should be directly involved in the event causing the original injury," such as seeing or hearing the accident or arriving at the scene of it while the injured party is there; (3) the mentally injured party must also have "an especially close emotional attachment to the directly injured person."[27]

McDonald's opinion drew four supporting votes, including Overton, another justice commonly on the defendants' side, and Ehrlich. The others were Boyd and Shaw. Adkins did not join McDonald's opinion, but his short concurring opinion merely proposed a modest extension of McDonald's view. Adkins would have included claims when a plaintiff first saw the injured loved one in a hospital, not just at the accident scene, and would have allowed unrelated loved ones to sue as well. That was, of course, beyond the scope of the case at hand.

Alderman, the most dependable vote for defendants among the seven, approved the result but wanted to proceed on more of a case-by-case expansion. McDonald had stressed that "a claim for psychic trauma unaccompanied by discernible bodily injury . . . remains nonexistent,"[28] but that was not limitation enough for Alderman. Alderman was joined by Shaw, who implicitly found nothing in Alderman's opinion directly contradicting McDonald's opinion, which he also supported.

On the day the opinion was originally released, the court decided a separate "impact rule" case, which underscored McDonald's point that there still would be no claim in the absence of physical manifestations of injury. McDonald wrote this opinion as well and emphasized that *Champion* had "modified, in limited situations, the requirement of an impact." The second case was *Brown v. Cadillac Motor Car Division.*

Harvey Brown had accidentally struck and killed his mother as she got out of his Cadillac. The jury in Dade County found that the Cadillac manufacturer was liable for his mother's death because of a defective accelerator, and then also found that Cadillac was responsible for Brown's own psychological trauma even though he showed no physical injury. The estate of the dead mother, Florence Winkler Brown, was awarded $9,000. Harvey Brown was awarded $1.5 million, and his wife Gayl was awarded another $250,000 over the traumatic loss of her mother-in-law. In a per curiam opinion, Judges Norman Hendry, Thomas H. Barkdull Jr., and Natalie Baskin of the Third DCA had overturned the verdicts for the Browns "because there was no impact upon which damages for mental distress could be awarded."[29]

At the Supreme Court, even Adkins agreed.

14

DIVORCE AND FAMILY LITIGATION

Till the Judge Do Us Part

John M. Canakaris was a beloved doctor in Bunnell in Flagler County for most of his ninety years. For a long time he was the town's only doctor. He delivered more than three thousand babies in that county, and even at age seventy-seven he returned to medical practice and started a medical clinic for the poor. But in the legal world, it was his first wife, Elaine, who made a difference. Her effort to hold on to a share of the wealth accumulated during their marriage led to a new legal standard for all wives who had helped build their husbands' careers and found themselves divorced after many years of marriage. Justice Overton, on behalf of a unanimous court in *Canakaris v. Canakaris* in 1980,[1] brought the realities of modern life to the award of property in divorce cases with the concept of "equitable distribution" of property.

Elaine was seventeen and a college freshman when John, a twenty-one-year-old first-year medical student, married her.[2] She dropped out of college and supported him through medical school and military service, and they had a son in 1944. The family ended up in Bunnell in 1950, where Mrs. Canakaris worked without pay as receptionist and assistant as her husband started his medical practice. The practice grew into a small clinic in 1953, became the sixty-bed Bunnell General Hospital in 1960, and then moved into a new eighty-bed Community Hospital of Bunnell, eventually acquired by Hospital Corporation of America.

In 1963 Mrs. Canakaris first sought "separate maintenance" on the grounds of extreme cruelty and adultery. "Separate maintenance" was a concept going back centuries to a time when ecclesiastical courts of England did not approve actual divorce. A divorce was not granted until 1976.

It was a period of great change in the relationships of men and women, from women's "liberation" to the increase in couples living together as well as a higher divorce rate. In 1971 the Florida Legislature passed a "no-fault divorce," eliminating the need to allege and prove wrongdoing, like adultery or extreme cruelty, and replacing it with the relatively simple allegation that the marriage was "irretrievably broken." The law was passed over the objections of Governor Askew, who thought it would turn Florida into a divorce mill. Representative Donald L. Tucker, the future House Speaker, countered that no-fault divorce would avoid having "little children read that their mother goes out and commits adultery . . . or that their father is a dope addict or has an ungovernable temper." Askew signed the law only after it was changed to allow a spouse to contest whether the marriage was irretrievably broken and to allow judges to order marriage counseling.[3]

Dr. and Mrs. Canakaris continued to litigate over the property settlement. Dr. Canakaris had annual income during the 1970s of at least $130,000 and a stated net worth of about $3.7 million, much of it from assets acquired before their breakup in 1963. He remarried after the divorce was granted and moved to a new $430,000 home on eighty acres. Circuit Judge J.T. Nelson awarded the first Mrs. Canakaris jewelry and a share of their jointly held properties of just under $300,000. Applying a long-standing concept called "special equity" to supersede the husband's formal title to property, the judge awarded her $50,000 plus full ownership of their longtime residence valued at $75,000, and she retained her one-half interest in the Bunnell General Hospital real estate.[4]

Although his wife ended up with less than a fifth of his stated net worth and income, it was Dr. Canakaris who appealed. Represented by Isham W. Adams of Daytona Beach, he asked the First District Court of Appeal to overturn the award of $500 a week in alimony as well as the $50,000 lump sum alimony and the award of his share of their longtime residence. In an opinion by First DCA Judge Tyrie A. Boyer, joined by Judge Woodrow M. Melvin, the court agreed with Dr. Canakaris and rejected the "special equity" in the home based on an unspecific "review of the record." Boyer then said the "record before us does not sustain" Mrs. Canakaris's need for $500 a week and directed the trial judge to determine, "based upon evidence, the needs of the wife." The district court also overturned the requirement that Dr. Canakaris pay his ex-wife's attorney fees and said she already had the ability to pay them herself. As temporary alimony, Boyer said, the $500 a week—$26,000 of her husband's $130,000 in annual income—was "generous."[5]

Judge Guyte P. McCord Jr., son of the longtime clerk of the Florida Supreme Court, dissented and set the stage for the Supreme Court's review. Mrs. Canakaris was a "faithful wife" who had given up college and career, done everything from scrub hospital floors to entertain doctors and others to boost her husband's career, while the husband had affairs and separated from his wife because of one such relationship. "This activity of the husband" should be considered in the property distribution, McCord said, adding that he found no "error or abuse of discretion" in anything except the award of attorney fees.

The Supreme Court used the wife's appeal in the Canakaris case to undertake a fresh examination of property arrangements in a divorce, as it had recently done in other areas of the law, including Justice Adkins's cleaning of the Augean stables of legal confusion over products liability in *West v. Caterpillar Tractor* (chapter 13). Not only was there confusion and inconsistency in applying long-standing concepts like "special equity," but as with changes in tort law, some concepts of property distribution in divorce were inconsistent with a society putting greater emphasis on equality. "Special equity" itself had developed as a way around the law that alimony could not be awarded to an adulterous spouse, the rule that was so awkwardly prominent in *Firestone v. Firestone* (chapter 12). It also was a way around a law that, until 1947, did not allow lump-sum alimony and then, until 1963, forced trial judges to choose between lump-sum alimony and more traditional periodic alimony.

In 1955 Justice Roberts had noted the movement of women into the workforce as a reason to deny permanent alimony to wives who had stayed at home during the marriage. In affirming a denial of alimony in *Kahn v. Kahn*,[6] Roberts applied some armchair sociology:

> Until recent years, a divorced wife had little prospect of being able to work and earn a livelihood, and it was essential to a well-ordered society that she be appropriately maintained by her estranged husband so that she would not become a charge on the community. Times have now changed. The broad, practically unlimited opportunities for women in the business world of today are a matter of common knowledge. Thus, in an era where the opportunities for self-support by the wife are so abundant, the fact that the marriage has been brought to an end because of the fault of the husband does not necessarily entitle the wife to be forever supported by a former husband who has little, if any, more economic advantages than she has.

Roberts, whose legal prominence was built in part on winning a nasty divorce case for tycoon Ed Ball, exacted a price for women's newfound opportunity. He went on to say: "We do not construe the marriage status, once achieved, as conferring on the former wife of a ship-wrecked marriage the right to live a life of veritable ease with no effort and little incentive on her part to apply such talent as she may possess to making her own way."

Roberts's observation in 1955 was sometimes said to be the beginning of the concept of "rehabilitative alimony," which was incorporated into the no-fault divorce law of 1971. It led some lawyers and judges to the conclusion that, especially after no-fault divorce, there was no such thing as permanent alimony anymore. There would be temporary "rehabilitative" alimony to allow the stay-at-home wife to make a transition into the workplace. And there might be some "special equity" to give her full rights to the marital residence regardless of legal title.

The onset of no-fault divorce in 1971 made it easier for spouses to separate—which often meant making it easier for husbands to leave. Despite language about judges' need to consider "any factor necessary to do equity and justice between the parties," there was still a widespread resistance among judges to women's sharing in the economic benefits accumulated during the marriage.

As illustrated by Boyer's bemusement at Mrs. Canakaris's $500 a week, the system generally treated the husband as the owner of the financial capacity from which was extracted some minimal "need" of the ex-wife. Judges brought their own notions of fairness, and often they lapsed into more traditional notions of the relationship of husbands and wives. Not every husband, of course, had the wealth that Dr. Canakaris had. In some cases, even before the separation the couple was living on very limited income with few assets other than their house. The husband's "ability to pay" was a significant limitation on whatever degree of sharing judges might have been inclined to approve.

Four years before the Canakaris case was decided at the First DCA, Judge John Rawls of that court undertook his own "in-depth consideration of the law of alimony in Florida" after the no-fault divorce law passed in 1971. Whether the wife has stayed at home and maintained the household and raised children or has been "gainfully employed in the market place and pays a housekeeper to rear the children and keep house" does not matter, Rawls said. What matters is "each spouse's contribution to the marital partnership."

In that particular case, *Brown v. Brown*, in which the wife was a registered nurse and real estate "saleslady," the divorce judge had awarded "rehabilitative" alimony of $500 a month for six months and $250 a month for another year. That was fine, Rawls said, but the wife had been "shortchanged" by receiving only "a pittance of the material assets accumulated in the husband's name during 21 years." He also objected to a decision to let the children as teenagers choose which parent to live with—something he said "invites them to play one parent against the other" and was "not in the best interest of the child."[7]

Judge Boyer, dissenting in that case, echoed Roberts's views about all this new egalitarianism. "Alimony came about during the era that women in general and wives in particular were placed on a pedestal by male chauvinists," Boyer wrote sarcastically. "Women apparently found being worshiped on a pedestal to be distasteful and commenced a virtual worldwide drive to be removed from their place of superiority to a position of equality." Four years later, in the majority this time, Boyer rejected the property allocation to Mrs. Canakaris as too generous.

Mrs. Canakaris appealed the First DCA decision to the Supreme Court. Justice Overton's 5–0 opinion on January 31, 1980, broke with tradition and declared that fairness—"equitable distribution," in his words—should be the primary goal in property distribution. While the goal was not to "equalize the financial position of the parties," Overton said, "a trial judge must ensure that neither spouse passes automatically from misfortune to prosperity or from prosperity to misfortune." The lump sum alimony Dr. Canakaris was challenging "was justified as part of an equitable distribution of the property . . . acquired during their marriage."[8]

Overton made a point about the award of attorneys' fees in divorce. The issue should not be whether the wife could afford legal counsel, Overton said, but "to ensure that both parties will have similar ability to secure competent legal counsel." The Canakarises' financial position was not equal, and Dr. Canakaris "has a superior financial ability to secure and pay counsel." Overton supported the requirement that the doctor pay the wife's attorney fees. With his typical deference to trial judges, Overton added, "It is important that appellate courts avoid establishing inflexible rules that make the achievement of equity between the parties difficult, if not impossible." Adkins, Boyd, England, and Alderman joined the opinion, and Sundberg concurred in the result. McDonald, on the court only three months, did not take part in the case, since his vote was unnecessary.

But when Overton referred to equitable distribution, what did he mean? A separate case the same day went into some detail about what "special equity" meant,[9] but Overton did not elaborate at all on what "equitable distribution" meant. That question began to consume the district courts. Overton's use of the term sounded to some like merely an offhand phrase rather than the legal term of art with its rich and detailed meaning. As a result, the *Canakaris* opinion sowed new confusion. What principles determine what is "equitable"? Does the behavior of the parties matter? If divorce is to be "no-fault," would allegations like adultery find their way back into the case in determining what was "equitable" in sharing the property? Does it matter that the husband was paying rent on an apartment for his mistress? All Overton had said was that the court "may consider any other factor necessary to do equity and justice." That's not much to go on.

An example of the confusion was in the Second District Court of Appeal, which later that year said *Canakaris* "confirms the fact that marriage may indeed be a partnership,"[10] but turned around two years later and said "equitable distribution" would not be considered "an independent vehicle" for deciding how to allocate property, separate from traditional approaches such as alimony and "special equity."[11] A similar thing happened in the Fourth District, which declared equitable distribution to be "an independent vehicle" and then said it wasn't and then sat en banc, with all the judges, and again said it was.[12]

The confusion brought the court's attention to the significant workload and inconsistency in divorce cases, which accounted for about a third of all the civil cases in the Florida circuit courts—87,131 of them filed in 1981. Sundberg as chief justice created a "Matrimonial Law Commission" in 1982 and appointed Overton as its chair. Its first recommendation reflected a long-standing effort by Overton to extend court-ordered mediation throughout the court system. It urged creation of state-supported mediation for custody and visitation issues, though not for property and support issues. In fact, the commission identified widespread problems from mixing custody and property issues as the spouses used one as leverage for the other. Trial judges were urged to decide custody and visitation early in the proceedings and appoint guardians ad litem to protect the interests of the children if necessary.

Perhaps most significantly, it took an important step toward enforcing child support and alimony payments. It would become a major issue, as federal welfare laws imposed more and more requirements on states to enforce collections on behalf of families receiving federal benefits, such as Medicaid and the welfare program—then known as Aid to Families with Dependent Children (AFDC)—but doing so without jailing the delinquent parent and actually diminishing their ability to pay. The commission also developed standard forms for use throughout the court system, a step that coincided with the court's implementation of "no-lawyer divorces" for couples with no children who had been married less than five years (chapter 9).

Three months before the *Canakaris* decision, Parker Lee McDonald dramatically affected the law on family relationships in *Raisen v. Raisen.* The case was not about the state of the couple's marriage but about the state of their automobile insurance.

Ruth Raisen, injured in a car accident with her husband driving, wanted to collect damages from Philip Raisen's insurance company, the Insurance Company of North America, but the insurance company wouldn't pay because of a long-standing rule that spouses could not sue each other. That "spousal immunity" extended to the spouses' insurance companies as well. Denied insurance coverage for her injuries in the lower courts, Mrs. Raisen appealed to the Supreme Court.

Justice Hatchett drew the case assignment. As his opinion circulated, he gained the support of Adkins, England, and Sundberg to overturn this long-standing doctrine on a 4–3 decision.[13] Hatchett concluded that, after passage of Florida's Married Women's Property Act of 1943, women were clearly authorized to enter into their own business and contract arrangements separate from their husbands. So Mr. Raisen and his insurance company were liable to Mrs. Raisen just as they would have been to any other passenger in the car. The old doctrine grew out of a time when a marriage was viewed as one entity and the woman was the husband's chattel.

As Hatchett's draft opinion circulated among the justices, Alderman jotted a note on the internal vote sheet: "If this opinion gets a majority, I will write a dissent." He was new enough on the court that the vote sheet form still listed Fred Karl's name, not Alderman's. His handwritten note continued, "This assault upon the doctrine of interspousal immunity is nothing more than an attempt to reach the pocket book of an insurance company. Without the prospect of collecting against an insurance company, there would be no reason for one spouse to sue the other for personal injuries arising out an accident." Boyd and Overton shared Alderman's view. It was May 16, 1979.

On July 18, with the case still unannounced, Hatchett resigned on short notice after the U.S. Senate confirmed his appointment by President Carter to the federal court of appeals. That left the vote on *Raisen* 3–3. Governor Graham, in his first appointment to the court, selected McDonald to replace Hatchett. One of the first things McDonald did after his arrival on October 26 was focus on *Raisen*. He quickly joined Alderman's side. The majority for eliminating spousal immunity became a minority. Alderman's dissenting opinion would now be the majority opinion.[14] It was released December 20.

In 1950 the court had rejected the idea that the Married Women's Property Act had changed a long tradition that spouses could not sue each other. Now, three decades later, Alderman rejected the idea again. He expressed concern about collusion between spouses to get money from an insured spouse's insurance company. If the lawsuit did not create a fissure in the marriage, it would be because their interests were aligned against the insurer, Alderman said; and if the lawsuit did create a fissure in the marriage, then it was against public policy.

McDonald's reasoning was different, but the result was the same. "It has been suggested that if the doctrine of interspousal immunity is retained, the application thereof should be relaxed to allow an action for tort when the tortious conduct is covered by liability insurance," wrote McDonald in a separate opinion. "Reasonable men may agree that this is a viable alternative, but I agree that should this distinction be made, it should be done by the legislature rather than this court."[15]

England, Adkins, and Sundberg adapted Hatchett's draft for their dissenting opinion. They considered it beyond reason that Mr. Raisen "purchased this insurance policy to protect all other wives and children but not his own."[16] Their dissent noted, "At least 28 jurisdictions have recognized the need to make a change in permitting one spouse to maintain an action against the other."

Two and a half years later, Alderman's majority held when Sheilah Hill sought to sue her husband for $800,000 over an intentional wrong, as opposed to an accident.[17] She said her husband had humiliated her, damaged her good name, held her against her will in a hospital, and forced her to have psychiatric examinations. An array of organizations lined up on Mrs. Hill's side, including the National Organization for Women, the Florida Women's Political Caucus, the Florida Association of Women Lawyers, the Academy of Florida Trial Lawyers, the American Civil Liberties Union and the Dade County Advocate for Victims.

"If there ever was a marriage which was devoid of marital harmony and peace which could be destroyed or impaired by the instituting of a civil lawsuit by one spouse against the other, then that is surely the set of facts which you're about to hear about," Mrs. Hill's lawyer, Sharon H. Tanner of Jacksonville, told the seven married white males who constituted the Supreme Court at the oral argument in February 1981.[18] But all of the amici and all of Tanner's reasoning didn't change the vote of any of the four justices who had turned down Ruth Raisen in 1979.

The Hills were married in 1972 and had a child in 1973. There were already two children from Mrs. Hill's previous marriage. Thomas Jefferson Hill was a deacon in the First Baptist Church, while his wife was a charismatic who spoke in tongues. The Hills separated in 1978. Mrs. Hill took their five-year-old daughter with her, then Mr. Hill physically took the daughter back. The same cycle happened again. The third time, Mrs. Hill took the girl to a charismatic religious camp in Tennessee. Mr. Hill got a subpoena to see his wife's bank records, tracked her down, and brought his daughter home. When Mrs. Hill followed to retrieve her daughter, Mr. Hill petitioned a court to have her declared mentally incompetent—a use of the legal process not barred by the doctrine of spousal immunity because he wasn't suing her for a tort—and then had her held overnight for evaluation. The psychiatrist released Mrs. Hill the next day.

Mr. Hill filed for divorce. Mrs. Hill filed a separate lawsuit for false imprisonment, malicious prosecution, and abuse of the legal process. Tanner argued that letting spouses sue over intentional wrongs "would have the beneficial effect of deterring harms done by spouses to each other." Only sixteen states, she said, retain the old rule. As far back as 1967, Justice Ervin in a dissent had argued for exceptions to the immunity for intentional torts committed during the marriage, but he was the lone voice.[19]

Rejecting the argument, Overton's opinion for the majority said the situation of Sheilah and Thomas Jefferson Hill actually "illustrates the need to retain the present immunity doctrine." If the couple is already going through divorce proceedings, Overton said, "it makes no sense" for two different court proceedings to deal with their differences. "We choose not to place lawyers, judges, litigation costs, and the full trappings of an adversary tort system into a family dispute while the parties remain married." Boyd, Alderman, and McDonald joined his opinion. Sundberg and Adkins dissented, without an opinion this time.

Another case that day, *West v. West*,[20] demonstrated how Overton saw the system working in broken marriages. The Supreme Court blocked a lawsuit by Virginia West against her husband, Richard B. West, on a claim that he caused a triple fracture of her ankle by intentionally throwing her onto the floor. The Wests, too, had gone through a divorce. The trial judge in the divorce case had directed the husband to pay all doctor, medical, and hospital bills that were not covered by insurance and retained jurisdiction to award permanent alimony for "any disability the wife may have that is directly related to the injuries she sustained during her marriage to the husband." That was the way the legal system should handle these things, Overton said.

The day of the *Hill* and *West* decisions, April 29, 1982, could have been called "Immunity Day" at the court. Half a dozen cases on the issue came out that Thursday morning. *Roberts v. Roberts*[21] made clear that the court was not interested in allowing lawsuits over one spouse's intentional harm to the other, even when the husband was dead and the wife was suing his estate. "To allow a tort claim against the decedent spouse's estate would only add a unique factor to probate of an estate which would not be allowable if the decedent party were living," wrote Overton. "This could adversely affect dependent family beneficiaries, particularly minor children." Again, Adkins and Sundberg dissented.

Ard v. Ard[22] was the first breach in the old wall. McDonald and Overton shifted into the plaintiffs' column alongside Adkins and Sundberg to create an exception to parent-child immunity "to the extent of the parent's available liability insurance coverage." Parents without liability insurance or whose children were not protected under the policy would remain immune from suit. It was also technically a switch for Adkins, who in an aberrational vote his second year on the court had sustained parent-child immunity. That case, in 1970, had been a lawsuit on behalf of a child killed in the crash of a private plane flown by his father.[23]

In the *Ard* case, the child was an infant, seriously injured after his mother removed him from a car and put him on the ground beside the car. The car ran over him. McDonald elaborated on what he had said in *Raisen* about his lack of concern about collusion and fraud in accident lawsuits between family members. McDonald figured that when insurance companies were involved, there would be plenty of scrutiny for the possibility of fraud. He also noted that recovery from insurance "is more likely to ease the financial difficulties" than create a source of disharmony. McDonald reaffirmed that parents without liability insurance or whose children are not protected under the policy would remain immune from suit. Unable to obtain another vote for abolishing both parental and spousal immunity outright, Adkins concurred in the decision.

The dissenters, Boyd and Alderman, expressed their continued dismay with the concept of tort lawsuits among family members. "Parents may insure against the possibility of injuries to their children," Boyd wrote for the two of them. "They may seek financial protection from the consequences of accidental injuries in the form of hospitalization, casualty, and disability insurance coverages." But liability insurance is "awkward and unnecessary," Boyd said, in light of "the infinite range of possible accidents that . . . are inextricably intertwined with parental conduct both reasonable and negligent."[24]

Joseph v. Quest[25] was about comparative negligence and a defendant's effort to cast blame for a child's injury back on the suing child's own parent. Ten-year-old Daren Joseph had been struck by a car driven by Marion Quest. Daren's father sued Quest for negligence. Quest turned around and sued Daren's mother and claimed her negligent supervision of her own son contributed to his injuries. If Quest prevailed, the payment for Daren's injuries would come partly from his own mother, which was equivalent to suing his own parent.

The jury awarded $150,000 in damages to young Daren Joseph and $17,000 to his father, then allocated much of the blame to Daren's parents: 10 percent to Daren, 10 percent to Daren's father, and 25 percent to Daren's mother. That left 55 percent of the blame for the original defendant, Marion Quest. The Josephs argued that the portion of the judgment blaming Mrs. Joseph violated the spousal immunity rule, so Quest should have to pay the entire amount.

This issue had come up before. In 1977, in an opinion written by Alderman predecessor Fred Karl, the court had allowed a defendant to apportion blame and financial liability to a plaintiff's spouse.[26] Justice Karl said the Contribution Among Tortfeasors Act prevailed over the common law doctrine of spousal immunity. McDonald, who wrote the opinion in *Ard*, wrote the opinion in *Joseph v. Quest* as well and applied the same reasoning to allocate responsibility among the defendants.

Why was parent-child immunity different from spousal immunity? "The situation is completely different for a minor child," McDonald wrote. Since a child must rely on his parents to bring a lawsuit on his behalf, a parent is unlikely to bring such a lawsuit against himself. But that consideration doesn't apply when there is insurance to pay the damages. Sundberg and Overton, along with Adkins, joined the opinion. Boyd, in dissent, saw no difference in the reasons for parent-child and spousal immunity. Both were about preserving family relationships, he said. Alderman also dissented.

At the end of Immunity Day, spouses couldn't sue each other even when one intentionally injured the other or when there was insurance to cover the costs of an accident, but children could sue their parents as long as there was insurance.

The next year, the court breached the barrier for lawsuits between spouses for the first time—but only after both were dead, which meant that the litigants were their estates. F. Eugene Tubbs and his wife, Carole A. Tubbs, had been flying together in their private airplane piloted by the husband when it crashed and killed them both. Tubbs, who as a medical student at the University of Florida had worked with Gatorade inventor J. Robert Cade, was a physician and a former Republican state legislator who ran unsuccessfully for insurance commissioner in 1974. As a legislator he was a major force behind state funding for the burn unit at Shands Hospital. The couple had four children, two of whom were from Mrs. Tubbs's previous marriage.

One of Mrs. Tubbs's children, as representative of her estate, sued the representative of Mr. Tubbs's estate, James R. Dressler, and Mr. Tubbs's insurance company. The author of the Supreme Court's opinion was as notable as the breach in the wall of immunity: Justice Raymond Ehrlich, whose career in private law practice had heavily emphasized the defense of insurance companies.

The Fifth District Court of Appeal, in considering the Tubbs case, had seen what was coming after the Immunity Day cases: "Since oral argument here, the Supreme Court has decided a series of cases which, although they do not directly address the precise factual circumstance before us here, nevertheless indicate to us a change of thinking by that court, and a modification of the doctrine," wrote Fifth DCA Judge Melvin Orfinger. Ehrlich proved him right: "This action for wrongful death is not barred by the doctrine of interspousal immunity," Ehrlich wrote, because "there is no longer any marital unit to preserve." Florida's Wrongful Death Act was a specific law that allowed the heirs to bring the suit, Ehrlich said. Boyd switched to the majority and left Alderman alone in dissent. Justice Leander Shaw, who had replaced Sundberg, was also in the majority.

Again in March of 1984 a specific statute was used to pry open the shell of immunity. Foster and Dean Burgess were divorced, but Mrs. Burgess alleged that while the divorce was pending, her husband had sneaked back into the house, gone into the attic, spliced a tape recorder into the telephone line, and recorded her conversations. Mrs. Burgess said her husband had violated the state's wiretapping law, which made it a third-degree felony if someone "willfully intercepts, endeavors to intercept, or procures any other person to intercept any wire or oral communication."[27] The law also allows "any person" who is wiretapped to receive damages of $100 for each day of the violation. Mrs. Burgess wanted not only the $100 for each day she was wiretapped but also $100,000 in punitive damages. Mr. Burgess said he "never did" wiretap his wife.[28]

Circuit Judge Erwin Fleet dismissed the wife's case because of spousal immunity. The First District Court of Appeal reluctantly upheld the dismissal and said it had "no choice" under the rule of Raisen v. Raisen. Judge Klein Wigginton in dissent said a "departure" from that rule should be permitted when the "traditional reasons" for the rule, the "promotion of peace and harmony in the home, and the avoidance of fraudulent or collusive claims," are not present or "are overshadowed by a more compelling statutorily created interest or constitutionally protected right."

Hitting a spouse had never been a sufficient basis to depart from the immunity rule, but the court decided that wiretapping was. Adkins, writing the majority opinion, noted that the wiretapping statute allowed "any person" to sue. He called that "positive and unambiguous" evidence of the legislature's intention to allow lawsuits among spouses about a tapped phone. More likely, the legislature never even thought about the matter, and if it had, the legislation probably would have stayed buried in committee, but it was enough to win Ehrlich over and produce a bare majority along with Overton and McDonald. Clearly, any broader decision against immunity would have cost Adkins a majority.

Adkins did manage to insert one morsel for future use: "A rule of law which leaves such repugnant behavior unsanctioned can hardly be said to preserve the marital unit." Boyd and Alderman dissented. Boyd scoffed at the idea that the words "any person" showed a "positive and unambiguous" intention of creating an exception to the tradition of spousal immunity.

Seventeen months later, Boyd wrote another 4–3 decision reaffirming spousal immunity in another husband-wife automobile accident. In this one, *Snowten v. U.S. Fidelity & Guaranty Company*,[29] Ehrlich was back on the side of Boyd, Alderman, and Shaw. The case was more notable for its dissenters. Overton wrote a one-sentence dissent, joined by McDonald, saying they would apply the *Ard* case, breaching parent-child immunity to the extent of insurance, to spousal immunity as well. It was a remarkable and unexplained departure from *Raisen*, where the two had been in Alderman's majority, with McDonald as the late-arriving tie-breaker. Adkins, of course, also dissented in *Snowten*, without opinion.

Soon after leaving the court along with Boyd under mandatory retirement rules in January 1987, Adkins noted in his memoir that, with the departure of Alderman in 1985 and now Boyd, "I am confident that the Florida Supreme Court will abolish the doctrine of spousal immunity at the next opportunity."[30] Governor Bob Martinez, who had succeeded Bob Graham the same day the Adkins and Boyd terms expired, appointed Circuit Judge Gerald Kogan of Miami to replace Boyd and Second DCA Judge Stephen H. Grimes to replace Adkins. Generally, Kogan voted Adkins's way and Grimes voted Boyd's on the issue of spousal immunity. The key difference was the earlier replacement of Alderman with Fourth DCA Judge Rosemary Barkett. A case simply had not come along before Adkins left.

Fifteen years after the replacement of Hatchett by McDonald had preserved spousal immunity in *Raisen v. Raisen*, the decision was undone by the replacement of Alderman by Barkett.

One of Kogan's first opinions, in 1988, had declared that the spousal immunity doctrine "no longer is applicable when the public policy reasons for applying it do not exist," but the pronouncement was effectively negated when the court said the insurance policy involved, purchased in New York, did not cover the accident anyway.[31] Then in 1993 Kogan rephrased a certified question to say: "Does the doctrine of interspousal immunity remain a part of Florida's common law?" His answer? "We find that both public necessity and fundamental rights require judicial abrogation of the doctrine." Thirty-two states had already eliminated the rule by then.

Kogan had a compelling set of facts to work with. Joyce Waite was seeking recovery under her homeowner's policy for substantial injuries she and others in her family sustained in a machete attack by her husband, who was eventually convicted of attempted murder. She divorced him and also sued him.

One other factor got only modest attention from Kogan and the court, but was an obvious and compelling basis for the decision: the legislature had explicitly abolished spousal immunity for intentional torts in 1985. "The ability of a person to sue another person for the intentional tort of battery shall not be affected by any marital relationship between the persons," the law said.[32]

But Kogan swept beyond the statute and the facts of *Waite v. Waite* to include accident cases as well. He saw "no reason to believe that married couples are any more likely to engage in fraudulent conduct against insurers than anyone else." The court "and its advisory commissions"—apparently a reference primarily to the recent commission on gender bias in the legal system, created by Ehrlich as chief justice—had reviewed the issues over the years and "now find that there no longer is sufficient reason" for the doctrine.

Shaw changed sides. Abandoning his previous support for immunity, he and Barkett joined Kogan's opinion. McDonald and Overton, the only justices left from the winning side of the *Raisen* and *Hill* decisions, joined the result in *Waite* simply because the legislature had abolished the doctrine in such cases. They noted that the legislature had not abolished it for accident cases. "Had the Legislature felt it desirable to completely abolish the doctrine, it could have done so then," McDonald wrote. He said he had been willing to consider "in a given situation whether an exception to this historical doctrine should be made," as in *Snowten* in 1985, but the "unfettered ability of one spouse to sue another," or even threats to do so, could strain a relationship.

The newest justice, Major B. Harding, who had replaced Ehrlich, wrote a concurring opinion with a perspective on marriage and lawsuits reminiscent of Hatchett's original opinion in *Raisen*. Eliminating the immunity, Harding wrote, "will not damage what the marital relationship is designed to be—a special relationship between partners who share love, common interests, concerns, hopes, and endeavors." Limiting litigation has never been the point of the doctrine. A spouse can already file a criminal complaint and under the 1985 law can sue over intentional harm, and those things are much more likely to create marital discord than a claim over an accident, Harding said. As for concern about collusion and fraud, "the remedy should be to expose the fraud rather than to discard all the honest claims along with the bad ones."

Down in Miami, England, by then more than a decade into the practice of appellate law, had only one criticism for his old Miami friend Kogan: couldn't you have cited the perceptive dissent of England, Adkins, and Sundberg in *Raisen v. Raisen*?

Divorce appeals kept coming, too, of course, though most of them stopped at the district court level. One was the appeal of Roxanne Pulitzer and her nationally celebrated divorce lawyer, Marvin Mitchelson, over the divorce judge's decision to award custody of her sons to ex-husband Herbert "Peter" Pulitzer Jr., a hotel executive and publishing heir. Circuit Judge Carl Harper, after an eighteen-day trial, had produced an eighteen-page final judgment noting "flagrant adultery and other gross marital misconduct" by Mrs. Pulitzer and said she often left the twin boys Mac and Zac with nannies while she went to nightclubs. The Fourth District Court called the case "a nonnoteworthy one insofar as novel or complex legal problems are concerned" and upheld the decision. The Supreme Court in October 1984 refused to review it.[33]

A more serious and consequential issue arose from a small flurry of cases over a divorced parent's obligation to pay for education expenses after a child turned eighteen. It was one of those unforeseen consequences of the successful effort to lower the voting age to eighteen during the 1970s and the Vietnam War, which had led Florida to also lower the age of legal adulthood from twenty-one to eighteen as of July 1, 1973. At twenty-one, most children of a broken marriage had nearly finished college, but at eighteen, they were just beginning. In fact, some had not even finished high school.

Dr. Bertram Grapin, a millionaire internist in North Miami, was ordered as part of the 1982 divorce to pay the expenses of his adult daughter's college education. Grapin insisted that he would send his children to school, but "under his terms and his conditions" and not under a court order. He appealed to the Third District Court of Appeal. Judge Natalie Baskin, joined by Judges Norman Hendry and James R. Jorgensen, upheld the rest of the divorce judgment but overturned the order that Dr. Grapin pay for college unless the daughter were "legally dependent," generally meaning mentally or physically disabled. Only if there were a "binding legal contract" during the marriage to pay the college expenses could a court order a father to pay for an adult child's education, Baskin wrote in a brief opinion.

At the Second District, Judge Grimes had come to a different conclusion. When Dr. William R. Nicolay and his wife Jacquelyn, of Winter Haven, were divorced in 1974, Mrs. Nicolay was awarded custody of their two daughters, and Dr. Nicolay was ordered to pay $500 a month in permanent alimony and $500 in child support until the youngest reached age eighteen. The court reserved jurisdiction to modify the awards, particularly with respect to higher education.

When the oldest daughter graduated with excellent grades, Mrs. Nicolay sought a court order for help with college expenses and said grants and scholarships had been denied because of Dr. Nicolay's income. After first agreeing to contribute $3,500 (at a time when tuition levels were a tenth the level of thirty years later), Dr. Nicolay asked for a reduction in the alimony and child support payments. The circuit judge terminated the child support because the daughters had reached adulthood. Mrs. Nicolay, who was working as a nurse in Winter Haven, came back with a request for higher alimony because of her need to pay for the daughters' college education, and the judge granted her an $85-a-month increase, to $585. Dr. Nicolay appealed to the Second DCA.

Grimes wrote an extensive review of the case law through the years, including the effect of the lower age of adulthood.

He also noted that the Supreme Court had addressed the issue shortly after the age of adulthood was lowered, in *Finn v. Finn*,[34] and upheld an order for payment of college expenses under a provision of the adulthood law that said the change "shall not affect the rights and obligations existing prior to July 1, 1973." Since the divorce order in that case was entered before July 1, 1973, the husband lost. But the Supreme Court at the time indulged the temptation to go beyond the case. It declared its belief "upon reflection" that "the legislature did not intend to deprive worthy children of the funds needed to attend college" and that it "would be inclined to hold that . . . a court could find a child under the age of twenty-one dependent by reason of attendance at college and order one or both of his parents to provide support."

The "Supreme Court" in *Finn* included three circuit judges filling in for recently retired Ervin and two justices caught up in impeachment hearings, Dekle and Boyd. The opinion was written by Circuit Judge Ben Willis, joined by Adkins, Roberts, and Overton as well as McCain, who would resign within a month. Even with its substitute justices and its hypothetical holding, it was still a Supreme Court opinion, and Grimes relied on it in saying the higher alimony to help Mrs. Nicolay pay for college "was indeed proper."

Now, in 1984, the Supreme Court was facing the conflict between the Grimes view and the Baskin view in the appeal of *Grapin v. Grapin*.[35] The court was unanimous. Grimes's reliance on that "dictum" in *Finn* was "misplaced," McDonald wrote for the court, because the comment simply referred to "the societal ideal of continued parental support." McDonald approved Baskin's holding that Grapin had "no legal duty" to support his adult daughter in college.

McDonald then engaged in a little dictum of his own. He endorsed a dissent by Circuit Judge Edward Cowart, sitting in on a Fifth District panel, saying that the rule also should apply to protect a father ordered to pay $30 a week until his eighteen-year-old son finished high school. Cowart had called Willis's comment in the Supreme Court's *Finn* decision "idealistic dicta."[36]

15

ENVIRONMENT AND GROWTH

Property Rights and the Public Good

Robert B. Troutman Jr. came to Florida from Atlanta in 1969 with a dream of building a high-rise development of 30,000 condos for 73,000 residents on the beautiful northern rim of Estero Bay in Lee County. He would build a 7.5-mile-long bulkhead, or seawall, to straighten out the jagged coastline, then fill in behind it with 17 million cubic yards of fill, incorporating submerged lands and islands, to create 1,100 new acres for development. The fill would come from digging twenty-seven lakes, a twelve-foot channel through the seagrass beds, and more channels for residents' boats. And to ensure the best possible panoramic views for the residents, he would cut down many of the mangrove trees.

Troutman was from a prominent, wealthy, and well-connected Atlanta family. His grandfather and father headed a major law firm, which became known as Troutman Sanders after its merger in 1971 with a firm headed by one-time Georgia Governor Carl Sanders. The Troutman firm represented Georgia Power Company and railroads and other businesses. Young Troutman himself went to Harvard Law School and was a roommate of Joseph P. Kennedy Jr., older brother of future President John F. Kennedy. In 1962 he was on a presidential commission to encourage businesses to hire blacks voluntarily, without (and, it was often said, to fend off) government mandates in those days before the 1964 Civil Rights Act banned discrimination in employment and commercial services. Troutman had bought up air rights over downtown Atlanta property and collected royalties as high-rises were developed, and he helped clear the way for approval by President Kennedy's Interstate Commerce Commission for a merger of two railroads operating in Georgia.

With dredge-and-fill riches already being made along the west coast in Tampa and St. Petersburg and Sarasota, Troutman on November 26, 1972, announced his purchase of 5,240 acres of land on Estero Bay from the Windsor Trust. Windsor had already fought with the state and settled over the high-water boundary delineating public and private ownership, though there would be later claims that the survey was grossly wrong in Windsor's favor. The settlement, negotiated under Governor Claude Kirk but actually signed by Governor Reubin Askew, allowed the owner of the land to have a bulkhead line along the high-water boundary and to receive a dredge-and-fill permit to build not only a canal fifty feet wide just inside the bulkhead line but also navigational channels. A lot of the boundary was guesswork, but the state signed the deal anyway out of fear of losing even more in court.

The Windsor deal was made before the Florida Legislature passed the first in a series of laws to deal with Florida's soaring population growth and burgeoning development. The Florida Environmental Land and Water Management Act in 1972, often referred to by lawyers simply as Chapter 380 of the Florida Statutes, began the shift of authority over large-scale development from local governments to the state level. This larger state role was already happening in a few other states, and a study of those states that influenced Florida policymakers referred to this as a "quiet revolution" in the law of planning and zoning.[1]

Chapter 380 created two primary ways of guarding against serious environmental damage. First, certain large regions would be designated as Areas of Critical State Concern and become subject to statewide management. Many in local government were willing to give up their autonomy in exchange for the state grants for water and sewer facilities that accompanied the designation. Second, large individual developments, described as "developments of regional impact," or DRIs, would be reviewed at the state level by the Department of Community Affairs, with developers having a possible appeal to the Governor and Cabinet in their role as the Land and Water Adjudicatory Commission.

More legislation followed to broaden state controls and authorize impact fees and other measures. The goal was to impose on developers and new residents, rather than existing residents, the costs of new roads and schools and other infrastructure to support new developments. The real estate industry and developers lobbied strenuously against the legislation as an encroachment on property rights, and they would be strong supporters of the legal challenges that followed.

Troutman was the assignee of the Windsor settlement that predated the legislation, and he thought the path was now clear for development of the property by his company, Estuary Properties. In June 1975 he filed his application with the Lee County Commission seeking approval of a "development of regional impact" on the Windsor tract and adjacent property, including his planned new dredge-and-fill acreage. A few days later, on July 1, 1975, two large blue binders labeled "The Estuaries" landed on the desk of a twenty-four-year-old environmental engineer named David Burr, just out of graduate school at the University of South Florida and working at the Southwest Florida Regional Planning Council. The binders included drawings of waterways to intercept runoff from development. The plan was that the area with red mangroves would be deeded to the state. The black mangroves, which were described as less environmentally significant, would be destroyed—1,065 acres of them.

Burr concluded, among other things, that Estuary Properties had inadequate evidence and no pilot project or other demonstration to show beneficial effects the canals might have in replacing the natural tidal action. Burr doubted the unproven assumptions of Troutman's experts and found serious environmental impact. He recommended the project not be approved. In the meantime, as word of Troutman's project got around, citizens of the area rose up in opposition. Based on the opposition and Burr's recommendation, the Lee County Commission rejected Troutman's project. In keeping with Chapter 380, the commission outlined what Estuary would have to change about its proposal to gain approval. The most significant elements were that he needed to cut the scale of the project in half, to fewer than 13,000 residential units, and leave the mangroves undisturbed. Troutman argued that made the project not financially feasible.

Estuary Properties appealed. The Florida Land and Water Adjudicatory Commission upheld the Lee County Commission. Then Estuary Properties turned to the courts. Troutman said his property was essentially confiscated by the government without compensation and wanted the courts to recognize his right to do what he wanted with his property.

At the same time, the other part of Chapter 380, the part about Areas of Critical State Concern, was also under challenge in court but on much more theoretical grounds. On July 16, 1974, the state's Administration Commission, one of the several entities that are really just the Governor and the elected Cabinet, used the authority of the new law to designate the Green Swamp northeast of Tampa as an Area of Critical State Concern. On June 17, 1975, it imposed new strict regulations on land development there.

In between, on April 15, 1975, after a long hearing in Key West, virtually all of the Florida Keys were declared an Area of Critical State Concern. Cross

Key Waterways Inc. in the Keys challenged the state actions on highly technical grounds focusing not only on Chapter 380 but also on the steps and time-
tables required for administrative action and the applicability of the separate
Administrative Procedure Act. To deal with a drawn-out timetable, the Governor and Cabinet had made the designations in "Emergency Rules." Local
governments and developers also challenged the process. The First District
Court of Appeal overturned the rules on one simple basis: the emergency
rules, hop-scotching over many of the procedural requirements, were not effective because there was no proof of "immediate danger to the public health,
safety, or welfare."

When *Askew v. Cross Key Waterways Inc.* reached the Supreme Court, the
justices focused on a more basic but still very legalistic objection. Although
the challengers of Chapter 380 ultimately could not make the case of a substantive constitutional violation, a confiscation of their property, they managed to get all three branches of government caught up in a do-over of the
legislation and launched a long line of cases over unconstitutional delegation
of legislative powers.

The Florida Constitution not only divides state government into the traditional three branches but also adds, "No person belonging to one branch
shall exercise any powers appertaining to either of the other branches unless
expressly provided herein."[2] To Sundberg, writing for the court, "determining
which geographic areas and resources are in greatest need of protection" was
a "fundamental legislative task."

The law the Legislature passed basically left executive branch people to do
this task. It "does not establish or provide for establishing priorities or other
means for identifying and choosing among the resources the act is intended to
preserve," Sundberg wrote. "When legislation is so lacking in guidelines that
neither the agency nor the courts can determine whether the agency is carrying out the intent of the legislature in its conduct, then, in fact, the agency
becomes the lawgiver rather than the administrator of the law."

The court said that the legislature, having created this program, could not
leave the specific designations to be made by a body made up of the governor
and Cabinet members elected statewide rather than the forty senators and 120
legislators elected from local districts.

The problem, as Sundberg saw it, was that the law treats as "fungible" the
"disparate categories of environmental, historical, natural and archeological
resources" of the state or local regions. He anticipated a runaway process. The
Cabinet, he said, "is empowered to supersede as it chooses the local governments regulating development in historic Pensacola or St. Augustine, or at the

shores of the Atlantic and Gulf of Mexico to a depth of a thousand feet, or in all acreage on the Suwannee and St. Johns and their tributaries or, indeed, in all the Florida Keys," Sundberg wrote. "If Cedar Key, Ybor City, Palm Beach and the path of the King's Road are found to be historic resources of satisfactory importance, they too may be designated."

The executive branch had not done that, of course. It had simply designated a handful of areas of enduring and very real concern. Sundberg, though, had been a warrior in the water wars of the Tampa Bay area, and he was particularly attuned to the idea that regionalization of resources was a way for those that did not have water, like Pinellas County, to lay a claim on the resources of those who did, like Pasco County. Who held power often made the difference in who won the substantive struggle.

England, shortly before joining the court, had been a principal draftsman in rewriting the state's Administrative Procedure Act establishing a meticulous process for decision-making within the executive branch. He wrote a concurring opinion arguing that the line Sundberg was drawing between legislative and executive was highly significant. "Justice Sundberg has revitalized a vastly more important doctrine, one that guarantees that Florida's government will continue to operate only by consent of the governed. He is saying, quite simply, that whatever may be the governmental predilections elsewhere, in Florida no person in one branch of our government may by accident or by assignment act in a role assigned by the Constitution to persons in another branch."

Sure enough, the Sundberg opinion seeded a fertile field of litigation over unlawful delegation of authority by the legislature to government agencies. The decision was only a temporary setback for Chapter 380, however. The legislature had followed the normal rule that you don't identify specific targets of legislation but identify standards that the executive branch applies. But if the court thought the legislature should designate the areas, well, the legislature was happy to do so. It promptly designated the Keys and Green Swamp and other areas as Areas of Critical State Concern.

In part because of the extended local review process, Troutman's case, *Graham v. Estuary Properties Inc.*,[3] was not resolved by the Supreme Court for six years after the *Cross Key* decision. It proved to be the major substantive test of Chapter 380.

Like the consolidated case of Cross Key and Green Swamp, Estuary Properties' challenge went through a district court of appeal and likewise scored a victory there. "The position of the Planning Council is that a private landowner has no private right to use his property unless he can prove that such will not impair a public benefit," said the long per curiam opinion signed by Judges E. R. "Dick" Mills Jr., Anne C. Booth, and Larry G. Smith of the First District Court of Appeal.[4] They were disdainful of the review process and said it did not properly balance the state and landowner interests. The clear intention of protecting the mangrove areas, the judges said, should have launched a condemnation process and payment to the landowner, which would have been a huge cost to the state and a blow to the whole process of regulating development.

Unlike the *Cross Key* case, the First DCA decision in *Estuary Properties* was not readily surmountable by a procedural do-over. The governor and Cabinet were given thirty days to give Estuary Properties permission for the development, "which shall include the use of the black mangrove acreage" for dirt fill that would obliterate it. The only alternative allowed was that Lee County, within thirty days, could choose to commence condemnation proceedings and buy the mangrove acreage it most wanted to protect.

The First DCA decision, pending since Askew was in office, came at the end of Governor Graham's first year in office, a week before Christmas in 1979. It was unthinkable that the Supreme Court would decline to review such a decision, and sure enough, it took the case.

The Supreme Court's decision eighteen months later was as much a victory for environmental protection as the First DCA's had been for developers. People don't have a right to do whatever they want with their property if it creates harm to the public or other property owners, said the court in a 6–1 opinion, written by Justice McDonald and including the conservative rancher, Justice Alderman. "There was ample evidence for the commission to find that destruction of the mangroves and creation of the waterway would result in an adverse impact on the surrounding area," McDonald wrote. "The owner of private property is not entitled to the highest and best use of his property if that use will create a public harm."

Condemnation and compensation are invoked if the government acts to require a landowner to create an affirmative benefit to the public, he added, not when the government is constraining a use that would create public harm. McDonald noted that compensation was required in an earlier case in which property was being incorporated into a game preserve, which meant that the owner could no longer hunt there.

Adkins was the lone dissenter on the side of Estuary Properties, and said simply that he would approve the opinion of the First DCA. A law clerk had handwritten a dissenting opinion for Adkins, but it relied heavily on a dissenting opinion in a U.S. Supreme Court case, which wasn't strong legal authority.[5] The draft, never published, made Adkins's position clear: "By denying the DRI application, the county and the adjudicatory commission deprived Estuary of the beneficial use of almost three-quarters of its property. This area, encompassing some 4,600 acres of red mangroves and black mangroves, is preserved for the public at the expense of the individual landowners."[6]

The robust holding of the Supreme Court, however, was not the last word. Thomas Pelham, who would serve as secretary of the Department of Community Affairs under two different governors, Bob Martinez and Charlie Crist, recalled being invited by a friend to drop in and meet Troutman one day not long after the *Estuary Properties* case was decided. They drove up to his house, and Troutman was outside his garage. After a short, cordial conversation, Pelham said, Troutman picked up a chain saw and put it in the back of his truck. "Excuse me, gentleman, I'm going to continue one man's fight against big government." He headed for the mangroves.[7]

The fight continued for another ten years. Howard Rhoads, Troutman's primary lawyer and one of those on the appeal to the Supreme Court, said in an oral history interview that he finally went back to the Lee County Commission and told them they would continue filing development plans year after year.[8] But since the state clearly wanted to preserve the property, Troutman would sell the property to the state.

Environmentalists realized early on that victories like Estuary Properties were ephemeral victories in long wars of attrition fought by developers like Troutman. Governor Graham had begun programs for purchases of environmentally sensitive lands, known as Save Our Rivers and Save Our Coasts. Governor Martinez turned them into a more permanent program called Preservation 2000, then Governor Bush, after taking office in 1999, renamed it Florida Forever. Estimates were that nine million acres of land were purchased under these programs.

The state's growing regulatory system that began with Chapter 380 brought more landowners to the negotiating table and probably moderated land prices, but outright purchase proved to be less contentious, more politically acceptable, and more effective at permanent preservation.

And so it ended. The mangroves and natural tidal flows of Estero Bay were preserved with compensation to the owner, and Troutman moved on to less contentious development projects nearby.

Before there was a statewide structure for managing growth, there was local politics. Residents saw growth not only as a threat to quality of life and urban sprawl but as increasingly costly to existing residents, as fees for municipal services rose to pay the cost of extending services to new subdivisions.

Growth was driving real estate profits and business revenues, but local tax revenues were lagging well behind the cost of creating the new roads, schools and utility lines that were needed as soon as new residents arrived. Private utilities could raise prices, and those that were regulated often got approval from remote regulators in Tallahassee. Government-run services, however, were far more vulnerable to political opposition when they wanted to raise fees. In some ways growth resembled a pyramid scheme, where the cost was immediate but the payback was extended and uncertain. When downturns happened, as in the early 1970s, local governments that had built out their infrastructure were stuck with costs for developments that never materialized.

Local governments sought relief in "impact fees," assessed as part of the process of approving development plans. No specific state legislation authorized impact fees; governments relied on their general "home rule" powers in the Florida Constitution and state laws. It fell to the courts to establish the boundaries of what local governments could do, just as they had established the constitutional dimensions of state government's role.

The first major case to reach the Florida Supreme Court was from Dunedin. The Contractors and Builders Association and various local contractors, represented by longtime developer attorney John T. Allen, challenged Dunedin's 1972 impact-fee ordinance as an illegal tax. On top of the cost of the physical connection itself, the city imposed a fee of $325 for a new water connection and $375 for a new sewer connection "to defray the cost of production, distribution, transmission and treatment facilities." The concept "strikes a sympathetic chord," Circuit Judge B. J. Driver said, but he decided the city had no authority to impose the fee.

In the city's appeal to the Second District, Judge Grimes wrote the opinion. Cases in other district courts had overturned impact-fee ordinances. Grimes turned to cases in Indiana, Illinois, and Utah, all upholding similar types of fees. "While many parts of this country are experiencing growth due to the population explosion, at the present time no state is more imminently faced with the problems inherent in population increase than Florida," Grimes wrote.[9]

When existing water and sewer facilities would serve current inhabitants, he said, "it seems unfair to make the existing inhabitants pay for new systems when they have already been paying for the old ones." The question was whether the new "connection charges," well in excess of the actual cost of the connection itself, were legal.

The circuit court had declared the fee a tax and said it was illegal because it was neither an ad valorem tax nor a tax authorized by state law. But in 1971, Grimes noted, the Florida Supreme Court had said that "the power to construct, maintain and operate the necessary facilities" was inherent in the power to operate municipal services. Therefore, said Grimes, "where the growth patterns are such that an existing water or sewer system will have to be expanded in the near future," the fee can be charged as long as it "does not exceed a proportionate part of the amount reasonably necessary to finance the expansion and is earmarked for that purpose."

While the Dunedin ordinance did not specifically earmark all the fees collected for the construction of the utility facilities, the city had done so in its accounting. So the fee stood. Judges Edward Boardman and John Scheb joined Grimes's opinion. On denial of rehearing, they cleared the way for an appeal by certifying the issue to the Supreme Court as one of great public interest.

The contractors opposing the fee took hope from a decision by the Fourth District Court of Appeal rejecting Broward County's imposition of a "land use fee" to pay for future road development. That case, *Broward County v. Janis Development Corp.*,[10] said there were "no specifics provided . . . as to where and when these monies are to be expended for roads."

But Justice Hatchett, writing for a unanimous five-justice panel in *Contractors and Builders of Pinellas County v. City of Dunedin*,[11] said that was different. Dunedin had a specific use for the funds, Hatchett wrote—"to expand the water and sewerage systems, so as to meet the increased demand which additional connections to the system create." He added, "A private utility in the same circumstances would presumably do the same thing, in which event surely even petitioners would not suggest that the private corporation was attempting to levy a tax on its customers." Roberts, Adkins, Overton, and England joined the opinion.

The Dunedin fee, while thought of as an "impact fee," was really more like a utility fee for municipal services. Other charges imposed around the state sought to deal with the effects of subdividing property and the resulting greater impact from the more intensive use. It was the Third District Court of Appeal, not the Supreme Court, that rendered the most influential decision in this field not long after the Supreme Court's decision in the Dunedin case.

Wald Corporation had been required to dedicate canal rights-of-way and maintenance easements as a condition of approval for a proposed subdivision. Wald wanted the ordinance authorizing those conditions to be declared unconstitutional. Judge Raymond G. Nathan wrote the opinion for a unanimous Third DCA panel that also included Judges Daniel S. Pearson and Norman

Hendry.[12] Instead of just upholding the trial judge's dismissal of the challenge, Nathan outlined in some detail what he called "a moderate standard" of assessing such an "exaction" from developers. There had to be a "rational nexus" between the anticipated needs of the community, including the owners of the individual parcels in the subdivision, and the property rights of the developer.

"The Wald property is located in a 'glade area' of Dade County which has been subject to periodic flooding," Nathan wrote. "Although the subdivision parcel itself is slightly above flood level, other parts of the glade both upstream and downstream from the parcel are lower, and are thus subject to runoff from the Wald subdivision." The resulting periodic flooding, both within and beyond the new subdivision, justified the canal requirements. And the requirement actually made the property more attractive to prospective buyers, who presumably would rather not have their homes flooded periodically.

Wald sought review at the Florida Supreme Court, but the court declined.[13] This case was much more of an "impact fee" case than the Dunedin one, which really was about the operation of municipal utilities and services, but both cases had a fundamental philosophy that existing residents should not have to bear the financial burdens created by new residents. The district courts continued to refine the "rational nexus" standard, and the Supreme Court denied review and let those decisions become the law statewide.

As with the other growth management policies created in the 1970s, the sound and fury of developers came to signify nothing, as growth continued at a feverish pace. Between 1970 and 1980, the state's population grew from 6,851,168 to 9,840,309, a 30 percent increase on top of 37 percent growth in the preceding decade. Growth slowed in percentage terms, but Florida continued to add about three million people each decade through 2010.

What none of the court decisions did was create significant discretion for localities to use fees as a mechanism to reflect anything other than direct economic costs. There was no room for other community values about growth and the quality of life or to reflect the additional financial and other burdens of the booms and busts of Florida real estate development. When future economic downturns hit, local governments would often suspend or reduce their impact fees as some incentive for developers but had no authority to do the opposite at times of peak development activity.

In fact, by focusing so heavily on the evidence supporting the linkage between the fee and direct costs, the courts' decisions simply shifted the starting point in negotiations between developer and the local government over the entire package of approvals, including zoning and site plans as well as impact fees and other exactions. Determined developers, with capital to pay lawyers and experts, had far more staying power than local neighborhood groups and more determination than local governments, which hated saying no to a major business activity.

Growth also meant new highways, including new interstates, and new interstates meant sharp increases in the value of land near those highways. Condemnation for right of way was a major activity.

One such proceeding initiated by the Florida Department of Transportation was for right-of-way for Interstate 75 through Manatee County. Robert and Lionel Nalven owned as trustees about a thousand acres in the area, and DOT wanted 91.5 of them. In the condemnation case that began in February 1977, DOT argued that "full compensation" for the property, the standard set by the Florida Constitution, should not require it to pay for the increase in value that resulted from the DOT's own plans to build the highway. Recent sales of nearby land were at $2,350 an acre, almost twice the sales price before the anticipation of the interstate construction. The ultimate question was whether DOT had to pay $133,525 or $217,914, a difference of about $85,000.

The trial judge, Acting Circuit Judge James S. Parker of Manatee County, told the jury that the amount should not include the enhanced value from the state's own project, so the jury awarded the Nalvens $133,525. They appealed. Grimes wrote the opinion for the Second DCA and reluctantly sent the case back for a new trial.[14] In 1912, he said, the Supreme Court had ruled that "full compensation" included the enhanced value from the project itself. Grimes called this "a minority view" and said most other states exclude that increase, but he was bound by it, even though the decision dated back seventy years to a wholly different era. The entry of the government into the market "distorted the market." He said the result would be "windfall gains" to some landowners. "The government, when pursuing public benefits through its condemnation power, should not have to spend more for property than would a reasonable and willing private purchaser," Grimes wrote. "Why do we labor this point? Because it may be that the State of Florida is paying more for property than it should be."

Grimes and fellow judges Edward Boardman and Monterey Campbell asked the Supreme Court to reconsider.

It did, but stuck to the old rule. It was once again the former real estate lawyer, Boyd, who wrote the opinion in *Department of Transportation v. Nalven*.[15] He said that the words "full compensation" meant the same thing in 1984 that they meant to the court in 1912. He noted that the law implementing that provision stated that the amount "shall be determined as of the date of trial, or the date upon which title passes, whichever shall occur first." The alternative would produce great complexity. When, for example, was there awareness of the government project? Even "general knowledge" of a highway before its exact route is known "could have and probably did cause a general increase in land values." It is therefore "very difficult to determine where to the draw the line against value enhancement due to project anticipation."

Justices Alderman, Adkins and Shaw joined him. Overton, a consistent protector of the public fisc, and Ehrlich "strongly" dissented. "Regrettably, this opinion will have a major fiscal impact for years to come because it will require the state to pay untold millions as a premium in for increases in property value caused solely by the government's proposed improvement for which the property was taken," Overton wrote. This decision "will possibly thwart the development of some public projects because of the decline in available taxpayer funds with which to pay the increased compensation required."

McDonald also wrote a dissent. "This case presents us with the opportunity to correct a gross inequity in the law of eminent domain. We should accept the suggestion of Judge Grimes of the Second District Court of Appeal to do so."

One of the weirdest and most complicated fights over control of Florida's natural resources reached the Supreme Court in 1985. The underlying facts revealed not only some egregiously bad title work in the earlier days of Florida's history but also a cavalier attitude of the state, including the Governor and Cabinet, in the stewardship of the state's lands from the earliest days of statehood through the 1960s.

The case of *Coastal Petroleum v. American Cyanamid Company*[16] illustrates that one of the most significant effects of a reapportioned legislature in the 1960s and the arrival of the progressive Askew administration in 1971 was to wrest political control of the state's natural resources from the agrarian, landholding interests and speculators that found favor with the legislature's "Pork Chop Gang."

The issue in a myriad of lawsuits was whether the State of Florida, perhaps inadvertently, had given away its rivers and other precious waters in the early days of statehood. By mid-1983, it was looking like the answer would be yes. Basically the state was starting to look like just another swamp peddler, leasing exploration and mineral rights to land it had already deeded away to others. By 1985, only the Supreme Court could pull the state's bacon out of the fire and reject what came to be known as the "I have a deed" rationale for claiming title.[17]

The state had recently granted twelve-thousand-year mining leases of mineral rights under state rivers to a little company called Coastal Petroleum

Corp., but the leases were worthless if the state had already given full title to its navigable rivers to others. Coastal had also bought up other exploration and mining rights, including rights to explore for oil in Florida's coastal waters of the Gulf of Mexico based on a lease from the state in 1941. In 1977 Coastal filed federal lawsuits against a number of companies, including American Cyanamid and Mobil Oil, for taking phosphate from land under the Peace and Alafia Rivers that Coastal said it controlled under the state's lease. The phosphate companies, much preferring to be in state rather than federal courts, filed suits in 1982 and 1983 to "quiet title"—to confirm their clear title—to the rivers. The major cases came through the Second District Court of Appeal in Lakeland, which was the heart of phosphate country and near the ancestral home of the phosphate companies' primary Florida law firm, Holland & Knight.

The state was essentially on Coastal's side against the big drilling and phosphate companies. Governor Graham and Attorney General Smith filed amicus briefs at the Second DCA to underscore the significance to them and to the state. The American Cyanamid case, they said, "will decide the ownership of the Peace River from Bartow to Fort Meade. Whether the people of Florida have a right to any mineral interest along this stretch of the river and whether the people have an unfettered right to use of this river for fishing, boating and other recreation purposes will be decided by this court." The Mobil case dealt with about twelve miles of the Peace River.

Back in the nineteenth century, the state had deeded away large swaths of swamp and other "overflow" lands with deeds and maps that did not exclude the rivers running through them. The law makes a distinction between these "swamp and overflow lands," conveyed by a specific act of Congress in 1850, and "sovereignty lands," which were inherent in statehood and include so-called navigable waters on the rivers and coasts.

The phosphate companies' claim was simple and persuaded the district courts of appeal: They had deeds that included the rivers in question, and any question about the title ended in 1963, when the legislature passed the Marketable Record Title Act saying that any deed more than thirty years old was no longer subject to challenge. In 1970—arguably a little late to affect the old deeds—the Legislature proposed and the voters approved a constitutional amendment saying that "sovereignty lands" were "in trust for all the people."[18]

Justice Boyd had written a decision in 1976 that was a major arguing point for those who held those old deeds. After the new Second DCA ruling for the phosphate companies, Coastal Petroleum appealed to the Supreme Court, and Boyd wrote an opinion reaffirming his view from 1976. The answer now was regrettable but clear, he said: "The essential fact upon which this case turns is that the lands were conveyed into private ownership without reservation of those portions underlying navigable waters." In the years since the deeds were executed in 1883, owners of the land have engaged in mining or other visible activities using the disputed property. "If the Trustees [the Governor and Cabinet] disputed the respondents' title, they should have taken action. . . . The law should not come to the aid of one who is not diligent in asserting his own rights."

Boyd did say that people had an inalienable right to actual use of the rivers, even if the state did not retain legal title. And he acknowledged the harshness of his view. "Many have suggested that the courts are being asked to give away state-owned lands. The truth is that the lands in question here . . . were legally conveyed by authorized state officials. It may very well be that . . . [they] failed to exercise care and diligence on behalf of the public. But the fact that decisions . . . were unwise is no reason to now penalize innocent purchasers who paid market value and relied upon state officers' authority to sell."

But this time, Boyd's view did not prevail. Only one justice, McDonald, joined Boyd's opinion.

It fell to Justice Shaw to rescue the state from the morass it created, and he did it with a simple concept supported by Adkins, Overton and Ehrlich, who formed the 4–2 majority. A "public trust doctrine," first applied by the Supreme Court in 1908 and 1927 and later cases, said that the navigable rivers, which he defined to include the Alafia and Peace, were "inalienable." The Supreme Court had never varied from holding that swamp deeds did not convey sovereignty lands, because the state could never deed them away, at least without an explicit deed to do so, and certainly not by implication. Shaw quoted the 1927 case to say that if conveyances of sovereignty lands were made "by mistake or otherwise," the conveyances "are ineffectual for lack of authority."

Shaw also had a sharp critique of Boyd's opinion in 1976—the one the phosphate companies had relied on. That case, *Odom v. Deltona Corp.*,[19] was about small lakes and ponds that were "non-navigable, non-sovereignty lands." But the opinion, said Shaw, "unfortunately . . . went on to answer irrelevant arguments put to us by the parties" on the effect of the Marketable Record Title Act. Even McDonald said he didn't agree with Boyd that the act controlled the disposition of sovereignty lands.

The ruling did not bring the battle to an end. Fourteen years later some legislators were proposing a bill known as the "Florida Land Title Protection Act" to overturn the Supreme Court's American Cyanamid decision and convey the lands in question to those who had tried to win them through the litigation.[20] Their argument was essentially Boyd's argument. Decried by newspaper editorials as a "land grab," the bill failed.

16

DEATH PENALTY

The Long Last Mile

At seven o'clock on the morning of May 25, 1979, the justices of the Florida Supreme Court gathered in the living room of Chief Justice Arthur England's house in Tallahassee's Waverly Hills subdivision.

At midnight it had seemed a near-certainty that John Spenkelink would be executed the next morning in Florida's electric chair. But Scharlette Holdman, a fearless and tireless advocate for death-row inmates who rounded up volunteer lawyers by badgering and shaming if necessary, had recruited Florida State University Law Professor Steven Goldstein and former Askew aide Howell L. Ferguson to make one more pitch to the Florida Supreme Court. Ferguson was a former assistant attorney general, had worked with England in Askew's office, was from the rich and well-known Lykes family, and had managed Justice Hatchett's successful election campaign in 1976. Ferguson called England, woke him up at 2 a.m., and asked for one final argument on Spenkelink's behalf.

"Fine," England said, "be at my house at seven o'clock." England hung up, promptly regretted what he had groggily committed to, but called research aide Michael Rosen and told him to arrange for "coffee and pencils." Then he called the other justices.[1]

It was a Friday. It had been seven long and frenzied days since Governor Graham signed Spenkelink's death warrant. No one had ever seen anything quite like this exaggerated and frantic application of the process of habeas corpus, the centuries-old writ for challenging the legality of someone's imprisonment. Florida had not used its electric chair for fifteen years, since two men were executed on May 12, 1964.[2] That was an entirely different time in criminal law—just a year after *Gideon v. Wainwright*,[3] the landmark 1963 burglary case out of Panama City that established a nationwide right to counsel for defendants in felony cases. The famous ruling on questioning suspects, *Miranda v. Arizona*,[4] was still two years away. In 1967 a formal national moratorium on executions had begun as a result of decisions in lower federal courts, including Florida's.[5]

This day in May in 1979 was about to end that moratorium and mark the return of the death penalty to America. Two years earlier Gary Gilmore had been executed by firing squad in Utah, but he had dismissed his lawyers and insisted on execution. Spenkelink had a platoon of lawyers and advocates fighting for his life.

His appeals set the pattern for hundreds of death warrants nationwide over the next quarter-century. The war of attrition made the death penalty one of the most expensive and frustrating of all the matters under the jurisdiction of the courts.

Growing up in California, John Spenkelink had been a bright and happy kid who looked up to his father, a decorated World War II veteran. But one day when he was twelve, John went into the garage and found his father dead from suicide, with a hose running from the exhaust pipe of the car. Soon John began a string of juvenile crimes and ended up in San Quentin at age eighteen. At twenty-three, serving time for armed robbery, he escaped and headed east. During a Nebraska snowstorm he picked up a hitchhiker, Joseph Szymankiewicz, a bigger, older man with a long career of violence and prison. They wound up in room 4 of the Ponce de Leon Motel in Tallahassee.

Spenkelink claimed the guy sodomized him, forced him to play Russian roulette, and took $8,000 from him. Spenkelink went out, got a gun, and came back for his money while Szymankiewicz was sleeping, as Spenkelink later recounted the events. As he was leaving with the money, Szymankiewicz saw him. They fought, and the gun went off. Spenkelink claimed self-defense. Prosecutors countered that Szymankiewicz was lying on his bed asleep when Spenkelink shot him in the back of the head. There was no corroboration for any forced sex; even by Spenkelink's account, it happened a week or more before the killing, and the two continued on to Florida together. After killing Szymankiewicz, Spenkelink took off for California. He was soon arrested as a suspect in an armed robbery there. The murder weapon from Tallahassee was found in his California apartment. He was brought back to Tallahassee for a murder trial.

Second Circuit Judge John A. Rudd encouraged a plea bargain. As defense lawyer Brian T. Hayes later recalled, the judge told the lawyers, "One drifter kills another: That's not worth two weeks of the court's time."[6] The prosecutor, Ken Davis, suggested a plea to second-degree murder, which carried a maximum life sentence and a prospect of parole in a few years.

Spenkelink turned it down. Hayes, a respected lawyer from Monticello, told him he was making a mistake and even made him acknowledge in writing that acquittal was unlikely and the death penalty was a possibility. Years later, celebrated death-penalty lawyer Millard Farmer estimated that three-fourths of those executed in America had at one point been offered a plea bargain to avoid the death penalty.[7] Even the most notorious serial killer executed in Florida's electric chair, Theodore Bundy, was once offered a life sentence for a plea.

On the witness stand making the case for self-defense, Spenkelink showed the same tough-guy dismissiveness about the charges as he had about the plea deal. He was convicted of first-degree murder. The jury recommended a death sentence, and on December 20, 1973, Judge Rudd imposed it.

By law, there was an automatic appeal to the Florida Supreme Court.

It was the sixth death sentence the Supreme Court had considered under a new death-penalty system created in December 1972, five months after the old death-penalty laws were declared unconstitutional by the U.S. Supreme Court. In the case of Joseph Taylor, an accomplice in a liquor-store robbery, the Supreme Court reduced the sentence to life because the judge gave no apparent consideration to the jury's recommendation of life.[8] Michael Paul Lamadline's death sentence was overturned because no sentencing jury was empaneled after his guilty plea.[9] The court upheld death sentences in the next three cases. Robert A. Sullivan got death for holding up a Howard Johnson's, abducting the assistant manager, driving him to a remote place, striking his head with a tire iron, and then firing both barrels of a shotgun into the back of his head.[10] Clifford Hallman was convicted of cutting the throat of a barmaid with a broken bottle.[11] Learie Leo Alford was convicted of raping and killing a thirteen-year-old girl he abducted from a bus stop.[12]

On February 19, 1975, the court upheld Spenkelink's sentence, 6–1.[13] Justice Boyd, who had previously called the law unconstitutional and dissented in the Sullivan and Hallman cases two months earlier, abandoned that view without explanation and wrote the majority opinion. This apparently was the first death case assigned to him. It was sometimes speculated that Spenkelink's homosexuality repulsed Boyd, who was a pious man and later voted against admitting a gay lawyer to the Florida Bar. It is also possible that, with ethics charges pending against him, Boyd abandoned the political boldness of a death-penalty dissent in favor of a tough majority opinion. Whatever Boyd's feelings, a material difference was that Spenkelink's lawyers had not challenged the constitutionality of the death penalty, as the previous cases did. Boyd wrote that Spenkelink's crime was "premeditated, especially cruel, atrocious, and heinous, and in connection with robbery to secure return of money."[14] He was joined by Adkins, Roberts, Overton, and McCain as well as Hillsborough Circuit Judge Harry Lee Coe, substituting for Dekle.

In a solitary dissent, Justice Ervin noted that the constitutionality of the death-penalty law remained a "live, unsettled" issue. He noted that both victim and defendant were "underprivileged drifters" with "foreign and strange surnames" and no connections in the community. Those were "the ingredients for invidious parochial discrimination" against "the poor and ignorant."[15]

Nineteen months passed as death-penalty challenges moved through federal courts for the first time. On September 12, 1977, Governor Askew had six black-bordered death warrants in front of him, one of them for Spenkelink. Three of the men under consideration were part of a pending case challenging the lack of standards in the grant of clemency. Spenkelink had not joined that case. A fourth case, Hallman's, was complicated by a civil settlement indicating that hospital negligence contributed to the victim's death. Governor Graham would later commute Hallman's sentence to life. Only two of the six men had cases with no procedural complications. One warrant was for Charles William Proffitt, whose case at the U.S. Supreme Court in 1976 had upheld Florida's new death statute.[16] Proffitt had only a burglary on his previous record. Spenkelink's criminal record was longer. Both men were white, and so were their victims.

Askew picked Spenkelink. His execution was set for the following Monday. A federal court stayed the execution indefinitely, but the warrant was enough to make Spenkelink a national *cause célèbre*. David E. Kendall, a Rhodes Scholar and Yale Law graduate who two decades later would represent President Bill Clinton in impeachment proceedings, stepped in to represent Spenkelink. Kendall had worked for the Legal Defense Fund but had just moved to the prestigious Washington firm of Williams & Connolly, which was contributing Kendall's time for free.

Kendall built his appeal around two major points. First, he had statistics showing racial bias in deciding who dies. Although most murder victims in America were black, most of the people on death rows in America had killed white people. That issue never got very far in a Florida Supreme Court case. Second, Kendall had a ruling from the U.S. Supreme Court a year earlier, in *Lockett v. Ohio*,[17] which made clear that states could not limit the types of mitigating factors in a defendant's life that juries and judges could use in considering leniency.

The *Lockett* issue would produce new sentencing hearings for a number of Florida inmates, but not for another eight years. On March 2, 1979, the U.S. Supreme Court refused to consider the issue.

A few days after the appeal was rejected, Kendall and others went to see Graham, who was just two months into his governorship, and asked for clemency. Graham was noncommittal. Then at 6:46 a.m. on May 18, a Friday, he signed a new death warrant, authorizing Spenkelink's execution anytime between then and the following Friday at noon. It was set for 7 a.m. the next Wednesday.

When the Florida Supreme Court opened Monday morning, Kendall was there with a petition for a stay. Assistant Attorney General Raymond Marky filed an immediate response. At 5:15 p.m., without a hearing, the Supreme Court denied a stay. With little hope left, Kendall drove to Starke to be with Spenkelink at the execution.

At the attorney general's office, Marky was close to winning his first execution. This short, skinny chain-smoker with black-rimmed glasses was a tenacious streetfighter of a lawyer with an encyclopedic memory of cases and a tart response to adversaries. He had spent his teenage years in the home of his uncle by marriage, Justice E. Harris Drew, who had inspired Ray to become a lawyer. Now he was in charge of capital appeals for the Florida attorney general. In private, Marky considered Spenkelink "probably the least obnoxious on death row in terms of the crime he committed."[18] But Marky was contemptuous of stays. "While I understand why lawyers do what we do, the judiciary should not let lawyers do what we do," he said.

But it wasn't over, after all.

Tuesday morning, Kendall got a call from Millard Farmer, a fearless, provocative combatant in southern civil rights litigation. Farmer had grown up in Newnan, Georgia, as a rich kid, heir to a fertilizer fortune. He and Marjorie Hames of the American Civil Liberties Union in Atlanta, who among many legal battles had successfully argued the companion case to *Roe v. Wade* at the U.S. Supreme Court, wanted to take over the case and argue that Spenkelink got ineffective representation from the very beginning—Kendall included. This was Spenkelink's last hope. Kendall agreed to focus on issues at the prison and turned the appeals over to Farmer and Hames, who filed new petitions in federal courts. They recruited to the defense team former U.S. Attorney General Ramsey Clark, whose father had been a justice of the U.S. Supreme Court.

The lawyers failed to get stays on Tuesday from three judges on the Fifth Circuit U.S. Court of Appeals. Late that night, Clark and Farmer arrived at the Atlanta home of Senior Judge Elbert P. Tuttle, one of the lionized judges on the Fifth Circuit whose rulings advanced the civil rights movement in the 1950s and 1960s. Semi-retired and eighty-one years old, Tuttle told Clark he had not granted a writ of habeas corpus in a dozen years. Why should he do so now? Clark replied that this first contested execution in years, under new statutes and court rulings, was raising untested issues that were unlikely to get proper consideration from the judges who rejected the earlier petitions. "We needed a very courageous, very independent, open-minded and fair judge," Clark said.[19]

Tuttle signed a stay. It was nearly midnight. Execution plans were halted. Spenkelink had already been allowed a final hug and kiss with his girlfriend and his mother. Marky and his boss, Assistant Attorney General George Georgieff, still in their offices at the state capitol, were shocked. What authority did this senior judge have?[20]

Marky went home but was back at his office well before dawn, drafting new appeals on a legal pad. Wednesday afternoon, after the documents were typed, he and Florida Attorney General Jim Smith held a press conference, then boarded the state jet and flew first to New Orleans to file at the headquarters of the Fifth Circuit, then to Washington to file at the U.S. Supreme Court. Although the nation's highest court had denied a stay two days earlier,[21] overturning another judge's stay was a different matter. The justices wouldn't do it. In dissent, Justice William H. Rehnquist cited "six years of litigation" and called Tuttle's stay "a clear abuse of the writ of habeas corpus."[22]

Attention turned to a three-judge panel of the Fifth Circuit, assembled to consider Marky's appeal there. Two of them held a telephone conference with the lawyers Thursday evening. One was Judge James P. Coleman, a former state attorney general and governor of Mississippi appointed to the court by President Lyndon Johnson. The other was Judge Alvin Rubin of Louisiana, appointed by President Jimmy Carter. Afterwards, Rubin wanted to sustain the stay, and Coleman wanted to dissolve it. They called Judge Peter T. Fay of Miami, who had been elevated from the district court to the circuit court by President Gerald Ford, and he voted with Coleman. At 11:40 Thursday night, the stay was dissolved and the execution was back on.[23]

The prison superintendent, David Brierton, set the execution for 10 a.m. Friday. Governor Graham's death warrant would expire at noon.

Brierton was a newcomer to the Florida prison system, a big man from Illinois who had a tough management style but also had a wine cellar and a management certificate from Harvard, read poetry, and loved classical music. Brierton had restored order to a violence-prone prison.[24] Brierton and his top deputy, Richard Dugger, were worried about Spenkelink's restiveness as the execution neared. "We talked about tranquilizers, but we didn't feel drugs were appropriate," Dugger recalled in 1984.[25] "We asked Spenkelink if he wanted a drink, and he said, 'Sure.'" Brierton pulled out a bottle of Jack Daniel's whiskey, and Dugger took it to the death-watch cell. Spenkelink took two shots.

The gathering of the Florida Supreme Court at England's house Friday morning looked like the last round. Unwilling to listen to Kendall on Monday, the justices now were up at sunrise to hear from new lawyers. Smith and Marky were there for the state. As England remembered it, lawyers in New Orleans made their case by phone. England's house had only one phone line with one extension phone. There was no cordless phone, no speakerphone, and nobody had cell phones in 1979. England and another justice listened to the defense lawyers and relayed the points to the other justices. Then Marky made his case. Everyone but the justices then went outside, and the justices began conferring privately.

The governor's office, meanwhile, "was going nuts," as England put it, because England's phone line had been busy. Brierton needed to know how to proceed, and Graham wanted to be sure a phone line to the justices would be open until the execution was over. A state trooper arrived to pick up Jim Smith; other troopers simultaneously picked up Smith's daughters at school as a result of death threats. As the justices talked, England got up and looked out a window and saw Marky the street-fighter, now so close to victory, standing by his car crying.

Sitting in the living room, the justices spoke in their usual order, beginning with Boyd, who retained the case assignment because he handled the original appeal. Boyd defended the original decision. Adkins was a predictable vote against stays. Sundberg was skeptical about the fairness of the death penalty but also had little patience with post-conviction appeals. Alderman, a newcomer as Askew's final appointee to the court, leaned toward defendants in civil cases and against defendants in criminal cases. He, too, opposed a stay. He and Adkins later wrote that the appeal was "an abuse of the judicial process."[26] Overton was in touch by telephone but did not participate in the decision. He had joined Boyd's original opinion.

England and Hatchett had been troubled by the death sentence during an earlier Spenkelink appeal, in 1977. England wrote then that he "cannot help but share many of counsel's stated and unstated concerns" about the death sentence. But he decided the 1977 appeal did not meet the technical requirements for post-conviction relief.

Hatchett's concurring opinion in the 1977 appeal described cases where death sentences had been reduced to life even though the crimes seemed much worse than Spenkelink's. In one, the victim was severely beaten, then tied up so that efforts to free herself would strangle her; in another, the victim had been beaten with an iron bar and the corpse cut into pieces; in a third, the victim was shot and bled to death as the killer kept others from helping her. "It is apparent to me that the death penalty under the Florida statutory scheme is being administered in an arbitrary and capricious manner," Hatchett wrote in

1977, but "this issue was apparently foreclosed" when the U.S. Supreme Court upheld Florida's statute in 1976.[27]

They had all voted against Spenkelink in 1977, and none of them saw any reason to stop the execution now. At 9:38 a.m. they denied a stay. At 9:50, the U.S. Supreme Court rejected a final plea from Ramsey Clark.

At the prison, Spenkelink's head had been shaved to accommodate the wet sponge and wired metal helmet where the electricity would enter his body. An electricity-conducting cream was applied to his lower right leg where an electrode would be attached to conduct the electricity out of his body. A few minutes before ten o'clock, white prison vans pulled up to a door at the north end of Q Wing, and thirty-two official witnesses and journalists were led into the twenty-two-by-twelve beige-walled witness room. In front of them was a large plate-glass window, but the blinds on the other side were closed.

At ten o'clock, Spenkelink was led down the prison corridor to the death chamber. The witnesses heard movement beyond the blinds. At 10:11 a.m., Graham by telephone gave Brierton the final approval. The blinds were raised. Spenkelink was already strapped tightly into the chair, little more than his eyes visible between the metal helmet and a black jaw strap. "For maybe 30 seconds, this trussed and immobile figure stared into the waiting room," wrote witness H. G. "Buddy" Davis, a journalism professor at the University of Florida who had won a Pulitzer Prize for his editorials in the *Gainesville Sun*.[28]

A hood was lowered over Spenkelink's face, and the executioner threw a red switch. There was a loud thump. A jolt of electricity, 2,300 volts at 9.5 amps, enough to power the floodlights at a minor league ballpark, zapped Spenkelink for eight seconds, then cycled down, then up again, then down, then up, then down. Everyone waited. Finally, a man with an insulated glove checked for a pulse.

Spenkelink was dead.

At England's house, the TV was on with news updates. There was "an immobile silence for five or ten minutes," England recounted. "Nobody on the court wanted to go into the office and decide cases."

Seven years before, on June 29, 1972, the U.S. Supreme Court had effectively struck down every capital-punishment law in America. The decision in *Furman v. Georgia*[29] was 5–4, but only Justices William J. Brennan Jr. and Thurgood Marshall considered capital punishment fundamentally unconstitutional. Justices William O. Douglas, Potter Stewart and Byron White carried the day with their view that it was the selection process, not the execution itself, that made the death penalty "cruel and unusual" in violation of the Eighth Amendment. It was a time when the court was on high alert over racial discrimination. The death penalty fell disproportionately on minorities and lower-class citizens, the three justices concluded, and decisions were inconsistent and arbitrary.

Three months before *Furman*, the Florida Legislature had amended Florida's capital statute to provide for life imprisonment without parole if the death penalty were ever held unconstitutional.[30] The legislature had carelessly made the new law effective on October 1, 1972, rather than immediately, so its life-without-parole standard was not in effect when *Furman* was decided on June 29. On July 17 the Florida Supreme Court ruled in *Donaldson v. Sack*[31] that the state's capital punishment statute had the same constitutional deficiencies as those of Texas and Georgia, which were the focus in *Furman*.

The court then had to deal with a hundred people on death row whose death sentences were no longer valid. Since the new law was not in effect, prisoners retained a chance at parole. A few of the hundred were already being resentenced to life by local trial judges. If some were not resentenced until after October 1 and were not given the same chance at parole, there would be extended litigation over equal protection.

On September 8, in *Anderson v. State*,[32] on a petition from Attorney General Robert L. Shevin, the court in one fell swoop resentenced to life in prison the twenty-seven convicted murderers with death sentences still on appeal. Two weeks later, over the attorney general's objections, the court did basically the same thing in *In re Baker*[33] for the sixty death row inmates whose appeals had already ended. Among those sixty were Freddie Lee Pitts and Wilbert Lee, who three years later would be pardoned after another man confessed to the crime.[34] Another thirteen men on death row, convicted of capital rape rather than murder, had to be resentenced by the trial judges, since it would be possible for them to receive a sentence less than life imprisonment.

By the time the "life without parole" statute took effect on October 1, 1972, it was pointless.

Governor Askew's legal staff and the legislature scrambled to draft a death penalty law for future cases that would meet the U.S. Supreme Court's approval. Askew established a Governor's Committee to Study Capital Punishment, chaired by retired justice Drew. Separately, the Judicial Council, chaired by Chief Justice Roberts, who would later rule on the law's constitutionality and on individual capital cases, weighed in with political support for the death penalty and said, "If it saves one life, it is worth having."[35] Committees in the House and Senate also went to work. They all had to guess what approach might satisfy the U.S. Supreme Court. In 1971, in *McGautha v. California*,[36] that court had said discretion in capital sentencing was not a problem. A year later, in *Furman*, it said discretion was the root of the problem, but the nine separate opinions sowed great confusion over acceptable alternatives.

What Florida lawmakers eventually cobbled together, with Askew's signature on December 8, 1972, made Florida the first state to reinstitute the death penalty.[37] Retaining a concept from the pointless capital statute passed earlier, the new statute[38] created a separate mini-trial on sentencing, with the same jury, immediately after the defendant's conviction of a capital crime. The jury and judge were required to weigh specific aggravating and mitigating factors, which the legislature viewed as critical to counter the unacceptable, arbitrary discretion that Furman had found unconstitutional. The jury's recommendation would be by majority vote, not unanimous—a critical point making Florida more death-prone in its sentencing decisions, since most states require unanimity or a super-majority to recommend a death sentence. Just as the judge could override a jury recommendation of death, the judge also, for the first time, could override a jury recommendation of life. The judge had to explain the final decision in writing. A death sentence was automatically appealed to the Florida Supreme Court.

Aggravating factors to be considered in sentencing included the heinousness or cruelty of the crime and prior convictions for violence. Mitigating circumstances included mental illness and emotional disturbance, which for centuries have been viewed as diminishing the criminality of a person's actions.

Florida and eventually many other states made a legislative determination that the death penalty remained morally appropriate and legally sustainable if it were applied in an orderly, rational, consistent way. Rigorous analysis, governed by evidence and specific criteria, would replace prejudice and vengeance in handing down death sentences. That might frustrate the "eye for an eye" supporters of capital punishment and the desire of victims' families for vengeance without mercy, and it might remain anathema to those morally opposed to capital punishment. But moral judgments on policy are for legislatures; the courts' role was to make the justice system fair and even-handed, to ensure "due process" and "equal protection of the laws."

No one seemed to imagine, as 1972 came to a close, that it would take six more years for the first execution to occur in Florida, that nearly five years would pass after that before the second execution, or that for the next thirty years, the criminal-justice system would be processing death cases with the same lurching, drawn-out, frustrating, unpredictable, and unsatisfying process that preceded the execution of John Spenkelink.

"No longer will one man die and another live on the basis of race, or a woman live and a man die on the basis of sex," Justice Adkins declared as the Florida Supreme Court upheld the new capital-punishment law by a 5–2 vote on July 26, 1973. "Only the most aggravated and unmitigated of most serious crimes" would be punished by death. "Review by this Court guarantees that the reasons present in one case will reach a similar result to that reached under similar circumstances in another case," because the Supreme Court can review a case "in light of the other decisions and determine whether or not the punishment is too great." Sentencing, Adkins said, "becomes a matter of reasoned judgment rather than an exercise in discretion at all."

The case was not an appeal of a death sentence. It was a consolidation of five cases from three counties where judges had delayed murder trials until the new death law could be tested on appeal. None of the five defendants was ever sentenced to death. The case was known as *State v. Dixon*.[39]

The soaring rhetoric and unbridled optimism were quite unusual for a Supreme Court opinion. Adkins said in his 1986 memoir that he "spent many sleepless nights" analyzing the *Furman* opinions and the legal arguments and "became convinced" that the law was constitutional.[40] The one clear standard from *Furman,* he said, was that judicial discretion in capital sentencing has to be "reasonable and controlled, rather than capricious and discriminatory."[41] The new law, he said, provided for that. That, "coupled with the fact that the majority of the court, myself included, favored capital punishment, allowed us to uphold the statute."

Once actual death cases started arriving at the court, the aspirations of *Dixon* were never heard from again. One line in the *Dixon* opinion contributed more than any other to the dilution of the standards. "When one or more of the aggravating circumstances is found," Adkins wrote, "death is presumed to be the proper sentence unless it or they are overridden by one or more of the mitigating circumstances."

The law passed by the legislature says nothing about presuming anything. Adkins's memoir reports, "I had to fight hard to keep this interpretation of the statute in the opinion and I am thankful that this is still the law." Adkins claimed his interpretation called for a "reasoned evaluation of all the circumstances in a case" rather than "merely adding and subtracting" circumstances." but his words seem to say the opposite.

Joining Adkins in the *Dixon* opinion were Carlton, McCain, Dekle and a circuit judge filling in for Roberts, Ben Willis of Leon County. Two justices dissented.

Boyd, who faced reelection the following year and was taking some political risk in this high-profile cause, objected that the new law actually made discretion worse, because judges now could overrule juries' votes for mercy. "With the same objectivity as a merchant measuring cloth," Boyd wrote, "I have compared the new Florida capital punishment statute with federal constitutional standards, and find said law to be unconstitutional."[42] Boyd's post-retirement memoir in 1987 noted his role in the Spenkelink case, professed his "mixed emotions, both on religious and on practical grounds," about the death penalty, and said he had "no authority to substitute my judgment for that of the people on this policy question."[43] His memoir doesn't mention his dissent in *Dixon*.

Ervin also dissented. He too said the law left too much discretion. The listed circumstances were "vague and overbroad," and it wasn't clear what "sufficient" means in weighing them.[44] He wondered "what weight" the appellate court might give to a jury recommendation of life that a judge overruled. He noted that the law did not require judges to explain decisions to choose life sentences, and those cases did not go to the Supreme Court anyway, so there was no way to compare death cases the Supreme Court sees with similar cases that might have produced a life sentence. (Adkins, addressing this issue in his opinion, directed trial judges who impose life sentences to explain those decisions in writing, but the court never collected those orders and has never referred to one.)[45]

Ervin said discretion exists not just in sentencing but from the very beginning of any murder case, including "(1) the inevitable discretion in making factual determinations [on guilt of a capital crime]; (2) the decision of the grand jury [to indict for capital murder]; (3) the decision of the prosecutor to bring charges, what charges to bring, and what penalty to ask for; (4) the jury's decision to convict of a lesser included offense; (5) executive clemency."[46] Ervin then launched into his own oratory. He said the legislature had been "under the influence of archaic and atavistic impulses and the whip of public furor stirred by national and local political opportunism." He said "the hallmark of a civilized progressive people is their appreciation that infliction of cruel and unusual punishment disproportionately upon the underprivileged and mentally incompetent is the antithesis of a fair and humane society and can be one of the elements leading to anarchy and revolution."[47]

It was 1976 when the U.S. Supreme Court finally considered the new statutes that were enacted around the country after *Furman*. One case was from

Florida, in the appeal of Charles Proffitt, the inmate whose death warrant later would be on Askew's desk the morning he chose to sign Spenkelink's instead.

By the time Proffitt's case was decided by the U.S. Supreme Court in mid-1976, a third of the death sentences imposed by Florida trial judges had been overturned by the Florida Supreme Court. The two most common reasons were that the judges had rejected jury recommendations of life without giving adequate justification and that the trial judges had misapplied those aggravating factors that Adkins had described as readily understandable.

Proffitt had been convicted of murdering Joel Medgebow, a high school wrestling coach in Tampa, who was sleeping in his bed with his wife beside him when an intruder broke in through a sliding glass door of the apartment just before 5 a.m. on March 21, 1974. The intruder stabbed Medgebow once with a butcher knife. When Mrs. Medgebow awoke and saw her husband propped on a pillow holding what turned out to be the knife, the intruder punched her and fled. Coach Medgebow died.

Proffitt had no record of violent crime, though he had a conviction for breaking and entering seven years earlier. The night of Medgebow's murder, Proffitt had been drinking with someone until about 3 a.m. He got home to his two-bedroom trailer around 5:30 a.m. and, according to a renter in the other bedroom, told his wife he had stabbed a guy and punched the man's wife. Proffitt's wife called police. Proffitt waited there for them.

In the sentencing trial after Proffitt's conviction, a jail physician testified as a state witness that Proffitt had come to him seeking psychiatric help because of what Proffitt called an uncontrollable desire to kill that had already resulted in the death of one person. The doctor said Proffitt posed a danger to others, though his problem could be treated. The jury recommended a death sentence, and Hillsborough Circuit Judge Walter N. Burnside Jr. imposed it.

Burnside's order, which is important to what happened later in the case, cited four aggravating circumstances: (1) the murder was committed in the course of a burglary, one of the felonies listed in the statute as an aggravating factor; (2) Proffitt "has the propensity to commit the crime of which he was convicted" and is "a danger and menace to society," factors not listed in the statute; (3) the murder was "especially heinous, atrocious and cruel," another listed aggravating factor; and (4) Proffitt's actions "created a great risk of serious bodily harm and death to many persons." The "enumerated mitigating factors are primarily negated," the judge added, without elaborating on the evidence that negated them.

Proffitt's appeal to the Florida Supreme Court was argued by Assistant Public Defender Robert T. Benton II, who would soon become a law clerk at the court and later an appellate judge. In a unanimous per curiam opinion in *Proffitt v. State* on May 28, 1975, the court recited Burnside's listed factors and declared, "We must obviously conclude that no error was committed [by the judge]."[48] That posed a problem that would follow the case through another twelve years of litigation in state and federal courts: Judge Burnside was, in fact, quite obviously in error.

Most obvious was declaring that the murder posed "a great risk . . . to many persons." Medgebow was stabbed once with a butcher knife that probably came from, and was left in, the victim's home. The wife was punched. There was no one else in the house. Who were the "many persons," and what exactly was the risk? Beyond that, neither "propensity" to commit murder nor danger to society is mentioned in the statute, which says the factors to be considered are "limited" to the ones listed. And Proffitt's case would turn out to be the only one in which the court ever found that a single stab wound, without additional acts of abuse or torture, made a crime "especially heinous."

Judge Burnside was correct, then, on only one of the four aggravating factors, the murder during a burglary. The fact that he was pretty obviously incorrect on the other three wasn't even noticed by the Florida justices. It would take a decade of litigation and a federal court ruling before the Florida Supreme Court revisited that flawed decision.

The U.S. Supreme Court accepted Proffitt's case as part of its first major reconsideration of the death penalty since *Furman*. Five new statutes from five states were considered in separate cases. The new statute from North Carolina had what Florida's attorney general, Robert Shevin, had unsuccessfully recommended for Florida: mandatory death sentences for certain crimes, without discretion. The court struck that one down, 7–2.[49] Louisiana's law was largely mandatory as well. The Texas law was troublesome to the centrist justices, but in the internal negotiations, they struck down the Louisiana law and upheld the Texas one. The approach in Georgia seemed the soundest because of the consideration of individual circumstances, and that law was upheld 7–2.[50] It became the lead case among the five opinions released on July 2, 1976.

Florida's statute was a lot like Georgia's. A majority had decided to uphold Florida's law, but as the opinions came together, the justices in the center were troubled by loose applications of the statute by the Florida Supreme Court in several cases, including Proffitt's. Those justices—Potter Stewart, Lewis Powell, and John Paul Stevens—basically shrugged off the weaknesses in implementing the law. How to explain the use of non-statutory aggravating circumstances, for example, when the statute said they were limited to the ones listed? They settled for saying that "it seems unlikely" the Florida court would uphold a death sentence that "rested entirely on nonstatutory aggravating circumstances."[51] Adkins' hard-fought "presumption" satisfied Stewart's need to explain away his concern.

On a 7–2 vote in *Proffitt v. Florida*,[52] Florida's new statute was upheld.

Florida had scraped by—not because it was applying the statute rigorously but because the fragmented and shaky alliances among the justices in Washington led them to uphold the most palatable of the new statutes and worry about details later. While Florida's justices did not adopt the constitutional minimalism that seemed to allow any aggravating circumstances to be considered as long as at least one was listed in the statute, the aspirational language about thoughtful "weighing" aggravating factors against mitigating ones ended up becoming almost a mathematical formula: $1 > 0$. The zero in that equation showed up frequently, as case after case found "no" mitigating circumstances, without any expression of concern about whether people really had "no" mitigating factors in their lives.

In 1981, Justice Sundberg suggested in *Elledge v. State*[53] that if the Supreme Court found that a trial judge had improperly applied some of the factors, then as long as one listed factor was found, the death sentence would still be upheld if there were no mitigating circumstances. Before long, that "zero" didn't have to be quite zero. Shortly after the *Elledge* decision, the court reversed an aggravating circumstance but upheld the death sentence when the judge had plenty of evidence to find mitigating circumstances but did not.[54] Four years later, the court rejected some aggravating factors but upheld the death sentence when there were "only" two mitigating circumstances: youth and the absence of a criminal record.[55]

Eventually the federal appeals court expressed dismay at the Florida court's forgiving attitude toward trial judges' loose and inconsistent standards. "Guarding against the arbitrary and discriminatory imposition of the death penalty must not become simply a guessing game played by a reviewing court in which it tries to discern whether the improper nonstatutory aggravating factors exerted a decisive influence on the sentence determination," the U.S. Fifth Circuit declared in 1981. "The guarantee against cruel and unusual punishment demands more."[56]

Figure 1. *Before the Reformation:* Vassar Carlton (*center*) was chief justice when the Supreme Court entered a time of scandal in 1973. Carlton resigned under personal stress and negative press attention on March 1, 1974. The least senior justices, David L. McCain (*to Carlton's far right*) and Hal P. Dekle (*to his far left*) resigned amid impeachment hearings in early 1975. *To Carlton's immediate right:* Justices B. K. Roberts and James C. Adkins Jr. *To Carlton's immediate left:* Justices Richard W. Ervin and Joseph A. Boyd Jr. Photo November 15, 1972. Courtesy of the State Archives of Florida, Florida Memory Collection.

Figure 2. *First Merit Selection:* Ben F. Overton was the first justice appointed under Askew's merit selection system, replacing Carlton. At an investiture held in St. Petersburg because of Overton's ailing mother, Overton is congratulated by Governor Reubin Askew as Overton's son and future circuit judge William Overton looks on happily. Courtesy of the State Archives of Florida, Florida Memory Collection.

Figure 3. *First Black Justice:* Joseph W. Hatchett takes the oath of office on September 2, 1975, as Court Clerk Sid White holds a Bible. Justices Boyd and Arthur J. England Jr. are in the background. The empty seat to England's left was Hatchett's. Courtesy of the State Archives of Florida, Florida Memory Collection.

Figure 4. *Proudest Moment:* For the rest of his life, Governor Askew said his appointment of Hatchett was his best decision as governor. At the investiture, Askew joins Hatchett's family—wife Betty Lue and daughters Cheryl and Brenda. Courtesy of the State Archives of Florida, Florida Memory Collection.

Figure 5. *Court in Transition:* Chief Justice Adkins (*seated center*) presided for two years as four new justices, creating a new majority, took their seats in 1974 and 1975. Seated by seniority, B. K. Roberts (*to Adkins's immediate right*) and Joseph Boyd (*to Adkins's immediate left*) remained after the 1974–75 scandal. New justices (*to Roberts's right*) were Ben Overton and Alan C. Sundberg and (*to Boyd's left*) Arthur England and Joseph Hatchett. Courtesy of the State Archives of Florida, Florida Memory Collection.

Figure 6. *First Passover*: Overton (*seated center*) became chief justice in 1976 when the court passed over Boyd (*seated to Overton's left*). That fall, Frederick Karl (*far right*) became the last justice to join the court through election. Others (*from left*): Hatchett, England, Adkins, then Boyd and Sundberg. Standing are Court Clerk Sid White and Marshal Tony Smilgin. Courtesy of the State Archives of Florida, Florida Memory Collection.

Figure 7. *Evolution:* Arthur England (*seated center*) engineered a second passover of Boyd to become chief justice in 1978. Karl's resignation gave Governor Askew one last appointment to the court, James E. Alderman (*far right*). Others (*from left*): Hatchett, Overton, Adkins, Boyd, and Sundberg. Courtesy of the State Archives of Florida, Florida Memory Collection.

Figure 8. *New Governor:* Chief Justice England administers the oath of office to Governor Bob Graham on January 2, 1979, as Graham succeeds Reubin Askew. *Clockwise from Graham's left*: daughters Gwen, Suzanne, and Cissy, and First Lady Adele Graham. Courtesy of the State Archives of Florida, Florida Memory Collection.

Figure 9. *Jousting over Jurisdiction*: England's advocacy for a constitutional amendment on Supreme Court jurisdiction led to a rare and dramatic news conference on February 29, 1980. England illustrated the court's heavy caseload by lining up files of pending death cases. Courtesy of the State Archives of Florida, Florida Memory Collection, Mark Foley, Associated Press.

Figure 10. *Becoming the "Askew Court:"* Alan Sundberg (*front center*) was the third of the Four Horsemen of the Reformation. He followed England as chief. Adkins and Boyd are seated beside Sundberg. *Standing, from left*: Alderman, Overton, England, and McDonald. Courtesy of the State Archives of Florida, Florida Memory Collection.

Figure 11. *Consolidating Change:* The departure of three of the five Askew-era justices brought new faces but did not change the progressive spirit. In this official photo in the lawyer's lounge of the court building, 1983, Chief Justice James E. Alderman is perched in the center. *Clockwise from left,* Adkins, Ehrlich, McDonald, Overton, newest justice Leander J. Shaw Jr., and Boyd. Courtesy of the State Archives of Florida, Florida Memory Collection.

Figure 12. *First Woman Justice:* Rosemary Barkett became the first woman to serve on the Supreme Court when Governor Graham appointed her. Here she takes the oath on November 15, 1985. Courtesy of the State Archives of Florida, Florida Memory Collection.

Figure 13. *First Contested Retention:* Florida Supreme Court Justices Leander J. Shaw Jr., *left,* and Raymond Ehrlich, answered questions on a Tallahassee talk show on November 5, 1984, as they sought to retain their seats on the Supreme Court in the statewide election the next day. Courtesy of the State Archives of Florida, Florida Memory Collection, Mark T. Foley, Associated Press.

Figure 14. *Across the Years:* Justices meet with Florida State University law students in 1986, shortly before the retirements of Chief Justice Boyd, *center*, and Adkins, to Boyd's right, both of whom joined the court in 1969 and served eighteen years. At far right is the newest justice, Rosemary Barkett, appointed in 1986. Other justices, *from left*, are Shaw, McDonald, Overton, and Ehrlich. Overton had the fifth-longest tenure of any justice, retiring in 1999 after nearly twenty-five years. Courtesy of the State Archives of Florida, Florida Memory Collection.

Figure 15. *A Most Convivial Court:* As justices arranged themselves for a group photo in 1987, the first woman justice suggested she take Justice Ehrlich's lap. *From left*, Overton, McDonald, and new justices Steve Grimes and Gerald Kogan share the fun. Courtesy of the State Archives of Florida, Florida Memory Collection.

Figure 16. *Order in the Court:* After their raucous start, the justices of 1987 adopt a more formal pose. *Seated from left*, Overton, Chief Justice McDonald, Ehrlich; *standing from left*, Grimes, Shaw, Barkett, and Kogan. Courtesy of the State Archives of Florida, Florida Memory Collection.

17

THE MACHINERY OF DEATH

From five original appeals of death sentences decided by the Florida Supreme Court in 1974, the number grew to seventeen in 1976 and to twenty in 1979 and 1980, then leaped to forty cases in 1981. A decade after the new law passed, justices estimated that capital cases were 40 percent of the court's workload. Over the twenty-five years following passage of the 1972 law the court would handle 1,900 death cases,[1] an average of six every single month. Direct appeals started backing up. Joseph Spaziano's case, filed in August 1976, wasn't decided until January 1981,[2] and after a resentencing ordered by the Supreme Court, the case was at the court for another sixteen months until the death sentence was upheld on May 26, 1983.[3]

With Governor Graham signing two death warrants per month in the 1980s as part of his popular anti-crime campaign, the post-conviction caseload was growing along with original appeals. A study in 2011 showed that the average time to decision for direct appeals of death sentences between 1968 and 1997 was 2.5 years, ranging from a minimum of three months to a maximum of just under twelve years, the latter in a case decided in 2002.[4] With post-conviction proceedings following the direct appeal, inmates spent an average of 12.68 years on death row. Spaziano, for example, stayed on death row for twenty years before a circuit court vacated his death sentence in January 1996 after a federal appeal.[5]

Richard Ervin, who retired in January 1975, was no longer on the court persistently challenging the reasoning or consistency of the opinions, as he had done in those first cases in 1974. Boyd, the other dissenter in *Dixon*, had been transformed into one of the most reliable votes for death. Even Hatchett, the former civil rights attorney, eschewed the role of consistent death-penalty dissenter taken on by the first black U.S. Supreme Court justice, Thurgood Marshall.

"Everything was new," Overton recalled in 2012. "From 1974 to '84 or '85, we were in many ways breaking new ground on legal issues." Once when he was chief justice, with new death appeals coming at the rate of twenty a year, Overton scheduled a special conference of the justices with twenty-five capital cases on the agenda, all held up by one or more of four issues. One issue was a U.S. Supreme Court decision on the defense right to see pre-sentence reports used by the trial judge in sentencing.

The Florida Supreme Court was a microcosm of the wider social ambivalence about capital punishment. Polls showed strong support in general for the death penalty, but support diminished as other factors were added to the poll questions—killers who were teenagers or mentally ill, doubts about guilt, the inequities inherent in plea bargaining. Those were the sorts of factors the 1972 death-penalty law tried to take into account.

For some people, of course, the focus on guided discretion in sentencing is just liberal intellectualism that ignores a terrible crime against someone who had no chance to argue anything in self-defense. From this perspective, there is nothing "cruel" about the death penalty, and it wouldn't be so "unusual" if the courts would just get out of the way. Supporters of capital punishment therefore simply tried to shut off post-conviction proceedings as much as possible. But when the U.S. Supreme Court struck down death-penalty laws in 1972 and approved new ones in 1976, the concern was not the execution itself but the haphazard selection of which killers would receive it.

Everyone, including the justices, fumed about the capital punishment system. Reform commissions, constitutional amendments, and legislative constraints all were tried in an effort to rein in serial appeals. A Capital Collateral Appeals office was created, with Attorney General Jim Smith arguing that it would actually speed up the appellate process by providing better staffing for defendants' counsel, but that office came to be viewed by death-penalty supporters as part of the problem.

Capital cases were different from other cases at the Supreme Court. The traditional role of an appellate court is to focus on a key legal issue in a case and determine a legal principle that resolves it in a manner consistent with other decisions. Capital cases, by contrast, are highly fact-specific. The Supreme Court acted more like a sentencing review board assessing procedural compliance and facts justifying the sentence. The court rarely articulated any comprehensive assessment or synthesis among seemingly disparate cases, as it had done with manufacturer liability in *West v. Caterpillar Tractor* or with post-divorce property distributions in *Canakaris v. Canakaris*.

After England and Sundberg arrived in 1975, the court was trying to fine-tune procedures to establish some procedural guidelines to simplify decisions and react to U.S. Supreme Court standards. "Arthur and I were being extremely careful" to avoid letting personal views on the death penalty get in the way of applying the law, said Sundberg in an interview with the author in 1983. "It took us maybe three years to flesh that statute out," Sundberg said. "Once we got over those hurdles, we didn't agonize over those issues anymore."

The case law changed as personnel on the court changed. McCain voted to uphold every death sentence he considered in 1975; his successor, Hatchett, voted to uphold just 13 percent of the death sentences he considered in 1976. Roberts voted to uphold more than 75 percent of death sentences on original appeal in 1976, his last year on the court. England and Sundberg, who joined the court in 1975, during 1976 voted to affirm 38.5 and 46 percent, respectively. The proportion of death sentences upheld declined from 59 percent in 1976 to 47 percent in 1977.

Spinkellink (the court system's original spelling of the name) was Boyd's only vote in favor of a death sentence in 1975. But Boyd supported 40 percent of the death sentences in 1976. By 1979, he was supporting death sentences in half the cases. He explained in an interview with the author in 1982 that "when a red file comes in," meaning a death case, he would "sit down like a scientist in a laboratory" to assess it. But he also said the U.S. Supreme Court had decided "Mr. Spenkelink's crime was worthy of death . . . I figure if they [other cases] are as bad as Spenkelink's crime, I don't see a particular reason philosophically to reduce it." Then he added, "However, I measure each one by what I think the statute provides, and the Constitution." Boyd also said in that interview, "I have never found any reason to feel I was wrong in my *Dixon* view, but the case went to Washington and they said there was nothing wrong with the statute, and I did not sing that song any further."

As Boyd's votes for death were reaching new highs, Overton's were moving in the other direction. He had joined Adkins's opinion in *Dixon* and went on to affirm death sentences in two-thirds of the cases during 1975 and 1976. But in 1978, as the U.S. Supreme Court began tightening the rules on capital punishment, Overton became more selective about upholding death sentences. When Justice Parker Lee McDonald arrived in 1979 to replace Hatchett, he and Overton were often dissenters on what they considered the court's inadequate attention to mitigating circumstances, especially the mental condition of the defendants. Overton supported fewer than half the death sentences in 1979 and fewer than a third in 1980.

McDonald was the clear leader on the importance of mitigating circumstances. By 1981 he was setting more exacting standards for both the guilt phase and the sentencing phase, and later was a frequent dissenter, often with Overton, favoring reversal of death sentences because of mitigating circumstances. He was far ahead of the other justices in taking diminished mental capacity seriously; he usually found himself on the dissenting side.

In *Harich v. State*,[6] McDonald in a dissent said a psychologist had given uncontroverted testimony that Roy Harich was under the influence of extreme mental or emotional disturbance and had substantially impaired capacity to appreciate the criminality of his conduct. The trial judge had ignored this evidence and failed to address nonstatutory circumstances that Harich offered. The majority opinion ignored the issue, and Harich was executed on April 24, 1991. In *Spaziano v. State*, McDonald in dissent noted that evidence of Spaziano's mental condition was an adequate basis for the jury's recommendation of life. Then, alluding to the case name in the original appeal, "Joseph Robert Spaziano, a/k/a Crazy Joe, Appellant," McDonald memorably added, "After all, Spaziano was known as Crazy Joe."[7]

In *Fitzpatrick v. State*,[8] McDonald cited the defendant's dull-normal intelligence, a juvenile record reflecting a lack of conformity to rules, his age (twenty), and testimony about a schizoid personality. Fitzpatrick considered himself a genius, invented things and sought patents, rode a bus to commit a bizarre bank hold-up he planned, went into a realty office to find a hostage to use as a shield, and was interrupted by a delivery boy. He ended up killing a police officer who stormed the place. McDonald said Fitzpatrick was dangerous and "should never be on the streets again," but dissented from his colleagues' agreement with the trial judge that there were no mitigating factors.

One of the biggest surprises about the new death-penalty structure created in 1972 was the significant number of death sentences imposed by trial judges after juries recommended life. Before the 1972 statute, a jury vote for life would have been final. Now it was often being given little weight at all.

The Supreme Court tried to draw a bright line for trial judges in *Tedder v. State*[9] on November 19, 1975. It was a per curiam opinion, but it was in fact written by England, who as a new justice was struggling to bring some order out of what he viewed as the chaos of past death-penalty decisions. Mack Tedder was convicted of killing his mother-in-law in Hernando County, and the jury recommended a life sentence. The judge overrode that recommendation and imposed a death sentence. On appeal, the court upheld the conviction but reversed the death sentence. "Great weight" needs to be given to jury recommendations of life, the court said. "In order to sustain a sentence of death following a jury recommendation of life, the facts suggesting a sentence of death should be so clear and convincing that no reasonable person could differ."[10] To impose death, the trial judge was being asked to declare that the jurors, who had just unanimously convicted the same defendant of first-degree murder "beyond a reasonable doubt," were "unreasonable" in setting a sentence. It seemed to be a very high standard indeed.

As it turned out, *Tedder* had only a marginal effect on trial judges and even at the Supreme Court itself. Before Tedder there had been twenty overrides of life recommendations by trial judges—an average of 6.7 per year. The Supreme Court upheld about a fourth of those, less than half the rate for affirming cases in which juries recommended death.

In the twenty-five years after *Tedder*, trial judges overrode 145 more "life" recommendations—an average of 5.8 per year. The Supreme Court continued to uphold about a fourth of these, even though some clearly did not meet the test articulated in *Tedder*, that "no reasonable person" could have decided as the jury had.

The *Dixon* case provided no analysis of the aggravating and mitigating factors listed in the statute. The national Model Penal Code, the source of many of the factors, offered abundant elaboration and examples of each factor, but Adkins didn't mention it. One aggravating factor, for example, was that the defendant "knowingly" created a "great risk of death or bodily harm to many persons." Said Adkins: "We feel that a man of ordinary intelligence and knowledge easily conceives the concepts involved." Although he offered no examples as guidance, circumstances like a bomb at a major venue or a shootout on a crowded sidewalk come to mind.

It would not be long, however, before the court would apply "great risk to many" in the *Proffitt* case when a man was stabbed once while in bed with his wife, with no one else in the house except the killer.[11] From there the court zigged and zagged. In March 1979 in *Kampff v. State,* faced with a shooting in a donut shop where two customers were present but uninjured, the court rejected the factor by saying "a great risk to many persons" means "more than . . . some degree of risk . . . to a few persons."[12] But eleven weeks later in *Lucas v. State,*[13] which was pending when *Kampff* was decided, the factor was applied to a "raging" gun battle that injured the two bystanders present. Eighteen months after that, without a mention of *Lucas*, the factor was rejected for a gun battle with three people present.[14] In a 1980 case, Amos Lee King, after brutally raping and killing a sixty-eight-year-old woman who lived alone, had set her house on fire. The court said the fire posed a "great risk to many persons,"[15] such as neighbors and firefighters.

In 1984 in *Lusk v. State,*[16] three justices said a prisoner's stabbing of another inmate in a prison lunchroom posed a great risk to many because it might have resulted in a prison riot, and they noted the *King* case had "modified" the definition used in *Kampff*. A majority of justices rejected that factor but upheld the Lusk death sentence on other grounds despite a jury recommendation of life. The 4–3 split on "great risk to many," a full decade after the first death sentences came to the court, demonstrates the continuing internal disagreement over the meaning of the phrase. In 1987, after a federal court ordered a new sentencing hearing for Amos King, the Supreme Court said the case was "a far cry from one where this factor could properly be found."[17] (King's death sentence was upheld on other grounds, and King was executed on February 26, 2003.)

Another aggravating factor, "previous conviction of a felony," might seem clear enough in focusing on repeat criminals, but for a time the court said it included felonies that happened at the same time as the capital murder being tried. The first such ruling was in *Hardwick v. State* in 1984 on a 4–3 vote, with Justice McDonald writing a dissent saying the legislature did not intend for "contemporaneous behavior to be counted as a prior history of violence."[18] In 1988, in *Perry v. State*, the court unanimously decided to "recede" from its earlier view,[19] but continued to count as a "previous conviction" a simultaneous felony involving other victims in the same episode, such as the shooting of a police officer as the defendant left the scene of a murder.

The most subjective factor in the statute was that the murder was "especially heinous, atrocious or cruel." A memorable example is, again, the Amos King case, *King v. State*, where the killer had torn the elderly victim's vagina with knitting needles and inflicted burns, bruises, a brain hemorrhage, stab wounds and a broken neck.[20] Another was *Rutledge v. State*,[21] where the evidence included a twenty-three-minute tape recording made by a telephone operator when a victim called for help. The mother and her three children are screaming and begging for mercy as the killer taunts them and butchers them, and then the father comes in and is obviously wandering from room to room wailing over what he found. Jesse Ray Rutledge's death sentence was upheld. England dissented without explanation. In 1983 Governor Graham commuted Rutledge's sentence to life because of evidence he was not the one who committed the crime.

Adkins had noted in *Dixon* that people might find almost any murder "heinous, atrocious or cruel" but said the statute (which requires that the act be "especially" so) is designed to have a narrower application. What would that be, exactly? The court upheld a finding of heinousness in one case when a victim suffered before dying[22] and reversed it in another case when a victim suffered before dying.[23] Heinousness was found when a victim was asleep[24] but not when a victim was waking from a nap.[25] It was heinous when Lenson Hargrave fired a third, fatal shot into a store clerk[26] but not when Antonio Menendez fired two fatal shots into a jewelry store owner.[27] A beating might,[28] or might not,[29] make a murder heinous. Sometimes heinousness would be based on suffering or anticipation of death.[30] If death was instantaneous, heinousness might be based on the "execution style" of the murder.[31]

In the earliest days, actually, the court all but ignored the law's limitation on aggravating factors. On the same day the court first upheld Spenkelink's death sentence in 1975, the court also upheld the death sentence of Anthony Eugene Sawyer, whose gun had gone off during a liquor-store holdup and killed the owner's son. A jury convicted him of murder but recommended a life sentence. The judge imposed death, and Overton wrote an opinion upholding that sentence. Overton properly noted the commission of the robbery as an aggravating factor, but he also cited factors not listed in the statute: thirteen arrests with no conviction, Sawyer's drug habit, and Sawyer's threats of reprisal against participants in his trial. Overton took no notice of the statute's specific list of factors. He also attached no significance to the jury recommendation of life, even though the *Taylor* case, decided a few months earlier, had cited the failure to consider a life recommendation as the reason for overturning a death sentence.[32]

Six years later, England commented that Sawyer's death sentence "in all probability would today be vacated."[33] England called it a "change of law." In fact, even at the time, *Sawyer* was clearly at odds with the words of the statute, with the rationale in *Dixon,* and with the precedent in *Taylor.* When England made the comment, Sawyer was still on death row awaiting execution. There was no procedure for the Supreme Court to reopen an old case except through post-conviction appeals, and the court quickly made clear it was not going to apply new refinements to old sentences. When other justices would say of Spenkelink's case what England said of Sawyer's, Boyd would often respond, "What do we do, go out and dig up Spenkelink?"

Armed with England's opinion, however, Sawyer's lawyer went to the trial judge and filed a "motion for mitigation of sentence." The judge reexamined the case and reduced the death sentence to life. It was a simple procedure. The Supreme Court soon outlawed it.

Boyd law clerk Randall Reder tried to create a database of death cases noting which aggravating and mitigating factors were found in each case, but it does not appear to have been used outside Boyd's office or maintained.[34] Another Boyd law clerk, Jim Logue, took up the challenge of more clearly defining the aggravating and mitigating factors. Logue had a heavy role in drafting Boyd's opinions. Boyd and Logue co-authored a law review article that did what *Dixon* should have done: define the listed factors and illustrate their application.[35] Instead of oratorical flourishes like Adkins's "never again" hyperbole in *Dixon*, the circuit judges and lawyers around the state needed specifics, and needed them in some organized presentation that promoted consistent practice. It never happened. The Boyd-Logue analysis never made its way out of the law review article and into any opinion, even Boyd's.

In his very first opinion in a death case, *Alvord v. State*,[36] in September 1975, England reviewed the capital cases of the previous three years. "These cases range from love triangle deaths to execution type slayings," he wrote. "Perhaps it would be possible to analyze each of these cases, together with the life sentences we have never reviewed, and conclude that Florida's trifurcated sentencing procedure [trial, sentencing, and appellate review] exhibits a non-discriminatory pattern consistent with the dictates of *Furman*. I cannot, however."[37]

England later referred to that opinion as "a letter to the U.S. Supreme Court to tell us this is constitutional." That court responded, as England put it with a touch of sarcasm, "You're doing a great job in Florida. You're narrowing it nicely."[38]

Less than five months after upholding the Florida statute in *Proffitt*, the U.S. Supreme Court heard oral arguments in *Gardner v. Florida*. Daniel Wilbur Gardner had been convicted of brutally murdering his wife after a day-long drinking spree. He had pulled hair from her head and sexually assaulted her with a broomstick. The next morning, he sought help when his wife could not be revived, wept when he realized she might be dead, and waited for police to arrive.

The jury, after weighing the aggravating and mitigating circumstances presented, recommended a life sentence. The trial judge, however, ordered a presentence investigation by the Probation and Parole Commission. Without showing a "confidential" section of the report to Gardner's lawyers, the judge overruled the jury, declared that there were no mitigating circumstances to weigh against the heinousness of the crime, and sentenced Gardner to death. Gardner's lawyers never asked to see the confidential portion, but the lawyers on appeal argued that the defendant's inability to see and challenge the information deprived him of "due process of law."

The Florida Supreme Court didn't even mention the issue in its per curiam opinion,[39] issued February 26, 1975, one week after the *Spinkellink* case. Perhaps the majority considered the issue waived by the defense lawyer's failure to ask to see the report. But Ervin, joined by Boyd, wrote a dissenting opinion. The defendant's drunkenness, they said, clearly established a mitigating factor, that "the capacity of the defendant to appreciate the criminality of his conduct or to conform his conduct to the requirements of the law was substantially impaired." Ervin said "a crime of passion in a marital setting in which the excessive use of alcohol was a material factor . . . traditionally has not resulted in the death penalty in this state."[40]

Ervin also said the confidential portion of the report included law enforcement statements calling the defendant a "menace to society" and noted a record of convictions, none of which was for a violent crime as the list of aggravating factors required. The defendant had been given no opportunity to challenge the accuracy or legal effect of the information. If the jury's advisory role is going to be meaningful, Ervin said, the judge cannot base his decision on something the jury didn't consider.

The U.S. Supreme Court, with only Justice Rehnquist dissenting, said the Florida Supreme Court had failed to meet its own announced standard of care in reviewing death sentences. The sentencing process, not just the trial, must follow standards of due process, Justice John Paul Stevens wrote. "It is of vital importance to the defendant and to the community that any decision to impose the death sentence be, and appear to be, based on reason rather than caprice or emotion." He also noted that the confidential part of the report wasn't even in the record on appeal that the Florida Supreme Court considered. "Without full disclosure of the basis for the death sentence," the Florida capital sentencing procedure would be just as capricious as the one struck down in 1972.[41] Justice Marshall went further and said the Florida court had "engaged in . . . [a] 'cursory or rubber-stamp review' that . . . *Proffitt* trusted would not occur."[42]

The court rejected the argument by Assistant Attorney General Wallace Allbritton that, since the *Gardner* case happened before the *Proffitt* decision, the U.S. Supreme Court should not apply the *Proffitt* standards of careful review in reviewing Gardner's appeal. Allbritton's argument echoed the "change of law" theme the Florida Supreme Court used to rationalize weaknesses in past decisions.

Gardner's original appeal had been a perfect opportunity for the Florida Supreme Court to examine the relationship of aggravating and mitigating factors—in this case, the mental condition of the defendant as a contributor to the heinousness of the crime—as well as the importance of the jury recommendation, which might well reflect that relationship. Obvious as the mitigating factors apparently were to Gardner's jury, the Supreme Court's opinion offered nary a word on the matter.

The U.S. Supreme Court's reversal of Daniel Gardner's death sentence was something of a shock. The Florida court had been deferring a great deal to trial judges. As far as most trial judges were concerned, all the Supreme Court seemed to require under the 1972 statute was that they let a jury vote first and then write a sentencing order that checked off, without elaboration, factors from the statute. And the U.S. Supreme Court in *Proffitt* seemed to be saying that was okay.

The Florida court responded to *Gardner v. Florida* by issuing a series of so-called *Gardner* orders to trial judges to reconsider death sentences if undisclosed information had been used the first time. Gardner himself was resentenced by the trial court to life in prison.

Three years after the U.S. Supreme Court in *Gardner* had objected to the Florida court's nonchalance about judges' use of evidence defense lawyers had not seen, the Florida Supreme Court itself was caught routinely soliciting psychological reports on capital defendants without any notice to defense counsel.

The practice was discovered when Overton referred to one of the reports during an oral argument in the spring of 1979 in the case of Paul Magill. "We have a copy of a psychological screening report," Overton said to the assistant attorney general, "and [it] says in part that he [Magill] feels very limited control in stressful situations . . . and then also shows that he will become possibly suicidal." Magill's lawyer, Margaret Good, said she didn't know of the report. When she asked for a copy the next day, the clerk's office told her it had been "stricken" from the record of the case.

Overton's question at oral argument and a subsequent story in the *St. Petersburg Times*[43] led to a mass appeal by 123 death row inmates challenging the practice as a violation of *Gardner*. Margaret Good even urged Spenkelink's lawyers to add the issue to their last-minute effort for a stay, but David Kendall declined because there was no indication the court had obtained a psychological profile on Spenkelink.

Overton's comments in the first *St. Petersburg Times* article as well as his later handwritten draft opinion in the case show clearly that the court intentionally sought the profiles in question. Overton implied that it was a reaction to the fact that the presentence report and psychiatric profile on Gardner himself had not been included in the original Gardner appeal file, so the court undertook to get them directly from the Probation and Parole Commission. By Overton's account, the court clerk who wrote the request asked for the "latest" report, not necessarily the one the trial judge had used. And a request possibly intended just for Gardner became a routine.

It does not appear to have been a secretive request; Overton asked about a report in oral argument, after all. It is entirely plausible that the documents seemed to him to be simply from the trial judge's sentencing. The psychological profiles might have offered some additional information about a defendant's mental state. But it was at least as likely that the information on Magill and others would be used as Gardner's own psychological information was— to justify a death sentence, ensuring that someone so unbalanced would have no chance to be on the loose again. Either way, the use seemed inconsistent with the *Gardner* requirement of giving the parties a chance to address the information.

The challenge became known as *Brown v. Wainwright*; Joseph Green Brown was the first challenger alphabetically, and Louie L. Wainwright was head of the state prison system.[44] The court's ruling, in a per curiam opinion, appears to have been a cobbling-together of a partial explanation from Overton, who was chief when the court first requested the profiles, and a rhetorical counterattack against critics by Sundberg, who was chief when the opinion was issued. A draft of a section for the opinion, in Overton's handwriting, was in his confidential files on the case, which were made available by the court on request in 2013. Nothing about the case was in Sundberg's files at the court, but many of the passages reflect Sundberg's vocabulary and style. In interviews for this book, Justices Overton, England, McDonald, and Alderman all said they no longer remember the drafting of the opinion.

The controversy seemed to frustrate the justices intensely. They had little tolerance for post-conviction motions anyway, and this broad attack by 123 death row inmates could lead to another round of *Gardner* hearings, this time focused on the Supreme Court's own error. Instead of just confessing an honest misunderstanding, however, the court's published opinion was a broadside attack on defense lawyers and the media coverage and gave a self-contradictory account of its own actions. The opinion was petulant and internally inconsistent in rejecting the challenge without ever explaining factually how the court came to be collecting the psychological profiles, why it did so, or how it had used them. The opinion referred to defense lawyers' "assertion" that the profiles were collected, to the "alleged impropriety" of doing so, and to "strident characterizations of our receipt of these materials."

"Regrettably, the thunderous emanations of this great debate, and the manner in which this joint petition was presented to the court, have cast a pall on the integrity of the painful process by which the court attempts to deal with the responsibility it has been assigned," the opinion says. "It seems to us both unwarranted and unseemly to vilify those who endeavor to follow the constitution; we are, after all the messengers, not the message."[45]

The court cited a Kentucky case that distinguished between "individualized information, pertaining to the defendant personally, which is to be considered by a trial judge," and "impersonal data" such as law review articles and philosophical or religious materials "that may be used by an appellate court."[46] It is an odd passage, because the issue in Brown was "individualized information," not material from a library. "A remaining question is whether the reading of non-record documents would so affect members of this court that they could not properly perform their assigned appellate functions. Plainly, it would not."

Having declared that it "plainly" did not consider anything it shouldn't consider, the court inserted a passage from Overton that the challenged information "was, as counsel concedes, in every instance obtained to deal with newly-articulated procedural standards." But which was it? Did the court disregard the material because it was outside the record, or did it use the material to comply with new standards? If the court didn't realize the material did not belong in the record, how would it know to disregard it? In another twist, the court said it didn't need the information anyway—and indeed, the day after the Magill argument, the court started sending back any new reports it received from probation officials.

In contrast with the aspirational assurances of Dixon and declarations about its assessment of the "total record" of a case,[47] Brown declared that the Supreme Court's role is limited. It didn't matter if the court had reviewed the profiles, because its role was not to "reweigh" evidence but only to look for "procedural regularity" and proportionality among death sentences.[48] "The issue, as in Brown, was, is it the function of the Supreme Court to weigh aggravating and mitigating circumstances," Sundberg said in an interview shortly after the decision. "I concluded no. It is never the appellate court's function to reweigh evidence."

"Proportionality," though, has never been given any serious definition or analysis by the court in its opinions. How does one choose the cases to compare? If there are two identical crimes, one by a middle-aged killer on a crime spree and another by a twelve-year-old altar boy, is it "proportional" to give them the same sentence? What if one victim was a drifter and the other a prominent and beloved civic leader? Is Boyd's Spenkelink standard really the benchmark?

And what is "procedural regularity?" How free is a trial judge to ignore uncontroverted evidence of mitigation? Must a trial judge explain the applicability of the factors and how they are weighed?

The U.S. Supreme Court turned away an appeal in *Brown*. Two years later, the issue reached the U.S. Eleventh Circuit Court of Appeals in a separate post-conviction appeal, *Ford v. Strickland*.[49] Chief Judge John C. Godbold noted the "intractable ambiguity" of the *Brown* opinion and said the court should have provided a direct statement of whether and how it had used the materials it collected. But the federal court declared itself powerless to inquire into the internal workings of Florida's highest court. The vote was 6–5, with an abstention by Judge Hatchett, who had participated as a Florida justice in Ford's original appeal.

Joseph Green Brown himself later came within fifteen hours of execution on his conviction of raping and killing thirty-four-year-old Earlene Barksdale, who had five children and owned a Tampa clothing shop. Brown was to be executed on October 17, 1983, and had been fitted for a burial suit and rejected a last meal when a federal judge ordered a stay. The main state witness at Brown's trial, who had denied on the witness stand that he had gotten a deal from the prosecution, was now saying he lied. He now said he and Brown had held up a Holiday Inn but did not kill the woman in the dress shop. There was no other evidence linking Brown to the murder—no fingerprints, no blood matches, no ballistics evidence. The bullet that killed Mrs. Barksdale could not have come from the gun used in the hotel robbery, but the prosecutor had told jurors that gun was the murder weapon.

The federal judge ordered a new trial. Lacking evidence, prosecutors in Hillsborough County set Brown free. For two decades afterward, Brown went around giving motivational speeches in churches and civic groups. Mixing religion and opposition to capital punishment, he told people to live right and stay out of jail. He even testified before a congressional subcommittee. Then, on September 13, 2012, Brown's wife of twenty years, Mamie Brown, was found dead in their apartment in Charlotte, N.C., The next day, Joseph Brown was charged with first-degree murder, a capital offense. He eventually pleaded guilty to second-degree murder and was sentenced to 15–19 years in prison.[50]

18

THE "E" SEAT

Ervin to England to Ehrlich

Arthur England and Alan Sundberg both left the court after less than eight years, both pressured by personal financial challenges as their children entered their college years. Each departure prompted a new nominating process.

England left on August 9, 1981, and returned to law practice in Miami, in appellate practice rather than tax law. He needed the money, but he was also feeling that eight years of dramatic change in the courts and the case law were giving way to a less exciting era. He joined his former firm, Steel, Hector & Davis, though later he became managing partner of friend Martin Fine's law firm, Fine Jacobson, and finally joined Greenberg Traurig.

Soon after leaving the court England divorced his first wife and lived in spartan bachelor quarters in Miami as his finances slowly recovered. One day at a gas station he ran into a former Sundberg law clerk, Deborah Miller, who had been lured to Miami from Orlando to take on some of prominent litigator Tobias Simon's cases after his death. He asked her out. She had to get used to not calling him "Justice England." They were married March 31, 1988, and had two children, Rachel and Aaron, in addition to the four girls England had from his previous marriage.

One of the members of the nominating commission to fill the England vacancy was James Apthorp, who had been Governor Askew's chief of staff, then became an executive of a development company. Apthorp had worked in the gubernatorial campaign of John E. Mathews Jr. in 1964 and become a friend of one of Mathews's law partners, Raymond Ehrlich, who had since become a prominent and highly regarded lawyer in Jacksonville. Now, seventeen years later, Apthorp called Ehrlich and urged him to apply for the opening on the Supreme Court. Ehrlich dismissed the idea. Apthorp called again. Ehrlich thought about it some more. On the deadline, he sent in his application.

There were thirty-eight applicants, the best known of them being University of Florida Law Professor Robert T. Mann, former legislator and judge and recent chairman of the Public Service Commission. Nine district court judges, including Stephen Grimes, Alan Schwarz and Harry Lee Anstead, applied. So did sixteen circuit judges. Two of the thirty-eight were black and six of them women. Charlotte Hubbard, chair of the commission, said she had a stack of a hundred letters advocating one applicant or another. Three women's groups had written her to urge that a woman be selected. "This is a process of merit selection, and we're going to choose on the basis of merit," she declared. The names we submit will be deemed to be fully qualified. We were not elected by anybody. If he (the governor) wants to use other considerations, that's up to him."[1]

In his interview with the Judicial Nominating Commission in late August, one of the first such sessions open to the public, Ehrlich addressed his lack of judicial experience by saying he "would be short on administration, but I hope I would be long on judgment, humility and compassion." Surprisingly, in light of his career representing insurance interests, Ehrlich expressed admiration for U.S. Supreme Court Justices Oliver Wendell Holmes and Benjamin Cardozo, both of whom were considered liberals and supporters of change. Although he thought the interview did not go well (Apthorp agreed with that, but still urged his selection), the commission nominated him along with appeal court judges Grimes and Schwartz.

As always, the governor received an abundance of letters about the nominees. Lawyers representing accident victims were strongly for Schwartz. Lawyers representing corporations and insurance companies split between Grimes and Ehrlich. There were a lot of letters from Jacksonville urging the Ehrlich appointment and saying that Jacksonville had been under-represented on the court. While Adkins, from Alachua County, already satisfied the new requirement of a justice from the First Appellate District, Jacksonville lawyers argued that the only justice from Jacksonville since the elder John E. Mathews died in office on April 30, 1955, had been Joe Hatchett, serving 1975–79, and he seemed to identify more with Clearwater, his hometown. Sundberg had been born in Jacksonville and went to high school there, but his professional life had been in St. Petersburg, so for the Ehrlich advocates, Sundberg didn't count either.

Ehrlich's parents, Ben and Esther Ehrlich, were Russian Jews who fled Czar Nicholas's pogroms before the Marxist revolution. When they arrived in the United States, they pursued the one thing they knew: selling merchandise.

They wound up in Swainsboro, a country town in southeast Georgia between Macon and Savannah, where they ran a dry goods store. Ray was born there on February 2, 1918—Groundhog Day, he liked to note. "Ray Ehrlich was a child of freedom," Ben Overton said many years later.

The family soon moved to Florida in pursuit of the greater financial promise of the Florida boom and settled in an even smaller town, Crescent City, on U.S. 15 southwest of St. Augustine and south of Palatka. It was a town with no dry goods store. Benny Ehrlich joined with a man named Jack Warner to start E&W Store on Central Avenue. The family moved into a stucco house on Prospect Avenue. "The state of morality was such in Crescent City that you couldn't really do much without the whole town knowing about it," Ray Ehrlich told the local newspaper years later after his nomination for the court.[2]

When the Depression hit, times were tough. Ray, who had worked in the store during high school, lost his $68 savings when the local bank failed. Ray set a goal of learning a new word every day and was valedictorian of his Class of 1935 at little Crescent City High School, though he noted modestly that there were only "eight or nine" in the class and only one or two others went to college.

At age seventeen, he went off to the University of Florida. His older brother Matthew had gone to the University of Pennsylvania, but times were harder now. His parents put a high value on education. Ray studied, avoided playing around, and helped friend Stephen C. O'Connell, the future justice and UF president, run for student government president. Despite taking a semester off to run the family store when his father fell ill, he graduated on time with high honors in 1939. His father eventually sold the store but still would show up there every morning at 7:30 and work a full day without pay.

Ray's early interest was not law but medicine, traceable to a chemistry professor in high school. He majored in chemistry at the University of Florida but had other interests as well—politics, even the International Relations Club and the Anti-War League. After disappointing himself with a B in chemistry, he decided he didn't like chemistry so much after all and turned to law. At UF law school, it is said, he was known as "the brain."[3] He got his law degree in 1942, shortly after the United States entered World War II, then joined the U.S. Navy.

After his discharge as a lieutenant commander in 1946, he was looking for a job. His last interview in Jacksonville one day was with J. Henson Markham, who offered Ehrlich a salary of $125 a month to join Osborne, Copp & Markham. Ehrlich took it. "He liked to talk, and I perceived that part of my job was to listen to him. He wanted a sounding board," Ehrlich told an interviewer with the Samuel Proctor Oral History Project in 1990. Markham believed in his client's causes and worked seven days a week, billing ten dollars an hour in those days before highly compensated law firms.

Markham put a premium on professional ethics. He was "utterly intolerant of lawyers that deviated from the strict code," Ehrlich said. "He indelibly impressed on me what it was to be a lawyer." His work for Markham was important in another way. Ehrlich left law school wanting to be a trial lawyer, but he had not anticipated representing corporations and insurance companies. "That was not my philosophy," Ehrlich said years later, but that's who Markham's clients were: Liberty Mutual Insurance, CNA predecessor Continental Insurance, Zurich Insurance, and others. The firm, though not Markham himself, also represented Southern Railway and oil and mining companies. By 1951 the firm was known as Osborne, Copp, Markham & Ehrlich.

After a heart attack, Markham's health gradually declined, and Ehrlich began trying his cases, though he continued calling Markham "the boss." In 1956 a young lawyer friend of Ehrlich's, John E. "Jack" Mathews Jr., son of the late justice, was elected to the legislature and would need some help in his law practice. He talked to Ehrlich about practicing law together. Markham told Ehrlich to "go on and do what you want to do," and Ehrlich could have simply left and taken many of the clients with him. "I am not going to leave you," he told Markham. Mathews went into partnership with John McNatt instead.

But McNatt decided he wanted to be a judge, and Mathews figured he could help because of his family's relationship with the governor, LeRoy Collins. That would leave young Mathews back where he started, in need of a law partner, so Mathews went back to Ehrlich and to Henry Osborne Jr., another young lawyer in the firm and son of the senior partner, Henry P. Osborne, who was easing toward retirement. Ehrlich agreed this time, but insisted that Markham come with them. "He was my friend and he gave me a job when there were not many jobs around," Ehrlich said. "I was loyal to him, and I could never walk away. He stayed with us until he died in 1964. He was a philosophical guy. He was not a money grubber, ever. . . . He never had any money. I learned an awful lot from him. He was a mentor, particularly in the law. . . . I have given a lot of young lawyers, or law students, counsel, and I have done nothing more than pass on to them what he gave me."

The senior Osborne came, too. It was a great arrangement. Mathews inherited McNatt's insurance clients, brought political connections, and had an explicit agreement with his partners that he could take time off for politics.

Osborne got his father's corporate clients, such as Texaco, Gulf Oil, Equitable Life, and Sun Life. Ehrlich got Markham's insurance clients. They became Mathews, Osborne & Ehrlich, often referred to by other lawyers as MOE.[4] Mathews served in the House of Representatives and went on to run for governor in 1964, losing to Jacksonville Mayor Haydon Burns, and in 1970, losing to Askew. In between, Mathews served in the Florida Senate and was Senate President for 1969–70.

Ehrlich had a reputation as a tireless worker: he was in the office before anyone else and still there when others had gone. Nobody made real money representing insurance companies, Ehrlich said later. "It is like a barber. The only way you can make money is you have to cut more heads of hair. We had to work longer hours, because they did not pay you the same rate. It was always a reduced rate."[5]

The serious law student who rarely went to parties had become an eligible and seemingly determined bachelor. By 1967, when Ehrlich was forty-nine, his father had died and his mother was in the River Garden nursing home in Jacksonville. One Sunday when he arrived for a visit, he was joined in the elevator by an attractive woman a decade younger than he. She was there to visit her uncle, and before leaving that day, Ray found out from the nurses that she was Mickey Bettman and that she visited her uncle there on Saturdays, though this one time she had come on Sunday instead. Ehrlich began visiting his mother on Saturdays. One Saturday he finally invited Mickey to dinner that evening, and she said she would go but would have to bring along her four children. He learned that Mickey's first husband, Henry Bettman, had been a stockbroker and Mickey had been a stay-at-home mom and a substitute teacher. After her husband died suddenly of an aneurysm at age thirty-eight, she was left to support and raise their four children. Her husband's employer, Thomson-McKinnon Securities, offered her a job. "Maybe they thought I'd keep some of his accounts, which I did," she told the *Florida Times-Union* years later.[6] In fact, she had about four hundred clients by 1981.

Ehrlich soon became a regular part of her life and her family. The youngest child, Carol, was nine. "I grew up thinking of him as my dad," she said. But the two busy people did not decide to marry until Carol was heading off to college. They struggled to set a date when both would be free. Ehrlich was in the midst of defending the City of Jacksonville and the Duval County Sheriff in a federal lawsuit filed by the surviving children of convicted murderer Ernest Dobbert, later executed for abusing and killing his daughter. The Dobbert children said the authorities were negligent in investigating reports of the abuse, and the high-profile case was settled halfway through the trial for $1 million. The couple managed to find one date they would both be sure to be off duty: Thanksgiving Day in 1975. Ehrlich was fifty-seven.

MOE was prospering. Mathews left politics after serving as President of the Florida Senate and losing his second run for governor, and turned his full attention to the law firm, which began commanding premium rates to non-insurance clients. The practice of law was becoming far more competitive, but Ehrlich refused to engage in sharp practice or play games with opposing counsel, like flooding the other side with pretrial discovery demands. When another MOE lawyer did that, Ehrlich told him, "How would you like it if I did that to you?"

By 1981 the firm had grown to two dozen lawyers, including one of Mickey's sons, Jack Bettman. He recalled the large, immaculately neat office with a spacious adjoining conference room occupied by Jack Mathews, and his step-father's more modest office, with files covering the desk as well as the floor, though Ehrlich knew where every file was. Ehrlich brought lunch from home, ate at his desk, then allowed himself a never-to-be-disturbed nap of twenty or thirty minutes on the couch in his office.

In failing health, Mathews retired from the law firm in 1981. The place wasn't the same to Ehrlich after that, and he did not relish the administrative responsibilities of senior partner. When Apthorp called about the England vacancy, Ehrlich was sixty-three and ready to turn the leadership over to the next generation of lawyers in the firm. He would take a pay cut. The annual salary of a justice then was $61,500.

In late August, after becoming one of the three nominees, Ehrlich was in Houston taking depositions for a case on behalf of Blue Cross Blue Shield. As he climbed the stairs with two bags in hand, he began feeling chest pains. He would carry his bags a hundred feet, then set them down to rest. As he went through the depositions, he got a call saying Graham wanted to interview him that evening when he got back to Jacksonville. He dropped his bags at his office, then went straight to meet Graham at the Old Orleans Restaurant. Ehrlich saw it as a pleasant interview, including the question about his favorite judges. He said nothing to Graham or his partners about his medical worries. The next day he called his doctor, who ordered tests. Five arteries were blocked. The doctor told Ehrlich he had a 100 percent chance of being dead in five years without bypass surgery.

Ehrlich said he told the others at his law firm he was going out of town and went into the hospital for the surgery, a quintuple bypass. Two hours before the surgery was to begin, he called Graham to tell him, said he would be "very obliged" if the governor would wait "and see whether I come out, whether I am going to live through this thing," but would certainly understand if he didn't want to wait. Five days later, Graham called the doctor, who told him Ehrlich was doing fine. Another three days passed, and Graham called the doctor again. "That made me very appreciative, that he was considering it." Ehrlich went home, heard nothing more for a few days, then was told the governor was on the phone. He picked up and said, "I have a lot of prankster friends, so is this really the governor?" Graham said yes, asked if Ehrlich were still interested, and said he was prepared to offer the appointment. Ehrlich said he was prepared to accept. It was October 14, 1981. Since Ehrlich wanted six weeks to recover and Graham was to be on a trip to Japan in November and wanted to be at the investiture, they set December 3 as the date Ehrlich would join the court.

After hanging up, Graham announced his decision in a press statement. While all three nominees "have exemplary preparation and qualifications," Graham said, Ehrlich "possesses those qualities of integrity, intellect and temperament which I consider essential for a person who sits on the state's highest court." He told a *Miami Herald* reporter that the court needed another practicing lawyer in its midst.

Interviewed by a reporter the evening his appointment was announced, Ehrlich at first didn't quite believe that an announcement had been made just an hour or so after he accepted the job. Assured it was official, he declared that his clients' interests would end when he put on the judicial robe. "No lawyer worth his mettle would take with him to the bench, under his robe, the cause of his clients. This is a new day. They know it. They know me."[7]

Ehrlich became the third "E" justice in that line of succession, replacing England, who had replaced Ervin. None of those three had been judges before joining the court. Ehrlich also was Jewish, replacing the first Jewish justice on the court. At sixty-three, Ehrlich was one of the oldest new justices in the state's history. "The sun was shining on my side of the street," he said of his appointment. "Grimes is a superb jurist. Schwartz is the best. I was the luckiest, that is all. I was the luckiest."[8]

The delay for surgery ended up giving Ehrlich an additional two years of service on the court before mandatory retirement. The Constitution requires that judges stand for a public retention vote at the next general election occurring at least one year after appointment,[9] so his December appointment meant he could skip the November 1982 general election and stand for retention in November 1984. His new six-year term therefore began in January 1985 and ended in January 1991. The Constitution requires retirement of judges by age seventy except "to complete a term, one-half of which has been served."[10] Ehrlich turned seventy in 1988, with slightly less than three years left in the six-year term. Had his retention vote been in 1982 for a term beginning in January 1983, he would have had to retire at the end of a term ending in January 1989, rather than 1991.

Small-framed, still gaunt, and wearing his trademark bow tie, Ehrlich showed up at the Supreme Court driving his 1973 Oldsmobile 98 convertible. The Jacksonville Bar had heavyweight representation at the investiture of this justice its leaders had lobbied so hard for: Florida Bar president-elect James C. Rinaman Jr. of Jacksonville and Jacksonville Bar president Stephen D. Busey. Another speaker at the event was not from the insurance defense side but the plaintiffs' side: Walter H. Beckham Jr. of Miami. As the room quieted just before the justices entered, longtime gadfly and activist Jim Fair stood up and waved a lawsuit he had filed in federal court that day. "What we have here is Fair vs. Ehrlich," Fair said. It complained that the courts were dominated by utilities and noted Ehrlich's connections to Florida Power & Light and other large companies. But Fair stopped and sat down before anyone intervened.

In his own remarks at the end of the program, after taking his seat at Chief Justice Sundberg's far left, Ehrlich spoke of his longtime law partner, the best man at his small wedding. "Jack Mathews touched my life more than any other person," he told the people in the crowded courtroom. "I would never be where I am today if I had not been professionally associated with Jack." He closed by saying to the crowd, "From the bottom of my heart, with its many bypasses, I thank you."

Recovery time was over. The next week, Ehrlich and his six new colleagues faced seventeen oral arguments, ten of them in capital-punishment appeals. There were ten other pending cases on which the vote was 3–3, with majority and dissenting opinions all written, with Ehrlich's vote determining which was which. Half of those were death cases. The court already had decided twice as many original capital appeals that year as it had in 1980. Ehrlich ended up voting on sixteen of the forty original capital appeals decided in 1982 and affirmed five death sentences, the lowest percentage of any of the justices in a year when the court as a whole upheld just over half the death sentences. In the first seven months of 1983, however, he voted on seven death cases and upheld five death sentences, more than any other justice except Adkins.

Early in 1982 the Ehrlichs moved into Killearn Estates across Tyron Circle and a couple of houses down from Overton, who was a couple of houses away from Alderman on the other side. Longtime law clerk Marguerite "Ditti" Davis, who clerked for Roberts, Karl and finally Alderman and was later a First District Court of Appeal judge, also lived nearby. When Grimes joined the court five years later, his backyard backed up to Overton's, and they even cut a gate in their fences to facilitate visits. They jokingly called their short circular street "the compound." They would sometimes carpool, but Ehrlich required that they leave no later than 7:10 a.m. and would not want to leave the court until after 6:30 in the evening. Overton recalled days when he would call his wife to say he would be late because he was riding home with Ray. Often, then, the morning carpool would not include Ehrlich, who had already left. Bypass or no bypass, Ehrlich was not changing his workaholic habits.

He struck up a close and admiring friendship with Sundberg, another brainy justice who also had been a trial lawyer rather than a judge before joining the court. Both had a mischievous sense of humor. Ehrlich, though always gentlemanly, confessed that he as well as Sundberg would sometimes resort to off-color comments—"muleskinner language," he called it—in conferences with other justices. Though he was a millionaire, Ehrlich was also tight with his money, in the way of people who lived through the Great Depression. Perhaps no other chief justice would have counted among his accomplishments his blow for practicality and surprising cost savings in abolishing the use of legal-sized paper in the Florida court system, by an order effective January 1, 1990.

Ehrlich would refer to female law clerks—and later to the first female justice, Rosemary Barkett—as "little lady." But in 1986 he wrote a bold opinion in *Marr v. State* striking down Florida's long-standing practice of instructing juries in rape cases that they should "rigidly scrutinize" the testimony of the victim if there is no other witness to the rape.[11] As chief justice, one of his most prominent initiatives was to create a Gender Bias Study Commission to identify and correct discrimination in the Florida legal system. At a news conference about the findings, he was asked if he had ever engaged in gender discrimination, and he said that he did call the first female justice "little lady." It was a perfect news conference answer—funny, self-effacing, quotable, candid, while totally avoiding the harder issue.

"Ray tried really hard not to do that," Barkett once said, "and he would generally do it when he was being really earnest . . . and trying to convey something." She added with amusement that Ehrlich showed "absolutely no gender bias in terms of whom he chose to tell his jokes to." Barkett was an unabashed admirer. "He was so smart, and he was so thoughtful, and he was so caring," she said. "He was able to bring people together and was so calm about everything he did. At the same time, he had this wicked sense of humor. He would write me notes on the bench, such as, 'Your mother would be very disappointed by how you are treating that litigant.'"[12]

An oft-told story is about the day the justices were posing for a group photograph, some standing, some sitting. Ehrlich asked where they should sit. Barkett flippantly replied, "I should just sit on your lap." "Come on!" Ehrlich said, and not to be out-bluffed, she did. "It is one of the wonderful memories I have of this court," Barkett said later in an interview, "because if you look at the picture, you will see Parker Lee laughing like crazy and Ben laughing like crazy, and Ray laughing. It was a wonderful moment which reflected the collegiality of that particular court."

19

ACCEPTING GAYS

The court took a significant step in advancing gay rights on June 18, 1981, but kept it a secret and even told the lawyer who won not to say anything about it. The court admitted a gay applicant to the Florida Bar and told the Board of Bar Examiners that private consensual sexual conduct was not a proper subject for Bar investigation of moral fitness to be a lawyer. The vote was 5–2, and the philosophies behind the majority and dissenting opinions were still echoing three decades later in the national debate over gay marriage.

The applicant, referred to as N.R.S. to protect his identity, had reported a "4-F" classification under the military draft's Selective Service System. The draft classification meant that a person was "not acceptable" for military service because of "physical, mental or moral" standards, and while the category covered a large number of physical infirmities, local draft boards sometimes used it to reject draft-age men they identified as gay, since the military at the time prohibited gays from serving. The classification was enough to arouse the suspicion of the Florida Board of Bar Examiners.

Summoned for questioning, N.R.S. "admitted a continuing sexual preference for men but refused to answer questions about his past sexual conduct," the court said. After he passed the bar exam, he was called back for more questioning but refused to show up. The examiners rejected his application on moral grounds, and his lawyer appealed to the Florida Supreme Court.

By a 5–2 vote, the court ordered N.R.S. admitted.[1] "Private, noncommercial sex acts between consenting adults are not relevant to prove fitness to practice law," the court said in a per curiam opinion. "The board suggests that an applicant's past homosexual acts are relevant to determine whether past conduct will prevent him from achieving the social acceptance necessary to enable him to discharge his professional responsibilities and whether the applicant intends to disobey the laws of Florida which he seeks to be sworn to uphold," the court said before rejecting that position. The board's inquiries must "bear a rational relationship to an applicant's fitness to practice law."

Still, the court allowed the board to make N.R.S. answer more questions "if, in good faith, it finds a need to assure itself that the petitioner's sexual conduct is other than noncommercial, private, and between consenting adults."

The court regularly issued "confidential" rulings about Bar applicants, and this was one of them. In July, however, a gay-oriented newspaper in Miami and the ACLU of Florida newsletter revealed the opinion, and on September 21, it was reported in the *St. Petersburg Times*.[2] On October 1, at the request of the lawyer for N.R.S., Robert F. Eimers, the court released it to the public.[3]

Eimers himself had been denied admission by the Bar Examiners three years earlier because of his "admitted homosexual orientation" after the board received a letter from out of state about Eimers's sexual orientation. With the help of the ACLU of Florida, Eimers won a Supreme Court order admitting him on a 6–1 vote.[4] Eimers, as the court put it, "is a graduate of an accredited law school, is certified for admission to the Pennsylvania Bar, and has passed all parts of The Florida Bar examination." The Florida Bar Examiners found him qualified "with the possible exception that he may fail to meet the 'good moral character' standard for admission due to his homosexual preference."

The majority for Eimers included all five of the new Askew-era justices—Overton and England, though they concurred only in the result, as well as Sundberg, Hatchett, and Karl. The sixth was Adkins. The court left open the possibility of a different decision if evidence showed that someone actually engaged in homosexual acts. A *New York Times* article said the decision "was believed to be the first in the United States concerning a homosexual's right to practice law, but mainly because other states did not routinely question applicants on the subject."[5] The *Times* article—a copy of which Sundberg kept in his files—also said the American Bar Association had surveyed state bar organizations across the country in 1976 about whether they considered sexual orientation in applications, and forty-five of them responded that they did not. Six states, including Florida, did not respond. Eimers's ACLU attorney, Terry DeMeo, was quoted in the article as saying that Florida applicants often simply lie when asked, because "they were not willing to risk careers to come out of the closet."

Florida's Bar Examiner files on applicants do not become public, but disbarments do, and the Florida Bar clearly had been hostile toward gays. In 1957 the court disbarred Harris L. Kimball, who had been caught one night on a dock at Lake Lorna Doone in Orlando having oral sex with another man. The criminal charge was dropped on the condition that Kimball leave town. Back then he was a young lawyer known for helping blacks accused of crimes in the days before public defenders, but he left town as required. That was not enough for the Bar, however, and the Supreme Court disbarred him on a 5–0 vote. Kimball then held a variety of jobs in New York, and finally, with full disclosure of the episode in Florida, won the right to practice law in New York.[6] He later sued for readmission in Florida, but the Supreme Court required that he first take the Bar exam again. He apparently did not.

In 1970 there was another disbarment over gay sex. The lawyer was convicted of indecent exposure after a police officer witnessed him having sex in the men's room in a public park in Fort Lauderdale. The court also cited "a lack of candor and serious conflicts" between the lawyer's testimony in the criminal case and the disbarment case. Ervin went along but expressed concern about the lack of "a substantial nexus between his antisocial act, or its notoriety, or place of commission, and a manifest permanent inability on respondent's part to live up to the professional responsibility and conduct required of an attorney."[7]

While the Eimers case was over admission to the Bar rather than disbarment, it was still a landmark in 1978. The dissenter was Boyd. "Applicant admits he is a homosexual," Boyd wrote. "I would remand this cause to the Board of Bar Examiners for an inquiry into whether he has committed homosexual acts of the kind criminally outlawed by Section 800.02, Florida Statutes. There should not be admitted to The Florida Bar anyone whose sexual life style contemplates routine violation of a criminal statute."

One problem with that landmark decision was that it did not seem to deter the Board of Bar Examiners. The N.R.S. case three years later was almost indistinguishable from Eimers's in 1978. So now the issue was back. Boyd's view had not changed since 1978, and this time Alderman had joined the court and expressed a similar view. "Because the legislature has chosen, on proper moral grounds, to prohibit homosexual activities, such activities involve moral turpitude as a matter of law," said Boyd. "A proclivity to commit criminal acts involving moral turpitude is clearly a proper basis for questioning whether an applicant has the moral qualifications for admission." He added, "Even without evidence of actual conduct, I am opposed to the admission of any person whose admitted "orientation" indicates a lifestyle likely to involve routine violation of a criminal statute."

Alderman did not join Boyd's dissent. He wrote his own, which Boyd joined, and equated consensual homosexual acts with shoplifting:

How deep should we look into the petitioner's life in order to determine if he is of good moral character? The fact that petitioner, in the past, may have committed homosexual acts would not necessarily exclude him from the practice of law. The same would be true, for example, if petitioner, while in high school, had been convicted of shoplifting. If he were otherwise qualified, if he acknowledges that his past conduct was improper, and if he establishes that he has no intention of repeating his past misconduct, he would not be denied admission because of his past mistake. On the other hand, if petitioner has a recent history of shoplifting and indicates that he plans to continue shoplifting because he sees nothing wrong with what he is doing, most certainly he would be denied admission. We should likewise deny admission to any applicant with a recent history of homosexual activity who indicates that he plans to continue this activity because he sees nothing wrong with what he is doing.

The court's decision in *N.R.S.* provoked the resignation of at least one member of the Board of Bar Examiners. Charles G. Edwards of Tampa, a longtime and respected member of the board, wrote that homosexuality is "considered reprehensible under every significant moral system, secular or religious." He said the decision is "incomprehensible to me" and "places me in a legal and moral dilemma" of having to "honor my oath to recommend only applicants with good moral character and at the same time obey the court's instructions." He resolved the dilemma by resigning.

The day before Edwards's resignation, the court had overturned the board's rejection of an applicant who the court said had shown full rehabilitation after a single cocaine conviction eight years earlier.[8] A Cuban refugee, he had worked his way through Florida State University Law School with high grades, and Sundberg had the view that if redemption and rehabilitation were going to mean anything in Bar admissions, this was the case. Sundberg actually administered the Bar oath to him a few days after the court's decision.

In a response to Edwards, Board Chairman Alexander L. Hinson of Quincy referred to "all of those board members who have for many months now expressed openly to me their sincere discouragement and frustration resulting from repeated reversals of board decisions by the court." Hinson referred to "difficult areas of social change, such as homosexuality and use of marijuana," and to cases based on applicant credibility in which "countless hours of actual and careful scrutiny on our part were seemingly rejected by what appeared to be only a cursory review of the final paper product." Hinson offered no specifics, but the court had been more generous than the examiners in recognizing "rehabilitation" of applicants in earlier opinions.[9]

Edwards's letter also expressed concern about the "confidential" label on opinions, again apparently referring to the *N.R.S.* case. Edwards thought the board would be left in a position of being unable to pursue certain questions without being able to explain why. In a separate response, board general counsel C. Graham Carothers said the board didn't have to explain why it did not ask questions. The opinion "broadens the scope of 'acceptable' conduct" by applicants, Carothers said. He acknowledged that counsel for that applicant favored in a confidential opinion "would enjoy a distinct advantage in representing other applicants" by having knowledge of a court decision that other lawyers did not know about. No one mentioned that other applicants might be deterred by fear of inquiries that were in fact no longer permitted.

Sundberg, as chief justice, received copies of all three letters and kept them in his files but apparently did not respond.[10]

It's not clear that the Board of Bar Examiners even then was fully deterred by the court's decision. Eimers alleged to the *St. Petersburg Times* at the end of September, as decisions from the July Bar exam results were drawing near, that even after the June decision in *N.R.S.*, the board continued to ask questions about homosexuality without any "good faith" belief that the applicant's conduct had been improper under the terms of the *N.R.S.* decision. That same month, Eimers said, a client had been asked whether he thought there was any connection between sex and morality. Carothers responded, while the opinion was still secret, that the board was "absolutely" not violating the court ruling but said he "would not read the purported opinion to mean we can't ask questions."[11]

It wasn't long before the court once again faced the issue of gay rights. The annual appropriations bill passed by the legislature on June 16 and 17 of 1981 contained a proviso that prohibited state funds for any university that "charters or gives official recognition or knowingly gives assistance to or provides meeting facilities for any group or organization that recommends or advocates sexual relations between persons not married to each other." The sponsors, Rep. Tom Bush of Fort Lauderdale and Sen. Alan Trask of Fort Meade, made clear that their intention was to keep gay rights groups off campus. Bush cited a brochure from "a homosexual organization" at Florida State University that "promoted homosexuality" through programs such as "Future Sex" and "Lesbian and Gay Rap Sessions."

The Trask-Bush legislation was languishing in committee until the two revived it as a proviso in the $9.3 billion appropriations bill. It passed after Trask dared fellow senators to cast an "anti-family" vote against it. While the governor has a line-item veto of appropriations, Graham said he did not have authority to veto a proviso as opposed to a spending item even though he opposed the measure.

In August, with the fiscal year already under way, Education Commissioner Ralph Turlington announced that he would challenge the proviso, and the defendants were fellow elected members of what was then a six-member Cabinet—Comptroller Gerald A. Lewis and Secretary of State George Firestone. Assistant Attorney General Thomas R. Tedcastle drew the assignment of defending the proviso, and among other things challenged Turlington's right to spend taxpayer money challenging the provision affecting his education budget.

Circuit Judge John Rudd in Tallahassee upheld the proviso. Trask boasted to a reporter that Rudd's ruling showed the provision was carefully drafted and added, "Contrary to what the gays might say, we are not a couple of Bible-thumping idiots who parked our brains outside of the Legislature before enacting this."[12] The First District Court of Appeal certified an immediate bypass of the appeal to the Supreme Court. The case featured two former presidents and one future president of the American Bar Association. Chesterfield Smith (ABA president 1973–74) and Tallahassee lawyer John Radey represented Turlington. W. Reece Smith (1980–81) and partner Sylvia H. Walbolt, whose husband was a vice president of the University of South Florida, represented USF president John Lott Brown as amicus. Sandy D'Alemberte (1991–92) joined the challenge as a trustee of Miami-Dade Community College and as a "citizen and taxpayer," with law partner Thomas R. Julin as co-counsel.

At oral argument on November 2, 1981, Chesterfield Smith strode to the lectern. If this was combat between Morality and Freedom, he was for Freedom. He began reading from handwritten notes drawn from the brief. "Free speech guarantees apply in Florida and in the United States to unpopular speech as well as popular speech," he said. "The Trask-Bush Amendment cannot be justified because the targeted communications appear to the majority of the Legislature, or perhaps even to the populace as a whole, offensive or sickening or disgusting or immoral."[13]

Boyd interrupted him. The U.S. Supreme Court in 1969 said speech could be prohibited only if it is "directed to inciting or producing imminent lawless action and is likely to incite or produce such action." So, said Boyd, "do you conclude that simply discussing this matter without suggesting immediate action fits the constitutional requirement?"

"When I was—yes, I do," said Smith. He launched into his oration again, but Sundberg stopped him. Maybe the state can't forbid speech, "but does that mean the taxpayers have to provide a forum for all different kinds of speech?" That was the point being pressed by Lewis and Firestone in support of the amendment. Lewis had already launched an investigation about violations of the amendment at the University of South Florida, but it was blocked by a federal court order. Smith responded that a system of higher education "has to permit . . . the right to advocate positions as to what the law should be."

Overton asked if the state could prohibit use of its facilities by a group advocating the use of heroin or cocaine. Not unless the group advocated immediate lawlessness, Smith replied.

Then Michael Coniglio of Lewis's office got up. He said Turlington had no standing to bring this litigation because he was an officeholder, and the state shouldn't have to pay for "the defensive and offensive teams as well as the referees." The justices told Coniglio they weren't interested in that argument and suggested he sit down and let his co-counsel argue the merits. Mitchell Franks of the secretary of state's office stood up and picked up the argument about Turlington's standing. Frustrated, Adkins interrupted. "We're going to get to the merits whether you want to argue them or not." So Franks argued them. He conceded the amendment was loose in its language, but he urged the court to give the amendment a narrow interpretation and uphold it.

It was after the end of the fiscal year, July 15, 1982, before the Supreme Court ruled in *Department of Education v. Lewis*.[14] A first glance at the author of the Supreme Court's opinion might have given them all pause: Joe Boyd. But this was not the same Joe Boyd who was outraged by homosexual conduct earlier that year in the Bar Examiners case. This Joe Boyd was the advocate of free expression and individual rights. The decision was unanimous, with Sundberg, Adkins, Overton, Alderman, McDonald, and Ehrlich all joining Boyd. His opinion, like the proviso itself, never mentions homosexuality. "Through a number of cases decided over many years this court has attempted to make clear to the legislature that, under our constitutional plan for the lawful exercise of governmental powers, an appropriations act is not the proper place for the enactment of general public policies on matters other than appropriations," Boyd wrote. "General appropriations bills should not be cluttered with extraneous matters which might cloud the legislative mind."

This proviso "is not directly and rationally related" to spending on universities and students, Boyd said. That ruling would have been enough to strike the proviso, but Boyd went on to discuss the issue of free expression. "The real purpose of the First Amendment is to protect also the expression of sentiments that the majority finds unacceptable or even unthinkable," he said. "While a state might choose not to establish any state-supported institutions of higher learning, once it has decided to do so, it may not make the privilege of attending contingent upon the surrender of constitutional rights." He invoked the memory of "those who fought in the American Revolution and adopted the Constitution and the Bill of Rights." "Ours is a nation rich in diversity," he said.

The proviso is "unconstitutional and void," Boyd concluded. "The Comptroller is directed to disregard it. The Secretary of State is directed to strike it from chapter 81–206."

20

REAPPORTIONMENT

Where to Draw the Lines

On a crisp and beautiful Saturday afternoon at the end of March in 1982, the Florida Supreme Court was in a special session about special sessions. The courtroom was filled with lawyers and the most powerful people in the Florida Legislature. Senator Dempsey Barron, the former Senate president whose official portrait shows him atop his palomino horse, was there in trademark attire of cowboy boots and a buckskin coat, and called it "a very solemn and important occasion."

As chairman of the Senate Reapportionment Committee, Barron was leading the effort for the court to order the House of Representatives to stay in session and debate the 1982 reapportionment plan instead of passing its version of a plan and going home—which is exactly what the House had done the day before, forcing the Senate to take it or leave it.[1]

The front row on one side of the two-story-high courtroom included House Speaker Ralph Haben of Palmetto in Manatee County and future House speaker and current House reapportionment chairman Lee Moffitt of Tampa. On the other side, the front pew was filled with reporters, and behind them were Barron and Senate President W. D. Childers, Senate president-designate Curtis Peterson of Lakeland, and the Senate's Republican and Democratic leaders, James Scott of Fort Lauderdale and Pete Skinner of Lake City. Representing the Senate that day was a tall, fifty-five-year-old Washington lawyer, Neal P. Rutledge, whose father, Wiley B. Rutledge, had been a justice of the U.S. Supreme Court, appointed by President Franklin D. Roosevelt in 1943.

Rutledge's job at the oral argument that March afternoon: convince at least four of Florida's seven justices that the Constitution's provision requiring a special session for reapportionment "which shall not exceed 30 consecutive days" did not allow the governor to call a session of just four days. Before 1968 the state constitution required the legislature to keep meeting until it came up with a plan. That had caused a mess in 1955–56 when the legislature, unable to agree for its entire two-year term, had its longest and least productive session in all of state history. The 1968 Constitution Revision Commission had tried to avoid that problem but had created a different one. Now, it appeared, the legislature didn't have to work at the problem very long at all. Rutledge said the goal was to "put a cutoff date on it" that would shift the burden of writing a plan to the Florida Supreme Court, but the session that could not exceed thirty days also could not be called for less than thirty days.

Justice Alderman wondered if the House could decide on its own, as it had on Friday, to just pass something and leave, regardless of how long the governor allowed for the session.

Rutledge said no.

But what if they are deadlocked?

"I don't think they're deadlocked. I think they're terribly close to passing the best reapportionment plan in the history of the state."

Boyd jumped in. "What law is it they're so close to passing?" The audience broke into laughter.

Governor Graham's general counsel, thirty-one-year-old Betty Steffens, who years later would become Justice Sundberg's second wife, stood up to defend the four-day special session the governor had called after consultation with House leaders Haben and Moffitt. The revision commission at one point, she said, had a draft that simply said "30 days," but that had been changed to "shall not exceed 30 days."

Justices Alderman and Boyd asked her if the governor could call a session lasting just one hour.

"I think that gets to the reasonableness of his act," Steffens replied.

But is the court to review the reasonableness of a governor's actions?, Alderman wondered.

She gave a complicated answer that sounded mostly like a "no."

Barry Richard, whose wavy dark hair was just beginning to turn gray as he marked his fortieth birthday that day, stood up to speak for the House, of which he had once been a member. He sought a middle ground. Graham did not have "absolute discretion," he said. "One hour, under most conceivable circumstances, would be an absurdity." But he added, in a shot at the Senate, "We face the same absurdity when one house of the Legislature . . . can handcuff three branches of government for thirty days."

For most of Florida's history, the Supreme Court had little to do with reapportionment. But after the U.S. Supreme Court, starting with *Baker v. Carr* in 1963, had made equal representation a matter of constitutional right, the Florida Supreme Court was given a role under the 1968 Constitution. The legislature would redraw the legislative districts every ten years after the federal census. The legislative plan would go to the Supreme Court, which would have thirty days to accept the plan or send it back for more work, and the congressional plan would go to the governor for signature or veto. If the legislature couldn't agree on a plan for legislative districts after a specified timetable, the Florida Supreme Court would draw the boundaries. That constitutional provision in effect created jurisdiction for the court to referee any constitutional issues that came up along the way.

Review of the 1972 reapportionment plan a decade earlier was the court's first serious involvement.[2] The court faced the first of a series of challenges to the practice of electing multiple legislators from one geographic district—a "multimember district," as it was called. Ninety-nine of the 120 House members were to be elected from multimember districts under the 1972 plan, as well as thirty-five of the forty senators. Proponents of these larger districts argued that they reduced parochialism by having legislators represent a more diverse population. Thirty members of the legislature intervened to challenge the dilution of minority voters through multimember districts, but the court voted 4–3 to set aside their objections.

Justice Adkins, writing for the majority, was very clear that the court's role in reapportionment would be limited: "Judicial relief becomes appropriate only when a legislature fails to reapportion according to federal and state constitutional requisites. . . . Even though we may disagree with the legislative policy in certain areas, . . . [we must] act with judicial restraint so as not to usurp the primary responsibility for reapportionment, which rests with the Legislature."[3] In three separate cases between 1966 and 1971, Adkins noted, the U.S. Supreme Court had agreed to multimember districts unless "designedly or otherwise" they "operate to minimize or cancel out the voting strength of racial or political elements of the voting population."[4] He noted that a requirement of single-member districts had failed during the Constitution Revision Commission sessions of 1967.

Adkins left open the prospect of a lawsuit in which plaintiffs could prove a racially discriminatory impact in violation of the Equal Protection Clause of the U.S. Constitution. Justices Roberts, Boyd, and Dekle joined Adkins's opinion. Justices Carlton and McCain wrote separate dissents, as did Judge Sam Spector substituting for Ervin. Carlton and Spector renewed the old fight over respecting county boundaries in legislative districting; they said the new apportionment "unnecessarily" ignores county lines. McCain's short opinion said there was "ample evidence" of "prejudice in and within certain districts" to justify rejection of the plan but did not say what the evidence was. "Computer results should not be substituted for the rights of the individual citizen to have fair and equal representation."

In 1977 two black NAACP leaders from St. Petersburg who had lost elections for the House in 1974 and 1976, Morris Milton and Charles Shorter, took the court up on its invitation in 1972 and filed a lawsuit claiming that multimember districts in southern Pinellas County diluted black votes. The lawsuit brought together a political odd couple—not just the two black leaders but also one of the state's leading Republicans, State Rep. S. Curtis Kiser, who was from a multimember district in whiter and more Republican northern Pinellas. A parallel case from Miami was filed by Republican Party leader Alberto R. Cardenas and Hispanic resident Frank Colunga, making a similar claim about the effect of multimember districts on Hispanic voting.[5] Most of the proceedings focused on the Pinellas case.

The U-shaped district in southern Pinellas County, which included predominantly black neighborhoods just south of St. Petersburg's downtown area, sent five white Republicans to the Legislature. Milton and Shorter wanted a chance to elect a black person from a single-member district dominated by those black neighborhoods. Kiser supported clumping black voters, who tended to vote Democratic, into such a district, with the result that white voters, more likely to vote Republican, were clumped in surrounding districts drawn to benefit Republicans.

Both the strategy and the likely consequences were very clear to both Kiser and Milton: for black voters, there would finally be a black legislator in Tallahassee—but at the price of diminishing blacks' influence in other legislative districts. For Republicans, who could remember a time a mere decade before when the Senate had just one Republican, St. Petersburg's C. W. Bill Young, and who still held only a fourth of the seats in either house of the legislature, Republican votes would no longer be diluted by black voters, and there could be more Republican legislators promoting more Republican policies.

Although the Milton-Kiser lawsuit focused on actual results in the elections statewide and the fact that there were still no blacks elected to the legislature, the Florida Supreme Court again rejected the statewide challenge to multimember districts. The court did, however, appoint Circuit Judge Victor Cawthon of Tallahassee as a special commissioner to hear evidence about racial discrimination in the south Pinellas district where Milton and Shorter had run unsuccessfully. Milton and Kiser along with Republican House member

Peter M. Dunbar were listed as counsel for the petitioners. Attorney General Robert Shevin and successor Jim Smith represented Secretary of State Bruce M. Smathers. As the case dragged on, Jack Mathews and Jack W. Shaw Jr. of the Mathews Osborne Ehrlich firm in Jacksonville came in to represent House Speaker Donald Tucker and Senate President Lew Brantley in support of multimember districts.

In December 1978 Cawthon recommended a rejection of the petition. About the same time, though, the U.S. Supreme Court agreed to review a case from Mobile, Alabama, in which a lower federal court had ordered that city to create single-member districts for the city commission. The court said at-large voting was discriminatory under the Fifteenth Amendment, which granted blacks the right to vote. The justices in Washington were having as much trouble with the issue as the justices in Tallahassee. The Mobile case was argued in Washington in March 1979, then reargued in October. On April 22, 1980, the U.S. Supreme Court reversed the lower court's decision and allowed multimember council districts but produced no majority opinion.[6]

The Florida justices also struggled to agree. The case was dramatically affected by the departure of Hatchett, the sole black justice, on July 18, 1979, after the case had been pending for two-and-a-half years. Hatchett had voted against dismissal of the case in 1977. In earlier oral arguments he had been, in Kiser's words, "friendly in the types of question he asked." On October 23, 1980, six months after the Mobile decision and with brand-new white justice McDonald voting in Hatchett's place, the Florida Supreme Court, 4–3, declared in *Milton v. Smathers* that the five-member district in Pinellas did not illegally discriminate against black voters.[7]

Alderman wrote for the majority that no "intentional" discrimination had been shown: "An examination of the record reveals that the reason black candidates have not been elected is not because of racial discrimination but rather because they run as Democratic candidates in a Republican area of the state." Citing the Mobile decision, Alderman added that proof of a discriminatory effect is not sufficient to invalidate multimember districts.

Boyd and McDonald signed on, as did Overton, who appeared to be the most reluctant of the four and may have been one cause of the delay. Overton wrote in a separate opinion that he was "bound" by the Mobile decision, but added that he supported single-member districts as a member of the 1978 Constitution Revision Commission. That proposal had been put on the ballot as Revision 3 to the Florida Constitution in 1978, but had lost in a sweep of "no" votes against all of the proposed amendments. Single-member districts had come the closest to voter approval, with 1.11 million opposed and 983,000 in favor. Once again leaving an issue open for further litigation, Overton said the decision in *Milton v. Smathers* applied only to the Equal Protection Clause in the Fourteenth Amendment, but the litigants had not addressed the Fifteenth Amendment question raised in Mobile. So a future case might still be brought on that basis.

Sundberg penned a dissent joined by England. The Mobile decision "evinces a lack of consensus as to whether a discriminatory purpose must be demonstrated in a proper Fifteenth Amendment case," Sundberg wrote. A mere statistical impact might not be enough to invalidate multi-member voting, he said, but it is asking too much of plaintiffs to require proof of actual "intent" to discriminate before invalidating multi-member districts.

Adkins wrote his own dissent, dissecting the multiple opinions in the U.S. Supreme Court's Mobile decision and examining evidence on the Pinellas elections. Adkins said the evidence was "sufficient to show a discriminatory purpose under the guideline as established by a majority of the justices" in the Mobile case. Approximately 12% of the population of the Pinellas districts was black, Adkins said, but no black has been elected to the legislature in Pinellas County in the twentieth century. Shorter had gotten 75% of the vote in nine adjacent precincts and more than 50% of the vote in 29 adjacent precincts, but those results were overwhelmed in other precincts, so he lost with 39,369 votes vs. 43,599 for the Republican. Two years later, a similar thing had happened with Milton, who lost with 9,651 votes against his opponent's 12,158. The Pinellas legislative delegation "consistently voted as a bloc" in the 1975 legislative session and thus were not effectively representing "divergent interests" in the district. Further, Adkins said, the "dual school system in Pinellas County was desegregated only pursuant to a court order." He noted "evidence of employment discrimination as well as [disparity] in municipal services, income level, and living conditions."

After the decision was announced, Kiser said the court had "reneged" on its commitment in 1972 to "go through a couple of elections and leave the door open" for a new challenge.[8]

But Kiser was not finished, and neither were the others seeking to end multi-member districts.

By the time the 1982 reapportionment session rolled around, the defeat of single-member districts at the polls in 1978 and the Supreme Court's decision of 1980 had been nullified in the evolving court of public opinion. Black organizations like the NAACP joined with liberal white voting-rights advocates and many newspaper editorial boards to push the Legislature it-self to end the practice of multimember districts. The cause was also taken up by the National Republican Party. Florida Republicans hired liberal icon Sandy D'Alemberte to push the concept. The math and the politics were irre-sistible: gerrymandering districts to embrace large numbers of black voters would also make remaining districts whiter and more Republican. And even as they increased their own advantages, Republicans also could win points with minorities.

University of Florida Political Science Professor Manning Dauer, the lead-ing academic on reapportionment in Florida, had warned in 1978 that an increase in minority representation would be accompanied by a big loss of influence for blacks in the legislature as a whole. Neither Dauer's warning nor the Republican enthusiasm gave the liberal advocates second thoughts. With Democrats solidly in control of the Florida Legislature in 1982, the symbolism of black officeholders prevailed over concerns of diminished power.

Some Democrats did foresee the political danger to their party, and two of them were the Democrats who chaired the House and Senate reapportion-ment committees, Rep. Lee Moffitt of Tampa and Sen. Dempsey Barron of Panama City. But as they held public hearings on reapportionment around the state, the pressure became irresistible. Just before the reapportionment ses-sion began in January 1982, they buckled. Florida would have single member districts for every legislative seat, and a special effort would be made to create "majority-minority" districts for black and Hispanic legislators.[9]

That decision made the line-drawing harder, as individual legislators struggled for political advantage in a very different apportionment system. Ambitious House members wanted Senate districts specially configured for them, and ambitious members of both houses wanted specially configured congressional districts. Every legislator wanted to be sure that the breakup of multi-member districts took account of where each legislator lived and avoided pitting one incumbent against another.

And so it was that on that beautiful Saturday afternoon of March 27, the House and the Senate were locked in combat over the tactical advantages of a shorter or longer special session.

Less than two hours after the oral arguments ended, the justices announced their decision, though deferring their explanation of it. By a 6–1 vote, the court adopted what Chief Justice Sundberg had described as "the concept of locking people in a room and making them reason together." Said the court: "We find the intent and purpose of the constitutional provision requires the Governor to reconvene the legislature in a special legislative apportionment session for a period of thirty days. We find that the Governor has no authority to limit the apportionment session to less than thirty consecutive days and his only discretion is to determine when the period will commence within thirty days after the regular session adjourns."[10] A week later, the court released a per curiam opinion.[11] While the governor had discretion to limit the duration of most special sessions, the court explained, that was not the purpose of the language about the reapportionment session, which was intended to avoid a repeat of the 520-day reapportionment session of 1955–56. The court noted that the summary of the amendment on the 1968 ballot said a failure to reapportion during the regular session means that the governor "is required to call a special 30-day session."

The ink on the formal opinion was barely dry when the two houses, with two special sessions on the same day, April 7, agreed on the 1982 legislative reapportionment plan. They would continue into June debating the congressional boundaries.

Before the plan could fall into place, the Supreme Court had to resolve an entirely new and quite prickly issue: What was to happen to the twenty senators elected to four-year terms in 1980? Were they entitled to serve their full four-year terms, even though their constituency had changed, or were their terms to be cut short when their districts changed in 1982? How did putting all forty Senate seats up for election in 1982 square with the Constitution's creation of staggered Senate terms, half elected every two years? The language of the Constitution read: "Senators shall be elected for terms of four years, . . . except, at the election next following a reapportionment, some senators shall be elected for terms of two years when necessary to maintain staggered terms." It made no mention of two-year terms for any of those elected before, rather than after, a reapportionment.

The plan passed on April 7 left that issue to the Supreme Court.

Senators had been concerned about the issue for more than a year. On May 12, 1981, a time of intense feuding between Childers and Barron over control of the Senate, Childers had asked Attorney General Smith for an official opinion, but Smith sided with Barron in favor of holdover terms. Childers, seeking any leverage possible against Barron, wanted all senators to have to run again. Childers also wanted Graham to ask the Supreme Court for an advisory opinion, but Graham said no. Steffens told Childers that the governor can seek advisory opinions only on matters "affecting his executive powers and duties." Childers already had an opinion from the Senate's general counsel, Steve Kahn, concluding that all senators had to run, though

Kahn agreed that it was not entirely clear. "The Florida Supreme Court is not beyond applying judicial magic to the plain language of the Constitution," Kahn wrote.[12]

Now the court faced the issue as part of its review of the entire reapportionment plan.

The oral argument lasted nearly four hours on May 4. One narrow issue focused on House District 27, composed of two parts of Volusia County connected by Interstate 4. Overton described it as having "one lane of I-4 in one district, one lane of I-4 in another district, and the median of I-4 in the third district." There were complaints about individual districts in Dade County where minority votes were diluted. And there were questions about the way Senate districts had been numbered—part of Barron's effort to let the senators elected in 1980 serve out their terms, by leaving them with their old district numbers even though they were out of north-to-south order on the reapportionment map.

During the oral argument, Overton was the most skeptical of the holdover Senate terms, while Sundberg repeatedly suggested that the law was on the Senate's side.

Toward the end of the long proceeding, the chairman of the 1968 Constitution Revision Commission, which had created the confusion, strode to the lectern in the big courtroom. "I don't know anything about what the framers of the Constitution intended," Chesterfield Smith intoned in his booming country-style oratory before going on to discuss that very topic. "The people were sick and tired of a Legislature that wouldn't reapportion itself," he said. Finally, a plan was passed under court order that required every legislator whose district boundaries had changed to run in a new election, even in the middle of their term. And that is what the members of the Constitution Revision Commission were thinking about when they wrote the section on reapportionment. It's a time-honored tradition "to kick the rascals out," he added. "There's nothing wrong with requiring people to refurbish themselves by going back to the people and submitting themselves to a vote again."

Smith wasn't an unbiased source of history, though. He was representing the League of Women Voters and the one senator squeezed out by the new boundaries, Miami Democrat Paul Steinberg. Barry Richard, again representing the House, agreed that all forty senators ought to be required to run again.

Neal Rutledge, the Washington lawyer back in the courtroom on behalf of the Senate, countered that holdover terms for senators were "absolutely consistent with the theory of representative government." That, he insisted, was what "the brilliant framers of the 1968 Constitution intended."

"One of the original framers is here and disagrees with you," Sundberg told him. Rutledge replied that Smith was simply being "an excellent advocate" for his clients.

On May 12, the court gave its answer: The reapportionment plan was valid, the court declared unanimously, but by a 5–2 vote the justices said the entire Florida Senate had to stand for reelection.[13] Overton wrote the majority opinion, joined by Boyd, Alderman, McDonald, and Ehrlich. "Let there be an election for all," McDonald declared in a concurring opinion. Overton based the majority opinion on "an interpretation of the words of the Constitution" and "a review of the history of our apportionment process during the last 27 years."

Sundberg looked at those very things and came to the opposite conclusion, with an elaborate dissection of the language and history of the provisions related to staggered Senate terms. "In spite of my emotional sympathies for the majority's position concerning the terms of senators, I believe in all intellectual honesty that its position is legally and rationally evanescent," he wrote. The senators were elected under a plan the court had declared valid, he said, and truncation of terms "has only been ordered by courts where senators were elected under an apportionment plan subsequently found by the court to be unconstitutional."

The assumption of the majority, "that we are personally represented and represented only by officials for whom we have voted, stretches too far the theory of representative government." Sundberg added, "Apparently the framers of the constitution thought that the desirability of maintaining a senate, of which at least one-half of the members are always experienced men or women, was more beneficial to the state after reapportionment than providing that each person in the state must be represented in the senate by a senator of their own choosing."

Adkins agreed with Sundberg's conclusion, but with his own very different but similarly detailed analysis. "It is sad," he concluded, "that we have warped the constitution with this strained construction."

21

SEARCH AND SEIZURE

Reshaping Constitutional Protections

So an undercover police officer walks into a Key West bar at happy hour on Valentine's Day. He walks up to a young woman sitting there with her boyfriend and tells her he'd like to buy some heroin. She steps away, consults with her boyfriend, then tells the undercover cop he can come to their trailer next door at 10:30 that night.

The undercover officer, Charles Hitchins of the Monroe County Sheriff's Department, goes back to the office, tells his superior officer, and gets wired with a body bug. In the four hours till the drug purchase, nobody bothers to get a search warrant from a judge. With Lt. Robert Santana and Sgt. Carol Key of the Key West Police Department monitoring the bugged conversation and other officers deployed nearby, Hitchins goes to the trailer and buys the heroin. The boyfriend, twenty-six-year-old Julian Sarmiento, is arrested.

That day, February 14, 1978, was just another routine day in the Florida drug wars, but this particular drug bust started a political and legal brouhaha that changed the Florida Constitution. It also put the Florida Supreme Court repeatedly at odds with the political branches of government over the balance between individual privacy and crime fighting. While the high-profile debate was about fighting crime, to Florida's justices it was a much simpler proposition: the Fourth Amendment to the U.S. Constitution calls for the police to get the approval of a judge, "a neutral and detached magistrate," whenever practical before searching a person's private property. The only effective way to ensure compliance with that principle has been to throw out any evidence seized in violation of the constitutional standard.

Often that means, as U.S. Supreme Court Justice Benjamin Cardozo so memorably put it in 1926, "the criminal is to go free because the constable blundered."[1] Or as Florida's Justice Drew once put it, in reversing a murder conviction and death sentence over a prosecutor's overzealous comments, "Many a winning touchdown has been called back and nullified because someone on the offensive team violated a rule by which the game was played. . . . Surely where life is at stake, the penalty cannot be less severe."[2]

At Sarmiento's trial on a charge of unlawful sale of heroin, his defense lawyer tried to have the recording of the bugged conversation excluded from evidence. Circuit Judge Bill G. Chappell refused, and Sarmiento was convicted. He appealed to the Third District Court of Appeal. Judge Phillip Hubbart wrote for a unanimous three-judge panel overturning the conviction because it was based on evidence from the "interception of private communications" in violation of the Florida Constitution's Declaration of Rights. Florida's provision on search and seizure went beyond the well-known Fourth Amendment to the U.S. Constitution, which sprang from the random searches of people's homes by British troops to find untaxed goods or forbidden muskets. Florida's Article I, Section 12 had additional language about "private communications." It said:

The right of the people to be secure in their persons, houses, papers and effects against . . . the unreasonable interception of private communications by any means, shall not be violated. No warrant shall be issued except upon probable cause, supported by affidavit, particularly describing the place or places to be searched, . . . the communication to be intercepted, and the nature of evidence to be obtained. Articles or information obtained in violation of this right shall not be admissible in evidence.

As Hubbart saw it, Sarmiento had a conversation in the privacy of his home. Sarmiento assumed the risk that Hitchins, the person he was talking to, might betray his trust and reveal the conversation but Sarmiento also had "a reasonable expectation of privacy that no one else was listening." The judge then launched into a panegyric:

We are unwilling to impose upon our citizens the risk of assuming that the uninvited ear of the state is an unseen and unknown listener to every private conversation which they have in their homes. That is too much for a proud and free people to tolerate without taking a long step down the totalitarian road. The home is the one place to which we can retreat, relax, and express ourselves as human beings without fear that an official record is being made of what we say by unknown government agents at their unfettered discretion.

Sarmiento was not exactly retreating, relaxing, and expressing himself as a human being as he swapped heroin for cash, but Hubbart was explaining why the home has special constitutional protection from "government agents" who take it upon themselves, without a judicial order, to intrude on that special place of privacy. As far back as 1966, the Third DCA had said the same thing in an opinion by Judge Thomas Barkdull and joined by Judges Norman Hendry and Richard H. M. Swann.[3] Now, a dozen years later, Hendry joined Hubbart's opinion in *Sarmiento*, as did retired judge Charles Carroll.

Hubbart brought to the decision a rich experience as a criminal defense lawyer as well as rich academic credentials. A graduate of Duke Law School with an LL.M. degree from Georgetown, he had been with the public defender service in Washington, moved to Miami and joined a private law firm, then became an assistant public defender before being appointed public defender in 1972. He had represented Wilbert Lee and Freddie Pitts in winning exoneration of a murder conviction and a pardon from Governor Askew in 1975. He ran unopposed for the Third DCA in 1976, the last election before merit selection took effect.

The recording of the conversation was particularly important in the Sarmiento case because Officer Hitchins's credibility was challenged by Sarmiento's lawyers. There was a separate criminal investigation of Hitchins himself, and the lawyers wanted to cross-examine Hitchins about whether his testimony against Sarmiento was part of a deal with prosecutors to close that investigation without charges. The judge in Sarmiento's trial had barred the defense tactic, but the Third DCA specifically said the cross-examination had to be allowed on a retrial. So the recording would have had extra importance in bolstering Hitchins's credibility.

Assistant Attorney General Paul Mendelson took the case to the Florida Supreme Court and said the ruling was inconsistent with another Third DCA decision shortly after *Sarmiento* that allowed use of taped conversations. Hubbart had been on the dissenting side that time. "I would afford our citizens greater rights under Article I, Section 12 of the Florida Constitution than that afforded by the Fourth Amendment," he said.[4]

The Florida Supreme Court's decision in *State v. Sarmiento*[5] on January 15, 1981, was a 5–2 per curiam decision in favor of Sarmiento. It appears that Sundberg, the chief justice at the time, was the major author, since the only archived background files on the case at the Supreme Court are from Sundberg's office. It was not a long opinion, and it mostly tracked Hubbart's, which might explain why Sundberg did not put his name on it. The interception of Sarmiento's conversation in his home, the court said, was "unreasonable" within the meaning of Florida's Declaration of Rights. Adkins, a persistent defender of rights against unreasonable searches, joined the opinion, along with Overton, England, and McDonald.

Boyd, who had not wanted to take the case and who took a lifelong pride in his dissents supporting constitutional rights, was now on the state's side. He joined a dissent by Alderman, who argued that the officers listening to the bugged conversation "were monitoring the conversations not only to obtain corroborating evidence" to support Hitchins's eventual testimony "but also for the protection of the undercover agent." Alderman found it "incredible and untenable" to say that Sarmiento had no reason to expect privacy in the conversation but would not expect outsiders to be listening. He cited a U.S. Supreme Court ruling in a criminal case against Teamsters Union boss James Hoffa that, as Alderman put it, "no matter how strongly a defendant trusts an apparent colleague, his expectations in this respect are not protected by the Fourth Amendment when it happens that his colleague is a government agent reporting regularly to the authorities."[6]

Not surprisingly, Mendelson petitioned for reconsideration. Sundberg law clerk George Meros explored his arguments and reported to Sundberg in a memo that there was "one well-taken point." Just three weeks before the oral argument in *Sarmiento*, the Supreme Court had upheld a Second District Court of Appeal opinion allowing use of a gun found during a "stop and frisk" and said, "We hereby adopt its opinion as our own."[7] Second DCA Judge Paul Danahy had concluded after considerable analysis that "the Florida Stop and Frisk Law was not intended to, and does not, impose any higher standard than that of the Fourth Amendment."[8] Mendelson's petition for reconsideration argued that the Supreme Court had failed to consider that decision in *Sarmiento*. Rather than explain that the interpretation of the Stop and Frisk statute was distinct from the constitutional provision for searches, the court simply denied rehearing.

The decision might have been just another decision in a minor drug case if "tough on crime" and a "war on drugs" were not such big political issues for Governor Graham and Attorney General Smith as their 1982 reelection campaigns approached. Law enforcement organizations also registered strong objection to legislators. By the time the legislative session of 1982 opened in January, Graham and Smith were joining legislators in supporting a constitutional amendment to overturn the *Sarmiento* decision and counter the idea that Florida would have greater constitutional protection against searches—or, as they put it, greater rights for criminals—than the U.S. Supreme Court recognized. The high court, with the arrival of new justices appointed by President Nixon to be "tough on crime," had begun relaxing the tough constitutional standards for police conduct that had developed during the 1960s. And now, it seemed, the Florida Supreme Court was going to thwart that trend by reading the Florida Constitution more generously for defendants.

The legislative session started in January rather than then-traditional April in 1982 because of reapportionment, and by the third week in June, after multiple extended sessions, the frazzled legislators were on an anti-crime spree. Already they had amended the drunk-driving law not once but twice to make Florida's one of the most punitive drunk-driving laws in the nation, with tougher punishment, easier gathering of evidence, and a higher threshold for excluding evidence.[9] On the last day of the session, June 22, they approved millions of dollars for more probation officers, new prison cells, more prison guards, and faster processing of new inmates. They also let state attorneys narrow the immunity granted to people who were compelled to give incriminating evidence; the so-called use immunity precluded use of any self-incriminating statements but let the person be prosecuted using other evidence. Legislators also restricted access to records of police internal affairs investigations until "probable cause" was found, and if no probable cause were found, the investigation would become public but the officer's name would not.

And by two-thirds votes, the legislature put two "anti-crime" constitutional amendments on the November 1982 ballot for voter approval. One would implement a proposal from a Criminal Justice Reform Commission that Attorney General Smith and Chief Justice Sundberg co-chaired even in the midst of disagreement over the *Sarmiento* case. The amendment would change the right to bail so that judges would have more leeway to deny bail to defendants considered dangerous to the community and at the same time also reduce the reliance on money bail for non-violent offenders as opposed to what is known as "their own recognizance.[10]

The other amendment was intended to undo the *Sarmiento* decision.

The proposed amendment had earlier failed 18–19 in the Senate, as opponents said Florida voters were putting state constitutional rights in the hands of the U.S. Supreme Court and foreswearing any interest in greater privacy protection. The leader of the opposition was conservative Democratic Senator Dempsey Barron of Panama City, a longtime defender of constitutional rights, but there were also Republicans among the opposition.

After losing the vote in the Senate, Governor Graham called a news conference and accused Barron of an "apparently relentless effort to make Florida a safe haven for criminals" by leading a "fight to prohibit prosecutors from using legitimately obtained evidence." Never mind that the issue in fact was whether the evidence was legitimately obtained, Graham then added: "The next time the people are alarmed because a rapist or drug smuggler takes a walk from prosecution, they have no one to thank but Senator Dempsey Barron—Senator Barron and the 18 other senators he led into this criminal-coddling vote." Attorney General Smith then called the other senators "a bunch of damn sheep."

Barron responded later that day that Graham had "issued the most irresponsible, scathing attack on the Senate that I have ever seen in my twenty-six years."[11] As the weeks passed, however, and the senators learned from the Supreme Court that they would all have to stand for reelection that fall (chapter 20), Barron joined a compromise. So did Senator Jack Gordon of Miami Beach, who spoke against the amendment before voting for it. A number of the forty senators took a walk; the vote was 32–0.

Like so many other proposed amendments to follow from the legislature and citizen initiatives, the wording on the ballot sounded like it was expanding a constitutional right rather than narrowing it. The amendment said: "This right shall be construed in conformity with the 4th Amendment to the United States Constitution, as interpreted by the United States Supreme Court. Articles or information obtained in violation of this right shall not be admissible in evidence if such articles or information would be inadmissible under decisions of the United States Supreme Court construing the 4th Amendment to the United States Constitution."

A week before releasing its decision in *Sarmiento*, the Florida Supreme Court heard oral arguments about the right of law enforcement, without a search warrant, to trample across a person's open land or fly over it to spy on it. That was as important to the war on drugs as wiring up undercover officers for drug purchases. What brought the matter to the court was the arrest of Frank J. Brady and two other men on a 1,800-acre ranch in Martin County after a raid that the trial judge later characterized as "reminiscent of Nazi Germany." Sheriff's deputies broke through a padlocked gate, walked three quarters of a mile across the property, and caught Brady and others unloading marijuana at a little airstrip. The officers knew thirty hours in advance that the pot plane was to arrive and invited an NBC news crew to join them on the raid. But they didn't get a search warrant from a judge. The trial judge ordered the evidence excluded from trial, which obviously put a very big hole in the prosecution's case.

As with *Sarmiento*, a search warrant would have taken care of the problem. That is often what the search-and-seizure cases are about. The warrant is a form, signed by a judge often after being filled out by officers, outlining the justification—the evidence giving rise to the suspicion—and, in the words of the Fourth Amendment, "particularly describing the place to be searched and the person or things to be seized." State and federal court decisions provide for "exigent circumstances" that don't allow time to find a judge and get the warrant before the crime occurs or the evidence disappears.

A lot of officers test the limits of the exigent circumstances, and their roll of the dice sometimes works because judges, who to some extent also live in a political world, excuse the warrantless search rather than ruin the chance to convict someone who is factually guilty. As a result, at both the federal and state level, the law of search and seizure was something of a mish-mash. There was much political advocacy for a "good faith" exception that would avoid the effects of officers' relatively innocent mistakes, but as Sundberg said in remarks to the Suncoast Tiger Bay Club in late 1981, "those are not particularly precise terms." His speech expressed concern that police would be tempted to break the rules too casually. "It will not appeal to the finest instincts of our law enforcement officials," Sundberg said.[12] Adkins, who also made civic club speeches about the 1982 amendment, liked to say that criminals don't wear "tails and horns" so that they can be readily identified. "Whatever you do to get them is also applicable to every individual citizen."

The U.S. Supreme Court had not, at that time, adopted a "good faith" exception, even though the rules on police behavior were clearly loosening. And even that exception would probably not have helped the police in *Sarmiento*. A good-faith exception would validate a warrant that was signed but for some reason turned out to contain errors or make up for an officer's legitimate belief that he did not need a warrant.

Frank Brady's case provided another example. As Judge Gavin Letts said in the Fourth District Court of Appeal decision upholding the trial judge's suppression of the marijuana evidence, "There was plenty of time to apply for a warrant here. It is claimed the deputies did not think they had probable cause to get one. Lack of probable cause cannot by itself be used to bolster forced entry, quite to the contrary."[13]

The issue turned on a legal concept called "curtilage," meaning the area surrounding a house that is effectively part of the residents' zone of privacy. That was in contrast with an "open field," which the U.S. Supreme Court decision in a moonshine case in 1924 had said was entitled to less constitutional protection because of the diminished expectation of privacy. As far as Assistant Attorney General Robert L. Bogen was concerned, the Fourth Amendment did not protect the Brady bunch out there in the open field.

But how do we determine, Overton and other justices wondered at oral argument, where the protected curtilage stops and the open field begins? What if it's five acres fenced in with a house in the middle?

"You can't take away the fact that it's an open field merely by constructing a fence around it," Bogen said.

Well, Brady had also dug a ditch around it and put up "no trespassing" signs. Still not enough, Bogen said.

"You're saying if you own more than one hundred acres or twenty acres, you can never have an expectation of privacy, even if you build a brick wall around it?" asked Sundberg.

"You're right, it's an open field," said Bogen.

Brady's lawyer, Steven Greenberg of Miami, invoked James Madison, who "said that the purpose of the Fourth and Fifth Amendments was to oblige the government to control itself." The Fourth Amendment protects people, not places, Greenberg said, referring to the leading U.S. Supreme Court decision on such things, *Katz v. United States* in 1967.[14] That case, a key factor in the *Brady* case, had called into question a hundred years of search-and-seizure precedents, including the moonshine case of 1924. Greenberg said Brady had a right to expect the police to get a warrant before they broke through his padlocked gate and walked three-quarters of a mile across his land.[15]

Nine months later, on October 15, 1981, the justices announced their decision in *State v. Brady*.[16] The author of the opinion was the first clue of the outcome: Adkins. After a long review of past cases at his own court and elsewhere, Adkins wrote, "We are not here sounding the death knell for the open fields doctrine—only for the blind, indiscriminate application thereof." The doctrine still applied "in a truly open field" or a public place. "There can be no reasonable expectation of privacy in a field open, visible, and easily accessible to others. That, however, was not the case here."

Alderman, whose family owned a sprawling ranch in nearby St. Lucie County, and Boyd, the other dissenter in *Sarmiento*, joined Adkins's opinion. So did Sundberg and Overton. England, part of the majority in *Sarmiento*, had left the court in August. McDonald, also part of the *Sarmiento* majority, was in dissent this time.

Adkins's opinion pointed to a 1980 case, *Norman v. State*,[17] in which the sheriff had gone to a farm, climbed a fence by a locked gate, and walked 250 yards to a barn, where he saw marijuana. That led to surveillance of the farm and eventually the arrest of Ray Norman, who was renting the farm and claimed he had no connection to the marijuana. The Supreme Court excluded the evidence. "If the owner or occupier of a field seeks to keep it private and demonstrates an actual intention to do so, and his expectation is one that society is willing to recognize as reasonable, then Fourth Amendment protections extend to activities in that field," Adkins wrote.

But that was the real question: was society prepared to recognize Brady's privacy as reasonable? "He went to great lengths to demonstrate that outsiders were not welcome on his property—certainly one could not have made it to the spot from which the drug transfer was observed without realizing that he was not to be there," Adkins said. "We think that respondent's expectation of privacy was a reasonable one."[18]

Even though the *Brady* decision was based on the Florida Constitution, the state appealed it to the U.S. Supreme Court, which granted review[19] but left the case hanging for two and a half years, until May 21, 1984.

There were similar decisions throughout 1981 and 1982. Three months after *Sarmiento*, for example, the court suppressed a recording from a bug used to convict former Surfside Mayor Louis Hoberman of bribery and unlawful compensation,[20] with Alderman and Boyd dissenting on the same theme as their *Sarmiento* dissent. And just a week before the vote on the constitutional amendment, the court suppressed marijuana seized from Debra Jayne De-Montmorency in Madison County after officers crossed a barbed-wire fence and walked three hundred feet into her woods to check out a tip.[21] On the other hand, in September 1982, in a case against a pawnbroker named Alex Morningstar who had been bugged in his store by two thieves-turned-informants, the court unanimously refused to extend to businesses the same protection Sarmiento had in his home.[22]

November 1982 brought the statewide vote on the amendment. It passed with 1,440,523 yes votes, 63.5 percent of the total. The pretrial detention amendment also passed, with 60.6 percent of the vote.

Six months later, Assistant Attorney General Ray Marky stood before the Florida Supreme Court and argued that the amendment made it legal for the police to tap any telephone conversation between a suspected marijuana seller and an informant. People should not expect privacy on their telephones, he said. Lines get crossed, some people have party lines (multiple residences sharing a phone line), or extension phones get picked up by others. "I just don't feel we as a society are ready to allow people to use the telephone without running a risk," he said. And the voters showed they agreed, he added, by passing the amendment to expand police powers to search and wiretap.[23]

Justice Adkins expressed shock. "Every voter that voted for that amendment, if you knocked on the door of their home and said, 'Do you expect your conversations on your phone to be private,' what would they say?"

"Some of them would probably say yes, and some would say no," said Marky. The question was whether the law was prepared to recognize their expectation.

The case arose before the amendment passed. The First District Court of Appeal had thrown out a recording of accused marijuana seller Patricia Williams of Jacksonville on the basis of *Sarmiento*. But now, on the state's appeal to the Supreme Court, Marky wanted the amendment applied retroactively to Williams and other older cases. Another case argued the same week was about using previously illegal evidence in revoking someone's probation.

Doesn't the new amendment "undermine your case substantially?" Boyd asked Williams's public defender, Joyce Reeves. The lawyer stumbled for a moment, then said, "I'm not sure the new constitutional amendment, if it does apply retroactively, which I argue it does not, has the effect of overruling *Sarmiento*."

"Certain people say that was the reason it was passed," interjected Overton.

Well, the language isn't so clear, Reeves began, then Adkins seized the opening and jumped in. "Do you think the majority of the people that voted ever heard of *Sarmiento*?" he asked her.

She thought there was a good chance they had not.

"All they wanted to do was stop crime," said Adkins, who had argued all along that it would be ineffective at doing that.

Marky later came back to that point. "I think if we're going to be loyal to the concept of democracy in proposing of amendments, we must presume an intelligent electorate," he said. "Otherwise, it's all a joke."

The Supreme Court, however, was not going to be stampeded by the amendment into turning its back on constitutional protections against search and seizure. The court was going to back off only when the U.S. Supreme Court had ruled clearly on the point. The retroactive effect was one of the first issues the court faced.

Most new laws apply only for the future. At least theoretically, people behave according to their understanding of the law at the time, and retroactively limiting what they can lawfully do is unfair. On July 7, 1983, the court refused to apply the new amendment retroactively. "It is a well-established rule of construction that in the absence of clear legislative expression to the contrary, a law is presumed to operate prospectively," Ehrlich wrote for a 6–1 majority in *State v. Lavazzoli*.[24] "Further, the amendment unquestionably alters a substantive right." Even Boyd abandoned Alderman to join the majority on that point, and Justice Shaw, who had replaced Sundberg, was also in the majority.

Alas, that did not help Patricia Williams. In her case, the conversation over the drugs was entirely by telephone, not between two people in the defendant's home. *Sarmiento* did not even apply, Boyd wrote for a unanimous court in December. The informant consented to the recordings, and that was enough under state law, which was not at odds with the Constitution. The recording of the phone conversation was admitted.[25]

A secret tape recording in another case caught the final words of Michael Phillips and then the gunshots that killed him. Phillips was found dead on the floor beside his desk in his office in Oakland Park, near Fort Lauderdale, where he had pretended to be a psychologist. He had come to Florida from California to escape grand larceny charges there, changed his identity from Earvin Herman Trimble, and ordained himself a minister of the First Church of Utilitarian Science so he could sponsor bingo. A bingo operator named Anthony Inciarrano, who had been put out of business by police, had put up $7,000 to support Phillips's bingo venture, but Phillips was backing out. They had an argument, which Phillips secretly recorded.

"We never had a deal," Phillips said.

"We never had a deal? Did we have a deal, yes or no?" says the other voice, which Inciarrano later said was his. And then there's the sound of five shots and Phillips's dying groans as the killer leaves.

Police never found a gun or anything else linking Inciarrano to the killing—just the tape, found when a detective followed wires from a pencil holder, where the microphone was hidden, to the recorder in the desk drawer. Inciarrano pleaded no contest to avoid the death penalty but reserved the right to challenge the admissibility of the recording, which was the only evidence against him.

Two earlier decisions seemed to support Inciarrano's argument. In 1981, in a long drawn-out murder case against a Tampa psychiatrist named Louis Tsavaris, accused of murdering his lover-patient, the Supreme Court had blocked use of a recording that the Hillsborough medical examiner had made when Tsavaris called him about the autopsy results.[26] Future justice Peggy Quince had argued that case as an assistant attorney general and lost. In 1978 the court had suppressed the secret recording an extortion victim made when the extortionist visited his home.[27] Both decisions turned on a state law in Chapter 934 that makes it a misdemeanor to "intercept" a private conversation without the consent of both parties and says "no part of the contents" or any "evidence derived therefrom may be received in evidence."

Judge George W. Hersey of the Fourth District Court of Appeal wanted to get around this problem and admit the evidence against Inciarrano, and he did so by redefining "intercepts." He compared a conversation to a pass in football. If the intended receiver catches it, that is a completed pass, not an "interception." It's an interception only if somebody you didn't want to catch it catches it. Hersey and his two fellow judges, including future justice Harry Lee Anstead, felt bound by the prior cases suppressing the telephone records and unanimously suppressed the recording but urged the Supreme Court to reconsider its prior decisions.[28]

"These are bad facts, and sometimes bad facts cause bad law," Adkins remarked when the case got to the Supreme Court for oral argument. "That's when we have to make up our minds whether we are a court of men or law." By that standard, it proved to be a court of men. Alderman wrote the opinion and said that neither of the earlier cases controlled the result in this one. The law in question prohibits the recording only when the other party has a "reasonable expectation of privacy," Alderman wrote. "One who enters the business premises of another for a lawful purpose is an invitee. At the moment that his intention changes, that is, if he suddenly decides to steal or pillage, or murder, or rape, then at that moment he becomes a trespasser and has no further right upon the premises. Thus, here, if appellant ever had a privilege, it dissolved in the sound of gunfire." Whatever expectation of privacy there was, in other words, society was not prepared to recognize it.

Adkins, who usually wanted to suppress such recordings, joined Alderman's opinion, as did Boyd, Overton and McDonald, though Overton separately stressed that the outcome would be different if the person being recorded were in his own home or office. Ehrlich, concurring only in the result, objected to Alderman's view that the commission of a criminal act waives any right of privacy. That would simply beg the question about constitutional protections. He borrowed Hersey's football analogy. "Once the conversation was directed to him, it was in his possession, whether through memory or recording," Ehrlich wrote. It would be more honest to simply admit error in the earlier cases and rule that this was simply not an "interception" under the statute. Shaw agreed with him.

In April 1984, while the Florida Supreme Court was beginning to ponder what to do about the secret recording in *Inciarrano*, the U.S. Supreme Court created a new twist in the *Brady* issue with a decision in *Oliver v. United States*.[29] The court resurrected the concept from the 1924 moonshine case that an "open field" was not entitled to constitutional protection. By that time, it had been six years since the arrest of the Brady bunch and the trial judge's suppression of the evidence.

A month after the *Oliver* decision, on May 21, 1984, the U.S. Supreme Court noted among its routine orders[30] that the prosecutor in Martin County had dropped the case against Frank Brady. The court remanded the case of Brady's co-defendants back to the Florida Supreme Court for reconsideration in light of *Oliver*. It took nine more months for the Florida Supreme Court to act. On February 28, 1985, Adkins wrote a two-paragraph opinion for a unanimous court declaring "that warrantless 'open field' searches are proper, and that evidence received as a result thereof should not be suppressed."[31] The same day, the court reversed itself in the *DeMontmorency* case, which had been pending on rehearing since 1982, and let the marijuana into evidence.[32]

Brady himself continued to be identified by authorities as a participant in drug-smuggling. In 1986, according to the *Palm Beach Post*, deputies arrived at the Brady ranch and seized a plane loaded with a thousand pounds of cocaine. After other arrests Brady eventually was sentenced to ten years in prison, though he testified against other smugglers and was released in 1991. Brady's son turned the ranch into a hunting business. And then, in 2008, Brady Sr. sold the entire 1,800 acres for $30 million to the Southwest Florida Water Management District, which planned to use it, along with an adjacent parcel, as a huge water-cleansing area in the restoration of Lake Okeechobee and the Everglades.[33]

The Florida Supreme Court lost the battle in the *Brady* case, but the war over search and seizure went on. The U.S. Supreme Court had not dealt with the matter of using planes and helicopters to spy on property from overhead when the Florida justices heard the appeal of Michael Riley, who had made his expectation of privacy perfectly clear. He was renting a mobile home on five acres in rural Pasco County, enclosed by a wire fence as well as bushes and shrubs, with a bold "Do Not Enter" sign in front of the mobile home. A few feet behind the mobile home was a greenhouse with a roof that was partly opaque and partly translucent. Tipped off that Riley was growing marijuana in the greenhouse but unable to see inside from the edge of the property, Pasco sheriff's deputies got a helicopter and flew over the greenhouse at about four hundred feet and shot pictures with a telephoto lens. The photographer claimed he could identify the marijuana through the translucent portions of the roof, so that was used as "probable cause" to obtain a search warrant and seize forty-four marijuana plants growing there.

Circuit Judge W. Lowell Bray Jr. rejected the evidence. He said the greenhouse was clearly part of the "curtilage" and there was "a reasonable expectation of privacy from aerial surveillance." The state appealed to the Second District Court of Appeal. Judge Grimes wrote for a unanimous panel overturning Bray's order and allowing the marijuana evidence. Citing the *Oliver* case, Grimes said the "non-harassing surveillance . . . struck an acceptable balance between society's interest in effective modern law enforcement and the individual's interest in the values protected by the fourth amendment." But the panel certified the issue to the Supreme Court.

Assistant Attorney General Candace M. Sunderland argued to the justices that the case was governed by two recent U.S. Supreme Court decisions allowing aerial surveillance, in one case by law enforcement officers in a plane flying at a lawful altitude of a thousand feet to look into a backyard surrounded by a ten-foot-high fence, and in the other case by government regulators getting around extensive security at a Dow Chemical plant by photographs taken from altitudes of 12,000, 3,000, and 1,200 feet.

By that time, Justice Rosemary Barkett had replaced Alderman. Maybe "naked-eye observations" from a fixed-wing aircraft at a lawful altitude are okay even when looking into the privacy of someone's backyard, but a helicopter hovering in place over people's homes at a much lower altitude and using a telephoto lens was quite different. "Purposeful surveillance from the air simply lays open everything and everyone below—whether marijuana plants, nude sunbathers, or family members relaxing in their lawn chairs—to minute inspection," Barkett wrote. "The usual steps one might take to protect his privacy are useless." She added, "We believe law enforcement can achieve its objectives without so infringing upon the privacy rights of Florida citizens." The court was unanimous: McDonald, Overton, Ehrlich and Shaw joined, along with Adkins, who had retired but was still counted on cases.

The state, knowing the U.S. Supreme Court was a more hospitable forum, appealed and with Justice Sandra Day O'Connor as the swing vote, won a 5–4 reversal in *Florida v. Riley*.[34] Attorney General Bob Butterworth had Miami lawyer Parker D. Thomson handle the appeal, and Marc H. Salton of New Port Richey still represented Riley. O'Connor's vote turned on one basic thing: Police observation of Riley's backyard from four hundred feet "did not violate an expectation of privacy that society is prepared to recognize as reasonable" in an era of "routine" overhead flights. A defendant, O'Connor said, has the burden of proving his expectation is reasonable.

Now it was back to the Florida Supreme Court, which was not giving up. Noting comments from other justices that were similar to O'Connor's about the burden of proof, Barkett wrote, "All nine justices of the United States Supreme Court agreed that the record lacked evidentiary development of Riley's claimed expectation of privacy." So the court sent the case back to the lower courts, where Riley would have a chance to produce evidence that helicopters flying over people's homes at four hundred feet are, in White's words, "sufficiently rare in this country to lend substance" to Riley's claim. Grimes, because of his earlier Second DCA opinion (essentially consistent with the U.S.

Supreme Court's decision), did not participate. McDonald thought the search issue had been disposed of with a determination that the marijuana should be admitted at trial. Ehrlich, Overton, Shaw and new justice Gerald Kogan agreed with Barkett.

While the *Riley* case was still pending at the U.S. Supreme Court, Florida's Supreme Court in 1988 considered whether the Florida courts were obligated to follow U.S. Supreme Court decisions made after the adoption of the 1982 amendment. The clear intent of the amendment was yes, and a majority of the court said so. Overton thought otherwise. "I believe the 1982 amendment simply requires this Court to interpret the Florida constitutional provision, section 12 of article I, in accordance with the United States Supreme Court decisions existing at the time the amendment was adopted," Overton wrote in *Bernie v. State*[35] in 1988. Then he softened the comment. "Although I do not believe we are bound by decisions of the United States Supreme Court rendered after November of 1982, I also do not believe we are in any way restricted in applying the principles of those cases. I would consider them as persuasive authority, but not mandated by the constitutional amendment."

Ehrlich thought Overton's approach was "an affront to the voters of this state." He said "nowhere" was there any indication that future high court decisions were not embraced by the amendment. "The very tenor of the ballot statement and other pre-election literature concerning the amendment supports a contrary conclusion." He was part of the 4–3 majority.

The case involved a package of cocaine sent by Emery Freight that broke open in transit. Barkett wrote that everyone was missing the point, because the actions of the police were a violation of a specific Florida statute, so there was no point in reaching any constitutional issue.

One argument never came up in the 1980s: what if one day everyone had drones with cameras that could fly over their neighbors' property?

22

PRIVATE LIVES AND PUBLIC VALUES
IN CRIMINAL LAW

Two days after the end of the long 1982 legislative session that produced the constitutional amendment on search and seizure, as political Tallahassee was escaping for the summer election campaigns, the Supreme Court weighed in yet again on the sanctity of the home, but in a wholly different context: domestic violence.

The case was *State v. Bobbitt*,[1] and it put Florida outside the national norm in its approach to the centuries-old "castle doctrine," the concept that a person can defend his home against intruders even if the intruders don't intend serious physical harm to the resident. "Self-defense" in a public place generally requires a person to retreat if practical rather than kill the attacker, but the "castle doctrine" does not require a person to retreat from his own home. The problem the court faced is what happens if both the initial victim and the initial attacker both have a right to be in the home, and the victim ends up killing the attacker.

As ten-year-old Tracy Bobbitt and her little brother watched through the doorway from the kitchen, their father, James William Bobbitt, drunk and angry, once again lit into his wife, Elsie. When she came home, he began beating her. This was nothing new. One time he had chased her with a hammer. This time, even before Mrs. Bobbitt got into the house, her husband confronted her in the yard, where a neighbor saw him visibly drunk and heard him threaten his wife. The neighbor left and called police but got a busy signal. The couple moved inside. Mr. Bobbitt's continuing attack seriously injured his wife's leg and broke her left cheekbone, perhaps with his fists but possibly with something like a baseball bat. As young Tracy described it to the jury, Mrs. Bobbitt twisted away from his grasp and backed into the kitchen. Her pocketbook, still hanging from her shoulder after she arrived home, had a gun in it that Mr. Bobbitt had given her for protection as she attended night classes. She pulled out the gun, and as her husband came toward her and was about six feet away, she fired once and killed him. Mrs. Bobbitt called the police. They came—and arrested her for second-degree murder.

At her trial, her public defender asked the judge to instruct the jury on the "castle doctrine" by saying that she had no duty to retreat from her own home before using deadly force in self-defense. What the defense wanted to tell the jury was this: "One unlawfully attacked in his own home or on his own premises has no duty to retreat and may lawfully stand his ground and meet force with force, including deadly force, if necessary to prevent imminent death or great bodily harm to himself or another, or to prevent the commission of a forcible felony." Instead, the judge offered only the usual instruction about self-defense—the duty to retreat if practical.

After the conviction, the judge reconsidered and agreed that he should have given the instruction Mrs. Bobbitt wanted, so he granted a new trial. The state appealed. The First District Court of Appeal, in an opinion by its first female judge, Anne Cawthon Booth, upheld the judge's grant of a new trial.

The prevailing case law at the time recognized the castle doctrine, first in defending against a trespasser[2] in 1892 and seventy years later in the case of a woman who shot her boyfriend as he moved threateningly toward her. The latter case, *Hedges v. State* in 1965,[3] had rejected the state's argument that the line should be drawn at intruders and that the castle doctrine should not apply in the case of guests, which was how the boyfriend was categorized. The court was expansive in its language. The rule is, the court said in 1965, "that when one is violently assaulted in his own house or immediately surrounding premises, he is not obliged to retreat but may stand his ground and use such force as prudence and caution would dictate as necessary to avoid death or great bodily harm."

It remained unclear, though, whether the castle doctrine would excuse the killing of an attacker who also was living in the house—like Mrs. Bobbitt's husband. Another appellate court, the Fourth District, had already said yes in a case in 1967 but then reversed itself eleven years later.[4]

The First District, on November 7, 1980, cited *Hedges* and said the doctrine should protect Mrs. Bobbitt's action.[5] She had no duty to retreat in her own home before acting in self-defense. "The test is whether a reasonably cautious and prudent person situated as she was would have believed, and did believe, that the use of such force was necessary to protect herself," Judge Booth wrote. "Here, defendant's evidence as to self-defense was sufficient to generate reasonable doubt as to guilt." She noted Mrs. Bobbitt's leg injury that made it difficult to escape. The decision was essentially two rulings: First, Mrs. Bobbitt's situation was covered by the castle doctrine, so she did not have to retreat from her husband. Second, even without the castle doctrine, retreat was impractical because of her injuries, and the shooting of her husband was reasonable self-defense.

Assistant Attorney General Wallace E. Allbritton wanted another shot at limiting the castle doctrine, and the Supreme Court granted his request for review. It took twenty months for the court to reach a decision.

While the *Bobbitt* case was pending, the court divided 4–3 on April 30, 1981, in allowing a husband to be tried for burglary for breaking into his wife's separate apartment. The couple in that case had split up, but the wife had never filed for divorce. The man, Leroy Franklin Cladd, went to his wife's apartment, broke through a locked door with a crowbar, struck his wife in the mouth, and tried to throw her over a second-floor stair railing, according to court records. He left but went back the next morning and tried to break in again. Cladd was charged with burglary and attempted burglary, but Circuit Judge David Patterson (later a judge on the Second District Court of Appeal) threw out the charges and said Cladd had a right to be with his wife. The Second DCA overturned the dismissal of the case.

At the Supreme Court, the lineup of justices on each side was a bit unusual. Alderman, the traditionalist on marriage and family issues, wrote for the majority in support of conviction. While stressing that the ruling had only narrow implications, he noted that the couple had been separated for six months. "In a society like ours, where the wife owns and holds property in her own right, where she can direct the use of her personal property as she pleases, where she can engage in business and pursue a career, it would be contrary to every principle of reason to hold that a husband could ad lib appropriate her property," Alderman wrote.[6] Justices Adkins, Overton, and McDonald agreed with him.

Boyd, as conservative as Alderman about moral and family issues, dissented. "Consortium is so basic as an incident of marriage that it should not be undermined except by a clear legislative statement of the public policy of this state," Boyd wrote.

Sundberg and England were also somewhat out of character as dissenters in staying with tradition. England, writing for the two of them, stressed that there was no charge of physical assault, no legal separation or divorce, and no effort to take the wife's separate property. The apartment, then, was no different from a vacation home or a garage workroom. "The effect of today's decision is to bring prosecuting attorneys into marital disputes in a way which is unprecedented," he said. "Like an anxious Pandora endeavoring to stuff the ills of the world back into her box, the majority endeavors to confine inter-spousal crimes to the factual situation of this case. As Pandora and the world sadly learned, however, once the box is opened there is no way to contain the ephemeral evils which escape." To let one spouse be charged with burglary against the other "has emanations which go far beyond this case."

Another year passed before the justices decided *Bobbitt*.

On June 24, 1982, Alderman wrote the decision for a majority that included Adkins, Sundberg, and McDonald. Mrs. Bobbitt lost. Alderman did little more than recite an opinion by his former Fourth DCA colleague, Judge Letts, who refused to extend the castle doctrine to a woman being attacked by her mentally ill son living in the house. The killer—the initial victim—could claim the ordinary rules of self-defense, but they required a retreat when possible.

Overton, who tended to defer to circuit judges, undoubtedly wanted to do so in this close case over whether Mrs. Bobbitt was a criminal or a victim. Joined by Boyd, Overton said the decision "does not recognize the realities of life." He could not understand why a woman who killed an attacking boyfriend could stand her ground but a woman who killed her attacking husband could not. He also couldn't understand why conviction of a woman who killed her nineteen-year-old son would depend on whether he lived with her or didn't. He expressed amazement that the Supreme Court would base a victim's duty to retreat on whether the attacker had legal title to the property. The court was holding that a woman under attack had to assess the property rights of her attacker before deciding whether to shoot.

The 4–2 decision went back to the First District, which stood its own ground. It had already said that Mrs. Bobbitt met any standard of self-defense, with or without the help of the castle doctrine. So despite Alderman's opinion, it upheld the trial judge's grant of the new trial.[7] Allbritton appealed once again to the Supreme Court, which let the First DCA decision stand.[8] It would be fifteen years before the Supreme Court reconsidered its own decision against the castle doctrine.[9]

The *Bobbitt* case and the castle doctrine complicated the reflexive liberal-conservative boundaries between aggressive enforcement of criminal laws and aggressive enforcement of individual rights. In domestic violence cases like *Bobbitt*, the attacker becomes the victim and the initial victim (usually the woman) becomes the person accused of a crime. The courts became the arbiter at this intersection of individual rights, public safety, equal protection, and changing community and cultural values. The further a case got from their own life experience and from familiar legal doctrines, the more uncomfortable the justices seemed.

The case of Richard Sylvester James will seem to many to be a grave injustice, letting a criminal go free on a technicality. But to the justices, it was all about a very familiar rule of evidence over hearsay and the basic constitutional concept of the right to cross-examine a witness against you.[10]

James was accused of sexually attacking and robbing Jeannette Reynolds, an elderly widow in poor health who lived alone in Orlando. A few months later, as is typical in the preparations for trial, Mrs. Reynolds gave a deposition in which she was questioned under oath by James's lawyer about what happened. She said that on January 3, 1978, shortly before midnight, a man she recognized as her yard man's helper came to her door and asked for jumper cables. She had none, but when she tried to close the door, the man pushed her inside, raped her, and stole $52 from her purse. A short time after the attack, police picked up James and a buddy, Daniel Newbury, and brought them to the hospital, where Mrs. Reynolds was being treated, and she identified James as the attacker.

Then, the day before James's trial started, Mrs. Reynolds died unexpectedly of poor health unrelated to the attack. That made the deposition critically important to the prosecution, because no one besides Mrs. Reynolds could identify her attacker or describe what happened. Because she was not in court to testify, her statements under oath at the deposition were read to the six jurors, who decided that beyond a reasonable doubt James was guilty of burglary, robbery, and attempted sexual battery.

James's lawyer, Bill Shepard of Orlando, appealed to the Fifth District Court of Appeal. He argued that a defendant has a constitutional right under the Sixth Amendment of the U.S. Constitution to confront witnesses against him and cross-examine them in front of the jury. The only exception is in specific circumstances, established in advance, when a deposition out of court is taken for the specific purpose of preserving a witness's testimony in case of unavailability at trial. Otherwise, under the Florida Rules of Criminal Procedure, the deposition can be used only to show inconsistency or unreliability of the witness's testimony, not to replace in-court testimony.

The Fifth DCA, in an opinion by Judge Orfinger, granted James a new trial, but certified the issue to the Supreme Court because of a recent U.S. Supreme Court ruling allowing testimony from a preliminary court hearing to be used at the trial itself.

In oral arguments in Tallahassee in April 1981,[11] Assistant Attorney General Barbara Ann Butler urged the justices to "balance the constitutional safe-guards afforded the defendant in criminal prosecutions with certain public policy considerations." After all, she said, James's own lawyer had asked all the questions at the deposition. "The attorney was free to pursue whatever line of questioning he desired," she said. "You can't hide behind the Sixth Amend-ment and say it's always applicable."

Adkins wasn't buying that argument. "There's a practical thing if I'm depos-ing a witness," he said. "I don't want to cross-examine that witness. I want to wait till I get in the courtroom. I don't want to train the witness. I don't want to show my hand." McDonald, who had already been assigned to write the court's opinion, noted that in addition to the Sixth Amendment, the Florida Constitution gives a right "to confront at trial adverse witnesses."

Cross-examination was so important because James insisted it was a case of mistaken identity. There were two people who worked for her yard service. On cross-examination Mrs. Reynolds might not have been sure about the identifi-cation. James's brother testified that James was with him until after midnight. James suggested that the attacker might have been Newbury, who also once worked in her yard. Newbury, on the other hand, testified that shortly after midnight he had run into James, who told him he had made a "hit" on "GG," which was the nickname for Mrs. Reynolds, who had a citizens band radio "handle" of "Golden Girl."

So now the justices faced the question of "great public importance" posed by the Fifth DCA: Could the deposition be used when the witness has died or is otherwise unavailable?

"The answer is no," McDonald wrote for a 5–2 majority. "We hold that discovery depositions may not be used as substantive evidence in a criminal trial."

The attacker, whoever it was, had outlived the evidence. But the court's decision was in effect ratified two decades later by the U.S. Supreme Court in *Crawford v. Washington*.[12]

Forty years before the fatal confrontations between black people and police that were continuing news throughout 2015 and 2016, the killing of a young black man in Pensacola led the Florida Supreme Court to confront the crimi-nality of a protest that followed the shooting of a young black man by a police officer in December 1974.

A grand jury decided that the officer acted in self-defense. That prompted three weeks of protests by about two hundred black demonstrators, who called the officer a murderer and demanded his firing. The leaders of the protest were Rev. Hawthorne K. Matthews, head of the Northwest Florida chapter of the Southern Christian Leadership Conference, which had been Martin Luther King's organization, and Rev. B.J. Brooks of the local chapter of the NAACP.

An account by a black-oriented newspaper many years later recounted the episode and, not surprisingly, two very different versions of what happened in the killing.[13] Sheriff's Deputy Doug Raines said that after a chase he pulled over a car driven by Wendel Sylvester Blackwell, twenty-three. Blackwell was ordered out of the car and put his hands on his head. Raines said he saw something shiny in Blackwell's hands and shot him dead with his .357 magnum. Witnesses said a small gun, apparently a derringer, was in Blackwell's hands clutched to his head even after he fell, but someone riding with the deputy moved it away. Matthews later said he believed the gun was never in Blackwell's possession and was planted afterward.

Matthews said that the next day, a woman called him and told him she had been in the car with Blackwell, that she and the deputy had been lovers, and that the deputy saw them getting into the car at a night club and chased in anger. She said she got away. Matthews told authorities about the call. A few days later the woman, Deborah Jones, was found strangled under an overpass. All this time, there was considerable racial tension in the community over an effort to get rid of the high school's team nickname, the Rebels, and the Confederate flag and school song, "Dixie," that went with the nickname.

On January 24, 1975, two days after the grand jury cleared Raines, about four hundred protestors marched to the Escambia courthouse. Nightly protests followed until February 24, when the crowd stepped up its rhetoric and began chanting, "2-4-6-8, who shall we assassinate? Doug Raines, Sheriff Untreiner, Askew, and the whole bunch of you pigs." The newspaper account claims the word used was "incarcerate," not "assassinate." Deputies with clubs broke up the assembly, arrested a number of adults and juveniles, and later charged Matthews and Brooks with felony extortion on the basis that they were threatening injury to the sheriff unless he fired Raines. The two were convicted, which for purposes of appeal meant that the court assumed the word used was "assassinate." Matthews was sentenced to five years. Brooks got five years of probation on the condition that he not participate in any demonstrations anywhere in Florida.

The first stop for the appeal was the First District Court. The focus was a U.S. Supreme Court decision, *Watts v. United States*,[14] overturning the conviction of a defendant from a Washington protest against the military draft who declared, "If they ever make me carry a rifle, the first person I want in my sights is LBJ," referring to President Lyndon Baines Johnson. The court said a "true threat" has to be distinguished from "political hyperbole."

Matthews and Brooks argued that the chanting tone and the laughter of protesters as well as "the improbability of the message itself" left a reasonable doubt that they expected "all Escambia County lawmen to capitulate rather than be killed along with the governor," as Judge Robert P. Smith Jr. described the argument. But accepting that as so, Judge Smith went on, he described testimony that people in the crowd had "weapons," including "several sticks or clubs," a golf club shaft with the head removed, and a steak knife "being passed from one demonstrator to the other." And Matthews, Smith said, went beyond that, with personal remarks to individual law-enforcement officers, such as "that goes for you, too." The First DCA upheld the conviction of Matthews but reversed the conviction of Brooks, whose participation did not go beyond "the bounds of permissible expression."[15]

At the Supreme Court, Justice Sundberg wrote the opinion in *Matthews v. State*[16] and said that the First DCA had "inherently" ruled that the extortion statute was constitutional, even though Judge Smith did not address the issue. Sundberg said there was "competent evidence" to justify the finding of extortion and to determine that it was not "unconstitutionally applied" to Matthews. "It transcends the scope of our review to substitute our judgment for that of the jury, the trial judge and the district court of appeal," Sundberg wrote.

Boyd wrote a succinct one-paragraph dissent, referring back to the U.S. Supreme Court precedent. "If Watts' statement is protected speech, then I cannot see how the '2-4-6-8' chant at a public gathering to protest what the demonstrators felt was government wrongdoing is anything other than protected speech," he wrote.

Hatchett wrote a much longer dissent and added some facts not mentioned in other opinions. "Human relations meetings" between public officials and black leaders had failed to produce any agreement. There were no firearms among the demonstrators, and there were no arrests for possession of weapons. The chant had been going on for five nights of protest before the sheriff arrested Matthews and Brooks. It was only after protesters blocked police cruisers entering and leaving the police compound that the sheriff went to the state attorney.

"Was the 'assassination' cheer . . . directed to inciting, threatening, or producing imminent violence against the sheriff, Raines, Askew and others?" Hatchett wondered. "And were the cheers 'likely to incite or produce such lawless action?'" The court, Hatchett said, had not addressed those "two critical questions," which were required by U.S. Supreme Court decisions before criminal penalties could be imposed for peaceful protests.

"The protections of the First Amendment encompass all of our citizens, whether black militants or Ku Klux Klan members," Hatchett added. "Only by allowing our citizens to voice their political opposition to the fullest extent possible can we encourage the use of the open political forum and inhibit the growing tendency of clandestine violent attacks as a means of political change."

England, Adkins and Overton, however, joined Sundberg in upholding Matthews's conviction. The 2010 news report indicates that Matthews and Brooks both won clemency from Governor Askew after serving sixty-three days.

Boyd was a frequent dissenter in support of free expression and against vague and overbroad statutes, as in the *Matthews* case, and he had a majority with him five years later in striking down a law that he found susceptible to misuse. It was a law originally sponsored in 1951 by a state senator named LeRoy Collins, who would become governor a few years later, and it was aimed at unmasking the Ku Klux Klan. The law forbade anyone from going onto public property wearing a mask or hood to conceal the face.

Boyd's opinion striking down the law doesn't even mention the KKK or the defendant's role as, in his own words, "Titan of the Knights of the Ku Klux Klan." It is one of a multitude of Supreme Court opinions that is very light on the facts. This one is also light on the law. It consumes barely a page in the *Southern Reporter*. It cites three cases with no elaboration about any of them except that they support the court's ultimate determination: "Although the law is overbroad in its sweep and lacks a rational basis, its language is very specific. The statutory words are not susceptible of any limiting construction." Adkins, Overton, Sundberg, England and McDonald all joined the short opinion declaring it unconstitutional. Alderman dissented, but wrote no opinion.

So what was the case of *Robinson v. State*[17] about? The KKK held a rally in Pensacola's Seville Square on June 23, 1979, to protest a biracial couple's plan to marry. Members wore their white robes, but with the familiar KKK hood raised so their faces were visible. This was because of the 1951 law, which said: "No person or persons shall in this state, while wearing any mask, hood, or device whereby any portion of the face is so hidden, concealed, or covered as to conceal the identity of the wearer, enter upon, or be, or appear upon or within the public property of any municipality or county of the state." At some point, B. W. Robinson lowered the hood over his face. A police officer told him to remove it. Robinson refused, and he was arrested.

In September, the American Civil Liberties Union of Florida decided to take on Robinson's case and challenge the "hood law." ACLU executive director Eleanor Ginsberg was quoted in news items across the country as saying the law has exceptions that permit people to wear masks in public at masquerade parties but not as a means of political expression. Bruce S. Rogow of Fort Lauderdale, one of the ACLU's leading litigators, challenged the constitutionality of the statute. In December 1979, after Circuit Judge William Jones rejected the argument, Robinson pleaded no contest, got six months' probation plus court costs of $240, and reserved the right to appeal on the constitutionality issue.[18]

Rogow told the Supreme Court that the law could be applied to someone wearing bandages on his face, to protesters who wore Richard Nixon masks at demonstrations, or even to Santa Claus.

After the Supreme Court's decision striking down the law on December 18, 1980, Representative George Sheldon of Tampa and Senator George Stuart of Orlando proposed a revised version of the law, and Sheldon recruited LeRoy Collins himself to return to the Capitol and testify. The new law added provisions requiring evidence of bad motives, such as "the intent to intimidate, threaten, abuse, or harass any other person."[19]

The justices also had to deal with recurring issues about "indecency," ranging from nudity on the beaches to porn films in the theaters. In the early 1970s the court was intolerant of dirty movies. After the arrival of the Askew-era justices and after several U.S. Supreme Court reversals of Florida Supreme Court decisions, the justices had more tolerance for dirty movies and magazines, but still wouldn't tolerate topless sunbathing.

Even in 1986, and even on a beach that had been locally recognized as a nude beach and had been used as such by its owner before its donation to the state, the court nixed topless sunbathing. Belinda McGuire was arrested on May 14, 1982, for jogging topless on what was known as Air Force Beach in the John D. MacArthur Beach State Recreation Area in Palm Beach County. John D. MacArthur himself "not only tolerated it, but positively approved of the nude sunbathing," his son J. Roderick MacArthur said in a deposition in the case, adding that his father "had always been a skinny-dipper." Alas for Belinda McGuire, the prior owner's personal preferences were not part of the chain of title to the land. The state decided to ban nude sunbathing and posted signs to that effect.

McGuire's lawyer, James K. Green of West Palm Beach, argued that she was not nude, but rather was wearing a bikini bottom. "The mere sight of a female breast . . . does not constitute indecency." But there was also the matter of the Florida Administrative Code, which said, "In every bathing area all persons shall be clothed as to prevent any indecent exposure of the person," and attire "shall conform to commonly accepted standards at all times." All this led the court to some finely tuned exploration of exactly what had to be covered. "Have you seen *Sports Illustrated* lately?" Adkins asked Assistant Attorney General Joan Fowler Rossin. The justices wondered about skimpy bikinis and breastfeeding mothers. Rossin argued that it isn't difficult to understand that topless or nude sunbathing is not acceptable. "There is no constitutional right to nudity," she said.

In its opinion, on June 12, 1986, the court noted that it had recently upheld the conviction of a topless dancer in a bar in Daytona Beach. Declaring Daytona's local ordinance was not "overbroad," the court commented that "the right to dress as one pleases . . . has little or no First Amendment implications."[20] In McGuire's case, McDonald's opinion said nude sunbathing "is not associated with dance, literature or any other form of expression," without addressing whether McGuire would have been innocent had she been performing ballet instead of jogging.

The justices scoffed at McGuire's claim that the MacArthur beach rules were too vague to understand. "We find this contention remarkable because on April 28, 1982, well before her arrest on May 12, McGuire received an individual warning from the park manager against sunbathing topless at Air Force Beach," the court said in an opinion by McDonald. Boyd, Overton, and Ehrlich joined the opinion.

Adkins and Shaw dissented. The officer who arrested McGuire even acknowledged that the beach, by common practice, had a clothing-optional area, Adkins wrote. The park manager said "seashells would suffice" in place of a bikini top. As for what was "commonly accepted," two different witnesses had different "levels of tolerance" about beachwear. "I would note, too, that in this era of violent crime increasingly scarce police resources could be used in a far more productive manner than in arresting those whose only crime involves exposing themselves, in the proper locale, to the sea's breeze and Florida's sunshine. I take comfort in knowing that sometime in the future, people will read the majority opinion and chuckle that the state would actually forbid topless jogging or sunbathing in a small area which was widely recognized as clothing-optional."

The same debate had divided the court almost ten years earlier with a somewhat different set of justices. Donna Moffett and a female friend were out on the public beach in St. Lucie County and took off the tops of their bikinis. They were arrested and convicted for violating a Florida law that said, "Whoever commits such acts as are of a nature to corrupt the public morals, or outrage the sense of public decency . . . shall be guilty of a misdemeanor of the second degree." Justice Boyd's analysis in *Moffett v. State*[21] was about as skimpy as the ladies' beach attire. By contrast, Boyd had actually dissented when the court upheld a statute that outlawed "persons wandering or strolling around from place to place without any lawful purpose or object [and] habitual loafers." But an outrage to public morals was not too vague for him when it came to topless women.

"Since the beginning of civilization public nudity has been considered improper," Boyd wrote, quoting the biblical story of Adam and Eve using fig leaves to cover what the St. Lucie pair had failed to cover. "We are fully aware of the changing social values as expressed in new modes of dress, but are convinced that by enacting Section 877.03 . . . the Legislature intended to prohibit adult females from appearing in public places, including Florida's public beaches, with openly exposed breasts."

England couldn't resist a pun in his dissent, which had Adkins's support. "The bare facts in the record before us . . . simply do not establish the commission of a crime," England wrote. "Approximately 50 to 75 other people were present on the beach at the time. The arresting officer testified that some of the witnesses were personally offended by the presence of topless women on the beach; other witnesses testified that they had no objections. So far as the record indicates, no one left the beach or moved to a more remote section of the sandy expanse as a result of the women's choice of attire." England added that there was no sign of any disturbance, but one of the women "testified that a male made an amorous advance, which she ignored, but that like advances often occurred regardless of her state of attire."

The early 1970s also brought much ado about porn films, to the point that the justices felt obligated to watch them personally in the solitude of the court to determine whether they met constitutional standards of obscenity as they evolved in the U.S. Supreme Court. England remembered watching such a movie, which he said was *Deep Throat*, in "the basement" of the Supreme Court building. Boyd, he said, frequently shielded his eyes with his hand.

The high-profile case over *Deep Throat* was to determine whether one Sal Aiuppa should go to trial for distributing obscene material by showing the film in Pinellas County. The case had been certified directly from Pinellas County Judge Robert Shingler, skipping two layers of courts, to the Supreme

Court of Florida. As Justice Ervin put it in more stately terms, "A perplexed and sorely concerned trial judge in conscientiously attempting to carry out his constitutional duties seeks in these proceedings our advice . . ."

Deep Throat was produced for $25,000 by a hairdresser who got the idea for a film on a woman's view of sex after he kept hearing his female clients talk about the subject. Roger Ebert, the Chicago film critic who became part of the famous Siskel and Ebert duo on television, wrote soon after release of the film: "The movie became 'pornographic chic' in New York before it was busted. Mike Nichols [the director of path-breaking films such as *The Graduate*] told Truman Capote he shouldn't miss it, and then the word just sort of got around: This is the first stag film to see with a date."[22]

What Aiuppa had done, as the state attorney in Pinellas County put it, was distribute a film that was obscene "considered as a whole, applying contemporary community standards, having its predominant appeal to the prurient interest, being utterly without redeeming social value, and going substantially beyond the customary limits of candor." Dekle wrote for a majority in *State v. Aiuppa*[23] that Florida's obscenity statute refers to "sex," which "in the statutory context" means "sexual intercourse, or interplay, this being the indisputable basis of this obscenity matter." The words "shameful or morbid" modify "nudity" and "sex," Dekle went on. "We hold these to include cunnilingus, sodomy and fellatio, as charged in the information, for these acts render nudity and sex shameful or morbid."

Dekle's opinion on May 1, 1974, contains a touch of nerdy humor, almost surely intentional, when Dekle refers to the obscenity statute as containing a "copulative verb." For those who missed that English class, a "copulative verb" is not a verb about copulation. Sometimes called a "linking verb," it does not have an object but merely describes the subject of the sentence—"is" or "seems" or "become," for example. The obscenity statute begins, "Material is obscene if . . ." The point Dekle was making was not nearly as significant as the pun.

To Justice Ervin, the law-enforcement effort against *Deep Throat* harkened back to the efforts of one Anthony Comstock, who in the 1870s had influenced Congress to pass the Comstock Law banning delivery of "obscene, lewd or lascivious material" and any material related to abortion or to prevention of venereal disease or conception. Comstock had complained about George Bernard Shaw's play *Mrs. Warren's Profession.* Now, a hundred years later, Ervin said the film seizures and arrests reflected a "renewed Twentieth Century Comstockian effort to suppress 'obscenity.'" He decried "the history of prudery, fanaticism, inquisition and suppression generated in the name of social or religious morality extending from earliest times—all of which in time invariably failed in their objectives to suppress human expression of ideas. But to what avail to say more here?"

The other justices, however, had plenty more to say—often with Justice Dekle authoring the opinion.

In a case decided the same day about the movie *The Devil in Miss Jones*, the jury had acquitted the employee involved and couldn't reach a verdict against the company exhibiting the movie. State Attorney Richard Gerstein still wanted an injunction, and the trial judge denied it as "double jeopardy." Gerstein appealed, and the Supreme Court said the injunction was okay because it was "remedial" and not punitive. The law allowing suppression of the film was held to be valid. Ervin, Adkins and McCain dissented.[24]

The previous fall in *Rhodes v. State*,[25] Dekle had deflected the "missiles of constitutional attack" in upholding a conviction for showing *He and She* and *Sex Family Robinson* at the Navy Point Adult Theater in Pensacola. And just a month before that, in a 4–3 vote in *Erznoznik v. City of Jacksonville*,[26] Dekle, Roberts, Boyd, and Overton had refused, over the objections of Ervin, Adkins, and McCain, to review a decision of circuit judge and future justice Major B. Harding upholding a "public nuisance" ordinance against showing films containing nudity at a drive-in theater where the screen was visible from a public street. Both the First District Court of Appeal and the Florida Supreme Court rejected Richard Erznoznik's appeal without opinion, but former Jacksonville circuit judge William H. Maness took the case to the U.S. Supreme Court and won a reversal, because movies containing "nudity" were the only ones deemed "offensive."[27]

Six months after the *Deep Throat* and *Devil in Miss Jones* cases, in an opinion providing no facts whatsoever and no legal analysis except the citation of *Rhodes* and two other cases, the court upheld the obscenity statute in a case that (as the U.S. Supreme Court later said) was over the publishing of "certain comic strips and pictures." The defendants in *Bucolo v. State* won a summary reversal at the U.S. Supreme Court,[28] but Florida's Supreme Court could not bring itself to simply capitulate. On remand back to Florida, Boyd noted that when the Florida court had upheld Bucolo's conviction the previous October, it was before two major U.S. Supreme Court decisions five months earlier "were called to our attention."[29] The Florida justices found additional support in those cases and sent the case back for a trial, but charges were dropped "using prosecutorial discretion."

That wasn't good enough for the defendants. Saying there was no "discretion" about dropping the case because the U.S. Supreme Court decision had declared that the materials were not obscene, they sought to expunge the record and win a permanent discharge. They filed a mandamus action in the U.S. Supreme Court naming Chief Justice Adkins and other justices as defendants. The nation's highest court on March 8, 1976, noting that its earlier decision "requires full recognition by the state courts," chided the Florida Supreme Court: "We agree with petitioners that nothing in the state-court record, as it now stands, recognizes that the State was foreclosed by this court's decision from seeking to convict petitioners of obscenity violations."[30]

The court also had to cope with another kind of obscenity—cursing in public. In 1974, six months before the *Bucolo* case, the obscenity statute was challenged by one George H. Jones, who had been convicted of uttering the words (as McCain's opinion presented it) "G_ _ D_ _ Mother F_ _, F_ _ Pigs and Son of a B_ _." In a search incident to his arrest for bad language, police had found marijuana and charged him for that, too. The Jones conviction was upheld 4–1, with Adkins, Boyd, and Dekle joining McCain. Ervin, dissenting, said there was no provocation or harm to others. He called the majority opinion "a parochial *ipse dixit* conclusion expressing personal prejudice that indecent language spoken in public in and of itself is a crime."[31]

The issue arose again in 1976 in a case from Wakulla County, but now there were new justices.

"The complaint alleges that . . . Blannie Mae Spears did . . . publicly use or utter indecent or obscene language, to wit: SON OF A BITCH, BASTARD M.F. ETC.," as Justice Hatchett put it in his opinion. "Recent developments," Hatchett wrote for a majority on September 23, 1976, "militate in favor of reconsideration" of McCain's opinion in favor of suppressing speech in *Jones.*

The U.S. Supreme Court by then, Hatchett noted, had overturned a conviction of someone walking around a courthouse in a jacket that said "Fuck the draft" as well as convictions of people saying "you god damn m.f. police." Consequently, Hatchett said, expression could be suppressed only if it is "in some significant way erotic" or if the speaker "abused a particular person with these vulgarities, intending to incite him to violence." But *Spears v. State,*[32] said, Hatchett, was not such a case. Overton, Adkins, Boyd, England, and Sundberg all joined his opinion. Roberts dissented without explanation.

A year later, Hatchett turned his attention to dirty magazines in *Johnson v. State.*[33] Members of the local ministerial association in Hamilton County, in an effort to maintain the moral standards of the community, had gone to a local store and bought five magazines and then turned them over to law enforcement for prosecution. The store clerk was defended by future Sixth Circuit Judge David A. Demers. With Overton, Boyd, Sundberg, and Karl in agreement, Hatchett threw out four of the convictions against the store clerk but upheld one, for the magazine *Climax*. The justices never broached the question whether this overbroad attack was itself evidence of the vagueness of the statute.

Adkins, alone in dissent, compared some of the contents of *Climax* to respected works of art. "Just as the sculpture 'Bound Slave' by Michelangelo, and 'David with the Head of Goliath' by Donatello, the magazine contained pictures of men with their genitals completely exposed," Adkins wrote. "Just as Rembrandt's 'Danae,' the magazine contained pictures of a nude female stretched out in a sensuous position. Just as the movie *Carnal Knowledge*, recently declared not to be obscene . . . the magazine contained pictures which implied the act of sexual intercourse." Adkins added, "Granted, the magazine lacked serious literary, artistic, or scientific value, but this alone does not bring it within the rule prohibiting certain publications."

Boyd's decision in 1978 upholding a case against the First Amendment Foundation of Florida[34] did not even mention the names of the films, but the case was once again from that hotbed of prurience, Pinellas County. Demers again represented the defendant. The organization apparently showed a series of films, "knowing the obscene nature thereof," each of them viewed by a police officer who described them in an affidavit. The organization ultimately pleaded no contest to twenty-nine counts, resulting in twenty-nine fines of $1,500 each. Boyd provided about as sterile a description as could be imagined. It drew unanimous support, with even Adkins concurring in the result but not the reasoning.

Eight years later, little had changed in the court's outlook. Ehrlich wrote for the court in a case not over a criminal conviction but over a request that a judge enjoin a magazine distributor from distributing certain magazines.[35] The judge granted the injunction after denying the distributor's argument that there needed to be "expert testimony" about the "community standards of decency" that supposedly applied. The Supreme Court rejected the idea. "Such testimony is usually admitted for the purpose of explaining to lay jurors what they otherwise could not understand," Ehrlich wrote. Pornography, he added, quoting from the U.S. Supreme Court, "can and does speak for itself."

Ehrlich's opinion, joined by Adkins, Overton, and McDonald, drew an unexpected dissenter: Joe Boyd. "The concept of due process of law teaches us that to allow a lone judicial officer to make such a finding based only on subjective judgment is a dangerous precedent, however correct or well-exercised that judgment may have been in this particular case." Justice Shaw agreed with Boyd.

23

SHAW

From Descendant of a Slave to Chief Justice

Alan Sundberg's two-year term as chief ending in July 1982 was his last hurrah on the court.

He won the post without the drama that preceded the selections of Overton and England. Sundberg was known for his wit as well as intelligence and also for being unfailingly kind to court staff as well as fellow justices. Adkins told his clerks that Sundberg was the first of the new justices to come to his office to pay his respects, in contrast with Overton and England's avoidance of the tainted older justices. "Alan entered a room not in a stride but rather with a sort of lope, and, after you noticed his size, it was his face you saw, always bright and interested," longtime friend Sandy D'Alemberte said of him. Sundberg played tennis—Overton, England and Hatchett joined him in frequent foursomes—and on weekends would go to the family's house on Lake Talquin for family skiing or would go fishing and hunting "and be one of the guys and a redneck like the rest of us," as former attorney general and eventual law partner Jim Smith once said of him.[1]

As a result, his selection to succeed England as chief was almost a foregone conclusion, even though it meant another "Passover" for Joe Boyd. On the afternoon of March 24, 1980, two weeks after voters approved the new jurisdictional amendment (chapter 10), the justices gathered for their weekly Monday conference. At the 1:00 break, Boyd told them he was leaving for a funeral and would appreciate it if they would elect a new chief while he was gone. "When I got back, they had not voted," Boyd told a reporter later, so he nominated Sundberg himself. "I like Sundberg. He's my good friend." Boyd said it didn't bother him that he had not been chief. "I also haven't been vice president of the United States or ambassador to Spain."[2]

Sundberg viewed his tenure as chief as a time of consolidating the many changes of recent years, but he ended up heavily focused on crime issues, in part because of riots in the Overtown section of Miami in May of 1980 after four Miami-Dade police officers were acquitted in the beating death of black businessman Arthur McDuffie. After the unrest subsided, Governor Graham wanted to dig deeper into the causes of the breakdown in confidence in the criminal-justice system, said his general counsel at the time, Betty Steffens. He appointed the attorney general, Jim Smith, and the chief justice, Sundberg, to co-chair a commission. It was an unusual role for a judge, but the riots had made the topic one of great urgency.

Among other things, the commission pushed for alternatives to cash bail and to jailing people for misdemeanors as well as sentencing guidelines to reduce disparities in sentencing. Out of that grew a separate sentencing commission, where Sundberg again had a leading role. It made a meticulous circuit-by-circuit analysis of sentences and produced a "matrix" of sentences reflecting not only the crimes but a number of other factors and allowed judges to go outside the guidelines when justified. The commission avoided the more contentious issue of whether the length of the sentences should be longer or shorter; members focused simply on harmonizing existing practices. They all but eliminated parole. The application of new sentencing guidelines would dog the court for years afterward as old customs of sentencing gave way to the new and often complex guidelines.

At the Florida Bar convention at the end of June in 1982, Sundberg gave the traditional annual report as chief justice and then told the gathering that he would not seek retention and would leave the court when his term expired in early January. During August, the traditional vacation break for the justices, which also becomes an occasion to catch up on unfinished cases, Sundberg accelerated his departure to September 15. He said the departure of a justice is "always disruptive," but "the least disruption" would occur if he left in September. "Public life is very demanding upon a family," he added. "Mine has paid heavy dues these past seven years." Like England, Sundberg had a daughter in college and more approaching college age, and it seemed to some who knew him that the relative wealth of his wife's parents weighed on his sense of obligation to his children.

Sundberg joined the Tallahassee office of prominent Florida firm Carlton Fields, whose senior eminence was former Florida Bar and American Bar President W. Reece Smith Jr. and whose partners included friends Leonard Gilbert and Sylvia Walbolt. Sundberg represented governors and legislators as well as corporate clients. Tobacco companies were also among Sundberg's clients, and among the cases he argued on their behalf was one against a class action lawsuit by flight attendants seeking damages from the days when smoking was allowed on flights. He earlier represented tobacco companies in the highly publicized effort to overturn a law allowing the state to file a multimillion-dollar lawsuit for reimbursement of Medicaid money.

Walbolt remembers an occasion when Sundberg appeared at the court for oral argument and was on a roll in his argument when one of his former colleagues started to interrupt with a question. Sundberg held up his hand like a "stop" signal, finished his statement, then turned to the judge for the question. The justices laughed. "Only Alan Sundberg could get away with that," Walbolt said.[3]

Like England, Sundberg divorced his wife soon after leaving the court. He began seeing Betty Steffens, who had been Graham's counsel for death penalty cases and then general counsel. The two lived together for years and then married in 1993. In 1997 Sundberg left private practice with Carlton Fields to become general counsel at Florida State University after longtime friend Sandy D'Alemberte became FSU president. In 2000 Sundberg left FSU to join Jim Smith in Smith, Ballard & Logan, a lobbying and law firm that also included Smith son-in-law and lobbyist Brian Ballard and Bob Graham's then-son-in-law Mark Logan. In 2003 Steffens was appointed by FSU president T. K. Wetherell to be FSU's general counsel, the job Sundberg had held under D'Alemberte. Governor Jeb Bush appointed Sundberg to the FSU Board of Trustees. A longtime pipe smoker, Sundberg was diagnosed with lung cancer in July 2001 and died at the Mayo Clinic in his hometown of Jacksonville on January 26, 2002, at the age of sixty-eight.

To succeed Sundberg at the court in the fall of 1982, Governor Graham chose Leander J. Shaw Jr., who had been Joe Hatchett's friend from their days at Howard University. Shaw became the second black person to serve on the Supreme Court. His new parking place would be one block away from his previous one. He had served on the First District Court of Appeal for a bit more than three years, also as a Graham appointee. He had served, by appointment from Governor Askew in 1974, as one of three judges on the Industrial Claims Commission, hearing appeals of workers' compensation, until that commission was abolished as part of comp reform legislation in 1979. Workers' comp appeals thereafter went directly to the First DCA.

Shaw grew up amid the rigid segregation of the South. His great-grandfather had been a slave. He was born September 6, 1930, in Salem, Virginia, below the Blue Ridge Mountains just west of Roanoke. His family soon moved just up the road to Lexington, home of Virginia Military Institute and Washington and Lee College. The one black school, the Lylburn Downing School, served all grades, from elementary to high school, and his father, also Leander J. Shaw, was the principal. His mother, Margaret Shaw, was a teacher. As he grew up to be the tallest kid around, Lee became the center on the high school basketball team. He sold newspapers and shined shoes for the white students at Washington and Lee. After he finished high school in 1948, he knew he was expected to go to college, but he needed a little convincing. Working at a pulpwood shop with his uncle and pushing a wheelbarrow full of slushy concrete on a construction site persuaded him that his father was right about that college education. He went to all-black West Virginia State College, which his father had attended, in Charleston, West Virginia.

He took ROTC, then after graduation in 1952 was shipped out to South Korea as a second lieutenant in U.S. Army artillery. When he got out in 1954, he hung out in New York City for a time and eventually enrolled at Brooklyn Law School. There he met his first wife, Dolores, whose godfather was noted black congressman and minister Adam Clayton Powell Jr. They were married in his office on Capitol Hill in Washington.[4]

By then Shaw's father had become dean of the graduate school at Florida A&M in Tallahassee. The place to go to law school, his father told him, was Howard University. He was in his last year there when first-year student Joe Hatchett, just out of the U.S. Army artillery in Europe, enrolled there.

Shaw finished law school in 1957 and went to St. Louis briefly. One day his father called, said FAMU was looking for a law professor for its law school and wondered if he knew anyone who would be interested. The son was interested himself, and Dean Thomas M. Jenkins soon offered him the job. Shaw taught there for three years until he passed the Bar and moved to Jacksonville. He took the Bar exam in 1959, along with Hatchett, and put up with the segregation that denied them a room at the DuPont Plaza Hotel in Miami, where the exam was being administered. Shaw did not actually complete his admission to the Bar until 1960, and on a hot June day, he took the Bar oath in the courtroom where he one day would preside. Standing next to him for the group photo of new lawyers was Major B. Harding, who would join the Supreme Court eight years after Shaw and would serve with him for a decade that included the sensational cases of the 2000 presidential election.

At the time of the Bar admission ceremony, Shaw had just left the FAMU faculty to join Earl M. Johnson in private practice in Jacksonville. Johnson's clients included the NAACP's Legal Defense Fund, but much of their work was the ordinary matters of a small law practice, from criminal cases to wills and divorces. In court he would encounter police officers and others on the witness stand using offensive slang for black people without apology or even remonstrance from judges. Like Hatchett, Shaw represented civil rights demonstrators in St. Augustine during the period of the Martin Luther King visit there. At one point, when he was trying to get about fifty demonstrators out of jail, the court clerk would not accept a court filing on their behalf from Shaw, who says he resorted to calling the Supreme Court to intervene with the local judge.

After *Gideon v. Wainwright* in 1963 led to the creation of the statewide public defender system, T. Edward Austin was chosen as Jacksonville's first public defender. Despite objections, which he said came from twenty or more public officials who learned of Austin's intentions and tried to talk him out of it, Austin hired Shaw as an assistant public defender, at the same time that Duval County Solicitor Edward M. Booth Sr. hired a black assistant solicitor, Alfred R. Taylor. No black people had served in official positions in Duval County since Reconstruction, lawyer-historian Edward Booth Jr. later reported. Austin said later he does not remember any arrangement with Solicitor Booth over the timing of the announcement. "I'm just real glad he did it," said Austin. "Spread some of the risk around." But he said, "You pick a winner, you'll be all right." On the second floor of the Duval courthouse, though, Shaw and Taylor were required to use the "colored" rest room instead the adjacent "white" men's room, which was available even to criminal defendants.[5]

One day a prominent white civil rights lawyer and former circuit judge in Jacksonville, William H. Maness, invited Shaw to be his guest at the Jacksonville Bar Association luncheon in February 1966. Maness was perhaps the most forceful white advocate for integration in Jacksonville in the 1960s. The invitation struck Shaw as a spontaneous gesture, but it was in fact a carefully planned effort by Maness and association president Earl Hadlow to end the whites-only membership. The board had agreed to extend membership to Shaw's former senior partner, Earl Johnson, but Maness wanted a trial run with a mere guest to assess members' reaction. Shaw was Maness's "guinea pig."

Maness, who had flown Hellcat fighter planes in the Pacific in World War II, recalled that his heart was pounding as he and Shaw walked through the door of the Roosevelt Hotel and up the stairs to the meeting room. "A march from Selma to Montgomery couldn't be as long, it seemed to me," he wrote in a memoir later. Shaw knew the significance of the occasion, but as one whose legal career had included the advice from judges not to be in town after the sun went down, this was relatively tame. "All they could say is get your black ass out of here, and I had heard that before," Shaw, with a laugh, told *Florida Times-Union* columnist Mark Woods in 2011.

When they reached Maness's table in the middle of the room, several other prominent lawyers came over, shook hands, and sat down. That, too, seemed spontaneous, but Shaw learned that Maness had told the others, "Come over, we're not going to sit there like lepers."[6] Maness remembered, as he told interviewer Mark D. Killian of the *Florida Bar Journal* in 1990, that when he stood and introduced Shaw as his guest, the applause "was sustained long enough to tell me it was more than a courteous gesture."[7]

When Austin became state attorney in 1969, Shaw moved with him, and Taylor came along as well. Shaw became an assistant state attorney and headed the capital crimes unit, where he won convictions in all but three of his forty-two murder cases and twenty-four rape cases. In 1972 Shaw left Austin's office to co-found the first interracial law firm in north Florida—Harrison, Finegold & Shaw. That same year he ran for circuit judge against a white candidate whose campaign posters showed his own picture and the slogan, "Looks like a judge." Harding, who was himself a circuit judge by then, remarked to Shaw at a public program years later, "I often wonder what he thought when you became an appellate judge and ruled on his cases."[8]

Shaw left the law firm in 1974 when Governor Askew, seeking accomplished blacks for appointment to state offices, appointed Shaw as one of three members of the Industrial Claims Commission. In 1979 Graham appointed him to the First DCA. When Sundberg resigned from the Supreme Court, Shaw was among the applicants for the seat.

Fourteen applicants were interviewed in Tampa by the Supreme Court Nominating Commission, chaired by the black president of Florida A&M University, Walter Smith.[9] Two were black men—Shaw and Third District Judge Wilkie D. Ferguson Jr. Four were white women—Third DCA Judge Natalie Baskin, Fifth DCA Judge Winifred Sharp, University of Miami Law Professor Minnette Massey, and Rosemary Barkett, who was then a circuit judge. Among the white males, Fourth DCA Judges Gavin K. Letts and Harry Lee Anstead were again applicants, along with Third DCA Judge Alan Schwartz, already twice nominated.

Baskin noted a gap in scholarship since England and Sundberg left, then added, "I think there's a bigger gap. There is no woman on the court, and women do represent over half the population." She added that more than individual qualifications mattered. "Your obligation is to consider the *court*, and what will constitute the best *court*." Barkett, on the other hand, said, "I think you should look for the three best people, and I don't think it should matter."

White males were also asked about the importance of a black or a woman on the court. "I sit here a white male Protestant, but I have to acknowledge, I think, in an ideal world, in the best of circumstances, that's highly desirable," said Holland & Knight lawyer John K. Aurell, son-in-law of former Governor LeRoy Collins.

Shaw said a black judge on the court would improve its "image," especially with so many death appeals, but race or sex should not be "an overriding concern." He added, "I'm not sitting here because I'm black."

The nominating commission nominated Letts, Schwartz, and Shaw. Graham took longer than usual to make the appointment. He felt substantial pressure, more than three years after the departure of Hatchett, to appoint Shaw. All three nominees for the vacancy the previous year had been white males. His approach to judicial selection was said to go roughly like this: Does any nominee stand out as clearly superior to the others? That person should have the job. Does any person stand out as clearly inferior to the others? That person should not have the job. At that point, among roughly equivalent choices, the preference should go to the minority or the woman on the list determined by the commission to be among the three best qualified.

Finally, four months after Sundberg's departure, on December 17, 1982, Graham called Shaw and extended the appointment. Graham reached Shaw in Philadelphia, where his mother had died just a few days before. Graham told reporters later that he had spent "a considerable amount of my personal time" making the decision and the choice was "especially difficult" because of the "high caliber of the candidates."

"When the governor has a chance to appoint a black person to the court, it's hard not to do it," remarked James Apthorp, a commission member who had been Askew's chief of staff. Graham's press secretary, Steve Hull, said, however, that race had nothing to do with the decision. "The governor has always said his priority in filling Supreme Court appointments is based on the qualifications of that person," Hull said.[10] Asked after Shaw's investiture if he would appoint a woman to the court, Graham said he would apply "the same standards" as he did with Shaw but did not "see that on the horizon."[11]

Shaw's investiture was January 10, 1983. Among the speakers was W. George Allen, the first black graduate of the University of Florida Law School (Class of 1962), who had been denied the right to live in married student housing and received death threats after he enrolled. Warren H. Dawson of Tampa, another civil rights litigator who was president of the largest organization for black lawyers, the National Bar Association, also was among the speakers. So was U.S. District Judge Susan H. Black of Jacksonville, who said Shaw is "always ready to share, discuss and consider others' opinions" and added, "His patience is concentrated strength." The invocation was from human rights advocate Monsignor William A. Kerr, rector of the St. Thomas More Co-Cathedral in Tallahassee and later director of Florida State University's Center for Intercultural Dialogue, which was named for Kerr after his death in 2009.

Shaw's second wife, Vidya, handled the ceremonial robing and told reporters afterward, "I don't think the governor could have made a better choice." Shaw took the seat of the junior justice at the far left of Chief Justice Alderman, next to Parker Lee McDonald, and Ehrlich shifted to the opposite end of the bench, next to Overton. Adkins and Boyd were next to the chief. "My friends have been generous and lavish in their praise," Shaw told the room full of spectators. "I recognize the office brings a challenge and a responsibility to justify that confidence. I hope to vindicate that."[12]

In 1984 Shaw and Ehrlich faced their first retention election together. Their retention was strongly opposed by George Schulte, the leader of the Citizen's Choice constitutional initiative thrown off the ballot in March. Schulte had vowed revenge the day the amendment was rejected for violating the "one subject" limitation in the Florida Constitution (chapter 26). Now he was appearing on radio and television shows and political and civic luncheons around the state decrying the "seven mental dwarves" for depriving people of a chance to control government spending.

This was the first serious campaign against justices under the merit-retention system put in place after the 1976 elections. The judicial code of ethics allowed judges facing organized opposition to raise money and go out to campaign. Shaw said he refused to be "a sitting duck" for an attack like Schulte's. "I can't believe he would want a court that would have to test public sentiment before they start ruling," Shaw said.[13] The two justices raised about $90,000, largely from lawyers. The *Gainesville Sun* was one of many newspaper voices on the other side. "If a single vote, or even a handful of votes, constituted sufficient cause to unseat a judge, then the *Sun* . . . could readily climb onto the Schulte bandwagon." The newspaper cited its objection to a court decision in mid-October refusing to stop the legislature's secret meetings. But one decision was not a proper basis for assessing a judge. The *Sun* editorial called the rejection of the amendment "judicial courage."[14]

Shaw and Ehrlich campaigned together around the state. One stop was in Broward County, where local Bar president Terry Russell greeted their small private plane at the airport to take them around for two days. He watched Ehrlich emerge from the plane first, lean and no more than 5-feet-9, fluidly stepping onto the tarmac, followed by the one-time basketball center, at 6-foot-3 and more than 200 pounds, squeezing through the same door, legs first, then torso, then arms. Like the two justices, Russell also had Jacksonville roots. He had been in high school when Shaw was a new black lawyer in town and was not only a curiosity but was occasionally in the midst of controversial cases. The visit to Broward County would later prove to have an enduring impact on Shaw and Russell.

Ehrlich and Shaw won easily with 72 percent of the vote in November.

Six years later, in 1990, Shaw's turn as chief justice in 1990 made him the first black chief justice in Florida's history, and apparently only the second in the United States. It was a new court in important ways compared with 1983, when Shaw arrived. Alderman had been replaced by Rosemary Barkett, the first woman on the court. Adkins and Boyd had retired, replaced by Stephen Grimes and Gerald Kogan. Ehrlich would be leaving in a few months because of mandatory retirement, and would be replaced by Harding. By the end of his tenure as chief, Shaw was third in seniority behind Overton and McDonald.

But his first months as chief were heavily devoted to another retention campaign with organized opposition. Shaw was the sole campaigner this time. Ehrlich was retiring. Grimes and Kogan had faced retention without controversy two years earlier, though Kogan had a slightly smaller percentage of "yes" votes at 73.3 percent, compared with Grimes's 74.6 percent. Overton, McDonald and Barkett won retention in 1986, all with more than 76% of the vote. Now in 1990, Shaw had opposition from two angles that generated much more voter emotion than the Citizen's Choice amendment. And Terry Russell, who first met Shaw on that tarmac in Broward County six years earlier and who would become president of the Florida Bar in another year, was Shaw's campaign chairman.

The brother of a murder victim was leading a campaign against Shaw after the court overturned the conviction of a man convicted of the murder. The opinion was per curiam and unanimous, but Shaw was the one justice on the ballot. The victim, Sharon Zeller, nineteen years old, was kidnapped as she left work at Walt Disney World the night of December 30, 1978. Her beaten body was found six days later at a sewage pumping station on Sand Lake Road in Orlando. The night of the murder, a vacationing Army Ranger, Robert Cox, rushed into his parents' room at a Days Inn near the pumping station, bleeding because part of his tongue had been bitten off, something he said happened during a fight at a roller-skating rink. Cox became a suspect in the murder, but with little hard evidence against him, the investigation languished, despite a steady stream of letters to news media and investigators and prosecutors from

Sharon Zeller's family. Cox went overseas with the army and took part in the invasion of Grenada in 1983.[15]

In 1986, more than seven years after the murder, Cox pled guilty in California over two separate incidents of kidnapping and assaulting women with a deadly weapon. Obviously expecting that evidence of those crimes would give them the needed edge in prosecution, Florida authorities charged him with Sharon Zeller's murder and brought him back to Orlando for trial. Still, there was only the circumstantial evidence. The jury deliberated for fourteen hours, then on July 2, 1988, nearly ten years after the murder, convicted Cox of committing it. They went on to recommend the death penalty on a 7–5 vote, and Circuit Judge Richard Conrad imposed it.

Cox's lawyer on the appeal, Assistant Public Defender Larry B. Henderson of Daytona Beach, argued that the state had failed to identify "substantial, competent evidence" to support the verdict. "The failure of the state to do its job, i.e., set forth in its brief what evidence it contends is legally sufficient to meet its burden, does a gross disservice to this court," Henderson said.[16] The state said there was a bloody boot print, but the expert testimony could say only that it was "consistent" with boots like the ones Cox was said to be wearing that night. So were hair and blood samples.

The Supreme Court did itself no favors with an opinion less than two pages long, with just one paragraph summarizing the problems with the state's evidence. When all the evidence is circumstantial, the court said, the evidence "must not only be consistent with the defendant's guilt but it must also be inconsistent with any reasonable hypothesis of innocence."[17] Cox was ordered acquitted. He had to return to prison in California, but he was expected to be freed in a few months. Although it was rare for the Supreme Court to find evidence insufficient, the decision was consistent with the standards applied in other cases, such as Anibal Jaramillo's in 1981 (chapter 24).[18] Cox was later arrested for holding a gun on a twelve-year-old girl in Decatur, Texas, and was sentenced to life.[19]

It was not the police or the prosecution that got the blame for the reversal but the Supreme Court, especially the one justice who happened to be on the ballot that fall, Leander Shaw. The jurors in the murder case, contacted by the *Orlando Sentinel*, were outraged. "Don't think for a moment there weren't doubts," the jury foreman told the *Sentinel*. "But we went through everything very, very carefully. We asked the judge for more instructions on reasonable doubt so we could be sure."[20] The victim's brother, Steven Zeller, helped organize a group that campaigned against Shaw's retention and said Shaw represented "a liberal, activist court" that was "out of touch with the mainstream of Florida."[21]

Shaw also faced organized opposition from those opposing a decision he wrote in 1989 striking down a state law that required teenage girls to get a parent's consent before having an abortion. After the U.S. Supreme Court upheld an "informed consent" requirement for abortion under Pennsylvania law, Governor Bob Martinez called a special legislative session on abortion, and the result was a parental consent law for minors seeking an abortion. The law included a "judicial bypass," allowing the girl the alternative of persuading a judge that she is mature enough to make the decision herself.

An unwed and pregnant fifteen-year-old girl sought such a "bypass," said she feared physical or emotional harm if she consulted her parents and feared the effect of her pregnancy on her ill mother. The trial judge denied her request for the waiver. The Fifth District Court of Appeal declared the statute unconstitutionally vague and said it "permits the arbitrary denial" a girl's request. The court added that the statute did not meet standards set by the U.S. Supreme Court.[22]

Attorney General Bob Butterworth and Assistant Attorney General Gerald B. Curington appealed to the Supreme Court. Nearly five months after the DCA decision, on October 5, 1989, the court released its opinion in *In re T.W.*,[23] striking down the notification law. Shaw had written it, but for unknown reasons the opinion went out that Thursday morning as per curiam. Shaw immediately asked that he be identified as the author, in full expectation that it would be a campaign issue against him. While he approved the Fifth DCA decision, Shaw went further and invoked Florida's own right to privacy, the amendment passed in 1980: "Every natural person has the right to be let alone and free from governmental intrusion into his private life except as otherwise provided herein."

Shaw said the amendment had been "implicated" in cases ranging from donor information on AIDS-tainted blood supply to Bar admission questions on psychiatric counseling. "Florida's privacy provision is clearly implicated in a woman's decision of whether or not to continue her pregnancy," he wrote. "We can conceive of few more personal or private decisions concerning one's body that one can make in the course of a lifetime, except perhaps the decision of the terminally ill in their choice of whether to discontinue necessary medical treatment." That much was consistent with the U.S. Supreme Court's abortion decisions.

The question, Shaw went on, is whether the right extends to minors. "We conclude that it does, based on the unambiguous language of the amendment." It is "common sense" that a minor's rights are not absolute, but this statute "intrudes upon the privacy of the pregnant minor from conception to birth" and "is not necessary for the preservation of maternal health or the potentiality of life." He noted that a different statute lets a pregnant minor consent to medical or surgical care related to either herself or her child during pregnancy "no matter how dire the possible consequences."

There had been little or no mention of abortion at the time the privacy amendment was being considered in 1978 and before its passage in 1980. Most of the public discussion was about government access to information and prosecutors' concerns about use of surveillance. A key opponent was State Sen. Don Childers, a Democrat from West Palm Beach, who said the amendment might legalize homosexual relationships and use of marijuana in the home.

By making abortion subject to Florida's own constitutional provision, the court buffered Florida from rulings of the increasingly conservative U.S. Supreme Court on abortion issues. Justices Barkett and Kogan joined Shaw's opinion, and Ehrlich joined as well except for a difference over the definition of "viability" of the fetus. Overton, Grimes and McDonald said the court should specify any additional procedural standards needed rather than strike down the statute. "The statute need not die on this basis," McDonald wrote. "It may be a hard decision, but dislike and hardship do not translate into unconstitutionality. It is the duty of judges to make hard decisions. That is one reason we have them."

It was, then, effectively a 4–3 decision, though all the justices agreed the law was lacking in some important respects and was covered by the Florida privacy amendment.

Carole Griffin, a lobbyist for conservative organizations, helped organize the opposition to Shaw's retention. "They're criticizing us for going after him on one issue," she told Sarasota Herald-Tribune reporter Alan Judd. "Well, let's take Hitler. We don't remember Hitler for having built the autobahn. We don't remember Hitler for having industrialized Germany. We remember him for one thing: the people he killed." Jean Doyle of Florida Right to Life Inc. said Shaw "presents a real endangerment to the family structure, to parental rights."[24]

"The unfairness bothers me," Shaw said to Judd. "If one group that is dissatisfied with one opinion . . . can take a justice off the bench, then we've got a problem."

One of those who didn't like Shaw's decision was his own campaign chairman, Terry Russell. "I've got to tell you that I'm a pro-life Democrat, that rare combination," he said in 2001 as he began a term as president of the Florida Bar. He went on:

Leander Shaw and I are philosophically opposed on that issue, but I really do believe that he did his job and did it as he felt he needed to. So I found myself in that conundrum: really wishing he hadn't ruled that way, but recognizing that he was a wonderful jurist and somebody who clearly needed to be retained in office. And I was going to help him stay there. I believe in the independence of the judiciary and the need to maintain the integrity of the merit selection process. Leander Shaw did not deserve to be knocked out of office because somebody didn't agree with one opinion he wrote.[25]

The opposition knocked twelve percentage points off Shaw's election results compared with what other justices had received in recent elections, but he was retained on the court with 59.6 percent of the votes cast in the November 1990 election. Shaw's presence in the campaign as the first black chief justice clearly motivated black voters, and it is likely that those votes spilled over to help Democrat Lawton Chiles win the governor's race against incumbent Republican Bob Martinez.

Shaw's time away from court was spent near the water. He and Vidya and son Sean lived on the edge of Lake Iamonia, fifteen miles north of Tallahassee. In 1994 Shaw bought a house on American Beach on Amelia Island, a beach popular with blacks since its purchase in 1935 by a black millionaire, who set it aside for blacks at a time when they were not allowed on most of Florida's beaches. "My body tells me when it's time to relax," he told a journalist who interviewed him there in 1999. And if his body didn't tell him in time, Shaw said with a chuckle, Jean Hendry would. His judicial assistant for his entire tenure at the Supreme Court, she would sometimes say, in what Shaw called her syrupy southern voice, "Isn't it time to go to the beach?"[26]

Shaw's retention in 1996 also had some controversy. This time it was not organized opposition but largely self-inflicted. Shaw and his wife were caught up in a nasty divorce. Vidya Shaw accused him of "fraud, deceit, duress, coercion, misrepresentation" in his filing for a divorce just two months after she, in what she said was an effort to preserve their marriage, signed an agreement giving him most of their property and waiving alimony in the event of divorce. The two had been married for seventeen years, and they had one son, Sean, in addition to four children from Shaw's first marriage.[27]

Mrs. Shaw's lawyer, Paula Walborsky, said the agreement had been "a vain attempt to keep her long-term marriage together." Justice Shaw's lawyer, Stephen Slepin, said the claims were "a sham" designed to harass the justice in his retention campaign. The post-nuptial agreement was signed in March 1995;

the divorce was granted in June. She was forty-two; he was sixty-five. A few months later, Mrs. Shaw challenged the agreement and said she signed when he threatened to play for their son audiotapes of what he said was her lesbian tryst at the house on American Beach. She denied the affair but said the tapes could be misconstrued. Justice Shaw denied having any audiotape and said his ex-wife had signed the post-nup after he discovered she was pilfering money from an apartment-rental company they jointly owned.

The controversy became public in the spring of 1996, as Shaw faced a retention vote for the last time. Shaw asked that the case files be sealed, but withdrew the request after copies of the court papers were sent to reporters. All the circuit judges in Leon County recused themselves, and the case was heard by a retired circuit judge from Bartow, William Norris. In 1991, while Shaw was chief justice, the court had rebuffed a Judicial Qualifications Commission petition that Norris receive a public reprimand for drunkenness and behavior arising from despondency. Saying Norris had suffered a "one-time personal crisis," the court 5–0 imposed a private reprimand, meaning no public appearance at the court was required. The court said he had been "an outstanding public servant for twenty years."[28]

Norris upheld the Shaws' agreement. The decision was affirmed in 1997 by the First District Court of Appeal, essentially saying that Mrs. Shaw's failure to provide a trial transcript, which her lawyer suggested she couldn't afford, kept her from meeting an appellant's burden of showing trial court error. The panel included two judges who had been on the First DCA during Shaw's tenure there, Richard Ervin III and James Joanos, as well as Judge William Van Nortwick Jr.[29]

In the end, it was a very nasty divorce in which the wife carelessly signed away too much and the husband took full advantage. It left Shaw with their residence on the lake, the place on the beach, his Mercedes, a state pension worth $900,000, and a taint on his long service on the bench. Mrs. Shaw apparently received little or nothing.

Halfway through that last term on the court came the case that brought Shaw worldwide and lasting attention, *Provenzano v. Moore*.[30] After the execution of four-hundred-pound Allen Lee "Tiny" Davis on July 8, 1999, the Supreme Court had imposed a moratorium on executions in Florida until it could reassess whether the electric chair amounted to "cruel and unusual punishment" in violation of the Constitution. It was the third abnormal execution since executions resumed in Florida in 1979. Flames had spurted out of the heads of Jesse Tafero in 1990 and Pedro Medina in 1997.

The 1999 challenge to the death penalty was brought by another death-row inmate, Thomas Provenzano, who had walked into the Orange County courthouse to face disorderly conduct charges and opened fire with a small arsenal of weapons under his garments. His original death sentence was upheld despite concerns by two justices, McDonald and Overton, that his mental condition had not been properly taken into consideration in the sentencing. Now, in a post-conviction petition against the head of the Department of Corrections, Michael W. Moore, Provenzano's lawyer, Michael P. Reiter, wanted the electric chair declared unconstitutional. His argument was that there is pain both in the preparation for execution as well as during the execution, the electric circuitry had not been maintained and was unreliable, and the prison had failed to follow its written execution protocol.

The chief justice at the time was Major Harding, who as a circuit judge had sentenced Davis to death. Harding joined a per curiam opinion upholding the use of the electric chair, but wrote his own opinion, joined by Justice R. Fred Lewis, suggesting that the legislature consider lethal injection instead. They formed the 4–3 majority along with Justice Charles T. Wells, who had come to the court from private practice, and Justice Peggy A. Quince, a former assistant attorney general who had argued in favor of a number of death sentences. The standard for finding cruel and unusual punishment, their opinion said, had been articulated two years earlier after the Medina execution: "It must involve torture or a lingering death or the infliction of 'unnecessary and wanton pain." They added, "The record in this case reveals abundant evidence that execution by electrocution renders an inmate instantaneously unconscious, thereby making it impossible to feel pain. The record also contains evidence that the electric chair is and has been functioning properly and that the electrical circuitry is being maintained." Anstead wrote his own dissenting opinion and joined dissents by Justice Barbara J. Pariente and Shaw.

Shaw's dissent said the Florida Supreme Court had never made more than a "snapshot" review of electrocution as a penalty and the U.S. Supreme Court had not done so since 1890. Shaw reviewed various forms of execution, from disembowelment to the guillotine to the gas chamber, and noted factors including "undue pain" and "undue violence, mutilation and disgrace." The U.S. Supreme Court in the past had looked to "evolving standards of decency" in determining the constitutionality of punishment. The three executions that were now the focus of review "were marred by extraordinary violence and mutilation."

To emphasize his point, Shaw did the thing that drew worldwide attention: along with the opinions in the case on the Supreme Court's website, he posted photos of the Davis execution showing what he called "a ghastly post-execution scene." The visible part of the face "is bright purple and scrunched tightly upwards; his eyes are clenched shut and his nose is pushed so severely upward that it is barely visible above the mouth-strap." He noted the mouth strap covering part of Davis's nostrils. "A stream of blood pours from his nostrils, flows over the wide leather mouth-strap, runs down his neck and chest, and forms a bright red pool (approximately eight by twelve inches) on his white shirt. The scene is unquestionably violent."

Shaw said he would support carrying out Provenzano's execution by lethal injection and did not consider that replacement for the electric chair unconstitutional.

The legislature eventually enacted that change.

Years later, as a member of an eight-person review of Florida's death penalty by the American Bar Association, Shaw said that he opposed the death penalty. "I think it's a system that at the least needs improving. It's sort of a crap shoot, really. If you get a good lawyer, chances are better than if you had a bad lawyer, no matter what the evidence is."[31]

Shaw would participate in thousands of opinions over his twenty years on the court and author what some have said is the most-cited opinion the court has ever issued, *DiGuilio v. State*, prescribing the proper uses of "harmless error" in appellate review (chapter 29). But the abortion and execution opinions would have the most enduring fame.

One other thing among the hundreds of things he did as chief justice: in 1991, a quarter-century after breaking racial barriers in Jacksonville, Shaw went back to swear in his old boss, Ed Austin, as mayor of the city.

At the end of his term on January 6, 2003, Shaw was forced to leave the court by constitutional retirement rules, which Adkins had dubbed "constitutional senility." He was seventy-three. He had won retention votes in 1984, 1990, and 1996. His twenty years on the court put him among the ten longest-serving justices in Florida history, out of eighty who had joined the court up to that date, and he had served longer than any other justice he served with except Overton, whose twenty-five-year tenure from March 1974 to January 1999 was exceeded by only five other justices in history.

At the retirement ceremony on November 8, 2002, Shaw's first wife Dolores was there, and his five children, sons Leander III (known as Jerry, his middle name) and Sean, and daughters Sherri, Dione, and Dawn. Askew was there, too, acknowledged by Shaw as "the governor who brought me back to Tallahassee." Joe Hatchett remarked that Shaw "wrote carefully researched and well-crafted opinions" that "satisfy the most scholarly minds while at the same time being entirely accessible to readers of much more modest experience and ability." He also will be remembered, Hatchett added, "for his friendship, his grace, gentility and warmth."

The court at the time included the first black woman on the court, Peggy Quince; another woman, Barbara Pariente; two Jewish justices, Pariente and Kogan; the first Cuban-American, Raoul Cantero; and white Protestant males Harry L. Anstead and Fred Lewis. "We have moved from a time where the very right to study law could be denied because of somebody's mere external appearance to a time today where the very appearance of this court symbolizes the devotion to the principle of equal justice under law," said Anstead, the chief justice.

Shaw told the audience that the court had received about three thousand appeals over the previous year, and the justices authored more than 350 opinions, which made the court one of the busiest in the nation. "We are defined not so much by the work we do daily but by the few high-profile cases that, for whatever reason, draw media attention," Shaw said. Most of the work, he noted, is done outside public view, and justices are often not recognized. He said he was once crossing the street on his way back from lunch and was asked to join a picket line in front of the court. "It turned out that they were protesting an opinion that I had written," but not a single protester recognized him.[32]

24

DEATH PENALTY

Deciding Who Dies

Nearly eleven years after the new death-penalty law was signed by Governor Askew in 1972 and four and a half years after the Spenkelink execution, a second person was executed under authority of the 1972 statute. Robert A. Sullivan, who had spent ten years on death row (almost twice as long as Spenkelink), had robbed a Howard Johnson's in Homestead, abducted the assistant manager, driven him to a remote spot, hit him in the head with a tire iron, then fired both barrels of a shotgun into the back of his head. On November 20, 1983, on his second death warrant, 350-pound Sullivan drank scotch on the rocks with the warden, just as Spenkelink had done, and died in the electric chair with a .06 blood-alcohol level.[1]

The Supreme Court had upheld his sentence in an opinion by Justice Hal Dekle on November 27, 1974. A decade later, with execution imminent and a frenzied effort for a stay, the court rejected ineffective-counsel claims by agreeing with the federal Eleventh Circuit that his earlier lawyer's "failure to divine the judicial development of Florida's capital sentencing does not constitute ineffective assistance of counsel."[2]

Many predicted at the time that executions would finally begin with some regularity.

Sure enough, within two months, Anthony Antone was executed for the murder of Tampa detective Richard Cloud in what was described as a mob hit. Antone, protesting his innocence and declaring in his final words that "they know not what they do," was executed on January 26, 1984.

On April 5, Arthur Frederick Goode, molester and killer of young boys after escaping from a mental institution, whose parents had whipped him for doing wrong but said he never understood what he had done, had a final dessert of Neapolitan ice cream and was executed.

A month later, the state executed James Adams, the first black man to die in the electric chair since the return of capital punishment, also protesting that the state had convicted the wrong man.

In June, Carl Shriner, who grew up with beatings by his father but never got to tell jurors about it because of misperceived limitations on mitigating evidence, was executed for the murder of a clerk at a Majik Market in Gainesville shortly after finishing a five-year sentence for an armed robbery.

In July, David Washington was executed two months after losing 8–1 at the U.S. Supreme Court, in a ruling that Attorney General Jim Smith hoped would curtail "the merry-go-round of appeals based on ambiguous and vague claims of ineffective assistance of counsel."[3] The ruling said reviews of the claims must be "highly deferential" to the lawyer in question and required a defendant to prove a "reasonable probability" but not a "likelihood" that the lawyer's errors made a difference in the outcome.[4] Washington had stabbed three people to death in three separate robberies in Miami in 1976.

Ernest John Dobbert had heaped abuse on his four children over a four-year period, had beaten his daughter Kelly Ann, burned her hands, belted her across the cheek and held her head underwater, then after killing her supposedly buried her in the backyard, though her body was not found. His own mental illness had prompted the jurors to recommend life in prison instead of death, but they were overruled by Judge Hudson Olliff, and on September 7, Dobbert was executed.

Two weeks later, Henry James was executed.

Seven weeks after that, Timothy Palmes was executed.

Eight executions in one year would not happen again for thirty years. In 1985 there were three, then three more in 1986, and one in 1987. The surge in 1984 was a result of the same kind of last-ditch appellate process that had preceded the Spenkelink execution. The heavy volume of appeals was set in motion by Governor Graham's persistent signing of death warrants month after month, and followed by post-conviction hearings in the state and federal courts until there was nothing more to argue.

Death sentences kept coming to the Supreme Court even as executions settled back to two or three a year. In 1984, as eight death-row cells were emptied by executions, ten cells were occupied by new death row inmates who were still there thirty years later.

The justice who propounded the lofty aspirations of objectivity and consistency in State v. Dixon turned out to be the most consistent justice of all in upholding death sentences. Adkins voted to execute more than three-fourths of the capital defendants whose appeals came to the court over the next decade, more than any other justice.[5] In his thirteen years on the court after writing the opinion in *Dixon*, Adkins not once dissented from a decision upholding a death sentence. "I support capital punishment because it is a deterrent to future murders," Adkins wrote in his memoir, "I do not mean deterrence in the traditional sense. If a man is going to commit a murder, I don't think he is going to think about the chair and then decide not to carry out the act. . . . Many killers have 'murder in their heart,' as country people used to say, and would enjoy murdering again. Electrocution prevents these people from murdering again. . . . [R]attlesnakes should be killed and not kept as pets."[6]

Adkins once got himself specially assigned to preside over the trial of one of three men accused of murdering two couples—two teenaged sisters and two older men—after they stumbled onto a marijuana-smuggling operation in an area of Bay County known as Sandy Creek on January 23, 1977. The older man in the foursome was shot almost immediately, apparently after pulling his own gun on the ringleader who stopped their truck. The others were bound and gagged, driven to a sinkhole in Taylor County, and shot in the head. Their bodies were not discovered until August. The "Sandy Creek murders" became a big story.

Local Circuit Judge Fred Turner recused himself, because as a lawyer he had represented the estate of one of the victims. Adkins, after consulting Fourteenth Circuit Chief Judge Robert L. McCrary, asked Chief Justice Overton to give him a special assignment to preside over the case. His rationale was that it would be the first major trial under the court's one-year experiment with television cameras in courtrooms. Adkins told his law clerks later that Overton said no at first, but then Adkins told him he had better not leave the building, because, as the senior justice, he would become acting chief and appoint himself. Adkins's account apparently was playfully exaggerated. Overton laughed when told the story and said it didn't happen, but added, "He was bugging me about it. Remember, he had written [books] on criminal procedure before he was on the court. He wanted to see what it was like under the new [death penalty] law."[7] Overton finally gave Adkins the high-profile assignment he wanted.

The defendant in Adkins's trial, David Goodwin, was down on the beach with the smuggled marijuana when the victims drove up. He was not at the sinkhole where the three were later killed. He did fetch the rope used by the ringleader, Walter Gale Steinhorst, to tie the victims. Steinhorst was convicted in a different trial, with a different judge, of being the actual killer and was sentenced to death. (He died in a prison hospital in 1999 after twenty-two years on death row.[8]) In Goodwin's trial, the jury recommended life, but Adkins sentenced him to death.

On appeal to the Supreme Court, Adkins could not participate, of course, and Dade Circuit Judge Harold Vann was designated to fill in for him. On a 5–1 vote, with Boyd dissenting, Adkins's own court overturned the death sentence.[9] Judge Vann's opinion for the majority noted the jury's recommendation of life, Goodwin's absence from the scene of the murder itself, and evidence of his fear of Steinhorst. "The facts of this case do not warrant the ultimate penalty," Vann wrote.

The court would have a number of capital defendants who took on some measure of national celebrity—foremost among them Spenkelink and later serial killers Theodore Bundy and Aileen Wuornos (who inspired films including 2003's *Monster*, starring Charlize Theron). Among the lesser celebrities was a black poet and community organizer from Chicago named Delbert Lee Tibbs, who had his own unique journey through the Florida capital appeals process.

Even decades after the crime, the state attorney and police in Fort Myers still asserted that Tibbs was the man who, on February 3, 1974, picked up a white seventeen-year-old girl and a white twenty-seven-year-old man who were hitchhiking from St. Petersburg. The girl later said they were picked up by a black man in a green truck with no right door handle, a blinking oil light, and a round hood. A few miles south of Fort Myers, she said, the driver pulled into a field, shot the man to death as he begged for his life, then raped the girl. The killer ordered her to dress and get back in the truck then soon told her to get out and walk in front of the truck. She escaped.

Neither the green truck nor the gun was ever found. Delbert Tibbs was unquestionably in Daytona Beach, not Fort Myers, on February 2, the day before the crime. He claimed he was in Daytona the next three days as well, but the state produced a sign-in card with his name at the Salvation Army Center in Orlando on the night of February 4, the day after the crime. (Years later, an expert said the signature was a forgery.) On February 6, on the basis of the girl's description, Tibbs was stopped by police in Leesburg, 200 miles north of Fort Myers and seventy miles west of Daytona. He was released, then picked up in nearby Ocala on February 7. He cooperated, said he had been in Daytona on February 3, had a picture taken for police in Fort Myers, and was sent on his way.

Ten days later, the girl was called back to Fort Myers from St. Petersburg. She was shown the pictures of Tibbs and said that was the man. On March 13 Tibbs was picked up in Mississippi, waived extradition, and was taken to Fort Myers. The girl picked him out of a four-man lineup. Tried by an all-white jury, he was convicted with the help of testimony from a cellmate, an admitted perjurer, who said Tibbs had confessed to him. The jury recommended a death sentence, and Circuit Judge Thomas Shands imposed it.

As Tibbs sat on death row waiting for his appeal, folk singer Pete Seeger put on a concert to raise money for his defense. Angela Davis, a well-known black activist of the era, raised money, too. On July 28, 1976, the newest justices—England, Sundberg, and Hatchett—joined Boyd in overturning the conviction on a 4–3 vote and ordering a new trial. It was a rare case—one of only two in the entire first decade of the death penalty—in which the court overturned a conviction because the evidence overall was deemed inadequate to prove guilt.

The one-man photo lineup was suggestive, the justices said, and tainted the subsequent identification in the real line-up. The girl had used marijuana the day of the crime, which added more doubt to the precision of her memory. While the girl said it was daylight, other evidence suggested it was after nightfall. She had described her assailant as dark-skinned, and Tibbs had light skin. The justices gave "no credence" to the jailmate's claims. Boyd, writing separately, added that the girl's original description was of "a ruffian whose language, personality and physical appearance conflicted substantially with that of the appellant (Tibbs), who was identified at the trial by Chicago public officials and professional people as having a good reputation and being a law-abiding citizen." Boyd also noted that no evidence besides the girl's identification put Tibbs within 150 miles of Fort Myers that day.

Boyd thought Tibbs should be set free but went along with the other three in remanding the case for a new trial. Boyd argued that a new trial after a finding of insufficient evidence was double jeopardy. He made his case again a year later in *McArthur v. State*,[10] in which England, Overton, Hatchett, and Karl had found evidence against that defendant "consistent with a reasonable hypothesis of innocence" and ordered a new trial. (Alderman had been the trial judge in that case.) Boyd's view was largely adopted the following year by the U.S. Supreme Court. That court sent the *McArthur* case back to the Florida Supreme Court, which set the defendant free as Boyd had urged.[11]

What happened in the Tibbs case after the remand for a new trial was a jurisprudential mess. While the case was still awaiting trial, the U.S. Supreme Court ruled that an appellate court's finding of "insufficient evidence" was the same as a jury's.[12] Had the jury, rather than the justices, perceived a "real possibility" of innocence and acquitted Tibbs because of "reasonable doubt," he could never be tried again because of the "double jeopardy" rule. (The U.S. Constitution forbids being tried again after an acquittal. Errors in procedures, by police or the court system, are considered different from weaknesses in the evidence itself, so retrials are allowed after reversals for procedural errors.)

So when Tibbs finally came up for retrial in Lee County, Circuit Judge Jack Schoonover ruled there could be no second trial and dismissed the case entirely. The state appealed to the Second District Court of Appeal. Judge Edward F. Boardman, joined by Judges Stephen Grimes and Herboth S. Ryder, cited a number of Florida cases overturning convictions because of inadequate evidence—most of them remanded for a new trial, as the majority in *Tibbs* had done. Boardman said it would be "an anomaly . . . if an appellate court could not reverse and remand for a new trial if it was of the opinion that the evidence . . . was so far from convincing as to require a new trial in the interest of justice."[13]

Tibbs went back to the Florida Supreme Court, and this time he wanted to stop that second trial and win outright acquittal. It was now 1981. B. K. Roberts, a dissenter in Tibbs's first appeal, had retired at the end of 1976, but Hatchett, who had supported the remand, was gone, too. Two new arrivals, McDonald and Alderman, both former trial judges in conservative counties, joined former trial judges Overton and Adkins to produce a 4–3 decision against Tibbs. Showing no concern for the "anomaly" that concerned Boardman, the four justices said the court had no business second guessing the original jury and should have upheld the conviction. The girl's testimony provided legal "sufficiency" for the verdict, and once the court determined legal "sufficiency" for a conviction, that was it. The earlier majority, they said, had engaged in "clearly improper" reweighing of the evidence. Tibbs's conviction should have been upheld, they said.

So what to do now? The court could take back its decision of five years earlier and reinstate the conviction and even the death sentence, "but that would prejudice Tibbs for our improper reweighing of the evidence." Another option was to just let Tibbs go, but that could be done only by declaring the evidence "insufficient," which the new majority thought was "stretching the point." So as a "compromise" they would not uphold the original conviction and would not let him go but would order a new trial.

The three justices remaining from the original majority were not happy, even though a new trial was exactly what they had called for the first time. They agreed that courts shouldn't "reweigh" evidence but said the original opinion had really declared the evidence "insufficient." England said he would simply "direct his discharge in the interest of justice." Sundberg, writing separately, said the weight-sufficiency distinction was "useless." Just three months earlier, though, in *Brown v. Wainwright* over the court's use of psychological profiles on inmates, both had declared that the court had no role in weighing evidence, only in protecting "procedural regularity" (chapter 16). Boyd stood by his original view that a new trial, with a chance for more evidence against Tibbs, amounted to double jeopardy in violation of the Constitution.

The U.S. Supreme Court took Tibbs's appeal. On June 7, 1982, the court upheld Florida's latest 4–3 decision that a retrial was not double jeopardy after a reversal on the weight, as opposed to sufficiency, of evidence.[14] A month after the U.S. Supreme Court decision, however, State Attorney Joseph D'Alessandro decided against a retrial. The victim, he said later, had "progressed from a marijuana smoker to a crack user and I could not put her on the stand." He dropped the charges on September 3, 1982. Assistant Attorney General Ray Marky later called Tibbs "the unworthy recipient of intellectually dishonest judicial officers."[15] The Death Penalty Information Center, however, lists Tibbs among its "Cases of Innocence." As of 2011, Tibbs had never been arrested for anything again.[16]

A few months later, things turned out far more simply in another death case where the evidence seemed wholly inadequate to prove guilt. Alderman wrote for a 5–1 majority declaring the evidence against Anibal Jaramillo "insufficient" and ordering the defendant freed.[17] Alderman noted that Jaramillo had been able to explain his fingerprints in the house where the murders occurred, so the state had failed to establish that the fingerprints could have gotten there only at the time of the murder. Other testimony said the victims' nephew, not Jaramillo, was the one seen in the vicinity near the time of the murders. The case had been tried before Circuit Judge Ellen Morphonios Gable in Miami.

This time, instead of insisting on a retrial, Alderman and McDonald joined Boyd and Sundberg as well as Ehrlich, who had replaced England, in setting Jaramillo free. Only Adkins dissented. Jaramillo was freed and later deported to Colombia, where he was murdered.[18]

The justices never tolerated any challenge to the death penalty based on racial disparity[19] and gave little attention to problems of excluding blacks or death-penalty opponents from juries. The U.S. Supreme Court, whose *Furman* decision in 1972 had been heavily motivated by racial disparity, sidelined the issue after 1976 with its confidence in the new standards in the new statutes. Soon the focus had shifted to differences in punishment based not simply on the race of the defendant but on the race of the victim. William Middleton, who joined more than 125 others on Florida's death row on September 30, 1980, seven years after the bold assurances in *Dixon*, was the first white defendant in Florida sentenced to death for the killing of a black person.[20] By 1984, of a dozen death row inmates viewed by the attorney general as most likely to be executed, only one had killed a black person.

Also rare was the overturning of a death sentence because of errors or ineptitude of prosecutors or defense lawyers. Those almost always worked against the defendant. Defense lawyers' oversights, such as failures to object to inadmissible evidence, were treated as "tactics" or simply "waivers" rather than blunders, so those were assessed against the defendant. Prosecutors' excesses or procedural errors might draw a remonstrance but were treated as "harmless" error in light of other evidence.

"We are deeply disturbed as a court by the continuing violations of prosecutorial duty, propriety and restraint," the justices wrote in *Bertolotti v. State*[21] in 1985. Closing arguments "must not be used to inflame the minds and passions of the jurors so that their verdict reflects an emotional response to the crime or the defendant rather than a logical analysis of the evidence." The prosecutor "clearly overstepped the bounds of proper argument on at least three occasions," including one "fairly susceptible of being interpreted as a comment on the defendant's exercise of his right to remain silent."

Did this clear error produce a new trial? No. Instead of focusing on the impairment of a fair trial, the justices in the unanimous per curiam opinion made the remarkable comment that professional misconduct by prosecutors during trial should "not be punished at the citizens' expense, by reversal and mistrial, but at the attorney's expense, by professional sanction."[22] They referred to the jury recommendation of a sentence as "advisory only," a dramatic departure from traditional emphasis on the importance of the jury recommendation.

When the defense attorney was identified as the culprit in *Francis v. State*[23] two months earlier, Alderman had written that the jury's recommendation of life, which the judge overrode and the Supreme Court rejected, had "no reasonable basis" and "perhaps" was "a result of the highly emotional closing argument of defense counsel" just before Easter Sunday about "the cup of forgiveness."[24]

In Sullivan's case, the prosecutor had intentionally gotten a witness to talk about Sullivan's lie-detector test, a stark violation of the rules of evidence, but the court said it was harmless because there was plenty of other evidence. Even a prosecutor's repeated references to a black defendant as an "animal" were approved in *Darden v. State*[25] because the defense lawyer "waited until the fifth time" to object.

Willie Darden came very close to a reversal of his conviction for killing a furniture store owner in Lakeland. Darden was tried in Citrus County and was the third person sentenced to death in Florida after restoration of the death penalty, behind Spenkelink and Sullivan. As of the date of oral argument, July 2, 1975, Sundberg was writing a majority opinion reversing Darden's conviction and death sentence on the basis of the prosecutor's remarks. Sundberg's vote tally from the justices' conference immediately afterward, contained in Sundberg's confidential files at the court,[26] shows that only Adkins and Roberts favored upholding the conviction, while Boyd, Overton, England, and Circuit Judge John Ferris, substituting on the case, all supported Sundberg's view that the prosecutors' remarks "were such that the issue of appellant's guilt or innocence was lost in a flood of these other overshadowing charges and accusations."

It was a gruesome crime. It began with the holdup of the wife of the furniture-store owner, and when her unarmed husband entered the room, he was shot between the eyes. A young store assistant who went to his aid was shot three times. A short time later, a short distance away, Darden wrecked his car during a rainstorm—that was what led police to him. A gun identified as "probably" the murder weapon was found thirty-nine feet from the car. Darden was on a furlough from prison after previous convictions.

"We have considered all the points raised on appeal by the appellant and conclude that only one merits consideration for reversal," Sundberg wrote in longhand on a yellow pad as he drafted what he thought would be the majority opinion. The prosecutor's argument, he said, "was so inflammatory and abusive as to have deprived the appellant of a fair trial." Sundberg said "strenuous advocacy . . . of the facts and evidence" helps a jury "arrive at that most desired result in our system—the truth." But this prosecutor was out of line. Over two separate pages of his legal pad, Sundberg listed, by transcript page number, the offending comments, first noting defense counsel's own use of "animal" in describing the killer's actions (while denying it was Darden):

Δ [shorthand for defendant] refers to vicious animal at p. 717. act on young boy was "work of an animal—p. 732. "I wouldn't do what you are being asked to do on that evidence." P. 734.
State—I was convinced that Willie Jasper Darden is a murderer . . . I will be convinced of that the rest of my life. P. 748.
. . .
p. 758—wish decedent had shotgun and had blown Δ's face off. I wish I could see him sitting there with no face, blown away by a shotgun.
p. 759—I wish someone had walked in back door & blown his head off at that point.

p. 765—Δ and his keepers, Division of Corrections on trial.

p. 766—If hadn't had accident would still be in public on his furloughs, visiting his family, shooting his pool, selling his gun, drinking his whiskey.

p. 774—I wish Δ had used pistol on himself.

. . .

p. 779—The only thing he hasn't done that I know of is cut his throat. objection by Δ.

But somewhere between Sundberg's draft opinion of August 26, 1975, and the final decision on February 18, 1976, Sundberg lost all the votes except England's. Boyd was shifting dramatically in 1975 from his initial dissents in capital cases in 1974 to affirming death sentences at a high rate, just as Adkins did. Overton, who had generally voted to uphold death sentences in 1975 and 1976 and had not yet begun to show more skepticism toward capital sentences, tended to give the benefit of the doubt to circuit judges and may have concluded that the defense lawyer did not make timely objections to the clearly improper argument. Those two, along with Adkins and Roberts, produced a majority against Darden. Judge Ferris shifted as well.

Boyd ended up writing the majority opinion affirming Darden's conviction. Released one year after the *Spenkelink* decision, Boyd took language from Sundberg's draft in elaborating on the prosecutor's comments, but concluded: "A careful examination of the record leads this court to conclude that, although the prosecutor's remarks under ordinary circumstances would constitute a violation of the Code of Professional Responsibility, in this particular case they amount to harmless error when the totality of the record is considered in these uniquely vicious crimes."

On March 15, 1988, after a record seven warrants, Darden was executed.

Once it upheld a death sentence, as it did in about half the original appeals, the Supreme Court clung to its decision. It reversed itself only after multiple challenges and usually under pressure of more stringent federal court reviews without ever acknowledging any inadequacy on its own part in identifying the issue from the outset. The court reflexively showed disdain for defense lawyers who pressed post-conviction claims. The justices in *Arango v. State* wrote a blistering criticism of 11th-hour appeals and the tarnishing of the reputations of a defendant's previous lawyers—and then upheld the defendant's claims. [27]

Two months after the Spenkelink execution, six of the seven justices lambasted defense lawyer Larry Spalding for his post-conviction effort to show ineffectiveness of the trial counsel representing Virgil Lee Douglas. Alderman even questioned Spalding's professional ethics.[28] Five years later, shortly after the U.S. Supreme Court decision in David Washington's case set a mid-level standard for showing ineffectiveness, Spalding prevailed at the federal Eleventh Circuit, which said in a 2–1 decision that the trial counsel's "ineffectiveness cries out from a reading of the transcript."[29] Twelve years after chastising Spalding about his professional conduct, the Florida Supreme Court in effect agreed with his position. The justices declared that there were mitigating circumstances to support the jury's original recommendation of life and overturned the trial judge's death sentence.[30]

The justices also failed to notice, or shrugged off, deficient lawyering that happened right in front of them. In *Wilson v. State*, the defense lawyer at oral argument first acknowledged there was sufficient evidence to prove his client guilty, then said that if he was guilty, the death penalty was probably appropriate. The justices, who say repeatedly that they scrutinize the entire record of a case, upheld the death penalty, and not a single one mentioned this cringeworthy level of advocacy until a post-conviction appeal two years later arguing ineffective representation. At that point, the court noted the "unique role" of the defense lawyer and said its own "judicially neutral review of so many death cases, many with records running to the thousands of pages, is no substitute for the careful, partisan scrutiny of a zealous advocate."[31] The same lawyer appeared in *Maxwell v. State* and took no issue with the judge's findings on the aggravating and mitigating factors. The Supreme Court reversed two of the factors on its own, but still upheld the death sentence under the *Elledge* Rule, again with no mention of any substandard legal representation.[32]

In a Jacksonville murder where two black defendants were tried together for the racially motivated murder of a white man, the jury recommended death for Jacob Dougan and life with a twenty-five-year minimum for Elwood Barclay. The trial judge sentenced both to death. At the Supreme Court, the same lawyer represented both men even though their interests were clearly in conflict because of their different sentences. The lawyer's brief was incomplete, contained no mention of Barclay after the title page, and offered nothing to support the life recommendation the trial judge had ignored. None of the justices, apparently, considered these omissions significant as they upheld Barclay's death sentence.[33]

Barclay had the misfortune to be tried in front of Circuit Judge R. Hudson Olliff, who sent five men to death row, four of them despite life recommendations from the jury. One indication of Olliff's judicial temperament was that in 1976, when Chief Circuit Judge Major B. Harding (the future justice) transferred Olliff from criminal to civil cases, Olliff held a press conference in his judicial robe and denounced Harding. Olliff even got an audience with Chief Justice Overton (to whom Harding was mailing the news clippings) before finally apologizing publicly for his "injudicious" comments.[34] In a study by the local newspaper, Olliff handled half again as many criminal cases as the other criminal judges and imposed only one-fourth as many sentences of probation.[35]

Olliff was the same judge who sentenced Ernest Dobbert to death despite a jury recommendation of life. He was given to expressing his personal outrage as he imposed death sentences. He spiced his rulings with references to his experiences as a paratrooper in World War II and seeing "friends blown to bits." He would add that he is "not easily shocked—but this was an especially shocking crime." Applying the factor of a previous crime of violence to Barclay's earlier breaking-and-entering conviction, Olliff said "it is not known" whether there was any violence, but even without evidence Olliff deemed it sufficient that a break-in "can and often does involve violence or threat of violence." The Supreme Court expressed no concern about such points of reference outside the record or the absence of evidence to support an aggravating circumstance.

In its original review of Barclay's case, the Florida Supreme Court said only that if Barclay got life, two perpetrators (Barclay and Dougan) "who participated equally" would have disparate sentences. The court did not mention—because it apparently did not know—that two other participants in the crime, who had actually committed a second murder as well, got life with no restrictions on their possible parole.[36]

After multiple appeals spanning seven years, including an affirmance from the U.S. Supreme Court, prominent lawyer Sandy D'Alemberte took on Barclay's case and persuaded the Florida Supreme Court that Barclay had "ineffective appellate counsel." The court reduced Barclay's sentence to life *in Barclay v. Wainwright*.[37] Dougan, as of the end of 2015, was sixty-eight years old and remained on death row, where he had been for more than forty years, longer than all but four other men.

The justices were not simply rubber-stamping death sentences. During the first dozen years under the new death statute, half the death sentences were reversed at the Supreme Court—overturned outright in about a fourth of the cases, remanded for resentencing in another fourth. That meant that even by the Supreme Court's deferential standards, only half the trial judges presiding over capital cases were applying the law correctly. The pattern continued year after year. Half the new death sentences were overturned in 1981, the same percentage as in 1974 and 1975. That rate of reversals doesn't count later reversals by federal courts on post-conviction petitions.

But a 50 percent reversal rate in 1974 was just four cases, and was understandable when the court was just beginning to apply the statute. By 1981 the caseload was five times larger, and a 50 percent reversal rate meant twenty cases were decided wrongly at the trial level and were reviewed unnecessarily. If the justices had any inclination to pause and reflect on the quality and consequences of their work on capital cases, it was subsumed by the urgency to go faster and faster in disposing of more and more cases. Not only had the justices created an expansive reading of the capital statute to begin with, but the absence of analytical rigor and consistency gave trial judges even more latitude to use death sentences to show they were tough on crime in a high-profile case. Better to be reversed than to be too lenient toward a killer in their community. Locally elected prosecutors could indulge themselves rhetorically with little concern about reversal because of the court's indulgence of "harmless error."

Defense lawyers had every reason to keep rolling the dice with more post-conviction appeals, even if the odds weren't good. They never knew when they might hit the jackpot. Delay might not only delay an appointment with the executioner but actually allow time for the law to "evolve" in their favor and produce a new sentencing hearing. Many more years would pass before the Supreme Court required that capital cases be assigned only to trial judges who had received special training and handled only by lawyers certified as knowledgeable and experienced in death cases.

The court's frustration with the lawyers handling post-conviction appeals grew steadily. By the mid-1980s, with more death warrants and a growing backlog of cases, the legislature reluctantly funded an office of Capital Collateral Review, or CCR, to replace the small, underfunded non-profit effort that Scharlette Holdman had run for years in tracking cases and warrants and recruiting volunteer lawyers. Attorney General Smith took some criticism for seeming to acquiesce in this system of multiple drawn-out appeals, but he recognized that many judges would not deny a stay to an inmate without counsel and viewed the new CCR as a way to bring more order to the process and perhaps speed it up.

But Governor Graham and later Governor Bob Martinez, who took office in 1987, continued to sign warrants in increasing numbers, and even CCR was overwhelmed. The court began to see defense briefs that were clearly cut-and-paste briefs, even without changing the names of the defendant in the text. CCR lawyers looked at the court's own sloppy review and saw their role as forcing justices' recognition of their errors. The lawyers were sleeping in their offices trying to keep up with the load, while the justices viewed the cut-and-paste work as repetitively raising issues previously rejected.

The court attempted to deal with the flood of cases by imposing time limits and limitations on multiple appeals. One goal was to also cut off access to federal courts by harnessing long-standing federal rules of deference to state courts. Something the Supreme Court did not do was move any of this process to the District Courts of Appeal. Its constitutional jurisdiction was over "final judgments of trial courts imposing the death penalty," and no one seemed interested in limiting that phrase to original sentencings, perhaps because it was unthinkable that an execution would proceed without Supreme Court review anyway. But the effect was to turn the court into a death panel, as opposed to the concept in the 1980 jurisdictional amendment that the court should deal with important questions of law, not justice in individual cases.

It was said in 1972 that having all death cases go to the Supreme Court was the only way to assure uniformity. The five District Courts of Appeal, which often rule differently on points of law, have no role in capital cases. In other areas of the law, these intermediate courts often instigate reconsideration of settled principles. Through conflicts among the districts and certifications to the Supreme Court, they crystallize important issues that need the Supreme Court's attention. They identify outdated concepts or areas of confusion, as occurred with the pivotal ruling on comparative negligence in *Hoffman v. Jones.*

With more sifting in the District Courts of Appeal, the Supreme Court would have been under more obvious pressure to bring a greater sense of reality to what was happening in the evolution of death-penalty litigation, to take the statutory language seriously from the beginning, and to provide clear refinement and direction to the lower courts. The Supreme Court might have been more focused on managing a capital system and a body of case law instead of processing individual cases. The absence of this sifting process in death cases meant that the Supreme Court's only cues of weaknesses and inconsistencies in its death-penalty jurisprudence came from sources the justices viscerally resisted—the federal courts and the defense lawyers.

The factors in aggravation and mitigation, which seemed so balanced, in fact were heavily tilted against defendants. The aggravating factors are relatively easy to prove, often through an official document or a few moments of testimony. Perhaps the most commonly used aggravating factor is that the murder was committed in the course of any of seven listed felonies, including rape, battery, burglary, or robbery. Those require no additional proof at sentencing. Autopsy testimony at trial or even a defendant's own confession often forms the factual basis for heinousness.

Mitigating factors, on the other hand, are complicated to prove, and even harder to make convincing to jurors. The statute lists, for example, the "influence of extreme mental or emotional disturbance" or a "substantially impaired" capacity to "appreciate the criminality of his conduct or to conform his conduct to the requirements of law." Those factors call for professional evaluations that are often complex, expensive, and ambiguous. Evidence of mental illness sometimes frightens jurors more than it evokes sympathy; it sometimes even tips jurors off to a defendant's previous wrongdoing that might otherwise be withheld from the jury as too prejudicial to be admitted as evidence.

Even seemingly simple mitigating factors, like "age," are complicated and inconsistent in practice. What does "age" mean exactly, since everybody has one? Paul Magill was seventeen years and ten months old when he kidnapped, raped, and killed a twenty-five-year-old convenience store clerk. The court referred to Magill as "nearly 18"[38] and didn't mention age at all after a court-ordered resentencing, despite a dissent from Boyd noting "society's special concern for its juveniles" that should give the age factor "great significance."[39] In *Gafford v. State*, about the same time as Magill's first appeal, the court upheld a trial judge's finding that age nineteen was a mitigating circumstance.[40]

The Supreme Court routinely deferred to trial judges who would hear a lot of evidence about mitigating factors and still find "no mitigating circumstances." In *James v. State*,[41] the court said the defense "presented a considerable amount of testimony in an attempt to mitigate his sentence," but it was rejected with the Supreme Court's approval. In *Johnson v. State*,[42] the defense similarly offered testimony about his family background and supporting testimony from friends, relatives, and neighbors; however, a finding of no mitigating circumstances was upheld.

Three years after the U.S. Supreme Court's *Proffitt* decision in 1976, and three weeks after Spenkelink was executed, Governor Graham signed death warrants on Charles Proffitt and Robert A. Sullivan. A round of appeals similar to Spenkelink's began immediately for each man. It took another four and a half years, but on November 30, 1983, Sullivan was the second person executed in Florida under the 1972 law.

Proffitt's appeals, however, continued. Twice he had been runner-up for the electric chair and lived to fight another day. Proffitt's lawyers focused on the problems in Judge Burnside's original sentencing order back in 1974—the one the Florida Supreme Court had called "obviously correct."

In 1978 and again after a death warrant was signed in 1979,[43] the Florida Supreme Court rejected Proffitt's new appeals. The court's attitude was that as long as one of the aggravating factors was good, those overlooked errors didn't matter anyway, and there was no reason to reconsider the finding of no mitigating circumstances. But in 1982 the federal Eleventh Circuit found fault with the past proceedings and ordered a new sentencing hearing for Proffitt.[44]

Despite continued state resistance to the order, Hillsborough Circuit Judge John P. Griffin eventually held a hearing and handed down a new death sentence, this time based on the one correct aggravating factor from the first trial—that the killing happened in the course of a burglary—and on a new factor added by the legislature in 1979, that the murder was "cold, calculated, and premeditated." There were also mitigating factors, which had been equally applicable twelve years earlier, but defense lawyers had learned over the past twelve years how to present them. Although the judge found a number of mitigating factors this time, Proffitt again was sentenced to death.

The case went up on appeal again to the Florida Supreme Court, which coyly said the federal Eleventh Circuit had ordered resentencing "in light of errors which that court cited had occurred in the 1974 sentencing proceeding."[45] The justices then said in a per curiam opinion, "There have been multiple restrictions and refinements in the death sentencing process, by both the United States Supreme Court and this Court, since this matter was first tried in 1974 and affirmed in 1975, and we are bound to fairly apply those decisions." It cited none of them. The court added that the new hearing produced different evidence, including "more mitigating evidence."[46]

Even the state conceded that "a murder committed during a residential burglary, without more," cannot be considered cold and calculating. Then the court reviewed the mitigating circumstances in more detail. Proffitt had been employed and a responsible worker. He had been drinking, made no statements about any criminal intentions that evening, had no weapon when he entered the premises, and stabbed the victim only once. He did not attempt to kill the wife. He went home, confessed, and voluntarily surrendered. "To hold, as argued by the state, that these circumstances justify the death penalty would mean that every murder during the course of a burglary justifies the imposition of the death penalty," the court said.[47] Looking at other cases it considered similar, the court rejected the death penalty and reduced the sentence to life in prison with no parole for at least twenty-five years.

Only Overton and Adkins were still around from 1975. Overton switched his position and joined the new decision. Adkins was retiring. On his way out, he registered his dissent without an opinion.

The lead counsel for Proffitt, Irwin J. Block (working without pay), was a law partner of Arthur England, who had been on the court when the first Proffitt appeal was decided but as a new justice did not participate in it.

The court's decision on July 2, 1987, was exactly eleven years after the U.S. Supreme Court upheld Proffitt's death sentence and Florida's death-penalty statute in *Proffitt v. Florida*. In the meantime, sixteen men had been executed in Florida, all of them sentenced before May 1978[48]—that is, before most of those refinements in the law and the more skillful defense presentation on aggravating and mitigating factors that saved Charles Proffitt. In a few months, on an unprecedented seventh warrant, the state would execute Willie Darden, who had arrived on death row about the same time as Proffitt. Seventeen more men from trials of that era remained on death row even in mid-2013. By the time Proffitt won a reduction of his sentence to life, the Florida Supreme Court also had reversed approximately 200 death sentences in original appeals since the 1972 statute was passed and had affirmed about that many more.

So Charles Proffitt, who had lost the landmark U.S. Supreme Court case that restored Florida's death penalty, whose death warrant had been lying next to the one Askew signed on John Spenkelink and the one Graham signed on Robert Sullivan, and who had lived to pursue post-conviction appeals for a dozen frustrating years, was now off death row for good.

A stark example of the wide variance in sensitivity to mitigating factors comes in the multiple appeals of a single inmate, Carl Ray Songer, convicted and sentenced to death in Citrus County of killing a state trooper. His death sentence went to a Supreme Court in turmoil during 1975, where three circuit judges sat in for the three justices involved in the 1974–75 court scandal. Circuit Judge John J. Crews was assigned to write the majority opinion.[49] He listed among the aggravating circumstances "recognized by statute" Songer's previous conviction for stealing a car, which was not in fact recognized by the statute because it was not a crime of violence. Crews also said Songer had escaped from the Oklahoma prison system and was a fugitive. And the trooper when shot "was in uniform, on active duty, and making a routine inspection of an apparently abandoned vehicle, all of which was a lawful exercise of a governmental function."

Crews then wrote, "In relating the statutorily enumerated mitigating circumstances to the instant case, even Appellant admits there are only three which possibly apply, i.e. youth, intoxication and insignificant prior history of criminal activity." After rejecting all three, Crews said, "We agree with the trial court that there are no mitigating circumstances." Songer's lawyer apparently did not claim any others. The reference to "statutorily enumerated" mitigating factors would become a critical issue.

Years later, Songer won a new sentencing in a rare en banc decision from the federal Eleventh Circuit Court of Appeals (with Judge Hatchett recused).[50] Songer's lawyer then was Deval L. Patrick, the future head of the U.S. Civil Rights Division of the Justice Department under President Bill Clinton and later governor of Massachusetts. Future Florida Supreme Court Justice Peggy Quince, then an assistant attorney general, represented the state. It was Songer's second trip through the federal system, after four appearances at the Florida Supreme Court. "During proceedings held in late January 1985, the state trial judge made statements, for the first time, indicating that he interpreted [the statute] limiting consideration of mitigating evidence to those enumerated items," the federal court said.[51]

Consideration of only the listed mitigating factors and no others was a clear violation of two U.S. Supreme Court decisions, *Lockett v. Ohio* in 1978[52] and *Eddings v. Oklahoma* in 1982,[53] which said courts in a death case had to consider "the character and record of the individual offender and the circumstances of the particular offense."[54] But at least before *Lockett*, and in some cases afterward, a lot of people involved in Florida capital cases, including defense lawyers as well as prosecutors and judges, clearly were under the same impression as Songer's trial judge.

In fact, the year after Songer's death sentence was upheld in 1975, Florida's justices themselves in *Cooper v. State* had seemed under the same misimpression. In approving exclusion of evidence that Vernon Cooper had not been the triggerman and was capable of rehabilitation, the court said, "The Legislature chose to list the mitigating circumstances which it judged to be reliable . . . and we are not free to expand the list."[55] That was a 7–0 decision that included all four of the new Askew-era justices. The justices would spend years denying that they meant what they said.

The unacknowledged truth is that the court really wasn't attaching much significance at all to mitigating circumstances unless the trial judge or the jury had done so. Overton and Adkins, both former trial judges themselves, had a strong sense of deference toward trial judges. If a trial judge limited the mitigating circumstances, that was okay with them. Perhaps a low point of appellate diligence came in *Darden v. State*,[56] where the Supreme Court declared there were no mitigating circumstances even though the trial judge had actually found two nonstatutory ones and given them little weight. This oversight is not apparent from the opinion; it was discovered by defense counsel during preparation of a post-conviction appeal.[57] The court denied the appeal and made no mention of the error.

It was 1980 before the Florida court conceded "apparent misconstruction" of the *Cooper* decision—not by its own justices, but by trial judges.[58] In 1981, in the case of Sonia Jacobs, the first woman sentenced to death since 1972, the court noted the judge's "mistaken belief" about mitigating circumstances. Then, noting that the jury had recommended a life sentence, the court actually proceeded to speculate on some mitigating factors that might apply and then used those to justify a reduction of her death sentence to life in prison.[59]

The Supreme Court never took any responsibility for contributing to the many mistaken beliefs. Opinions claimed unconvincingly that *Cooper* had been about the relevance of the specific evidence offered, not the admissibility of it. In January 1985, a decade after the original decision, the court refused to reconsider the Songer death sentence when presented with a juror's testimony that she had been under the same misimpression. The court declared it would not allow inquiries into jury proceedings.[60]

So it was left to the federal Eleventh Circuit to convert these mistaken impressions into a determination of injustice for Songer. The decision among the Eleventh Circuit's eleven participating judges was unanimous, though four judges wanted a new sentencing jury as part of the resentencing rather than leaving it to the trial judge's discretion.[61] Four more years passed before Songer made his final appearance at the Florida Supreme Court, which was still refusing to acknowledge that mitigating circumstances had ever been limited.

Finally, at the U.S. Supreme Court, in the case of *Hitchcock v. Dugger*,[62] none other than Justice Antonin Scalia, a combative defender of the death penalty, expressed incredulity at the Florida Supreme Court's failure to acknowledge reality. At oral argument in 1986, Justice John Paul Stevens remarked to defense lawyer Craig Barnard that the error seemed obvious and the case seemed very simple. Barnard drew laughter when he replied, "I agree that it's that simple, but we haven't been able to convince other courts that it's that simple."[63] On April 22, 1987, Scalia wrote for a unanimous court, "We think it could not be clearer that the advisory jury was instructed not to consider, and the sentencing judge refused to consider, evidence of nonstatutory mitigating circumstances."[64] Scalia noted that the legislature in 1985 eliminated the phrase "as enumerated" from the statutory provision requiring the jury and the judge to consider mitigating circumstances, and he cited the Eleventh Circuit's decision in *Songer*.

The Florida Supreme Court capitulated after the Eleventh Circuit decision in *Songer*, but parceled out resentencings one case at a time for some two-dozen affected cases. The attorney general's office still fought each one. Scalia himself noted two Florida Supreme Court cases that had followed the Eleventh Circuit decision. One was *Harvard v. State*[65] in February 1986, another of Barnard's cases. The judge who originally sentenced Harvard testified at a post-conviction hearing that he had thought the factors were limited. And in *Lucas v. State*[66] a few months later, the third time the Florida court sent the case back for resentencing, the Florida Supreme Court noted that in the original trial the judge had told the jury it "may not go outside the specifically enumerated" factors. In neither case had the Supreme Court noted the error during the original appeal.

When the Florida Supreme Court granted Harvard a new sentencing hearing, Attorney General Jim Smith's office was horrified. It sought rehearing and said there were "close to 40 other inmates on Death Row" sentenced before *Lockett* and before the court's restatement of the law in *Songer* shortly afterward. First District Judge Anne C. Booth, a former Supreme Court law clerk sitting as a substitute justice, wrote that she did not want to reopen old cases and saw no requirement to apply *Lockett* retroactively. The problem with her position on *Lockett* was that the Florida Supreme Court was insisting that the *Lockett* standard had been the law in Florida even before the *Lockett* case was decided. Rejecting the Attorney General's argument and Booth's dissent, the justices denied rehearing.[67]

As for Lucas, who was originally sentenced in 1977, his death sentence was reversed four times before finally being upheld on his fifth direct appeal, and he was denied post-conviction relief in 2003. As of late 2016, he was still on death row. James Hitchcock, whose original appeal to the Florida Supreme Court in 1977 had taken the court five years to resolve, was eventually resentenced to death and likewise was still on death row as of late 2016.[68]

In Songer's new sentencing hearing ordered by the Eleventh Circuit in 1985, with no limitation on mitigating evidence, a jury still unanimously recommended a death sentence, and visiting Circuit Judge John W. Booth imposed it. Songer had another automatic appeal to Tallahassee. In a per curiam opinion, the Supreme Court unanimously reduced Songer's sentence to life in prison.

Overton, the only justice left from the original Songer death appeal, joined his colleagues. The court focused on "seven factors" in Songer's favor: "Songer's sincere and heartfelt remorse, his chemical dependency on drugs, which caused significant mood swings; his history of adapting well to prison life and using the time for self-improvement; his positive change of character attributes, as manifested in a desire to help others; his emotionally impoverished upbringing; his positive influence on his family despite his incarceration; and his developing strong spiritual and religious standards." The unmentioned irony is that many of these mitigating circumstances existed simply because of Songer's long tenure in prison as a result of his many appeals. He had lived through three death warrants. Had the state and the court squarely dealt with the *Lockett* problem from the beginning, Songer probably would have been executed after the Supreme Court affirmed his second death sentence following a *Gardner* hearing in 1982.[69]

By 1989, however, in contrast with the usual anguish justices expressed over killings of law-enforcement officers, the Supreme Court barely mentioned the circumstances of Songer's case. The killer had pumped four rapid-fire shots into the trooper as he leaned through the car window. The only aggravating factor recognized was that Songer had been under sentence of imprisonment, and even that factor was diminished by the fact that he simply walked away from a work-release site. The Supreme Court concluded: "Our customary process of finding similar cases for comparison is not necessary here because of the almost total lack of aggravation and the presence of significant mitigation."[70]

The court announced its decision on May 25, 1989, the tenth anniversary of the execution of John Spenkelink, who had urged the *Lockett* issue in his final appeals, but lost.

25

SOVEREIGN IMMUNITY

Suing City Hall

Orla Ralph was sunbathing on Daytona Beach late on a Sunday afternoon when Cheryl Ann Fetsko ran over her with her Buick.

Driving on the beach was a long and cherished tradition in Daytona Beach. Its hard-packed sand made it favorable for automobiles and occasional amateur car races from the earliest days of the automobile at the end of the nineteenth century. The first "Daytona Beach Road Course" race was in 1936 and included both road and beach segments. Bill France Sr. started NASCAR in 1948 and in 1959 opened the Daytona International Speedway, where the museum still offers old photographs of those races on the beach, which were replaced by the Daytona 500. But there was still something about driving free along the beach that appealed to visitors, and the tradition continued. The City of Daytona Beach had a charter provision making the beach between the high and low water mark a public highway.

Orla Ralph, born in County Cork, Ireland, was on a cultural exchange program with two friends after finishing postgraduate work in linguistics at Polytechnic of London. She planned to stay for three months, and the three young women got jobs as waitresses at the International Inn near the intersection with U.S. 92. Ralph had traveled to South America, India, and Nepal and had climbed peaks in the Himalayas. Now, while she was just lying on Daytona's beach outside the motel, this car ran over her abdomen and ruptured her stomach, spleen, and small intestine. It was around 4:50 p.m. on August 28, 1977. She was in the hospital for three months, ran up more than $22,000 in medical bills (it was 1977, after all), and couldn't work for a year and a half.

Ralph of course sued Cheryl Ann Fetsko, a nurse, but she also sued the City of Daytona Beach over its policy of letting people drive on a beach where people were sunbathing. As she put it in an interview years later, allowing driving on the beach is "the craziest thing I've ever heard of."[1] Volusia Circuit Judge Robert P. Miller dismissed her lawsuit against the city, however, because Florida limited the immunity of local and state government for accidents. Ralph appealed to the Fifth District Court of Appeal, which upheld the dismissal of the lawsuit in a 2–1 decision.

Next stop: the Florida Supreme Court.

The court had been struggling for years to delineate exactly when Florida's government entities were protected by so-called sovereign immunity and when they had to compensate for injuries. Sovereign immunity grew out of the early idea that you can't sue the king, but in twentieth-century America it came to focus more on preventing government, and ultimately the people, from paying damages every time some government action or inaction contributes to someone's injury. Since the Florida Constitution of 1868,[2] the legislature has had the power to waive the state's immunity, but the first broad legislation did not happen until 1973. In the absence of legislative action, the Supreme Court had been applying its own ideas about compensating individuals for the wrongful actions of government employees. The result was the same kind of Augean mess that Adkins found in the case law of products liability (chapter 13) and that the court was trying to clean out in other areas as well.

The case law divided government activities into "governmental" ones, which were immune from lawsuits, and "proprietary" ones, which were not immune—but the terms were defined mostly case by case. Police and fire protection, issuing permits or licenses, and maintaining jails were "governmental," for example, while maintaining streets and parks and sidewalks was "proprietary."[3] But there were exceptions, such as some "special relationship" the courts would find to justify an exception to "governmental" immunity.

It was a legislative statute rather than a dramatic court ruling that created an upheaval in the law of sovereign immunity. The Florida statute in 1973, adapted from the Federal Tort Claims Act of 1946, said government agencies and subdivisions would be liable "under circumstances in which the state or such agency or subdivision, if a private person, would be liable."[4] That was hardly specific guidance and did little to bring order out of the chaos of past decisions. So the new justices who arrived after the 1973 statute was passed tried their hand but soon found the effort similarly frustrating because of ever-shifting court majorities.

Two separate cases after the 1973 law illustrate the challenge. In the first case, a tractor-trailer owned by Commercial Carrier Corporation went through an intersection that had once had a stop sign, struck another vehicle, and killed the occupants. Sued on behalf of the victims, the trucking company in turn sued Indian River County for failing to replace the missing stop sign and also sued the Florida Department of Transportation (DOT) for failing to paint the word "STOP" on the roadway itself. Commercial Carrier argued that the new statute was "a total waiver of sovereign immunity," but the Third District Court of Appeal cited multiple cases preceding the new statute and unanimously said it is "not actionable negligence against an individual that a governmental authority has failed to maintain a traffic control device at a given time and place."[5] In other words, private citizens didn't put up stop signs, so that was not something government was liable for.

The second case also arose out of a traffic collision, five weeks after the one in Indian River County. The defendant in that second lawsuit, William Walden Cheney, blamed the accident on a malfunctioning traffic light and brought the Dade County government into the litigation over its failure to fix the light. Again the case ended up at the Third DCA, and ten months after its unanimous decision against Commercial Carrier, that court again ruled for the government entity. The judges said there was no special duty to any individual but only a general obligation to fix the traffic signal,[6] and the government couldn't be sued over a general obligation.

Assigned to the appeal at the Supreme Court, Justice Alan Sundberg tried to reframe the law of sovereign immunity. By a 5–2 vote in a 1979 opinion by Sundberg in *Commercial Carrier Corporation v. Indian River County,*[7] the Supreme Court reinstated both claims against the government entities. Sundberg largely abandoned the old delineations, particularly the requirement that only those owed some "special duty" by the government could make a claim. He suggested it was "circuitous reasoning" to say that there was "a duty to none where there is a duty to all."

Sundberg concluded that the Legislature could not have intended that the old standards continue unchanged, because there was so much "severe criticism from numerous courts and commentators."[8] Borrowing from the California Supreme Court, he prescribed a checklist of questions courts should ask in granting immunity: whether the government function at issue was a "basic governmental policy, program, or objective," whether the act or omission was "essential" in pursuing that basic goal, whether the act or omission required "the exercise of basic policy evaluation, judgment, and expertise," and whether the government body had the authority and duty to act.

He added that the 1973 law "evinces the intent of our legislature to waive sovereign immunity on a broad basis," but "certain 'discretionary' governmental functions" remain immune, because under the concept of separate branches of government, they "may not be subjected to scrutiny by judge or jury as to the wisdom of their performance."[9] He distinguished between "planning" and "operational" decision making. Maintaining a traffic light or a stop sign is "operational level activity," so the government could be sued over it. It "does not fall within that category of governmental activity which involves broad policy or planning decisions."

Adkins, England, and Hatchett, who often voted in favor of claimants in personal injury cases, joined Sundberg's opinion. So did Alderman. Overton, on the other hand, wrote a dissent, and Boyd joined him. "The effect of the majority opinion is to allow negligence claims against the state and counties for failure to properly maintain miles of interstate and primary state and county road," Overton wrote.[10] "Common sense dictates that the maintenance of thousands of miles of public roadways is not the kind of activity which private individuals engage in, but is uniquely governmental in nature." So fixing traffic lights and stop signs are not circumstances "for which a private person would be liable," as the statute requires. Furthermore, "the use of funds for the maintenance of public roadways is a discretionary function and, therefore, immune from liability." It is a matter of allocating public funds, according to Overton.

A change of justices subtly shifted the balance on the court. Just two years later, Sundberg found himself on the dissenting side of another sovereign immunity case, with Overton writing the majority opinion, now joined not only by Boyd but by Alderman and the newest justice, McDonald, in place of Hatchett. England also swung over to Overton's side, though he did not join Overton's reasoning. So it was now just Sundberg and Adkins in favor of the latest claim against government.

The case was brought by Cheryl M. and Cecil Cauley against the City of Jacksonville.[11] Mrs. Cauley was injured when the right front wheel of her automobile dropped off the pavement into "a long-existing and dangerous depression in the road shoulder," went out of control, and collided with another car. The Cauleys claimed that the city knew about the dangerous condition and breached its "duty to exercise reasonable care in the repair and maintenance of the roadway" and to warn about the danger. A jury put the damages at $400,000 plus another $200,000 for Mr. Cauley for loss of consortium, but held Mrs. Cauley 75 percent responsible for the accident. The $150,000 left as the city's responsibility was then reduced to $100,000, the maximum allowed under the sovereign immunity statute.

Overton traced the Florida Supreme Court's long line of cases waiving sovereign immunity, going back to 1850. But the issue was not whether the city was immune, but whether municipalities were protected by the cap on payments, which at the time was $50,000 per claimant or $100,000 per incidence (those caps were later doubled). Sundberg argued that the caps did not apply to municipalities; Overton declared that they did. The problem with Sundberg's dissent is that the statute specifically listed "counties and municipalities" together in the list of entities covered; the statute's comprehensive definition appeared to try to harmonize the law for all government entities.

A pair of cases from the Tampa Bay area the next year, on September 14, 1982, again showed Overton and Sundberg disagreeing over how broadly to read the statute. The lead case, *Department of Transportation v. Neilson*,[12] was over the design and construction of the intersection of West Interbay Boulevard and Westshore Boulevard and the adequacy of the traffic control devices. Patricia Neilson's car had collided with a truck owned by Belcher Oil Company as she crossed Westshore. She sued Belcher, DOT, the City of Tampa, and Hillsborough County. Overton, again joined by Boyd, Alderman, and McDonald, said government generally is not liable for "defects inherent in the overall design of a public improvement" unless the entity created "a known dangerous condition" not apparent to others. Obviously, if the maintenance of a particular traffic signal was immune, then surely the design of the intersection was. Overton did say that the failure to warn of a known dangerous condition could be subject to government liability. Sundberg, in dissent, said that determinations on whether this was a "planning" level decision should be made case by case, not through a general categorization.

Plaintiffs won, however, in the other two cases that day. One was a lawsuit filed by Bert Collom of St. Petersburg after his wife Judith and daughter April, walking across private property during a torrential rainstorm, unknowingly stepped into a storm sewer drainage ditch on a city easement, were sucked into a pipe, and drowned. Collom said the city had failed to place screens, bars, or other protective devices over the opening of the pipe and to post warnings about the dangerous condition. In the other case, also from St. Petersburg, Lula Mae Mathews's twenty-month-old daughter Kasandra had been playing in a public park, fell into Booker Creek, and drowned. Notably, the concrete barrier that lined the creek as it flowed through that portion of the park had holes for fencing but no fence installed. In both cases, the trial judges dismissed the suits and said the claims involved "planning" rather than "operational" decisions.

At the Second District Court of Appeal, Judge T. Truett Ott wryly observed in the *Collom* case about sovereign immunity law, "Everything has changed, yet nothing has changed. Claimants now tend to paint everything 'operational,' but the governments say it is almost all 'planning.' And as always, the courts must draw the lines."¹³ Joined by Judge Monterey Campbell and future justice Stephen Grimes, Ott said the city had "a disturbing notion" in believing that "some of the safety features in a sewer system . . . might have to be eliminated solely because the city couldn't afford them." He compared that to a homeowner's economizing by building a wooden chimney. Ott was also on the three-judge panel in the Mathews case, along with judges Edward Boardman and T. Frank Hobson Jr. "While the city had the discretion to decide whether to alter the natural state of Booker Creek," Boardman wrote, "once it decided to do so, the alterations had to be designed and performed in a reasonable manner."¹⁴

The two cases were consolidated at the Supreme Court, and Overton again wrote the opinion. This time he upheld the lawsuits against the city, though he rejected Ott's "broad language of governmental liability," which he said "implies governmental liability for defects inherent in plans for improvements."¹⁵ It was a unanimous decision, although Adkins, Sundberg, and new arrival Ray Ehrlich did not join Overton's narrower construction of the legal categories.

More lack of precision and clarity from the legislature brought confusion and a rare confession of error by the court in *Rupp v. Bryant*, a tragic case of a student at Forrest High School in Jacksonville whose spinal cord was severed and who suffered permanent paralysis as a result of hazing by a school-sponsored organization.

The issue was the extent to which public employees are individually liable for negligence in the performance of their duties. The focus was on teachers and their duty to supervise students. What made the case more dramatic in terms of teacher and school system responsibility is that the organization, the Omega Club, had "a known propensity for violating school board policy" and was not allowed to meet off campus without the principal's approval or to have any meeting at all without the advisor, Robert E. Rupp. At a meeting Rupp did not attend, the "hazing ceremony" happened with the resulting severe injury to the student, Glenn Bryant.

The legal challenge for the justices sprang from an earlier case, in 1980, over a student's injury on a trampoline in physical education class. The instructor, said to have minimal training in acrobatics and trampoline safety, ordered a student to do a flip, and when the student refused, physically picked him up, put him on the trampoline, and twice again ordered him to do the maneuver. The student, Robert Talmadge, tried to do a flip and injured his knee and teeth. When Talmadge sued, coach Sonny Walters said the state's sovereign immunity law immunized him from the lawsuit. The trial judge agreed, but the Second District Court of Appeal said the law did not immunize the coach from being sued; it simply provided for the state to cover any individual damages.[16] There were conflicts among the district courts on the point, and the Supreme Court sought to resolve them by taking the appeals by Walters and the school board.

It appears the trampoline case first was assigned to Boyd, but his opinion drew no support and ended up becoming a dissent. England, then the chief justice, took on the task of creating a majority opinion. He faced one section of the law saying that no officer or employee of the state acting in the scope of his employment shall be liable for damages unless he "acted in bad faith or with malicious purpose or in a manner exhibiting wanton and willful disregard of human rights, safety, or property." But the next part of the statute, added a year later, "appears to be inconsistent," England said, in providing for the state to pay any judgment up to the limits of the waiver of sovereign immunity, which was then $50,000. Boyd viewed the provision as allowing lawsuits against employees for negligence, and the state would pay those amounts, but if the employee were sued for bad faith or malicious actions, the state would not pay.

England's opinion said it had always been possible to sue employees for negligence, even before the state waived its sovereign immunity, and the statute limited only the state's liability. That decision in *District School Board of Lake County v. Talmadge*[17] on February 14, 1980, galvanized legislators, who said that wasn't at all what they meant. The legislature passed a new provision that clearly relieved state employees of lawsuits for negligence and made the provision retroactive for all pending lawsuits.

But could the legislature take away the right to sue that the *Talmadge* case said had always been there? In a word, no. The court had just said so in a case the previous year,[18] and it reaffirmed that decision when the hazing-paralysis case arrived. The harder question is what right Bryant had to sue before the 1980 amendment.

Once again the chief justice, this time Sundberg, took on the opinion. On July 15, 1982, with England gone and in one of his own last opinions, Sundberg forthrightly said, without pointing at England in particular, that the court had been "regrettably overbroad" in saying the employees had always been subject to negligence lawsuits over their actions as employees and that the waiver of immunity in 1975 had not changed that. Basically, that had been one of the ways around government immunity. Sundberg once again described the tortured path of permitting and restricting lawsuits, this time not just against governments themselves but against its employees who were doing the work. He differentiated between discretionary and "ministerial" actions.

The continued confusion was reflected in Sundberg's assessment of the parties' own arguments, which were "at either extreme" of interpretation and relied on "equally suspect" cases. "The Bryants claim absolute liability of the principal and teacher, who in turn claim absolute immunity. . . . Neither party is totally correct. Not only was *Talmadge* overbroad in its assessment of complete liability of public employees, but it also relied upon a case which did not explicitly involve the issue of official immunity." The employees, though, relied on an "equally suspect" decision from the First DCA, also "misguided."

Finally, though, Sundberg was offering some clarity on the issue. The role of a faculty member in supervising students or even in teaching, while certainly involving judgment, was "ministerial" and therefore subject to a lawsuit. It was not a "planning" or "discretionary" activity, as a policy decision would be. The principal and the faculty advisor in the hazing case were indeed subject to a lawsuit. The only problem was that Bryant had not claimed that the actions met the words of the statute even in its earlier version. He said the actions were "gross and in reckless disregard" of Bryant's safety, while the statute used the words "wanton and willful disregard." So, subject to amendment or other correction back at the trial level, the Bryants had not stated an enforceable claim. The school board, however, which would inevitably have to pay anyway up to the limits of sovereign immunity, was still subject to the lawsuit.

And then came Orla Ralph's case over driving on the beach. By the time her appeal reached the Supreme Court, Sundberg had left and joined the Carlton Fields law firm, which was now representing Ralph in the appeal. Sundberg himself was barred from appearing before his former colleagues for two years, and Cynthia S. Tunnicliff was handling the appeal.

Adkins asked Tunnicliff at oral argument if she were claiming "the rights of sunbathers are superior to the rights of motorists."[19]

"No, your honor, I'm not," she replied, but Ms. Ralph was using the beach for its intended purpose of sunbathing. "It's not the same as telling somebody they're not supposed to lay down in the middle of I-4."

"Is there any limitation on the power of government to make a planning type decision . . . when anyone with common sense knows it's going to be disastrous?" wondered Boyd.

"When a city does something and they know it is dangerous, they must then warn the public," said Tunnicliff, citing the *Collom* case in St. Petersburg. "At a minimum," the city should have put up signs.

Alderman pushed back. "When you go to Daytona Beach, the cars are *zip zip zip* all over the place on that beach," he said. "How could you go to Daytona Beach and not be aware of automobiles on the beach?"

Alfred A. Green, who along with City Attorney Frank B. Gummey III was representing Daytona Beach, later took up Alderman's point and said the risk from automobiles was "readily apparent to anyone who uses the beach."

But the city "invited this lady to use their beach as a recreational area," said Ehrlich. Shouldn't the city tell her which part she's invited to use?

"She's invited to use all of it," said Green.

So a city can create a danger, Ehrlich said, and then "sit back and say anh-anh, this is all planning?"

Green said cities should be able to make decisions "they deem appropriate without worrying about possible allegations of negligence."

Ehrlich wrote the opinion in *Ralph v. City of Daytona Beach*,[20] and in it he harkened back to Overton's cautionary remark in the *Neilson* case that a lack of a proper warning about a known dangerous condition could subject a government entity to a lawsuit. "While the fact of vehicular traffic on the beach was widely known, it was not readily apparent to sunbathers invited to use the beach for sunbathing that this lethal mixture of cars and reclining persons was inadequately supervised." Overton joined Ehrlich's opinion, as did Adkins and Boyd. Alderman and McDonald dissented without an opinion.

The decision on February 17, 1983, created a proliferation of lawsuits over local governments' failure to warn about one thing or another, including more beach-driving cases. Injured sunbathers often were looking for an institutional defendant with money instead of beach drivers with small insurance policies. For reasons not clear, but undoubtedly reflecting an outpouring of dismay from local governments and growing division within the court over tort cases, the Supreme Court held the case on petition for rehearing for more than two years, until June 27, 1985. At that point, Daytona Beach decided to ban beach driving at night, when most of the accidents happened. Two years after that, the city approved a settlement for Orla Ralph for $45,000, about half covered by the city's insurance, in addition to $25,000 from Fetsko's insurance.[21]

But there were limits to the court's acceptance of these lawsuits about inadequate warnings. Later in 1983 the court declared the Escambia County School Board immune from a lawsuit over the placement of bus stops. It had been sued by John F. Harrison after his son, Frederick Coley Harrison, had stepped into the highway and been struck by a car and killed as he walked to the bus stop.[22] McDonald's majority opinion, after noting that the boy was not actually at the bus stop when the accident happened and that the school board did not guarantee safety on the way to the bus stop, said it would be difficult to select bus stops that held no potential danger for some student. "The decision as to where to locate bus stops necessarily requires the utilization of governmental planning and discretion." Boyd, Overton, Alderman, and new justice Leander Shaw joined the opinion. Adkins and Ehrlich dissented.

The decision was another turning point. The St. Petersburg and Daytona Beach cases had followed the Sundberg concept of expanded liability, but now the court, with a different majority, was focusing on the limits of that liability.

The new focus became obvious in 1985 in the case of *Trianon Park Condominium Association v. City of Hialeah*.[23] Overton wrote the majority opinion in this 4–3 decision awarding immunity to the city in a claim that building inspectors had been negligent in inspecting the plaintiffs' condominium building. Three years after Hialeah issued a certificate of occupancy, the roof of the sixty-five-unit building caved in during a rainstorm and damaged forty-nine of the units. There was also evidence of structural flaws in unit entrances, combustibility of walls, and other defects that violated the city building code. The verdict, against the city and the developer, was $290,939.

The Supreme Court overturned the plaintiffs' claim against the city and left them with a $153,000 settlement against the developer. Overton said there could be no lawsuit to enforce a government's police powers, which included inspections. The waiver of immunity in the statute was for traditional torts for which private individuals could be sued. Overton resurrected the "public duty doctrine" that Sundberg had strongly criticized. He offered some new categories to replace Sundberg's checklist of questions. Two categories were immune from lawsuits: (1) legislative, permitting, licensing, and executive officer functions, and (2) enforcement of laws and the protection of public safety. Two others had to be analyzed, he said, for whether they are discretionary or operational: (3) capital improvements and property control operations; and (4) providing professional, educational, and general services for the health and welfare of citizens.[24]

This time Shaw was a dissenter, joined by Adkins. Shaw said Overton "commingles" the separate issues of immunity and the traditional notions of duty under tort law. Ehrlich also dissented, again joined by Adkins, and said the court was "receding" from Sundberg's approach in *Commercial Carrier*.

A group of cases on April 4, 1985, made it another "Immunity Day," as with family immunity two years earlier (chapter 14). *Reddish v. Smith*[25] declared a prisoner transfer was immune from liability when the prisoner escaped and shot someone. *Carter v. City of Stuart*[26] protected a city from a lawsuit over its failure to enforce its dog-control ordinance. *Daytona Beach v. Palmer*[27] declared a city immune from a lawsuit over a firefighting decision.

The most dramatic of the day's decisions was *Everton v. Willard*,[28] which decided that a deputy sheriff's decision not to arrest a motorist for driving under the influence was immune from liability for a subsequent fatal accident caused by the possibly intoxicated motorist. Azor Everton was injured and Renee Trinko was killed in a two-car collision when the car they were in was hit by a car driven by Marion Willard. Ten or twenty minutes before the accident, a Pinellas sheriff's deputy, C. W. Parker, stopped Willard and gave him a ticket for an improper U-turn and in the course of that incident could tell that Willard had been drinking, as Willard actually admitted. As he observed Willard, the deputy decided not to charge Willard with DUI and let him drive away.

Everton and Renee Trinko's father, Anton Trinko, sued Pinellas County as well as Willard. Overton cited the *Trianon Condominium* case in saying that it was the kind of discretion exercised by many types of public officials. "There has never been a common law duty of care owed to an individual with respect to the discretionary judgmental power granted a police officer to make an arrest and to enforce the law," Overton wrote. "This discretionary power is considered basic to the police power function of governmental entities and is recognized as critical to a law enforcement officer's ability to carry out his duties." Shaw registered a strong dissent, and Ehrlich wrote his own.

The court's support for tighter limits on lawsuits lasted until yet another change in the court's makeup, the arrival of Rosemary Barkett to replace Alderman in 1985.

26

CONSTITUTIONAL AMENDMENTS

Tinkering with Democracy

The first time Arthur England returned to the Supreme Court as an appellate lawyer, he had to defeat not only the lawyer on the other side of the case but also his own opinion as a justice eight years earlier.

It was 1984, nearly three years after his resignation, and he was asking the court to remove a proposed citizen initiative from the ballot. England was representing longtime friend Martin Fine, a prominent lawyer who headed his own firm in Miami. Fine had his own partners working on the case but enlisted this former justice, who would know perhaps better than just about any other lawyer in Florida how to overcome his own precedent and win the support of the current justices.

The initiative, known as "Citizens' Choice," drew on the wave of sentiment for smaller government that had helped propel Ronald Reagan to the presidency in 1980 and was now boosting his reelection campaign. The Florida initiative was inspired by a successful effort in California, known as Proposition 13, approved by the voters there in 1978.[1] The Citizens' Choice amendment in Florida, if passed, would have a severe financial impact on all levels of government and on virtually every tax and fee collected by limiting the overall growth in government revenues to two-thirds of the rise in the cost of living.

The citizen initiative was a fairly new thing in Florida, a creation of the Constitution Revision Commission of 1967. For the progressive urban reformers who were the leading force in government and in constitution revision, a majority of "the people" were in metropolitan areas that recognized the need for better roads and schools and city services as well as for broader social services and attention to matters of racial and ethnic equality. The drafters of the era also seemed to assume this viewpoint was Florida's inexorable political future.

The initiative process, approved by voters as part of the new Constitution of 1968, let individuals "propose the revision or amendment of any portion or portions" of the Constitution. Petitions had to bear signatures of 8 percent of past voter turnout statewide and in half the congressional districts. As with other forms of amendment, the citizen initiative would not appear on the ballot with its full wording but only with a ballot summary. Another provision referred to amending "any section" of the Constitution.

Two years after the initiative was created, in 1970, the Supreme Court, in *Adams v. Gunter*,[2] rejected an initiative for a unicameral legislature, which was proposed by State Senator and future Congressman and State Treasurer Bill Gunter. In an opinion by Justice Drew, the court noted the Constitution's reference to "any section" and said an amendment could change only one section of the Constitution. The creation of a unicameral legislature would require reinterpretation of any number of provisions in the Constitution, Drew said. Boyd's dissent, joined by Ervin, said that whatever citizen initiatives were approved, it became "the duty of the legislative, executive and judicial branches of government to make such adjustments as may be required to comply with the will of the people."[3]

At the instigation of the legislature, voters reworded Article XI, Section 3, the citizen initiative provision, to limit amendments to "one subject and matter directly connected therewith."

The first citizen initiative after that was championed by the First Citizen of Florida, Governor Askew, promoting what was known as the "Sunshine Amendment," requiring elected officials to disclose their personal financial interests and imposing new rules of ethical conduct, including limitations on lobbying by former officeholders. Askew had gathered the signatures needed to get his "Ethics in Government" proposal on the 1976 ballot, but a former Republican state senator from Broward County named Charles H. Weber filed a lawsuit in circuit court against Secretary of State Bruce A. Smathers, the supervisor of elections in Florida, arguing that the amendment should be stricken as a violation of the "one subject" provision. Weber and Askew had met on the electoral battlefield four years earlier. Weber had co-sponsored the statewide straw vote against busing to achieve school integration, and despite its non-binding nature, Askew had mounted a campaign of conscience against it—and lost badly in the voting, while winning public respect. Weber did not run for reelection to the Senate in 1974. "My ambition was to make government more like business," he explained. "I have failed miserably."[4]

The court by then included three Askew appointees and an elected justice who had worked for Askew. Chief Justice Overton, the first of Askew's appointees, wrote the opinion in *Weber v. Smathers*.[5] "There is no showing by the appellant Weber that the instant amendment is clearly and conclusively defective," Overton wrote. It "will not conflict with other articles and sections of the Constitution, and the wording that is to appear on the ballot is legally adequate." Furthermore, Overton said, the change in the "one subject" standard in 1972 "was designed to enlarge the right to amend the Constitution by initiative petition." Adkins, Boyd, and Askew appointee Hatchett joined the opinion. It was a relatively short opinion, but the language saying it was not "clearly and conclusively defective" seemed to set a very high standard for challengers.

Justice Roberts, who would end up resigning from the court before the amendment took effect, was the only dissenter.

England went even further in a concurring opinion joined by Adkins and Sundberg. England had drafted a 1971 constitutional amendment putting into place Askew's major campaign promise, a corporate profits tax, and later worked for Askew as his consumer affairs counsel. "With a concern for future cases where the right of initiative may be exercised," England wanted to "express my understanding of the term 'one subject' in this provision of the Constitution."

The rewording in 1972, England said, meant that "the power of initiative was consciously extended to multi-section and multi-article revisions short of a complete reworking of the entire document." The limitation is "functional," as opposed to a limitation to one section or article. England then added an idea that would haunt his argument in 1984:

Perhaps, as Justice Roberts infers, the Constitution will be subject to potentially devastating effects from multiple initiative petitions having subjects framed as broadly as the mind can devise. There remains to protect against that, of course, the very formidable procedural requirements for sustaining an initiative drive. But beyond even that, the simple fact is that in 1972 the people of Florida made it clear that they no longer wanted their initiative rights confined in the 1968 straight jacket (the "any section" limitation), and the wisdom of their decision is simply irrelevant to our task.

Eight years later, England's expansive view came up against a tax-cut plan devised by the conservative mind of a balding, bespectacled, friendly but scrappy man named George Schulte and the Floridians for Tax Relief in 1983. By then England would no longer be a judge but an advocate for a determined opponent.

Two years after allowing Askew's "Ethics in Government" amendment on the ballot, the Supreme Court faced another amendment and another effort to remove it. This time the proposed amendment would allow casino gambling along the waterfront of Broward and Dade counties, with the casino taxes earmarked for law enforcement and public schools. The proposal was vigorously opposed by Askew as well as by most of the state's newspapers, which took the extraordinary step of giving money in addition to their editorial support to the anti-casino campaign. Former Third District Court of Appeal Judge and reapportionment crusader Richard H. M. Swann, with Hall & Swann in Coral Gables, led the representation for Floridians Against Casino Takeover in the effort to remove the proposition from the November 1978 ballot.

The Supreme Court's opinion was per curiam, but the old files are in boxes from Sundberg's office, suggesting that he originally was assigned responsibility for the case and was a major contributor to the opinion. The court noted that the ethics initiative had been approved despite its effect on "several classes of people, several types of disclosures, and several kinds of penalties." Just as those were "within the ambit of a single subject, ethics in government, so is the generation and collection of taxes and the distribution thereof part and parcel of the single subject of legalized casino gambling," the opinion said. The various elements "flesh out and implement the initiative proposal." The justices then echoed England's words from 1976 equating the Constitution's "one subject" requirement with a similar one for legislation, which allowed "widely divergent rights and requirements."

The court took back its 1976 reference to "conflict with other articles and sections" and said that concept "has no place in assessing the legitimacy of an initiative proposal" after the 1972 change in the language. Established practices of judicial construction could deal with any problems. The court said the challengers of the casino amendment did not prove it was "clearly and conclusively defective."

Alderman was the lone dissenter. He said the casino amendment was the kind of "logrolling" that the one-subject requirement was designed to prevent. "The interest of those citizens who favor casino gambling," Alderman wrote, "is not necessarily the same as the interest of those citizens who seek additional tax revenues for the support and maintenance of free public schools and local law enforcement." He said the amendment was thus "clearly and conclusively defective" and should be removed from the ballot.

Boyd, while concurring that the amendment should remain on the ballot, objected to the expansive language of the majority opinion. The ethics amendment in 1976 was more "offensive to the single subject requirement" than this one, he said, so why all this language expanding the range of acceptable amendments? While other justices' unnecessary philosophizing would come back to haunt them in future cases, Boyd would get no credit for hewing most closely to the strictures of sound common-law decision making, focusing on the facts and the narrow application of precedents to those facts.

The vigorous and successful "no" campaign against the casino amendment had a devastating effect on a far more significant set of constitutional amendments, the proposals from the 1977 Constitution Revision Commission.[6] Unlike the casino proposal, which was basically just an end-run of the legislature with legislation masquerading as a constitutional provision, the Revision Commission, chaired by Sandy D'Alemberte, had enlisted some of the most influential thinkers about government and produced a series of proposals for changing the Constitution. One of those was elimination of the Cabinet form of government, the single most contentious element of constitutional revision. The combination of opposition to that, by the various constituencies of each of the Cabinet members, and the campaign against casino gambling sank the entire collection of Revision Commission proposals. "No" was the order of the day.

In November 1980, eleven different constitutional amendments passed, many of them retrieved by the legislature from the wreckage of the Constitution Revision proposals of 1978. They included the change in the Supreme Court's jurisdiction (chapter 10), a privacy amendment Overton had championed (chapter 26), and an increase in the homestead exemption to $25,000.[7] The only amendment defeated that year was a legislative proposal to abolish the Constitution Revision Commission, which meets every twenty years. No amendments were removed from the ballot by the court.

In 1982 the Supreme Court got a taste of a new kind of problem with constitutional amendments on the ballot: the deceptive ballot summary. The proposal this time was not a citizen initiative but a legislative one. What it did and what the ballot summary said it did were two different things. What it did was eliminate the Sunshine Amendment's provision that kept former legislators from lobbying for two years after they leave office. The ban was replaced by a requirement that they disclose their lobbying activities. The ballot summary's spin on the change read, "Financial Disclosure Required Before Lobbying by Former Legislators." The 1982 proposal was passed on the next-to-last day of the 1982 legislative session.

An irony was that two years earlier, the legislature had passed a statute requiring that ballot summaries be "printed in clear and unambiguous language" on the ballot, but the statute went on to say that the requirements of ballot language do not apply to the legislature's own amendments.[8]

Askew, now four years out of the governorship, personally filed a lawsuit in circuit court in Leon County seeking to get the amendment off the ballot because of the deceptive summary. He was joined by Common Cause and the League of Women Voters and was represented by Albert J. Hadeed, John K. McPherson, and Terri Wood of Southern Legal Counsel in Gainesville. Circuit Judge Ben Willis ruled that the amendment met the constitutional requirements.

On October 21, 1982, less than two weeks before election day, the Supreme Court in *Askew v. Firestone* overturned Willis's ruling in a 5–1 opinion written by Justice McDonald.[9] He looked back to a 1954 decision saying that the ballot must "be fair and advise the voter sufficiently to enable him intelligently to cast his ballot."[10] McDonald went on, "Simply put, the ballot must give the voter fair notice of the decision he must make." A constitutional amendment, he added, quoting from a case back in 1912, "is a highly important function of government that should be performed with the greatest certainty, efficiency, care and deliberation." Legislators and voters alike are entitled to "a fair notification in the proposition itself that it is neither less nor more extensive than it appears to be."

If the amendment were not replacing something else, the ballot language would be fine, McDonald said. And if the legislature wanted to modify the existing prohibition, that's fine, too. However, he added, "A proposed amendment cannot fly under false colors; this one does. The burden of informing the public should not fall only on the press and opponents of the measure—the ballot title and summary must do this."

Everyone except Chief Justice Alderman wrote a separate opinion, though everyone except Adkins concurred in McDonald's. Adkins in dissent said the majority "seems to impute fraud and deceit to the legislature." That body, in his view, had done "all the legislature is required to do" in the wording of the summary. Boyd, who objected to the expansive language in the *Casino* case, now said he joined "with reluctance" in removing the amendment because he thought courts should not remove issues from the ballot "without compelling constitutional reasons."

Overton wrote an opinion joined by McDonald and Ehrlich, saying that the language "conclusively misleads the public" but also saying he was "concerned with the substantial power this Court is exercising in removing from the ballot a constitutional amendment which has been placed there by the legislature of this state on a vote of 29 to 6 in the senate and 96 to 15 in the house." He said the legislature and the Supreme Court "should devise a process whereby misleading language can be challenged and corrected in sufficient time to allow a vote on the proposal." Ehrlich, the former law partner of a Senate president, said he did "not intend to imply" that the legislators "intentionally set out to mislead or deceive the voters" and even said that was "undoubtedly not the case," but "the end result of their well-intentioned efforts was not in compliance" with the constitutional standard.

The decision on the Orwellian ballot language was the first indicator that the court was rethinking its broad tolerance of constitutional amendments and its abiding faith in voters' understanding of the consequences of their decisions. McDonald even had an interesting way of citing *Weber,* the Sunshine Amendment decision from 1976. His citation was followed by "disapproved on other grounds sub nom *Floridians Against Casino Takeover v. Let's Help Florida."* No one at the time saw the *Casino* opinion as "disapproving" the *Weber* decision. In fact, what it had disapproved was the confining language about effect on multiple sections.

Every election year seemed to push the boundaries of constitutional change. The effort in 1982 to undermine the Sunshine Amendment coincided with an effort targeting the court itself in a campaign led by Governor Graham and Attorney General Smith to overturn "liberal" court decisions on constitutional protections against searches without a warrant and reasonable cause (chapter 20). The proposed search-and-seizure amendment had passed in the same last-minute flurry of legislation that had produced the lobbying amendment.

The 1982 case on ballot language left the justices bogged down in their recent deference to voters' wisdom at the same time they had invented a new protective standard focused on deception in the ballot language. McDonald's concurring opinion had only hinted at a cohesive approach to the Constitution's language about amendments: "The ballot must give the voter fair notice of the decision he must make." Despite the lack of clarity or specificity about ballot summaries or the single subject requirement, there is a discernible philosophy: amendments are to be focused enough to be accurately summarized on a ballot for people to read and consider during their time in the voting booth. To achieve that, the "one thing" that an amendment is intended to do must be reasonably self-contained and understandable to someone in a voting booth trying to cast a meaningful vote.

Into this fragile jurisprudence came George Schulte and Floridians for Tax Relief in 1983. They claimed to have gathered half-a-million signatures, almost twice the 256,000 required, to put their Citizens' Choice proposal on the ballot. As described in its ballot summary, the initiative would limit the state and every local government and other taxing unit "to 1980–81 revenue dollars" plus ad valorem taxes on subsequent new construction and annual adjustments of two-thirds of the Consumer Price Index "up to a maximum of 5%," with exceptions to be approved by voters "for specified purposes, amounts and periods." If revenues exceeded the cap, they would go into an escrow account and the amounts would be made up in lower taxes the following year.

Their campaign was a reaction to tax increases supported by Governor Graham during his first term, which added $1 billion to the state's annual revenues. State spending had grown from $6.2 billion in 1979–80 to $11.9 billion in 1983–84. Graham declared he would beat the Citizens' Choice amendment at the polls. Martin Fine filed his court challenge and argued that the proposal violated not only the Florida Constitution but also due process under the U.S. Constitution.

On Fine's behalf, England filed a petition for mandamus with the First District Court of Appeal to order Secretary of State George A. Firestone to remove the amendment from the ballot. Robert E. Gibson of Tallahassee, representing Citizens' Choice, argued that there was indeed just one subject. "The sole purpose is to limit the amount of people's money that can be taken from them," Gibson told the First DCA in oral argument, as protesters outside waved signs like "HONK IF YOU HATE TAXES."[11] England countered that the proposal was many amendments rolled into one and that voters have a right to have proposed amendments "put to them one at a time."

Not only did England lose 3–0, but Judge Winifred Wentworth instructed him that he should have filed the case in circuit court to introduce evidence of the facts behind his claims.[12] A *Tampa Tribune* article picked up the theme in an article headlined, "Is legal fight against tax cut flawed?" It cited Wentworth's opinion and questioned whether England "made a serious blunder" in his strategy. England responded in the article that the issues were not factual ones requiring a circuit court trial but strictly a matter of the language of the proposed amendment and of the Constitution.

The First DCA certified the issues to the Supreme Court.

It's not that former justices always win when they return to argue at their old court, but they have spent many hours debating legal issues with some of the justices who will decide their case, and they know far more than opinions reveal about what motivates each justice. The returning justice also brings credibility and familiarity. While Ehrlich and Shaw had arrived after he left, England had served for seven years with Adkins, Boyd, and Overton and overlapped four years with Alderman and two with McDonald. That was an important advantage. But then there was that matter of the opinion that England had written and Adkins had joined.

Overton was a traditional conservative, but one thing he was not was radical. Throughout his years on the court he was progressive and even paternalistic toward government, continually in search of improvement but ultimately a protector of its institutions. All the justices of the Supreme Court were fundamentally establishmentarian and Madisonian, believers in a republican form of government and alternately believers in popular sovereignty and suspicious of the tyranny of unchecked majorities. Adkins was occasionally provocative and decidedly populist, but he also liked to say, not entirely in jest, that "the law is what I say it is." Boyd, who had been a real estate lawyer in Miami and a Marine in the Pacific during World War II, held the Constitution in high regard as a protection against tyranny and shared the founders' view of a government as the way people governed themselves, "one nation under God." Alderman, the most conservative in his support of property rights and moral standards and the interests of business, was still no Tea Party radical (a term not in the lexicon then) but had banned alcohol at Supreme Court receptions after investitures and other ceremonial events.

England's argument emphasized the scope and radicalism of Citizens' Choice and took the bloom off the rose of the court's love affair with citizen initiatives. The power of voter decisions no longer held the charm it had in *Weber* and *Casinos*. Overton, who had written the majority opinion in *Weber*, wrote a majority opinion in the Citizens' Choice case that was like *Adams v. Gunter* all over again, almost as if *Weber* and *Casinos* had never happened.

"There is no question but that this proposal addresses at least three subjects which affect separate, distinct functions of the existing governmental structure of Florida, and substantially affects multiple sections and articles of our present constitution which are not in any way identified to the electorate," Overton wrote in *Fine v. Firestone*.[13]

First, it applies to all types of taxation at every level of government. Second, it restricts the operation and expansion of services based on user fees, such as municipal water, sewer, garbage, and power services. And third, it affects the capital funding of government infrastructure, including separate constitutional provisions for bond financing. "In our view," Overton wrote, "the single-subject restraint on constitutional change by initiative proposals is intended to direct the electorate's attention to one change which may affect only one subject and matters directly connected therewith, and that includes an understanding by the electorate of the specific changes in the existing constitution proposed by any initiative proposal."

Overton took back what the court said in *Casinos,* that courts can just apply rules of statutory construction to handle any conflicts with other constitutional provisions. The court shouldn't "be placed in the position of redrafting substantial portions of the constitution by judicial construction." Overton added, without citing any authority, that any initiative "should identify the articles or sections of the constitution substantially affected." In response to Judge Wentworth's opinion, Overton said no fact-finding was necessary. He went on to strike the amendment from the ballot.

England had overcome his old opinion as well as the critics of his litigation strategy.

McDonald in his concurring opinion reached back to, of all things, the *Weber* dissent of B. K. Roberts. "Justice Roberts counseled against hasty constitutional amendments and reminded the court of its responsibility as judicial officers. I heartily concur with him." The broad accommodating language of the casinos case "does not take into account a proposed amendment, such as here, which is simply too broad."

Shaw's concurring opinion vaguely echoed McDonald's from 1982. Citizens' Choice failed both purposes behind the one-subject limitation as he saw it:

1. Ensuring that initiatives are sufficiently clear so that the reader, whether layman or judge, can understand what it purports to do and perceive its limits.
2. Ensuring that there is a logical and natural unity of purpose in the initiative so that a vote for or against the initiative is an unequivocal expression of approval or disapproval of the entire initiative.

After release of the court's decision on March 27, 1984, Schulte decried "the anarchy of government against the citizens" and declared that he would use the coming retention vote on Ehrlich and Shaw to "destroy the Supreme Court governor-crony appointment system."[14] In June he announced a campaign against their retention (chapter 23). "They're going to pay for this," he said.[15] He also filed a lawsuit in federal court and said the group's First Amendment and Due Process rights had been infringed. The federal district court and later the Eleventh Circuit dismissed the challenge.[16]

That fall brought confirmation that the Citizens' Choice decision was no aberration. Another ballot proposal was aimed at substantially curtailing jury verdicts in civil cases. Once again England, who by then had actually joined Martin Fine's firm, was representing the challenger, along with Barry Richard of Roberts, Baggett, LaFace, Richard & Wiser, which later merged into Greenberg Traurig. The other side of the case had its own cast of luminaries, including Chesterfield Smith and Julian Clarkson of Holland & Knight, former attorney general Robert Shevin, then in private practice, and future Florida State Law Dean Donald W. Weidner.

The amendment would limit non-economic damages in lawsuits—primarily "pain and suffering" damages—to $100,000. It also encouraged summary judgments in lieu of trials and overturned a long-standing rule on joint and several liability, which held that all defendants could be held responsible for the full damages even if they bore only a fraction of the fault. The ballot summary included the headline, "Citizens' Rights in Civil Actions." In *Evans v. Firestone*,[17] the court unanimously declared the proposal to contain multiple subjects. The justices also said the summary was deceptive and, like the one in *Askew*, turned the effect of the amendment on its head by saying the amendment "establishes" a "full recovery of all actual expenses." In fact, the amendment added nothing to plaintiffs' recovery, and the effect was to protect defendants.

Again, there were multiple concurring opinions—by Overton, McDonald, Ehrlich, and Shaw, some of them also concurring with each other.

Overton repeated his plea for a process where misleading language can be corrected after a successful challenge, so that striking the full amendment is not the only remedy.

He got his wish. In 1986 the ballot included a proposal from the legislature directing the attorney general to ask the Supreme Court for an advisory opinion on any initiative petition and added those cases to the court's jurisdiction.[18] The amendment passed overwhelmingly, 1,988,841 to 759,691.

But the initiatives kept coming, in growing numbers for decades to come, with recurring debate over ballot summaries and numbers of "subjects." The issues often seemed narrow, even trivial, much to the consternation of those who thought the Constitution should be limited to fundamental matters of government and not be subject to special interest petitions and the moods of transient majorities. But the court did not screen for triviality.

27

OPEN GOVERNMENT AND PRIVACY

The Forsberg Saga

"For your information," Justice McDonald told lawyers out of the blue at an oral argument on June 5, 1984, "we've had a raging internal debate on whether there is such a thing as a federal constitutional right of privacy."[1] By that time, the court had been struggling with the question for more than seven years. The court's oldest pending case was *Forsberg v. Housing Authority of Miami Beach*, in which two residents of a public housing project claimed that their housing files were protected by a constitutional right of privacy even though the records were supposed to be public under the state's Public Records Law.

The case had arrived on July 11, 1978. The motto on the court's official seal is "*Sat cito si recte*," literally translated from Latin as "soon enough if correct" and basically saying, "Take your time and get it right." But six years is a very long time. Every year or so the lawyer for Dean Forsberg and Walter Freeman, the lead plaintiffs in the tenant class action, would write asking the court to please rule.

"Before any case gets out, it takes four people to agree," Chief Justice Alderman explained to a newspaper reporter a few days before oral argument in the case in 1983. "Whether it takes one year or five years, you've still got to have four."[2] Alderman was brand new at the court when the case arrived in July 1978. He had risen by seniority to chief justice, and the case was still pending.

The *Forsberg* case grew out of a request in 1976 from the *Miami Herald*, which was investigating whether the people receiving taxpayer-supported housing were entitled to it. The director of the housing authority refused to provide the records and asked for an opinion from Attorney General Shevin, who replied in 1977 that the records were public.[3] Forsberg and Freeman then organized a class-action lawsuit, handled by Legal Services of Greater Miami. Dade Circuit Judge William A. Herin turned them down, and they appealed. Freeman was eighty-four years old at the time. He had died by the time of oral arguments at the Supreme Court on October 4, 1983. Forsberg, disabled and living on Social Security benefits in Rebecca Towers, carried on.

The Forsberg saga is the story of the justices' struggle between a strong commitment to open government and the commitment of one justice in particular, Ben Overton, to creating a right of privacy for the people of Florida.

Throughout the 1970s, the court had shown extraordinary zeal for open government and giving reporters access to records and meetings, despite a contingent of skeptical justices who occasionally gained a majority.

As with changes in tort law (chapter 11), the court's favorable attitude toward open government started under the leadership of Justice Adkins soon after his arrival on the court in 1969—well before the arrival of Governor Askew's appointees. "Government in the sunshine" was a political and editorial crusade that coincided with the flow of urban Democrats and anti-government Republicans to the legislature in the 1960s. Their expansive legislation was made more expansive through court decisions.

One of the court's most important early decisions was to stop the Broward County school board from holding backroom meetings, with the public excluded, to discuss issues before resuming a formal public meeting to vote. The board allowed some reporters to remain while requiring others to leave. Opening up the backroom meetings further, one board member said, would have "no stopping point" and "even the P.T.A. would want to attend." During such a meeting on April 17, 1968, the board had discussed salaries and had a preview of other issues that were on the agenda for its formal meeting the next day. Such a preview meeting was routine until a citizen advocate named Barbara Doran, represented by Tobias Simon and others, asked a circuit judge to enjoin the practice.

The school board responded that the Sunshine Law was unconstitutionally broad and vague and delegated legislative authority to the judiciary. A case in 1950 had declared that an open-meetings law at the time applied only to formal meetings, but the new Sunshine Law in 1967 declared that "all meetings" of boards and commissions "at which official acts are to be taken are declared to be public meetings open to the public at all times." To Adkins, brand new to the court when he wrote the opinion in *Board of Public Instruction of Broward County v. Doran*,[4] there was no need to declare "all meetings" to be "public" unless the legislature wanted to overrule the 1950 case and make "all" meetings, not just formal ones, public meetings. "The obvious intent was to cover any gathering of the members where the members deal with some matter on which foreseeable action will be taken by the board," Adkins wrote.

Rejecting the school board's arguments for a narrower construction, Adkins launched into a robust oratory, even extending beyond the terms of the 1967 law to suggest an "inalienable" right of his own invention—not only to be present but to "be heard" at public meetings. "No one noticed until years later that I had raised this right almost to the level of a constitutional right," he said in his memoir.[5] And boosted by a reference to "hanky panky," that passage became "probably the most quoted paragraph I have ever written":

> The right of the public to be present and to be heard during all phases of enactments by boards and commissions is a source of strength in our country. During past years tendencies toward secrecy in public affairs have been the subject of extensive criticism. Terms such as managed news, secret meetings, closed records, executive sessions, and study sessions have become synonymous with "hanky panky" in the minds of public-spirited citizens. . . . Regardless of their good intentions, these specified boards and commissions, through devious ways, should not be allowed to deprive the public of this inalienable right. . . . Statutes enacted for the public benefit should be interpreted most favorably to the public.[6]

Ervin, Roberts, Drew, Carlton, and Boyd all joined Adkins's opinion.

Two years later, in *City of Miami Beach v. Berns*,[7] four of those justices reaffirmed the application of the law to informal meetings or conversations of two or more members. Drew dissented without opinion, and Roberts did not participate. "It is the law's intent that any meeting, relating to any matter on which foreseeable action will be taken, occur openly and publicly," Adkins said, and the court should "block evasive techniques." Going well beyond the facts of the case at hand, he said informal conferences of any two members "permits crystallization of secret decisions to a point just short of ceremonial acceptance." Whether there should be exceptions to the requirement of open meetings was a matter for the legislature, he said. In the meantime, the Sunshine Law should be "construed as containing no exceptions."

That broad statement was undercut less than eighteen months later in *Bassett v. Braddock*,[8] which carved out an exception for a school board's discussions about labor negotiations with the Dade Classroom Teachers Association. It was Justice Dekle's first significant sunshine case, and he was joined by Roberts, Carlton, McCain, and retired Justice Drew.

Dekle noted that the legislature had considered but failed to pass a sunshine exception for collective bargaining in the three legislative sessions after a constitutional amendment allowed collective bargaining by state employees.

Dekle expressed hope that the legislature would pass such an exception, and in the meantime he upheld the one created by the lower court.

Adkins's dissent focused on why open negotiating sessions were almost inherently contemplated in the collective bargaining process under the Constitution. Because strikes by public employees were prohibited, public scrutiny really was the only leverage left for public unions. "In fact, it may be said that bad faith emanates from closed doors," Adkins wrote, with Boyd joining him. "There is no case cited which requires that collective bargaining negotiation must be behind closed doors; therefore, for the court to make this an exception to the government in the sunshine law would be legislation."

The next year, 1973, in a case that had defied resolution for three years, Dekle and Adkins were once again on opposite sides of the sunshine issue, but Adkins had his majority back. Ervin was on the case instead of Drew, and McCain had returned to the side of sunshine. By a 4–3 vote, the court said the sunshine law applies to boards "acting in a quasi-judicial capacity"—in this case, the Alachua County school board's suspension of a student from high school because of long hair in October 1968. After Michael Canney's father said he would not require his son to cut his hair, the principal at Gainesville High School suspended Michael for ten days. Michael sought a public hearing at the school board. His attorney argued that the school system had to prove that his hair style disrupted the educational process. The board recessed the hearing and considered its decision in private after Canney's attorney remarked that the board was "in a position of being a quasi-judicial administrative agency at this point."

At the First District Court of Appeal, Judge John S. Rawls declared that the legislature "is not empowered . . . to prescribe the conduct of the . . . judicial branch."[9] To him, apparently, a "quasi-judicial function" by a non-judicial entity such as the school board made that entity the constitutional equivalent of the judicial branch, at least temporarily, so the Sunshine Law did not apply.

It took another three years for the Supreme Court to resolve Canney's appeal. The *Miami Herald*, the *Gainesville Sun* and the *Florida Times-Union* all filed amicus briefs, and so did Deputy Attorney General Barry S. Richard on behalf of Attorney General Robert L. Shevin, who had taken office in 1971 as a strong advocate of open government.

Calling a process "quasi-judicial" does not make the school board into a judicial body, Adkins said in *Canney v. Board of Public Instruction of Alachua County*.[10] Adkins again expressed impatience with the "devious ways" that boards and agencies were trying to "circumvent the plain provisions" of the Sunshine Law "in the hope that the judiciary will read some exception into the law." Although it was long after Michael Canney had lost his chance to go to school with long hair, the court ordered the suspension vacated because of the Sunshine Law violation.

The next year brought the issue of whether citizen advisory boards had to be open to the public. Even though their decisions are not binding on a town council, Adkins said in *Town of Palm Beach v. Gradison*,[11] they are subject to the Sunshine Law. Adkins said advisory boards, like citizen boards, could be the venue for working out all the issues and making "recommendations" that set up a largely perfunctory vote by the elected body. Again Adkins was joined by Ervin, Boyd, and McCain, while Roberts and Dekle argued that a town council is always free to reject an advisory recommendation.

The arrival of Askew's Four Horsemen in 1974 and 1975 did not immediately open wide the curtains to let the sunshine in.

In an advisory opinion in 1976, the court unanimously said functions established by the Constitution, such as dispensing pardons and clemency through the combined Governor and Cabinet, were not subject to legislative requirements such as the Sunshine Law.[12] A year later, in an opinion by England, the court said the Sunshine Law was not violated when members of the Public Service Commission (PSC), without discussion among themselves, adopted a staff recommendation for a 20 percent increase in electric rates charged to Florida Power Company customers, including challenger Occidental Chemical Company. "Nothing in the Sunshine Law requires each commissioner to do his or her thinking and studying in public," England wrote.[13] Adkins and Boyd dissented, but Askew appointees Overton, Sundberg, and Hatchett agreed with England. Karl, who as public counsel had appeared regularly at the PSC against utility companies, did not participate.

In 1979 Askew's last appointee, Alderman, wrote an opinion joined by the other four Askew-era justices affirming a statutory exemption allowing a teacher disciplinary hearing to be closed at the teacher's request.[14] Even this explicit exception created by the legislature wasn't good enough for dissenters Adkins and Boyd, who said the law amounted to unlawfully delegating the authority to close a public meeting to one individual without any standards.

For the most part, however, the court continued to reject efforts to circumvent the Sunshine Law. One "devious" attempt, to use Adkins's description, was the Lee County Commission's use of "pseudonyms or cloaked references" when the Lee County Commission discussed the termination of a department head for cause. Judge Grimes of the Second District Court of Appeal wrote an opinion in 1975 upholding the commission's approach. Citing cases from before the 1967 Sunshine Law amendments but not more recent cases, Grimes declared that access to personnel records would "make a mockery of public employees' right of privacy." If personnel information were made public, "the public will be prejudiced by the inability of its agencies to attract qualified personnel."[15] He cited no evidence or policy supporting that assertion.

Grimes's judicially created exception led to a clarification by the legislature: In 1975 it passed a law stating that exceptions to the public records law were limited to those "provided by law," rather than the more general "deemed by law to be confidential." It was a clear rebuke to the Grimes point of view, and when the Supreme Court finally decided the appeal two years later, even Roberts was won over (Dekle had resigned by then). The Supreme Court unanimously reversed the Grimes decision in *News-Press Publishing Company v. Wisher*.[16] Grimes's narrow application of open-government laws would haunt his effort to win appointment to the Supreme Court; Governor Bob Martinez finally appointed him on his third nomination, a dozen years later.

The court system was not immune to the strong open-government sentiment. In 1976, even as the cameras-in-court petition was pending (chapter 8), the Supreme Court was ahead of the nation's highest court in overturning the unilateral closing of a courtroom by a judge.

Companies accused in a high-profile case with selling unregistered securities filed a "motion to control prejudicial publicity," served only the other parties to the case, and won an order from Circuit Judge Russell H. McIntosh barring media from reporting on any evidence presented without the jury unless the judge ordered it admitted. The order also barred anyone involved in the case, including subpoenaed witnesses, from any interviews or public communications. A few months before McIntosh's order, on June 30, 1976, the U.S. Supreme Court had decided *Nebraska Press Association v. Stuart* and declared in a unanimous decision that "plainly a whole community cannot be restrained from discussing a subject intimately affecting life within it."[17] When media companies learned of the order, they unsuccessfully asked McIntosh to rescind the order then filed an emergency appeal to the Fourth District Court of Appeal, which denied a writ of prohibition two days later, as jury selection was ending.[18]

Eleven days later, the media petitioners went to the Florida Supreme Court and won an emergency hearing but failed to get the trial judge's order lifted immediately. The court instead set a two-week briefing schedule with oral arguments on November 17, 1976, a month after the original gag order was imposed. At that point, the feverish pace ended. More than eight months passed before the Supreme Court, in a groundbreaking opinion by Boyd, gave the media a substantial victory in *State of Florida ex rel. Miami Herald Publishing Company v. McIntosh*.[19]

The Supreme Court was unanimous. Adkins, Overton, and Hatchett joined Boyd's opinion, Roberts agreed with the result, and both England and Sundberg wrote separate concurring opinions. Boyd's majority opinion had an extended discussion about the balance between free press and fair trial. "This case is really quite easy, it seems to me," wrote England in a concurring opinion. McIntosh's order was one "least capable of withstanding constitutional scrutiny" because it "imposes a prior restraint on reporting a public trial without notice to the media or any opportunity to be heard, and without any factual foundation demonstrating a need for the restraint." Sundberg noted that there could be "some limitation upon the right of the press to publish some portions of judicial proceedings," but said the judge needs to find "a clear and present danger" or "serious and imminent threat" to the "fair administration of justice in the cause" that cannot be alleviated by alternative methods.

While there were already plenty of U.S. Supreme Court precedents barring gag orders against media coverage of the courts, the Florida Supreme Court's decision was ahead of the high court's major case on closure of courts to reporters, *Gannett Company v. DePasquale*.[20] Decided unanimously in 1979, the case declared that the Sixth Amendment right to a "public" trial does not bestow on the media a right to attend trials. Afterward, reporters covering courts carried what were called "Gannett cards" containing a brief formulaic objection and request for a hearing, to be recited if reporters found themselves suddenly barred by a judge's order. Later, in *Richmond Newspapers v. Virginia*,[21] the U.S. Supreme Court recognized a First Amendment right of the public to attend trials, subject to "reasonable limitations" imposed by a particular judge.

But how can the media attend evidentiary hearings convened to decide whether the media should be precluded from access to that very same evidence? That was the question in 1982 after a fourteen-year-old boy charged in the murder of a four-year-old girl had given the police four self-incriminating statements. "The details of the search, the killing, and Bellay's confession were widely reported by the press," Adkins wrote in his opinion for the court in *Miami Herald Publishing Company v. Lewis*.[22] "The public was virtually inundated with information detailing the crime," he said. "Where prejudicial information already has been made public, there would be little justification for closing a pretrial hearing in order to prevent only the disclosure of details which had already been publicized," he wrote. The decision was 6–0, with England not participating.

In 1981 the Supreme Court ruled 5–0 that the files of the Florida Bar, which is an arm of the court for regulatory purposes, were not subject to the Sunshine Law and that records of investigations of unauthorized practice of law were not public records.[23] With the shoe on its own foot, the court was much more protective of the subjects of meetings and records. To open the investigative files "might allow adverse and harmful publicity to focus on persons innocent of any wrongdoing but who, nevertheless, are subject to an unfounded complaint," said the per curiam opinion. The records are open once probable cause is found.

Access to the Supreme Court's own records has been extremely confined. Briefs and other filings with the court are public, as are the court's written orders and opinions, but the court never has allowed the public into internal conferences on cases, and when England was chief even banned law clerks from attending. Adkins occasionally advocated opening up most of the conferences. First in a commencement address at the University of Florida and then (because no one wrote about the speech) in conversation with a newspaper reporter, Adkins remarked as the 1973–75 scandals came to an end, "It's one way of reinstating a little more confidence in the court's processes."[24]

Drafts of opinions and vote sheets circulated among the justices are treated as confidential. The court has no written policy on availability of documents other than the formal filings and dispositions of cases. While later justices left most of their files, Justice Hatchett not only took his with him but declined to provide access for research on this book; he said he had promised to give them to Florida A&M University, his alma mater. England said he "burned" many of his files after his departure. Overton, who after retirement taught at the University of Florida Law School, took many of his files with him but then "donated" them back to the court. He put no restriction on access, but the court continued to bar outsiders' access to so-called confidential files unless the justices themselves first reviewed them and approved access.

On the other hand, the court was a pioneer in electronic availability of briefs, orders and opinions almost contemporaneously with filing. It even maintains a special page listing formal documents in any case that attracts media interest. Overton was a pioneer on this, and Gerald Kogan as chief justice 1996–1998 established the public information officer position and established the court's website. The court already had pioneered broad access for cameras and audio recordings and had begun working with Florida State University to maintain a video archive of oral arguments.

Two cases in 1979 and 1980 demonstrated how far the Supreme Court was willing to go to give full effect to openness in the state and local government agencies despite more serious challenges over the privacy of third parties.

Wait v. Florida Power & Light Company was a public records case, not an open-meetings case, and the most surprising element may have been its author: Alderman, clearly the most conservative and traditional of all of Askew's appointees. B. W. Wait III was director of utilities for the City of New Smyrna Beach, which was challenging FP&L's development of nuclear power plants, and FP&L wanted to see New Smyrna's internal documents related to its municipal power utility. This was still early in the effort of major corporations to use the Public Records Law as part of discovery and to use discovery to discourage the pursuit of litigation against them; the case undoubtedly propelled the trend.

Wait argued it had an attorney-client privilege. The trial court as well as the First DCA rejected Wait's position. The justices eventually rejected it as well and said the legislative amendment passed in response to Grimes's opinion in *Wisher* had the "obvious" intention of precluding "judicially-created exceptions." The court did add a footnote that kept alive a spark from Grimes's opinion in *Wisher*: "Whether or not there is a constitutional right of privacy which limits the Public Records Act is not presented, and we do not consider that issue in the present case."

The opinion led to an outburst of concern from police and prosecutors that the broad rejection of judicially created exceptions posed a threat to confidentiality of criminal investigative records. Overton wanted to grant rehearing and ensure that the decision did not go beyond the specific facts of this case, but only Adkins joined him. Then the legislature passed a public records exemption for "all criminal intelligence and criminal investigative information received by a criminal justice agency." It was specifically retroactive to the time "prior to January 25, 1979," the date of the *Wait* decision. *Wait* itself, however, was not overridden.

Even broader was the court's approach to records of public business in the hands of private entities. In *State ex rel. Schellenberg v. Byron, Harless, Schaffer, Reid & Associates Inc.*,[25] the court opened access to the records of a private consulting firm hired by a municipal power agency, the Jacksonville Electric Authority (known as JEA), to recruit a new managing director. The consultant, the Byron Harless firm (the case name erroneously includes a comma in the name of the pioneer in organizational psychology, Byron Harless), promised candidates confidentiality and actually destroyed notes about candidates who withdrew.

Robert W. Schellenberg, general manager of Jacksonville's dominant television-news station WJXT, the Post-Newsweek station, asked to look at the consultant's papers, and the firm refused. Joined by Attorney General Shevin's office, WJXT won an order from a circuit judge, but the judge impounded the papers pending the consultant's appeal.

The papers identified prospects, their current positions, biographical material and comments on the candidates' "personalities, personal strengths and weaknesses, aspirations, work and living habits, and families." The JEA agreement with the consultants was that they would submit a final public written report on the candidates, including their identity and biographical information, and JEA would finally make its selection in public. The consulting firm was told by Jacksonville's general counsel that its internal notes for the "exclusive use and eyes" of its own personnel would not be public records.

As is so often claimed in high-level recruitments, the public agency wanted to avoid prospects' concern about "dire consequences" to their careers if the information got out.

At the time, the controlling court precedent was a 1974 decision from the First DCA declaring that the "work product" of a consultant hired by a school board for a superintendent search, if never delivered to the school board, was the "private property" of the consultant. The Florida Supreme Court declined to review that case.[26] But in 1975, once again responding to restrictive application of the Public Records Law, the legislature had amended the law to extend the definition of a public "agency" to include a "business entity acting on behalf of any public agency." That change had led to Schellenberg's request for the Byron Harless records on March 24, 1976.

More than a year later, with the case now at the First DCA, the court of appeal summarized the papers, omitted identifying information, and made the summary public. The First DCA appointed attorney Delbridge L. Gibbs to represent the candidates' interests and sought additional filings on the privacy claims. Lawyers were given access to the papers on condition that the information not be revealed to others. At one point, Shevin's office, reflecting the considerable professional controversy over Harless's psychological profiling of prospective employees, offered the unusual suggestion at oral argument that public agencies should not be collecting such information and that the papers should never have been created and ought to be destroyed.[27] The appellate court described the suggestion as a "*cri de coeur*" rather than a real legal position, and Shevin's office did not pursue the idea in its written briefs.

In deciding whether the 1975 amendment compelled the disclosure of the papers, the First DCA fretted that the broad definition of a "record" and the expansion of the coverage "will require more government warehouses than wastebaskets." But even though the law "may create paper mountains, stifle creative pencilwork and exhilarate warehousers," Judge Robert P. Smith Jr. said, "The legislature is entitled to put Florida on that course for good or ill." The consultant's handwritten notes were public records because "they were made 'in connection with the transaction' of the public business contracted to the consultant." But then Smith turned around and found an overriding constitutional right of privacy. "We hold that Florida has no compelling or overriding interest in exposing, for the edification of the public, the information in the consultant's papers," he wrote.

Shevin appealed to the Florida Supreme Court. It took another eighteen months for a decision. Alderman wrote the opinion and began with the privacy issue: "In essence, the district court formulated a general federal right of privacy, the core of which is described as the 'inviolability of personhood.' We find that the district court's conclusion is unsupported by either the decisions of this court or those of the Supreme Court of the United States."

Alderman wrote that there were basically two types of constitutional privacy—a protection against government surveillance and intrusion into private affairs, and a protection against government interference in private decisions, such as marriage, contraception, procreation and child-rearing. This case, on the other hand, was about "disclosural" privacy, and Alderman said that is not as broad as Judge Smith's opinion had said. In fact, shortly before the First DCA decision, the Florida Supreme Court had declared in *Laird v. State*[28] that there was no general state constitutional right of privacy.

But then Alderman went back to the definition of "public records" and wound up excluding some of the most personal information, not because the information was "private" but because it was in the consultant's handwritten notes intended only for his own use in preparing a report. Boyd, Sundberg, and McDonald joined the opinion.

Adkins, normally a staunch opponent of judicially created exceptions to the law, dissented and argued for an exception this time. There was "highly personal and sensitive information . . . representing the intimate feelings of the applicants toward family members, close friends and themselves," and said that should be "protected against involuntary disclosure notwithstanding the provisions of Florida's Public Records Law," Adkins wrote. "The public revelation of the information given would most certainly threaten the present liveli-hoods of many of the applicants questioned."

England likewise objected to a "categorical rejection of a general right of privacy under the federal and Florida Constitutions."

Overton, who had pushed a state constitutional right of privacy as a member of the 1977 Constitution Revision Commission, was more definitive. "I must disagree . . . with those portions of the opinion which categorically reject a constitutional right of disclosural privacy," Overton wrote. "However, I find that such right of disclosural privacy as may exist does not apply to public records as defined in this cause."

By the time of the decision, of course, JEA's selection was in the distant past. The information Schellenberg first sought was no longer news.

More cases tested the line between openness and confidentiality, and for the most part, the court held firm on openness unless a statute specifically made an exception. In 1983, the court in *Wood v. Marston* applied the Sunshine Law to meetings of a 10-person faculty committee that University of Florida president Robert Q. Marston was obligated to consult in the search for a new dean of the law school. As it happened, the dean stepping down was Joseph Julin, the father of media lawyer Thomas R. Julin, who had once been editor of the campus newspaper, the *Alligator*, and was one of the petitioners in the case and later the lead counsel.

Terri Wood, editor of a law school publication *The Verdict* and a former reporter at *Cocoa Today*, was the lead petitioner. Chesterfield Smith was arguing on behalf of President Marston and told a friend that he was hoping the UF loyalties of some of the justices would bolster his case. Alas, as Smith stood before the court making his argument, UF law grad Ray Ehrlich mischievously interrupted to tell Smith that the court understood his position, "but in the event that we disagree with you," what would he propose as attorney's fees to the prevailing side?

Ehrlich wrote the opinion for a 6–1 majority rejecting the secrecy. Noting concern about public discussion of candidates, Ehrlich said they were no different from the challenges facing other groups subject to the sunshine laws. "We note that the dean search did take place entirely in the sunshine and that the faculty and the committee were more than equal to the challenges of the situation." Overton (another UF alum) noted in a concurring opinion that this was the first time the court had applied the law to commissions established by the executive branch rather than by legislation, but he joined the majority. Implicitly taking back Adkins's broad declaration in the *Doran* case, the court specifically said "nothing in this opinion gives the public the right to be more than spectators." Smith's side did get one vote, from UF alum McDonald.

As for attorney's fees, the parties stipulated to an award of $70,000 in fees, of which $50,000 would be donated to the law school for the study of open-government law. The law faculty, however, said its academic freedom would be infringed if winning litigants could dictate the curriculum. So the money instead went to the journalism school to establish the William C. Steel Media Access Fund for the study of open government, named for the recently deceased partner of Steel, Hector & Davis, the law firm Tom Julin joined after law school graduation. The rest of the money went to Sandra Bieber, the young lawyer who had represented Wood and Julin before they were admitted to the Bar.[29]

Wood v. Marston was about meetings, not records, but the *Wood* case was fundamentally about the same concern for reputations of applicants that had been present in the *Byron Harless* case.

There was one place the Florida Supreme Court would not tread when it came to open government: the Florida Legislature itself. After several years of escalating tension between capitol reporters and the legislative leadership, thirteen Florida newspapers joined in a lawsuit in the reapportionment year of 1982 against the leaders of the House and the Senate. The lawsuit focused on a budget meeting in the 1981 session. The petitioners said the closed meeting violated the legislature's internal rules, state law, and the Constitution—which pretty much covered everything.

"It is the final product of the Legislature that is subject to review by the courts, not the internal procedures," Adkins wrote for a 4–3 majority.[30] "Just as the Legislature may not invade our province of procedural rulemaking for the court system, we may not invade the Legislature's province of internal procedural rulemaking." Alderman, Ehrlich, and Shaw agreed.

McDonald wrote a partial dissent, joined by Boyd and Overton. He agreed with Adkins's broad proposition but said that if the legislature actually violates the law or the Constitution, as opposed to its internal rules, the courts can intercede.

The *Forsberg* case, the court's oldest case, was still pending. When it arrived at the Supreme Court in 1978, the court was entering a new period of turnover in its membership. Fred Karl had just left after his fourteen-month tenure, to be replaced by Alderman. Then McDonald replaced Hatchett. In 1981 and 1982, England and Sundberg, both supporters of releasing the records in *Byron Harless* but expressing different views about a right to privacy, were replaced by Raymond Ehrlich and Leander Shaw. Boyd and McDonald were the only justices left from the four who joined the main opinion in the *Byron Harless* decision. Adkins, the dissenter in *Byron Harless* over the privacy issue, was still on the court as well.

The information sought in the *Forsberg* case was at least as intrusive for the poor people in government housing as for the executive candidates in the JEA case. As hundreds and hundreds of cases were decided on other issues, the justices had been unable to agree on where to draw a line between the Public Records Law and some undefined but overriding constitutional right to privacy.

Overton was the strongest advocate for the Constitution Revision Commission's proposed constitutional amendment on privacy in 1978, before the *Forsberg* case reached his court. Overton's interest grew after seeing a report on the CBS news magazine *60 Minutes* about companies' abuse of credit and insurance information. Many members of the revision commission, while wanting to constrain government collection of information, saw constitutional protection from private entities as a quagmire. Overton persisted. "I would rather see the Constitution Revision Commission or the Legislature really be involved with this . . . rather than have it end up . . . decided by four men on the Supreme Court," he told a reporter in October 1977.[31]

All of the commission's proposals, including the privacy amendment, were rejected by the voters in November 1978. But House and Senate leaders Hyatt J. Brown and Philip D. Lewis revived the best of the commission's ideas for legislative consideration, and the privacy amendment returned to the ballot as a legislative proposal in 1980. Its focus was on government collection of information; it contained a specific statement that the new provision "shall not be construed to limit the public's right of access to public records and meetings as provided by law."

Two weeks after the voters approved the amendment on this second try, Overton law clerk Pat Alexander wrote a memorandum to Overton on the *Forsberg* case outlining "two possible ways in which the result desired in this case could be reached."[32] Overton's desired result clearly was to protect the tenants' information. One way would be to take an expansive view of existing legislative exceptions and say that the intent was to protect "the types of information" covered by those exceptions, even though there was no specific exception for the tenant records. Among the types "expressly made confidential by statute," Alexander's list included "birth records; records of treatment and services provided retarded persons; records detailing treatment of alcoholism and drug abuse; . . . records of adult protective services and adult corrections . . . [and] vocational rehabilitation services." Alexander gave examples of housing authority forms seeking highly personal information, including a "preliminary social behavioral" screening, and said the authority "is, apparently, not limited in the amount and type of information it may request from an applicant or tenant."

It would be consistent with the *Byron Harless* case, Alexander wrote, to say that "the confidentiality of these records is necessary to fully implement the legislature's effort to protect [a person's] intimate personal details." But that might inspire every government agency to make subjective decisions about whether some piece of information was part of the legislative "intent." Some might even have to create a "duplicate filing system" for protected and unprotected information.

The second approach would be to do what the *Byron Harless* case didn't do, which was to find a constitutional right of privacy applying to disclosure of personal information. "The majority opinion in *Byron Harless* presents a very ambiguous analysis of the federal right of privacy," Alexander wrote. It wasn't clear whether the court was saying that there was no right to privacy or that the right existed but was outweighed by the public interest in disclosure. "This ambiguity will allow the *Forsberg* majority to bar disclosure of the files of applicants for . . . tenants in public housing."

That second section of the memo is filled with notes and edits in Overton's handwriting, as if he were using this part of the memo to formulate an opinion protecting the tenants' records through a right of privacy. "We in effect applied a balancing test in Byron Harless," he scribbled in the margin, "and determined that under the facts a constitutional protection of privacy interests was not present." The *Forsberg* case would be another "balancing" between public access and private information, and the balancing this time could lean toward privacy. Overton underlined a passage suggesting that the 1980 constitutional amendment created a "right to challenge the government's need to collect information of an intimate and personal nature."

It was August 1981 before Overton finished a draft opinion for other justices to consider.[33] His strong concern about government collection of private information was coming up against his conclusion that the Housing Authority actually had some reason to collect all that information on tenants. He also recognized the importance of public records in holding government accountable, as the amendment itself provided for. The *Miami Herald* request in the *Forsberg* case was appropriate, in his view. Still, Overton disliked the prospect of private companies scarfing up data for their own marketing and sales.

Overton's draft opinion called for the Housing Authority—and by extension any other government agency facing a similar request—to create "some method of protection and vindication for the improper use of tenant information." The authority "must require persons examining or making use of authority records to certify, in writing, that the examination of the records is for the purpose of ensuring governmental accountability and . . . is not intended for private use."

That was a big, unprecedented step. And then he took another one. If the information were used for these "private" purposes, "the offending person is subject to tort liability for civil invasion of the right of privacy." While other cases had rejected lawsuits against media companies for invasion of privacy when the information was a public record, "we reject this generalization" extending that principle to these private companies making profits off public data. "We deem a suit for invasion of privacy entirely appropriate for vindication of personal privacy rights when there is no public benefit."

It would have been a dramatic landmark decision, a bold application of Florida's initiative on privacy. But no other justice supported it. The vote sheet that circulated with the opinion shows that Alderman, Adkins, and McDonald initially supported the opinion, but Adkins and McDonald then crossed out their initials. Alderman soon followed.

"Seems to me that you have tried to divide the baby," Sundberg wrote in longhand. "I don't see your rule on private use vs. governmental responsibility as being workable." The amendment specifically says it should not be used to limit public access to records, Sundberg noted. "Haven't you used it to do just that?" The privacy amendment should be interpreted as requiring a "compelling state interest" to collect information, but the amendment "is not implicated here because public records are expressly exempt."

There was a new complication. The draft opinion circulated with a note from Chief Justice Alderman that *Forsberg* was "traveling with" a Bar Examiner case, No. 60550, in which an unidentified Bar applicant was objecting to questions about any previous "regular treatment for amnesia, or any form of insanity, emotional disturbance, nervous or mental disorder." The applicant was being represented by longtime mental-health advocate Parker D. Thomson, who was representing the *Herald* in *Forsberg* but had no way of knowing that the court had paired the two cases and thus positioned him on both sides of the issue.

Alderman had drafted an opinion in that case citing Overton's draft opinion in *Forsberg;* he said the applicant's privacy rights indeed were implicated but the waiver of those rights was appropriate as a condition of practicing law, which is a privilege and not a right. All the justices except Adkins agreed with that result, but Sundberg noted on the vote sheet, dated September 14, 1981, "Since I don't see the *Forsberg* test as being any test at all, I can only concur in result." Adkins, though, was supportive of the applicant's concerns. He wrote, "I don't see how we can overcome a clear constitutional provision coupled with a statutory privilege between patient and psychiatrist."

In March 1982 Overton responded to Sundberg's criticism by saying Sundberg's view "would make the constitutional amendment meaningless because it allows private information which is necessarily available to the public to be used [for] private purposes and private gain." He added, "I ask if this view prevailed, when if ever could this privacy amendment be applied?"

In June 1982 Boyd circulated a draft dissenting opinion in response to Overton's draft in *Forsberg*. He, too, focused on the 1980 privacy amendment. "This new constitutional provision restricts the power of government to intrude into the private lives of persons," Boyd wrote. "It does not, however, require the state to maintain the confidentiality of personal or intimate information it may have concerning individuals." That balance, he said, is for the legislature to determine. Boyd added, "The provision operates directly against government; there is no indication that it was intended to create any new rights or liabilities among private persons." Boyd agreed with Sundberg that the amendment required a "compelling state interest" for the state to require disclosure of personal information, but said there was "no question of the state's authority to obtain personal and financial information about public housing tenants."

The Bar admission issue itself was held up for two more years while the struggle over privacy continued within the court: it was finally resolved without waiting for *Forsberg*. In a different Bar Examiner case released on November 3, 1983—one being pressed by Tallahassee lawyer Steven M. Goldstein—the court in a 6–1 decision written by Alderman allowed the Bar Examiners to ask about mental-health history.[34] Ideas and passages from Alderman's draft opinion in No. 60550 (both cases were in the anonymous title of "Applicant") were in the new opinion. Adkins in dissent conceded there was a "compelling state interest" in getting the information on prospective lawyers but said the mental-health questions were "overbroad." A week later, the court released a simple per curiam decision in No. 60550 and simply cited Goldstein's case from the previous week.[35] There was no longer any mention of *Forsberg*, which was still a year away from a decision.

The two Bar cases clearly had been separated from *Forsberg* at or before the justices' conference a month earlier, after oral argument in *Forsberg*. The conference discussion must have made it clear that *Forsberg* would not be resolved soon or at least would not be a useful precedent for the Bar cases, which already had a clear majority and could proceed independently of *Forsberg*.

At the *Forsberg* oral argument, Overton pressed the issues from his two-year-old draft opinion. He asked Assistant Attorney General Mitchell Franks what the new constitutional provision meant if it does not protect people from disclosure of private information. "It's directed to the collection of information," said Franks on behalf of the housing authority. "Once the information is collected and legitimately so, it becomes a public record."

No limitation on who can see it?

"That's correct, your honor."

Overton also questioned Legal Services attorney Lester C. Wisotsky, representing Forsberg. "How could individuals know whether an agency was operating properly—is accountable—if the records were not open?"

The "legitimate interest" of the public, Wisotsky replied, has to be balanced against the tenants' privacy. He urged the court to set "standards" for agencies and lower courts to use in "deleting material that has no relevance" to the purpose of the agency.

"That seems inconsistent," interjected Alderman, who was outspoken about making the records available. "Why isn't it also relevant for the public to see that if they want to monitor the housing authority's performance?"

Wisotsky said a tenant's request for emotional counseling might be important to the agency but is "not the type of information" the public needs.

As other justices weighed in with a similar concern, Parker Thomson, representing the *Herald*, suggested that a tenant might seek money damages from someone who misuses the records.

Overton also noted that poor people have to disclose the information as a condition of receiving government housing, then observed, "The poor end up without any privacy, but the rich can protect their privacy." Thomson replied that the law has "the same rule" for rich and poor, and noted that the JEA applicants in *Byron Harless* had been executives.

Eight months after the oral argument, *Forsberg* was still undecided.

And now there was another case up for argument on privacy vs. access. *Tribune Company v. Cannella* focused on a much narrower issue, but as a practical matter the answer depended in part on whether the *Forsberg* case would identify a privacy right that overrode the Public Records Law. The afternoon affiliate of the *Tampa Tribune*, the *Tampa Times*, had asked for the files of three Tampa police officers who had been involved in the shooting death of a suspect the night before the request. The city said it had a policy of delaying such requests for seven days. When the seven days were up, the city said, well, wait until Monday. That Monday, the city said come back in the afternoon. That afternoon, the three officers obtained a restraining order to stop the release of the records. By the time of the hearing in the local circuit court, the officers had also obtained a federal restraining order on constitutional grounds. Complicating things even further, Chief Assistant State Attorney Norman Cannella subpoenaed the officers' personnel records, and the city turned them over without retaining a copy. Cannella then claimed the records were criminal investigative files exempt from disclosure under the statute.[36]

In all, it took twenty-two days of "intricate legal maneuvering," as the Supreme Court later described it, for the newspaper to get the records. The Second District Court of Appeal, in a rare en banc consideration, referred to a "shell game" over the records but ruled 5–4 that a forty-eight-hour waiting period would be permissible.

Local governments themselves could not raise privacy claims as a basis for denying records, but the waiting period gave employees a chance to raise the issue themselves. Gregg Thomas, representing the Tampa newspaper, said that is not what the legislature had in mind when it directed "immediate access" to all public records. "Every time a person wants a record in the state of Florida, there's going to be a privacy claim—every time," Thomas told the justices.

The lawyer for the City of Tampa, Luis G. Figueroa, said it was not "frivolous" for the city to provide for "the assertion of any possible right by an individual."

"Is it your argument," Alderman asked him, "that somewhere out there unidentified may be some inchoate constitutional right that hasn't been recognized yet, and you want to give the employees a chance to come in and claim it?" Figueroa wouldn't have put it quite that way, but he said rights "evolve" over time and might one day protect public employees.

"Who places the burden upon the city, though, to be the guardian of the employee, to give him the opportunity to raise this privacy right of his?" Alderman asked.

"We say the legislature does," answered Figueroa, by saying records are to be inspected "at reasonable times and under reasonable conditions."

Alderman kept pressing. "'The reasonable condition' is related to making sure the file is in a proper room and there's proper security, so somebody doesn't steal things out of the file or mutilate it."

"I think that's very narrow," said Figueroa. "We have decided that allowing . . . the employee to participate in the disclosure process is reasonable."

This was the oral argument in which McDonald mentioned the "raging internal debate" about privacy. While there is no indication in the available files, it seems likely that Chief Justice Alderman afterward said enough is enough on *Forsberg*. There wasn't any raging debate, really; it was just Overton, troubled but alone in trying to limit the after-effects of releasing the records.

Nearly three months later, on August 30, 1984, after six years and the "raging internal debate," and with the *Cannella* case going through a final review inside the court, the justices announced a decision in *Forsberg*.[37] It was unanimous in favor of releasing the tenants' records. A per curiam decision just five paragraphs long was signed by Boyd, Alderman, McDonald, Ehrlich, and Shaw. Adkins concurred only in the result. "Our examination of the statutes has brought to light no exemption pertaining to the records involved in this appeal," the per curiam opinion said. "There is, likewise, no state constitutional right of privacy which would shield these records." There was no mention of a federal right of privacy.

Overton joined his colleagues on the release of the records to the media, as he was willing to do back in 1981, but objected in a concurring opinion that the majority should "explain why we cannot address in this case the assertion that this court should protect the privacy of the poor who must use public facilities such as public housing or hospitals." Forsberg and Freeman "submitted information of a personal and confidential nature concerning their family status and relationship, income, expenses, assets, employment and medical history, as a condition to obtaining decent, safe and sanitary housing at a price that they could afford." Now they were facing "humiliation and embarrassment, needless invasion of their personal privacy, denial of their right to be let alone, harassment and other adverse consequences, if information concerning their personal lives is subject to public inspection."

Overton acknowledged it was "absolutely necessary" for a housing authority serving low-income and disabled persons to collect that information, so the new constitutional provision was not violated. And "the public's right to know about the housing authority's operations, including the selection of tenants, is paramount to the individual tenant's right of nondisclosure of personal information." Perhaps, Overton said, picking up from his earlier draft opinion, tenants could sue "persons who use personal, intimate information contained in tenant files for strictly private purposes totally unconnected with governmental accountability," such as insurance evaluations and credit histories.

A week after deciding *Forsberg*, the justices issued a unanimous decision in *Cannella*, written by Ehrlich, banning the waiting period for records.

Later, in *Michel v. Douglas*,[38] the court refused to create an exemption for the personnel records of employees of a mental hospital, who asserted a danger from former patients. The court again said there is no federal or state constitutional right to "disclosural privacy." But McDonald, writing for the court, also said the right of access is "not the right to rummage freely," and urged that agencies' information-gathering focus on information actually relevant to employees' employment or qualifications.

Again the majority included Boyd, Alderman, Ehrlich, and Shaw, and again Overton wrote a separate opinion. Still probing for some benefit from the privacy amendment, Overton wanted additional briefs on whether a constitutional right of privacy protects against disclosure of records if there is a danger of physical harm.

28

CHIEF JUSTICE BOYD

The Passover Ends

Passed over four times for chief justice after an ethical reprimand, Joe Boyd was selected as chief justice of the Florida Supreme Court on April 30, 1984, and took office on July 1. It had been his turn in 1976, after Jimmy Adkins, who was elected along with Boyd and Carlton in 1968, but he still bore the taint of scandal from the year before. In 1978, in 1980, and in 1982, Boyd was again passed over in favor of a justice from the Askew era, which was widely seen as a period of ethical reformation on the court.

Boyd had argued in 1976 that his reelection by the voters in 1974 showed they had put the past behind them, so the other justices should, too, but the election had been before Boyd's reprimand in early 1975. Justice England engineered the selection of Overton (chapter 6). In 1978 England engineered his own selection as the next-senior justice behind Overton (chapter 10). The selection of universally liked Alan C. Sundberg was almost inevitable in 1980. That November Boyd survived another statewide vote to retain him on the court, and once again he thought this should end his period of penance; however, in 1982, he was passed over again, and the last Askew appointee, Jim Alderman, was selected chief.

Each time, Boyd endured the journalists' phone calls for his comment on being passed over once again. A religious man, he sometimes wryly referred to it in private as his "Passover." In public, he put on a brave face. Even in private, "He didn't wallow in resentment," said longtime senior law clerk James Logue, who arrived in 1977 and stayed the rest of Boyd's tenure and then some.[1] Boyd would say it was his opinions that mattered, that he was going to do his best for the people of Florida. If pressed on the scandal that kept blocking his path to chief, he would call it "a conspiracy to destroy me," and say that he prayed for his enemies and tried to love them, as the Bible instructed.

But it wasn't just the scandal that deterred the justices from choosing Boyd.

It was also Boyd's internal relationships. Boyd was not thought of as an administrator or a leader, not enough of a "detail guy" to be an effective chief, even though he had been chairman of the Dade County Commission before his election to the court and had served during World War II as a Marine sergeant, among the first to enter Nagasaki in Japan after its destruction by the Americans' atomic bomb.

Boyd also was not the intellectual that Ivy Leaguers England and Sundberg were. He had grown up in a country town in northeast Georgia and had put himself through college and law school selling various goods from Bibles and brushes to appliances and automobiles. Boyd was much more the politician than England and Sundberg, and it was a standing joke about Boyd's familiar greeting to everyone, extending his hand and saying, "Hi, I'm Joe Boyd." England and Sundberg would ask each other how a particular opinion would "play in Perry," another small city, but Boyd instinctively understood how opinions would play in Perry, because he had grown up in a town like that. He shared that trait with Adkins, who often would talk about "Levy County justice."

Boyd's take on cases was instinctual and philosophical and even populist. He liked being the source of common sense that cut through the complex legal arguments, but he also felt the others did not see him as a real judge, only as a politician. He would say to his clerks on a tough issue, "Let one of those smart judges figure this out."

Boyd did not write easily and did not like to do legal research. Every now and then he'd pull law books off the shelf and open them to the precedents for a pending case, but that was rare. Boyd relied more heavily than other justices on his law clerks, primarily senior aide Jim Logue. He was later joined by Randall Reder, who worked for Adkins before joining Boyd for the longer term. They would do the research and combine it all into well-crafted opinions that bore Boyd's name. It had been one of his earlier law clerks, drafting an opinion in a utility case, who first noticed the improper memo that led to Boyd's reprimand. In oral arguments, Boyd was more willing to indulge side issues in cases and was known for asking odd questions or posing off-the-wall scenarios in oral arguments. To him they weren't side issues; they were a different perspective on the case.

Boyd had a civil liberties streak—a reverence for "due process of law." That instinct had led Boyd to some resounding dissents that became landmark majority opinions at the U.S. Supreme Court. His lone dissent to strike down a "right of reply" to newspaper articles became a unanimous decision of the U.S. Supreme Court in *Tornillo v. Miami Herald Publishing Company*[2] (chapter 12). He and Ervin dissented when the court ignored a capital defendant's right to see presentence investigation reports, another viewpoint that won acceptance at the U.S. Supreme Court.[3] And *Argersinger v. Hamlin*,[4] a U.S. Supreme Court decision extending the famous right to counsel to anyone facing jail time, followed Boyd's dissent. Boyd was given to quoting the Bible or Shakespeare, but the line that resonated in his *Argersinger* dissent was purely his own. "There is no magic yardstick by which we can determine liberty is more precious to one person than to another," he said, then added: "From the inside all jails look alike."[5]

It was hard to not like Joe Boyd. Just saying hello would lead to a visit and more than one old story. Until England shut off public access to the justices' floor, Boyd would invite people he met to drop by his office. Unfortunately, he could be talkative in the justices' conferences, too. "He can't be around anybody without talking," Ehrlich once said of him. Adkins, the one closest to him among the justices, would sometimes have to rein in Boyd's chatter. Boyd confided in his wife, Ann, the anchor in his life and "my secret weapon," and in his longtime law clerks. He and Ann would spend free time at his house on the Gulf of Mexico at Shell Point, where his favorite activities included jet-skiing. His law clerks would often join them.[6]

Justices almost never dropped in to talk about cases with Boyd, and he did not drop in on them. His loquaciousness surely made his social isolation from the other justices all the more difficult for him.

But one day in the spring of 1984, something different happened. Boyd went to lunch with law clerk Randy Reder, and they talked about the chief justice selection. Boyd had always accepted the "passover" gracefully, but today it was eating at him. "Adkins is right," Reder told him. Adkins had always said, "Anybody who's a member of that court is qualified to be chief justice." And the court had changed. England, who had been a key lawyer in the case involving the unethical memorandum, was gone. So was Karl, the prosecutor at the impeachment committee. And so were Sundberg and Hatchett, who had voted in the past to skip Boyd. The Askew justices had all had their turn as chief, and there were new justices now. Only McDonald and Overton remained from the days when the scandal was a preoccupation. Reder urged Boyd to talk to each justice and tell them he wanted the job.[7]

The two returned to the court building, and Boyd as usual took the elevator to the top floor. This time he did not turn left toward his office but turned right. He went from office to office, visiting each justice. Ehrlich was noncommittal. Shaw, the newest justice, had not been involved in a chief selection before but figured that Boyd had passed muster with the voters in 1980 and saw no reason to depart from the seniority system. Alderman, the current chief, was noncommittal. McDonald, Boyd told Reder later, leaned back in his chair with his hands behind his head and said that he appreciated Boyd's visit but could not support him for chief. During the interview process for appointment as a justice in 1979, McDonald had stated that he would never support Boyd for chief, and he stuck to that commitment. Adkins was supportive, of course, but Overton was not. With Boyd's own vote, that still was only three of the seven.

Ditti Davis, Alderman's law clerk, whose tenure at the court went back to B. K. Roberts, liked Boyd and encouraged Alderman to support him. Whatever else you might think of Boyd, she told Alderman, he is a good politician, and maybe that is what the court needs right now. Alderman, who had joined the "passover" in 1980 and 1982, decided to support Boyd this time. That was the key switch. Boyd now had Adkins, Shaw, and Alderman—four votes, including his own, out of seven.

The decision was on the conference agenda later than in past years, on April 30, 1984. "I nominated Joe, and I got enough votes," Adkins said afterward. "The public respects Joe Boyd a good deal. He's popular all over the state."[8]

Said McDonald: "The folks finally felt it was time for him to have a chance."

Boyd brought a different personality to the chief's office. Alderman had been quiet and reserved—so quiet that Adkins once quipped, "I don't think he even talks to himself." Boyd was something of a loner too, but he loved to talk. Expectations for Boyd were low, but he substantially exceeded them. He viewed himself as actually better suited to organizing tasks and projects within the court than sitting in an office reviewing cases. His opinion load was reduced as chief, because the chief focused on motions and more routine petitions that often were decided by the chief alone. Logue took much of the caseload of the office, while Reder took on the administrative details.

An early visible move was to put pads on the bare wooden pews in the courtroom and to put chillers on the water fountains and water heaters in the bathrooms. "In the space age, I think the court should provide some comforts," Boyd told Linda Yates of the *Florida Bar Journal*. "I'm a taxpayer too, and I hate to see money wasted. I intend to make each dollar count."[9] One of his initiatives was to establish time standards for how long each type of case should take, which later became part of the court rules.

Boyd also came up against some major policy issues. The legislature wanted more efficiency and technology in the court system, and that meshed with Boyd's own populist notions about efficient government. There was also new federal legislation that required states, as a condition of Medicaid funding, to institute a child-support enforcement system to collect child-support payments from Medicaid and welfare recipients—a major program that would involve the court system. While some other justices and judges groused about kowtowing to the legislature, Boyd pushed those ahead by administrative order. He didn't worry much about consulting the other justices. He never had much of a relationship with them anyway. He was going to prove himself to all the doubters with what he accomplished.

Perhaps the best indicator of his seriousness of purpose was his selection of Overton, a consummate administrator, to head a new, relatively high-profile Judicial Management Council to carry forward the technology and management initiatives the legislature wanted. Adkins, his longtime supporter, went to Boyd and wondered why he had not been recognized for that loyalty with this visible role. Overton was never a supporter of Boyd and often was brusque toward him. Adkins was admired for many things, but organizational discipline was not among them. Overton, Boyd told him, was simply the right person for the job.

McDonald succeeded Boyd as chief in 1986. The seniority system remained unbroken for thirty more years.

29

CRIMINAL LAW

To Establish Justice

Jack Neil was just another defendant in just another shooting in Miami until his lawyer raised the objection that made his case a national landmark: Blacks were being systematically excluded from the jury.

It was a highly sensitive issue in Miami in January 1982, when Neil was brought to trial. A series of verdicts had produced outrage among blacks in Miami because of the all-white makeup of juries. In May 1980 an all-white jury in Tampa had acquitted four Dade County police officers in the beating death of Arthur McDuffie, a black businessman. Riots followed. Another all-white jury had acquitted a Hispanic police officer in the shooting death of Nevell Johnson Jr., a twenty-year-old black male. Again, there was racial violence. On the other hand, the black superintendent of Dade County schools, Johnny L. Jones, had been convicted by an all-white jury over misuse of school funds in what was known as the "Gold Plumbing Case."

"The Florida courts are beset with problems relating to the use of peremptory challenges," said a brief prepared by Donald A. Middlebrooks, the future federal district judge who was representing the ACLU of Florida and Common Cause in Jack Neil's later appeal to the Florida Supreme Court. Peremptory challenges let the lawyers on each side reject potential jurors without giving a reason. A *Miami Herald* poll of black residents after the riots showed that 77 percent thought the state attorney's office was biased against black defendants and 88 percent said it was impossible for a black person to get a fair trial in Dade County.

Neil, who was black, had been charged with second-degree murder and unlawful possession of a firearm after the shooting of a black Haitian immigrant. Neil's mother worked at Palm Springs General Hospital, where Paul A. Louis was outside counsel. The hospital administrator called Louis on her behalf to get his help. Louis had been a B-26 pilot, was shot down over Europe in World

War II, and had been a prisoner of war. He came home, went to the University of Miami Law School, was a prosecutor for a time, then organized a small firm with a wide-ranging practice in Miami. Louis took Neil's case and focused on self-defense, which put a premium on having a juror who would be sensitive to the dynamics of two different black communities as well as the pressure felt by an eyewitness who was an illegal immigrant summoned to testify for the government.

On the day of trial, only four out of a panel of thirty-five prospective jurors were black. Three of them were among the first group of seventeen prospects brought forward for the questioning process known as "voir dire." One was married and a government secretary who opposed individuals possessing handguns in their homes. One was a plumber's assistant, and one was an elementary schoolteacher. They gave the same general answers as white prospects about their lack of criminal records and ability to decide impartially, but all three blacks were dismissed.

That evening, with jury selection unfinished, Louis went home and fumed, said longtime law partner John L. Zavertnik.[1] Louis called a lawyer friend, Joseph Beeler, who handled federal appellate cases, and Beeler told him about two recent cases in California and Massachusetts that had curtailed the use of peremptory challenges to exclude minorities. In court the next day, Louis challenged the prosecutor's actions. "Is this whitey's law?" he asked Circuit Judge Morton Perry. "This man is entitled to be tried by a jury of his peers, not a systematic exclusion."[2]

For the moment, the judge took no action. Another ten jury prospects came forward for the voir dire. None of them were black. Louis began using his peremptory challenges to strike all of the white prospects in an effort to get to a third panel with the last black prospect. Realizing Louis's purpose, Judge Perry granted additional peremptory challenges to both sides. But by the time the last black juror came up, the only seat left was for an alternate. So Neil's jury consisted of a mortgage broker from Coconut Grove, a realtor from North Miami, a developer from South Miami, an electronics salesman, the owner of a towing company in Hialeah, and a computer systems analyst for Florida Power & Light. Four men, two women, all white. Neil was convicted.

Louis took the case to the Third District Court of Appeal. On the three-judge panel was James R. Jorgenson, a former Dade police officer who had just finished his LL.M. thesis at the University of Virginia Law School on the subject of jury discrimination. A law review article based on that thesis, published after the *Neil* case was finished,[3] was critical of the reasoning behind the court decisions in California and Massachusetts that Louis had relied on. Those states "gutted the peremptory challenge system without giving thought to alternative methods which would enhance minority participation on trial juries," Jorgensen wrote in his article. He rejected the idea that U.S. Supreme Court cases calling for a "fair cross-section of the community" in jury trials had anything to do with peremptory challenges.

Judges Jorgensen, Thomas Barkdull and Phillip Hubbart were unanimous in affirming Neil's conviction. "Neil's reliance on those cases is misplaced," the per curiam opinion said. "Defendants are not entitled to a jury of any particular composition. . . . Neil's argument . . . is simply not compelling. . . . When peremptory challenges are subjected to judicial scrutiny, they will no longer be peremptory."

Neil got one break from the Third DCA: The judges certified the case as one of "great public importance" and sent it on to the Supreme Court for an answer to this question: "Absent the criteria established in *Swain v. Alabama* . . . may a party be required to state the basis for the exercise of a peremptory challenge?"

Swain was a U.S. Supreme Court case from nearly twenty years earlier that had rejected a challenge to all-white juries resulting from peremptory challenges. Robert Swain was a black man, convicted of rape and sentenced to death by an all-white jury in Talladega, Alabama, after eight blacks in the original jury pool were dismissed—two because they were exempt from jury duty and six because of the prosecutor's peremptory challenges. It was rare to have a black person on any jury in Talladega County, but that was not enough for the Supreme Court to find systemic discrimination and grant a new trial for Robert Swain. "The presumption in any particular case must be that the prosecutor is using the state's challenges to obtain a fair and impartial jury to try the case before the court," wrote Justice Byron White.

The headlines and public protests in Miami against exclusion of blacks from juries had become so sensitive that State Attorney Janet Reno, the future U.S. attorney general, had proclaimed a policy against discriminatory use of peremptory challenges. She told the chief judge that if any trial judge believes a prosecutor is systematically excluding jurors because of race, she will have the prosecutor announce the reasons for the exclusion, begin jury selection again, and allow jury selection to continue until the judge is satisfied.[4] In a case against black school principal Solomon Barnes, a defendant along with superintendent Jones in the Dade schools' "gold plumbing" scandal over the alleged use of school funds to purchase fancy plumbing for personal use, Circuit Judge Marvin U. Mounts had been so dissatisfied with the jury selection process that he threatened to declare a mistrial. Reno personally appeared, said she recognized the need for a jury "totally representative of the community," and asked that jury selection start over with the prosecutor voluntarily stating reasons for any peremptory challenge. The jury ended up with five whites and one black. They convicted Barnes.

The problem cut both ways. In one of the cases against white Dade police officers, it was defense counsel who continually rejected blacks as jurors. Judge David Gersten threw out the entire first jury panel, started over, once again faced rejections of black jurors by the defense and ended up with an all-white jury, which convicted the officer. The defense lawyers appealed the judge's rejection of the first panel.

Miami had struggled with the racial balance of juries before, and that issue had also gone to the Florida Supreme Court.[5] At first the focus was on the original jury pools. Starting in the late 1960s, jury commissioners charged with individually selecting the jury venire—the large initial group called for jury duty—had tried to ensure that 15 to 19 percent of the pool was black and that there was roughly an equal balance of men and women. George A. Silva, a defendant in a rape case, challenged that system. The Supreme Court, in an opinion by Justice Adkins, "reluctantly" struck down this system of "proportional racial limitation."[6]

Adkins could not get around a twenty-year-old U.S. Supreme Court decision overturning, without opinion or elaboration, a Florida conviction in which jurors had been selected on the basis of "racial proportionate representation which limited the numbers of Negroes serving on juries."[7] The Florida court had upheld that conviction and was not going to be overturned on the same issue again. Silva also challenged the exclusion of people eighteen to twenty years old, who had recently won the right to vote under the Twenty-sixth Amendment. The Supreme Court said the new right to vote for those between eighteen and twenty did not affect the Florida statute stating that jurors must be twenty-one or over—and noted that it had followed that same principle in 1939 after the Nineteenth Amendment gave women the right to vote in 1920.[8]

Chief Justice Roberts as well as Carlton, McCain, and Boyd joined the Adkins opinion in *State v. Silva*. Ervin dissented in the exclusion of the eighteen-to twenty-year-old voters from juries. Justice Dekle dissented on the racial considerations in the jury pool. "An improved more equally balanced jury venire is a strange basis for its disqualification," he said. "We lose our perspective in our eager efforts for equality."[9]

Neil was now raising a different aspect of the problem. Often the pools had disproportionately few minorities, but the focus now was on the exclusion of blacks from the jury itself.

Three months behind Neil's case at the Third DCA was another case raising the same issue. The Third DCA again upheld the conviction, again with Jorgensen on the panel, but Judge Wilkie Ferguson wrote a separate opinion. A black judge who had grown up in the Liberty Square public housing project, Ferguson had been a U.S. Army paratrooper in the 1960s and later served on a presidential commission that investigated the Liberty City riots in 1968. Appointed by Governor Askew as the first black circuit judge in Miami, his official biography said he "made a landmark ruling precluding the systematic exclusion of blacks from juries" even before his appointment to the Third DCA by Governor Graham in 1980. (President Bill Clinton later appointed him to the federal district court.)

Now facing the jury discrimination issue as an appellate judge, Ferguson concurred with Jorgensen and Judge Lenore Nesbitt only because he felt bound by the decision in *Neil*, but he found that decision "oblivious to the immediate social impact." He said the *Neil* decision "raised the peremptory challenge, a procedural tool without constitutional foundation, to a position of such jurisprudential eminence that it now transcends the right of any minority group not to be systematically excluded from participation in the administration of criminal justice—a right which is constitutionally guaranteed."[10]

Louis wanted reinforcements for Jack Neil's appeal to the Florida Supreme Court. He recruited Jesse McCrary, a prominent black lawyer from Miami who had become the first black member of Florida's Cabinet since Reconstruction when Governor Askew appointed him to a vacancy as secretary of state. Louis also recruited the ACLU of Florida and Common Cause, which were represented by Don Middlebrooks of Steel, Hector & Davis.

On May 11, 1984, Paul Louis and Assistant Attorney General Diane E. Leeds stood in the courtroom of the Supreme Court for oral argument. Louis, who had been on the Supreme Court Nominating Commission that recommended McDonald for the court, was passionate in attacking the discrimination, but some of the justices sympathetic to his argument occasionally felt the need to interject more succinct answers to their colleagues' questions. Attorney General Jim Smith, a Democrat at the time, passed up the chance to take a position like Janet Reno's. Instead, Leeds clung to tradition and asserted that the standard set in *Swain* was not "really that hard a standard to meet." All a defense lawyer had to do, she said without any sarcasm, was look up each Dade prosecutor on the county computer, find which cases he handled, check court records of the jury pools, get voter registration records to discover their race, and from that prove systematic exclusion. "Just because it has not been met in many cases does not mean it cannot be met," she said.[11]

The justices' questions and comments made it pretty clear that Shaw, the only black justice, and McDonald were on Neil's side, and Ehrlich and Overton seemed to lean that way as well. Alderman, Adkins, and Boyd were all supportive of the traditional peremptory challenge.

In the closing moments of the argument, McCrary stepped to the lectern for rebuttal on Neil's behalf. His argument was simple and direct: whatever you think of the tradition of peremptory challenges, he said, "on the basis of race, you cannot discriminate against black people."

Even though the justices seemed to have made up their minds, it took multiple conference discussions to resolve the case. The four former trial judges were split, but "we'd seen what went on as far as striking blacks was concerned," McDonald said years later.[12] He remembered that in his own Ninth Circuit a deputy sheriff would draw names for the jury pool out of a box, and if he drew a name from a black precinct and thought the judge wouldn't notice, he would simply lay it aside. In some places, county commissioners would send over the names for the jury pool. All were very much aware of the many headlines about all-white juries in Miami. Two of the four former circuit judges, Adkins from Gainesville and Alderman from St. Lucie County, nonetheless felt too strongly about "the sanctity of the peremptory challenge," as McDonald put it, to support Neil's position and noted Louis's use of peremptories to strike white jurors.

None of the justices, McDonald said, thought about how far out in front of the country Florida was going to be by ruling in Neil's favor. It was really unheard of for the Florida Supreme Court to step out ahead of the U.S. Supreme Court in expanding constitutional rights. *Swain* had rejected an argument like Paul Louis's even in the liberal era of Chief Justice Earl Warren, and that was so recent that the justice who wrote it was still on the court. There were only those two cases from liberal California and Massachusetts to bolster Louis's position. Florida's Supreme Court had every excuse to duck the issue.

On September 27, the justices lined up in a 4–3 decision exactly as the oral argument had indicated. McDonald wrote the opinion in *State v. Neil*[13] and rejected the state's argument that a decision for Neil would "open a Pandora's box of problems, including quota juries and an undesirable fundamental alteration of the jury system." McDonald echoed Judge Ferguson's view. "The right to peremptory challenges is not of constitutional dimension," McDonald wrote. "The primary purpose of peremptory challenges is to aid and assist in the selection of an impartial jury. It was not intended that such challenges be used solely as a scalpel to excise a distinct racial group from a representative cross-section of society. It was not intended that such challenges be used to encroach upon the constitutional guarantee of an impartial jury."

Joined by Overton, Ehrlich, and Shaw, McDonald briefly outlined a procedure for trial judges to use, although there had been little in the arguments about how that would work exactly. "A party's peremptories cannot be examined until the issue is properly presented to the trial court and until the trial court has determined that such examination is warranted. If such occurs, the challenged party must show that the questioned challenges, but no others, were not exercised solely on the basis of race." Neil won a new trial. A week later, on the same 4–3 vote, so did Oscar Andrews, the defendant whose case had produced Ferguson's concurring opinion.[14] But back in Miami, the witnesses against Neil had disappeared, and the state attorney simply dropped the charges.

It would be two more years before the U.S. Supreme Court took a similar step. Kentucky's Supreme Court, unlike Florida's, had clung to tradition and the impossible standard of *Swain*, but in *Batson v. Kentucky*,[15] the high court voted 7–2 to adopt a process similar to what McDonald had put forward in the *Neil* case.

The process McDonald outlined was a narrow one and relatively simple. Nearly four years after the *Neil* decision, Florida's justices decided that process was not strong enough. By then, Alderman, a conservative both economically and socially, had been replaced by Rosemary Barkett, a former nun who would be known as one of the most liberal justices. When a "*Neil* objection" is made, the judge cannot simply accept the state's reasons, Barkett wrote in *State v. Slappy*,[16] one of three cases on the issue that were released March 10, 1988. The lawyer's reasons had to refer to answers from the jury prospects and have some other basis in the record of the proceedings, and there had to "clear and reasonably specific" racially neutral explanations. That was too much for McDonald and Overton. They dissented and expressed concern that judges would end up conducting a "mini-trial" over the issue. But Ehrlich and Shaw, the other two in the *Neil* majority, stood with Barkett, and Justice Stephen H. Grimes, who had replaced Adkins, provided the crucial fourth vote.

Six days after the three cases were published, Grimes made a speech as the first Huber Hurst Distinguished Lecturer at the University of Florida Law School. In response to a question about "the extent to which you and the other justices allow policy considerations to enter your decision-making as opposed to strictly legal considerations," Grimes mentioned the trilogy of cases just released on peremptory challenges. "We know that our decisions may have the effect of reducing, if not ultimately eliminating, the use of peremptory challenges if our rationale is extended," he said. "We were ahead of the United States Supreme Court on this issue. So, we are certainly making policy decisions in some cases."[17]

The next year Grimes wrote the opinion in *Kibler v. State*[18] when the court overturned a lower-court ruling that only black defendants could challenge the exclusion of black jurors. The *Batson* case had suggested that the defendant had to show the jury challenges were directed to a racial group of which he was a member. Grimes said Florida's Constitution guarantees a right to an "impartial jury," and anyone is entitled to a jury reflecting a cross-section of the community. "We recognize that this opinion places further limitations on the ability to exercise peremptory challenges. However, we are unable to fashion any other rule which will maintain the credibility of our criminal justice system. The right of an accused to an impartial jury cannot be fully guaranteed when the peremptory challenge is used to purposefully exclude members of a cognizable racial group, regardless of the race of the defendant." McDonald agreed, though he thought the state had adequately explained its exclusion of the black jurors for non-racial reasons.

The other two former trial lawyers on the court were divided. Barkett went along with Grimes but expressed "great ambivalence." The decision was adding yet another complication in assessing whether a jury was fair, but she said she would err on the side of prohibiting discrimination or the appearance of it "regardless of the cost."

Ehrlich struggled as well, but came down on the other side. "The picking of a jury is an art, not a science. There are as many techniques or "systems" for picking a jury as there are trial lawyers. . . . In our endeavor to rid the courtroom of prejudice in the selection of jurors, we have dulled, if not obliterated, the edge of the one weapon best suited to ensure that the jury is fair and impartial." People will be left on juries, Ehrlich predicted, "even though the trial lawyer's instincts and experience tell him that the challenged juror is a 'ringer,' that is, the juror is not going to be fair and impartial."

Three weeks later the court unanimously overturned a death sentence in *Roundtree v. State*[19] after the prosecutor in Jacksonville had excluded ten black prospects on what the court called an "obvious pretext," including such things as the jurors' clothing that was in fact nothing out of the ordinary and exclusion of several unmarried black jurors even though unmarried white jurors were retained.

A few weeks after that, on August 31, 1989, McDonald wrote an opinion that seems so strikingly obvious it makes you realize one of the reasons discrimination and other such manipulation of juries could have happened: The judge must stay in the courtroom during the jury selection.[20]

The decision did not help the defendant, since there was not a claim about racially motivated exclusion of jurors and the defense lawyer had actually waived the judge's presence. But that would not be enough in the future. "If a party exceeds the bounds of proper examination or misstates the law, a judge can immediately alleviate the prejudice by means of a curative instruction," McDonald wrote. "It is more important than ever for the trial judge to be present during all parts of voir dire to assure that selection of jurors is free from racial prejudice."

As with Jack Neil's case, the case of Angelo John DiGuilio in Volusia County started out as a fairly typical case of its type, a drug bust. The trial produced an all-too-common blunder when the arresting officer testified that DiGuilio, being questioned after the bust, refused to provide personal information and said he wanted to talk to an attorney.

The testimony was a clear violation of rules against telling a jury about a defendant's exercise of his right to remain silent. The rule exists because the exercise of a constitutional right should not be considered by jurors as a sign of guilt. Suspects in custody, like DiGuilio, receive a "Miranda warning" about the right to remain silent, as DiGuilio did. People may simply remain silent out of caution.

The Supreme Court's ultimate decision, an opinion by Justice Shaw, exposed flaws in earlier decisions by the Supreme Court, including one that overturned a conviction of mob boss Santo Trafficante Jr. in the 1950s.

The exchange between the prosecutor and the police officer in DiGuilio's trial went this way:

Q: Did Mr. DiGuilio make any statements to you at that time?
A: Only to the effect that the driver of the car picked him up at his home and he had come directly to the Howard Johnson's. That he lived in South Daytona. He refused to give me an address. He refused to identify the name of the driver. He also indicated to me that the driver had parked the car and walked north to the southeast doors to the motel and

had entered. After that, he advised me he felt like he should speak to his attorney. And there was no further questioning.

Before DiGuilio's case, and certainly before "Miranda warnings" protected a person's right to refuse to answer police questions, such a forbidden statement was often treated as "harmless" in light of significant other evidence of guilt. Adkins recounted the erratic history of this doctrine in his memoir. As the court's law clerk in 1939, he said, he had worked on an opinion saying that a comment on a defendant's failure to testify was always reversible error. That decision was overruled 28 years later when the court treated such a comment as "harmless error." Then in 1978, Adkins, by then a justice, wrote an opinion in *Willinsky v. State*[21] that reinstated the 1939 rule. But a few weeks later, the court declared, over Adkins' objections, that the error was waived if the defense did not object at the time.[22]

Adkins saw the rule as a matter of creating incentives for good behavior by prosecutors in an area rife with mischief. When reversal of convictions was inevitable after a comment was made, "very few comments were ever made," Adkins said. A "harmless error" exception invites more appeals. "In all of these appeals, the appellate courts will ultimately decide that the error was harmless if they want the defendant to go to prison and harmful if they want the defendant to walk," Adkins said in his memoir. "Appellate law will become increasingly full of inconsistencies as courts attempt to apply the harmless error analysis to the forthcoming flood of cases."[23]

In the DiGuilio case, defense lawyer John W. Tanner, who in 1988 would be elected the state attorney in the Seventh Circuit, first did what any good defense lawyer would do when the officer testified: he stood up and objected. He asked that the jury be excused and then asked the judge for a mistrial because of the clearly improper comment on the defendant's exercise of his Fifth Amendment right to remain silent. Seventh Circuit Judge McFerrin Smith III denied the mistrial, and the trial went on. DiGuilio was convicted of conspiracy to traffic in cocaine.

The circumstances of DiGuilio's arrest demonstrate the harmful effect of the police officer's comment. DiGuilio was not the target of the undercover drug deal. A man named Rosa was, and he was to bring the cocaine to the undercover officer in a motel room. When Rosa arrived, he told the officer the cocaine was with another man in a motel room across the street. He got in the officer's undercover rental car, drove across the street, and returned in a few minutes with a passenger, DiGuilio, who continued sitting in the car while Rosa took the cocaine to the officer in the motel room. Officers moved in and arrested both men. The two men were left alone in the back seat of the rental car for a while, then moved to a police car, where their conversation was bugged. DiGuilio, as Justice Shaw later put it in his opinion, "indicated he knew something of what had happened," though the recording quality was so poor that the conversation could hardly be understood.

At trial, the prosecution argued that the remarks proved DiGuilio was guilty of conspiracy to traffic in cocaine. The jury found DiGuilio not guilty of trafficking but guilty of conspiring to traffic.

Tanner appealed to the Fifth District Court of Appeal over the officer's testimony about DiGuilio's limited response to questioning in the police car. "I argued that this could never be harmless error," he recalled decades later. "There's no way to know what weight that carries with a jury. Even if the evidence seems overwhelming or clear—yeah, that may be true to appellate court judges, but how about to six or twelve lay citizens? They may not think it's clear at all." Appearing unresponsive taints the jury's view of the defendant, as Tanner saw it.[24]

Tanner commented later, "Shame on us [prosecutors] if we don't have our officers prepared and have our semi-annual session with police on the requirements in these situations and let them know that you have to bite your tongue," Tanner said.

Fifth DCA Judge Melvin Orfinger saw the prosecutor's question as the root of the problem. "When the prosecutor asked the officer if defendant indicated whether or not he would answer any questions, he should have known what the answer would be," Orfinger wrote for a 3–0 panel. He said silence or the desire to talk to a lawyer should not be "used as evidence against him when he has been told, as he must be, that he has those rights."

Assistant Attorney General Richard B. Martell then sought rehearing and argued that in January, while DiGuilio's case was pending at the Fifth DCA, the Florida Supreme Court had changed the rules once again in a case called *State v. Murray*.[25] The request for rehearing was rejected. *Murray* was not about a comment on the defendant's right to remain silent in the investigation, Orfinger said, but on the defendant's right not to take the witness stand. So, Orfinger concluded, it is not clear that the Supreme Court had in fact changed the standard to be applied to DiGuilio.

The *Murray* opinion had been written for a unanimous court by Justice Shaw, who said, "Prosecutorial error alone does not warrant automatic reversal of a conviction unless the errors involved are so basic to a fair trial that they can never be treated as harmless." The issue, he said, is whether the error committed "was so prejudicial" that it infected the outcome of the trial. Shaw said the lower court, the Fourth District Court of Appeal, "focused entirely on the prosecutor's conduct" without any "recitation of the factual evidence on which the state relied, or any conclusion as to whether this evidence was or was not dispositive" of the entire case.

The state appealed the Diguilio case to the Supreme Court. In *State v. DiGuilio*,[26] Shaw decided to revisit the whole history of cases on the subject. He would eventually identify the opinion as one of his most significant. It is said to be the most cited of all Supreme Court opinions.

Shaw began with the little-known fact that once upon a time, a defendant was not even allowed to testify in his own defense. That did not change until federal legislation in 1878 and Florida legislation in 1895. Florida law made one thing clear: "nor shall any prosecuting attorney be permitted before the jury or court to comment on the failure of the accused to testify in his own behalf." Accordingly, in 1903, the Florida Supreme Court had reversed a conviction because of a prosecutor's comment. In all the cases through the first half of the twentieth century, the court had ruled that the 1895 statute barring comment on the defendant's decision not to testify was independent of a separate law that said convictions were not to be overturned if an error had been "harmless." Violation by the prosecutor "cannot be cured by the court instructing the jury to disregard his comment."[27]

In 1941 the legislature passed a new "harmless error" law, which by its terms applied to all errors, including a prosecutor's comment on the right not to testify. Yet the state attorney general's office—that would have been Attorney General Richard Ervin—had not included any reference to the statute in three different unsuccessful arguments to keep the Supreme Court from overturning convictions.

One of those cases, *Trafficante v. State* in 1957,[28] had overturned the 1954 bribery conviction and five-year sentence of reputed organized-crime boss Santo Trafficante Jr. of Tampa and his younger brother, Henry Trafficante. Among a number of arrests of Santo Trafficante in the 1950s, this was the only case in which there had been a conviction. The prosecutor in his closing argument had referred to the testimony of prosecution witnesses as being "uncontradicted, uncontradicted, by these two Trafficantes."

The other two cases had defendants named Way and Gordon. "There is no reference in *Way, Trafficante,* or *Gordon* to section 924.33 [the 1941 harmless-error law]," Shaw wrote in footnote 8 in the *DiGuilio* case. "A review of the briefs filed in these cases shows that the state did not rely on, or even recognize the existence of, section 924.33."

In *Trafficante*, the state had simply argued that the prosecutor's closing argument should not be interpreted as a comment on failure to testify. The crucial effect of the state's failure to cite the statute is suggested in Justice Campbell Thornal's concurring opinion in *Trafficante*: "The Legislature had made this [reversal of conviction because of a comment] a rule of law by statute. We are not permitted to change it by judicial decree." The rule had in fact been changed by legislative decree fifteen years earlier, but the Supreme Court clearly didn't realize it. The justices "were feeling considerable discomfort at our rule of per se reversal," as Shaw put it later, but felt confined by their interpretation of a statute that was no longer valid.

If the court had applied the overlooked 1941 "harmless error" statute in 1957, it is very possible that the mob boss would have gone to prison.

A separate line of cases, Shaw said in *DiGuilio*, dealt with comments on the accused person's decision not to talk to police after being taken into custody. That is what the famous U.S. Supreme Court decision in *Miranda v. Arizona* in 1966 was about. And once again, Shaw reported, the Florida Supreme Court seems to have misunderstood the law. After *Miranda*, in 1967, the U.S. Supreme Court in *Chapman v. California* said a comment on an accused person's silence does not always mean the trial as a whole was not fair. But the Florida Supreme Court in 1975, in an opinion by Adkins espousing his long-held view, declared in *Bennett v. State* that such comments required reversal in all cases.[29]

"Although we cited *Chapman* in *Bennett*, we overlooked its holding that automatic reversal of a conviction is only appropriate when the constitutional right which is violated vitiates the right to a fair trial," Shaw wrote in *DiGuilio*. "It was not until we issued *State v. Marshall* [1985] and *State v. Murray* [1984][30] that we adopted the correct rule . . . that constitutional errors, with rare exceptions, are subject to harmless error analysis." It had taken yet another U.S. Supreme Court decision, *Hastings v. United States* in 1983,[31] to alert the Florida Supreme Court to this approach.

Shaw's comments were an unusually explicit confession of lapses on the part of the Supreme Court. Alderman's opinion in *Murray* had obscured the problem of ignoring the *Bennett* case; Alderman merely said "we agree with the recent analysis" in *Hastings*. McDonald's opinion in *Marshall* went a little further by noting that despite *Chapman*, "the courts of this state . . . have persisted in applying a per se reversal rule to comments on a defendant's failure to testify, in spite of Florida's harmless error statute."

McDonald's opinion in *Marshall* was a victory for prosecutors. He went on at some length about the justification for the dramatic change in doctrine:

First, comments on silence are no longer considered to be fundamental error.[32] . . . Second, the United States Supreme Court has held that the harmless error rule is consistent with the federal constitution. . . . Third, the harmless error rule is a preferred method of promoting the administration of justice. It makes no sense to order a new trial, because of a nonfundamental error committed at trial, when we know beyond a reasonable doubt that the defendant will be convicted again. Our trial courts are already excessively burdened. An additional and unnecessary trial in such an instance might affect the rights of others to a fair and expeditious trial. Finally, we should consider legislative intent. Section 924.33, Florida Statutes (1983), adopts the harmless error rule for appeals of criminal convictions.

The new rule, McDonald wrote in *Marshall*, was this: "Any comment on, or which is fairly susceptible of being interpreted as referring to, a defendant's failure to testify is error and is strongly discouraged. Such a comment, however, should be evaluated according to the harmless error rule, with the state having the burden of showing the comment to have been harmless beyond a reasonable doubt."

The decision in *Marshall* was 4–3. Boyd, Alderman, and Shaw joined McDonald. Adkins and Overton dissented without opinion. Ehrlich's dissenting opinion in a companion case, *State v. Kinchen*,[33] was joined by Overton. Said Ehrlich:

The presumption of a defendant's innocence, the state's burden of proving his guilt beyond a reasonable doubt and the defendant's concomitant right to stand mute before his accusers without conceding guilt in any way are fundamental underpinnings of due process. To permit equivocal or indirect comments on the defendant's silence so long as any other reasonable interpretation is possible significantly erodes the protection this state has traditionally afforded its citizens. . . .

The per se rule has served the citizens of Florida quite well. I am not as optimistic about the new rule that the Court is adopting. I am apprehensive that it is an open invitation to prosecutorial overreaching.

The decisions in *Marshall* and *Kinchen* did little to settle the confusion on the issue. Appellate courts that had chafed at the obligation to grant new trials even if the evidence made another guilty verdict very likely now gave way to broad confusion in applying a vague new standard for when a comment was or was not "harmless" in the trial.

No wonder Shaw in *DiGuilio* stepped back for a long historical analysis of the two lines of cases, one on a defendant's silence at trial and the other on silence during an interrogation after arrest. Shaw tried a whole new approach that formed a middle ground. After all, he had been both a public defender and a prosecutor.

First, he noted that the comments at issue often were not "clear-cut violations where the prosecutor directly comments on the accused's silence," but indirect remarks, sometimes cleverly intentional, sometimes inadvertent, sometimes, as Tanner would say, simply a result of poor trial preparation, occasionally made not by prosecutors but by lawyers for other defendants. All those "are lumped together in an amorphous mass," Shaw said. "No bright line can be drawn around or within the almost unlimited variety of comments that will place all of the harmful errors on one side and the harmless errors on the other, unless the circumstances of the trial are considered."

Shaw undertook to get the incentives right, so that prosecutors could not sneak in a reference but get away with it as harmless error while defense lawyers could not turn every possible comment into an excuse for a mistrial. The rule of per-se reversals "substitutes mechanics for judgment." Instead Shaw blended a rule focusing on comments that were "fairly susceptible" of being viewed as an improper comment with a prosecutor's obligation "to show beyond a reasonable doubt that the specific comment(s) did not contribute to the verdict."

Shaw got rid of the traditional approach that as long as there was a lot of evidence against the defendant, any comment was deemed "harmless." Evidence may seem overwhelming, Shaw was saying, but "an error that constituted a substantial part of the prosecution's case may have played a substantial part in the jury's deliberation and thus contributed to the actual verdict reached."

When the *DiGuilio* decision was first released with a remand of the case to the Fifth DCA, people were still confused by how the lower courts were to make that decision. So on rehearing, Shaw undertook the analysis as he thought it should be done in DiGuilio's case. "Because we wish to make it clear that the harmless error test is to be rigorously applied, we examine the record ourselves rather than remanding. We conclude that the error was harmful and the conviction should be quashed."

The guilt or innocence of DiGuilio was a closer case than it seemed, Shaw said. "The fact that Rosa returned shortly with DiGuilio and the cocaine does not show beyond a reasonable doubt that DiGuilio was a cohort who was holding the cocaine," Shaw explained. "DiGuilio could have been present in the motel room and not known of the impending drug deal or of the cocaine.

Rosa's statement to the purported drug buyer about a cohort could have been false, a precautionary measure to dissuade strong-arm tactics. Violence, suspicion, and lying between drug dealers is common."

The not-guilty part of the jury verdict suggests the jurors were not convinced beyond a reasonable doubt that DiGuilio had possessed the cocaine, Shaw went on. "Indeed, under the circumstances, it is plausible that DiGuilio had learned of the drug deal after the arrest by observing the events or in an unrecorded conversation with Rosa [in the rental car] and that DiGuilio's recorded remarks were based on knowledge obtained after his arrest."

So what does all that have to do with the officer's comment that DiGuilio, when questioned, exercised his right to remain silent? "It put before the jury the fact that DiGuilio declined to offer any plausible explanation at the time of his arrest for his suspicious presence in the midst of a drug deal," Shaw said. "Further, at least indirectly, it also highlighted for the jury the fact that DiGuilio was not testifying at trial and still had offered no plausible explanation." A defendant is not obligated to offer a defense, and the state bears the full responsibility of removing all reasonable doubt.

And so, with yet another standard now in place for harmless error—not the per se rule of before, but still theoretically high—the reversal of DiGuilio's conviction by the Fifth DCA was affirmed.

Suddenly, the relaxed standard from McDonald's opinion in *Marshall* did not seem so relaxed. Shaw's opinion in *DiGuilio* signaled that the standard of finding a comment "harmless" should still be very high. And without saying so, Shaw was debunking an approach to harmless error that the Florida Supreme Court itself had been using for years to uphold convictions, including that of serial killer Ted Bundy and many others on death row.[34]

30

"ROSEMARY THE FIRST"

When Leander Shaw was sworn in as the second black justice in January 1983, Governor Graham was asked by a reporter when he might appoint a woman to the court. Graham said he did "not see that on the horizon."[1] He might have seen no appointments at all on the horizon. His two most recent appointees, Ehrlich and Shaw, were likely to win retention in 1984 for six more years. Overton, McDonald, and Alderman all were career judges and were likely to win retention in 1986. It would be four years before Adkins and Boyd faced mandatory retirement in January 1987, the beginning of the next governor's term.

A little more than two years later, however, Jim Alderman asked for a private meeting with Graham, "just between the two of us," as Graham later put it. Alderman told the governor he would soon resign from the Supreme Court to take over his family ranch because of his father's heart attack a few months earlier. His father, B. E. Alderman, was no longer able to run the 9,000-acre ranch west of Fort Pierce near Yeehaw Junction. His grandfather had made the first purchase of land back in 1937, at $2 an acre. Three earlier generations had been ranchers in Florida going back to the 1830s. Young Jim, who had gone into law because his grandfather and father did not need him in the operation when he was in his twenties, now was stepping down from the pinnacle of the legal profession, barely a year after completing a two-year term as chief justice, 1982–1984. He was going to practice law, and joined a firm based in St. Lucie County.

The other justices already knew of his father's condition and weren't surprised when Alderman announced his decision at the weekly conference the following Monday, April 29, 1985. His public announcement that afternoon did not say exactly when he was leaving other than he would not seek retention in the 1986 election. He said he would time his departure in consultation with the other justices. As with Sundberg, that ended up being the end of the summer recess, the month for catching up and taking vacations. He left, at the age of forty-eight, on August 31, 1985. In 2014 this very traditional man still had no Internet in his two-story home and did not use e-mail.

Once Alderman set the date, the nominating process started. The new justice had to be from the Fourth appellate district, and the process drew a flock of sitting judges. Among them were Fourth District Court of Appeal Chief Judge George Hersey and Judge Hugh Glickstein and Circuit Judges Frank Orlando, William C. Owen Jr., and Charles E. Smith. All three who were nominated were Fourth DCA judges. It was the third time on a nomination list for Harry Lee Anstead, the second time for Gavin K. Letts. Both had become Fourth DCA judges by election rather than appointment. A newcomer to the nomination list was Rosemary Barkett, whom Graham had appointed to the Fourth DCA the previous year. Appointing the first woman to the Supreme Court was enticing on its own, but it also would be important the following year if Graham, as everyone expected, challenged the first female U.S. senator from Florida, incumbent Republican Paula Hawkins.

No other justice had anything like the roundabout route Rosemary Barkett took to the Supreme Court. Her parents were from Syria and set out in the mid-1920s to follow other family members to the United States. Stymied by immigration quotas, they got only as far as Mexico. Her father became a peddler but eventually owned a dry goods store. Rosemary was born on August 29, 1939, in Ciudad Victoria, Mexico, 200 miles southwest of the U.S. border at Brownsville, Texas, where the Rio Grande empties into the Gulf of Mexico. One more sibling came along behind Rosemary. Though her mother had fourteen pregnancies, only seven children survived as Rosemary moved through her grade-school years. Four of them were girls. Her sister, Irma Barkett Elder, ten years older, noted that their mother liked to show off Rosemary's precocious ability to whistle before she was a year old.[2]

Rosemary went to a Catholic pre-school, but in January 1945, the family set out for Miami. As they came through immigration, the family name was changed from "Barakat" to a spelling already used by relatives who arrived previously, "Barkett." Her father opened a grocery store near the old Orange Bowl stadium in Miami and later acquired avocado groves out near Homestead. Rosemary spoke no English on her first day at school, but she again learned quickly. She remembered no language problems in school. With her parents working late at the store, she and her sisters would have dinner alone together often and would talk about different subjects—politics, movie stars, all sorts of things. "It was always interesting, made us our own thinkers," sister Irma recalled.

In junior high, kids would give Christmas presents to each other at school, and her sister said Rosemary would buy extras and give them to girls who didn't get gifts. In 1958 she became a naturalized American citizen. As college approached, she applied to Catholic University, got in, but then began worrying about finances. Suddenly she announced that she was going to enter the convent "because I want to do something for other people." Her parents were not enthusiastic. Her father wasn't even Catholic, and her mother wanted grandchildren. Barkett became Sister St. Michael among the Sisters of St. Joseph Convent, taught elementary school in different locations around the state, and was sometimes called "the fun nun"—roller-skating and playing ball with the children. After eight years, she left, "because I think I can do so much good outside the convent."

Barkett went to Spring Hill College in Mobile, Alabama, graduated summa cum laude, then went on to the University of Florida Law School and got her law degree in 1970. West Palm Beach lawyer Joseph Farish interviewed her at law school and came back and told his partners, "I hired someone you're all going to love." Farish had a reputation for hiring great lawyers. Both Barkett and future justice Harry Lee Anstead worked there.

Barkett was the first female trial lawyer in Palm Beach County. She was liked even by her adversaries. "She took her cases seriously, but she never took herself seriously," said friend and future justice Barbara Pariente, who arrived in West Palm Beach four years after Barkett. She once represented former governor Claude Kirk in a divorce case against his wife, Erika, the famously mysterious "Madame X" companion at his inaugural ball in 1967 before they were married. Pariente represented Mrs. Kirk. Under their powerful cross-examinations, as Pariente told it later, the couple suddenly reconciled in mid-trial and remained married until death did them part. Pariente later represented Barkett in a lawsuit against Farish over fees due at her departure from his law firm.[3]

In 1979, around the time Alderman was joining the Supreme Court, Barkett decided to apply for a circuit judgeship on the Fifteenth Circuit Court, and Graham appointed her. She was the first female circuit judge in Palm Beach County. In the manner of other successful lawyers who tempered their lifestyles after moving to the bench, Barkett traded her cream-colored Mercedes SL convertible for a Mustang. In 1984 she became the first woman on the Fourth District Court of Appeal, joining Anstead and Letts there. Her friends began calling her Rosemary the First. "She's very open, yet she knows her own values," Fourth DCA Judge Daniel Hurley said of her. "She doesn't retreat, but she doesn't beat you over the head with her views either."[4] Barkett had been on that court barely a year when Alderman resigned.

When Graham selected her, he created a special show about his appointment of the first woman justice. As Askew had done with the appointment of Joe

Hatchett ten years earlier, Graham scheduled a press conference instead of simply issuing a written announcement. Barkett secretly flew into Tallahassee the night before and stood beside Graham on Wednesday morning, October 2, 1985—the first time an appointee had been present at a governor's announcement. "Judge Barkett stands on a record of humanity, service, legal talent, professionalism and demeanor, which speaks for her own qualities," Graham said. "Her childhood experiences of growing up in another country, expressing herself in a different language, functioning in another culture have given her an awareness of the full range of human experience."

Barkett said the appointment "means a little more to me because it comes from someone I admire." She kissed the governor on the cheek, another first in the recorded history of Supreme Court appointees.[5] Less noticed at the time was that she was also the first justice of Arab ancestry and the first who was a native of Mexico (or any other country outside the United States).

In another novelty after the press conference, Graham escorted Barkett from the capitol across Duval Street to the Supreme Court building. Ehrlich, working in his office, recalled hearing "a lot of racket" and walked into the corridor as the elevator door opened and "out popped the governor and Rosemary." Chief Justice Boyd greeted them. One of the most obvious challenges the court faced with the first woman justice was the one restroom marked "Justices," which was at the far end of the north corridor. The restroom became perhaps the most famous aspect of the story of the first woman justice. Marshal Tony Smilgin promptly commandeered a restroom at the south end of the corridor and converted it into a restroom he thought suitable for a woman justice, complete with a shower and a makeup mirror, which in Ehrlich's later puckish retelling had "a thousand lights." Other women in the justices' offices used it as well.

Although Barkett's tenure formally began at the end of October, her investiture was November 15. Sister Mary Victor, who had taught with Barkett in a Catholic school in St. Augustine and gave the invocation, beforehand walked down the corridor lined with photographs of the white-haired men who had been justices. "I wonder how they feel," she said to *Orlando Sentinel* reporter Craig Crawford.[6] "It's about time, after 140 years," said former state legislator Lois Frankel, who was then president of the Palm Beach chapter of the Florida Association of Women Lawyers. Chief Justice Boyd remarked in opening the ceremony, "While several of the good ol' boys were in the robing room, one asked why there's such a big crowd out there. When some of us were sworn in, we were lucky to fill the seats." In fact, when Boyd and other more senior justices were sworn in, before the introduction of cameras in courtrooms, the swearing-in of a new justice was a small, private event.

Two trial lawyers spoke. "She will be less conservative," said Russell Trout-man of Orlando. Added Christian D. Searcy, president-elect of the Academy of Florida Trial Lawyers (later known as the Florida Justice Association), "In the past, too many justices have come from law practices where they defended business." He said Barkett "will respect individual rights without worrying about whether it hinders the progress of business."[7] Barkett herself read a letter from a fourth-grade boy, who congratulated her and added, "If I was the first man on the Supreme Court of Florida, I would be so proud."

At her first weekly conference of the justices, she encountered, as every new justice does, a collection of pending cases where the other justices were tied 3–3. One of the cases that day was a rehearing petition for a case decided on a 4–3 vote, with Alderman in the majority. Other justices urged Barkett not to disturb the outcome of previously published cases on what was normally a routinely denied request for rehearing. Adkins, however, told her that she was one-seventh of the court and should vote her conscience. The 4–3 decision was reversed.

Not long after her arrival, *Tallahassee Democrat* reporter Judy Doyle ar-rived to interview the new female justice on a very rainy day. She entered the office and found garbage cans in the middle of the office to catch the water leaking through the ceiling. She ended up writing a story on the condition of the building. The problem had gone on for years, but the court had never gotten an appropriation to fix it. The thirty-year-old elevator was unreliable, just to take one additional example. This time, the money came, not only for roof repairs but for a major renovation and expansion of the building. Less inclined than "the boys" to acquiesce in the condition of the place, Barkett got Boyd's appointment as chair of the "house committee" to oversee renovation of the leaky old building. During the major renovation and expansion, which continued through Ehrlich's tenure as chief, Barkett patrolled the construction areas in a hardhat and brought the project in on time and on budget.

Barkett worked at a feverish pace from the start. She told her early law clerks that she would demand more from them because she could not expect to get away with mistakes or shortcuts that "the boys" might get away with. She often was at her office late at night after others had gone and would often be up before dawn for a run. The floor of her office was a major part of her filing system. It also was a place she and clerks would sit to draw diagrams of the issues and alternatives in pending cases.

She was still "the fun nun." On one occasion she announced to her law clerks that they deserved an "afternoon off," which actually began at 4 p.m. They and a newspaper reporter all drove down to Wakulla Springs for a boat ride at the state park followed by oysters and beer at a rustic bar, where Barkett joined in the singing when Patsy Cline's "Crazy" came on the jukebox.[8] "She could party with the best of them," said Ehrlich. "She could play a mean guitar and she could dance. She always thought she could sing but really couldn't, but we played like she could."[9]

Her October appointment meant that she had barely a year before going through a retention election. Overton and McDonald, both retained in 1980, were on the ballot as well. There was little opposition to any of them, and all won with more than 76 percent of the vote.

Six years later, however, Barkett was again on the ballot, again with Overton and McDonald as well as Major B. Harding in his first retention election. Barkett became chief justice in July 1992, and like Shaw two years earlier, had to devote the first few months of her term fending off opposition. By the mid-year campaign-finance reporting, she had raised more than $200,000. She added another $100,000 before the campaign was over.

The opposition garnered plenty of media attention by challenging Barkett's votes on criminal cases, including death-penalty cases, and privacy cases like her vote to join the Shaw opinion in the T.W. parental-notification abortion case in 1989. The coalition of opponents had learned from the 1990 experience and now had a broader attack, focusing on the entire court and on a broader set of opinions.

The court "has become a liberal activist court bent on furthering its own political agenda, a court out of touch with the mainstream of Florida," said Tallahassee lawyer Tim Warfel, executive director of Citizens for a Responsible Judiciary. Also among the opponents were Steve Zeller, who led opposition to Shaw in 1990, and Orange County State Attorney Lawson Lamar, who said Barkett "seems to look for any reason at all to put aside the recommendations of death." Their organization complained she had voted "against law enforcement" in nearly three-fourths of her criminal-justice opinions, including the *Cox* case over the murder of Zeller's sister (chapter 23).[10] The National Rifle Association also was among the opponents. Five other state attorneys, sixteen sheriffs and forty-eight police chiefs also were listed among the opposition.

Barkett's campaign assembled analyses showing that her decisions were consistent with statutes and case law and also rebutting exaggerated claims about the effects or reasoning of the cases. On the T.W. case, for example (chapter 23),[11] an analysis released by law professors from six Florida law schools said that "contrary to the impression given" in a newsletter from the opposition, the case has never been used "to strike down child pornography or statutory rape laws." Florida State Law Professor Steven Gey, who closely followed the Florida Supreme Court, had law students analyze 3,013 written opinions issued by the court during Barkett's tenure up to that point. He said she voted with the majority in 91 percent of the cases, including 88 percent of the criminal cases.[12] The basic theme of Barkett supporters was that she followed existing case law and was well within the mainstream of the court. Opponents thought that proved their point that the whole court was too "liberal."

The dueling case analyses were incomplete on both sides. The opposition exaggerated the impact of decisions, but Barkett's depiction of herself as a regular part of the majority obscured the fact that often it was a majority because of her. As Troutman and Searcy predicted at her investiture, she clearly was more "liberal" than the conservative she replaced. She continued to use rehearing petitions to reverse the outcome of 4–3 votes. Her view was, "If I'm here, I'm going to vote."[13]

She shared McDonald's determination to give more attention to mitigating circumstances in death-penalty cases but often disagreed with him on personal-injury cases. Her personal views on the death penalty were significantly different from Alderman's, but she voted more than 200 times to uphold death sentences. The murder of Steve Zeller's sister was brutal and ghastly, but the court was unanimous, including conservative former trial judges Overton and McDonald, in deciding that the evidence did not meet the fundamental standard of being "beyond a reasonable doubt."

Barkett also had a greater empathy than Alderman in cases where defendants were caught by police through intrusions on privacy, especially random sweeps and stops. Her opponents in 1992 highlighted a 1991 case, *Bostick v. State*,[14] determining whether law-enforcement officers can board a Greyhound bus in search of drug couriers. The issue was whether officers could single out for questioning any citizen on the bus without any basis for believing that particular person had violated any law, and whether a passenger's consent to a search of his belongings was truly voluntary rather than compliance with legal authority. The Broward Sheriff's Department called this "working the buses," and it was designed to find drug couriers.

Judge Letts, a more conservative judge than Barkett, described the situation this way in his opinion before the case reached the Supreme Court: Two Broward sheriff's deputies, "complete with badges, insignia and one of them holding a recognizable zipper pouch containing a pistol," boarded a Miami-to-Atlanta bus during a stop in Fort Lauderdale. "Eyeing the passengers, the officers, admittedly without articulable suspicion, picked out the defendant passenger and asked to inspect his ticket and identification." The papers matched and were handed back, but then the deputies told the passenger, Terrance Bostick, that they were narcotics agents and wanted to inspect his luggage. They found cocaine and arrested him for drug trafficking.

Barkett said the case presents "the perpetual conflict between, on the one hand, the right of an individual to be free from governmental interference and, on the other hand, the need of government to ensure the safety of its decisions." She added, "When the state has reason to believe that an individual has committed a crime, the state has the power to interfere with that individual's autonomy through a seizure or a search. However, this power must be exercised within certain constitutional constraints."

The U.S. Supreme Court, she noted, had allowed police to briefly stop and question people "reasonably suspected of committing or about to commit a crime." The state argued that the encounter on the bus was merely "a consensual encounter." Barkett disagreed. The sheriff's procedure of "working the buses" included an officer standing in the aisle so that the passenger was blocked from exiting, and Bostick could not leave the bus because the stopover was only a brief one. The passenger would reasonably feel he could not leave or disregard the officer's questions.

"Government has exceeded its power," Barkett concluded. Then, in words that her opponents said "compared Florida law enforcement officers with Gestapo police in Nazi Germany and communists in Soviet Russia and Cuba," but in fact drew on a theme in the trial judge's order, Barkett noted: "Roving patrols, random sweeps, and arbitrary searches or seizure would go far to eliminate such crime in this state. Yet we are not a state that subscribes to the notion that ends justify means." Her opinion declared the "working the buses" procedure inherently a violation of the constitutional right against unreasonable searches and seizures. It was a 4–3 decision, and the dissents illustrate the different weight judges give to the contending arguments. Ehrlich, Shaw and Gerald Kogan, who joined the court along with Steve Grimes in January 1987, agreed with Barkett.

"To many the practice of police boarding a bus seeking evidence of transportation of drugs is distasteful," wrote McDonald in dissent. "I can accept that, but find nothing illegal about it so long as there are no overt acts of threat or intimidation in the procurement of a consent to search. The entire war on drugs is distasteful and society should accept some minimal inconvenience and minimal incursion on their rights of privacy in that fight." Overton and Grimes agreed with him. Grimes separately expressed "a certain amount of discomfort in the prospect of the police routinely boarding stopped buses to inquire of the passengers whether they will consent to a search of their luggage," but "I know of no legal principle which would justify this court in declaring the practice to be per se illegal."

The state appealed to the U.S. Supreme Court, which reversed the decision in an opinion by Justice Sandra O'Connor, the first woman on that Supreme Court. She said the Florida court was wrong in its broad rejection of "working the buses" and in focusing on whether Bostick was "free to leave" the bus. Since his bus was about to depart, Bostick "would not have felt free to leave the bus even if the police had not been present," so his movements were confined not by the deputies but by his decision to take the bus. O'Connor said each encounter under the bus program had to be evaluated by "whether the police conduct would have communicated to a reasonable person that the person was not free to decline the officers' requests or otherwise terminate the encounter."

Applying that standard on remand, Barkett and two other justices still felt a "reasonable person" would not have felt free to terminate the encounter, but a majority disagreed. Barkett's critics said her dissent was "almost as an act of defiance," but her supporters said O'Connor had left it to the Florida court to evaluate the encounter under the standard O'Connor established.

In the final days of the campaign, the National Rifle Association mounted an advertising blitz saying Barkett "coddles killers." As with the Shaw challenge two years earlier, the opposition appeared to knock down the support for all four justices up for retention, but all survived with comfortable margins. Barkett took a little bigger hit. Overton, McDonald, and Harding drew about 65 percent of the vote, more than ten percentage points below the support Overton and McDonald had six years earlier. Barkett had 60.9 percent.

She later reflected on the disadvantages of the merit-retention process. "It's not a perfect system," she said. "People have this ridiculous false view in their head that if they unretain somebody, they will get somebody who is perfect, who is going to agree with them on every level. . . . You're running against a phantom thing, a phantom person."[15]

With the retention campaign behind her four months into her term as chief, Barkett threw herself into her chief justice duties. Less than a year later, however, she had a much more welcome distraction. On September 24, 1993, President Bill Clinton nominated her to replace Judge Paul H. Roney of St. Petersburg on the Eleventh Circuit Court of Appeals, the same court on which Hatchett served.

There was a strong Republican campaign against her confirmation that echoed the 1992 retention campaign in Florida. In fact, before the Senate vote on her confirmation on April 14, Republican Senator Strom Thurmond, the oldest and longest-serving senator going back to his days as a segregationist "Dixiecrat" in the 1940s, gave a long speech that itemized the same cases and rhetoric that had been used against her in 1992, including the *Bostick* case. Thurmond criticized Clinton for saying in his State of the Union address that he wanted to attack crime and then nominating Barkett. "She has issued a series of search and seizure decisions which if implemented would severely hamper the ability of the police to enforce laws against drug trafficking and other crimes," Thurmond said, according to the Congressional Record. "This liberal lady judge," he said, "has attempted at every turn to make excuses for the acts of brutal criminals."

The Senate confirmed her to the life-tenured federal judgeship by a 61–37 vote. Barkett resigned from the Florida Supreme Court on April 21, 1994, and Steve Grimes, next in seniority for chief, stepped into the role ten weeks early. Grimes and his successor, Kogan, split the extra weeks of the two-year chief justice term. Grimes served as chief until May 31, 1996, then Kogan became chief June 1 rather than July 1 in 1998.

Barkett shunned the traditional authoritarianism of a federal judgeship. "Like Madonna and Elvis, she is known everywhere by her first name," Pariente once said of her. "People feel they know her and feel they are her friend."[16]

Barkett served on the Eleventh Circuit court until Sept. 30, 2013, when she was named by the U.S. State Department to be a judge of the Iran-United States Claims Tribunal in The Hague in the Netherlands. The nine-member court was created as part of the deal signed on election day in November 1979 to release American hostages from Iran. The United States agreed to terminate litigation against Iran and release frozen assets in exchange for an escrow account and the creation of this alternative tribunal to adjudicate private and government claims between the countries. Nearly thirty-five years later, the court was still in operation. Barkett became the only woman among the nine judges. She had just passed her seventy-fourth birthday.

31

VIRGIL HAWKINS

Crossing the Bar

Virgil D. Hawkins was dead when he was readmitted to the Florida Bar on October 20, 1988, but he had plenty of supporters, now, when they were no longer much good to him. Five years earlier, fighting disbarment over his handling of some clients' cases, he had told the Florida Supreme Court, "When I get to heaven, I want to be a member of the Florida Bar." But he resigned, and by the time the court let him back in, it was after St. Peter's deadline.

After his long struggle to become a lawyer, Virgil Hawkins was, at the end of his eight years as a member of the Bar, simply another lawyer who had fouled up cases and couldn't account for client funds. He was reprimanded and finally forced to resign from the Bar. In death, however, Hawkins became an icon of the civil rights struggle, a man who had spent the last half of his eighty-one years trying and failing and trying again to become a member of the Florida Bar. On October 20, 1988, he became the only American ever readmitted to the practice of law after his death, according to his lawyer and friend who urged the honor, Harley Herman, who added that the only other man in the world to receive such an honor was another man of peaceful and determined protest, Mohandas Gandhi. (On March 16, 2015, the California Supreme Court posthumously admitted Hong Yen Chang to the California Bar after his denial under the Chinese Exclusion Act 125 years earlier.)[1]

Now, with Hawkins's posthumous readmission to the Bar, the institutions that had stood in his way and begrudged everything he got from them could hardly do enough to honor him for what they had put him through.[2] His original lawsuit seeking admission to the University of Florida Law School in 1949 had prompted the creation of the "separate but equal" Florida A&M Law School. His success at integrating Florida law schools contributed to the demise of FAMU Law (it was resurrected in Orlando in 2002) in favor of a new law school at Florida State. Now that Hawkins was dead, things were named for him—an Inn of Court, the Legal Clinic at the UF Law School, and at FSU Law School a scholarship and a collection of books moved from across the tracks when the FAMU law school was closed. The University of Florida even awarded Hawkins an honorary degree in 2001, first in the main university graduation and then at a law school ceremony. Hawkins's sister, Harriett Livingston, accepted the award, and his niece, Halle Williams, remarked, "Justice delayed is still justice."[3]

Born in the small black community of Okahumpka near Leesburg in Lake County in 1907, Hawkins was the son of a preacher and as an adult moved into teaching in local schools and then into public relations at Bethune-Cookman College. Harley Herman, the lawyer who sought Hawkins's posthumous readmission, wrote that Hawkins had wanted to be a lawyer ever since he saw black defendants in his home county sentenced to six months on the chain gang for playing penny-ante poker.[4] But Hawkins did not pursue that goal until after World War II, when the U.S. Supreme Court was first beginning to order blacks admitted to universities. When Thurgood Marshall and the NAACP Legal Defense Fund decided to target Florida graduate schools, Hawkins became one of five who filed applications at Florida professional schools that did not have Negro analogs in Florida's "separate but equal" system. Hawkins's application prompted the legislature and the Board of Control, which governed Florida universities, to create a "separate but equal" law school for blacks at Florida A&M. (More details on desegregation efforts in Florida are in the previous volume of this history series.)[5]

Turned down by the University of Florida Law School, Hawkins sought a writ of mandamus from the Florida Supreme Court against the Board of Control, which later morphed into the Board of Regents. Alex Akerman Jr. initially represented him. Akerman was also working with Thurgood Marshall on the defense of the "Groveland Boys" in Lake County during that era.[6]

The Hawkins petition was soon bolstered by a U.S. Supreme Court decision on June 5, 1950, in another of Thurgood Marshall's challenges, *Sweatt v. Painter*,[7] which rebuffed Texas' strategy to avoid integration of the University of Texas Law School by the rapid creation of a separate black law school. That was exactly what Florida was doing in authorizing a new FAMU law school. Instead of following the ruling of the higher court, Florida's Board of Control just ignored it and offered to either pay for Hawkins to attend a law school out of state or let him attend a new law school being created at Florida A&M.

The Florida Supreme Court, likewise ignoring the *Sweatt* case, produced a unanimous opinion written by Justice Harold L. "Tom" Sebring, who had been a prosecutor in the Nuremberg war crimes trials of Nazis after World War

II, approving an "alternative plan" that would enroll Hawkins at the nascent FAMU law school but let him attend classes at UF law school until the FAMU school was ready. That would get Hawkins the UF law school education he wanted, but would deny him a diploma from the University of Florida and would defeat the goal of admitting blacks to that program. The plan "conforms as nearly as it can, with due regard to the requirements of the paramount Federal law, with the long established policy of the State of Florida that there shall be a system of segregation of the races in the state school system but that impartial provision shall be made in the schools for white and Negro students alike," Sebring wrote.

B. K. Roberts was the junior member of the unanimous court. Richard Ervin, who was Roberts's roommate during law school at UF and became attorney general in January 1949, was defending the Board of Control and its segregation policy. The court was unanimous in approving the "alternative plan."

Hawkins rejected it.

There was another opinion in 1951, now with Horace Hill representing Hawkins. Yet another rejection by the Florida court in 1952 sat at the U.S. Supreme Court until being vacated in 1954 alongside *the Brown v. Board of Education* decision. In an opinion by Roberts in 1955, the court stalled once again by appointing a special master to study the "numerous adjustments and changes" that would be necessary and exploring the dangers of violence if a black person were admitted to the university.

The 1955 decision is notable not only for its defiance of the U.S. Supreme Court after the *Brown* decision but also for two separate opinions. One, by Justice Glenn Terrell, remarked upon "the diverse moral, cultural and I.Q. or preparation response of the white and Negro races" and went on to say that segregation was "the unvarying law of the animal kingdom." The opinion explained, "Place the horse, the cow, the sheep, the goat and the pig in the same pasture and they instinctively segregate." After more such examples Terrell added: "When God created man, he allotted each race to his own continent according to color, Europe to the white man, Asia to the yellow man, Africa to the black man, and America to the red man, but now we are advised that God's plan was in error." Terrell did not go into why there were so many white people on the continent allotted to the red man.

The other opinion was the first break in the unanimity of the Florida Supreme Court against integration. Sebring, joined by Justice Elwyn Thomas, wrote that, since the U.S. Supreme Court in *Brown v. Board of Education* had now "expressly repudiated the longstanding principle established in *Plessy v.*

Ferguson," the 1896 case permitting segregation, "our judicial duty" is to "give effect to this new pronouncement . . . whatever may be our personal views and desires." It is plain, Sebring added, that the principles in *Brown* applied not just to elementary and high schools but to "public schools at all levels," including higher education.

The majority, though, continued to block Hawkins's admission to UF, as did another round between the Florida and U.S. Supreme Courts in 1957. Roberts resurrected long-dead states' rights theories from before the Civil War in rejecting a U.S. Supreme Court directive to integrate the University of Florida Law School. Roberts predicted "violence in university communities and a critical disruption of the university system . . . if Negro students are permitted to enter the state's white universities at this time."[8] A federal lawsuit finally produced the settlement in 1958 that opened the law school to blacks but only on the condition that Hawkins withdraw his own application. The honor of being the first black student went to George H. Starke Jr., who lasted three semesters before dropping out for a career in finance in New York. The first black law graduate was W. George Allen, a native of Sanford and a graduate of Florida A&M, in the Class of 1962.

Hawkins moved to Boston, drove a cab, worked at Boston Red Sox games, waited tables at the Parker House hotel, and cleaned restrooms at the Harvard Club to support himself at the New England School of Law, where he was one of two blacks in the class.[9] The choice of that law school was an incredibly ill-informed decision, because the school was not accredited by the American Bar Association at the time and thus did not qualify a graduate to become a member of the Florida Bar. So once again Hawkins hit a dead end.

And then an entirely unrelated event gave Hawkins a new chance.

Benjamin H. Ervin, brother of Justice Richard Ervin and former Florida Bar president Robert Ervin of the prominent Tallahassee firm of Ervin, Varn, Jacobs & Odom, had failed the Florida Bar exam four times after graduating from the University of Miami Law School in February 1956. But Joseph C. Jacobs of the Ervin firm filed a petition on Ben Ervin's behalf nearly two decades later, asking that the Supreme Court admit him to the Bar anyway under an old "diploma privilege," which allowed graduates of Florida law schools to be admitted without taking the Bar exam as long as they showed good moral character.

The diploma privilege was created in 1925 for "a student in any law school chartered by and conducted within this state or approved by the Supreme Court." The privilege was eliminated, except for students already enrolled, as of July 25, 1951, which just happened to be as the new FAMU law school was starting up and as Hawkins pressed his case for admission to UF. There was a provision that "time spent in military service" was "not to be reckoned" in the time limit for those enrolled to complete their degree. The law was repealed entirely in 1955.

How did that privilege apply to Ben Ervin, who graduated in 1956? Because, he said, he had "a firm and abiding determination" to enter the University of Miami Law School for the summer session beginning June 14, 1951, before the diploma privilege ended, but was recalled to active military duty on June 5 as the Korean War continued. He produced a sworn statement from former U.S. Senator Claude Pepper and two of his staff members attesting to that intention. If not for military service, he would have qualified for the diploma privilege without taking the Bar exam, Jacobs argued.

Justice Richard Ervin did not take part in the case, of course, but the case went to four other justices who served with him—Boyd, Carlton, Dekle, and McCain, all subjects of ethics investigations at the time—as well as First District Court of Appeal Judge Dewey M. Johnson, a well-connected political figure who had been president of the Florida Senate in 1959. Bar cases went to five-justice panels then, and Adkins and Roberts did not take part, for reasons not disclosed. The court issued its decision on January 30, 1974, the day before Chief Justice Carlton's resignation took effect. The vote was 4–1 to admit Ervin, with Boyd dissenting.[10]

"This court has issued certificates to practice law pursuant to the diploma privilege in several cases involving similar fact situations," said the opinion, citing four cases decided in 1964, 1966, and 1967. One applicant claimed rehabilitation of character after an initial denial on character grounds when he originally qualified for the diploma privilege. One had gotten his law degree in 1939, returned home to Cuba, then returned to Florida in 1965; he was admitted without any expression of concern whether he still had competent knowledge of Florida law after twenty-five years out of the country. In a third, In re Bennett,[11] Justice Thornal in dissent noted, "It is clear that he intended to enter law school in the fall of 1951. However, it is equally clear to me that he was not 'enrolled' prior to the critical date." It had been ten years since his graduation, and he also had failed the exam twice, Thornal noted.

In Ervin's case, Carlton wrote a short opinion agreeing with Thorrnal's reasoning in Bennett but also concurring in Ervin's admission. "I see no equitable reason for loosely interpreting any exceptions to the requirement of passing the Bar Examination, particularly in the case of an applicant who graduated from law school eighteen years ago," Carlton said. "Nevertheless,

I am of the opinion that, once the rules have been stretched to accommodate one applicant, other applicants similarly situated should be treated in like manner."

Boyd's dissent focused on the wording of the diploma privilege in the statute: "There is nothing in the record to indicate that he [Ervin] communicated in any manner with any approved law school on or before July 25, 1951. If the statute had provided for waiver of the bar examination for those who 'intended' to attend, but who were precluded by such circumstances as war, the petitioner would clearly be eligible. Regrettably, the statutory provision extends the diploma privilege to those 'enrolled' . . . and I do not believe that I have the authority to construe the word 'enrolled' to mean 'intended to enroll,' as the majority has done in this case."

Ben Ervin was admitted, and he joined his brother's law firm.

To Virgil Hawkins, who was sixty-seven years old by then, that precedent was an opening. He, too, "intended" to enroll in a Florida law school before July 25, 1951, and he had reams of documents and even U.S. Supreme Court opinions to prove it. If Ben Ervin could qualify for the diploma privilege on the basis of intent, why not Hawkins? Represented by James A. Shook of Ocala, Hawkins filed a petition for admission to the Florida Bar under a similarly expansive application of the diploma privilege.

The court's original draft opinions in the case were never published but were found in the secretary of state archives by Harley Herman. They disappeared from the state files after Herman quoted them extensively in an article.[12]

Justice Arthur England, apparently assigned the Hawkins petition when it arrived at the court, drafted an opinion noting that the Hawkins story "constitutes a regrettable chapter in the history of this court." England quoted some pointed sarcasm appearing in the Florida Bar brief, written by Bar general counsel Richard C. McFarlain, a widely respected lawyer known for his sharp and sometimes caustic wit. Referring to the early 1950s decisions against Hawkins, the brief said the Supreme Court would have left the issue open until Hawkins "agreed to go to Florida Agricultural and Mechanical College or, in the alternative, turned white." After the U.S. Supreme Court order in 1954, McFarlain's brief said, the Florida Supreme Court's opinion meant that to get the benefit of that order, Hawkins "no longer had to turn white. He merely had to prove that the Ku Klux Klan and other assorted yahoos would not burn down Gainesville."

England also expressed concern about Hawkins's competence to practice

law. His draft opinion waived the requirement of graduation from an accredited law school but still required Hawkins to take the Bar exam for admission.

> There is no controversy between Mr. Hawkins and the Bar as to the mag-
> nitude of the injustice caused Mr. Hawkins by acts of this court. No one
> triumphs in the fact that we are now given the opportunity to rectify that
> injustice, to some degree. The Bar aptly reminds us, however, that any
> enthusiasm we may have to right this wrong must be considered in light
> of our ongoing responsibility to the public. . . . The Bar suggests that it
> would compound earlier errors to accommodate Mr. Hawkins without
> proper concern for his present fitness to provide legal services to the
> populace. The record before us . . . does not show that Mr. Hawkins
> has ever practiced law or endeavored to retain his legal acumen. . . . We
> cannot overlook these facts in considering his request for immediate
> admission to the practice of law. . . .

> We are left, then, in the difficult position of having before us an injus-
> tice of our own making, having the exclusive power to rectify it, having
> no prescribed method or precedent to do so, and having a competing
> public concern which militates against individual relief.

England's opinion apparently drew the support of five other justices—Roberts,
Adkins, Boyd, Overton, and Sundberg.

Hatchett, the first black justice, wrote a blistering dissent detailing the sor-
did history of Hawkins's quest. Ordinarily, Hatchett's unflappable persona was
reflected in his opinions—analytical, sometimes reflective, but not passionate.
The dissent about Hawkins was passionate. "It is necessary to understand the
injustice members of this court once willfully wrought in order to appreciate
the significance of a decision further compounding that injustice," Hatchett
wrote. Noting the 1955 opinion by Roberts, who was now standing in the way
of Hawkins's admission to the Bar, Hatchett assailed the "implausible and insufficient reasons for the majority's illegal refusal to follow the mandate of
the Supreme Court of the United States." He concluded: "If the law does not
allow this court to salvage even the remaining fragment of a career truncated
by the illegal actions of its own members, then the law must nevertheless be
followed. . . . We can never restore to Hawkins the opportunity to serve as a
lawyer during the important period of Florida's history."

According to England in an interview for this book, Roberts was alarmed
at the prospect of such a sharp and high-profile assault on the court and his
own legacy in his last year. Roberts came into the justices' conference and
declared that he had changed his mind and wanted to admit Hawkins without

the exam requirement—and in fact wanted to author the opinion himself. Hatchett, according to England, began to rise out of his chair in anger over Roberts's attempt to take the credit for Hawkins's admission, but England and Sundberg restrained him. (Hatchett declined to discuss the Hawkins case; all the other participants in that conference have died.)

The compromise decision, published in the last month of Roberts's tenure, on November 12, 1976, was almost embarrassingly bland in light of the penitence it might have shown. Perhaps as a price of compromise and unanimity, the per curiam opinion deemed it "unnecessary to recite in detail the historical chronology" and buried the Hawkins case history in footnoted citations. The justices unanimously ordered Hawkins admitted once the Board of Bar Examiners confirmed his moral fitness. He would not have to take the Bar exam. But the court imposed two conditions if Hawkins were to actually practice law. First, he had to take the "Bridging the Gap" seminar that was then optional and is now required for all new lawyers. And second, he had to serve an "internship" for at least six months under the supervision of a member of the Bar.

Formally admitted to the Bar on February 8, 1977, in his seventieth year, Hawkins did not follow the path of Ben Ervin to a big firm headed by an older brother with experienced lawyers and a strong administrative structure. Hawkins went back to Leesburg in his home county, a county with a long tradition of racial discrimination and black poverty, and set up a law practice catering to people who couldn't afford a lawyer. None of the lawyers around him had supported his application for the Bar, Herman said in his detailed retrospective on Hawkins's career, and there were few resources or experienced support staff in town. He was like an invisible man.

While Hatchett had bristled at the idea of obstacles that might continue to keep Hawkins from the Bar, England's draft accurately anticipated the difficulty Hawkins had in dealing with the realities of law practice. Herman's detailed account of Hawkins's law practice, including the cases that led to his reprimand and ultimate resignation, puts blame on the court and the Bar for not providing real supervision of Hawkins's early law practice, in the manner of supervising a third-year law student. The internship "did not provide a mechanism for Hawkins to actually practice law under the supervision of a Florida lawyer, but rather allowed Hawkins to view another in the practice of law," Herman wrote. Hawkins obviously also bears blame. He did not accurately assess his own "abilities and limitations," at his age and in declining health. Herman cites a magazine article about Hawkins by Dudley Clendinen in the *St. Petersburg Times* Sunday magazine saying that Hawkins "was ill and weak in bed" in January 1974.

Herman's assessment was this:

> During the decades that Hawkins fought for his right to an education to become a lawyer, his perseverance, and refusal to accept the impossibility of his goals, allowed him to succeed when others would have given up. However, this same characteristic would be a disservice to Hawkins as he made his initial decisions about how to begin his practice. His youthful goal of helping people in his hometown might have been attainable if he had become a lawyer in his mid-forties when clients were more likely to resolve disputes with their lawyers in a neighborly manner, rather than through grievance proceedings and malpractice suits and the practice of law had not reached the rapidly changing fast-paced level of modern practice.

In particular, Hawkins proved unable to provide the time-consuming and thorough representation needed in a felony case and a divorce case he took on. He ended up disciplined in two separate proceedings. In January 1984, the Supreme Court censured him and put him on probation for two years. The next year, facing two more complaints, he resigned. The court accepted the resignation on April 18, 1985.[13]

"Hawkins had more than a claim on the court's conscience," argued Herman. The court had "derailed Hawkins' opportunity for a legal career in the prime of his life" and had "an obligation to remediate the damage it caused," not just by imposing an "internship" as a condition of practice but by calling on the Bar and the University of Florida to provide the same kind of attentive oversight and clinical instruction they provide to third-year students. The court anticipated the problem, but could not think beyond its role as a "regulator" to address the problem. With support and supervision, Herman said, "Hawkins could have made a valuable contribution to the legal needs of the poor during the remainder of his life."

Soon after resigning from the Bar, Hawkins was interviewed by Barbara Stewart of the *Orlando Sentinel*. "I know what I did," he said. "I integrated schools in Florida. No one can take that away from me."[14] It was his last public statement. A few weeks later he suffered a stroke, and nine months after that, on February 11, 1988, at the age of eighty-one, Hawkins died of acute kidney failure.[15]

Herman wrote a letter to the court urging Hawkins's posthumous reinstatement. The court asked the Florida Bar for its view. Florida Bar President

Rutledge R. Liles of Jacksonville, Bar President-elect and future American Bar Association President Stephen N. Zack, and Bar Executive Director John F. Harkness were all on the Bar's brief saying the matter was technically beyond its purview but "special recognition of the unique contributions of Virgil Darnell Hawkins in opening the practice of law in Florida to persons of all races is quite appropriate and timely."

With no further concern about Hawkins's ability to practice law, the court could afford to be magnanimous. In its 7–0 opinion on October 20, 1988,[16] the court noted that Hawkins would have been eligible to apply for readmission himself after April 18, 1988, three years after his resignation. They recognized "that while the actions that led to Hawkins' resignation are not condoned, the denial of an equal education, the years elapsing from Hawkins' graduation from an unaccredited law school until the time he began to practice law, and the difficulties involved in attempting to practice law as a sole practitioner, without prior experience and at an advanced age, substantially diminished Hawkins' ability to successfully practice law, and in all probability, substantially contributed to his errors in judgment."

The justices added, in the tone of a proclamation:

> The survival of democracy and justice in this country and the world requires individuals to take action at various times in history, similar to those taken by Hawkins, and . . . recognition of his noble efforts through posthumous readmission to The Florida Bar can serve to motivate others to allow the good of the many to outweigh individual needs, and to sacrifice the pursuit of happiness, so that others will enjoy a better world. . . .
>
> Upon consideration, this court has determined that the petition for reinstatement should be granted. This decision sets no precedent because it is unique. Hawkins' struggle for equal justice under the law should be memorialized. Hawkins is entitled to be recognized for his contribution to our state in the manner that he would have most desired had he lived.

A decade later, a new generation of justices felt the urge to take yet another step, delivered in formal ceremony in the large courtroom, with an audience far larger than the one that was there when Joe Hatchett sat in as a college sophomore watching quixotic Horace Hill tilting at the windmills of segregation. On Tuesday, May 25, 1999, the fiftieth anniversary of the filing of Hawkins's lawsuit, the court had a ceremony, complete with a documentary film. In the film, then-Congresswoman Carrie Meek, who had become Florida's first black state senator along with Arnett Girardeau in 1982, noted her acceptance of the state's segregationist alternative to allowing blacks in its law schools then—payment of tuition for black Floridians to enroll in another state. "I'm sorry I took the handout they gave me and went to the University of Michigan," she said.

Chief Justice Major B. Harding, on behalf of the court, issued what was described as an apology to Hawkins. "Ladies and Gentlemen, you have heard about a regrettable and poignant moment in the jurisprudential history of this court," he said. "We must learn from the lessons taught . . . hatred and discrimination will not triumph."[17]

"This case involved a lot of hate," Horace Hill said. "It took a lot of strength and moral courage for this court to admit wrong." Said Hawkins's niece, Harriet Livingston, whose daughter had graduated from the UF Law School, "He never gave up."

NOTES

These endnotes have a style and abbreviations based primarily on *The Blue-book* citation standards, developed by the law reviews of Columbia, Harvard, and Yale universities, as well as the University of Pennsylvania. This standard is normally used for legal publications for citing court cases and legal periodicals such as law reviews. The standards have been slightly modified for utility and clarity in the context of this book. For Florida Supreme Court cases during the period 1972–87, the full date of the opinion, rather than just the year, is included in the citation so that the reader will have an accurate chronology of the cases.

The official reporter of appellate cases for Florida is the West Publishing Company *Southern Reporter*, part of the West Publishing Company National Reporter System for the state and federal courts in the United States. The West reporters are all numbered chronologically by publication but occasionally start over in a new series. So there is a *Southern Reporter* (abbreviated "So."), *Southern Reporter* Second Series (abbreviated "So.2d"), and *Southern Reporter* Third Series (abbreviated "So.3d"). Most cases cited here are in the "Southern Second" series. The citation in the Notes section gives the name of the case (the petitioner or appellant bringing the case to the court is first, the "v." stands for "versus," and the respondent or appellee follows). Then comes the Southern Reporter volume number, the name of the volume, and the page, as in Shepherd v. State, 46 So.2d 880 (Fla. May 16, 1950). "Fla." standing alone in parentheses refers to the Florida Supreme Court. A Florida District Court of Appeal is indicated with the district number, so that the Florida Second District Court of Appeal is shown as "Fla. 2nd DCA," followed by the year of the decision. Readers should note that the official publication of an opinion may have occurred well after the original date of the released opinion because of motions for rehearing, which most times are denied but may result in modifications of the opinion that replace the original (which is then no longer publicly available). Original versions of the opinion may be available through

Florida Law Weekly. Dates shown for opinions, whether in notes or text as well as the chronology, are the date of publication of the original opinion unless otherwise noted.

Federal cases, similarly, are cited to the *West Federal Reporter*, the federal equivalent of the Southern Reporter. The *Federal Reporter* Second Series is abbreviated "F.2d." The parenthetical after the citation of volume and page shows the number of the circuit (so that the Eleventh Circuit U.S. Court of Appeals, whose jurisdiction includes Florida as well as Georgia and Alabama, is shown as "11th Cir.")

U.S. Supreme Court cases are cited to its official reporter volume, United States Reports, abbreviated "U.S.," as in 436 U.S. 447 (1978), and not to the West or any other reporting volume.

A number of references in the footnotes are to articles written by the author for the *St. Petersburg Times*. Many of these are from individual clippings contained in "byline files" for each writer and in subject-matter clips, and not all include the headlines or page numbers. In such event, only the date of the newspaper is shown, which will facilitate access through microfilms, Google News, or other collections. Most articles from the period of this book are not available on the Internet. In newspaper articles, which are not itemized in the Bibliography, "Skene" refers to Neil Skene unless otherwise noted, and "Dyckman" refers to Martin Dyckman. In some cases citation is to an interview the author conducted years ago; where remaining notes are undated, the footnote includes the approximate date.

The *St. Petersburg Times* is now known as the *Tampa Bay Times*. Other newspapers have also altered their names over the years, often dropping any individual city name. *Sun-Sentinel* is the newspaper based in Fort Lauderdale. The *Sentinel* is based in Orlando. The *Florida Times-Union* is based in Jacksonville.

Books are cited by the author's last name and a shortened title. The full information is in the bibliography.

Website URLs were current at the time of the research but may no longer be "live" links.

Public documents in court cases, including briefs, are normally available in the State Archives in the R.A. Gray Building in Tallahassee. They are not available by *Southern Reporter* citation; the library relies upon the court's docket number, which appears in the report of the case (and on the digital reporting services). The Florida Supreme Court archivist organizes and catalogs the files of the justices after their departure from the court, creates an index that is publicly available, and makes the files available under procedures established by the court. These are organized by the justice's name, then in one or more Series, then by box number, and then by individual folders within the boxes, including one or more folders on each case. Some of these files, containing drafts of opinions or other material deemed "confidential," may be accessed only with the consent of the court. Confidential drafts cited in this book were accessed with the permission of the court, reportedly after specific review by the justices.

"L.J." and "L. Rev." are abbreviations in the names of a "Law Journal" or "Law Review."

Other abbreviations for frequently cited sources:

MH	*Miami Herald*
SPT	*St. Petersburg Times*
FSU L. Rev	*Florida State University Law Review*
UF L. Rev.	*University of Florida Law Review*

Chapter 1. Four Horsemen of the Reformation

1. The account of the Hatchett investiture is derived from interviews and informal conversations with Judge Hatchett, primarily an interview on Oct. 25, 2011, and from Dyckman, "Hatchett Takes Oath as Florida Justice," *SPT*, Sept. 3, 1975, p. 1-B.

2. Dyckman, "Hatchett Takes Oath as Florida Justice," *ibid.* .

3. Shepherd v. State, 46 So.2d 880 (Fla. May 16, 1950).

4. For more on the court's resistance to integration, including Roberts' role, see Walter W. Manley II and Canter Brown Jr., *The Supreme Court of Florida, 1917-1972* (Gainesville: University of Florida Press, 2006), 241-274. See also Sylvia H. Walbolt and Andrew D. Manko, *From Chattel to Justice* (Florida Supreme Court Historical Society), accessible at http://www.flcourthistory.org/From-Chattel-to-Justice.

5. B. K. Roberts, "Law Practice in the Depression Decade of the 1930s," *Florida Supreme Court Historical Society Review* I.1 (1984). See also Roberts' closing remarks on the videotaped ceremony in the Supreme Court courtroom, "Justice B. K. Roberts Oral History Program" (Oct. 30, 1986).

6. Unless otherwise indicated, quotations of Justice Hatchett are from an interview by the author on October 25, 2011.

7. Susan Denley, *SPT*, July 3, 1975, Pinellas Times p. 1.

8. Quoted in *SPT*, May 4, 1998.

9. Hawkins cases at the Florida Supreme Court, all styled State ex rel. Hawkins v. Board of Control, were, in chronological order: 47 So.2d 608 (1950) (7-0 opinion by Justice Harold L. Sebring); 53 So.2d 116 (1951), *cert. denied*, 342 U.S. 877 (1951); 60 So.1d 162 (1952) (7-0 opinion by Sebring), *cert. granted*, 347 U.S. 971 (1954), *mandate recalled and vacated and cert. granted*, 350 U.S. 413 (1956); 83 So.2d 20 (1955) (on remand after *Brown*) (5-2 opinion by Roberts, dissents by Sebring and Thomas); 93 So.2d 354 (1957) (5-2 opinion by Roberts asserting state sovereignty, concurrence by Terrell, dissents by Thomas and Drew), *cert. denied without prejudice for petitioner to file federal complaint*, 355 U.S. 839 (1957). *See also* 162 F. Supp 851 (N.D. Fla. 1958), *rev'd and remanded*, 253 F.2d 752 (11th Cir. 1958).

10. Compiled from *Florida's First Black Lawyers, 1969–1979*, by the Virgil Hawkins Chapter of the National Bar Association, June C. McKinney and Janeia R. Daniels, eds. (2009).

11. William C. Kidder, *The Struggle for Access from Sweatt to Grutter: A History of African American, Latino, and American Indian Law School Admissions, 1950–2000*, Harvard Black Letter Law Journal, Vol. 19, p. 1 (2003).

12. Martin Dyckman, *SPT*, July 13, 1975, page 1-B, 3-B.

13. Chesterfield Smith speech on Hatchett retirement. From "Hatchett" folder, Box 128, Chesterfield Smith Papers, Smathers Library, University of Florida.

14. *The Supreme Court of Florida, 1917–1972* contains a detailed account of this period in Chapter 14, "A Peaceful Revolution of Earthquake Proportions." Full biographies of the justices investigated during the scandal, including their comments, appear in that chapter.

15. Peter D. Webster, *Selection and Retention Of Judges: Is There One "Best" Method?* 23 FSU L. Rev. 1, 29 (1995).

16. Martin Dyckman, *A Most Disorderly Court* (Gainesville: University Press of Florida, 2008), 76.

17. The court scandals of 1973–75 are recounted in detail in Dyckman, *Disorderly Court*. See *The Supreme Court or Florida, 1917–1972*, Chapter 14. The account here is drawn from those sources and from interviews with the following people: Martin Dyckman on August 31, 2009; Randall Reeder on July 10, 2012; Judge Marguerite Davis on Aug. 29, 2012, and Sept. 19, 2012; Ben Overton on November 15, 2009 and June 19, 2012, and Talbot D'Alemberte on June 5, 2010 and June 21, 2012.

18. Dyckman, *Disorderly Court*, 53–54.

19. A full biographical history of Justice Carlton is in Manley and Brown, *Supreme Court of Florida, 1917–1972*.

20. Dyckman, *Disorderly Court*, 20.

21. Interview with Fred Baggett on May 30, 2012.

Chapter 2. 1974: Overton and England

1. This passage on Justice Overton and his selection as justice is based on interviews with Justice Overton on November 15, 2009, June 19, 2012, and (by telephone) November 5, 2012, as well as the following: Interview of Ben Overton by Samuel Proctor. University of Florida College of Law Oral History Collection, October 28, 1994. http://ufdc.ufl.edu/UF00006381/00001, accessed November 4, 2012.; Dyckman, *Disorderly Court*, 68–69; *Ben F. Overton: Chief Justice of the Supreme Court*, 50 Fla. B. J. 194 (April 1976). Quotations are from the author's interviews unless otherwise indicated.

2. Talbot D'Alemberte speaking at memorial service for Ben Overton at the Supreme Court, January 7, 2013.

3. Interview of Ben Overton by Samuel Proctor.

4. Information in this and the next few paragraphs comes from Interview of Ben Overton by Samuel Proctor.

5. Martin Dyckman, *Floridian of His Century: The Courage of Governor LeRoy Collins* (Gainesville: University Press of Florida, 2006), 255–56.

6. State Bd. of Trustees of Internal Improvement Trust Fund v. Ball, 300 So.2d 741 (1st Fla. Dist. Ct. App. 1974).

7. See Florida Bar v. Mason, 334 So.2d 1 (Fla. Jan. 15, 1976).

8. Gulf Power Co. v. Bevis, 289 So. 2d 401 (Fla. Jan. 30, 1974).

9. Gulf Power Co. v. Bevis, 296 So. 2d 482 (Fla. June 13, 1974).

10. Arthur J. England Jr., interviews Oct. 25, 2009 and Nov. 6, 2012. This account is drawn from those interviews, from Dyckman, *Disorderly Court*, 77–81; and from Spector v. Glisson, 305 So.2d 777 (Fla. 1974).

11. Spector v. Glisson, 305 So.2d 777 (Fla. 1974). The date of the opinion is Dec. 4, 1974, with rehearing denied Jan. 17, 1975.

12. See Smith v. Brantley, 400 So.2d 443 (Fla. June 18, 1981).

13. Florida Laws Ch. 71-49, Sec. 1; Fla. Stat. Sec. 105.021 (1971).

14. Martin Dyckman, *Reubin O'D. Askew and the Golden Age of Florida Politics* (Gainesville: University of Florida Press, 2011), 51–52, 56–57.

15. England interview on Nov. 6, 2012.

16. In Re: Advisory Opinion to the Governor, 243 So.2d 573 (Fla. Jan. 21, 1971).

17. *SPT*, August 7, 1974, p. 1-B, 13-B.

18. Supreme Court Session for an Oral History of Arthur J. England, Mar. 11, 1988.

Chapter 3. 1975: Sundberg and Hatchett

1. State *ex rel.* Turner v. Earle, 295 So. 2d 609 (Fla. Feb. 27, 1974).

2. Austin v. State *ex rel.* Christian, 310 So.2d 289 (Fla. Feb. 10, 1975).

3. Dyckman, *Disorderly Court*, 74–75.

4. Katherine Gazella, "Judge Robert Mann, known for his integrity, dies at 77," *SPT*, 4-B, Feb. 27, 2002.

5. Fla. Stat. § 112.313 (4) (2012).

6. Dyckman, *Disorderly Court*, 87.

7. Ray Reynolds, "17 Equal Pieces," Filmed interview accessible at https://www.youtube.com/watch?v=36qIYlrJ7jE&feature=youtu.be

8. In re Dekle, 308 So.2d 4, 5 (Fla. Feb. 4, 1975).

9. In re Dekle, 308 So.2d 5, 11 (Fla. Feb. 4, 1975).

10. *Id.* at 12.

11. *Id.* at 11 (DuVal dissenting).

12. In re Boyd, 308 So.2d 13 (Fla. Feb. 4, 1975).

13. *Id.* at 20.

14. *Id.* at 21.

15. *Id.* at 21.

16. Dyckman, *Disorderly Court*, 104.

17. Dyckman, *Disorderly Court*, 103.

18. Manley and Brown, *Supreme Court of Florida*, 335.

19. Dyckman, *Disorderly Court*, 115.

20. Dyckman, *Disorderly Court*, 117, quoting *SPT*, March 6, 1975.

21. Linda H. Yates, "The New Chief Justice–Alan C. Sundberg," *Florida Bar Journal*, October, 1980, 585.

22. Richard Sundberg interview on November 11, 2012.

23. Martin Dyckman, "Sundberg's contributions to Florida," *SPT*, January 30, 2002.

24. Note from Dyckman to the author.

25. Report dated May 29, 1975 regarding examination of Joseph W. Boyd May 13–16, 1975,

attached to Richard Earle letter to W.J. Rish, dated June 16, 1975, from Martin Dyckman summary of papers in Florida State Archives, Supreme Court, House Impeachment Investigation, Series 19, Carton 355, folder 1.

26. McCain v. Select Committee, 313 So.3d 722 (Fla. 1975).

27. Baggett interview on May 30, 2012.

28. D'Alemberte interview on June 5, 2010.

29. John Newton interview on Jan. 11, 2012.

30. Dyckman, *Disorderly Court*, 133.

31. Dyckman, *Disorderly Court*, 134.

32. Florida Bar v. Thomson, 310 So.2d 300 (Fla. Jan. 29, 1975).

33. The Florida Bar v. McCain, 361 So.2d 700 (Fla. June 15, 1978).

34. David von Drehle, "McCain Had It All–And Lost It," *MH*, Nov. 24, 1986, p. 1A.

35. David von Drehle, "Daughter Took Care of Fugitive," *MH*, Nov. 14, 1986, p. 1A.

36. See Lucy Morgan, "Authorities Are Satisfied that Body Was Fugitive Former Justice McCain," *SPT*, Nov. 14, 1986, at 1-B. A more complete biography of David L. McCain appears in Manley and Brown, *Supreme Court of Florida 1917–1972* at 326.

37. David von Drehle, Nov. 24, p. 1A.

38. Hatchett interview on October 25, 2011.

39. Telephone interview with Robert L. Parks on Feb. 22, 2012.

40. Dyckman, *Askew and the Golden Age*, 51.

41. Caroline Heck, "DuVal Backs Off from Charge on Hatchett Choice," *SPT*, Aug. 14, 1976, p. 11-B.

42. Martin Dyckman, "Askew Expected to Name New Justice Today," *SPT*, July 3, 1975, 2B.

43. Dyckman, "Askew Expected to Name New Justice Today."

44. Chesterfield Smith speech on Hatchett retirement from 11th Circuit U.S. Court of Appeals, from "Hatchett" folder, Box 128, Chesterfield Smith Papers, George Smathers Library, University of Florida.

45. U.S. House of Representatives, Office of History and Preservation, "Black Americans in Congress." Washington, D.C. http://history.house.gov/People/Detail/23324?ret=True. See also Peter D. Klingman, *Josiah Walls: Florida's Black Congressman of Reconstruction*. Gainesville: University Press of Florida, 1976.

46. Askew's comments are assembled from multiple accounts of his announcement, including Martin Dyckman, "Askew Picks Black for High Court," *SPT*, July 9, 1975, 1A; and Martin Dyckman, "Joe Hatchett: A Lawyer's Lawyer," *Daytona Beach News-Journal*, July 13, 1975, 1D.

47. United Press International, *SPT*, July 17, 1975.

48. Dyckman, "Hatchett Takes Oath as Florida Justice," *SPT*, Sept. 3, 1975, 1B.

Chapter 4. Article V: Architects of Change

1. 369 U.S. 186 (1962). The case arose after the Tennessee legislature had refused to reapportion itself for half a century.

2. See Neil Skene, "Reapportionment in Florida," in Allen Morris and Joan Morris, eds., *The Florida Handbook*. The chapter traces legislative and congressional apportionment in Florida from the first territorial legislature in 1822 and continues through the reapportionment of 2012.

A comprehensive revision of the chapter is in the 2014 edition of the book, now published by the Clerk of the Florida House of Representatives.

3. There were three major U.S. Supreme Court decisions on Florida apportionment during this period, styled as Swann v. Adams: 378 U.S. 210 (1965); 383 U.S. 210 (1966); 385 U.S. 440 (1967). See also 385 U.S. 997 (1967).

4. Roy D. Wasson, "The Judges of the Third District Court of Appeal," in Kathleen M. O'Connor and Edward M. Guedes, eds., *Florida's Third District Court of Appeal: 50 Years 1957–2007*, p. 39 (Centennial Press 2007).

5. Judicial Council of Florida, Eleventh Annual Report, June 30 1966, p. 2.

6. Interview with Governor Bob Graham, approximately May 1981.

7. Oral History Interview of Claude R. Kirk Jr. by Sid Johnston, pp. 3–4, December 16, 1986, University of Florida Oral History Program. http://ufdc.ufl.edu//UF00007670/00001.

8. Oral History Interview of Chesterfield H. Smith by Julian Pleasants, January 14, 2000, and March 9, 2000, p. 3, University of Florida Oral History Program. http://ufdc.ufl.edu//UF00006389/00001.

9. Chesterfield Smith Oral History Interview, p. 15.

10. Chesterfield Smith Oral History Interview, p. 32.

11. A more detailed account of the commission's work appears in Supreme Court History Vol. II, pp. 295–297.

12. Oral History Interview of Richard T. Earle Jr. by Denise Stobbie, p. 3 (words in parentheses appear in the transcript, words in brackets were added by author), December 16, 1986, http://ufdc.ufl.edu//UF00007675/00001.

13. Talbot D'Alemberte, *The Florida State Constitution*, p. 12 (Oxford University Press, 2011).

14. Journal of the Senate, April 12, 1977, p. 130.

15. HJR 4-X, Journal of the Florida House of Representatives (Extraordinary Session 1967), January 9, 1967, pp. 2, 4–17.

16. Journal of the Florida House of Representatives (Extraordinary Session 1967), January 11, 1967.

17. The full text of his remarks is in the Journal of the Florida House of Representatives (Extraordinary Session 1967) pp. 19–21, for January 10, 1967.

18. Richard Earle Oral History, p. 5.

19. Judicial Council of Florida, Sixteenth Annual Report, April 1, 1971, p. 3.

20. Adkins, "Yesterday," Florida Supreme Court Historical Society Newsletter, Undated copy in author's files.

21. Interview with D'Alemberte, June 21, 2012.

22. Associated Press, "'Candidate' Returns to Work," SPT, Jan. 18, 1982, p. 2B.

23. Craig Basse and Lucy Morgan, "Dempsey Barron Dead at 79," SPT, 1-A, July 8, 2001.

24. Journal of the Florida Senate (Extraordinary Session 1971), November 27, 1971, pp. 1, 4.

25. Florida Laws Ch. 78–346, Fla. Stat. Sec. 34.021 (1972).

26. Florida Laws. Ch. 71–49, Fla. Stat. Ch. 105 (1972). See also of the Florida House of Representatives May 11, 1971, p. 474.

27. Journal of the Florida House of Representatives (Special Session 1971), December 9, 1971, pp. 115–116; Journal of the Florida Senate (Special Session), December 9, 1971, p. 69.

28. Remarks of Reubin Askew at "A Day with the Florida Governors," Spring 2006 sympo-

sium, the Lou Frey Institute of Politics and Government at the University of Central Florida, March 27, 2006. Notes in Martin Dyckman's personal files.

29. Remarks by Bob Graham and Reubin Askew at Annual Dinner of the Florida Supreme Court Historical Society, January 31, 2013. Recorded by the author.

Chapter 5. The Third Branch

1. The account of Judge Peel's assistance appears in Bruce R. Jacob, *Memories of and Reflections about Gideon v. Wainwright*, 33 Stetson L. Rev 181, 215 (2003). Jacob attributes the story to Fred L. Turner, the lawyer (and future judge) who represented Gideon in his retrial. Jacob, who represented Florida as an assistant attorney general in Gideon's appeal at the U.S. Supreme Court, was dean emeritus and professor of law at Stetson when he wrote the article for the fortieth anniversary of the *Gideon* decision.

2. Associated Press, "CIA Man Gets Job of Running Courts," *SPT*, June 1, 1972.

3. Office of State Courts Administrator, "Memory Book: 40th Anniversary Office of State Courts Administrator," July 2012.

4. Larry C. Berkson and Steven W. Hays, "The Unmaking of a Court Administrator," 60 Judicature No. 3 (October 1976), p. 135.

5. United Press International, "State Courts Administrator Resigns," *SPT*, May 20, 1975.

6. Martin Dyckman, "Supreme Court's Credit Card Used by Administrator," *SPT*, June 19, 1975, p. 8-B.

7. Office of the Auditor General, Audit of Supreme Court of Florida for fiscal years ending June 30, 1976, and June 30, 1977, quoting audit for fiscal year ending June 30, 1975.

8. Dyckman, *Disorderly Court*, p. 129.

9. Arthur England Remarks, Arthur England Oral History (videotape), Mar. 11 1988.

10. *Florida Bar News*, April 15, 1999.

Chapter 6. The Spirit of 1976: Reformers Take Control

1. Dyckman, *Disorderly Court*, p. 137.

2. Dyckman, *SPT*, Jan. 15, 1976, p. 1-A.

3. Mike Baxter, *MH*, Mar. 28, 1976 (clipping found in *St. Petersburg Times* news library clippings on Florida Supreme Court).

4. Martin Dyckman, "Adkins, on Handing Over the Gavel," *SPT*, Feb. 29, 1976.

5. Virginia Ellis, *SPT*, Mar. 2, 1976.

6. Interview with John F. Harkness Jr. by the author, Sept. 22, 2013.

7. State ex rel. Jack M. Turner v. Earle, 295 So.2d 609 (Fla. Feb. 27, 1974).

8. HJR 3911, Journal of the Senate, May 29, 1974, p. 670 (36–0 vote); Journal of the House of Representatives, May 29, 1974, p. 1070 (91–9 vote). See Fla. Const. Art. V. Sec. 12(a)(1).

9. Martin Dyckman, "Merit Retention Issue Returns this Year for Another Try," *SPT*, March 28, 1976.

10. Conversation with Donald C. Tucker, Nov. 27, 2015.

11. Frederick B. Karl, *The 57 Club: My Four Decades in Florida Politics* (University Press of Florida, Gainesville, FL, 2010), Chap. 14.

12. "Roberts: Appointment of Judges is an Issue in the Running," *SPT*, Feb. 8, 1976.

13. Martin Dyckman, *SPT*, June 13, 1976, p.1-B.

14. Interview with Robert T. Benton II by the author, Dec. 19, 2011.

15. Dyckman, "Askew to Campaign Openly for Justice Hatchett, Aide Says," *SPT*, July 15, 1976, p. 2-B.

16. John Van Gieson, Associated Press, "Normally Staid Race for Court Becomes Slugfest," *SPT*, Aug. 1, 1976, p. 2-B.

17. Martin Dyckman, "Bar Grades Court Candidates," *SPT*, August 24, 1976, p. 1-B. Other poll results cited in this chapter are from this article.

18. Interview of Robert Parks by the author, Feb. 22, 2012.

19. Karl, *The 57 Club*, p. 248.

20. Juanita Green, *MH*, March 22, 1964, p. 4-F.

21. 323 U.S. 214 (1944).

22. Janet Zink, The Buzz, *Tampa Bay Times*, March 22, 2011, http://www.tampabay.com/blogs/the-buzz-florida-politics/content/fred-karl-accepts-award-his-mother-gov-rick-scott/2036845, accessed June 22, 2014.

Chapter 7. Unexpected Replacements: Alderman and McDonald

1. Karl, *The 57 Club*, p. 262.

2. Ibid., p. 264.

3. Ibid., p. 269.

4. Interview with Overton, June 19, 2012.

5. Virginia Ellis, *SPT*, February 10, 1978.

6. Biographical information is derived primarily from the author's interview with Alderman at his ranch, January 24, 2013, from the author's interviews with Marguerite Davis, who was Alderman's law clerk, August 29, 2012, and September 19, 2012, and from Nancy Dale, *The Legacy of the Florida Pioneer Cow Hunters: In Their Own Words* (2011), Chapter 1.

7. Charles Stafford, *SPT*, June 26, 1979.

8. Gary Lee Blankenship, *Parker Lee McDonald: Chief Justice of the Supreme Court*, 60 Fla. Bar Journal 11, 16 (1986).

9. Ibid., p. 15.

Chapter 8. Playing Chicken with Courtroom Cameras

1. Wolfgang Saxon, "W. E. Arnow, Judge in Antiwar Trial, Dies at 83," *New York Times*, Dec. 1, 1994, accessible at http://www.nytimes.com/1994/12/01/obituaries/w-e-arnow-judge-in-antiwar-trial-dies-at-83.html.

2. Estes v. Texas, 381 U.S. 532 (1965). The case summarizes the development of the cameras issue over the years.

3. 381 U.S. at 552 (Burger concurring).

4. 381 U.S. at 544.

5. 381 U.S. at 550.

6. E-mail to the author from Joseph R. Klock, Aug. 28, 2015.

7. U.S. v. Columbia Broadcasting System Inc., 497 F.2d 102 (5th Circ. 1974) (overturning bans on sketch artists) and 497 F.2d 107 (5th Circ. 1974) (overturning contempt conviction). See also

Denise Caffrey, *United States v. CBS: When Sketch Artists Are Allowed in the Courtroom, Can Photographers Be Far Behind?*, 1975 Duke Law Journal 188.

8. Katharine Graham, Personal History (1997). The incident is cited in an online excerpt from the book at http://www.washingtonpost.com/wp-srv/national/longterm/watergate/stories/graham.htm (accessed Sept. 29, 2013).

9. Interview with Sandy D'Alemberte, June 5, 2010.

10. Petition of Post-Newsweek Stations, Florida, Inc., for Change in Code of Judicial Conduct, 327 So.2d 1 (Jan. 28, 1976).

11. Petition of Post-Newsweek Stations, 337 So.2d 804 (Sept. 17, 1976) (Post-Newsweek II).

12. Arthur J. England Jr., "Cameras in Courts: Driving from Failure toward Success," Florida Bar Journal, April 2009.

13. Karl, p. 268.

14. Petition of Post-Newsweek Stations, 347 So.2d 402 (April 7, 1977) (Post-Newsweek experiment order).

15. Chandler v. State, 366 So.2d 64 (Fla. 3rd DCA 1978).

16. Handwritten draft, Sundberg Series 1, Box 6 File No. 326, Supreme Court Archives.

17. Petition of Post-Newsweek Stations, 370 So.2d 764, 780–781 (Fla. Apr. 12, 1979) (Post-Newsweek final order).

18. 370 So.2d at 776.

19. *SPT,* April 13, 1979, p. 1-B.

20. Richmond Newspapers Inc. v. Virginia, 448 U.S. 555 (1980).

21. 427 U.S. 560 (Jan. 26, 1981).

22. 427 U.S. at 574–575.

23. State v. Green, 395 So.2d 532 (Fla. Mar. 5, 1981).

24. State v. Palm Beach Newspapers Inc., 395 So.2d 544, 548–549 (Fla. Mar. 5, 1981).

25. See generally Radio Television Digital News Association, Cameras in the Court: A State-by-State Guide, http://rtdna.org/article/cameras_in_the_court_a_state_by_state_guide_updated, last accessed Aug. 15, 2014.

26. See generally "The Courtroom Sketch Artist," May 14, 2014. http://documentary.net/courtroom-sketch-artist/, accessed Aug. 15, 2014.

27. Robert H. Giles and Robert W. Snyder, Covering the Courts: Free Press, Fair Trials & Journalistic Performance (Transaction Publishers, 1999).

28. "Judiciary Approves Pilot Project for Cameras in District Courts," Sept. 14, 2010. http://www.uscourts.gov/news/2010/09/14/judiciary-approves-pilot-project-cameras-district-courts, last accessed Aug. 15, 2014.

29. Associated Press, "TV Okayed for Florida Supreme Court," *SPT,* Nov. 15, 1984.

Chapter 9. Access to Legal Services: Who Will Serve the Poor?

1. Interview with England, October 26, 2009.

2. The "Levinson Report," led by University of Florida Law Professor Harold Levinson, was co-sponsored by the university and the Florida Bar and released in 1970.

3. The history of the Interest on Trust Accounts program is assembled primarily from the following sources: the opinions of the Florida Supreme Court in 1978 and 1981, In re Interest on Trust Accounts, 356 So.2d 799 (Fla., 1978), and In the Matter of Interest on Trust Accounts,

402 So.2d 389 (Fla., 1981); Arthur J. England Jr. and Russell E. Carlisle, "History of Interest on Trust Accounts Program," *Florida Bar Journal*, February 2001, p. 101; Florida Justice Institute video, "Interest on Lawyers' Trust Accounts, http://www.floridajusticeinstitute.org/wp-content/uploads/2013/11/IOLTA_HISTORY.mp4 (accessed December 13, 2014); interviews and conversations with Arthur England and Randall C. Berg Jr.; William A. VanNortwick Jr., Kent R. Spuhler Jr. and Paul C. Doyle, "Pro Bono Services in Florida," *Florida Bar Journal*, April 1999, p. 30; Talbot D'Alemberte, "Tributaries of Justice: The Search for Full Access," *Florida Bar Journal*, April 1999, p. 12; and Linda K. Rexer, "The History of IOLTA: Lessons for the Future," *Dialogue* (No. 3, Summer 2010).

4. 402 So.2d at 391.

5. *Bigelow v. Virginia, 421 U.S. 809 (1975).*

6. *Virginia State Board of Pharmacy v. Virginia Citizens Consumer Council, Inc., 425 U.S. 748 (1976).*

7. Bates v. State Bar of Arizona, 433 U.S. 350 (1977).

8. In re Primus, 436 U.S. 412 (1978).,

9. Ohralik v. Ohio State Bar Association, 436 U.S. 447 (1978).

10. Florida Bar Re: Amendment to Code of Professional Responsibility (Advertising), 380 So.2d 435 (Fla., 1980).

11. 380 So.2d at 442.

12. Florida Bar v. American Legal & Business Forms, Inc., 274 So.2d 225 (Fla. Feb. 28, 1973).

13. Florida Bar v. Stupica, 300 So.2d 683 (Fla. July 17, 1974).

14. Florida Bar v. Brumbaugh, 355 So.2d 1186 (Fla. Jan. 10, 1978).

15. Florida Bar v. Furman, 376 So2d 378 (Fla. May 10, 1979).

16. Matter of Interest on Trust Accounts, 372 So.2d 67 (Fla., May 24, 1979).

17. 402 So.2d at 393.

18. L. David Shear, "The Interest on Trust Accounts Program: The Quest Now Is Implementation," *Florida Bar Journal*, February 1982, p. 104

19. Philips v. Washington Legal Foundation. 524 U.S. 156 (June 15, 1998).

20. Brown v. Legal Foundation of Washington, 538 U.S. 216 (2003).

21. Florida Bar In Re Emergency Delivery of Legal Services to the Poor (Mandatory Pro Bono), 432 So.2d 39, 41 (Fla. May 12, 1983). See also Judson H. Orrick, "Court Rejects Mandatory Pro Bono Petition," *Florida Bar News*, June 1, 1983, p. 4.

22. Florida Bar v. Furman, 451 So.2d 808 (Fla. Apr. 26, 1984).

23. Florida Bar Re: Amendment to Florida Rules of Civil Procedure (Dissolution of Marriage), 450 So.2d 817 (Fla. May 3, 1984). See also Skene, "Court Eases Divorce Rule in Florida," *SPT*, Dec. 9, 1983, p. 1-A.

24. Skene, "Florida Considering 'No-lawyer' Divorces," *SPT*, Feb. 11, 1983, p. 1-A.

25. Florida Bar Re: Amendment to Florida Rules of Civil Procedure (Dissolution of Marriage), 450 So.2d 810 (Fla. Dec. 8, 1983).

26. Laurel Tielis, "Rosemary Furman Fights to Bring Justice to All at a Price All—Except Lawyers—Can Afford," *People*, Dec. 17, 1984, http://www.people.com/people/archive/article/0,,20089408,00.html, accessed Dec. 2, 2014.

27. The Florida Bar re Amendment to Rules Regulating the Florida Bar (Chapter 10), 510 So.2d 596 (Fla.1987). See Dunn v. Florida Bar, 889 F.2d 1010 (11th Circ. 1989) (denial of attorney fees).

28. See Talbot D'Alemberte, *The Role of the Courts in Providing Legal Services: A Proposal to Provide Legal Access For The Poor*, 17 Fla. State U. Law Review 107 (1989–1990), which includes the petition.

Chapter 10. "Save the Supreme Court"

1. Arthur J. England Jr., Eleanor Mitchell Hunter, and Richard C. Williams Jr., *Constitutional Jurisdiction of the Supreme Court of Florida: 1980 Reform*, 32 UF L. Rev. 153 (Winter 1980).

2. Supreme Court of Florida, 1979 Report on the Florida Judiciary, http://www.floridasupremecourt.org/pub_info/documents/1979_Report_On_The_Judiciary.pdf.

3. David Powell, "Arthur England is Named New Chief Justice," Associated Press, published in *SPT*, March 28. 1978, p. 1-B.

4. See Senate Journals for Court of Impeachment, excerpts for April 18, May 12, May 26, and September 13–15, 1978.

5. 103 So.2d 639 (Fla. 1958).

6. 103 So.2d at 643.

7. 177 So.2d 221 (Fla. 1965).

8. 177 So.2d at 225.

9. 168 So.2d 749 (Fla. 1964).

10. Rosenthal v. Scott, 131 So.2d 480 (Fla. 1961).

11. Foley v. Weaver Drugs, Inc., 172 So.2d 907 (Fla. 3DCA, 1965).

12. 177 So.2d at 233.

13. 347 So.2d 408, 409 (Fla. April 21, 1977) (England dissenting).

14. 336 So.2d 545 (Fla. May 12, 1976).

15. Edwards v. National Airlines Inc., 307 So.2d 244 (Fla. 4th DCA 1975).

16. Transcript, Memorial Service for Alan C. Sundberg, Supreme Court of Florida, January 29, 2002, accessible at http://wfsu.org/gavel2gavel/transcript/pdfs/SundbergCerem.pdf. (The names of speakers do not appear in the transcript and reflect the author's observations at the event. The event is also on video.)

17. Telephone Interview with Sharyn Smith, April 25, 2015.

18. In re Advisory Opinion to Governor Request of June 29, 1979, 374 So.2d 959, 971–972 (Fla. June 29, 1979).

19. Florida Industrial Commission v. Neal, 224 So.2d 774 (Fla. 1st DCA 1969).

20. In re Florida Workmen's Compensation Rules of Procedure, 285 So.2d 601 (Fla. Nov. 14, 1973). A useful narrative and anecdotal history relied upon in this summary of workers' compensation in Florida is Creston Nelson-Morrill, *Workers' Compensation in Florida 1935–1995: The History, People & Politics*, Florida Workers' Compensation Institute and HealthTrac Books (1995). A history that is more oriented to legislation and case law is Timothy A. Watson and Michael J. Valen, *A Historic Review of Workers' Compensation Reform in Florida*, 21 FSU L. Rev. 501 (1993–1994).

21. 279 So.2d 281 (Fla. June 6, 1973).

22. 307 So.2d 166 (Fla. Oct. 24, 1974).

23. Department of Agriculture and Consumer Services v. Bonanno, 568 So.2d 24 (Fla. Sept. 27, 1990).

24. 362 So.2d 926 (Fla. Sept. 14, 1978).

25. Amendments to the Florida Rules of Workers' Comp. Procedure, 891 So.2d 474 (Fla. Dec. 2, 2004).

26. Ben F. Overton, "Relieving an Overworked State Supreme Court: Florida Asks its Courts of Appeal to Assist in Screening Cases," *Judicature* Vol. 66, p. 371 (March 1983).

27. Journal of the Senate, November 28. 1979, p. 11–12; *Journal of the House of Representatives*, November 28, 1979, p. 23–24.

28. Cramp v. Board of Public Instruction of Orange County, 268 U.S. 278 (1961).

29. See Karl, *The 57 Club*, p. 103–105.

30. Sam Miller, United Press International, "Chief Justice and Chief Antagonist Debate Caseload," *Tallahassee Democrat*, Feb. 29, 1980.

31. 385 So.2d 1356 (Fla. June 26, 1980).

32. Arthur J. England Jr. and Richard C. Williams Jr., *Florida Appellate Reform One Year Later*, 9 FSU L. Rev. 221 (No. 2, Spring 1981).

33. Fred Schneyer, "High Court Rules Give Finality but Some Think Justice is Lost," *Ft. Lauderdale News and Sun-Sentinel*, May 29, 1983, p. 1G.

Chapter 11. Personal Injury: A Collision of Interests

1. 280 So.2d 431 (Fla. July 10, 1973)

2. Interviews by telephone and e-mail with Sammy Cacciatore. The background of the case is based on those exchanges, supplemented by briefs of the parties.

3. Thomas L. Shaffer, Remarks, Symposium, *Faith Tends to Subvert Legal Order*, 66 Fordham L. Rev. 1089, 1089 (1998), available at http://ir.lawnet.fordham.edu/flr/vol66/iss4/3/. See also Michael I. Swygert and W. Gary Vause, *Florida's First Law School*, at 351 (Carolina Academic Press, Durham, N.C.: 2006).

4. Louisville & Nashville R.R. Co. v. Yniestra, 21 Fla. 700 (1886).

5. 239 So.2d 76 (Fla. 4th Dist. 1970).

6. Jones v. Hoffman, 272 So.2d 529 (Fla. 4th Dist. 1973).

7. Connolly v. Steakley, 197 So.2d 524, 537 (Fla. 1967).

8. Waller v. First Savings & Trust Co., 138 So. 780 (Fla. 1931).

9. Randolph v. Randolph, 1 So.2d 480 (Fla. 1941).

10. Hargrove v. Town of Cocoa Beach, 96 So.2d 130 (Fla. 1957).

11. Supreme Court Archives, Adkins Files Series 2, Opinion Files Box 5, File No. 589.

12. Adkins, *Eighteen Years*, at 6.

13. 280 So.2d at 437.

14. Georgia Southern & Florida Railway Co. v. Seven-Up Bottling Co., 175 So.2d 39 (Fla. 1965).

15. Adkins, *Eighteen Years*, at 7.

16. Connolly v. Steakley, 197 So.2d 524, 525 (Fla. 1967).

17. Li v. Yellow Cab Company of California 13 Cal.3d 804, 812 (1975).

18. Author's Interview with James C. Adkins, 1983.

19. 247 So.2d 40 (Fla. Apr. 7, 1971).

20. Ripley v. Ewell, 61 So.2d 420. at 423 (Fla. 1952).

21. United Press International, "Wife Awarded Damages in Unusual Suit," *Florida Times-Union*, Nov. 4, 1971.

22. 5 U.S. 137 (1803).

23. 285 So.2d 397 (Fla. Oct. 10, 1973).

24. 281 So.2d 1, 4 (Fla. July 11, 1973).

25. Adkins, *Eighteen Years*, at 3.

26. Georgia Southern & Florida Railway Co. v. Seven-Up Bottling Co. of Southeast Georgia, 175 So.2d 39 (Fla., 1965).

27. Williams v. Seaboard Airline Railroad Co., 283 So.2d 33 (Fla. July 31, 1973).

28. 318 So.2d 386 (Fla. July 30, 1975).

29. *Id.* at 389 (citing Duval v. Thomas, 114 So.2d 791 (1959))

30. 318 So.1d at 391.

31. Fla. Stat. §768.31.

32. Fla. Stat. §768.31.

33. *Ocean Telegraph Co. v. Saunders, 14 So. 148 (Fla. 1893).*

34. See a student case note, David Richard Lenox, *Should the Florida Supreme Court Replace the Impact Rule with a Foreseeability Analysis?*, 11 FSU L. Rev. (Spring 1983).

35. 271 So.2d 466, 472 (Fla. 4th DCA 1972).

36. 291 So.2d 593 (Fla. Jan. 10, 1974).

Chapter 12. Media Law: Satyrs, Beer Trucks, and Teachers

1. Time Inc. v. Firestone, 424 U.S. 448, 449 (March 2,1976), and Firestone v. Time Inc., 305 So.2 d 172, 174 (Fla. Dec. 11, 1974).

2. 305 So.2d at 174.

3. Dyckman, *Disorderly Court*, p. 130–131.

4. Transcript, Florida House of Representatives Select Committee on Impeachment: Inquiry into Justice McCain, Vol. III, April 10, 1975, p. 257–259. Copy in Files of Martin Dyckman.

5. Firestone v. Firestone, 249 So.2d 719 (Fla. 4th DCA 1971).

6. Transcript, Florida House of Representatives Select Committee on Impeachment: Inquiry into Justice McCain, Vol. III, April 10, 1975, p. 257. Copy in Files of Martin Dyckman.

7. E-mail from Marguerite Davis to the author, Aug. 16, 2015.

8. Dyckman, *Disorderly Court*, p. 30.

9. Firestone v. Time, Inc., 231 So.2d 862 (Fla. 4th DCA 1970).

10. Time, Inc. v. Firestone., 237 So.2d 754 (Fla. Apr. 29, 1970).

11. 376 U.S. 254 (1964).

12. Curtis Publishing Co. v. Butts, 388 U.S. 130 (1967).

13. Time Inc. v. Hill, 385 U.S. 374 (1967).

14. Rosenbloom v. Metromedia Inc., 403 U.S. 29 (1971).

15. 271 So.2d 745 (Fla. Dec. 20, 1972).

16. Martin Dyckman, "Justice McCain's Vote on Friend's Appeal is Eyed," *SPT,* Dec. 22, 1974, p. 1-B

17. 271 So.2d at 752.

18. Time Inc. v. Firestone, 279 So.2d 389 (Fla. 4th DCA 1973).

19. Time Inc. v. Firestone, 424 U.S. 448, 457 (March 2, 1976).

20. 287 So.2d 78 (Fla. July 18, 1973).

21. Time, Inc. v. Hill, 385 U.S. 374, 389 (1967).

22. Red Lion Broadcasting Co. v. FCC, 395 U.S. 367 (1969).

23. Columbia Broadcasting System Inc. v. Democratic National Committee, 412 U.S. 94 (1973).

24. Miami Herald Publishing Co. v. Tornillo, 418 U.S. 241 (1974).

25. Dyckman, *Disorderly Court*, 76.

26. Katie Skene, "Lucy Morgan," in Sherri Winsett, ed., *Treasures of Our Past*, Lawton Chiles High School, May 22, 2009, p. 55.

27. Morgan v. State, 309 So.2d 552 (Fla. 2nd DCA 1975).

28. Morgan v. State, 325 So.2d 40 (Fla. 2nd DCA 1975).

29. 408 U.S. 665 (June 29, 1972).

30. New York Times v. United States, 403 U.S. 713 (1971). The *Washington Post* case was consolidated with the case against the *New York Times*.

31. 337 So.2d 951 (Fla. July 30, 1976).

32. 337 So.2d at 955–956.

33. M. David Shapiro, *Case Note: Private Citizens Need Only Show Negligence in Defamation Actions Against Media Defendants*, 13 FSU L. Rev. 159 (Spring 1985).

34. 458 So.2d 243 (Fla. Sept. 13, 1984).

35. 456 So.2d 462 (Fla. Sept. 13, 1984).

36. Compare Gibson v. Maloney, 231 So.2d 823 (Fla., 1970).

37. George K. Rahdert & David M. Snyder, *Rediscovering Florida's Common Law Defenses to Libel and Slander*," 11 Stetson L. Rev. 1 (1981).

Chapter 13. Personal Injury: A Wrong Finds a Remedy

1. 336 So.2d 80 (Fla. July 21, 1976).

2. Interview with Philip Freidin, January 23, 2016.

3. West v. Caterpillar Tractor Co., Inc., 504 F.2d 967 (5th Cir. 1974).

4. Adkins, *Eighteen Years*, p. 8.

5. 336 So.2d at 90.

6. 547 F.2d 885 (5th Cir. 1977).

7. 451 So.2d 447 (Fla. Apr. 12, 1984).

8. Brown v. Kendrick, 192 So.2d 49 (Fla. 1st DCA 1966)

9. Lafferty v. Allstate Ins. Co., 425 So.2d 1147 (Fla. 4th DCA 1982)

10. 425 So.2d at 1150–1151.

11. Insurance Co. of North America v. Pasakarnis, 425 So.2d 1141, 1142 (Fla. 4th DCA 1982).

12. Skene, "Court: Lack of seat belt may cut money damages," *SPT*, April 13, 1984, p. 1-A.

13. 451 So.2d at 451.

14. 451 So.2d at 455, citing Fla. Stat. Sec. 316.613 (3).

15. Laws of Florida, Ch. 86–49, codified as Fla. Stat. Sec. 316.614(10).

16. Belcher Yacht, Inc. v. Stickney, 450 So.2d 1111 (Fla. May 3, 1984).

17. Jones v. Utica Mut. Ins. Co., 463 So.2d 1153, 10 Fla. L. Weekly 159 (Fla. Mar. 7, 1985). Although initially released on May 3, 1984, the case was held up on reconsideration and finally published on March 7, 1985.

18. Skene, "Dog Day at the Court," *SPT*, May 4, 1984, p. 1-B.

19. 463 So.2d at 1159.

20. Mapoles v. Mapoles, 350 So.2d 1137 (Fla. 1st DCA 1977).

21. 474 So.2d 783 (Fla. May 16, 1985, amended on denial of rehearing, Aug. 29, 1985).

22. Mary C. Williams, "Susan Von Stetina, In Coma for 13 Years After Accident," *Sun-Sentinel*, July 16, 1993.

23. This account is drawn from the two appellate opinions in the case and from an Associated Press article, "Child is Killed: Mother Dies from Shock," *Palm Beach Post*, September 7, 1980, p. B17. (The article also appeared with different headlines in other newspapers, including the *Lakeland Ledger*, September 3, 1980, p. 4B.)

24. 291 So.2d 593 (Jan. 10, 1974). See Chapter 11.

25. Champion v. Gray, 420 So.2d 348 (Fla. 5th DCA 1982).

26. 478 So.2d 17 (Fla. March 7, 1985).

27. 478 So.2d at 20.

28. 478 So.1d at 22 n. 4.

29. Cadillac Motor Car Division v. Brown, 428 So.2d 301, 302 (Fla. 3rd Dist. App. 1983).

Chapter 14. Divorce and Family Litigation: Till the Judge Do Us Part

1. 382 So.2d 1197 (Fla. Jan. 31, 1980).

2. The history of their marriage is drawn from the opinions in the First DCA and Supreme Court opinions, including Judge McCord's dissent, and from obituaries of Dr. Canakaris, one in the *Daytona Beach News Journal*, Dec. 7, 2012 (accessible at http://www.legacy.com/obituaries/news-journalonline/obituary.aspx?pid=161524738), and one at Flagler Live, "John Canakaris, Father of Flagler County Medicine and Humanitarian, Is Dead at 90," Dec. 4, 2012 (accessible at http://flaglerlive.com/47716/john-canakaris-obituary/).

3. Dyckman, *Reubin O'D Askew and the Golden Age of Florida Politics*, p. 86.

4. The details of the property division are from the court opinions in the case.

5. Canakaris v. Canakaris, 356 So.2d 858 (Fla. 1st DCA 1978).

6. 78 So.2d 367 (Fla. 1955).

7. Brown v. Brown, 300 So.2d 719, 725 (Fla. 1st DCA 1974).

8. 382 So.2d at 1204.

9. Duncan v. Duncan, 379 So.2d 949 (Fla. Jan. 31, 1980).

10. Neff v. Neff, 386 So.2d 318, 319 (Fla. 2nd DCA 1980).

11. Powers v. Powers, 409 So.2d 177, 178 (Fla. 2nd DCA 1982).

12. Compare Bird v. Bird, 385 So.2d 1090 (Fla. 4th DCA 1980), Sangas v. Sangas, 407 So.2d 630 (Fla. 4th DCA 1981), and Tronconi v. Tronconi, 425 So.2d 547 (Fla. 4th DCA 1982) (en banc). See also Melinda S. Gentile, *Property Distribution Upon Dissolution of Marriage: Florida's Need for an Equitable Distribution Statute*, 8 Nova L. J. 71 (1983).

13. Drafts and vote sheets are in Florida Supreme Court archived file, Sundberg Files Series 1, Box 6, File No. 361 *Raisen v. Raisen*.

14. 379 So.2d 352 (Fla. Dec. 20, 1979).

15. 379 So.2d at 355.

16. 379 So.2d at 359.

17. Hill v. Hill, 415 So.2d 20 (Fla. Apr. 29, 1982).

18. Skene, "Ex-wife Asks High Court to Let Her Sue Spouse," *SPT*, Feb. 10, 1981, p. 1-B.

19. Bencomo v. Bencomo, 200 So.2d 171, 174 (Fla. 1967).

20. 414 So.2d 189 (Fla. Apr. 29, 1982).

21. 414 So.2d 190 (Fla. Apr. 29, 1982).

22. 414 So.2d 1066 (Fla. Apr. 29, 1982).

23. *Orefice v. Albert,* 237 So. 2d 142 (Fla. 1970).

24. 414 So.2d at 1070–1071.

25. 414 So.2d 1063 (Fla. Apr. 29, 1982). See also Woods v. Withrow, 413 So.2d 1179 (Fla. April 29, 1982), released the same day and consistent with *Joseph.*

26. Shor v. Paoli, 353 So.2d 825 (Fla. Nov. 17, 1977).

27. Fla. Stat. Sec. 934.03(1).

28. Skene, "Court Says Woman Can Sue Ex-spouse over Taped Phone Calls," *SPT,* March 16, 1984, p. 1-B.

29. 475 So.2d 1211 (Fla. Aug. 29, 1985).

30. Adkins, *Eighteen Years,* at 5–6, fn. 15.

31. Sturiano v. Brooks, 523 So.2d 1126 (Fla. Mar. 24, 1988).

32. Fla. Laws Ch. 85–328, Fla. Stat. Sec. 741.235.

33. Pulitzer v. Pulitzer, 449 So.2d 370 (Fla. 4th DCA 1984), review denied, 458 So.2d 273 (Fla. Oct. 22, 1984). See also Mike McQueen, Associated Press, "State Supreme Court Turns Down Appeal of Pulitzer," *SPT,* Oct. 26, 1984.

34. 312 So.2d 726 (Fla. Mar. 26, 1975).

35. 450 So.2d 853, Fla. May 17, 1984).

36. Owens v. Owens, 415 So.2d 855, 858 (Fla. 5th DCA 1982).

Chapter 15. Environment and Growth: Property Rights and the Public Good

1. See Nancy Stroud, *A History and New Turns in Florida's Growth Management Reform in Symposium: 40th Anniversary of the Quiet Revolution in Zoning and Land Use Regulation,* 45 John Marshall Law Review 397 (Winter 2012), referring to Fred Bosselman and David Callies, "The Quiet Revolution in Land Use Control," Council on Environmental Quality, Washington, D.C. (Dec. 1971).

2. Fla. Const. Art. II, Sec. 3.

3. 399 So.2d 1374 (Fla. Apr. 16, 1981).

4. Estuary Properties Inc. v. Askew, 381 So.2d 1126 (Fla. 1st DCA. 1979).

5. Adkins's draft quoted Justice Brennan's dissent in San Diego Gas & Electric Co. v. City of San Diego.

6. Handwritten document beginning "Adkins, J., Dissents," in Supreme Court Archives, Adkins Papers, Series 2, Opinion Files, Box 5, File No. 549.

7. Interview with Thomas Pelham by telephone, May 15, 2015.

8. Howard Rhoads interview by Mary Evans, Undated, Southwest Florida Oral History Project, "The Battle for Estero Bay 1959–1980," Florida Gulf Coast University. http://ruby.fgcu.edu/courses/jkent/81180/Main%20oral%20history%20project/estero/Rhodes/rhoades.htm, last accessed May 15, 2015.

9. Contractors and Builders Association of Pinellas County v. City of Dunedin, 312 So.2d 763 (Fla. 2nd DCA 1975).

10. 311 So.2d 371 (Fla. 4th DCA 1975).

11. 329 So.2d 314 (Fla. Feb. 25, 1976).

12. Wald Corp. v. Metropolitan Dade County, 338 So.2d 863 (Fla. 3rd DCA, 1976).

13. Wald Corp. v. Metropolitan Dade County, 348 So.2d 955 (Fla. May 27, 1977).

14. Nalven v. Department of Transportation, 409 So.2d 166 (Fla. 2d DCA 1982).

15. 455 So.2d 301 (Fla. Apr. 19, 1984).

16. 492 So.2d 339 (Fla. May 15, 1986).

17. See Monica K. Reimer, "The Public Trust Doctrine: Historic Protection for Florida's Navigable Rivers and Lakes," *Florida Bar Journal* vol. LXXV No. 4 (April 2001), p. 10.

18. Fla. Const. Art. X, Sec. 11, proposed by House Joint Resolution HJR 792 (1970).

19. 341 So.2d 977 (Fla. Nov. 30,1976).

20. See Reimer, "The Public Trust Doctrine."

Chapter 16. Death Penalty: The Long Last Mile

1. Interview with Justice England on October 26, 2009, supplemented by Justice England's detailed description of the events of that morning during a seminar at Yale Law School on April 18, 1985. A transcript of his remarks is quoted at length in Robert A. Burt, "Disorder in the Court: The Death Penalty and the Constitution," *Faculty Scholarship Series,* Paper 804 (1987). http://digitalcommons.law.yale.edu/fss_papers/804 (last accessed December 12, 2012).

2. The website of the Florida Department of Corrections has a list of executions, one for those through 1964 (http://www.dc.state.fl.us/oth/deathrow/execlist2.html), and one for those under the 1972 statute, beginning with Spenkelink (http://www.dc.state.fl.us/oth/deathrow/execlist. html).

3. 372 U.S. 335 (1963). The famous decision was an appeal from the Florida Supreme Court's denial, without opinion, of Clarence Earl Gideon's habeas petition, sub nom. Gideon v. Cochrane, 135 So.2d 746 (Fla. 1961), on remand *sub. nom.* Gideon v. Wainwright, 153 So.2d 299 (Fla. 1963). Gideon was acquitted in his new trial.

4. 384 U.S. 486 (1966).

5. Adderly v. Wainwright, 272 F.Supp. 530 (M.D. Fla. 1967).

6. Telephone conversation between Brian T. Hayes and Albert W. Alschuler, Professor of Law at Northwestern University, dated only "1984," quoted in Alschuler, *Plea-Bargaining and the Death Penalty,* 58 DePaul L. Rev. 671, 672–673 (2009). Hayes died April 30, 2011.

7. Quoted in Welsh S. White, *Litigating in the Shadow of Death: Defense Attorneys in Capital Cases,* 145 (2006), cited in Alschuler at 672.

8. Taylor v. State, 294 So.2d 648 (Fla. May 15, 1974).

9. Lamadline v. State, 303 So.2d 17 (Fla. Nov. 6, 1974).

10. Sullivan v. State, 303 So.2d 632 (Fla. Nov. 27, 1974).

11. Hallman v. State, 305 So2d 180 (Fla. Dec. 11, 1974).

12. Alford v. State, 307 So.2d 433 (Fla. Jan 29, 1975).

13. Spinkellink v. State, 313 So.2d 666 (Fla. Feb. 19, 1975).

14. 313 So.2d at 671.

15. 313 So.2d at 673–674 (Ervin dissenting).

16. Proffitt v. Florida, 428 U.S. 242 (July 2, 1976).

17. 438 U.S. 586 (July 3, 1978). *See also* Eddings v. Oklahoma, 455 U.S. 104 (Jan. 19, 1982).

18. Michael Mello, *Dead Wrong: A Death Row Lawyer Speaks Out Against Capital Punishment* (University of Wisconsin Press, 1999), at p. 115. Marky made a similar observation in conversations with the author of this history in the mid-1980s.

19. Ramsey Clark, "Spenkelink's Last Appeal," *The Nation,* Oct. 27. 1979, at 385, *quoted in* Burt, *Disorder in the Court,* at 1808–1810.

20. David von Drehle, Among *the Lowest of the Dead: The Culture of Capital Punishment* (New York: Times Books, 1995), at pp. 81–84.

21. Wainwright v. Spenkelink, 442 U.S. 901 (May 24, 1979).

22. 442 U.S. 1301 (May 22, 1979). The statutory authority for the writ is at 28 U.S.C. §1651.

23. Skene and Dyckman, "Path is Cleared for Execution." *SPT*, May 25, 1979, p. 1-A.

24. Von Drehle, *Among the Lowest of the Dead*, p. 41–43.

25. Skene, "Sullivan Shared Scotch with Prison Chief Before His Death," *SPT*, Feb. 7, 1984, p. 1-B.

26. Spenkelink v. Wainwright, 372 So.2d 927 (Fla. May 25, 1979).

27. Spenkelink v. State, 350 So.2d 85, 87–88 (Fla. Sept. 16, 1977).

28. H.G. "Buddy" Davis, "The Witness Room: An Air of Grimness and Finality," *SPT*, May 26, 1979, p. 1-A. His account of the witness room and the execution is supplemented by the author's observations at executions of Anthony Antone and Arthur Frederick Goode in 1984.

29. 408 U.S. 238 (June 29, 1972).

30. Ch. 72-118, 1972 Fla. Sess. Laws 258, *amending* Fla. Stat. § 775.082 (1971). *See generally* Charles W. Ehrhardt and L. Harold Levinson, *Florida's Legislative Response to Furman: An Exercise in Futility?*, 64. J. Crim. Law & Criminology 10 (Mar. 1973).

31. 265 So.2d 499 (Fla. July 17. 1972).

32. 267 So.2d 8 (Fla. Sept. 8, 1972).

33. 267 So.2d 331 (Fla. Sept. 26, 1972).

34. See Jim Wooten, "It's Over for 2 Wrongly Held 12 Years," *New York Times*, Sept. 20, 1975. See also "Nightmare Ends for 2 Wrongly Accused," *MH*, May 1, 1998, describing the legislative claims bill granting each man compensation of $500,000. The exoneration largely resulted from the work of *Miami Herald* reporter Gene Miller, whose book won a Pulitzer Prize. Gene Miller, *Invitation to a Lynching* (New York: Doubleday 1975). On September 20, 1975, Governor Askew and the required three members of the elected six-member Cabinet signed the pardon.

35. Jere Moore Jr., Associated Press, "Judicial Council Favors Death Penalty," *SPT*, November 4, 1972.

36. 402 U.S. 183 (1971).

37. "Askew Signs Bill Restoring Death Penalty," *SPT*, Dec. 9, 1972, p. 12-B.

38. Ch. 72-724, 1973 Fla. Sess. Laws, amending Fla. Stat. § 921.141 (1971).

39. 283 So.2d 1 (Fla. July 26, 1973).

40. Adkins, *Eighteen Years*, 11 Nova L. Rev. at 14.

41. 283 So.2d at 7.

42. 283 So.2d at 26 (Boyd dissenting).

43. Boyd, *Looking Back*, 11 Nova L. Rev. at 34–35 (1986).

44. 283 So.2d at 18 (Ervin dissenting).

45. 283 So.2d at 8.

46. 283 So.2d at 19 (Ervin dissenting).

47. 283 So.2d at 22 (Ervin dissenting).

48. 315 So.2d 461, 466–467 (Fla. May 28, 1975).

49. Roberts v. Louisiana, 428 U.S. 325 (July 2, 1976), and Woodson v. North Carolina, 428 U.S. 280 (July 2, 1976).

50. Gregg v. Georgia, 428 U.S. 153 (July 2, 1976).

51. 428 U.S. 242, 251 (1976). See also Woodward and Armstrong, *The Brethren*, at pp. 430–441.

52. 428 U.S. 242 (July 2, 1976).

53. 346 So.2d 998 (Fla. Apr. 7, 1977).

54. Hargrave v. State, 366 So.2d 1 (Fla. June 30, 1978).

55. Vaught v. State, 410 So.2d 147 (Fla. Jan 7, 1982).

56. Henry v. Wainwright, 661 F.2d 56, 60 (5th Circ. 1981), vacated on other grounds, 457 U.S. 1114 (1982), adhered to on remand, 686 F.2d 311 (5th Circ. 1982).

Chapter 17. The Machinery of Death

1. Michael Mello, *In the Years When Murder Wore the Mask of Law: Diary of a Capital Appeals Lawyers (1983–1986)*, 24 Vermont L. Rev. 583, 657 (2000).

2. Spaziano v. State, 393 So.2d 1119 (Fla. Jan. 8, 1981).

3. Spaziano v. State, 433 So.2d 508 (May 26, 1983).

4. Commission on Capital Cases, "Appellate Time Frames: A Comprehensive Statistical Examination (May 13, 2011), accessible at http://www.floridacapitalcases.state.fl.us/Publications/Appellate%20Time%20Frame%20Statistics%20&%20Appendix2.pdf.

5. State v. Spaziano, 692 So.2d 174 (Fla. Apr 17. 1997). See Commission on Capital Cases, Statistical Appendix, accessible at http://www.floridacapitalcases.state.fl.us/Publications/Appellate%20Time%20Frame%20Statistics%20&%20Appendix2.pdf.

6. 437 So.2d 1082, 1087 (Fla. Aug. 25, 1983).

7. 433 So.2d 508, 512 (Fla. May 26, 1983).

8. 437 So.2d 1072, 1079 (Fla. July 21, 1983).

9. 322 So.2d 908 (Fla. November 19, 1975).

10. 322 So.2d at 910.

11. Proffitt v. State, 315 So.2d 461 (Fla. May 28, 1975), *aff'd sub nom.* Proffitt v. Florida, 428 U.S. 242 (July 2, 1976).

12. 371 So.2d 1007, 1009 (Fla. Mar. 29, 1979).

13. 376 So. 2d 1149 (Fla. June 14, 1979).

14. Johnson v. State, 393 So.2d 1069 (Fla. Dec. 11, 1980).

15. King v. State, 390 So.2d 315 (Fla. May 8, 1980).

16. 446 So.2d 1038 (Fla. Jan. 26, 1984).

17. King v. State 514 So.2d 354, 361 (Fla. Sept. 24, 1987).

18. 461 So.2d 79, 82 (Fla. Nov. 21, 1984).

19. 522 So.2d 817, 821 (Fla. Mar. 10, 1988).

20. 390 So.2d 315 (Fla. May 8, 1980).

21. 374 So.2d 975 (Fla. July 26, 1979).

22. Mason v. State, 438 So. 2d 374 (Fla. Sept. 8, 1983).

23. Teffeteller v. State, 439 So. 2d 840 (Fla. Aug. 25, 1983).

24. Breedlove v. State, 413 So. 2d 1 (Fla. Mar. 4, 1982).

25. Middleton v. State, 426 So. 2d 548 (Fla. Dec. 22, 1982).

26. Hargrave v. State, 366 So. 2d 1 (Fla. June 30, 1978).

27. Menendez v. State, 368 So. 2d 1278 (Fla. Jan. 25, 1979).

28. Scott v. State, 411 So. 2d 866 (Fla. Mar. 11, 1982).

29. Rembert v. State, 445 So.2d 337 (Fla. Feb. 2, 1984).

30. Washington v. State, 362 So. 2d 658 (Fla. Sept. 7, 1978), and Routly v. State, 440 So.2d 1257 (Fla. Sept. 22, 1983).

31. Harvard v. State, 375 So. 2d 833 (Fla. Apr. 7, 1977).

32. Taylor v. State, 294 So.2d 648 (Fla. May 15, 1974).

33. Witt v. State, 387 So.2d 922, 931 (Fla. July 24, 1980) (England dissenting).

34. Interview with Randall Reder, Mar. 20, 2012.

35. Boyd and Logue, *Developments in the Application of Florida's Capital Punishment Law*, 34 U. Miami L. Rev 441 (1980).

36. 322 So.2d 533 (Fla. Sept. 17, 1975).

37. 322 So.2d at 542.

38. Interview with England, October 26, 2009.

39. Gardner v. State, 313 So.2d 675 (Fla. Feb. 26, 1975), *reversed sub nom.* Gardner v. Florida, 430 U.S. 349 (Mar. 22, 1977).

40. 313 So.2d at 679.

41. 430 U.S. at 361.

42. 430 U.S. at 367.

43. Kelly Scott. "Justices Saw Confidential Psychological Profiles of Death Row Inmates," *SPT*, Aug. 19, 1980, at 1-B. (Photocopy in author's files.)

44. 392 So2d 1327 (Fla. Jan. 15, 1981).

45. 392 So.2d at 1333.

46. 322 So.2d at 1333.

47. Swan v. State, 322 So.2d 485 (Fla. Sept. 3, 1975).

48. 392 So.2d at 1331.

49. 696 F.2d 804 (11th Cir. 1983).

50. Cleve R. Wootson Jr., "Brown Sentenced to Prison for Strangling Wife in 2012," *The Charlotte Observer*, Sept. 13, 2013, p. B-1.

Chapter 18. The "E" Seat: Ervin to England to Ehrlich

1. Skene, "Applicants for Supreme Court Vacancy Total 38 as Deadline Passes," *SPT*, Aug. 11, 1981, p. 2-B.

2. "Former Resident on High Court List," *Putnam County Courier*, Sept. 24, 1981, p. 1.

3. Lucy Morgan, *SPT*, Oct. 11, 2005, quoting Justice Overton at a memorial service for Ehrlich.

4. Transcript, Ray Ehrlich Oral History Interview with Denise Stobbie, Dec. 20, 1990, p. 6–8, Samuel Proctor Oral History Program Collection, P.K. Yonge Library of Florida History, University of Florida.

5. Oral History Interview with Ehrlich, p. 9.

6. Norm Going, "Stockbroker Going to Capital Office Employer to Open," *Florida Times-Union*, January 19, 1982, p. B-5.

7. Skene, "Lawyer Named to High Court," *SPT*, Oct. 15, 1981, p. 1-B, 4-B.

8. Oral History Interview with Ehrlich, p. 20.

9. Fla. Const. Art. V, Sec. 10(a).

10. Fla. Const. Art. V, Sec. 7.

11. 494 So.2d 1139 (Fla. Sept. 25, 1986).

12. Rosemary Barkett Interviewed by Hank Coxe, Florida Supreme Court Historical Society Dinner, January 30, 2014.

Chapter 19. Accepting Gays

1. Florida Board of Bar Examiners Re: N.R.S., 403 So.2d 1315 (Fla. June 18, 1981).

2. Skene, "Gays Can be Admitted to Bar, Supreme Court Secretly Rules," *SPT,* Sept. 27, 1981, p. 1-B.

3. Skene "Secret High Court Ruling on Gays is Made Public," *SPT,* Oct. 2, 1981, p. 1-B.

4. In re Florida Board of Bar Examiners in re Eimers, 358 So.2d 7 (Fla. March 2, 1978).

5. Jon Nordheimer, "Florida High Court Upholds Right of Homosexuals to Practice Law," *New York Times,* March 21, 1978, p. 25.

6. State ex rel Florida Bar v. Kimball, 96 So.2d 825 (Fla. 1957). See also Florida Bar in re Petition of Harris L. Kimball for Reinstatement, 425 So.2d 531 (Fla. Dec. 16, 1982), and Skene, "Lawyer Once Disbarred for Homosexual Act Seeks Reinstatement Without Taking Exam," *SPT,* Oct. 10, 1982.

7. Florida Bar v. Kay, 232 So.2d 378 (Fla. 1970).

8. In Re Petition of Diez-Arguelles, 401 So.2d 1347 (Fla. July 30, 1981).

9. See, for example, Florida Board of Bar Examiners in re Questions of Law Certified, 350 So.2d 1072 (Fla. Sept. 29, 1977); In Re Florida Board of Bar Examiners, 341 So.2d 503 (Fla. Nov. 24, 1976). See also In Re Application of VMF, 491 So.2d 1104 (Fla. July 10, 1986).

10. Florida Supreme Court archives, Sundberg Files Series 5 Chief Justice Files Box 3 File 94.

11. Skene, *SPT,* Sept. 27, 1981, and *SPT,* Oct. 2, 1981, *ibid.*

12. "Florida Curb on Homosexuals Survives a Test," *New York Times,* Oct. 4, 1981, accessible at http://www.nytimes.com/1981/10/04/us/florida-curb-on-homosexuals-survives-a-test.html.

13. Skene, "Trask-Bush Debate in High Court Pits Morality Against Freedom," *SPT,* Nov. 3, 1981.

14. 416 So.2d 455 (Fla. July 15, 1982).

Chapter 20. Reapportionment: Where to Draw the Lines

1. The account of the oral argument and background of the case is from Skene, "30 More Days," *SPT,* March 28, 1982, p. 1-B.

2. For earlier periods, see Manley and Brown, *Florida Supreme Court 1917-1972,* p. 280.

3. In re Apportionment Law Appearing as Senate Joint Resolution No. 1305, 1972 Regular Session, 263 So.2d 797, 800 (Fla. 1972).

4. Citing Burns v. Richardson, 384 U.S. 73 (1966).

5. Milton v. Smathers, 351 So.2d 24 (Fla. June 30, 1977); Cardenas v. Smathers, 351 So.2d 21 (Fla. June 30, 1977).

6. City of Mobile v. Bolden, 446 U.S. 55 (1980).

7. 389 So.2d 978 (Fla. Oct. 23, 1980).

8. Skene, "Court: 5-member Pinellas House District Not Biased Against Blacks," *SPT,* Oct. 24, 1980, p. 1-A, 11-A.

9. A more detailed compilation of the history of reapportionment in Florida may be found in the biennial *Florida Handbook,* formerly published by Allen and Joan Morris, and now published by the Florida House of Representatives. See Skene, "Reapportionment in Florida," *Florida Handbook* (2013-2014 ed.), p. 247.

10. Florida Senate v. Graham, 412 So.2d 359 (Fla. Mar. 27, 1982).

11. Florida Senate v. Graham, 412 So.2d 360 (Fla. Apr. 6, 1982).

12. Skene, "Graham Won't Ask Court for Reapportionment Ruling," *SPT,* June 11, 1981.

13. In re Apportionment Law Appearing as Senate Joint Resolution 1E, 1982 Special Reapportionment Session, 414 So.2d 1040 (Fla. April 26, 1982, and "on the merits" May 12, 1982).

Chapter 21. Search and Seizure: Reshaping Constitutional Protections

1. People v. Defore, 150 N.E. 585, 587 (N.Y. 1926).

2. Grant v. State, 194 So.2d 612, 616 (Fla. 1967).

3. Hajdu v. State, 189 So.2d 230 (Fla. 3rd DCA 1966).

4. Franco v. State, 376 So.2d 1168, 1171 (Fla. 3rd DCA 1979).

5. 397 So.2d 643 (Fla. Jan. 15, 1981).

6. 397 So.2d at 646, citing Hoffa v. United States, 385 U.S. 293 (1966).

7. Hetland v. State, 387 So.2d 963 (Fla., Sept. 11, 1980), affirming State v. Hetland, 366 So.2d 831 (Fla. 2nd DCA 1979).

8. Supreme Court Archives, Sundberg Files Series 1, Box 6, File No. 435.

9. Florida Laws Ch. 82-155 and 82-403, codified at Fla. Stat. Section 316.193. See also Mark Dobson, *Florida's New 'Drunk Driving' Laws: An Overview of Constitutional and Statutory Problems,* 7 Nova Law Journal 179 (1983).

10. Skene, "Legislature adjourns after anti-crime spree," *SPT,* June 23, 1982, p. 1-B.

11. Skene, "Governor, Senators Exchange Insults," *SPT,* March 17, 1982, p. 1-B.

12. Editorial, "Making things worse, not better," *SPT,* Dec. 5, 1981.

13. State v. Brady, 379 So.2d 1294, 1296 (Fla. 4th DCA, 1980).

14. 389 U.S. 347, 350–352 (1967)

15. Description of the oral argument is taken from Skene, "Where's My Curtilage? Who Cares? Oh, the Court," *SPT,* Jan. 7, 1981.

16. 406 So.2d 1093 (Fla. Oct. 15, 1981).

17. 379 So.2d 643 (Fla. Jan. 24, 1980).

18. 406 So.2d at 1098.

19. Florida v. Brady, 456 U.S. 988 (1982).

20. Hoberman v. State, 400 So.2d 758 (Fla. Apr. 30, 1981). See also Williams v. State, 421 So.2d 512 (Fla. Oct. 28, 1982),

21. DeMontmorency v. State was not finally released for another three years as it was pending on rehearing, but the original decision was reported at 1982 Florida Law Weekly 485 (Fla. Oct. 28, 1982). See also Skene, "Police Tactics Prompt Successful Appeals," *SPT,* Oct. 29, 1982. But see DeMontmorency v. State, 464 So.2d 1201 (Fla. Feb. 28, 1985).

22. Morningstar v. State, 428 So.2d 220 (Fla. Sept. 23, 1982).

23. The account of the oral argument is derived from Skene, *SPT,* May 7, 1984, p. 1-B.

24. 434 So.2d 321 (Fla. July 7, 1983).

25. State v. Williams, 443 So.2d 952 (Fla. Dec. 8, 1983).

26. State v. Tsavaris, 394 So.2d 418 (Fla. Feb. 12, 1981).

27. State v. Walls, 356 So.2d 294 (Fla. Mar. 2, 1978).

28. Inciarrano v. State, 447 So.2d 386 (Fla.4th DCA 1984).

29. 466 U.S. 170 (Apr. 17, 1984).

30. Florida v. Brady, 467 U.S. 1201 (May 21, 1984).

31. State v. Brady, 466 So.2d 1064 (Fla. Feb. 28, 1985).

32. DeMontmorency v. State, 464 So.2d 1201 (Fla. Feb. 28, 1985). See footnote 21 above.

34. 488 U.S. 445 (Jan. 23, 1989).

35. 524 So.2d 988, 994 (Fla. Jan. 7, 1988).

Chapter 22. Private Lives and Public Values in Criminal Law

1. 415 So.2d 724 (Fla. June 24, 1982).

2. Wilson v. State, 11 So. 556 (Fla. 1892).

3. 172 So. 2d 824 (Fla. 1965).

4. The Fourth DCA cases were Watkins v. State, 197 So.2d 312 (Fla. 4th DCA 1967), and Conner v. State, 361 So.2d 774 (1978). An extensive history of the castle doctrine and a charmingly thoughtful assessment of Florida's cases can be found in a student case note written by Thomas Katheder after the Bobbitt decision, *Lovers and Other Strangers: When Is a House a Castle*, 11 Florida State Law Review 465 (Summer 1983).

5. State v. Bobbitt, 415 So.2d 724 (Fla. 1st DCA 1982).

6. Cladd v. State, 398 So.2d 442 (Fla. April 30, 1981).

7. State v. Bobbitt, 420 So. 2d 362 (Fla. 1st DCA 1982).

8. State v. Bobbitt, 429 So. 2d 7 (Fla. Mar. 25, 1983).

9. Weiand v. State, 732 So.2d 1044 (Fla. March 11, 1999).

10. State v. James, 402 So.2d 1169 (Fla. July 23, 1981).

11. Skene, "Dead Victim's Statements Brought Conviction—But Was It Justice?," *SPT*, April 13, 1981.

12. 531 U.S. 36 (2004).

13. Ryne Ziemba, "A Cycle of Injustice?," *Independent Weekly*, Vol. 19, No. 5, Mar. 25, 2010, accessible at http://www.inweekly.net/article.asp?artID=11293.

14. 394 U.S. 705 (1969).

15. Matthews v. State, 336 So.2d 643 (Fla. 1st DCA 1978).

16. 363 So.2d 1066 (Fla. July 27, 1978).

17. 393 So.2d 1076 (Fla. Dec. 18, 1980).

18. The background of the case is summarized from an Associated Press item, headlined "Civil Liberties Unit to Assist Klansman," found via Google News in *The Day* newspaper of New London, Connecticut, Sept. 20, 1979, p. 27, and "Klan Leader Pleads No Contest," *Palm Beach Post*, Dec. 6, 1979, p. 2A.

19. Fla. Laws Ch 81–249, Fla. Stat. Sec. 876.155.

20. City of Daytona Beach v. Del Percio, 476 So.2d 197 (Fla. Aug. 30, 1985).

21. 340 So.2d 1155 (Fla. Oct. 14, 1976).

22. Roger Ebert, "Inside *Deep Throat*," February 10, 2005, http://www.rogerebert.com/reviews/inside-deep-throat-2005.

23. 298 So.2d 391 (Fla. May 1, 1974).

24. State ex rel. Gerstein v. Walvick Theatre Corporation, 298 So.2d 406 (Fla. May 1, 1974).

25. 283 So.2d 351 (Fla. Sept. 19, 1973).

26. 294 So.2d 93 (Fla. Apr. 25, 1974).

27. Erznoznik v. City of Jacksonville, 422 U.S. 205 (June 23, 1975).

28. 303 So.2d 329 (Fla. Oct. 16, 1974), reversed, 421 U.S. 927 (May 20, 1975).

29. Bucolo v. State, 316 So.2d 551 (Fla. July 9, 1975).

30. Bucolo v. Adkins, 424 U.S. 641 (March 8, 1976).

31. Jones v. State, 293 So.2d 33 (Fla. Apr. 10, 1974), cert denied, 419 U.S. 1081 (Dec. 23, 1974).

32. 337 So.2d 977 (Fla. Sept. 23, 1976).

33. 351 So.2d 10 (Fla. June 9, 1977).

34. First Amendment Foundation of Florida, Inc. v. State, 364 So.2d 450 (Fla. Oct. 12, 1978).

35. City of Miami v. Florida Literary Distributing Corp., 486 So.2d 569 (Fla. Apr. 3, 1986).

Chapter 23. Shaw: From Descendant of a Slave to Chief Justice

1. Transcript, Memorial Service for Alan C. Sundberg, Supreme Court of Florida, Jan. 29, 2002, accessible at http://wfsu.org/gavel2gavel/transcript/pdfs/SundbergCerem.pdf. (The names of speakers do not appear in the transcript and reflect the author's observations at the event. The event is also on video.)

2. Patrick McMahon, *SPT*, March 25, 1980,

3. Sylvia Walbolt, "Twenty Tips from a Battered and Bruised Oral-Argument Veteran," *Litigation*, Vol. 37, No. 2, p. 1, at p.2 (American Bar Association, Winter 2011). Interview with Sylvia Walbolt, July 26, 2012.

4. Kim I. Eisler, "New Justice Started Career as a Curiosity," *Tampa Tribune*, p. 1-A. Clipping in Randall Reder files in Supreme Court archives from January 1982.

5. U.S. Rep. Corrine Brown, Extension of Remarks, *Congressional Record*, Vol. 157, No. 114, July 27, 2011, pp. e1417-e1418.

6. The account of the luncheon is from Mark Woods, "How a Tense Moment Let City Progress in Race Relations," *Florida Times-Union*, Oct. 23, 2011, accessible at http://jacksonville.com/opinion/blog/401820/mark-woods/2011-10-23/mark-woods-how-tense-moment-let-city-progress-race.

7. Mark D. Killian, "Chief Justice Shaw," *Florida Bar Journal*, p. 12 (October 1990).

8. Transcript, Leander Shaw Retirement Ceremony, Nov. 8, 2002.

9. This account of the commission interviews is from Skene, "Supreme Court Candidates State Views Before Nominating Board," *SPT*, Oct. 21, 1982.

10. Skene, "Governor Names Black Appeal Judge," *SPT*, Dec. 18, 1982, p. 2-B.

11. Madelyn Miller, Associated Press, "Supreme Court Gets Second Black Justice Ever," *SPT*, Jan. 11, 1983.

12. Ibid.

13. Diana Smith, Associated Press, "Florida's High Court Justices Take to the Streets to Save Jobs," *Gainesville Sun*, Oct. 28, 1984, p. 2D, accessible at https://news.google.com/newspapers?nid=1320&dat=19841028&id=eDxWAAAAIBAJ&sjid=xukDAAAAIBAJ&pg=1791,4300152&hl=en.

14. "Retain Ehrlich and Shaw," *Gainesville Sun*, Oct. 25, 1984, p. 14A.

15. Associated Press, "Man Awaiting Florida Execution Is Ordered Acquitted in '79 Killing," *New York Times*, Dec. 22, 1989, accessible at http://www.nytimes.com/1989/12/22/us/man-awaiting-florida-execution-is-ordered-acquitted-in-79-killing.html.

16. Reply Brief of Appellant Cox, filed July 11, 1989, Florida Supreme Court archive at Florida State University Law School, Case No. 73150, accessible at http://archive.law.fsu.edu/library/flsupct/73150/73150rep.pdf.

17. Cox v. State, 555 So.2d 352 (Fla. Dec. 21, 1989), rehearing denied, Feb. 12, 1990.

18. Jaramillo v. State, 417 So.2d 257 (Fla. July 8, 1982).

19. Florida Commission on Capital Cases, Florida Capital Cases, accessible at http://www.floridacapitalcases.state.fl.us/Documents/Case_updates/Htm/113377.htm.

20. Bob Levenson, "Murder-case Jurors Shaken by Reversal of Guilty Verdict," *Orlando Sentinel*, Jan. 4, 1990, accessible at http://articles.orlandosentinel.com/1990-01-04/news/9001043996_1_zellers-tongue-cox.

21. Alan Judd, "Victim's Brother Targets 'Liberal' Judge," *Ocala Star-Banner*, Sept. 11, 1990, p. 2B, accessible at https://news.google.com/newspapers?nid=1356&dat=19900911&id=rowxAAAAIBAJ&sjid=IgcEAAAAIBAJ&pg=5869,258315&hl=en.

22. The court cited Planned Parenthood of Central Missouri v. Danforth, 428U.S. 52 (July 1, 1976) and Planned Parenthood Association of Kansas City, Missouri v. Ashcroft, 462 U.S. 476 (June 15, 1983).

23. 551 So.2d 1186 (Fla. Oct. 5, 1989).

24. Alan Judd, "Abortion Ruling Signals Battle," *Sarasota Herald-Tribune*, Apr. 16, 1990, p. 1-A, 10A-11A. Accessible at https://news.google.com/newspapers?nid=1755&dat=19900416&id=h64cAAAAIBAJ&sjid=e3oEAAAAIBAJ&pg=6979,291231&hl=en.

25. Jan Pudlow, "Terry Russell: President of the Bar," *Florida Bar Journal* vol. LXXV, No. 7, p. 10 (July/August 2001). Accessible at http://www.floridabar.org/DIVCOM/JN/JNJournal01.nsf/Author/DCA4D5083727394D85256B100071CDAF

26. Paul Jerome, "Judge of Justice," *Flavour* Magazine, Summer 1999, p. 18.

27. Information on the dispute over the post-nuptial agreement is derived from two newspaper articles: Associated Press, "Justice, ex-wife exchange charges," *Sarasota Herald-Tribune*, Apr. 5, 1996, p. 6B, accessible at https://news.google.com/newspapers?nid=1755&dat=19960405&id=eyAfAAAAIBAJ&sjid=7HwEAAAAIBAJ&pg=3535,4566582&hl=en; Randolph Pendleton, "Justice Shaw, His Ex-Wife Engaged in Court Battle," *Florida Times-Union*, Apr. 5, 1996, accessible at https://www.questia.com/newspaper/1G1-57519640/justice-shaw-his-ex-wife-engaged-in-court-battle; Noreen Marcus, *Sun-Sentinel*, Nov. 15, 1997, "Judge's Ex-wife Loses Appeal in Divorce," Nov. 15, 1997, accessible at http://articles.sun-sentinel.com/1997-11-15/news/9711150502_1_appeals-court-leander-shaw-1st-district-court; Noreen Marcus, "Scales of Justice Tip Toward Judge," *Sun-Sentinel*, Oct. 26, 1996.

28. In Re Inquiry Concerning a Judge—William A. Norris, 581 So.2d 578 (Fla. June 6, 1991).

29. Shaw v. Shaw, 704 So.2d 630 (Fla. 1st DCA 1997).

30. 744 So.2d 413 (Fla. Sept. 24, 1999).

31. Jan Pudlow, "Finding Chinks in the Death Penalty Machine," *Florida Bar News*, Nov. 1, 2006.

32. Transcript, Leander Shaw Retirement Ceremony, Nov. 8, 2002.

Chapter 24. Death Penalty: Deciding Who Dies

1. Skene, "Sullivan Shared Scotch with Prison Chief Before His Death," *SPT*, Feb. 7, 1984, p. 1-B.

2. Sullivan v. State, 441 So.2d 609 (Fla. Nov. 21, 1983) (published the day after the execution).

3. Skene, "Court Limits Appeals Based on Poor Counsel," *SPT*, May 15, 1984, p. 1-A.

4. Strickland v. Washington, 466 U.S. 668, 694 (1984).

5. Skene, *Review of Capital Cases*, at 271.

6. Adkins, *Eighteen Years* at 14.

7. Author's interview with Overton, June 19, 2012.

8. Lucy Morgan, "Condemned Man's Death is Sixth This Year Not In the Chair," *SPT*, Sept. 25, 1999, p. 5-B.

9. Goodwin v. State, 405 So.2d 170, 172 (Fla. July 30, 1981).

10. 351 So.2d 972 (Fla. Sept. 30, 1977).

11. Boyd, *Looking Back on Eighteen Years as a Justice of the Supreme Court of Florida*, 11 Nova Law Review 25, 33 (1986–87), citing McArthur v. Nourse, 369 So.2d 578 (Fla. Mar. 29, 1979).

12. Burks v. United States, 437 U.S. 1 (1978) and Greene v. Massey, 437 U.S. 19 (1978).

13. 379 So.2d at 387, quoting State v. Coles, 91 So.2d 200, 202 (Fla. 1956).

14. Tibbs v. Florida, 457 U.S. 31 (June 7, 1982).

15. Commission on Capital Cases Case Histories, p. 135.

16. Commission on Capital Cases Case Histories, May 2011, citing the National Crime Information Center.

17. Jaramillo v. State, 417 So.2d 257 (Fla. July 8, 1982).

18. Commission on Capital Cases Case Histories, May 2011.

19. One study of the subject is Michael L. Radelet and Margaret Vandiver, *The Florida Supreme Court and Death Penalty Appeals,* Journal of Criminal Law and Criminology, Vol. 74, p. 913 (1983). See also a symposium in the Stetson Law Review, Vol. XV, No. 2 (1986).

20. Skene, "Criticism of Death Penalty Centers on Victims' Race," *SPT,* May 13, 1984, p. 1-A.

21. 476 So.2d 130 (Fla. Aug. 15, 1985).

22. 476 So.2d at 133–134.

23. 413 So.2d 1175 (Fla. Apr. 15, 1982).

24. Francis v. State, 473 So.2d 672 (Fla. June 20, 1985).

25. 329 So. 2d 287 (Fla. Feb. 18, 1976).

26. Florida Supreme Court archived files, Sundberg Series 1, Box 2, File No. 92.

27. 437 So.2d 1099 (Fla. Sept. 1, 1983).

28. Associated Press, published in *Evening Independent* (St. Petersburg), July 23, 1979.

29. Douglas v. Wainwright, 739 F.2d 531, 533 (11th Circ. 1984).

30. Douglas v. State, 575 So.2d 165 (Fla. Jan 15, 1991).

31. Wilson v. Wainwright, 474 So.2d 1162 (Fla. Aug. 15, 1985), overturning Wilson v. State, 436 So.2d 908 (Fla. 1983).

32. See Skene, *Review of Capital Cases,* at 348 n. 507, referencing Maxwell v. State, 443 So.2d 967 (Fla. 1983). See Maxwell v. Florida, 479 U.S. 972 (1986)(Marshall, dissenting), denying review from Maxwell v. State, 490 So.2d 927 (Fla. May 15, 1986).

33. Barclay v. State, 343 So.2d 1266 (Fla. Mar. 17, 1977); reaffirmed after remand, 411 So.2d 1310 (Fla. June 4, 1981).

34. Michael Castengera, "Panel Investigating Olliff Press Conference," *Jacksonville Journal,* November 23, 1976, Letter from Chief Judge Major B. Harding to Chief Justice Ben F. Overton, November 19, 1976, in Harding's files (copy in author's files).

35. Michael Castengera, "Judges' Patterns Studied," *Jacksonville Journal,* Undated clipping in Harding files accompanying clipping noted in previous footnote.

36. Skene, "Shamefully Flouting the Law," *SPT,* July 10, 1983. (Photocopy in author's files.)

37. 444 So.2d 956 (Fla. Jan. 19, 1984).

38. Magill v. State, 386 So.2d 1188, 1191 (Fla. May 8, 1980).

39. Magill v. State, 428 So.2d 649, 654 (Fla. Mar. 10, 1983) (Boyd dissenting).

40. 387 So.2d 333 (Fla. June 12, 1980).

41. 453 So.2d 786 (Fla. May 24, 1984).

42. 465 So.2d 499 (Fla. Feb. 24, 1985).

43. Proffitt v. State, 360 So.2d 771 (Fla. June 29, 1978) and 372 So.2d 1111 (Fla. June 25, 1979).

44. Proffitt v. Wainwright, 685 F.2d 1227 (11th Cir. Sept. 10, 1982), modified, 706 F.2d 311 (11th Cir. 1982), cert. denied, 464 U.S. 1002 (1983).

45. Proffitt v. State, 510 So.2d 896, 897 (Fla. July 9, 1987).

46. 510 So.2d at 897.

47. 510 So.2d at 897.

48. See Florida Department of Corrections, "Execution List–1976 to Present," http://www.dc.state.fl.us/oth/deathrow/execlist.html.

49. Songer v. State, 322 So.2d 481 (Fla. Sept. 3, 1975).

50. Songer v. Wainwright, 769 F.2d 1488 (11th Cir. Aug. 16, 1985).

51. 769 F.2d at 1489.

52. 438 U.S. 586 (1978).

53. 455 U.S. 104 (1982).

54. Lockett v. Ohio, 438 U.S. 586 (1978), quoting Furman v. Georgia, 408 U.S. at, 304 (1976).

55. Cooper v. State, 336 So.2d 1133, 1139 (Fla. July 8, 1976).

56. 329 So.2d 287 (Fla. Feb. 18, 1976).

57. Skene, *Review of Capital Cases*, at 324 n. 377, citing appendix to petition for writ of habeas corpus, Darden v. Wainwright, Florida Supreme Court Case No. 67,555, 1985.

58. Perry v. State, 395 So.2d 170, 174 (Fla. Dec. 18, 1980).

59. Jacobs v. State, 396 So.2d 713, 718 (Fla., Mar. 26, 1981)

60. Songer v. State, 463 So.2d 229 (Fla. Jan. 31, 1985)

61. Songer v. Wainwright, 769 F.2d 1488 (11th Cir. Aug. 16, 1985)

62. 481 U.S. 393 (Apr. 22, 1987), reversing Hitchcock v. Wainwright, 770 F.2d 1514 (11th Cir. 1985) (en banc).

63. Hitchcock v. Dugger, author's notes from oral argument, Oct. 15, 1986. See also Hitchcock v. Dugger, The Oyez Project at Chicago-Kent College of Law, http://www.oyez.org/cases/1986/85-6756, accessed January 15, 2015.

64. 481 U.S. at 397.

65. 486 So.2d 537 (Fla. Feb. 6, 1986). The original appeal was upheld in Harvard v. State, 414 So.2d 1032 (Fla. Apr. 15, 1982).

66. 490 So.2d 943 (Fla. July 3, 1986).

67. 486 So.2d at 537.

68. Hitchcock v. State, 413 So.2d 741 (Fla. Feb. 25, 1982). See also Hitchcock v. State, 991 So.2d 337 (Fla. May 22, 2008).

69. Songer v. State, 544 So.2d 1010 (Fla. May 25, 1989)

70. 544 So.2d at 1011.

Chapter 25. Sovereign Immunity: Suing City Hall

1. Mike McKee, "Driving on Beach 'The Craziest Thing I've Ever Heard of,'" *Orlando Sentinel*, Aug. 4, 1985, accessed online at http://articles.orlandosentinel.com/1985-08-04/news/0320060247_1_daytona-beach-beach-driving-beach-shores.

2. Fla. Const. Art IV, Sec. 19 (1868).

3. An excellent recounting of the history of sovereign immunity in Florida is by Eleventh Circuit Judge Gerald T. Wetherington of Miami-Dade and Eleventh Circuit court administrator Donald I. Pollock, "Tort Suits Against Governmental Entities in Florida," 44 UF L. Rev. 1 (Jan. 1992).

4. Fla. Stat. 768.28.

5. Commercial Carrier Corp. v. Indian River County, 342 So.2d 1047, 1049 (Fla. 3rd DCA 1977)

6. Cheney v. Dade County, 353 So.2d 623 (Fla. 3rd DCA 1977).

7. 371 So.2d 1010 (Fla. Apr. 19, 1979).

8. 371 So.2d at 1016.

9. 371 So.2d at 1022.

10. 371 So.2d at 1023.

11. Cauley v. City of Jacksonville, 403 So.2d 379 (Fla. July 16, 1981).

12. 419 So.2d 1071 (Fla. Sept. 14, 1982).

13. Collom v. City of St. Petersburg, 400 So.2d 507 (Fla. 2nd DCA 1981).

14. Mathews v. City of St. Petersburg, Fla., 400 So.2d 841 (Fla. 2nd DCA 1981).

15. City of St. Petersburg v. Collom, 419 So.2d 1082 (Fla. Sept. 14, 1982).

16. Talmadge v. District School Board of Lake County, 355 So.2d 502 (Fla. 2nd DCA 1978).

17. 381 So.2d 698 (Fla. Feb. 14, 1980).

18. Department of Transportation v. Knowles, 402 So.2d 1155 (Fla. June 25, 1981).

19. The account of the oral argument is from Skene, "Injured Visitor Attacks Idea of Cars on Sands of Daytona Beach," SPT, Dec. 10, 1982.

20. 471 So.2d 1 (Fla. Feb. 17, 1983)

21. Al Truesdell, "Daytona, Woman May Settle Beach-driving Suit Today," Orlando Sentinel, June 3, 1987, accessible at http://articles.orlandosentinel.com/1987-06-03/news/0130280206 _1_florida-supreme-fetsko-ralph.

22. Harrison v. Escambia County School Board, 434 So.2d 316 (Fla. July 7, 1983).

23. 468 So.2d 912 (Fla. April 4, 1985).

24. 468 So. 2d at 919.

25. 468 So. 2d 929 (Fla. April 4, 1985).

26. 468 So. 2d 955 (Fla. April 4, 1985).

27. 469 So. 2d 121 (Fla. April 4, 1985).

28. 468 So. 2d 936 (Fla. April 4, 1985).

Chapter 26. Constitutional Amendments: Tinkering with Democracy

1. Proposition 13 is the focus of Nordlinger v. Hahn, 505 U.S. 1 (June 18, 1992), in which the U.S. Supreme Court rejected claims that Proposition 13 violated the federal Constitution.

2. 238 So.2d 824 (Fla. July 30, 1970).

3. 238 So.2d at 836.

4. Obituary: "Charles H. Weber, Ex-state Senator," Sun-Sentinel, May 13, 1989, accessible at http://articles.sun-sentinel.com/1989-05-13/news/8901240951_1_mr-weber-wilton-manors-fort-lauderdale-board.

5. 338 So.2d 819 (Fla. Oct. 11, 1976).

6. The list and results of initiatives are available from the Florida Secretary of State in the elections database, available at http://dos.elections.myflorida.com/initiatives/.

7. See Osterndorf v. Turner, 426 So.2d 539 (Fla. Dec. 16, 1982), striking down a five-year wait for the higher exemption.

8. Fla. Laws Chap. 80-305; Fla. Stat. Sec. 101.161 (1).

9. 421 So. 2d 151 (Fla. Oct. 21, 1982).

10. The case cited was Hill v. Milander, 72 So.2d 796 (Fla. 1954).

11. Skene, "Citizens' Choice Day in Court: Is It One Subject or Many?" *SPT,* Sept. 29, 1983.

12. Fine v. Firestone, 443 So.2d 253 (1st DCA 1983).

13. 448 So.2d 984 (Fla. Mar. 27, 1984).

14. Skene, "Citizens' Choice Thrown Off Ballot," *SPT,* Mar. 28, 1984, p. 1-B

15. Skene, "Citizens' Choice Backers Want Justices Removed," *SPT,* Jun 7, 1984.

16. Gibson v. Firestone, 741 F.2d 1268 (11th Cir. 1984).

17. 457 So.2d 1351 (Fla. Oct. 3, 1984).

18. Ballot Amendment 4, General Election 1984.

Chapter 27. Open Government and Privacy: The Forsberg Saga

1. Skene, "Court Again Considers Issue of Privacy, Public Records," *SPT,* June 6, 1984.

2. Skene, *SPT,* Oct. 2, 1983.

3. Attorney General Opinion 77-69.

4. So.2d 693 (Fla. 1969).

5. Adkins, *Eighteen Years,* 11 Nova L. Rev. at 19-20.

6. 224 So.2d 699.

7. 245 So. 2d 38 (Fla. Jan. 27, 1971).

8. 262 So.2d 425 (Fla. May 17, 1972).

9. Canney v. Board of Public Instruction of Alachua County, 231 So.2d 32 (Fla. 1st DCA 1970).

10. 278 So.2d 260 (Fla. Apr. 6, 1973).

11. 296 So.2d 473 (Fla. May 1, 1974).

12. In re Advisory Opinion to the Governor, 334 So.2d 561 (Fla. June 23, 1976).

13. Occidental Chemical Co. v. Mayo, 351 So.2d 336, 342 (Fla. July 14, 1977).

14. Tribune Company v. School Board of Hillsborough County, 367 So.2d 627 (Fla. Feb. 1, 1979).

15. Wisher v. News-Press Pub. Co., 310 So.2d 345, 348 (Fla. 2nd DCA, 1977).

16. 345 So.2d 646 (Fla. Feb. 25, 1977).

17. 427 U.S. 539 (June 30, 1976).

18. State ex rel. Miami Herald Publishing Co. v. McIntosh, 320 So.2d 861 (Fla. 4th DCA 1975).

19. 340 So.2d 904 (Fla. July 30, 1976).

20. 443 U.S. 368 (July 2, 1979).

21. 448 U.S. 555, 581 fn. 18 (July 2, 1980).

22. 426 So.2d 1 (Fla. Sept. 2, 1982).

23. The Florida Bar In re Advisory Opinion Concerning the Applicability of Chapter 119, 398 So.2d 446 (Fla. Apr. 30, 1981).

24. Dyckman, "Adkins Would Open Court Conference," *SPT,* June 19, 1975.

25. 379 So.2d 633 (Fla. Jan. 17, 1980).

26. State ex rel. Tindel v. Sharp, 300 So.2d 750 (Fla. 1st DCA 1974), *cert. denied,* 310 So.2d 745 (Fla. March 20, 1975).

27. See the First DCA's opinion in the case, 360 So.2d 83, 86 (Fla. 1st DCA 1978).

28. 342 So.2d 962 (Fla. Feb. 10, 1977).

29. Interview with Tom Julin, June 12, 2015.

30. Moffitt v. Willis, 459 So.2d 1018 (Fla. Oct. 18, 1984)

31. Virginia Ellis, *SPT,* Oct. 16, 1977.

32. The memo is in the Supreme Court archives in a large folder from Overton's office labeled "Privacy."

33. The draft opinions and vote sheets are in the Supreme Court archives from Sundberg's office, Sundberg Series 1, Box 4, File No. 193.

34. Florida Board of Bar Examiners Re: Applicant, 443 So.2d 71, No. 63161 (Fla. Nov. 3 1983).

35. Florida Board of Bar Examiners Re: Applicant, 443 So.2d 77, No. 60550 (Fla. Nov. 10, 1983).

36. See footnote 1 of the Cannella decision, 458 So.2d 1075, 1079 (Fla. Sept. 6, 1984).

37. 455 So.2d 373 (Fla. Aug. 30, 1984).

38. 464 So.2d 545 (Fla. Feb. 21, 1985).

Chapter 28. Chief Justice Boyd: The Passover Ends

1. Author's interview with James Logue, Dec. 28, 2011.

2. 287 So.2d 78 (Fla. July 18, 1973), reversed, Miami Herald Pub. Co. v. Tornillo, 418 U.S. 241 (1974).

3. Gardner v. Florida, 430 U.S. 349 (1977), reversing Gardner v. State, 313 So.2d 675 (Fla. 1975).

4. Argersinger v. Hamlin, 407 U.S. 25 (1972), reversing State ex rel. Argersinger v. Hamlin, 236 So.2d 442 (Fla. 1970).

5. State ex rel. Argersinger v. Hamlin, 236 So.2d 442, 445 (Fla. June 3, 1970).

6. See also Manley and Brown, *Florida Supreme Court 1917–1972,* pp. 320–325.

7. Author's interview with Randall Reder, March 20, 2012.

8. Skene *SPT,* May 1, 1984, p. 1-B.

9. Linda H. Yates, "In the Chief Justice's Office," *Florida Bar Journal* p. 497, 499 (October 1984).

Chapter 29. Criminal Law: To Establish Justice

1. Author's interview with John L. Zavertnik, May 5, 2015.

2. The description of the circuit court proceedings is taken from the briefs filed at the Florida Supreme Court and from the author's interview with John L. Zavertnik.

3. James R. Jorgensen, "Back To The Laboratory With Peremptory Challenges: A Florida Response," 12 FSU L. Rev. 559 (1984–85). The author's footnote says, "This article incorporates substantial portions of the author's thesis submitted for an LL.M. degree in Judicial Process received in 1984 from the University of Virginia."

4. Petitioner's Initial Brief on the Merits, Neil v. State, Case No. 63899 and 63933, p. 32. The descriptions of the cases are drawn from this brief.

5. A detailed history of the Florida Supreme Court's tolerance of all-white juries is in Sylvia H. Walbolt and Andrew D. Manko, *From Chattel to Justice* (Florida Supreme Court Historical Society), accessible at http://www.flcourthistory.org/From-Chattel-to-Justice.

6. State v. Silva, 259 So.2d 153 (Fla .Feb. 22, 1972).

7. Shepherd. v. Florida, 341 U.S. 50 (1951), reversing Shepherd v. State, 46 So.2d. 880 (Fla. 1950). The basis for the reversal is discussed in *Silva*, 259 So.2d at 158.

8. Hall v. State, 136 Fla. 644 (Fla. 1939).

9. 259 So.2d at 164.

10. Andrews v. State, 483 So.2d 480 (Fla. 3rd DCA 1983).

11. Skene, "Do Away with Discrimination in Jury Selection," *St. Petersburg Times*, May 13, 1984.

12. Author's interview with Justice Parker Lee McDonald, May 5, 2015.

13. 457 So.2d 481 (Fla., Sept. 27, 1984), clarified as applying to then-pending cases that had raised the issue, State v. Castillo, 486 So.2d 565 (Fla. March 20, 1986).

14. Andrews v. State, 459 So.2d 1018 (Fla. Oct. 4, 1984).

15. 476 U.S. 79 (Apr. 30, 1986).

16. 522 So.2d 18 (Fla. Mar. 10, 1988). See also two other cases decided the same day: Tillman v. State, 522 So.2d 14 (Fla. Mar. 10, 1988) and Blackshear v. State, 521 So.2d 1083 (Fla. Mar. 10, 1988).

17. Stephen H. Grimes, *Distinguished Law Week Lecture: Judicial Decision-Making in Florida's Appellate Courts*, U. Fla. Journal of Law & Public Policy, vol. 1, p. 3 (1987).

18. 546 So.2d 710 (Fla. June 15, 1989).

19. 546 So.2d 1042 (Fla. July 6, 1989).

20. State v. Singletary, 549 So.2d 996 (Fla., Aug. 31, 1989).

21. 360 So. 2d 760 (Fla. Apr. 5, 1978).

22. Clark v. State, 363 So. 2d 331 (Fla. July 28, 1978).

23. Adkins, *Eighteen Years*, at 12–13.

24. Author's interview with John W. Tanner, May 22, 2015.

25. 443 So.2d 955 (Fla. Jan 12, 1984).

26. 491 So.2d 1129 (Fla. July 17, 1986).

27. Rowe v. State, 98 So. 613, 618 (Fla. 1924).

28. 67 So.2d 321 (Fla. 1957).

29. 316 So.2d 41 (Fla. July 15, 1975).

30. Citations are omitted from the quoted passage.

31. 461 U.S. 499 (May 23, 1983).

32. McDonald cited Clark v. State, 363 So.2d 331 (Fla. July 28, 1978) as well as Chapman v. California. Citations are omitted from this quotation of the passage.

33. 490 So.2d 21 (Fla. Aug. 30, 1985).

34. See discussion of the *DiGuilio* case in Tom Stacy and Kim Dayton, *Rethinking Harmless Error*, 88 Colum. L. Rev. 79, 126 (1988).

Chapter 30. "Rosemary the First"

1. Madelyn Miller, Associated Press, "Supreme Court Gets Second Black Justice Ever," *St. Petersburg Times*, Jan. 11, 1983.

2. Elements of Barkett's childhood were from Irma Barkett Elder's remarks at a Ceremonial Session of the Florida Supreme Court for an Oral History of Rosemary Barkett, Apr. 19, 1996.

3. Pariente spoke at a Ceremonial Session of the Florida Supreme Court for an Oral History of Rosemary Barkett, Apr. 19, 1996.

4. Deborah Petit, "She Traded Nun's Habit for Robes of a Judge, And It Suited Her Well," *Ft.*

Lauderdale Sun-Sentinel, Oct. 3, 1985, accessible at http://articles.sun-sentinel.com/1985-10-03/news/8502110786_1_rosemary-barkett-robes-farish.

5. Linda Kleindienst and Deborah Petit, *Ft. Lauderdale Sun-Sentinel*, Oct. 3, 1985, accessible at http://articles.sun-sentinel.com/1985-10-03/news/8502110836_1_rosemary-barkett-gavin-letts-high-court.

6. Craig Crawford, For State Supreme Court 1st Woman Justice Takes Oath," *Orlando Sentinel*, Nov. 16, 1985, accessible at http://articles.orlandosentinel.com/1985-11-16/news/0340370044_1_barkett-justices-court-of-appeal.

7. Crawford, ibid.

8. Charles Fishman, "Rosemary Barkett: The Supreme Court Justice Who Mixes Law, Patsy Cline Tunes and Limpkins," *Orlando Sentinel*, March 18, 1990, accessible at http://articles.orlandosentinel.com/1990-03-18/news/9002282331_1_rosemary-barkett-wakulla-springs-court-justice.

9. Ehrlich's comments were from a Ceremonial Session of the Florida Supreme Court for an Oral History of Rosemary Barkett, Apr. 19, 1996.

10. Cox v. State, 555 So.2d 352 (Fla. Dec. 21, 1989), rehearing denied, Feb. 12, 1990.

11. 551 So.2d 1186 (Fla. Oct. 5, 1989).

12. Linda Kleindienst, "Justice's Record On Bench Gets Attention From All Sides," *Ft. Lauderdale Sun-Sentinel*, Oct. 21, 1992, accessible at http://articles.sun-sentinel.com/1992-10-21/news/9202240748_1_justice-barkett-three-other-justices-chief-justice.

13. Author's Interview with Rosemary Barkett, Aug. 25, 2013.

14. 554 So.2d 1153 (Fla. Nov. 30, 1989).

15. Author's Interview with Barkett.

16. Ceremonial Session, April 19, 1996.

Chapter 31. Virgil Hawkins: Crossing the Bar

1. Jeffrey L. Bleich, Benjamin J. Horwich and Joshua S. Meltzer, "Righting a Historic Wrong," *California Supreme Court Historical Society Newsletter*, p. 2 (Spring/Summer 2015).

2. The Florida Supreme Court opinion admitting Hawkins, In Re: Florida Board of Bar Examiners, 339 So.2d 637 (Fla., Nov. 12, 1976), contained the following summary of the Hawkins litigation: State ex rel. Hawkins v. Board of Control, 53 So.2d 116 (Fla. 1950), cert. denied, 342 U.S. 8779 (1951); State ex rel. Hawkins v. Board of Control, 60 So.2d 162 (Fla.1952), vacated and remanded, 347 U.S. 971 (1954); Relief upon mandate withheld, 83 So.2d 20 (Fla.1955), mandate recalled and modified, cert. denied, 350 U.S. 413 (1956), relief upon mandate withheld, 93 So.2d 354 (Fla. 1957), cert. denied without prejudice, 355 U.S. 839 (1957).

3. "Browner Speaks at Graduation, Hawkins Awarded Honorary Degree, FlaLaw Online, June 4, 2001, accessible at http://www.law.ufl.edu/flalaw/2001/06/browner-speaks-at-graduation-hawkins-awarded-honorary-degree/.

4. Harley Herman, *Anatomy of a Bar Resignation: The Virgil Hawkins' Story: An Idealist Faces the Pragmatic Challenges of the Practice of Law*, 2 Florida Coastal L.J. 77 (Fall 2000).

5. Manley and Brown, The Supreme Court of Florida 1917–1972 (2006).

6. See Gilbert King, *Devil in the Grove* (New York: Harper Perennial 2012).

7. 339 U.S. 629 (1950).

8. State *ex rel.* Hawkins v. Board of Control, 93 So.2d 354, 359 (1957).

9. Herman, "Anatomy of a Bar Resignation," at p. 4, and note from Martin Dyckman re: his telephone interview with Charles Hicks (Hawkins classmate), June 13, 2013.

10. In Re: Florida Bd. of Bar Examiners In Re: Ervin, 290 So.2d 9 (Fla. Jan. 30, 1974).

11. 168 So.2d 318 (Fla. 1964).

12. The draft opinions are quoted at length in Herman, "Anatomy of a Bar Resignation."

13. Florida Bar v. Hawkins, 467 So.2d 998 (Fla. Apr. 18, 1985), which includes citations to earlier reprimands.

14. Barbara Stewart, "'The Law and Virgil Hawkins," *Orlando Sentinel* Sunday magazine, Mar. 8, 1987, 14 at p. 17, cited in Herman, "Anatomy of a Bar Resignation."

15. Associated Press, "Virgil D. Hawkins; Broke Color Barrier to Become Lawyer," *New York Times*, February 15, 1988.

16. In re Hawkins, 532 So. 2d 669 (Fla. Oct. 20, 1988).

17. Jo Becker, "State Court Honors Civil Rights Pioneer," *SPT*, May 26, 1999, p. 1-B.

BIBLIOGRAPHY

Primary Sources

Interviews

Adkins Jr., James C. Interviewed by Neil Skene, approximately 1983, Tallahassee, Florida.

Alderman, James E. Interviewed by Neil Skene, January 24, 2013, Alderman Ranch, Yeehaw Junction, Florida.

Anstead, Harry Lee. Interviewed by Neil Skene, October 28, 2013 and November 11, 2013, Tallahassee.

Askew, Reubin. Informal Conversations with Neil Skene, January 23, 2011, January 7, 2013, and December 4, 2013, Tallahassee.

Baggett, Fred. Interviewed by Neil Skene and Jennifer Skene, May 30, 2012, Tallahassee.

Barkett, Rosemary. Interviewed by Hank Coxe, January 30, 2014, Florida Supreme Court Historical Society Dinner, Tallahassee.

Barkett, Rosemary. Interviewed by Neil Skene, August 18, 2013, Coral Gables, Florida, and by telephone, July 15, 2015.

Benton, Robert. Interviewed by Neil Skene, December 19, 2011, Tallahassee.

Berg Jr., Randall C. Interviewed by Neil Skene, August 18, 2013, Coral Gables.

Burr, David. Interviewed by Amy Hilliard. Undated, Southwest Florida Oral History Project, "The Battle for Estero Bay 1959–1980." Florida Gulf Coast University. Last accessed May 12, 2015. http://ruby.fgcu.edu/courses/jkent/81180/Main%20oral%20history%20project/estero/Burr/burr.htm.

Cacciatore, S. Sammy. Interviewed by Neil Skene by telephone, July 9, 2013, and by e-mail, July 12, 2013, and May 27, 2014.

Cantero, Raoul. Interviewed by Neil Skene, October 27. 3009, Miami, Florida.

Conigliaro, Matthew. Interviewed by Neil Skene, July 11, 2012, St. Petersburg, Florida.

D'Alemberte, Talbot. Interviewed by Neil Skene, June 5, 2010, and June 21, 2012, Tallahassee.

Davis, Marguerite. Interviewed by Neil Skene, August 29, 2012 and September 19, 2012, Tallahassee, and August 16, 2015 by e-mail.

Dyckman, Martin. Interviewed by Neil Skene, August 31, 2009, Tallahassee.

Earle Jr., Richard T. Interviewed by Denise Stobbie. December 16, 1986. http://ufdc.ufl.edu//UF00007675/00001.

Ehrlich, Raymond. Transcript, Raymond Ehrlich Oral History Interview with Denise Stobbie, December 20, 1990, Samuel Proctor Oral History Program Collection, P. K. Yonge Library of Florida History, University of Florida, Gainesville.

England Jr., Arthur J. Interviewed by Neil Skene, October 25, 2009, October 26, 2009, and November 6, 2012, Coral Gables, and August 30, 2011, Miami, Florida.

Flagler Live, "John Canakaris, Father of Flagler County Medicine and Humanitarian is Dead at 90." December 4, 2012. Accessible at http://flaglerlive.com/47716/john-canakaris-obituary.

Freidin, Philip. Interviewed by Neil Skene, by telephone, January 24, 2016.

Graham, Bob. Interviewed by Neil Skene, approximately May 1981 (among multiple occasions), Tallahassee.

Grimes, Stephen H. Interviewed by Neil Skene, August 7, 2010, January 31, 2013, and January 17, 2015, Tallahassee.

Hall, Tom. Interviewed by Neil Skene, July 22, 2013, Tallahassee.

Harding, Major B. Interviewed by Neil Skene, August 7, 2010 and May 20, 2015, Tallahassee.

Harkness, John F. Jr. Interviewed by Neil Skene, Sept. 22, 2013. Tallahassee.

Hatchett, Joseph W. Interviewed by Neil Skene, October 25, 2011, Tallahassee.

Hicks, Charles. Interviewed by Martin Dyckman by telephone, June 13, 2013. Interviewer's notes provided to the author.

Julin, Tom. Interview by Neil Skene by telephone, June 12, 2015.

Kogan, Gerald. Interviewed by Neil Skene, October 27, 2009, Coral Gables, Florida.

Kirk, Claude R. Interviewed by Sid Johnston, December 16, 1986, University of Florida Oral History Program. http://ufdc.ufl.edu//UF00007670/00001.

Klock, Joseph R. Interviewed by Neil Skene through e-mail, August 28, 2015, Tallahassee.

Logue, James. Interviewed by Neil Skene, December 28, 2011. Tallahassee.

Marky, Raymond. Interviewed by Neil Skene, 1986, Tallahassee.

McDonald, Parker Lee. Interviewed by Neil Skene, August 7, 2010, and January 17, 2013, Tallahassee, and by telephone, May 5, 2015.

Newton, John. Interviewed by Neil Skene, January 11, 2012, and August 6, 2014, Tallahassee.

Overton, Ben. Interviewed by Neil Skene, November 15, 2009, October 22, 2010, June 19, 2012, Gainesville, Florida, and by telephone November 5, 2012.

Overton, Ben. Interviewed by Samuel Proctor. Transcript in University of Florida College of Law Oral History Collection, October 28, 1994. http://ufdc.ufl.edu/UF00006381/00001.

Pariente, Barbara J. Interviewed by Neil Skene, January 30, 2014, Tallahassee.

Parks, Robert. Interviewed by Neil Skene by telephone, February 22, 2012.

Pelham, Thomas. Interviewed by Neil Skene by telephone, May 15, 2015.

Proctor, Martin. Interviewed by Neil Skene, January 11, 2012, Tallahassee.

Quince, Peggy A. Interviewed by Neil Skene and Hallee Moore, January 31, 2013.

Reeder, Randall. Interviewed by Neil Skene, March 20, 2012, Tampa.

Rhoads, Howard. Interviewed by Mary Evans. Undated, Southwest Florida Oral History Project, "The Battle for Estero Bay 1959–1980." Florida Gulf Coast University. Last accessed May 15, 2015. http://ruby.fgcu.edu/courses/jkent81180/Main%20oral%20history%20project/estero/Rhodes/rhoades.htm.

Richard, Barry. Interviewed by Neil Skene, July 18, 2014, Tallahassee.

Shlakman, Mark. Interviewed by Neil Skene and Jennifer Skene, June 24, 2011.

Smith, Chesterfield H. Interviewed by Julian Pleasants. Oral History Interview of Chesterfield H. Smith, pp. 3, 15, and 32. January 14, 2000, and March 9, 2000. University of Florida Oral History Program. http://ufdc.ufl.edu//UF00006389/00001.

Smith, William Reece. Interviewed by Neil Skene, March 21, 2012.

Smith, Sharyn. Interviewed by Neil Skene by telephone, April 25, 2015.

Steffens, Betty. Interviewed by Neil Skene, October 10, 2012, Tallahassee.

Sundberg, Richard. Interviewed by Neil Skene, by telephone, November 11, 2012.

Tanner, John W. Interviewed by Neil Skene by telephone, May 22, 2015.

Tucker, Donald C. Conversation with Neil Skene, November 27, 2015.

Walbolt, Sylvia. Interviewed by Neil Skene by telephone, July 26, 2012.

Wright, Wilson. Interviewed by Neil Skene, February 1, 2012, Tallahassee.

Zaiser, Kent. Interviewed by Neil Skene, June 28, 2012.

Zavertnik, John L. Interviewed by Neil Skene by telephone, May 5, 2015.

Manuscripts

Dyckman, Martin. Summary of papers of a report regarding an examination of Joseph W. Boyd, May 13–16, 1975, attached to a letter from Richard Earle to W. J. Rish, dated June 16, 1975. Summary in Florida State Archives, Florida Supreme Court, House Impeachment Investigation, Series 19, Carton 355, folder 1, Tallahassee.

Harding, Major B., Scrapbook (CD-ROM).

Smith, Chesterfield. Personal papers. Chesterfield Smith Papers, George Smathers Library, University of Florida, Gainesville.

Court Documents and Public Records

Adkins, James C. Adkins Files Series 2, Opinion Files Box 5, File No. 549 and 589. Florida Supreme Court Archives, Tallahassee.

Attorney General of Florida Opinion 77–69.

Commission on Capital Case Histories. http://www.floridacapitalcases.state.fl.us/Documents/Publications/casehistory05-13-11%20Report.pdf.

Cox v. State, Reply Brief of Appellant Cox, filed July 11, 1989. Florida Supreme Court archive at Florida State University Law School, Tallahassee. Case No. 73150, Accessible at http://archive.law.fsu.edu/library/flsupct/73150/73150rep.pdf.

Florida Commission on Capital Cases. "Appellate Time Frames: A Comprehensive Statistical Examination. (May 13, 2011). Accessible at http://www.floridacapitalcases.state.fl.us/Publications/Appellate%20Time%20Frame%20Statistics%20&%20Appendix2.pdf.

Florida Commission on Capital Cases, Florida Capital Cases. Robert Craig Cox. Report dated March 9, 2002. Accessible at http://www.floridacapitalcases.state.fl.us/Documents/Case_updates/Htm/113377.htm.

Florida Department of Corrections website list of executions through 1964. http://www.dc.state.fl.us/oth/deathrow/execlist2.html.

Florida Department of Corrections website list of executions under the 1972 statute. http://www.dc.state.fl.us/oth/deathrow/execlist.html.

Florida House of Representatives Select Committee on Impeachment: Inquiry Into Justice McCain, Vol. III. April 10, 1975 (Transcript). Copy in files of Martin Dyckman.

Florida Secretary of State, Ballot Amendment 4, General Election 1984.

Florida Secretary of State elections database. Available at http://dos.elections.myflorida.com/initiatives/.

Hitchcock v. Dugger. The Oyez Project at Chicago-Kent College of Law, Chicago. Accessed January 15, 2015. http://www.oyez.org/cases/1980-1989/1986/1986_85_6756.

Journal of the Florida House of Representatives

Journal of the Senate

Judicial Council of Florida, Annual Reports

Neil v. State, Petitioner's Initial Brief on the Merits, Neil v. State, Case No. 63899 and 63933, p. 32. In author's files.

Office of the Auditor General. Audit of Supreme Court of Florida for fiscal years ending June 30, 1976, and June 30, 1977.

Overton, Ben. Privacy folder. Florida Supreme Court Archives, Tallahassee.

Shaw, Leander. Transcript, Leander Shaw Retirement Ceremony. November 8, 2002. In Author's Files.

Sundberg, Alan C. Handwritten draft, Sundberg Series 1, Box 6, File Nos. 326 and 435. Florida Supreme Court Archives, Tallahassee.

Sundberg, Alan C. Sundberg Files, Series 1, Box 2, File No. 92. Florida Supreme Court Archives, Tallahassee.

Sundberg, Alan C. Sundberg Files Series 5, Chief Justice Files Box 3, File 94. Florida Supreme Court Archives, Tallahassee.

Sundberg, Alan C. Memorial Service for. Supreme Court of Florida, January 29, 2002 (Transcript). Available at http://wfsu.org/gavel2gavel/transcript/pdfs/SundbergCerem.pdf.

Supreme Court of Florida. 1979 Report on the Florida Judiciary. http://www.floridasupremecourt.org/pub_info/documents/1979_Report_On_The_Judiciary.pdf.

United States Courts. "Judiciary Approves Pilot Project for Cameras in District Courts." http://www.uscourts.gov/news/2010/09/14/judiciary-approves-pilot-project-cameras-district-courts September 14, 2010.

U.S. House of Representatives, Office of History and Preservation, "Black Americans in Congress." Washington, D.C. http://history.house.gov/People/Detail/23324?ret=True.

Secondary Sources

Books

Allman, T. D., Finding Florida: The True History of the Sunshine State, p. 302–305. New York: Atlantic Monthly Press, 2013.

Dale, Nancy. The Legacy of the Florida Pioneer Cow Hunters: In Their Own Words. iUniverse, 2011.

D'Alemberte, Talbot. The Florida State Constitution. Oxford University Press. 2011.

Dyckman, Martin. A Most Disorderly Court. Gainesville: University Press of Florida, 2008.

Dyckman, Martin. Floridian of His Century: The Courage of Governor LeRoy Collins. Gainesville: University Press of Florida, 2006.

Dyckman, Martin. Reubin O'D. Askew and the Golden Age of Florida Politics. Gainesville: University Press of Florida, 2011.

Giles, Robert H., and Robert W. Snyder. Covering the Courts: Free Press, Fair Trials & Journalistic Performance. Transaction Publishers, 1999.

Graham, Katharine. Personal History. New York: Alfred A. Knopf, Inc., 1997.

Karl, Frederick B. The 57 Club: My Four Decades in Florida Politics. Gainesville: University Press of Florida, 2010.

King, Gilbert. Devil in the Grove. New York: Harper Perennial, 2012.

Klingman, Peter D. Josiah Walls: Florida's Black Congressman of Reconstruction. Gainesville: University Press of Florida, 1976.

Manley II, Walter W., and Canter Brown Jr. *The Supreme Court of Florida, 1917–1972.* Gainesville: University Press of Florida, 2006. (Also cited as Supreme Court History Volume II.)

McKinney, June C. and Janeia R. Daniels, eds. *Florida's First Black Lawyers, 1969–1979.* Virgil Hawkins Chapter of the National Bar Association, 2009.

Mello, Michael. A *Death Row Lawyer Speaks Out Against Capital Punishment.* University of Wisconsin Press, 1999.

Miller, Gene. *Invitation to a Lynching.* New York: Doubleday, 1975.

Morris, Allen, and Joan Morris. *Florida Handbook 2011–2012.* Tallahassee: Peninsular Publishing Company, 2011.

Nelson-Morrill, Creston. *Workers' Compensation in Florida 1935–1995: The History, People & Politics.* Florida Workers' Compensation Institute and HealthTrac Books, 1995.

Skene, Katie. "Lucy Morgan," in Sherri Winsett, ed. *Treasures of Our Past, Lawton Chiles High School.* Tallahassee: Harvest Printing & Copy Center Inc., 2009.

Skene, Neil. "Reapportionment in Florida," in *The Florida Handbook* (2013–2014 ed.), published by the Florida House of Representatives.

Vause, W. Gary. *Florida's First Law School.* Durham, NC: Carolina Academic Press, 2006.

Von Drehle, David. *Among the Lowest of the Dead: The Culture of Capital Punishment.* New York: Times Books, 1995.

Wasson, Roy D. "The Judges of the Third District Court of Appeal," in Kathleen M. O'Connor and Edward M. Guedes, eds., *Florida's Third District Court of Appeal: 50 Years 1957–2007,* ed. Centennial Press, 2007.

West Publishing Company, *Federal Reporter.*

West Publishing Company, *Southern Reporter.*

Woodward, Bob, and Scott Armstrong, *The Brethren.* New York: Simon and Schuster, 1979.

Legal Periodicals

Adkins, James C. "Yesterday." *Florida Supreme Court Historical Society Newsletter.* Undated copy in author's files.

Adkins, James C., with Leonard K Samuels and Paul Hampton Crockett. "Eighteen Years in the Judicial Catbird Seat." 11 *Nova Law Review* 1 (1986).

Alschuler, Albert W. "Plea-Bargaining and the Death Penalty." 58 *DePaul Law Reiew* 671 (2009).

Berkson, Larry C. and Steven W. Hays. "The Unmaking of a Court Administrator," 60 *Judicature* (No. 3, October 1976).

Blankenship, Gary Lee. "Parker Lee McDonald: Chief Justice of the Supreme Court." 60 *Florida Bar Journal* 11 (1986).

Bleich, Jeffrey L., Benjamin J. Horwich, and Joshua S. Meltzer. "Righting a Historic Wrong," California Supreme Court Historical Society Newsletter, p. 2 (Spring/Summer 2015).

Bosselman, Red and Callies, David. "The Quiet Revolution in Land Use Control." Council on Environmental Quality, Washington, D.C. (December 1971).

Boyd Jr., Joseph A. "Looking Back on Eighteen Years as a Justice of the Supreme Court of Florida." 11 *Nova Law Review* 25 (1986).

Caffrey, Denise, "United States v. CBS: When Sketch Artists Are Allowed in the Courtroom, Can Photographers Be Far Behind?" 1875 *Duke Law Journal* 188.

D'Alemberte, Talbot. "The Role of the Courts in Providing Legal Services: A Proposal to Provide Legal Access for the Poor." 17 *Florida State University Law Review* 107 (1989–1990).

D'Alemberte, Talbot. "Tributaries of Justice: The Search for Full Access." *Florida Bar Journal*, (April 1999).

Ehrhardt, Charles W., and Harold Levinson, "Florida's Legislative Response to Furman: An Exercise in Futility?" 64 *Journal of Criminal Law & Criminology* (March 1973).

England Jr., Arthur J. Lecture at Yale Law School, New Haven, Connecticut, April 18, 1985. A transcript of his remarks appears in Robert A. Burt, "Disorder in the Court: The Death Penalty and the Constitution." Faculty Scholarship Series. Paper 804 (1987). Last accessed December 12, 2012. http://digitalcommons.law.yale.edu/fss_papers/804.

England Jr., Arthur J. "Cameras in Courts: Driving From Failure Toward Success." *Florida Bar Journal* (April 2009).

England Jr., Arthur J. and Russell E. Carlisle, "History of Interest on Trust Accounts Program." *Florida Bar Journal* (February 2001).

England Jr., Arthur J., Eleanor Mitchell Hunter, and Richard C. Williams Jr., "Constitutional Jurisdiction of the Supreme Court of Florida: 1980 Reform." 32 *University of Florida Law Review* 153 (Winter 1980).

England Jr., Arthur J., and Richard C. Williams Jr., "Florida Appellate Reform One Year Later." *Florida State University Law Review* 221 (Spring 1981).

Gentile, Melinda. "Property Distribution Upon Dissolution of Marriage: Florida's Need for an Equitable Distribution Statute." 8 *Nova Law Journal* 71 (1983).

Grimes, Stephen H. "Distinguished Law Week Lecture: Judicial Decision-Making in Florida's Appellate Courts." *University of Florida Journal of Law & Policy*, vol. 1 (1987).

Herman, Harley. "Anatomy of a Bar Resignation: The Virgil Hawkins' Story: An Idealist Faces the Pragmatic Challenges of the Practice of Law." 2 *Florida Coastal Law Journal* 77 (Fall 2000).

Jacob, Bruce R. "Memories of and Reflections About Gideon v. Wainwright." 33 *Stetson Law Review* 181 (2003).

Jorgensen, James R. "Back to the Laboratory with Peremptory Challenges: A Florida Response." 12 *Florida State Law University Law Review* 559 (1984–85).

Katheder, Thomas. "Lovers and Other Strangers: When Is a House a Castle?" 11 *Florida State University Law Review* 465 (Summer 1983).

Kidder, William C. "The Struggle for Access from Sweatt to Grutter: A History of African American, Latino and American Indian Law School Admissions, 1950–2000." 19 *Harvard Black Letter Law Journal* 1 (2003).

Killian, Mark D. "Chief Justice Shaw." *Florida Bar Journal* 12 (October 1990).

Lenox, David Richard. "Should the Florida Supreme Court Replace the Impact Rule with a Foreseeability Analysis?" 11 *Florida State University Law Review* 229 (Spring 1983).

Levinson, Harold. "The Levinson Report." Co-sponsored by University of Florida and the Florida Bar. (1970).

Mello, Michael. "In the Years When Murder Wore the Mask of Law: Diary of a Capital Appeals Lawyer (1983–1986)." 24 *Vermont. Law Review* 583 (2000).

Office of State Courts Administrator. "Memory Book: 40th Anniversary Office of State Courts Administrator"(July 2012).

Overton, Ben F. "Relieving an Overworked State Supreme Court: Florida Asks Its Courts of Appeal to Assist in Screening Cases," 66 *Judicature* 371 (March 1983).

Pudlow, Jan. "Terry Russell: President of the Bar." *Florida Bar Journal* (July/August 2001). Accessible at http://www.floridabar.org/DIVCOM/JN/JNJournal01.nsf/Author/DCA4D-5083727394D85256B100071CDAF.

Radelet, Michael L., and Margaret Vandiver. "The Florida Supreme Court and Death Penalty Appeals." *Journal of Criminal Law and Criminology* vol. 74 (1983).

Rahdert, George K., & David M. Snyder, "Rediscovering Florida's Common Law Defenses to Libel and Slander." 11 *Stetson Law Review* 1 (1981).

Reimer, Monica K. "The Public Trust Doctrine: Historic Protection for Florida's Navigable Rivers and Lakes," LXXV *Florida Bar Journal* 10 (April 2001).

Rexer, Linda K. "The History of IOLTA: Lessons for the Future," 14 *Dialogue* (No. 3, Summer 2010).

Roberts, B. K. "Law Practice in the Depression Decade of the 1930s." *Florida Supreme Court Historical Society Review* (No. 1.1, 1984).

Shaffer, Thomas L. Remarks, Symposium, "Faith Tends to Subvert Legal Order." 66 *Fordham Law Review* 1089. (1998). Available at http://ir.lawnet.fordham.edu/flr/vol66/iss4/3/.

Shapiro, M. David. "Case Note: Private Citizens Need Only Show Negligence in Defamation Actions Against Media Defendants." 13 *Florida State University Law Review* 159 (Spring 1985).

Shear, L. David. "The Interest on Trust Accounts Program: The Quest Now is Implementation." *Florida Bar Journal* 104 (February 1982).

Skene, Neil. "Review of Capital Cases: Does the Florida Supreme Court Know What It's Doing?" 15 *Stetson Law Review* 263 (No. 2, 1986).

Stacy, Tom and Dayton, Kim. "Rethinking Harmless Error." 88 *Columbia Law Review* 79 (1988).

Stroud, Nancy. "A History and New Turns in Florida's Growth Management Reform." In Symposium: "40th Anniversary of the Quiet Revolution in Zoning and Land Use Regulation." 45 *John Marshall Law Review* 397 (Winter 2012).

Symposium. *Stetson Law Review*, vol. XV, no. 2 (1986).

Unsigned. "Ben F. Overton: Chief Justice of the Supreme Court." 50 *Florida Bar Journal* 194 (April 1976).

Van Nortwick Jr., William A., Spuhler Jr., Kent R., and Doyle, Paul C. "Pro Bono Services in Florida." *Florida Bar Journal* (April 1999).

Walbolt, Sylvia. "Twenty Tips from a Battered and Bruised Oral-Argument Veteran." *Litigation*, vol. 37, no. 2, p. 1 (American Bar Association, Winter 2011).

Walbolt, Sylvia H. and Manko, Andrew D. "From Chattel to Justice." Florida Supreme Court Historical Society. http://www.flcourthistory.org/From-Chattel-to-Justice.

Watson, Timothy A. and Michael J. Valen, "A Historic Review of Workers' Compensation Reform in Florida." 21 Fla. St. U. Law Review (1993–1994).

Webster, Peter D. "Selection and Retention of Judges: Is There One 'Best' Method?" 23 *Florida State University Law Review* 1 (1995).

Wetherington, Gerald T. and Donald I. Pollock, "Tort Suits Against Governmental Entities in Florida." 44 *University of Florida Law Review* 1 (January 1992).

Yates, Linda H. "In the Chief Justice's Office," *Florida Bar Journal* 497 (October 1984).

Yates, Linda H. "The New Chief Justice—Alan C. Sundberg." *Florida Bar Journal* 585 (October 1980).

Magazines and News Websites

Clark, Ramsey. "Spenkelink's Last Appeal." *The Nation* (October 27, 1979).

Ebert, Roger. "Inside Deep Throat." http://www.rogerebert.com/reviews/inside-deep-throat-2005. February 10, 2005.

Flagler Live. "John Canakaris, Father of Flagler County Medicine and Humanitarian, is Dead at 90." Accessed December 4, 2012. http://flaglerlive.com/47716/john-canakaris-obituary.

Jerome, Paul. "Judge of Justice." *Flavour Magazine.* (Summer 1999).

Radio Television Digital News Association. "Cameras in the Court: A State-by-State Guide." http://rtdna.org/article/cameras_in_the_court_a_state_by_state_guide_updated#.UFFt7t0 × 2E. (Summer 2012).

Tielis, Laurel. "Rosemary Furman Fights to Bring Justice to All at a Price All—Except Lawyers—Can Afford." *People Magazine.* December 17, 1984, http://www. people.com/people/archive/article/0,,20089408,00.html. accessed Dec. 2, 2014.

Ziembe, Ryne. "A Cycle of Injustice?" Independent Weekly, Vol. 19, No. 5, March 25, 2010. Accessible at http://www.inweekly.net/article.asp?artID=11293.

Newspapers and Other Periodicals

Daytona Beach News-Journal
Evening Independent (St. Petersburg)
Florida Bar News
Florida Times-Union
Fort Lauderdale News and Sun-Sentinel
Gainesville Sun
Jacksonville Journal
Lakeland Ledger
New York Times
Ocala Star-Banner
Orlando Sentinel
Palm Beach Post
Putnam County Courier
Sarasota Herald-Tribune
St. Petersburg Times
Tallahassee Democrat
Tampa Bay Times
Tampa Tribune
The Charlotte Observer
The Day, New London, Connecticut
The Miami Herald

Videos

Barkett, Rosemary. Oral History of Rosemary Barkett at a Ceremonial Session of the Florida Supreme Court, April 19, 1996. Available from Florida Supreme Court Historical Society.

Florida Justice Institute. Interest on Lawyers' Trust Accounts. Last accessed December 13, 2014.

http://www.floridajusticeinstitute.org/wp-content/uploads/2013/11/IOLTA_HISTORY. mp4.

Supreme Court Session for an oral history of Arthur J. England Jr. March 11, 1988. Available from Florida Supreme Court Historical Society.

Justice B. K. Roberts Oral History Program. October 30, 1986. Available from Florida Supreme Court Historical Society.

Reynolds, Thomas R. "17 Equal Pieces." Filmed interview accessible at https://www.youtube. com/watch?v=36qIYlrJ7jE&feature=youtu.be.

Shaffer, Thomas L. Remarks, Symposium, "Faith Tends to Subvert Legal Order." Available at http://ir.lawnet.fordham.edu/flr/vol66/iss4/3/.

The Courtroom Sketch Artist. May 14, 2012. http://documentary.net/courtroom-sketch-artist/.

INDEX

Neil Skene's career has blended law, journalism, corporate management, and education. A member of the Bar in Florida and Georgia, he began covering the Florida Supreme Court for the *St. Petersburg Times* in 1980. In 1986 he became executive editor at Congressional Quarterly Inc., then served as president and publisher, 1989–1997. He wrote the Tallahassee column for *Florida Trend* 2005–2008 and was special counsel at the Florida Department of Children and Families 2008–2010. He is vice chairman of the board of MedAffinity Corporation and senior deputy director for strategy and innovation at the Illinois Department of Children and Family Services.